The Postcolonial Orient

Historical Materialism Book Series

The Historical Materialism Book Series is a major publishing initiative of the radical left. The capitalist crisis of the twenty-first century has been met by a resurgence of interest in critical Marxist theory. At the same time, the publishing institutions committed to Marxism have contracted markedly since the high point of the 1970s. The Historical Materialism Book Series is dedicated to addressing this situation by making available important works of Marxist theory. The aim of the series is to publish important theoretical contributions as the basis for vigorous intellectual debate and exchange on the left.

The peer-reviewed series publishes original monographs, translated texts, and reprints of classics across the bounds of academic disciplinary agendas and across the divisions of the left. The series is particularly concerned to encourage the internationalization of Marxist debate and aims to translate significant studies from beyond the English-speaking world.

For a full list of titles in the Historical Materialism Book Series
available in paperback from Haymarket Books, visit:
www.haymarketbooks.org / category / hm-series

The Postcolonial Orient

*The Politics of Difference and
the Project of Provincialising Europe*

By
Vasant Kaiwar

Haymarket Books
Chicago, IL

First published in 2014 by Brill Academic Publishers, The Netherlands
© 2014 Koninklijke Brill NV, Leiden, The Netherlands

Published in paperback in 2015 by
Haymarket Books
P.O. Box 180165
Chicago, IL 60618
773-583-7884
www.haymarketbooks.org

ISBN: 978-1-60846-479-1

Trade distribution:
In the US, Consortium Book Sales, www.cbsd.com
In Canada, Publishers Group Canada, www.pgcbooks.ca
In the UK, Turnaround Publisher Services, www.turnaround-uk.com
In all other countries, Publishers Group Worldwide, www.pgw.com

Cover design by Ragina Johnson.

This book was published with the generous support of
Lannan Foundation and the Wallace Global Fund.

10 9 8 7 6 5 4 3 2 1

Library of Congress Cataloging-in-Publication data is available.

Contents

Acknowledgements

The initial draft of this book was composed in Paris, in close, almost daily, conversations with Sucheta Mazumdar and Thierry Labica during the course of a semester-long seminar in 2008. I am most grateful to them for the insights they contributed to an evolving project.

I am deeply indebted to Sucheta Mazumdar for closely and exhaustively reading and discussing the various drafts of my earlier papers, book chapters, and now the manuscript of the book, and for sharing her work on modernisation theory and civilisational models of history that appear to be making something of a comeback at a moment when globalisation without borders is also being widely celebrated. Our collaboration goes back to 1981 when we started the journal, *South Asia Bulletin*, and has continued through three decades that include twenty volumes of the journal (in 1993 it was expanded and renamed *Comparative Studies of South Asia, Africa and the Middle East*) and two edited volumes, *Antinomies of Modernity*[1] and *From Orientalism to Postcolonialism: Asia, Europe and the Lineages of Difference*.[2]

I am much obliged to Thierry Labica for his theoretically incisive responses to my earlier writings on the subject of this book, for translating a 2004 article from English into French for *ContreTemps* that began our very fruitful scholarly association, which continued with *From Orientalism to Postcolonialism*, culminating in his translation of an abbreviated version of this manuscript into French for publication by Éditions Syllepse.

The book was further honed in debates during a weekly seminar held at Maison Suger in the autumn of 2008, involving Samir Amin, Daniel Bensaïd, Georges Labica, Jean-Jacques Lecercle, Stathis Kouvelakis, all of whom gave generously of their time, none more so than Jean-Jacques Lecercle. The seminar itself and the semester-long stay in Paris were made possible by a generous grant from the International Programme of Advanced Studies of the Fondation Maison des Sciences de l'Homme directed by Jean-Luc Racine. Additional facilities, including office space, were provided by the Columbia University Institute of Scholars at Reid Hall, with Danielle Haase-Dubosc at the helm. To all of them, my very special thanks.

To a wider group of scholars – Perry Anderson, Srinivas Aravamudan, Cemil Aydin, Timothy Brennan, Sebastian Budgen, Giancarlo Casale, Miriam Cooke, Steve Edwards, Jehanne Gheith, David Gilmartin, Rada Ivekovic, Ranjana Khanna, Roland Lardinois, Bruce Lawrence, Afshin Matin-Asgari, Matthias Middell, David Need, Chris Newberry, Firat Oruc, Matt Perry, Jacques Pouchepadass, Michel Prum, Mohamad Tavakoli-Targhi,

---

1   Kaiwar and Mazumdar 2003.
2   Mazumdar, Kaiwar and Labica 2009.

Willie Thompson, Achin Vanaik, Joanne Waghorne, and Richard Wolin – who have read and commented on my various papers, many thanks indeed, in particular to Srinivas Aravamudan, Cemil Aydin, and Afshin Matin-Asgari, who shared their considerable expertise in matters of cultural studies, Orientalism and postcolonialism with me. Finally, I am most grateful to the anonymous reviewers of this manuscript for their searching comments and suggestions for revisions, and to David Broder, Danny Hayward, Simon Mussell and Debbie de Wit at Brill for seeing the manuscript through the production stages.

Earlier versions of portions of the book were read to the Triangle South Asia Colloquium in 2002 and 2004, the conference on 'Cultures Impériales: perspectives transatlantiques sur les empires' at the Université Paris X-Nanterre in November 2005, the conference on 'Mapping Difference: Structures and Categories of Knowledge Production' at Duke University in May 2006, the Conference on 'World Orders Revisited' at the University of Leipzig in September 2008, and the conference on 'Actually Existing Globalisation and Its Challenges', co-organised by Columbia University Institute of Scholars and the International Programme in Advanced Studies, FMSH, in Paris in December 2008, in addition to seminars at the Maison des Sciences de l'Homme in 2003, 2005 and 2007. I wish to thank the organisers and participants at those conferences and colloquia for their valuable input. Earlier versions of some parts of the book appeared in *Historical Materialism* 12(2), under the title, 'Towards Orientalism and Nativism: The Impasse of Subaltern Studies'.

This book is dedicated to the memory of Daniel Bensaïd (1946–2010). Steadfast and committed in the struggle for social justice, lucid and eloquent in his brilliant exegeses on Marx and the politics of our time, an outstanding polemicist and one who never thought to trim his sails to fit the winds of a structurally adjusted world, he was also the most generous of friends.

Vasant Kaiwar
Durham, North Carolina

Preface

This book is an engagement with what is commonly understood nowadays by the term 'postcolonialism' in American and British universities and, to an extent, in the ex-colonial countries themselves. The 'postcolonial' might once have referred primarily to the agendas of development and distributive justice that informed the concerns of the first two generations or so of progressive thinkers and public figures with the end of the formal colonisation of a number of countries of what was once called the 'Third World'. That is, included in that definition would have been forms of thought, critique, and so on, that had sought to deal with the legacies of a specific kind of political-economic geography associated with the fallout of capitalist imperialism (the competition among the industrial/industrialising countries for markets, land and raw materials for their industries) often culminating in the outright annexation and sometimes occupation by settler populations from the imperialist countries of previously autonomously governed territories. Anti-colonialism, in the critical and programmatic senses, was very much part of what would have been included in a definition of postcolonialism to the extent that anti-colonialism also had an anticipatory element, a looking forward beyond the period of colonial rule by one or another metropolitan capital to a period when the specific articulations implied by colonialism would no longer exist. A concern with the present (or immediate past) served also as an anticipation of a future in which elements of that past could be made serviceable for a new kind of political economy and society.

Implicit in this thinking, therefore, one suspects, was the idea that European colonialism in the 'Third World' was part of a revolution betrayed;[1] it represented the conquest minus the bourgeois revolution that was supposed to come with the advent of capital, especially as its progressive results were visible in the European countries that had carried out a social transformation that could conveniently be captured under that rubric. What the Third World represented was, so to speak, the blood without the fruit. The huge challenge that theory and practice have tried to meet is to address the many problems left by the colonial legacy.

---

1 I will not be placing quotation marks around Third World hereafter, it being understood that the term has often been used in a polemic vein even if, at one time, it seemed as if some common features prevailed in colonies and ex-colonies which had come under the rule of countries undergoing more or less rapid capitalist development, a transformation denied the colonies for one reason or another. Despite these polemic uses, the term itself is still employed to refer to a broad spectrum of ex-colonial countries that otherwise share no readily identifiable common feature.

However, this is not the 'postcolonialism' one is likely to encounter in the Anglo-phone metropolitan universities nowadays.[2] What one is much more likely to find is a mode of thinking that eschews 'economism', focusing instead on Eurocentrism, resistance to its pretentious and empty universalism, difference grounded in cultural autonomy (however diminished it is now), and a conception that when European modernity was introduced into the Third World it took 'alternative' forms that did not replicate or attempt to emulate the original. An insistence on difference is the crux of the project of 'provincialising' Europe. This kind of postcolonialism – replete with incredulity towards the 'metanarratives' of capital and a range of other postmodernist gestures – has become the representative form of postcolonial thinking.

There are good reasons for rejecting 'economism', not least the tendency in ahistori-cal mainstream economics to exorbitate the place of some substantive entity called the 'economy', more or less deleting the historical novelty and specificity of capital-ism (the capital social form) by simply positing a universal set of economic laws and tendencies that operate across history, assigning it thereby the same value and place it holds in capitalism. This is the proper definition of economism: an ahistorical abstrac-tion involving *homo œconomicus*. For the most part, Marxists have been critical of this tendency.[3] But in some metropolitan postcolonial circles, this sort of historicising of economism seems to be of no interest at all. A critique of the term economism has become shorthand for a critique of any literature that still insists on focusing on the broad range of political-economic concerns having to do with the polarising impact of capitalism on the world scale.[4]

I suppose we could call this a metropolitan postcolonialism. In that case, of course, there is the very real possibility that the postcolonial critic will call into question the very use of the term 'postcolonialism'. Terry Eagleton is barely joking when he notes that there must be a 'secret handbook' for aspiring postcolonial theorists that calls on them to do just that, pointing in the process to the homogenisation, Eurocentrism, and so on, involved in the use of the term,[5] while retaining the substance of a critique that draws on a venerable body of European writing that is broadly consistent with phenomenological existentialism, whose politics range from far-right (Heidegger) to,

---

2 I use the term 'metropolitan' throughout this text in the sense in which Edward Said and a host of others have used it, namely, to signify the 'First World' heartlands of colonialism and imperialism. See, for example, Said 1993, p. 9, or Mansour 1992, p. 45. The term has always had both a cultural-political as well an economic significance, and nowadays the former aspect is likely to resonate more strongly than the latter.

3 Among modern-day theorists, Brenner and Wood have been among the most insistent on the specificities of capitalism, 'its very distinctive dynamics, in contrast to all other social forms and processes'; Wood 2007, p. 144. See Brenner 1976; 1982; 1986; and Wood 2002; 2007.

4 For a useful discussion of the concepts surrounding 'economism', see Mitchell 1998, p. 421.

5 Eagleton 1998, pp. 24–5.

at best, a liberal left (Derrida).[6] Its dominance in the ex-colonial countries is much less certain, for there a more complex reality supervenes in which the original concerns of postcolonial thought and programmes will not go away, and metropolitan postcolonialism's pretensions are themselves the subject of some suspicion.

This book is divided into six parts. Part I ('Introduction') sets the stage by means of an inquiry into the historic conditions of arrival and reception of postcolonial studies 'from the margins' in the United States. It makes the argument for the necessity of periodisation involving critical historical moments and passages of the post-Second World War period, further amplifying the point by examining the implications for the politics of knowledge production of major changes in immigration patterns, transformations in academic fields of study, the crisis and restructuring of capitalism, all culminating in the political waves generated by the collapse of a major component of the post-1917 world order in the years 1989–91. Part II ('Situating Postcolonial Studies') turns to the other side, as it were. It presents aspects of the rich spectrum of postcolonial thought via a case study of India, including a close look at the modernisation, Marxist and populist variants of it, attempting in the process to locate Subaltern Studies and its successor postcolonial form in a field of debates and polemics that emerged out of the legacies of colonialism. This perforce requires a proper understanding of colonialism and the divergent meanings of the 'post' in postcolonial-studies. Part III ('Colonialism, Modernity, Postcolonialism') reads two of the keywords of the postcolonial lexicon – *colonialism* and *modernity* – as periodising concepts and structuring categories that come together with significant effect in the compound 'colonial modernity'. This is a compound employed both to indicate the limits of a Eurocentric historicist perspective, and to provide the basis of an alternative narrative, which is, in all but name, itself a *grand récit*, but which is nonetheless limited by its failure to historicise either of its constituent terms adequately.

Part IV ('Provincialising Europe or Exoticising India') carries the arguments of parts I–III forward by examining two exemplary texts – Dipesh Chakrabarty's *Provincializing Europe* and Ranajit Guha's *Dominance without Hegemony* – which foreground the key historical and historiographical issues of the present 'metropolitan' moment of postcolonialism. This affords a vantage point from which to inquire more closely into the implications of the project of provincialising Europe, its potentialities and limitations for a critique of colonialism and imperialism, and for an understanding of the state of the world in our day. Part V ('Uses and Abuses of Marx') takes up several issues of enduring political-theoretical significance – modernity/modernisation, the transition to capitalism, labour, exploitation, hegemony, and historicism – that recur in various registers in postcolonial theory, and which have been vital

---

6   Brennan 2006, p. 264; Shatz 2012, pp. 11–4.

components of Marxist theory as it has sought to grapple with the concerns of the Third World. The aim here, as in the book more generally, is to read postcolonial texts against the horizon of late capitalism and with the still unrealised potentialities of Marxism in mind, remembering Sartre's assessment of Marxism as the 'untranscendable philosophy of our time'.[7] Part VI ('The Postcolonial Orient') concludes the book by exploring the politics of difference and the limits of a 'post-foundational' approach to explaining such issues as the fragmentation, dispersion, atomisation and heterogeneity that seem to mark the current moment of capital. The postcolonial Orient itself – conceptualised not as a geographic space so much as an arena in which cultural claims, political debate, not to mention polemical exchanges of the theoretical kind, converge – emerges in this context as a crystallisation of aspects of the post-1989 development of postcolonial thought. And, in that sense, it also reflects the workings of 'transformism', in the Gramscian sense, on the world of postcolonial intellectuals and the subsequent loss of a political will to grasp the workings of the capital system in its global totality within a properly historical-materialist framework.

In saying all of the above about the postcolonial Orient, I should note that I am not mainly interested here in entering the lists either with those who imagine that, as Said noted with reference to his position in *Orientalism*, 'interpretation is misinterpretation, there is no such thing as correct interpretation',[8] or those who maintain that Orientalism is a misrepresentation of the lives of the people of the 'Orient'. To an extent, Orientalism is misrepresentation if the agenda of such a form of thought is taken literally to be about the realities of places in the 'East' (or whatever gets drawn into this geographic commonsense) and their social, political and cultural developments over time. But much of it is so hackneyed that it is really about something else – for example, the political and moral right of the European ruling classes to dominate and improve the 'lesser' civilisations. It is not so much about the places themselves as what is wrong with them, what differentiates them from the 'West', and why it becomes necessary to see the world in such stark binary terms.[9] There is a politics of knowledge involved that is a discourse, but also an ideology, in that it enables the construction of

7 Sartre 1963, p. 34.

8 Bayoumi and Rubin 2000, p. 423 cited in Lazarus 2011, p. 196.

9 I am going to use 'West', by and large, not as a substantive 'civilisational' entity with definite qualities that play themselves out in the historical arena. I agree that the use of it is altogether, as Lazarus notes, 'amorphous and indeterminate', as I shall demonstrate at various points below, but it provides postcolonial studies a central category around which a polemic against all sorts of targets – but primarily the Enlightenment, and its supposed derivatives like Marxism – can be mounted.

political agendas, the mobilisation of a political constituency, not to mention fabrications invented to conceal the truth of one's intentions and the like.[10]

Perhaps it is this ideological dimension that has now come to roost in postcolonial circles, but one involving a neat reversal of the values associated with colonial-era Orientalism. It is also in this world of postcolonialism that we see some telling categorial and theoretical shifts – for example, from capitalism to modernity (and all its so-called hybridisations, alternatives, and so on), from class to civilisation, that is, from the struggles of often non-literate working populations over land and wages to those of intellectuals over culture, from Marx and Gramsci to Nietzsche and Heidegger, if not Foucault and Derrida. The historical conditions in which these shifts might have occurred and their political and theoretical implications are what this book, for the most part, aims to illuminate.

A more general argument underpinning the book is that notwithstanding the ambition to provincialise Europe, that is historically to decentre Europe and free its former colonies from the taint of inadequacy in relation to the West, the results fall well short. Indeed, in many respects, the dominant postcolonialism of our day can be seen as part of a longer history of what one might call, following Raymond Schwab, the 'Oriental Renaissance'.[11] Historically, it has involved, from the metropolitan perspective, the possibility of renewing Europe via an encounter with sources of wisdom from the East. The original Oriental Renaissance was a response to and refuge from the spreading influence of the Enlightenment and the French Revolution. It was a doctrine that sought the sources of a renewal of Europe in the 'Aryan Orient'. Europe distracted by the radical secularism of the Enlightenment and proletarian masses on the streets turned to the 'Orient' for the wisdom that would renew it, and found it in the classics of Persian and Sanskrit antiquity.

While the original Oriental Renaissance had but shallow roots in Europe and blew over with the repression and containment of the revolutions of 1848 and the consolidation of bourgeois Europe behind the ramparts of the integral state à la Gramsci, it has had a curious afterlife, an ever-present resource to be drawn on at times of crisis or moments when the agenda of muscular imperialism seems rather threadbare. This curious afterlife is no doubt what René Guénon, in his 1929 pamphlet *Autorité spirituelle et pouvoir temporel*, called upon when he drew a parallel between contemporary

---

10   That said, I entirely share Samir Amin's position that Orientalist thinking 'merits reproach' for producing false judgements, and Edward Said's argument that the 'first imperative is to find out what occurred and … why, not as isolated events but as part of an unfolding history' (Said 1999, p. 99 cited Lazarus 2011, p. 197). It is heartening to know that Amin and Said who might, in a limited context, be seen as in opposition, can weigh in on the merits of 'good' history. More on 'good' history in part IV of the book.

11   Schwab 1984.

India and medieval Western society to illustrate the 'universal supremacy of the spiritual over the temporal', even if the occasion for it was a French political 'crisis' involving
the authority of the Pope, Pius XI, vis-à-vis the monarchist and counter-revolutionary
l'Action Française.[12] Or, more broadly, it could be captured in the statement attributed to the inter-war race theorist, Houston Stewart Chamberlain: '[a] great human-
istic task has fallen to our lot to accomplish and thereto is Aryan India summoned'.[13]
Undoubtedly, this was also the spirit in which Foucault could write about 'two completely different discourses, belonging to two equally different kinds of society'. And
even if one had ruled the other for a century or more, their essences remained radically different, the East with its 'erotic arts' and its timeless 'political spirituality', the
West with its 'sexual science' and its modern (secular) concept of political revolution.
Presumably, the West needed to come into contact with the political spirituality, if
not the erotic arts, of the East so as to breathe some new life into its desiccated scientific secularism.[14]

From the perspective of the colonies, the Oriental Renaissance has had rather different valences. The ideas of conservative or reactionary European thought – whether
it originated with Orientalists like Guénon, Mircea Eliade, Louis Dumont, Henri
Corbin and Louis Massignon, or more generally with philosophers like Nietzsche and
Heidegger – even if not directly known or cited, have become general currency and
inspired among anti-colonial thinkers of a like stripe the possibility of asserting their
cultural autonomy vis-à-vis the West, demonstrating that actually a truer universalism
than the one that came in the wake of Europe's revolutionary tradition was already
available to the 'East', which it would be the task of a proper cultural nationalism to
develop. The parallel to Chamberlain's assertion of the 'great humanist task' is to be
found in the sentiment expressed by inter-war and post-war pan-Asianists and pan-
Islamists that Asian civilisations should not be regarded as inferior to Europe's on the
grounds that the priceless gifts of their own civilisations contributed to the European
Renaissance.[15] Logically, it would be the task of nationalists, if not pan-Asianists, to
develop this legacy on their own behalf.

---

12   Lardinois 1994, p. 30.
13   Cited in Pollock 1993, p. 86.
14   Foucault 1978, p. 119, cited in Afary and Anderson 2005, pp. 30–1. More broadly, on
       Foucault's Oriental 'subtext', see Schaub 1989, pp. 306–16.
15   The former theme is widely echoed in, or implicitly informs, the works of both anti-
       colonial and postcolonial writers in South Asia. On the influence of what he calls the
       'reactionary modernism' of Nietzsche, Ernst Junger and Heidegger on Iran, see Matin-
       Asgari 2004, pp. 113–23. Suitably reworked, the critique of the West by these 'reactionary'
       modernists could inform notions of national autonomism based on the greater historical
       antiquity and cultural difference of the East. The latter theme of a civilisational gift to the
       West is discussed in Aydin 2009, pp. 107–28.

A postcolonial expression of the civilisational gifts involved in the Oriental Renaissance is to be found in Chakrabarty's notion of an 'anti-colonial spirit of gratitude' to European thought,[16] and the latter's renewal 'from and for the margins',[17] itself a paraphrase of Jarava Lal Mehta's idea of a long journey through Europe, the 'foreign and the strange', before returning to one's home base.[18] All this no doubt serves well a 'Europe' facing fears of growing old, being swamped by immigration, and losing its way in endless battles over identity (Christian, post-Christian, secular).[19] And, equally or more so, an ex-colonial world in which the promised social outcomes of economic development and redistributive justice have turned very sour indeed. The Oriental Renaissance, in its postcolonial variant, then, is for a world in which the political tasks involved in bringing about certain outcomes seem very hard to imagine, shifting the debate not so much to culture as to civilisation. Culture is merely a somewhat compromised and 'hybridised' expression of an underlying civilisation with roots that extend far back beyond the onset of colonialism to some classical moment of authenticity. The postcolonial wisdom from the East, relocated now in the centres of Anglo-American higher education, offers its counsels not in a militant counter-revolutionary mode, but in a somewhat wistful, resignationist one. Without an understanding of this historical legacy it would be difficult to grasp the ways in which a sophisticated postcolonialism has sought to construct its civilisational narratives, or the reasons for its reception in the West.

Orientalism as a massive accumulation of thought in a variety of disciplines posits the 'Orient' as the adequate or only civilisational foil for Europe, which nonetheless remains the invariable place of the universal against the many particularities represented by the former.[20] Orientalism is renewed, reconstructed and given new form at moments of critical and extended political engagement.[21] Historically, the Orient appears as an inexhaustible source of inspiration and distractions for a self-identical Europe that needs the rest of the world to renew itself: it is Europe's birth-right.

16   Chakrabarty 2000, p. 255.

17   Chakrabarty 2000, p. 16.

18   Mehta 1976, p. 466.

19   I should point out that 'Europe' here is not limited to a Continental reference, separating it from the so-called 'Anglo-Saxon' world. The term is used to signify the historical 'West' or, in Etienne Balibar's characterisation, the space that might once have included Western Christendom; Balibar 2004, pp. 6–7.

20   This idea has been developed as the 'third coordinate of Orientalism' – the critical feature that structures the descriptive aspects of both the Romantic and Utilitarian versions of Orientalism, as commonly understood by Said and his interlocutors; see Kaiwar and Mazumdar 2009, pp. 28–32.

21   It is not surprising that Foucault, for example, should rework familiar Orientalist themes during the period of his uncompromising, if somewhat anguished, commitment to the Iranian Revolution; see, for example, Afary and Anderson 2005.

When the crisis passes, Europe moves on and the Orient sinks back into its provinciality or marginality until something else – predictably enough given capital's chronic proneness to crises and endemic uncertainties – brings it back into view. Europeans can never really become deracinated because their culture is Promethean and can take on any identity, wearing and discarding it as needs must. The many Orients have no such luxury: they are quickly deracinated by contact with Europe. Thus appropriating 'Oriental lore', in a shallow dilettantish manner ignoring the historicity if not political implications of ideas contained in that lore, in order to make political points vis-à-vis one's domestic interlocutors,[22] exoticising and admiring the East from afar while remaining a Westerner in one's own life does not seem to entail any liability for a European.[23] Indeed, it might signify the latter's graciousness in acknowledging the existence of the rest of the world.

In reverse, this simply produces the imagery of bestiality: the East 'aping' the manners of the West without comprehending its proper civilisational genius. The ape can only mimic the gestures of the human; the domain of the latter is simply beyond the former's reach. Enough said: we must consider the possibility that the East-West dichotomy is fundamentally racist and that operating within its parameters is already to succumb to racism. But this judgement is complicated by the issue of a threshold of audibility that the Third World theorist is expected to rise above, and this involves some acceptance – whether in an anti-colonial spirit of gratitude or something more pragmatic – of an essential divide between East and West.

It is odd how the philosophical nostrums of Europeans become the existential realities of the Orient – if not the present then the past, for example, Guha's Manusmriti via Nietzsche – which then come back in that form to propel a fresh round of 'deep thinking' in the West. Michael Hardt's verdict on *Provincializing Europe* – that it promises to take Marx beyond Marx, renew Marxism with the aid of postcolonial theory – is probably as clear an example as any.[24] It is a problematic assessment. The references to Europe in postcolonial thought – pretentious claims of universalism, floating signifier, and suchlike – come across as so many empty gestures, devoid of an understanding of the contradictions of Europe, the suppressions that have allowed Europe to emerge as a self-identical entity confronting the world as the place of the universal. There is always already an asymmetry in the relationship between the place of the universal and the places of particularities, and the civilisational narratives built around it.

In her introduction to an important volume on Marxism and postcolonial studies,[25] Crystal Bartolovich argues that Marxists should not become purely antagonistic to

22 Schaub 1989, p. 308.
23 Brinton 1967, p. 206.
24 Hardt 2001, pp. 243–9.
25 Bartolovich 2002, pp. 1–17.

postcolonial studies, listing several important contributions made by the latter that could potentially enrich Marxism. Among those are the extension of the discussion of subalternity and political representation in the non-metropolitan context, the contention that the 'master narratives' of nationalism, secularism and internationalism have been neglectful of difference, not to mention the detailed knowledge of particular local conditions, situations and texts, and the identification of Eurocentric concepts, practices, habits of thought, and so on.[26] Perhaps so, but it is worth pointing out that most of these contributions long antedate what Bartolovich and her fellow contributors to the volume identify as postcolonial studies. Indeed, many of these insights were contributed by Marxist or left-Keynesian political economists who might look askance at postcolonial studies. What is distinctive about the latter is the adaptation of a range of issues central to anti-colonial and anti-imperialist thought to a kind of poststructuralist idiom, heavily influenced by post-war Heideggerian quietism.

More promising, I think, is the approach advocated by Neil Larsen in the same volume. Larsen notes that all contemporary 'theory' with social implications can be shown to bear a 'necessary, if tensile' relationship to the thought of Marx, if one accepts Sartre's view expressed in his *Search for a Method*, that a 'going beyond Marxism' will be at best 'the rediscovery of a thought already contained in the philosophy which one believes he has gone beyond'.[27] This reminds one of a point Fredric Jameson makes with regard to 'second-order' philosophies that presuppose the totality they reject[28] – a notion that can well be applied to postcolonial studies. But a more important point made by Jameson is that Marxism can reveal the seam that other theories conceal,[29] which, once revealed, open the inquiry to history and to the social totality that it is the perhaps non-conscious vocation of other theories to occlude from view. It is in this spirit of dialectical critique that an engagement with postcolonial studies should proceed, not in the spirit of epistemic charity and ecumenical multiculturalism.

I would argue against the proposition, à la Robert Young or Benita Parry, that we should all somehow accept the postcolonial label as it is currently employed. Just as not all European theorists, for example, are expected to be 'postmodernists', so not all people from the ex-colonies should uncritically accept the postcolonial label. It cannot be used in this objectifying fashion. Postcolonial studies represents a political stance; postcolonial texts should be read in detail to highlight the kinds of omissions and amnesia that accompany their stated objective of developing a critique of Eurocentrism, and their less overtly articulated goal of establishing a safe distance from Marxism. They should be read, as noted, against the horizon of capital and with the still unrealised potentialities of Marxism in mind. When Stuart Hall states that

---

26   Bartolovich 2002, pp. 10–11.
27   Sartre 1963, p. 7, cited in Larsen 2002, p. 204.
28   Jameson 1981, pp. 52–3.
29   Jameson 1988, Volume II, p. 149.

something has changed, and that the world has somehow become postcolonial, he merely registers an appearance form of late capitalism.[30]

Postcolonial studies with its poststructuralist, post-modernist imbrications does not have the same value or valences as Marxism; to the extent that postcolonial studies has the ability or ambition to enrich Marxism, it must perforce become an aspect of Marxism, whose core theses it should be in the interest of Marxists to defend. At the heart of this line of thinking is the realisation that Marxism is not just a theory of capital – important though that is in the face of the arbitrary carnage wrought by the notion that it is some sort of metanarrative of progress. Marxism is also the 'anticipatory expression of a future society'.[31] Neither Marx nor the rich tradition of thought that his work inspires seek to construct Utopia in the sense in which a Fourier or an Owen might have done, but as the rich debates about Utopia make clear – and the work of Ernst Bloch has been one of the indispensable if neglected sources here – a Utopian horizon is indispensable to Marxism.

Marxism's categorial abstractions are profoundly historical, rooted not only in the social form of capital but also in the struggles to overcome that form. It should be in the interests of Marxists to develop this rich conceptual and political heritage, among them: the labour theory of value, its emphasis on the social form of capital rather than some quantitative physicalist reduction of it, the non-intuitive nature of an understanding of the capital relation and the ineluctable exploitation built into its core;[32] alienation and reification; totality, understood minimally as the imperative to totalise even if any particular form of it should be open to question and refutation;[33] the refusal of closure; and the centrality of class struggle, sometimes breaking out into mass rebellion and even revolution but often submerged, taking on board a variety of other struggles that are the displaced and transformed forms of it.

The question of *différance* should be applied not so much to language as to the question of revolution – a punctual rupture in the fabric of capital through which the future comes rushing in. Politics, no matter how mundane, takes place against the backdrop of that possibility and its endless and, in our time, seemingly interminable deferrals. But the question of revolution itself, it seems, will never disappear; it is constantly re-posed in different forms. And perhaps here we find a valuable reminder about history itself, refusing desire and setting 'inexorable limits to individual as well as collective praxis', which 'its ruses turn into grisly and ironic reversals of their overt intention'.[34]

---

30   Hall 1996, p. 246.

31   Jameson 1988, Volume II, pp. 175–7.

32   See, for example, Elson 1979, Harvey 2006, Jameson 2011.

33   Jameson 1981, pp. 52–3; Jameson 2011, pp. 5–6.

34   Jameson 1981, p. 102.

We are very far now from some ambiguous desire to make ourselves at home within the rule of capital, or rather advocate that as a final horizon of practical possibility. If some people should still insist on reaching out to postcolonial studies, my inclination would be to mine it for whatever insights it might offer – a sensitivity to difference, for example, but relocated from some cherished cultural legacy to the uneven-and-combined geographies of capital – to enrich Marxist theory and praxis. What makes Marxism so rich and able constantly to renew itself is its inexhaustible ability to take on board insights generated within very wide and seemingly unrelated fields of intellectual inquiry and subject them to the incomparable critical power of its core concepts and methods of analysis through collective work, polemical exchanges, and so on.[35]

This sort of undertaking assumes a degree of urgency because under the present 'globalisation' of capital something has been achieved that no earlier stage of capitalist development has been able to do, namely, making the overcoming of capital seem like an archaic and quixotic task. As Eagleton has pointed out, the tendency in some quarters of the left has been to concur with this assessment and trim their political sails accordingly.[36] The prolonged crisis of the capitalist economy, post-1974, has been a vital catalyst in a certain mode of representing the history of class struggles and revolutions in the past, as well as eradicating in some cases any mention of them in history texts. A good deal of evidence has had to be suppressed to pull off that narrative. The history of colonialism has not been exempt from this sort of revisionism. That is to say, a crisis of world capitalism has been a material precondition for the full flowering of postcolonial studies.[37]

In the process of addressing these issues, one might have to subject the starting point, that is, the self-identification of historians and social theorists with Europe or the 'margins', as the case may be, to critical scrutiny. A commitment to a transformative internationalism should mark the point of departure from which all identitarian positions on the one hand, and euphemisms such as 'globalisation' on the other, are subject to a critical appraisal. Marx's observation that 'labour in a white skin cannot emancipate itself where it is branded in a black skin', is truer now than in his

---

35   There is a very rich body of Marxist writing to draw on in developing a critical engagement with postcolonial studies. In addition to the classic works of Marx, Engels, Lenin and Gramsci, there are the contemporary interventions of Aijaz Ahmad, Samir Amin, Perry Anderson, Daniel Bensaïd, Timothy Brennan, Robert Brenner, Paul Burkett, Arif Dirlik, Terry Eagleton, David Harvey, Fredric Jameson, Neil Lazarus, Moïshe Postone, Sumit Sarkar, Tony Smith, Peter Thomas, Ellen Wood, Slavoj Žižek, to name but the most prominent. Chibber 2013 unfortunately appeared too late for me to draw upon its stimulating ideas.

36   Eagleton 1996, p. 23.

37   Lazarus 2011, pp. 1–20.

own time.[38] One sees little productive political space left for nationalism, and none whatsoever for Eurocentrism, even and especially if it claims to be of the left variety,[39] or for that matter for Third-Worldism, however disguised. Our political geography may have to come to terms with a world in which there will be no margins or centre in an increasingly turbulent world, no room for mystifications of history, only a clear-eyed historical materialism, which as Gramsci says is the 'absolute *"historicism"*, the absolute *secularisation* and *earthliness* of thought'.[40] Perhaps, once again, Jameson's call to historicise, rooted in a 'persistent human curiosity of a generally systemic – rather than merely anecdotal – kind' and pervasive anxieties about the larger fate and destiny of the system,[41] retains its political charge and perennial appeal. What the 'Utopian impulse' calls on us to do, then, is to account for the present from the perspective of the future, and in so doing asks us to 'recognise that the future is in our hands, which is to say, the future is now unfolding because of us, or else in spite of us'. This is what the slogan 'always historicise' means when it is 'turned around and made to look forwards, not backwards'.[42]

---

38   Marx 1977, p. 414.
39   I have in mind the misleadingly entitled article of 1998 by Slavoj Žižek. People may literally imagine this to be a plea for left 'Eurocentrism', despite it being nothing of the kind, and, moreover, imagine that Marxism is constitutively Eurocentric, although it is also nothing of the kind; see Žižek 1998.
40   Gramsci 1971, p. 465, emphasis added.
41   Jameson 1994, pp. xi–xii.
42   Buchanan 1988, p. 28.

CHAPTER 1

Introduction

In response to the question, 'When exactly does the "postcolonial" begin?', Arif Dirlik responds with admirable brevity – and, as he claims, only partly facetiously – that it does so when 'Third-World intellectuals have arrived in the First-World academy'.[1] Nowadays, the question runs the risk of being dismissed either as the reworking of an old historicist approach, seeking origins and absolute starting-points, or the reply itself is seen as merely rhetorical since the Third World itself has been declared defunct. Of course, that could in itself be a function of a certain kind of historical moment, the passing of a political aspiration, but more on that later. In the meantime, postcolonial studies of a certain genealogy and derivation has become securely institutionalised in any number of US and Anglophone universities in the British Commonwealth for reasons that have much to do with the complex politics of academic knowledge production, and it is perhaps the privilege of those on the inside, relatively speaking, not to want to rock the boat too much by looking into the conditions of possibility of their own academic practice.[2]

1.1 A Narrative of Arrival

That said, the question of beginnings is not so easy to discard. No fewer than two luminaries of the academic formation to which Dirlik refers seem to share a perception that the publication of Edward Said's *Orientalism*, in 1978, launched a new area of academic inquiry[3] that has subsequently been called postcolonial studies or some variation thereof. If so, 1978 must have been the *annus mirabilis* of postcolonial studies, for it was also the year of Foucault's visit to Iran, then on the cusp of a revolution to overthrow the Shah whose tyranny had become unbearable to large sections of the population of that country. In an interview with Baqir Parham, Foucault declared that in 1978 humanity was at 'point zero' insofar as political thought was concerned, and that Iran offered new possibilities of a concept of revolution that attempted to

---

1 The query was posed by Shohat 1992, p. 103, cited in Dirlik 1994, p. 328.

2 I am going to refer to postcolonial studies in the singular, taking the term to refer to a field of scholarly production and intervention, rather than discrete individual studies.

3 Bhabha 1992, p. 465; Spivak 1993, p. 56. This is discussed in Vieira 1999, pp. 273–4.

go beyond both liberalism and Marxism.[4] Just as Marxists regarded the Russian Revolution of 1917 as a new type of revolution that had 'gone beyond' the perspectives of the French Revolution of 1789, so too did Foucault seem to anticipate that the coming revolution in Iran would reduce the two centuries from 1789 to 1979 to a 'modernist parenthesis amid something far deeper and more permanent', namely, the phenomenon of an 'elemental and irreducible religious uprising'.[5] In retrospect, of course, Foucault was wrong in his anticipation. Unlike the French and Russian Revolutions, the Iranian Revolution, or counter-revolution, has not inspired many imitators. But it did usher in a period when religious issues of an elemental nature have become far more prominent in politics, a development fairly well documented in the directions taken by academic knowledge production as well.

The roots of this kind of reaction lie, to an extent, in the often violent politics of the Cold War, especially as it affected a range of poor and sometimes newly independent countries in, what one used to call without qualification, the Third World. The United States, as Brennan points out, made it its business to 'export counter-revolution', working ceaselessly, often covertly, to 'undermine, subvert and overthrow regimes and movements' it deemed in opposition to its interests and political philosophy.[6] The reach of the United States was truly global: in Latin American this included Cuba, of course, but also Guatemala, Nicaragua, Guyana, Grenada, Haiti, Venezuela, Peru and Chile (the locus of the first 9/11); in Africa, Angola, Mozambique, Congo, Libya, Ghana, not to mention the Horn of Africa; in the Middle East, Iran, Iraq, Syria, Afghanistan; in Southeast Asia, Vietnam, the Philippines, Korea, but also Indonesia, Cambodia and Laos. Coups and targeted assassinations were launched in Greece, Turkey, Iran and Pakistan.[7] This narrative would be incomplete without the participation of the US's then-satellite states in Western Europe and the actions of the USSR and its own satellite states in Eastern Europe.[8] The purges, the show trials, not to mention armed intervention on the streets of Budapest and Prague, were only the more overt and brutal manifestations of a logic of geopolitics that carried on where the more overt colonialism of the pre-war period left off. On both sides of the 'Iron Curtain', the left was subject to massive suppression, if not liquidation; the entire socialist agenda, or what had survived of it

---

4   Afary and Anderson 2005, p. 75.
5   Afary and Anderson 2005, pp. 132–3.
6   Brennan 1997, p. 33.
7   Lazarus 2011, pp. 5–6.
8   For graphic details of the events in Eastern Europe, see Judt 2011.

after Fascism and Stalinism, came to be thoroughly destabilised from within and without.

All this was happening even as the economy, after the economic depression of the interwar years and the ravages of World War II, entered a 'golden age', a long economic boom that lasted until the early-to-mid-1970s or so. It was during this period that the welfare state as we knew it was constructed in the prosperous West and the newly independent countries staked out a position that included economic development and political self-determination.[9] One can see that the goal of the superpowers was in fact a gigantic global operation of containment of these tendencies, limited only by their need for tactical and other alliances in their global confrontations. With the end of the post-World War II boom,[10] the world economy has reverted to a more familiar pattern of long drawn out recessions, followed by short-term and feeble recoveries often accompanied by various speculatively induced bubbles. The dynamics of this process lie entirely within the logic of capitalist competition itself, although the costs have been frequently visited upon workers demanding a living wage and a range of countries whose debts and financial obligations, piled up during the boom years, have now come home to roost.[11] In this period of slow growth, long recessions, evanescent booms and bubbles, the welfare state of the West is being rolled back, just as in the Third World the demands for development and economic justice have been discarded, sometimes under pressure from the multi-lateral agencies (the IMF and World Bank) and the indigenous ruling classes.

Postcolonial studies in the metropolitan countries, emerging as it did at the end of the 1970s and consolidating itself over the next decade-and-a-half or so, would seem to coincide with, if not follow, these developments rather closely. Foucault's critique of liberalism and Marxism, and his calling into question the emancipatory potentialities of the Enlightenment,[12] expressed in his assessment of the Iranian Revolution, could also have been the position of Jacques Derrida,[13] and would seem to be the direct inspiration for a great deal of postcolonial political thought. A periodisation of postcolonial studies in its emergence and consolidation as a 'field of academic inquiry' ought to involve both the critical passages of post-war history and the impression they leave on

---

9   Lazarus 2011, p. 2.

10   Henceforth, I will simply use post-war to signify post-Second World War.

11   The post-war boom and bust cycles of capital have been studied extensively by Brenner;
     see Brenner 2002 and 2006; Hobsbawm 1996c, pp. 257–86.

12   Afary and Anderson 2005, p. 16.

13   Ahmad 1999, p. 98.

theory, structuralist and poststructuralist.[14] If E.P. Thompson had a point in arguing that structuralism recapitulated some of the sense of powerlessness that many people felt in the face of the Cold War,[15] then poststructuralism, it might be argued, was a sign of the impasse of structuralism and of a renewed overtly imperial dominance,[16] the ensuing roll-back of the historic gains of the working people albeit at very different levels, the development of parasitic casino capitalism and the crushing of any sort of hope that capital as a social form could be transformed.

Postcolonial studies might be most usefully located in these political, theoretical and institutional cross-currents. That is, if the emergence of a field of postcolonial studies is traceable to a period when the economic boom of the post-war period came to an end – the mid-1970s – and the limits then placed on the programmes of modernisation and social transformation in the ex-colonial world; and the subsequent consolidation of that field can be seen in the 1980s and thereafter, coinciding with the entrenchment of a kind of market-fetishising ideology and its disciplining of working class and peasant populations to austerity, wage-cuts and so on, it still leaves room for considerable regional variations. Those would depend on the sites of emergence and consolidation, issues of intellectual formation, the size and diversity of the local intelligentsia, their exposure to critical bodies of thought including Marxism, migrations and diasporic settlements, not to mention the varying depths of the crises induced by the post-1970s economic slowdown. It should come as no surprise that Latin American intellectuals should develop their particular heritage of radical thought in the post-1970s conjuncture in particular directions, confronted by the immediate presence of the United States,[17] and that South Asian and African intellectuals should do so in other directions, influenced by their varying proximity to their erstwhile colonisers and, in some cases, to the Soviet Union or China. Harootunian's point that the Subaltern Studies people, in practice, tend to portray a 'putative relationship between the English [colonisers] and their Bengali subjects' as a stand-in for the relationship between coloniser and colonised everywhere, marked further by a 'psychological ambiguity that owes much to Hegel's master-slave dialectic', is well taken, but postcolonial studies is hardly alone in this manner of representing a particular situation in

---

14   Lazarus 2011, p. 1.
15   Thompson 1978, pp. 84ff.
16   On the impasse of structuralism and its *débouchement* into poststructuralism, see Anderson 1983, pp. 32–55; on the work of periodisation, see Lazarus 2011, p. 9.
17   Vieira 1999, pp. 273–4.

universalising terms.[18] Indeed, a case can be made that the 'postcolonial' arises when a range of political ideologies that went by other descriptions – for example, liberation theology, anarcho-Communism, Maoism, the Bandung spirit, Third-Worldism, pan-Asianism, Subaltern Studies, and so on and so forth – are captured under that singular heading.[19] But by and large, the postcolonial also seems to signify a de-radicalised reading of what many of the social movements stood for, a reworking into forms consistent with the keywords of today's academic production – hybridity, mimicry, liminality, migrancy, multiculturalism, transnationalism, globalisation, to name but the most prominent.

The result is sometimes a randomisation of history,[20] if not outright denial of the very historicity of the phenomena of postcoloniality itself. This is exemplified in Vieira's statement that if postcolonialism 'somehow' presupposes colonialism, any attempt to identify beginnings is doomed to failure, insofar as 'it has existed from time immemorial'.[21] Stuart Hall has his own version of history, but the randomisation goes beyond history to concepts themselves. Thus, in his view, colonisation has made 'ethnic absolutism' an increasingly untenable cultural strategy, and made the colonies diasporic in relation to their 'cultures of origin', although it is arguable that both ethnic absolutism and the notion of an original national culture to which modern identity politics ought to seek a return owe much to colonial rule.[22] Colonialism, in Hall's account, originating with the conquest of the New World and the arrival of the Portuguese in the Indian Ocean (both in the late fifteenth century), henceforth shifts everything so that the very idea of 'isolated or separate' identities has been obliged to yield to a 'variety of paradigms' designed to capture these

---

18   Harootunian 1999, p. 143.

19   Dirlik 1999, p. 287. A similar point is made by Vieira when she notes that the 'Orient-imported label' (postcolonialism) brings to visibility a Latin American body of postcolonial theory, *'even enabling its constitution as such'* (Vieira 1999, p. 274, emphasis added).

20   Anderson 1983, p. 48. Anderson considers the 'randomisation of history' as one of the three chief characteristics of poststructuralist thought, the others being the exorbitation of language and the attenuation of truth. All of which would lend some force to Lazarus's point about what he calls postcolonial studies' supplementarity to poststructuralism (Lazarus 2011, p. 1).

21   Vieira 1999, p. 273. I suppose we should treat this as some sort of literary joke, but elsewhere in the same essay, the author notes that the 'rhythms of colonialism, especially for Brazil' [why so?] can be dated back to the 'first intervention of the Trade Wind' that blew Cabral off course and into Porto Seguro' (Vieira 1999, p. 274). Time immemorial seems to begin in 1500.

22   This has been exhaustively discussed and debated in the Indian literature on religio-political communalism. For example, see Thapar 1969 and Chandra 1984.

'different but related forms of relationship, interconnection and discontinuity'. Yet it also seems that the Enlightenment, dominated by Science and the Social Sciences, imposes a single discursive system within which people are constrained to manoeuvre.[23] So, what is the relationship of the Enlightenment to colonialism? Does it put an end to colonial paradigms? Is the Enlightenment continuous with the Romantic-racialism of the nineteenth century, or is it simply another 'construction' whose historical co-ordinates are of no interest in comparison to its polemic uses?

One could go on, but the point is that any account of postcolonialism that does not seek to locate it in a historically identifiable modern-day colonialism, itself a product of the dynamics of capital as the modern world system, is likely to produce precisely the sorts of confusions that I have outlined above. It is therefore with some relief that one turns to Partha Chatterjee's outline of the emergence of the postcolonial moment of Subaltern Studies, or a Subaltern Studies-influenced postcolonialism. Chatterjee's brief but highly informative essay, 'India's History from Below', published in *Le Monde Diplomatique*,[24] a condensed version of an earlier essay,[25] might be read in part as a rebuttal of Dirlik's position on postcolonial studies, although Chatterjee himself nowhere indicates, nor is there reason to believe, that he intended it to be so. If Dirlik's position is thought of as 'externalist', the origin of postcolonial studies being a function of relocation or translocation of Third World intellectuals, Chatterjee's position is 'internalist'.

His narrative locates postcolonialism as a move beyond Subaltern Studies. The latter began with Gramsci-inspired studies of rural rebellions and insurrections by a group of historians under the leadership of Ranajit Guha. They launched a series of impressive volumes simply entitled *Subaltern Studies*, published by Oxford University Press in India from 1982 onwards. The first six volumes were edited by Guha himself between 1982 and 1989. These studies, Chatterjee informs us, by and large utilised the British colonial archives, reading them against the grain to arrive at an understanding of rebellions, insurrections, and the 'world' of the rebels themselves. But as he explains, from about 1987, and more so from about 1989, the participants in the group began to grapple far more seriously than they had earlier with the realisation that subaltern histories were 'fragmentary, disconnected and incomplete'.[26] The

23   Hall 1996, pp. 250–3.
24   Chatterjee 2006, pp. 12–3.
25   Published in 1998 in Bengali as 'A Brief History of Subaltern Studies', and republished in English translation in Chatterjee 2010.
26   Chatterjee 2006, p. 12.

project evolved from inquiry into subaltern 'autonomy' at moments of rebellion through representations of the subaltern in the colonial archives and in mainstream histories to a whole range of subjects connected to colonial governance, education, movements of religious and social reforms, the state and public institutions, modern ideas of rationality, science, regimes of power and related topics. At the same time, the question of modernity came into focus with the idea of alternative or hybrid forms of it, 'focusing on the dissemination of the ideas, practices and institutions of western modernity under colonial conditions'.[27] In a nutshell, this might be considered the postcolonial moment of Subaltern Studies.

If the narrative is taken at face value, what stands out is the statement that the 'internalist' transition is a function of a realisation of the inadequacy of subaltern histories that are 'fragmentary, disconnected and incomplete'. This would imply that the ambition of postcolonial studies now stands for something else – a move from anecdotal accounts of small-scale events to nothing less than a totalising interpretation of modernity itself, indeed, possibly even what one might call the development of a postcolonial 'metanarrative' consciously distanced, one might imagine, from those attributable to nationalism or Marxism. The focus is now on cultural continuities and ruptures, Eurocentrism and its pretentious universalism, authenticity, symbolic issues of identity and difference, and, of course, the whole vexed issue of multiple, alternative and hybrid modernities and the like. The idea of other modernities was developed to take aim at the facile Eurocentric universalism of the Enlightenment-inspired civilising mission and the pretension that European experience must stand as the normal line of development of all other histories. Chatterjee, like his colleague in the Subaltern Studies collective, Dipesh Chakrabarty, argues that to reveal the workings of these other modernities is to question this type of universalism and, in the process, 'provincialise Europe'.

In light of the above, Dirlik's response to the origins of the 'postcolonial' has come up against a spirited and, dare one say, totalising riposte, one that compresses aspects of a turbulent history in which the very meanings of 'post' undergo a complex series of transformations and transmutations corresponding to some of the deeper impulses working through the system. However, a little reflection will suggest that a good deal of history has been suppressed in this account. For instance, the pioneers of *Subaltern Studies* – including Ranajit Guha, Chatterjee, Chakrabarty and others like Sumit Sarkar who later left the collective – are Bengali intellectuals. Of course, one can object that *Subaltern Studies* has not only drawn into its fold intellectuals throughout

---

27   Chatterjee 2006, pp. 12–3.

India, but abroad as well, in Latin America and Africa, and there were always a few English contributors to the early volumes. But this is hardly a crippling objection; the originality of *Subaltern Studies* is traceable to a specific historic-geographic location. Here it ought to be salient that Bengal was not only the first major province of the former Mughal empire to be colonised by the British, but that, in Tapan Raychaudhuri's words, Bengalis – more expressly, middle-class Bengalis – were the first 'Asian group of any size whose *mental world was transformed* through its interaction with the West'.[28]

Their political perspectives were simultaneously transformed by their location on the cusp of massively traumatic fissures – one thinks now of 1905 and 1947 and the experiences of those two partitions of the province of Bengal, but also of 1971 and the war of independence in the former East Pakistan that resulted in the birth of the new nation state of Bangladesh and the accompanying sorrows of a large refugee population in Calcutta (Kolkata) and elsewhere in West Bengal.[29] One also thinks of a settling of political accounts in India itself with, for instance, the far-too rigid and bureaucratised Stalinist Communist parties, one of which, the CPM, had ruled West Bengal for almost 34 years until recently defeated at the polls, and the other, the CPI, which had earlier compromised itself via its complicity with the Emergency rule of Indira Gandhi in the mid-1970s.[30] There is also the legacy of the Naxal insurrections that had resulted in a broad stalemate, if not urban guerrillaism without a coherent ideology or programme by the early 1980s.[31]

Like their counterparts of the Scottish Enlightenment, Bengali intellectuals have been immensely productive of new social thought. Bengal's continued positioning on the forefront of methodological and theoretical innovations is a function of its history, and the intellectual vitality that began with the earliest encounters with European thought continues to this day. Ironically, then, at least one contributory factor to the immense output of intellectual innovation by Bengali intellectuals is explainable by the impact of the Enlightenment on Bengal, far greater than elsewhere in India, and by the ex-centric positioning of Bengal vis-à-vis the intellectual map of the world since the late-eighteenth century. So that while middle-class Bengalis experienced the 'furious oscillations

---

28   Raychaudhuri 1998, p. ix, emphasis added. This passage is cited in Chakrabarty 2000, p. 4, although it is unclear if Chakrabarty draws out the full significance.

29   Some of the implications of refugee settlement are discussed in Chatterjee 2004; the issue of multiple partitions and 1971 is discussed in Chatterjee 2010.

30   For example, see the discussion in Sarkar 1997, pp. 83ff.

31   Vanaik 1990, pp. 177–95; Bannerjee 1984; Ray 1992; see also Guha 1997b, p. xi on the Naxalite uprisings and the emergence of Subaltern Studies.

of modern times'[32] to which the Enlightenment gave expression, they did so as outsiders, even somewhat despised ones. The attraction towards, and the animus against, the Enlightenment are not hard to understand.

Some of the foregoing might also explain the early receptivity to Gramsci's work and its adoption into the history courses taught by Susobhan Sarkar at Presidency College, Calcutta,[33] where Ranajit Guha was a student of his. Intellectual filiations of this sort are immensely important at certain critical junctures and form part of any routine discussion of the works of European intellectuals and should form part of the discussion of Third World intellectuals as well. Intellectual history is not simply an exclusive prerogative of metropolitan intellectuals. In this case, a history with a very specific regional location can nonetheless illuminate some of the broadest global currents of reform and revolution, the relationship of the Third World and the West, losing neither the sense of the larger shaping forces, nor the concrete experience of individuals.[34]

A further set of affiliations, this time with Said and Gayatri Spivak in the US, signified a crucial development through which Subaltern Studies could position itself as an influential branch of the larger field of postcolonial studies. The 1986 publication of Chatterjee's *Nationalist Thought in the Colonial World*, which applied the Saidian view, expressed in *Orientalism*, about the 'overwhelming nature' of post-Enlightenment colonial power-knowledge to the case of the colonial Indian intelligentsia – no doubt a position Chatterjee arrived at as part of the re-examination of the limitations of the earlier Gramsci-influenced Subaltern Studies' commitment to studying peasant rebellion (alluded to above) – completed a rather felicitous circle: from Foucault's views on modernity to Said's views on colonialism, and now a comment on the possibilities and limitations of alternative modernities produced under colonial conditions.[35] The publication in the following year of *Selected Subaltern Studies*, including essays from the first four volumes of *Subaltern Studies*,[36] with a foreword by Said and an editorial note by Spivak, signified the moment of triumphant arrival.

Henceforth, subaltern historiography could lead a schizophrenic double life: in India itself as part of a field of debates about politics, gender issues, economic development and social justice, and in the US as part of postcolonial

---

32   Napoleon Bonaparte, cited in Rothschild 2001, p. 1.

33   De 1976; De 1983, pp. 3–15. For more detail on this subject, see Chaturvedi 2000, p. viii.

34   See Jameson 1993, p. 172, for a discussion of the different temporal and spatial frames needed for this.

35   Chatterjee 1986.

36   Guha and Spivak 1988.

studies with its interest in migrancy, fragments, and so on, the Third World intellectual as a sort of mildly insurgent presence within the solid structures of a still-Eurocentric academy. The combined influence of Said's literary humanism, French poststructuralism, and US postcolonial theory with its play of desires and the seduction of the commodity, and their combined lack of interest in exploring any social reality in historical depth, has no doubt taken its toll: Chakrabarty's claim to be 'writing some very particular ways of being-in-the-world', the Bengali past, 'into some of the universal, abstract, and European categories of capitalist/political modernity',[37] perhaps represents one result of this sort of immigrant positioning in the US academy. This could probably only happen in a country where postcoloniality can be represented as immigrant presence.[38]

In the US, where the term has the densest network of references, it more often than not refers to the impact on identity politics of the post-1965 immigration from outside the old European heartlands. That the massive new immigrant presence after 1965, coinciding with the end of formal colonialism in parts of Asia and Africa, the Vietnam War, and a phase of pitiless counter-revolutionary vigilantism by the US in Latin America and by its proxies in Southern Africa, should generate fields of study and polemics is not surprising. That postcolonialism should ultimately come to stand for a forgetting of those worldly processes of war, revolution and counter-revolution is perhaps the mystery. 'Post' in this sense might also stand for a successful operation of containment and redirection. Aijaz Ahmad's point that this intellectual formation has gone through two stages – 'Third-World cultural nationalism' followed by a postmodernistic celebration of 'fragments'[39] – is useful. But both actually co-exist, partly because of the very real disciplining that has made them the only apparently safe expressions of a politics that no longer speaks its name, and partly because the size and composition of the 'fragments' has become indeterminate. Indeed, when Chakrabarty states that we are in an 'unhistoricisable ... now',[40] he most probably means to refer to things and people that have fallen into this liminal zone. One might argue, then, that there are not two stages, but rather the progressive realisation of the potentialities of the first in

---

37   Chakrabarty 2000, p. 255.
38   See also Harootunian 1999, p. 142, on the armies of enthusiasts located in English departments who jumped on this bandwagon to show how literature, and more so culture, was complicit in imperial and colonial oppression.
39   Ahmad 1992, pp. 209–10.
40   Chakrabarty 2000, pp. 112–13.

the second. Ahistorical 'culture' and indeterminate 'fragments' express, as it were, the postcolonial *Geist*.

For Said, ironically, the initial interest in promoting Subaltern Studies was that here was a group of intellectuals from an ex-colony who represented a revolution in historiography, and were attempting to restore to Indian history the important role of the 'urban poor and rural masses'.[41] He must have recognised the broader political necessity of doing so at a time when the struggle for self-determination of the Palestinian people was heating up, and that anti-colonial and post-colonial struggles for social justice were neither things of the past nor mere discontinuous fragments. Perhaps he was also expressing this hope in the face of the inability of his colleagues in English departments, not to mention the number-crunching social scientists and post-foundational economists, to do so. What he did not recognise, and 1995 was quite late in the day already, was that the focus on the properly insurgent urban poor and rural masses that informed early Subaltern Studies had already been practically jettisoned!

1.2   1989 and All That

The shift in critical registers during this passage – from capital and its colonial manifestations and class struggles (albeit in inchoate forms) to a critique of Enlightenment rationality, from colonial archives read against the grain to literary sources (plays, novels, biographies, autobiographies) that afforded those with the proper language skills access to ways of being in the world that did not replicate a Western paradigm, 'from multinationals to Macaulay',[42] and so on – encountered, in the expansion of English studies, and more broadly cultural studies, in the US during the 1980s, one set of structural conditions of enablement. Part of this shift, Harootunian argues, is connected to a broader restructuring of the US academy, a function of the failure of area-studies to fully meet the challenge posed by Said's critique of knowledge production that was in collusion with imperialism, and the simultaneous overpopulation of the canonical fields of literature ('how many books on Keats do we need and what's left to edit?', he asks),[43] and 'Western civilization'.

All this created an opening that was seized by academics located outside those canonical fields, often in English departments, Said's home base, to

---

41   Said 1995, p. 5.
42   Sarkar 1997, p. 108.
43   Harootunian 1999, p. 142.

reposition themselves vis-à-vis this classical canon, and towards the literature produced under colonial and postcolonial conditions. One of the effects of the emphasis on English literature, and especially nineteenth-century writing, has been to give special prominence to the literature on India, especially Bengal, and to Indian Anglophone writers,[44] or translations from the vernacular into English for the purposes of illustrating certain aspects of those conditions. In retrospect, it is ironic that pioneering theorists like Césaire, Fanon and Lumumba, who from the vantage points of former French imperialist strongholds in Africa and the Caribbean made extensive and often militant interventions on issues of politics and culture in colonial and postcolonial contexts, have only belatedly if at all (in the case of Lumumba) been absorbed into the postcolonial canon, and often at the initiative of those opposed to the directions taken by postcolonial theory.[45] Nor yet have they, and other theorists like Memmi and Senghor whose interventions were perhaps less militant, provided the impetus to the development of a 'full-scale theory or discourse of postcoloniality' in either France or Western Europe,[46] although this may be changing as the impact of postcolonial studies diffuses outwards from the metropolitan Anglophone (especially the US) academy.

Be that as it may, one of the exceptions to the largely literary focus of postcolonial studies, Harootunian notes, has been Ranajit Guha's 'stable of subaltern specialists' who nonetheless have largely if not exclusively focused on Bengal.[47] Even here, one might argue, the force of our times has made itself felt in that the literary has trumped a more classically socio-political focus, literary texts becoming the privileged way into indigenous histories suppressed by the prose of world history and its narrative of progress.[48] One of the effects of the institutional capture of the field of postcolonial studies by

---

44   One of Aijaz Ahmad's points in his argument against Third World literature as a 'national allegory' was that a good deal of vernacular writing on South Asia that does not deal with either colonialism or nationalism as its primary registers never makes it to Anglophone metropolitan audiences; Ahmad 1992, pp. 102ff.

45   See, for instance, the discussions in Parry 2002, pp. 141–4, and Brennan 2002, pp. 190–2.

46   Harootunian 1999, pp. 142–3.

47   Harootunian 1999, p. 142. This is no longer entirely the case, of course, but see my arguments above.

48   Guha 2002, chapter 5 in particular, being only the most prominent recent example. The work itself recapitulates many of the ideas found in his earlier work of 1997, *Dominance without Hegemony*. What the later work adds to the earlier one is an extended polemic against Hegel's World-History in favour of a sense of historicality informed by a poetic sensibility. That particular emphasis is buttressed in the later work by recourse to the philosophy of Heidegger and his student Hans-Georg Gadamer, notably absent in Guha's

English literature and cultural-studies departments has been that the 'more modest associations with chronology and temporality', political economy and materiality that one would expect to see in any field that organises its own historicity around the term 'colonial' have been subordinated to a new identity serving an 'entirely new or different field of study and research', in which the emphasis would be textual, semiotic and generic.[49] The privileging of novelistic or poetic narratives had already been anticipated in Benedict Anderson's *Imagined Communities*,[50] which forged the connection between novel, modernity and nation, but this tendency found its full expression in Bhabha's *Nation and Narration*,[51] where the English model was 'forcefully restated' and the act of 'writing the nation' was made to look 'inconceivable without appealing to the novelistic narrative'.[52]

If US area studies 'inaugurally and lastingly' suppressed the role of capital in its curricular and research paradigms to emphasise the role of culture, and cultural difference, on the road to political and economic modernisation, postcolonial studies has followed suit, insisting on presenting capital as a mere narrative category that subserves a Western historiography of progress, as sheer economism and homogenisation of history. These gestures have become an intrinsic part of the post-foundational rhetoric of postcolonial studies.[53] There is a historic background to these gestures that needs to be remembered. Organisations like the Social Science Research Council and the Rockefeller Foundation poured money at home and abroad into the social sciences to prepare them for combat against the Cold-War enemies of the United States. During the Vietnam War, the Ford Foundation tried to support the study of Southeast Asia at Kyoto University, and had also been active in India and Indonesia.[54] Capital could hardly be framed for critical study in this environment, which was directed to combat the twin evils of Marxism and communism. Now that area studies has itself become a casualty of the post-Cold War moment, it would appear that the field has been vacated for a post-foundational postcolonialism to occupy, even if in the process capital is not actively

---

earlier work and thrown in, one assumes, to reinforce the focus on the writings of Rabindranath Tagore.

49   Harootunian 1999, pp. 130, 141–2.

50   Anderson 1983. It should be said in Anderson's favour that a greater sense of the materiality of political economy is retained than in the later postcolonial work on the subject.

51   Bhabha 1990.

52   Harootunian 1999, p. 143.

53   This is most eloquently expressed in Prakash 1992b, pp. 13–20, for example.

54   Harootunian 1999, p. 132.

promoted in academic study, but more or less silently suppressed as the central, indeed foundational, category of modern life. Some of the corporate concerns of the Cold-War moment have, in their turn, made their way into the rhetoric and positioning of postcolonial studies.

In fact, post-foundationalism seems to be a response to 1989, or more so 1989–91, the moment of collapse of the entire system that revolved around the Soviet Union and its satellite states. This is how I read Stuart Hall's statement that the world has become post-colonial in some very profound way and any interpretation of the contemporary world in post-foundational terms is also postcolonial.[55] The foundation for social thought in the post-war period seems to have been provided not so much by the colonial system or its historical aftermath as by the opposition of social forms that underpinned the Cold War: the US as the representative of capitalism in its global extension and the Soviet Union as the representative of something else seen to be in opposition to it. When the opposition disappeared, the foundation went with it, and we were dumped into a post-foundational world. This might lend some credence to Robert Young's point that the rise of postcolonial studies coincided with the end of Marxism as the 'defining political, cultural, and economic objective' of much of the Third World.[56] It is doubtful, of course, that Marxism ever had such a defining position in Third World political economy, but the point might be the larger one that most countries, in the immediate aftermath of their political independence, had at least the semblance of a choice between the western 'free-market demand economy' or the Soviet-style command economy, or a 'mixed economy', like that of India.[57] Most, of course, had very little room for manoeuvre and remained captive to their erstwhile colonial masters, but in the conceptual field such a juxtapositioning was very important to oppositional forces. With the collapse of the Soviet system, and the headlong rush of China to embrace capital, there is effectively no choice. For all practical purposes, there is only one single global system. As Young notes, with the collapse of the Second World, the Third World itself ceased to exist (not as a substantive entity, which it probably never was, but as a kind of political position of non-alignment or neutrality), or it moved from an affiliation with the Second World to the First. That is to say, postcolonialism is the moment when the Third World embraces US-style capitalism in a fit of absent-mindedness.

Stuart Hall seems troubled by the fall-out of post-foundationalism since it brings with it a forgetting of economics altogether. Hence his argument that in

---

55   Hall 1996, pp. 257–8.
56   Young 1998, p. 6.
57   Young 1998, pp. 6–7.

abandoning 'deterministic economism', alternative ways of 'thinking questions' about economic relations and their effects as the 'conditions of existence' of other practices have failed to materialise. Instead, we have a 'massive, gigantic and eloquent disavowal', a failure of theorisation so profound and so disabling that 'much weaker and less conceptually rich paradigms' have continued to flourish and dominate the field.[58] He suggests the possibility that there is 'some conceptual incompatibility' between a certain kind of post-foundationalism and the serious investigation of these 'complex articulations', partly an 'institutional effect' of the fact that, as outlined above, 'post-colonial work' has been most fully developed by literary scholars who have been reluctant to make the break across disciplinary boundaries required to advance the argument. But one need not assume that this is an 'unbridgeable chasm' since, in Hall's opinion, 'certain articulations' are either 'implicitly assumed' or 'silently at work' in almost all post-colonial critical work.[59] But such minimalism is hardly acceptable. After all, one of the most famous Marxist theorists of our day has brilliantly combined an interpretation of literary and philosophical texts with a searching analysis, even a dramatic reconstitution, of the understanding of the relationship between culture and economics.[60] The 'mutual cost' involved in isolating one from the other is hardly inevitable. In the final analysis, postcolonialism's failure in this regard is political.

Much discussion of the economic trajectory of the world under colonial and post-colonial conditions in Marxist, and Marxist-influenced, circles has been informed by the indubitable fact that the 'economic' instance under capitalism is far more prominent and more autonomous of customary ideological dominants than in previous epochs of social production. And while capital's dynamism has had dramatic effects, in consistently promoting output and more inconsistently human welfare, it has also brought about massive and unprecedented levels of global polarisation between rich and poor countries, and now increasingly social polarisation between classes. Discussions of polarisation have also turned to its political, social, cultural and environmental effects.

---

58   Hall 1996, p. 258. What these paradigms might be is anybody's guess: since the article is directed in part anyway against Dirlik 1994, we assume he has in mind Marxism. But then nobody would argue that in the late 1980s, much less the 1990s or the 2000s, anything resembling Marxism dominates the field of postcolonial studies.

59   Hall 1996, p. 258.

60   I am thinking now of Jameson's still growing corpus of work, his recent analysis of Marx's *Capital*, Volume I, being an example; see Jameson 2011. See also Jameson 1991 and 1994 for more explicit considerations of 'economy' and 'culture'. For an extended exposition of the significance of Jameson's 'Western Marxism', see Anderson 1998.

But this is far from an economic determinism that posits either self-sustaining growth without limits once the right preconditions are met, or a notion that economics always-everywhere determines other outcomes.

Indeed, these issues ought to be front and centre of postcolonial studies, as a means for considering not only its own trajectories but the realities of the times that have shaped the formations of fields of study. The high rates of growth in the immediate aftermath of the end of World War II was accompanied for a time by a distribution of the benefits to a much larger portion of the population than ever before, and sustained by progressive taxation on the rich. Those in turn paid for investments in infrastructure, institution building, comprehensive social security programmes,[61] and geographic alliances between labour and capital that led to a phenomenon widely known as labourism, whereby political parties representing organised labour assumed some of the tasks of managing working class demands on behalf of capital.[62] Beginning in the 1970s, however, this period of buoyant growth petered out, a function of overproduction and overcapacity in the advanced industrial countries,[63] a return to high and persistent unemployment, the fracturing of the geographically specific cross-class labourist alliances, attempts to export some of the costs of the economic crisis to the Third World,[64] a stringent regime of debt-collection from the latter by banks and governments sometimes euphemistically packaged as 'structural adjustment', and ferocious attempts to push through privatisation to levels that the Western countries would not have tolerated for themselves even in their chronically crisis-ridden state.[65] The last expression of '"Third World" solidarity', San Juan argues, was in 1973 with the demand for a 'New International Economic Order' staged at the United Nations in the wake of the oil crisis of 1973, not surprisingly a failure in the circumstances. By 1982, he suggests, the 'defeat' of the Third World bloc allowed the US-led Western bloc into a campaign against global Keynesianism. Despite occasional 'success' stories, the 'Third World' as an independent actor, with its own singular interests and aspirations, has virtually disappeared from the world scene.

For our purposes, the economic boom (especially in the US) was also the period of the vast expansion of the modern university system, securely tenured professorships, recruitment of non-traditional students (both from the working class and from abroad with extensive scholarship support) and teaching of

---

61   Leys 1996, p. 173; Habermas 2001, p. 48, both cited in Lazarus 2011, p. 2.

62   Miliband 2009.

63   See Brenner 2006, pp. 34–40, pp. 151–60, for a discussion of this.

64   Harvey 1982, p. 329.

65   Chang 2002; San Juan 2002, p. 238.

non-traditional subjects, not without a great deal of foot-dragging from vested interests. The downturn, for its part, has been accompanied by the promotion of a more utilitarian educational curriculum, a stress on number-crunching in disciplines like political science, sociology and economics with no real interest in investigating the actual causes of economic and social crises. To an extent perhaps the discourses of the 'post', as Hall calls them, have preserved from a completely opposite angle the same disdain for actual investigations of the socio-economic dimensions of today's culture, accompanied by a rather 'unhealthy disrespect for evidence' that might point to certain truths, however limited and contingent, 'beyond interpretation and construction'.[66] On the other side of the world, the boom and the bust have produced the stagnation and decline in countries like India of colonial-era university structures, some of which had attained high levels of academic excellence during and after the colonial period, while glittering new private institutes of science and technology have sprung up, in part financed from abroad and sustained by contract work from western corporations.

It is in this climate that 'post' theory came to the fore and indeed to 'command the heights', however not so much, as Lazarus suggests, 'against this increasingly chill sociological [political?] climate', but as he himself notes in some sort of heady, almost delirious, disavowal of the structural conditions of its own genesis and development.[67] It is a matter of puzzlement to some that postcolonialism tends to sidestep the issues opened up by this moment of history, and that it has remained 'silent on the relationship of the idea of postcolonialism to its context in contemporary capitalism'.[68] For the most part, Dirlik maintains, postcolonial studies makes no significant attempt to address the causes of the often dire socio-economic situation of former colonial peoples with the requisite depth and sophistication. He might be alluding to structural adjustment, environmental destruction, the dismal prospects for many of the working poor, chronic and indeed lifelong unemployment, not to mention the continuing predations of brutal regimes that took over from colonial rulers and have received generous support from them – aspects of the gale of 'destructive production' characteristic of the present phase of capitalism.[69]

But if postcolonial studies is to position itself in a 'properly oppositional role', or 'survive in any meaningful way', its sympathetic critics maintain, it will need

66   Dirlik 1999, p. 287.
67   Lazarus 2011, p. 186.
68   Dirlik 1994, p. 330.
69   For a brilliant Marxist analysis of the 'waste of people' and the broader sets of disorders produced by 'contemporary capitalism', see Mészáros 1995, pp. 170–87, 701–2.

to be far more absorbed with the contemporary world, in the process developing a 'substantive economic basis' for its critique.[70] Of course, this can be only
be a beginning: after all, a postcolonial theorist like Chatterjee does claim that
people like him, who maintain a close connection to – and, indeed, live for part
of the year in – their country of origin, need to be involved in the present-day
world, actively intervene in political debates, and manoeuvre themselves in
opposition to the political and economic projects of the modern nation state.[71]
However, one would need to have exceedingly modest expectations of postcolonial studies' oppositional stances to be satisfied with this. Liberal and even
conservative critics can have an oppositional stance towards present-day economic trajectories, especially those associated with cronyism, speculation, and
so-called vulture capitalism. Right and left can agree on many things, save the
essentials. At minimum, it seems the postcolonial theorists' disavowal of the
totalising impulses of Marxism are at the root of some of their unease with
it, rather than its supposed 'economistic, ideological and...reductionist'
aspects.[72] That these have been part of the history of Marxism, alongside more
sophisticated understandings of the inter-permeation of the economic and
the cultural, need not be denied.[73] What is missing, however, in postcolonial
studies, besides the 'imperative to historicise', is the equally critical imperative
to totalise. As Brennan notes, the postcolonial critic's project is always some
variant of a sweeping claim 'to break from historicism', and 'escape totalising
thought'.[74] An oppositional stance can certainly be built from elements such as
this, but what sort of opposition?[75]

Recall that in Chatterjee's narrative, the move away from the original
emphases of Subaltern Studies on rural class struggles was launched during the late-1980s, from about 1987 and more so from about 1989,[76] and that
it was the result of a collective rethinking of the limitation of that approach.
Questions arise when one takes into account the issue of timing: 1989, we all
know, is a year of some consequence, too much, so one assumes, to be men-

70   See Young 1998, p. 7; Loomba 1998, pp. 256–7.

71   Several of the essays in Chatterjee 2004 reflect this kind of involvement.

72   Hall 1996, p. 258.

73   Bartolovich 2002, p. 5.

74   Brennan 2006, p. 236.

75   As one of its less friendly critics notes, postcolonial studies has been, implicitly at least,
      complicit in the 'legitimation of contemporary forms of power' (Dirlik 1999, p. 286). But
      even assuming that there is a political spectrum within postcolonialism, it is still
      important to find out what is left out, cannot be spoken about, does not 'compute' in
      postcolonial studies.

76   Chatterjee 2006, p. 12.

tioned *en passant* in an account that largely – as in Chatterjee's – focuses on an
'internalist' evolution of an intellectual-academic project launched a few years
earlier (the early 1980s), but not so early as to have escaped the initial rum-
blings of the epochal events to come. For at last in 1989, and more in the years
1989–91, a whole host of local discontents, advances and retreats – described
above – had their global denouement in the collapse of the geopolitical divisions inaugurated by the Revolution of 1917 and its aftermath. The reverberations of those massively significant events were felt most acutely, needless to
say, in the Eastern bloc countries and the Republics of the ex-Soviet Union,
which experienced the shock of entering the capitalist world as now-under-
developed, virtually Third World entities. But the reverberations were also felt
strongly throughout the former colonial world and particularly in countries
like India that had developed a close relationship to the ex-Soviet Union. A
strange symmetry asserts itself in considering the moment of departure and
the moment of closure of a historic epoch encompassing the years 1917 to 1989.

The Russian Revolution taking place on the peripheries of the European
world certainly poses the question of an affinity with the anti-colonial movements already under way in the colonial world in the aftermath of World
War I.[77] The revolution was, as Eagleton describes it, 'ectopic as well as
untimely', pitched on the narrow ground between 'Europe and Asia, city and
country, past and present, the First World and the Third'.[78] It faced two ways:
towards Europe where it could be read as the harbinger of revolutions in the
economically more advanced countries that would consolidate it and lead to
world communism, and towards Asia, and the colonial world, where it could be
seen as an anticipation of anti-colonial revolutions. The lead up to the Russian
Revolution had also provided people in both Europe and the colonial world a
significant corpus of Marxist literature on imperialism, its relationship to capital and global polarisation that is relevant to our day. Lenin's *Imperialism*, for
example, had spelled out the link between capitalism and imperialism, the latter as the 'superstructure' of capitalism,[79] by which he meant that it was at the
same time a form of capitalism (the economic element), a form of class activity of the bourgeoisie (the social element), and a form of the state (the political
element), the whole being 'inseparably combined'.[80] It involved an immense
development of cartels, trusts, big banks, all implying the concentration of
production, the seizure of the sources of raw materials (at home and abroad in

---

77   Brennan 2006, p. 309, n. 13.

78   Eagleton 1997, p. 53.

79   Lenin 1963 [1917], <www.marxists.org/archive/lenin/works/1916/imp-hsc/>.

80   Lefebvre 1957, p. 236, cited in Labica 2007, p. 227.

the colonies) by the trusts and the financial oligarchy and the economic division of the world,[81] whether through the physical conquest of less developed
regions or their subordination through the mechanisms of finance, gunboats
and Maxim guns. Lenin also pointed to the profound hypocrisy of the 'most
liberal and radical of politicians in Great Britain' transforming themselves
when they became governors of India into 'real and proper Genghis Khans'.[82]
Echoing Marx and Engels, he noted the limits of 'bourgeois civilisation' taking
on respectable forms at home but going naked in the colonies.[83]

To arrive at our own day, the 'manic triumphalism' that accompanied the
collapse of communism coincides with a period when capital revealed prodigious new powers, penetrating and colonising the last precapitalist enclaves
(Nature and the Unconscious),[84] but also unleashing in the process brutal
regimes of accumulation based on sweatshops and Victorian-style discipline
in factories located in export-processing zones free of even minimal pretensions to regulation and organisation.[85] Capital finds itself today not only mired
in prolonged stagnation accompanied by massive unemployment and deep
cuts in wages and social welfare, but has become in the process as threatened
and threatening as it ever was during the high noon of imperialism.[86] However,
it was in the 1990s, with the slowing of growth in the core countries of capitalism, and the spectacular acceleration of growth in some ex-colonial and
post-revolutionary societies, that a momentous change, or at least the unmistakeable signs thereof, in the global distribution of capital really took shape,
giving rise to the BRICS group of nations. But these changes have come at a
price. The bold new world that the United States wished to usher in, as we now
know, has also resulted in widespread social inequalities and environmental

---

81   Labica 2007, p. 226.

82   Losurdo 2007, p. 242.

83   Losurdo 2007, p. 245. No doubt, the assumption of respectable forms at home was a
      function of the difficulty in getting away with great crimes at home, but that has never
      deterred capital from trying: in our day, the names of Exxon Mobil and British Petroleum
      might stand for great crimes of a certain order, and the whole business of 'austerity' in
      which governments collude with banks to scrounge on the biological vitality of the
      working people might stand for another.

84   Jameson 1991, p. 49. This can be summed up in two achievements: the 'industrialisation of
      agriculture' and 'the colonisation and commercialisation of the Unconscious or, in other
      words, mass culture and the culture industry' (Jameson 2002, p. 12).

85   See, for instance, Pilger 2003, Davis 2007.

86   Ahmad 1999, p. 96. This piece by Ahmad is an extended response to Derrida 1994a.

degradation, in the latter regard perhaps equalling the record of some of the former Communist countries.[87]

The spectacular collapse of communism has been accompanied not only by the equally spectacular collapse of the left in the West, particularly in its Latin European heartlands, but also by the rise of all manner of extreme right-wing, neo-fascist parties across the ex-communist countries and in the West where the weakening of left-wing forces has given 'licence to the ideologues of the far Right'. What Harvey calls 'the spatial libertarianism of market forces' has had deeply unsettling effects on the ex-colonial world, leaving for many only the 'secular spatio-temporalities of the free market' and the 'mythological time-space of religion and nationhood'.[88] Had Chatterjee's account made note of these world-shaking events in the formation of the postcolonial moment of Subaltern Studies, it might not be a stretch to assert that the neatly contained 'internalist' account would have broken down. After all, if 1917 pointed simultaneously West and East with radically different valences, so too did 1989. Globalisation, if that is how we wish to refer to post-1989, *is* the moment of difference *par excellence*, even if not in the precise sense that postcolonial theorists would have it.

A 'break from historicism' cannot, of course, excuse a randomisation of history. Postcolonial studies came into being and consolidated itself, Lazarus notes, during the 1980s in a relation of 'supplementarity' to 'post'-theory whose key positions included a hostility towards totality and systematic analysis, the adoption of epistemological conventionalism or constructivism, anti-foundationalism, and anti-humanism.[89] Relative to Marxism, we are now supposedly confronted with a critique that has been finally 'detotalised, refined, diversified, opened up to the questions of desire and intensity, to flux and signs and the multiple subject – in a word, the tools of a social critique *for today*'.[90] The refinements include a refusal of struggle-based models of politics and a preference for models that privilege 'difference', 'ambivalence', 'complexity', and 'complicity', the ensuing repudiation of Marxism, usually taking the form 'not of a cold war anti-Marxism but of an avant-gardist "post-Marxism"'.[91]

But the question that continues to pose itself is whether a critical postcolonialism can dispense with structures or foundational concepts? Critical

---

87   The market 'Utopianism' of the United States, and more broadly the Western powers, its
      limits, social and political consequences, have been discussed in depth in Harvey 2000.

88   Harvey 2000, p. 194.

89   Lazarus 2011, p. 186.

90   Cusset 2008, p. 330.

91   Lazarus 2011, p. 186.

foundational concepts – such as capital, class used not as a static sociological description, but as a relationship of forces around the production
of surplus value, and not least the concept of value itself in its historically
determinate form rather than in its transhistorical 'neoclassical' form – are
not intrinsically 'essentialist'.[92] Dirlik is right to insist that this is a 'bogeyman
designed to scare off the opposition', especially a Marxist opposition, and does
not reflect the ways in which these concepts are employed by critical thinkers.[93]
No doubt, all this is because revolutions are said to have failed, to have con-
sumed their own, and given us macabre caricatures. Some of this is true, but it
also involves serious amnesia. History will, of course, remind us that every revolution has been followed by massive counter-revolution, able to muster many
times more resources than anything a revolution could ever do. It is in this
historical context (a massively material, unmissable fact) that revolutions turn
on their own, that is when criticism from within seems to echo criticism from
without accompanied by the force of arms. No immaculate account of revolutionary self-devouring will do. Any opening to desire and intensity, to flux and
signs and the multiple subject that dispenses with the brute realities of capital,
and its counter-revolutionary tendency, can only be open to co-optation by
capital, the subject *par excellence* that in all its variety is entirely devoted to
one end: accumulation, the Moses and the Prophets.

For those who want to break from historicism, escape from totalising
thought, somehow a detotalised, refined and diversified critique of Marxism
has also ended up implicitly turning capitalism into the final, untranscendable horizon of human social existence.[94] It all came to a head in 1989, when
we were invited, in Galeano's memorable words, to the 'world historical burial
of socialism'.[95] The quickening pulse of history requiring a pugnacious confrontation with the political economies of the present seems to have elicited
a range of quixotic responses from the postcolonial theorists, who defend,
as it were, the right of social formations subject to pretentiously universalist Enlightenment designs to reject them in favour of a more authentic culture, but often in postures that appear quietistic if not entirely resignationist,

92   Dirlik 1999, p. 288.
93   Dirlik 1999, p. 288. There are by now simply too many examples of superb uses of these
      historically determinate, not essentialist, categories to give depth and political purpose to
      socio-economic analysis to continue to take this sort of labelling literally.
94   Bartolovich 2002, p. 2.
95   Galeano 1991, p. 250, cited in Bartolovich 2002, p. 2.

thereby rendering their odds of success even more insuperable than they might otherwise be.[96]

1.3   Postcolonial Difference

When Chatterjee writes that after some consideration the Subaltern Studies' focus on peasant rebellions was abandoned during the late 1980s, it was not because they had disappeared. If anything, Maoist rebellions in some sixty of India's 160 districts have intensified, seeing new levels of militant organisation. Similar trends are visible in many countries with still considerable rural populations. But now it is no longer possible to tell that story as part of the heroic resistance of a pre-capitalist community to the encroachment of an alien world of colonial capital, because by and large the subsumption of the peasant mode of production to capital is virtually complete. The peasantry – for all the predictions of its longevity – is finally disappearing into the ranks of the proletariat (a class of landless, surplus value producing workers on farms now owned or leased for long periods by transnational corporations). Class struggles – whether for better wages, a share of the resources on or under the land that people could once have called their own, or any other variation thereof – now pit workers against their capitalist employers. Of course, there is vast structural (near-permanent) unemployment, but this is part of the new configuration of the capital relation, a reserve army of often rural paupers.[97]

Their heroism and that of their ancestors seems to have spent itself in what appear as, in retrospect, futile gestures to hold back this tide. But Chatterjee's stated reason for the abandonment of the study of peasant rebellions has nothing to do with these historically significant socio-economic developments. Rather it has to do with the notion that peasant histories are 'fragmentary, disconnected and incomplete',[98] the abandonment coming just at the

---

96   The quintessential expression of this, at least among the prominent Indian theorists of subalternity and postcolonialism, is Chakrabarty 2000, but one can think of other attempts to elucidate the characteristic themes of 'hybrid, alternative' (plural) modernities, such as Chatterjee 1993, or even Ranajit Guha 1997a, whose 'Indian historiography of India' seems to have no room for class struggles. When these are discussed as in Guha's earlier work of 1983, *Elementary Aspects of Peasant Insurgency in Colonial India*, the antagonism almost always requires the presence of the foreigner.

97   For a discussion of this in relation to contemporary structural trends in capitalism and the ways in which they find their way into social theory, see Larsen 2002, p. 218 and Jameson 2011, p. 71.

98   Chatterjee 2006, p. 12.

moment when it should have been possible to start telling those histories in a less fragmentary, and more connected and complete form. In any case, why the champions of fragments should abandon a history because it is fragmentary is a mystery, unless one considers other temptations.

The study of peasant rebellions no doubt contained a Utopian surplus, a 'dream' of a revolution designed to wipe away aeons of scandalous exploitation and needless suffering, especially among those who did not go along with the reactionary historicist notion that the pain was worth it for the ultimate improvement of the human condition. That dream, one might say, died many small deaths with each encroachment of capital and each act of political repression, but its big death seems to have come with the winding down of the post-war economic boom, the determined steps taken by the leading powers and their allies in the ex-colonial countries to push through agrarian modernisation at all costs, not to mention the prodigious powers of recuperation shown by capital in its post-1989 phase to conquer every hitherto autonomous region of social life. For those who will have nothing to do with the narrative of capital's ruthless and final conquest of the world, including the last redoubts of autonomous peasant life along with Nature and the Unconscious, the temptation to shift ground in favour of studies of political spirituality, different ways of being-in-the-world, insanity, sexuality, governmentality, ethnoscapes, not to mention migrancy, marginality, fragments and anecdotes of all kinds, nicely filled out with the new buzzwords of postcolonial studies, must have been irresistible.[99] These have taken the place of peasant rebellion, which has been quietly consigned to a place of forgetfulness. Indeed, it seems the social life of the commodity is to be celebrated even as the social life of the peasantry no longer figures on the research agenda. A fragmentary history has been replaced by substantive fragments, held together conceptually by the notion of alternative, different, hybrid modernities and the framework of an institutional-realist postcolonialism,[100] coinciding with a lot of postmodernist-inspired culturalist *jouissance*.

---

99   All of these can also be studied in the framework of their relationship to different modes of production, or even to capital in its various phases from the formal to real ownership of the process of production, but that is not the postcolonial way. On the question of formal to real ownership of the process of production, see Marx 1977, pp. 943–1084.

100   On the new spirit of 'realism' in 'late' Subaltern Studies, see Sarkar 1997, p. 100; see also Chatterjee 2010, p. 298.

It was in the United States that the revised, 'late', Subaltern Studies first came to be articulated as a postcolonial project,[101] when the 'historical study of modern discourses and institutions of power in colonial India' fed into a growing literature on 'the production of hybrid cultural forms in many different regions of the formerly colonial world',[102] when a project originated in England and India by Ranajit Guha and a group of likeminded historians in the late 1970s, and developed via a close engagement with colonial-era primary sources relating to rural India, debouches into a larger, primarily US-based field of postcolonial studies. It does so from a special vantage point, the 'subaltern consciousness'. Here, the notion of a 'subaltern split' starts to assume some rather interesting new valences. Chakrabarty argues that subaltern histories will have a 'split running through them', constructed within the elements of the 'master codes' of secular history without ever granting them 'complete hegemony'. Subaltern history, Chakrabarty reminds us, remembers history as an 'imperious code' that accompanied the civilising mission of the European Enlightenment, inaugurated in the eighteenth century as a 'world-historical task', and that this history is neither 'natural' nor indeed hegemonic in the 'world of subaltern peoples'.[103] While in the colonial context the subaltern split would have referred to class issues, it was extended in the metropolitan context to rework arguments about contemporary cultures in the Western countries, instanced most immediately in the 'diasporic cultures of immigrants', but less obviously in the formation of Western modernity, 'even in its purportedly "original" form'.[104] In the process, Chatterjee explains, historical and social-science disciplines have tended to merge with the concerns of literary and cultural disciplines to 'break new ground'.[105] Here, the project of studying subaltern consciousness – a notion that can be and has been easily extended to embrace immigrants no matter how privileged – can overlap nicely with the study of US-born minorities regardless of their socio-economic standing.

And here, the 'supplementarity' of postcolonialism to poststructuralism takes a rather concrete form. That is, despite its initial reception as a form of 'apolitical idealism',[106] its hostility to totality and systematic analysis, its adoption of epistemological conventionalism or constructivism,

101 For examples, see Chakrabarty 1992, pp. 1–26; Prakash 1992b, pp. 8–20; Prakash 1994, pp. 1475–90; Chaturvedi 2000, p. xii.
102 Chatterjee 2010, p. 297.
103 Chakrabarty 2000, p. 93.
104 Chatterjee 2010, p. 297.
105 Ibid.
106 Young 1998, p. 7.

anti-foundationalism, and anti-humanism,[107] poststructuralist theory had been adapted in the 1980s to the peculiarities of the situation of the United States where class issues were seen as far less central than in either Europe or South Asia, and society itself was segmented into 'communities' and 'micro-groups'.[108] In a country that at least since the immigration reforms of the mid-1960s has seen a vast influx of immigrants from the former colonial world, any sort of emphasis on class contradiction, especially involving mostly the traditional Euro-American population, could be portrayed as a kind of 'ethnocentrism'.[109] For postcolonial studies, likewise, the emphasis on minorities, communities, micro-groups, and so on, involves playing down issues of class and nation, and a corresponding 'exaltation' of migrancy, liminality, hybridity and multiculturalism.[110]

Occurring in the wake of the more radical phase of the civil rights movement in the United States, postcolonialism arrived, as it were, at a moment when a liberal desire for formal equality (an opportunity to compete for a place at the table) coexisted with a libertarian desire for individual autonomy and freedom from constraints, coinciding in the latter aspect with the culture wars raging in the aftermath of the Vietnam War. Not so ironically, then, its critics have noted that postcolonialism has tended – in repudiating 'metanarratives', 'foundational categories', and the like, in favour of localised contingencies – to reproduce the essential lines of 'liberal and . . . libertarian empiricism', or a 'fetishised narcissism of small differences'.[111] That is, at least, one aspect of the narrative of arrival.

It is difficult in the context of all the valences – historical, theoretical, political – of postcolonialism to accept Peter Hulme's assessment that the term 'postcolonial' is (or should be) a descriptive, not evaluative, term.[112] Perhaps this is an opening to consider the kind of triangulation that Cusset employs for 'cultural studies': to paraphrase the Surrealists' formula, he states, cultural studies could be defined as the 'chance encounter between a recent British Marxist apparatus and a French theoretical umbrella, in the arena of American leisure

---

107   Lazarus 2011, p. 186.
108   Whether this is plausible in one of the most industrialised and capitalist countries in the world is debatable, but on the role of the impact of immigration on the question of class politics in the US, see the invaluable Davis 2000.
109   Cusset 2008, p. 134.
110   Lazarus 2011, pp. 186–7.
111   Dirlik 1999, p. 288; Harootunian 1999, p. 141.
112   Hulme 1995, p. 120. This is the case even leaving aside the question of whether there is description without evaluation, especially in such a contentious and politicised field as postcolonial studies.

culture', although on a 'less than sterilised operating table'.[113] Postcolonial studies can then be represented as the less-than-chance encounter between Third
World anti-colonialism and American cultural studies under the protective
umbrella of German phenomenological existentialism reworked by French
poststructuralism and thereby given its detotalised form, all taking place
within the sanitised precincts of the US university campuses.

   In privileging culture in the above sense – particularly cultural heterogeneity and 'hybridity' – in the readings of contemporary migrations and metropolitan settings, there might be an implication that a 'contrasting homogeneity'
might have existed in the past. Young suggests that the histories of slavery,
indentured labour and political exile refute such an idea.[114] At the same time,
the tendency towards an emphasis on heterogeneity or 'hybridity' ignores the
extent to which the contemporary cultural scene is marked by 'cultural, ethnic
and racial essentialisms',[115] or at any rate the tendency is to pass over these
essentialisms with a light touch within the cultural geography of nation states,
while emphasising 'hybridity' and the like in an immigrant context.[116] The indeterminacy of the 'fragment' noted earlier is most likely a function of the issue
of scale in the passage from one domain to the other. The privileging of culture over political economy was anticipated, as noted, by 'area studies', whose
essentialisms postcolonial studies would almost certainly repudiate. Arguably,
by a circumflex motion, culture has made a turn to history, minus a detailed
engagement with political economy, and with every potentiality of replacing
recognised essentialisms with unrecognised or denied variants.[117] The exemplary place accorded the novels, plays and short stories of the writer Pramodya
Ananta Toer in Benedict Anderson's account of the unfolding of Indonesian
nationalism, is also present in the works of the Subaltern Studies postcolonialists where one finds an exalted position for religious ritual, the novel and

---

113   Cusset notes that cultural studies initially came from Great Britain and the Centre for
      Contemporary Cultural Studies, founded in 1964 in Birmingham, and was inspired by the
      works of Hoggart (1957) and Williams (1961), both of which dealt with the 'traditions and
      cultural resistance of the British proletariat' (Cusset 2008, p. 133). For a brief overview of
      British cultural studies, see Turner 2003.
114   Young 1998, p. 6.
115   Dirlik 1999, p. 289.
116   This might be the point that Boehmer is making when she refers to the neglected
      'homogeneities', the 'binaries' that persist beneath the challenge to western dominance
      (Boehmer 1998, p. 20).
117   The manner in which *the* Muslim community is portrayed has definite essentialising
      potentialities, but this can be presented as a 'strategic essentialism', although in that case
      one might have to wonder what the strategy is. For example, see Chatterjee 2004, p. 126.

poetry in the making of Indian nationalism, all of which mark, as it were, the peculiarities of a national or – more likely where a subcontinent like India is involved – a regional formation, essential signifiers of cultural authenticity and (post)colonial difference.

If the genesis of any significant development and movement in the domains of ideas, politics, economy and culture can be traced to particular historical-locational factors, their continued import rests on the larger fields of concerns and interests they tap into. Subaltern Studies has had an impact not only on the Western academy, but also across Latin America, Asia and Africa.[118] This has been attained not by micro-studies or micro-histories, charming as those might be, and not by anything that might be construed as an empiricist 'defence of the fragment', but instead by engaging epochally significant bodies of theoretical thought. The attraction of the earlier Subaltern Studies' essays and monographs on peasant rebellions and insurrections lies not in garden-variety sociologies of peasant struggles, but in the centrality of Gramsci and the category of the subaltern. Later, the Marx-Heidegger dyad, around which Chakrabarty, for instance, organises his *Provincializing Europe* (undoubtedly the most important work to emerge out of the postcolonial phase of Subaltern Studies), corresponds to the two political registers in which the politics of the ex-colonial countries can be represented in universalist terms. This is ironic when one reflects on how vehemently Chakrabarty himself, and his colleagues-in-arms, polemicise against universalism and in favour of the many ways of being-in-the-world. The engagement with Eurocentric pretensions on the requisite levels of sophistication and scale, while made possible by extensive and intensive mining of major bodies of European thought – fully acknowledged by all the major theoreticians of postcolonialism – also makes possible a confrontation with, for example, the ideological legacies of Hegel and Weber. Therefore, any attempt to assess the import of postcolonialism requires going well beyond a provincial to a global archive of knowledge, informed centrally by European and, indeed, Eurocentric thought.

---

118   I have already referred to the Latin American example: for instance, Mignolo 2000. Of particular interest might be the chapter 'Are Subaltern Studies Postmodern or Postcolonial? The Politics and Sensibilities of Geohistorical Locations'. On the impact of 'Oriental import' into Latin American postcolonialism, see Vieira 1999. Studies of indigenism and the uprisings of indigenous peoples in Central America seem to draw inspiration from Ranajit Guha's *Elementary Aspects*, as James Scott suggests in his cover blurb to the 1999 Duke University Press edition of the book. Lee examines the influence of Ranajit Guha's 'On Some Aspects of the Historiography of Colonial India' on the African subalternist historiography; see Lee 2005, pp. 1–13.

The key terms of postcolonial studies (like Eurocentrism, colonialism, universalism, and so forth) are animated by debates that originated in the global moment of modernity and require thinking in large historically determinate abstractions.[119] Their vitality rests on the political moments outlined above, and by enabling conditions and opportunities intrinsic to actually existing globalisation, by revisions to immigration laws in Western countries for holders of general currency (like doctorates from major Western universities) that enable these individuals to secure employment in a global workplace of ideas, and to opportunities for publication in major outlets, some of which have been started by the same people.

Needless to say, in considering the histories of slavery and indentured labour, not to mention migration and exile, violence and resistance, and strategic political alliances of all kinds in the context of empires and nation states, the primary debate is not about 'homogeneity', the 'drive for shallow homogenisation', the 'totalising viewpoint of nationalism' and variants thereof *versus* 'heterogeneity' and the 'potentially richer definitions that a fragmentary point of view' might afford.[120] Other more pressing issues come into focus, namely, the political economy of capital, both in relation to its earlier forms, which gave rise to colonialism, and its contemporary forms of neoliberal globalisation. Common to both variants is the 'millennial toil' of countless numbers, the scandalous wasting away and destruction of human life to feed the engines of capital accumulation.[121] There is no formula involving postcolonial difference, or the 'irreducible heterogeneity of *différance*',[122] that can capture this continuous and continuing reality. *Pace* Stuart Hall, we have not moved from colonial difference to postcolonial *différance*. If difference refers to the entrenched structural properties of capital – its tendencies to separate, fragment, alienate, exploit, create societal crises of all kinds,[123] 'infinite divisibility of social relations',[124] and so on – then perhaps deferral should refer us to the question of overcoming. In fact, it should pose the question of a revolution that will have to attack head on the challenges created by the mode of production that has dominated social life for several centuries now, and that in its erratic

119   A practice not always adhered to; a casualty, one imagines, of the kinds of polemics postcolonial thought is drawn towards. This will become apparent in Part III.

120   Pandey 1991, p. 559.

121   Jameson 1988, Volume II, p. 162.

122   Anderson 1983, p. 50.

123   Smith 1990, p. 64.

124   Jameson interview, in Buchanan 2007, p. 36.

progress has created massive productive forces that should have enabled us to banish hunger and privation, exploitation and oppression of all kinds. That such issues are still with us – more urgently than ever – is perhaps testimony to both the inventiveness of capital itself and the failures, often tragic and grotesque, of past revolutions. But this is not to suggest that the latter have been wiped off the agenda and that we are now free to indulge the 'joyous affirmation of the play of the world and the innocence of becoming ... without fault, without truth and without origin',[125] the seduction of the commodity, and so on. These are exercises in futility.

---

125   Derrida 1978, p. 292.

Situating Postcolonial Studies

The preceding pages have tried to develop an overview of what we now understand by postcolonial studies with some careful attention given to global historical conditions and conjunctures. What follows in this part is an attempt to
place key terms like postcolonialism, Eurocentrism and universalism within
a set of historical coordinates, linking the Indian experiences of colonialism, decolonisation and economic development to each other. The different
moments of anti- and post-colonial thought constitute a broad zone of engagement that properly grounds the condition of possibility of postcolonialism
as understood in the preceding pages. In launching this line of thought it is
necessary to point out that the postcolonialism familiar to the metropolitan
academy is only the latest moment, and is by no means an exclusive representation of postcolonial thought, broadly conceived, past or present. Not only
has the specific Indian variant of postcolonialism had a complicated evolution out of Subaltern Studies, but it has also emerged from an involved engagement with ideas associated with modernisation and forms of populist thought,
even if that particular genealogy would be unrecognisable as such to postcolonialism's metropolitan adherents and interlocutors, or, indeed, would be of
little interest to most of them. Of course, this could be a function of the loss
of interest in history, particularly in that of the ex-colonial countries, even as
'breaking-down-area-studies' rhetoric flourishes. In order to correct this historical amnesia and myopia, a more complete, if still somewhat schematic,
consideration of the different moments of postcolonial thought will be necessary in order to illustrate their history and dynamics, internal and global, the
conditions in which they took shape, persisted, or gave way to other forms.
The point to remember is that these are not autarchic developments within
specific countries in relation to specific colonial experiences alone – although,
as mentioned at the outset, a proper historical grounding *is* important. Rather
they should be conceived of as forms of thought and action embedded in
the complex forces of the history of the second half of the twentieth century.
And so, the argument here will have two reference points: one, a history of
what might broadly be termed postcolonial thought in India; and two, a set
of political-theoretical coordinates within which Subaltern Studies-inspired
postcolonialism has framed that history and its own position.

2.1   Definitions: Colonialism, for Example

Whatever the other valences of postcolonialism, the point of departure has
to be an understanding of what is meant by colonialism. After all, crucial to
the whole project of 'unthinking' Eurocentrism,[1] and provincialising Europe,
which postcolonial studies sets forth as its main goals, is the issue of alternative and 'hybrid' modernities that result when aspects of European modernity
are introduced elsewhere under *'colonial conditions'*.[2] That is, the world is neither programmed to follow the European path, nor is it therefore somehow
to be considered defective. In the Indian context, colonialism in the common
parlance refers to the period of British rule, which began piecemeal in the
1760s and ended formally in 1947. The East India Company, chartered by Queen
Elizabeth on 31 December 1600, had been trading with various principalities
in the Indian subcontinent and apparently doing quite well by its sharehold-
ers for many decades before acquiring any sort of territorial aspirations. The
transition from trading company to Company Raj was triggered by a variety of
global and local factors – the silver famine, the disintegration of Mughal power,
Anglo-French rivalries from North America to South Asia, the rise of new principalities, especially the Marathas and Mysore under Tipu Sultan challenging
the Mughals and the British for a major share of the considerable wealth of
the subcontinent.[3] After massing armies throughout the subcontinent and following numerous pitched battles, from the last third or so of the eighteenth-
century to the end of the second decade of the nineteenth-century, the British
had not only acquired considerable territory in Bengal, but had also defeated
their European rivals the French, not to mention Mysore and the Marathas,
successfully occupied important arteries of trade, major centres of both artisanal and agricultural production, and gradually but systematically imposed
their own legal and administrative framework on the subcontinent, which
they welded during the decades that followed into an empire with its capital
first in Calcutta and then in Delhi.[4] In general, since the period of British rule
over India is referred to as the colonial period, what aspects of it are the keys
to the definition?

Often colonialism is narrowly understood to refer to the conquest by
European nation states of polities located outside 'Europe'. Deciding where

---

1   Shohat and Stam 1994.
2   Chatterjee 2006, pp. 12–13.
3   A compact textbook on the history of the East India Company is Lawson 1993.
4   The defeat of the forces of Mysore under Tipu Sultan by the East India Company army, led by
    Arthur Wellesley, is graphically described in Jasanoff 2005.

Europe ended and where non-Europe began could be at times a tricky business, as in the case of the Russian empire of the Tsars, or the Ottoman Empire,
but it was often accomplished with some degree of arbitrary finality by choos-
ing a mountain range or a body of water that could stand as a dividing line
when a surrounding ocean did not quite provide the line of demarcation.[5]
This was the predominant form when theories of imperialism and colonialism caught up with history, perpetuating two myths: one, that colonialism
required a Europe-Other binary; and two, that it had a cultural dimension,
which acted as a justification for the colonising venture.[6] At the simplest level,
this has allowed for a definition of colonialism that simply subsumes the prior
presence of Europeans in foreign waters to the subsequent completed form.
Thus, in Stuart Hall's definition, 'colonisation' is 'more' [less?] than direct rule
over certain areas of the world by the imperial powers. It signifies the 'whole
process' of 'expansion, exploration, conquest, colonisation and imperial hege-
monisation', which constituted the 'outer face' of European and then Western
capitalist modernity after 1492. The formulation is question-begging enough to
be useless for most purposes of scholarly definition, since colonisation seems
to include 'colonisation', but the notion of an 'outer face' of European modernity is interesting enough to debate. Does this exclude the colonisation of one
European country by another (for example, of Ireland by England)? After all,
Engels observed in a letter to Marx of 1856: 'Ireland may be regarded as the first
English colony and as one which because of its *proximity* is still governed in
exactly the same old way, and here one can observe that the so-called liberty of
English citizens is based on the oppression of the colonies'.[7]

By the same token, it would seem that cultural distance is not particularly
useful in defining colonialism either. As Cleary points out, the 'thesis' that
Ireland was an English colony does not at all rest on the assumption that the
country was somehow, 'culturally or otherwise', 'outside of Europe' and hence
part of the 'Third World'.[8] The major social, intellectual and cultural transformations that shaped Western Europe's society over several centuries – the
Reformation, Counter-Reformation, the Enlightenment and French repub-
licanism, the Industrial Revolution, not to mention German Romanticism –
were, as Cleary notes, 'decisive to the development of modern Irish society'.

---

5   Lewis and Wigen 1997; Kaiwar and Mazumdar 2009.
6   See, for example, the discussion in Kadam 2006.
7   Engels, cited in Deane 1991, pp. 118–119; Cleary 2002, p. 120.
8   Cleary 2002, p. 105. I did not know that being outside of Europe was necessary to be part of
    the 'Third World'.

The usefulness of the Irish example is that it puts paid to two rather unfortunate effects of conventional nationalist and postcolonial thinking. One is the continuation of the metageography of Inside/Outside that has not only inspired colonial-era ideologies (like Orientalism), but also the more contemporary notion of different regimes of truth in Europe versus the Outside (non-Europe). The other is a notion of modernity as always already inherent in Europe and its imposition on the Outside under 'colonial conditions'. Ireland – fully a part of Western European history and civilisation – was nonetheless a colony of another Western European country.

Can the argument about colonisation rest on foreign occupation, that is, the origins of the occupiers outside the pre-existing polity that they occupy and later administer? If that were so, it could be argued that India had been colonised many times before, and the Mughals could then be said to have preceded the British as a colonial power. While the Mughals may have originated as a self-consciously foreign occupation force, over time at least the ruling family became indigenised in a number of ways. But more significantly, the economy was not systematically subjected to the interest of an external metropolitan power that structurally subjugated and derived vital economic benefits from its relationship to the occupied land. Whatever the sources of inspiration for Mughal identity, courtly etiquette, dietary preferences, and so on, the 'economy' they presided over was centred in the subcontinent, and more so as time passed. Much of the surplus extracted as revenue was disbursed in the subcontinent, albeit often in the form of conspicuous consumption.[9] In many ways, therefore, over time the Mughals came to call Hindustan – the name they gave to the northern part of the subcontinent – their home.[10] They retained their Persianate, Afghani and Turkic connections, not only in the forms of elite culture, but more narrowly in terms of the administrators, advisers and institutional arrangements for surplus extraction, for instance, the *mansabdari system* and the jagir, whose Turkic inspiration has been commented on by a number of historians.[11] The resulting fusions, syncretism, and so on, are now generally referred to under the umbrella term, Indo-Islamic.[12]

The key point for my argument is that Hindustan was not subsumed to an external metropolis either in the ancestral lands of the Mughals (located in

---

9   This subject is extensively discussed in Raychaudhuri 1982, pp. 261–307, particularly pp. 288ff.

10 This point is nicely made in a recent book, Dalrymple 2008.

11 Habib 2000; Lapidus 2002, pp. 369ff. Perry Anderson goes so far as to see the Arab *iqta* as the predecessor of both the Ottoman *timar* and the Mughal *jagir* (Anderson 1974, p. 500).

12 A brief exposition of this term can be found in Bose and Jalal 1998, pp. 24ff.

present-day Uzbekistan), or any intermediate locus of power and attachment (either in Persia or Afghanistan). Even if one were to assume that this may have been Babur's original intention at the time that the Mughal empire was founded in the early sixteenth century, his successors had neither the means nor the capacity to do so.[13] The tendency to use the term 'colonialism' for foreign occupation is in fact loose and not particularly useful, either from a theoretical or historical perspective.

To cut a very long and complex story short, the most useful point of departure for our purposes is the development of capitalism. As the capital form developed, unevenly to be sure, in the European countryside, there was a drive to overcome the precapitalist modes of production that had been hitherto dominant. Historically, this has taken the form of a *separation*, the wresting away of the sources of subsistence, including land and other natural resources, from immediate producers by a class of people who were able to concentrate the often scattered holdings of the former and thus undertake large-scale production, often on an improved technical basis. For in agriculture unlike industry, small-scale production based on peasant possession of land and other means of production could not be overcome by starting parallel enterprises producing similar goods more efficiently at lower prices. As an indispensable condition of production and always in short supply, land had to be acquired by one means or another. Marx describes the entire process of eviction by legislation, force and fraud that cleared the English countryside for capitalism to take root,[14] summarising this process thus:

> To unleash the 'eternal natural laws' of the capitalist mode of production, to complete the process of separation between the workers and the conditions of their labour, to transform, at one pole, the social means of production and subsistence into capital, and at the opposite pole, the mass of the population into wage-labourers, into the *free 'labouring poor'*, that artificial product of modern history.[15]

Marx is clear that this process was attended by a great deal of violence, written in the 'annals of mankind in letters of blood and fire'.[16] As he puts it, if

13   So this is not a question of intentionality, but actuality.
14   See Marx 1977, chs. 27–9; see also Wood 1998, pp. 14–31, for an extended analysis of the forms taken by agrarian capitalism.
15   Marx 1977, p. 925.
16   Marx 1977, p. 875.

money 'comes into the world with a "congenital blood-stain on one cheek" ',[17] then capital comes 'dripping from head to toe, from every pore, with blood and dirt'. There was no peaceful evolution of capital in Europe out of 'the womb of feudalism'.[18]

Colonialism, then, follows a similar logic, the wresting away of the resources of immediate producers, now by conquest, occupation and brute force, and the transfer of land and other means of subsistence either into the hands of colonial rulers in areas dominated by plantations, or into the hands of a class of landlords who paid sizeable rents to the colonial state in return for their land deeds. In his writings on the conquest of India by the British, Marx emphasised the plunder of the subcontinent and its similarities to the 'brutalisation of Ireland'.[19] If the 'dawn of the era of capitalist production' was driven by the accumulation of resources on a worldwide scale, based in part on 'the discovery of gold and silver in America, the extirpation, enslavement and entombment in mines of the indigenous population of that continent', not to mention the conversion of Africa into a 'preserve for the commercial hunting of black skins',[20] its further consolidation required that the 'treasures captured outside Europe by undisguised looting, enslavement, and murder' flow back to the mother-country and be *turned into capital there*'.[21] There were, in brief, two aspects to the whole situation: the quantitative (the accumulation of resources, primitive or original accumulation in the Marxist parlance), and the qualitative (the transformation of those resources into capital, that is, into a specific social form based on the systematic competition among capitalists for raw materials and market shares). The brutality of colonialism was a direct expression of the horrors of capitalism, the 'profound hypocrisy and inherent barbarism of bourgeois civilisation' lying unveiled before our eyes, turning from its home, 'where it assumes respectable forms, to the colonies, where it goes naked'.[22]

The expropriated and subordinated indigenous elite of the various regions that came under European control had constituted the bases of their authority in the inheritance of 'ancient' cultures and states of more recent vintage, and in some cases had developed a high degree of collective consciousness

---

17   Augier 1842, p. 265, cited in Marx 1977, p. 926.

18   A view attributed to Marx by Stuart Hall. See, for example, Nimtz 2002, p. 69, citing an interview with Hall; Terry 1995, pp. 56–7.

19   Jani 2002, p. 87.

20   Marx 1977, p. 915.

21   Marx, 1977, p. 918, emphasis added.

22   Marx 1974, p. 324.

of their privileged place in the natural order of things. The discourses developed to symbolise this order, and the nostalgia produced by its passing, have left powerful legacies for some – the more conservative or romantic strands of anti-colonial and post-colonial thought. New battles have reached back for slogans and ideas extractable from old, now defunct social orders. To an extent, it might be useful to think of the 'bourgeois' revolution in Europe – at least in its negative valence as the overthrow of the old feudal regimes – and colonialism abroad together, even if the economic outcomes were vastly different in the short term. Counter-revolutionary thought in Europe, often based on an integralist Catholicism strongly supporting the concepts of 'social order and hierarchy',[23] has its anti-colonial reflections in the nostalgia for the Rani of Jhansi, or the Ranee [sic] of Sirmoor, or even for the Mughals, or at least some form of untouched, authentic civilisation. The themes of 'social order and hierarchy' recur in postcolonial thought in ways that might not be easily recognised in relation to its European counterpart, coming to the fore perhaps in the quest to locate the roots of an anti-colonial nationalism uncontaminated by the force of a colonising presence,[24] or in the unity of a community established by recognising the rights of subsistence of all sections of the population, 'albeit a differential right entailing differential duties and privileges.'[25] The lords in their palaces and the peasants in their thatched huts, all in their proper place before the advent of colonialism.

In thinking through the structural coordinates of colonialism, what is distinctive about British rule over the Indian subcontinent, for example, is not simple occupation or even outside rule, but that over time, at least until the interwar years, India was firmly tied to Britain as a subsidiary, dependent appendage of an outside power. With the development of modern technologies of transport, communication and banking, among others, it became possible to subsume the economy of a distant occupied land to that of a metropolitan ruling power.

With the advent of industrial capitalism and its ever-more insistent demands for resources for domestic industries, and for markets to which the resulting manufactures could be sold, the subsumption became ever tighter. A well-known Pakistani sociologist, Hamza Alavi, used this type of economic relationship to formulate his idea of a variation on the classic theme of capitalism, namely, the 'colonial mode of production'. Alavi saw the internal disarticulation and external articulation of the colony as the keys to his definition

---

23 This is presumably what Charles Maurras's Action Française, or René Guénon, and the Catholic Right in Europe more generally, was about; see Lardinois 1996, pp. 28–30.

24 Harootunian 1999, p. 130.

25 Chatterjee 2000, p. 17.

of this particular 'mode of production'. That is, the internal connections of differentiated economic activities in the colony are disrupted, and henceforth get disconnected from each other, and are only completed through links to economic activities in the colonising country.[26] The main sectors of the local economy are often more strongly linked with the metropolitan country than with the rest of the colonial economy. The circuit of value had to be completed via the metropolis, at least in key economic arenas such as agricultural production.[27] Over time, as new sectors of the colonial economy developed – for example, jute or cotton textile manufacturing using modern machinery, the expansion of railroads, or plantation-based tea production – these were also tied into colonial interests, either via the monopolist ownership by expatriates from the colonising power who were free to repatriate their profits to the home country; differential tariffs on imported machinery, spare parts, yarn or cloth from England, which kept domestic production dependent on metropolitan suppliers; guaranteed rates of return on invested capital; or a near-exclusive reservation of the best quality produce for export to the metropolitan market.[28]

This type of economic linkage is the nub of a proper definition of colonialism. A *specific kind of economic geography – not mere external occupation –* is implied in the definition. This echoes the experience of other colonised lands. In Ireland, for example, there was an exceptionally rapid and violent effort to control and redirect the society and economy in the interests of the colonisers. Thus, at the beginning of the seventeenth century, as Cleary points out, Ireland was 'a lightly settled, overwhelmingly pastoral, heavily wooded country, with a poorly integrated, quasi-autarchic and technologically backward economy'. By the century's end, all of that had changed, as the country was reoriented towards English mercantilist interests and concurrently integrated into the world of North Atlantic trade.[29] In all the colonial sites in the emerging Atlantic world, this 'precociously accelerated process of modernisation' was accompanied by what would 'ultimately' appear, from the perspective of a more fully developed nineteenth-century industrial capitalism, as 'economic and legal-juridical "archaisms"' – for example, the landed oligarchic estates system in Ireland, the Spanish *encomienda* and *hacienda* systems in South America, all of which came to be regarded as impediments to 'proper'

---

26   Alavi 1975, pp. 33–5; Alavi 1981, pp. 10–12.
27   Marx makes these points at great length. See, for example, Marx 1974, pp. 313ff. For a more recent study relating to the Arab countries, see Mansour 1992, pp. 44–5.
28   On some of the economic mechanisms, see Headrick 1988, pp. 85–6, pp. 365–8.
29   Cleary 2002, p. 112.

capitalist development.[30] Critical here, of course, is the fact that the process of transformation of productive forms, based on inter-capitalist competition, which ultimately drove the industrial revolutions, was absent in the colonial cases. Whether the colonial regimes were protecting their own settlers or their indigenous *compradors*, the situation that evolved was one of an initially rapid transformation of the external form of the economy, a dependent link to the metropolitan economy, and subsequent stagnation, which in effect condemned these societies to economic backwardness, endemic poverty and periodic famine.[31] One could find in colonial India any number of agrarian and industrial archaisms similar to the Atlantic cases – *zamindari* landlord-ism, indentured labour in plantations, debt-bondage of ostensibly free peasants by methods resembling serfdom,[32] or even the monopolistic practices of jute manufacturers, protected by the colonial state, that contributed little to overall capital accumulation in India.[33]

Other features may supervene, of course: cultural trauma,[34] racial domination, cultural, religious and linguistic diversity in territories joined by the colonisers for administrative purposes, and so on. More critically, economic backwardness may have manifested itself in the persistence of different modes of production articulated in such a way as to perpetuate it even after the removal of the colonial presence. Economic backwardness may also have been perpetuated by the persistence of a large and illiterate peasantry governed by 'traditional authorities' who might have been put in place by colonial authorities in

---

30   Cleary 2002, p. 112. Cleary quotes Whelan to suggest that Ireland did not have the 'long conditioning' process of other, non-colonised, European medieval societies. This is hardly the case: when capitalist development arrived, it was usually violent and rapid; see, for example, Weber 1976, for the case of France.

31   See, for example, Davis 2001; Kaiwar 2012. I refer to colonial-era famines in India as 'famines of structural adjustment'. On acute food shortages despite growing acreage under cultivation, see Roy 2002, p. 112.

32   Prakash 1990a.

33   Sethia 1996, pp. 71–99.

34   Dalrymple, for instance, hints at the loss of confidence in the existing educational system of classical Persian-language learning after the crushing of the 1857 uprising; see Dalrymple 2008. Cleary refers to the impetus lent to 'cultural nationalism' by the collapse of Gaelic as the spoken language of the people and its replacement by English in the wake of famine and demographic collapse. But in India, there was more restructuring than collapse, the rise of standardised vernaculars, a vernacular printing press and cultural nationalism(s) based on the rise of a lively literary production in the standardised vernacular. Not all colonial cases are identical in this respect: the proximity and relative demographic proportions of coloniser and the colonised play a significant role.

the interest of indirect rule,[35] a weak indigenous bourgeoisie unable to carry out transformative tasks and often subordinated to the aforementioned 'traditional' authorities, not to mention a 'scarcity of intellectuals', a legacy of the miserliness of colonial rulers in investing in modern educational curricula.[36] Of course, these are matters of gradation rather than absolutes, symptomatic features of social and economic backwardness and not entirely unique to colonies. Lenin would have recognised many of these features as integral to the late-Tsarist social formation in Russia, and Gramsci would have recognised the same in Sardinia before and after the Risorgimento.[37] What then defines a colonial situation in this gradation is a specific variety of economic dependence made possible by a political system of direct or 'indirect' rule in which the key levers of the economy are very much under the control of the colonising power, a structure within which the multiplier effects of economic activity accrue not to the colony, but to the colonising power, overdetermined by the replacement of indigenous systems of customary practices, law and administration by those of the colonisers' country, and some attempt to combine the former and the latter in ways advantageous to the latter, and some or all of the cultural features, including the linguistic trauma described above.[38]

Significantly, Alavi does not emphasise the violence involved in foisting this dependency on the colonised subjects as a distinctive feature of the 'colonial mode of production'. Indeed, this does not seem to be a significant part of Indian writings on the colonial mode of production or its variants. It is arguable that the 'transition' to capitalism was just as violent and far more comprehensive in the colonisers' own countries, for example, the United Kingdom. One thinks now not only of the enclosure movement in England, of which Marx wrote so eloquently in part VIII of *Capital*, Volume I, but also the Highland Clearances in Scotland.[39] Whether these events were any less violent than the conquest of Bengal, or the imposition of the Protestant Ascendancy in Ireland,

---

35   Heussler 1968; Nicolson 1969, pp. 124–79.

36   Parry 2002, p. 136.

37   Lenin 1974, pp. 245–7, for example; or Gramsci 1971, pp. 95–8.

38   David Lloyd suggests that the objective of colonialism was 'normally' the wholesale transformation of the colonised society, including the 'eradication of its indigenous structures of feeling' (Lloyd 1999, pp. 2–11). How this was to be accomplished, except as a consequence of institutional changes in systems of property, law and administration, not to mention exclusion from resources needed for a decent social life, to name only the most prominent mechanisms used by colonial rulers, is hard to see. It is most doubtful that colonisers, even the most resourceful, could have direct access to indigenous structures of feeling.

39   Marx 1977, pp. 873–940; Richards 1982.

ought to be a matter of sober debate rather than nationalist assertion. And whether the violence of the initial incorporation under metropolitan rule is invariably a predictor of the future status of the area brought under control is also debatable. By the 1840s, when Scotland was becoming, in Cleary's words, 'an advanced industrial and urban economy', Ireland remained an overwhelmingly agrarian country locked into a 'sustained economic crisis', culminating in the Great Famine, the last great subsistence catastrophe in Western Europe.[40] In this case, Scotland became a part of the metropolitan economy rather than remaining a colony.

With those contrasting cases in mind, the key to *colonial* capitalism is most likely to be the absence of the full development of the capital social relation that characterised advanced metropolitan structures of production. In the colonies, vestiges of older social relations were maintained to ensure a degree of dispersed social control and governance on the cheap, whose main aim was resource removal and market monopolisation. The Indian debate on this issue coincided with and was part of a much wider debate about the modes of production in colonial (and 'peripheral' capitalist) societies, that pitted the likes of Sweezy, Frank and Wallerstein on one side, and Laclau and Brenner on the other.[41] The former equated the penetration of market relations into a society with capitalism *per se* and argued that the necessary focus of attention needed to be on the 'unequal exchange' that obtained between 'core' and 'periphery'.[42] The latter tended to argue that the expansion of capitalist relations did not necessarily mean that the colonies were fully capitalist. In Brenner's summary of the latter position – a very influential one following a similar intervention in the European debates on the transition to capitalism – the argument of the former 'fail[ed] to take into account either the way in which class structures, once established, will in fact determine the course of economic development or underdevelopment over an entire epoch, or the way in which these class structures will themselves emerge'.[43]

Both the mechanisms of colonial extraction of resources and the establishment of a caricatural version of capitalist social relations were well known to Marx, who alludes to India under East India Company rule as a battlefield between the Lancashire industrial interests and the 'moneyocracy' and

---

40   Cleary 2002, p. 119. On the famine, see Kinealy 1994, written on the eve of the 150th anniversary of the famine.

41   Sweezy 1942; Frank 1969; Wallerstein 1974; Laclau 1977; Brenner 1977. For the Indian debate, see Bhaduri 1973; Alavi 1975 and 1978; Banaji 1978; Patnaik 1976 and 1978; Washbrook 1981.

42   On the 'unequal exchange' thesis, see also Emmanuel 1972; Amin 1978.

43   Brenner 1977, p. 27.

'oligarchy' of the Home Counties, who were more interested in extracting a goodly amount of revenue from India. Thus, writing in the early 1850s, he notes that the charges of the so-called Home Establishment amounted to three percent of the considerable agricultural revenue extracted from India, along with an additional 14 percent on interest charges for the Indian debt and dividends paid to Company officials and stockholders, along with military charges amounting to 66 percent. This contrasted with the expenditures on public works, which amounted to no more than three percent of the total revenue. Similarly, both zamindari and ryotwari land settlements in India were compared to, what came later to be known as, 'semi-feudal' relations involving a great deal of extra-economic coercion structured into the production relation, not to mention swingeing levels of debt imposed by moneylenders unrelieved by any form of capital investment.[44] The resulting structures were most likely sufficient to produce the vast economic polarisation of the metropolis and colony in terms of the productiveness of the overall social economy, per-capita output and income. What is not being argued for here is some vague transhistorical tendency of all societies to develop autochthonously towards the capital social form – a historical teleology built into much dependency theory – a potentiality that is then brought to a crashing halt by being 'incorporated' into the European economic circuit.[45]

---

44   Marx 1974, pp. 314–5, pp. 317–9.

45   It might be useful in considering the issues of social form versus the long-term dynamic to think of the related categories of capital and capitalism. Capital is, of course, the term Marx preferred to use, and it refers to a *relationship* between the immediate producers and the owners of the means of production, that is, the mediation of the primary production relationship via markets and money as immediate producers are required to constitute their means of subsistence by selling their capacity to labour (labour power) to owners of the means of production. Capitalism would then refer more broadly to the establishment of this relationship across a wide spectrum of social formations in the early modern and modern periods. In such a social formation, Marx argued that production took the form of a generalisation of commodity production, and a resulting vast multiplication of commodities that could be sold for a profit, the exchange ratios being dictated by the 'socially necessary labour' (the average time needed to produce in a society at a given level of technological development) contained in them. Colonial societies, with exceptions, for all the reasons spelt out above, did not necessarily incorporate the full capital relation across a wide spectrum of production, remaining more or less arenas of supply of cheap raw materials for metropolitan industry or markets for industrial manufactures, under the domination of others where such a relationship had advanced from a 'formal' to 'real' stage. For a full explication of these terms and the capital relation, see the above referenced 'Appendix: Results of the Immediate Process of Production', in Marx 1977, pp. 943–1084.

On the question of polarisation, Angus Maddison's calculations reveal that from the beginning of British conquest of territories in the subcontinent in 1757 to independence in 1947, per-capita income increased by no more than one third on the most optimistic reading, while in the United Kingdom itself there was a 'tenfold increase in per-capita income' over the same period.[46] In the agrarian sector, particularly food production, there was actually a secular downturn in output by something like 0.18 percent per annum between 1891 and 1941, and for the period 1921–41 it was around 0.44 percent per annum at a time of rapid population growth.[47] The more conservative sections of British opinion tended to blame the Indians for the economic calamities and regular famines that punctuated the period of British rule, culminating in the double strike of the 1896–97 and 1899–1900 famines that took around ten million victims.[48] An editorial in *The Times* noted, for instance:

> But for their listless acceptance of the worst miseries in the hand of fate, India would ages ago have been fertilised by a system of irrigation, and saved almost from the possibility of Famine. The Natives are one of the most improvident as well as helpless races on earth.[49]

Critical voices within the colonial administration knew better. Many of the small irrigation works that dotted the Indian countryside, especially in areas where monsoon run-off could be diverted to fields, were allowed to fall into disrepair, while the colonial administration concentrated on showpiece large-scale irrigation works.[50] Sir William Stampe, architect of several of those irrigation projects in Northern India, warned of the serious technical and environmental problems arising out of what he thought were issues endemic to the colonial administration's implementation of those works, particularly in relation to drainage, rising water-tables and soil salinity.[51] Others pointed to

---

46 Maddison 1971, p. 23, available at: <www.ggdc.net/maddison/>.

47 For details on regional declines in food production, see Roy 2002. For aggregate and district-wide figures on 'availability and productivity', see Blyn 1966, Tables 1.1, 1.2 and 5.3.

48 The 1896–97 famine took up to 5.1 million people, and the 1899–1900 famine up to 4.4 million. See, for example, Maharatna 1996, p. 15; Seavoy 1986, p. 242, Fig. 10; Visaria and Visaria 1983, pp. 530–1, App. 5.2. Two of the best regional studies of famines in India are Satya 1997 and Navtej Singh 1996. Far better known in the West is Davis 2001, which contains chapters on India, Brazil, China, Africa and Southeast Asia.

49 *The Times*, 23 January 1877, cited in Davis 2001, p. 450, n. 116. Similar or worse stereotypes were attached to the so-called 'potato-eaters' of Ireland.

50 Hardiman 1995, pp. 185–209.

51 Stampe 1944. See also Gilmartin 1995, pp. 210–36; Whitcombe 1995, pp. 237–59.

chronic problems of underinvestment in agriculture and fixed capital,[52] and
to extractive practices that amounted to mining the fertility of the soil and
the biological vitality of India's workers. Later works have borne out these
judgements.[53]

One would have to conclude that the failure of colonial 'improvement' or
'development' had little to do with the remnants of an age-old culture dragging
down the priceless gifts of European civilisation. Rather, colonial 'improvement' was not designed to succeed. As with other bureaucratic centralist forms,
aggravated by its own peculiarities, the colonial version had little potential for
either local initiative or efficient top-down management. The results were pre-
dictable enough. The *fin-de-siècle* famines were something like a turning point:
British colonisers were running out of fresh rationalisations for their presence
in India. In the immediate aftermath of World War I, it became apparent that
the British were in a holding pattern in India, with the initiative slowly but
surely shifting to the other side.[54] In colonies like India – administrative colonies, as Cleary calls them, more accurately perhaps colonies of extraction or
exploitation – the metropolitan society was a mere sociological 'bridgehead'
to colonial capital, with no 'Creole identity'. When the tide of nationalist resistance could no longer be stemmed, they simply packed up and left,[55] not without some considerable last-minute damage, as we shall see.

These considerations on the structural coordinates of colonialism are
salient to thinking about some of the elements of postcolonialism that this
work will consider later. The global capitalism of the post-1848 period has been
extremely cruel. It has left most of the world with no place to hide. The descendants of the vanquished have been forced to live alongside those whose ancestors had conquered and colonised them, and whose taunts continued to inflict
a great deal of psychological damage. Prefixes like neo- and post- come into
their own in circumstances like this. In the 1950s and 1960s, in Latin America,
even without the direct territorial occupation associated with colonialism,
the term 'neo-colonialism' nonetheless acquired a resonance within the politics of the Cold War, bringing about 'a political, economic, cultural and social
convulsion' akin to the concomitant anti-colonial movements in Africa and

---

52   The implications of this are examined in Kaiwar 2000, pp. 1–49.
53   Bagchi 1982, pp. 213–14; Davis 2001, p. 307.
54   For those in search of a symbolic moment, Gandhi's switch from being an empire loyalist
     to a staunch opponent, coinciding with the passage of the Rowlatt Act in 1919 granting
     emergency powers to the government, is probably as good an example as any.
55   Cleary 2002, p. 115.

Southeast Asia.[56] All kinds of phenomena that may or may not have had any direct relation to colonialism could be subsumed under the sign of a 'post', although the historicising of the 'post' itself is often vigorously denied. Thus, in Latin America, 'transculturation', 'hybridisation' (which Vieira suggests might be 'understood as a cultural strategy to undermine domination') and 'in-betweenness' (cast as a locus of enunciation), features of Latin American society that supposedly existed long before the postcolonial acquired any sort of theoretical cachet, could be resumed under that rubric.[57] This sort of arbitrariness, while common enough, is unfortunate. One might find faint traces of transculturation, and so on, in ancient societies, but to suggest that a 'postcolonial' moment always already existed in those societies is problematic. Secondly, to assimilate the turmoil of the world over the last half century or so to 'colonialism' and its aftermath, rather than to capital – given that colonialism and its 'post' form cannot be understood apart from capital – is to add a sheerly meretricious surplus to the already 'controversial shiftiness' of the prefix 'post' in postcolonialism.[58]

2.2   Postcolonial Modernisation

The growing self-assertion of a nationalist movement in India – still inchoate in many ways, but beginning to acquire firm outlines in the course of the first two decades of the twentieth-century – set in motion substantial political reforms after 1918. Decolonisation in some form – whether full political independence, or Dominion Status in the first instance – was not only on the cards, but proceeded on the ground in slow steps, starting with devolution to elected local councils and graduating to progressively greater power sharing with elected Indian officials at the provincial and finally central-government levels, Indianisation of the Civil Service, and so on.[59] The global context in

---

56 Vieira 1999, p. 275. The prefix 'neo' was a direct reference to US domination of Latin America, which brought with it, in addition to economic control, all manner of racist overtones, along both the cultural and somatic axes.

57 Vieira 1999, p. 274. Vieira attributes the popularisation of these terms to the Brazilian Silviano Santiago in 1978, long before Homi Bhabha made them popular in the Anglophone world.

58 Bhabha 2005, p. 1.

59 In this context, Hopkins proposes a distinction between the drive for self-government as opposed to full statehood (Hopkins 2008, pp. 211–47, specifically p. 216). Decolonisation seems to involve, in the first instance, some variation of the former, for example, Home Rule. For reasons to be discussed below, it seems to end with the latter, generally speaking,

which these significant forays into anti-colonial activism were launched
included, of course, the experiences of World War I and more so perhaps the
Russian Revolution. It is easy now to forget that the Russian Revolution had
significant resonances for anti-colonial activists in the inter-war and post-
World War II periods. Brennan reminds us that the first flush of the revolution
created a 'massive repertoire of images, tropes and vocabularies' that hovered
over everyone's thinking.[60] Facing west, the revolution represented, in Lukács's
view, the promise of 'community', the 'coming light' for Europe.[61] Facing the
colonised world, it created a political climate in which new political possibilities opened up, sowing the seeds of doubt 'in the minds of thinking people
about the validity of many things which they had accepted without question
from the West ... *quickening the pulse of the peoples of Asia'.*[62]

If external impulses acted to quicken the pulse, events closer to home were
unquestionably of equal significance. The massive famines of the last quarter
of the nineteenth century in India (alluded to above) were further overlaid
by the worldwide economic depression of the 1873–96 period, creating levels
of rural poverty, debt and endemic deprivation of basic necessities that even
colonial officials were forced to acknowledge. For example, an official inquiry
found that the weight of the average Bombay mill worker – perhaps among
the better paid of the urban proletariat – at the turn of the century was 99lbs,
and although their diet did not even meet the standard set by the Bombay
Jail Manual, the mill-workers were forced to 'save' money and send it home to

        although in the process the very geography and boundaries of the postcolonial state may
        undergo vast changes. This was the case even with a staunch Home Ruler like Tilak whose
        description of a voyage through Madras, Ceylon (Sri Lanka) and Burma (Myanmar)
        records his impressions of these regions. Tilak finds the spirit of 'hindutva' common to
        all these areas (!), but it is unclear as late as 1900 as to whether any one or more of them
        would be included in his idea of a 'Homeland'; see for example, Bal Gangadhar Tilak,
        Journey to Madras, Ceylon and Burma, translated from the Marathi and cited in Wolpert
        1962, p. 135.
60   Brennan 2002, p. 192.
61   Wiggershaus 1994, p. 178, cited in Brennan 2002, p. 192.
62   Panikkar 1959, p. 192; Brennan 2002, p. 194, emphasis added. Brennan goes on to point
        out, following Claudin, that the Comintern in its transformation into the Cominform
        developed a 'disdain' for local and national needs that alienated many activist
        intellectuals. However, he also remarks on the 'telescoping', which failed to register the
        conceptual breakthrough of the early Communist International. The point is easily lost
        within the 'end of history' scenarios following 1991 that tend to obliterate the impact of
        the Russian Revolution on the histories of colonial peoples.

keep their holdings intact.[63] A rapacious social order, sandwiched between the relentless demands for revenue by the colonial state and for interest payments by the money-lending capitalists, and the need to hold on to even an exiguous parcel of land in the event of unemployment or old age forced workers into the syndrome of overwork and underconsumption.

As in the case of their Latin American counterparts of a century earlier, it might be true to say of the emergent South Asian political elite that many if not all of their struggles that resulted in the independence movement were motivated as much by a fear of what would happen if the masses revolted as they were by dissatisfaction with imperial control. Concerned to insure against the prospect if not the looming certainty of such insurrection, and rather like the Creole elite of South America, the nationalist leadership of India seem to have concluded that the best course of action would be to take direct control of government.[64]

Some of the features of Creole nationalism, which Cleary alludes to, had their counterparts in India, although some were specific to the local situation. In 'many' instances it seems the attitude of the Creole elite towards Spain was indecisive, even after they had seized control from royal governors in the early nineteenth-century, and it was only the restoration of the Spanish monarchy in 1814, after the end of Napoleon's occupation of Spain, and its decision to return to the *status quo ante* that pushed many of them into opting finally for independence.[65] War and revolution, nearly a century later, may have played a similar role, quickening the pulse and hardening the political resolve. The British colonial government's decision to employ emergency powers after World War I to arrest and try *in camera* anyone suspected of political terrorism – the so-called Rowlatt Act – finally pushed Gandhi from loyalty to empire (and perhaps some vague commitment to Home Rule) to a more uncompromising stance for *Swaraj*.[66] It must be remembered that what sent Gandhi back to India from South Africa in 1915 was the development of a 'violent anarchist movement' directed against colonial officials and their proxies in the rural areas. While he may have believed, in all sincerity, in *ahimsa* and *satyagraha* as absolute principles, as the very 'breath of life', as he declared, he was also honest enough to confess that he placed it before the Congress and the country

63   Kooiman 1983, pp. 136ff.

64   Cleary 2002, p. 117.

65   Burkholder and Johnson 1994, pp. 290–334; Cleary 2002, p. 117.

66   Vohra 2001, p. 126.

as 'a political weapon to be employed for the solution of practical problems'.[67]
The practical problem in question was precisely an insurrectionary movement
with anarcho-communist tendencies.

In 1947, India became independent, but not before a bloody Partition had
taken place, to the satisfaction of some of the departing colonial officers for
whom the prospect of relocating units of the colonial army to Pakistan – with
the possible support of elements within the newly formed state of Pakistan –
was not too far-fetched. This was the Viceroy Wavell's so-called 'breakdown
plan' for the withdrawal of the British Army and officials to the Muslim provinces of the Northwest and Northeast of India, in the face of considerable agitation against British rule in 1946, leaving the rest of the country to the Indian
National Congress.[68] It should be pointed out that the seamless transition from
British to US dominance that characterised the situation of many ex-colonial
countries, including the white-settler Dominions, was not entirely replicated
in India, although the situation in Pakistan was rather different.[69]

Notwithstanding the fantasies of extremists in the British military, I think it
is fair to say, based on the Indian experience, that the process of decolonisation begins not just when the colonising power starts pulling its troops and
administrators out, but when the integral relationship of domination begins to
break down. In general, decolonisation has been a long and drawn-out process
in which the push for full and formal independence – the formation of new
nation states, forms of development characterised by the growth of indigenous
capital, and the disengagement from disarticulated relations – can be seen as
the final phase.[70] In the Indian case, this could be traced to the immediate
aftermath of World War I, although very few at the time would have visualised
an early exit for the British. Any definition of postcolonialism must refer to this
historic process of at least a formal reversal of the colonial relationship, and a
form of thought and action that attempted to chart a course that would repair
the harm caused by colonial rule. This involves, at minimum, addressing the
legacies of maldevelopment, the disarticulated economic relationships that

---

67   Speech at the All-India Congress Committee Meeting, Wardha, 15 January 1942; Gandhi
      1958–94, Volume 75, p. 220.
68   The best detailed history of this period is still Sarkar 1983. Sarkar concludes that this is
      evidence of 'the desire in some high official circles to make of Pakistan an Indian northern
      Ireland' (Sarkar 1983, p. 422).
69   Hopkins 2008, p. 247.
70   I agree with Stuart Hall's characterisation of the long drawn-out nature of the process
      and the combination of political and economic imperatives that guide it (Hall 1996,
      pp. 247–8).

originated with colonial rule and a critical engagement with the neglect during colonial rule of education, housing, welfare, women's rights, not to mention invidious laws, the use of racialising, ethnicising discourses directed towards the colonised population and specific groups therein.

With reservations that will vary by country, it should be possible to find agreement with Lazarus when he states that we must decisively register the 'sheer, irreversible advance' represented by decolonisation in the post-war years.[71] Notable among the achievements were the 'articulation and elaboration' of a national consciousness, the mobilisation of a popular will and the 'tempering' of this will in the 'fire of anti-colonial campaigns' for national liberation in the face of the hugely repressive response of the colonial governments, repressive efforts in which somehow the US managed to insert itself alongside or in place of the former colonisers. Vietnam would be the clearest case in point, but there are other more covert examples not only in the rest of Asia, but also in Latin America and the Great Lakes region of Africa. The energy, dynamism and optimism of the decolonising and immediate post-independence era have had to grapple with the enormous burdens left behind both by colonial rule and the massive disorders created during the decolonisation process. Perhaps the uneven geography of the ex-colonial world – the 'profound differences' between countries that some people have alluded to[72] – is a result of the specific disposition of forces, both internal and external, with which the transformational energies of each newly independent nation state have had to contend.

To the extent that nationalism may be considered the ideology of the classes that stepped up to assume those tasks, it is best thought of not as a restoration of the *status quo ante* in terms of law, administration and related superstructural aspects of society. In much of the ex-colonial countries, constitutions were framed so as to strike down bitterly resented colonial laws and edicts, and many equally resented precolonial customs and practices were 'officially scrapped or proscribed'.[73] The development of a secular constitution in post-independence India, for instance, along with the legal abolition of the obnoxious practice of untouchability, separate electorates for religious minorities institutionalised by the colonial rulers, not to mention the termination of princely privileges, speak to an embrace of the more progressive possibilities opened up by modernity, while developing economic policies adequate to the new order of politics. In other words, nationalism was not the restoration of a

71   Lazarus 2011, p. 3.
72   See, for example, Jameson 1986, p. 67.
73   Zeleza 2009, pp. 160ff; Lazarus 2011, p. 4.

self-identical cultural sphere disrupted by colonial rule, nor was it by and large a reactionary nativism or generalised xenophobia – although on the far right of Indian nationalism such tendencies did and still do exist. In fact, today we confront the paradox of ultra-nationalism in India as elsewhere that favours neoliberal globalisation on the one hand, and nativist and xenophobic cultural programmes on the other,[74] in an ironic recapitulation of elements of the colonial epoch.

But within the broad mainstream, nationalism represented a form of thought and a set of policies addressed to the limitations of colonial rule, its disarticulating and subsuming functions. For the leaders of the Indian National Congress, and for others including Indian economists who had mostly studied in England, the main tasks were to reconstruct the Indian economy, including the improvement of food production that had been left in a shambles by colonial mismanagement for many years, and to develop a system of education and basic industries to protect India's independence once formal decolonisation was complete. The Bombay Plan of 1944, drawn up by some of the leading industrialists of India, would be a good instance of the thinking involved in what one might call postcolonial modernisation. It visualised a doubling of the per-capita national income in 15 years through the development of basic industries, including coal and steel. Despite being drawn up by big industrialists, it was prepared to accept a 'temporary eclipse in the freedom of enterprise' in order to jump start economic development, and indeed it made a number of positive references to the 'Russian experiment', no doubt alluding to the Five Year Plans developed by the Soviet Union.[75] B.R. Ambedkar's position, articulated in 1945, that 'machinery and modern civilisation are indispensable for liberating humans from the life of a brute', would be another instance, in this case coming from a lawyer of untouchable background, who as the Chairman of the Drafting Committee of the Indian Constitution articulated many of the underlying principles of modern-day secular India.[76]

---

74   This could be a rough paraphrase of the Sangh Parivar's (BJP-RSS) position.

75   Sarkar 1983, pp. 407–8.

76   Ambedkar's advocacy of 'machinery and modern civilisation' was part of his polemic directed against Gandhi, and it appeared in a book on what he thought Gandhi and the Indian Congress had done to the untouchables (Ambedkar 1945, pp. 294–5). To an extent, perhaps Ambedkar's polemics were misdirected against Gandhi, who was both a secularist and in favour of social and economic progress. I have tried to sort through some of these issues elsewhere (Kaiwar 2007a, pp. 50–69). Krishna Kumar argues that Gandhi wished to see social and political empowerment precede and contain the development of capitalism in the interests of the people, rather than their being subjugated to unseen and little understood (from the popular perspective) forces (Kumar 1993, pp. 507–17).

Nationalists therefore had no issue with capital or modernity in the conventional sense of the development of the productive forces: indeed, they gave the impression of being all too eager to embrace both. Some nationalists may have claimed to be socialists as well, or at least liked it well enough at a theoretical level to keep their more conservative counterparts guessing. They could draw on a vast wealth of analysis coming from metropolitan critics of colonialism, who saw colonial rule itself as the source of the problems of ex-colonies.[77] A crucial part of the critique of colonialism related to the disarticulated development of colonial economies, manifested in a backward agriculture that nonetheless provided both food crops and commercial inputs (cotton, sugarcane, and so on) to industrial development mainly to the colonising metropolis, but with little in the way of fixed-capital investments in return. Much of the money extracted from agriculture went into further moneylending, or speculative activities in real estate, usury and hoarding.[78] This prompted the urgent development of policies designed to direct agriculture towards a more productive symbiosis with the urban sector, based on what Samir Amin called 'semi-autocentric development',[79] that is, economic transformation in which the immediate needs of the newly independent nation states would take priority over the needs of metropolitan ruling classes. Without agricultural growth of at least one percent per capita for several decades, Amin argued, no industrialisation, urbanisation and social development would be possible.[80] Several concurrent policies were needed to jump-start autocentric development, starting with an agricultural revolution involving appropriate kinds of equipment and inputs (water supply, fertiliser, and so on), the technical aspects of development, and economic policies of support (prices, income structures, finance, and so on), along with social administration (organisation of property, ground rents, agricultural wages, marketing, credit and producer co-operatives), a proper articulation with trade and industry, involving variously state holding, co-operation, local and foreign private capital.[81] Semi-autocentric development would then encompass 'within general parameters' a growth path that reflected previous

---

But arguably, the antinomies of Gandhi do not permit a simple conclusion, one way or the other.

77   Digby, for example, was only one in a long line of British critics of British colonialism. Digby's work was driven by his experience of working in Madras and Ceylon (now Sri Lanka); see Digby 1901.

78   Mandel 1983, pp. 502–3; San Juan 2002, p. 232.

79   Amin 1990, p. 1.

80   Amin 1990, p. 8.

81   Amin 1990, p. 9.

levels of development of the agricultural productive forces, previous levels of industrialisation, class forces, state formation, the history of colonialism, and so forth.[82]

The Intensive Agricultural Development Programme (IADP), launched by the Indian government shortly after independence to increase the productiveness of agriculture with aid and technology from the USA, together with lessons learnt during the late colonial period, was an instance of this sort of 'semi-autocentric development'. Altogether it was neither an adoption of Soviet-style planning nor a commitment to American-style capitalism, but a patchwork of pragmatic arrangements that were designed not to upset rural property holders or urban industrialists. Rather like modernisation initiatives elsewhere, whose primary objectives were to bring capital into a productive relationship to agriculture, while enabling the latter to provide food surpluses to feed a growing urban population and provide some crucial commercial inputs for national industrial development, the state was a crucial part of the initiatives. Envisaged was a kind of triangulation of state, rural and urban capital in a productive relationship.[83]

Alongside the application of a broad range of modernising initiatives – and these included basic literacy and adult education campaigns, political enfranchisement (including the vote for women), the construction and provision of hospitals and clinics, roads, and sewage facilities – there were lively debates informed by economic theories of both Keynesian and Marxist origins. In India, for example, newspapers and journals like the *Economic Weekly*, founded by Sachin Chaudhuri in 1949 and published since 1966 as the *Economic and Political Weekly* (EPW), attempted to assess the potentialities and limitations of India's development experience. Special issues devoted to Political Economy and Agriculture provided a forum for extended and detailed discussion. The founding of the *Journal of Peasant Studies* in 1973, and the *Cambridge Journal of Economics* in 1977 (begun by economists at SOAS and Cambridge, respectively), provided further opportunities for debate. Some of the economists, like Joan Robinson, who initiated and participated in these debates were British,[84] but many more were Indians trained at Oxford and Cambridge, the London School of Economics, not to mention the Delhi School of Economics founded in 1948. Indian economists were well represented on the academic staff of

---

82   Amin 1990, p. 32.

83   Tipps 1973, pp. 202ff.

84   Joan Robinson spent three formative years in India between 1926–9 before going on teach at the University of Cambridge, where a number of Indian economists wrote their doctoral dissertations under her supervision.

leading British and US universities, and indeed on the Planning Commission of India as well – one of them, Manmohan Singh, is the Prime Minister of India at the time of writing.[85] With variations, this sort of scenario was repeated elsewhere, for example, the critical work on planning and development that emerged from the Institution for Economic Management in Cairo, or the African Institute for Economic Development and Planning, and the Third World Forum in Dakar, Senegal.[86]

While for most people, modernisation was uniquely a Third World challenge – informed by their experience of colonial-era 'maldevelopment' – we must remind ourselves that it was occurring against the backdrop of several critical global developments: one was the absolute devastation during the Second World War of many of the metropolitan powers that still had colonies at the end of the war, and were forced to give them in the next two decades or so; another was the prolonged economic boom that succeeded the inter-war economic depression; and a third was the construction of welfare states in Western Europe, alongside the development of Soviet-style command economies with extensive state-directed welfare systems in place. There is no question that something resembling modernisation was also occurring in both Western and Eastern Europe, albeit at much higher levels of economic development and with a historic background of already fully capitalist social relations in the West and a Soviet-style bureaucratic centralisation in the East, and that the surpluses generated by the post-war boom sustained many of these welfare mechanisms. Thus, Habermas's point that in 'welfare-state democracies, highly productive capitalist economies were socially domesticated *for the first time*, and were brought more or less in line with the *normative self-understanding of democratic constitutional states*', seems entirely appropriate.[87] As Lazarus

85   Manmohan Singh is the seventeenth prime minister of India, the first Sikh, an economist who studied both at Cambridge and Oxford, worked for the International Monetary Fund, the Reserve Bank of India and the Planning Commission of India. His speech at Oxford on the occasion of his acceptance of a honorary PhD was not only controversial, but also a compendium of the stock themes of Indian developmental ideas in the years since independence. For a text of this speech, see <http://www.hindu.com/nic/0046/pmspeech.htm>. Many of the Indian economists who have participated in the debates about development and social justice are household names in India, none more so than Amartya Sen, whose works constitute a thorough engagement with the history of economic thought, deeply informed by concerns about social justice. A full bibliography of his works, extending back to 1962, is available at: <www.en.wikipedia.org/wiki/Amartya_Sen>. For an assessment of his work by a Marxist philosopher, see Cohen 1993.
86   Meier and Seers 1984.
87   Habermas 2001, p. 48, emphasis added.

notes, in commenting on Habermas's points, if the social gains achieved under the aegis of the welfare state in Europe or the so-called 'Great Society' in the US were made possible by a temporary truce between capital and labour, in the 'Third World' they were powered by the struggle for self-determination.[88] I think this underestimates the extent to which some form of truce between capital and organised labour was required in the Third World itself, a truce that has since broken down in ways not dissimilar to the more developed West, but also the extent to which European development was driven by self-determination against the post-war giants, the US and the USSR. However, what is critical here is that the economic boom and the profits it provided were the cushion on which all variants and manner of development agenda could rest.[89]

The first phase of post-colonial development inspired high, if in retrospect unrealistic, hopes and although nowadays this phase – dominant in the 1950s to the mid-1970s and by no means entirely moribund even now – may have been judged a failure, the reasons for that failure are rather complex. They relate very much to the ways in which a host of newly independent countries were drawn into the global economy under colonial conditions, the conditions of general economic backwardness within the countries concerned at the time of independence, and the challenges of developing a far-reaching programme of land reform or indeed public efficiency, both of which have posed insuperable problems in countries, like India, which have not undergone a social revolution and have an entrenched middle class that has grown rich through speculation, rentierism, and so on.[90] The spectre of rural uprisings and mass urban revolt has not disappeared in the postcolonial countries and has fuelled the diversion of scarce resources from development to repressive purposes, including the purchase of small arms for paramilitary forces and private armies. These conflicts have often taken priority over the interests of the often impoverished majority, and have indeed often been used as a pretext for violently

---

88   Lazarus 2011, p. 3.

89   Anti-Americanism was rife in many parts of Europe – France and Greece being only two prime examples. Judt documents the extent to which both anti-Communism and anti-anti-Communism informed a great deal of critical thought in France, perhaps an example of European non-alignment (Judt 2011). As for the Bandung 'spirit' – or whatever one wants to call it – it was sustained by a rhetorical non-alignment alongside a real anti-Communism and a looking westward for aid. Many Third World countries would have welcomed a Marshall Plan for the newly independent countries. I am indebted to Sucheta Mazumdar for drawing my attention to this. See also San Juan 2002, p. 221; Berger 2003, pp. 429ff.

90   These issues have been well analysed in the case of India; see Bardhan 1999; Chibber 2003.

suppressing their entirely legitimate demands. This situation is hardly unique to any one region of the ex-colonial world.[91]

Of course, overlying these domestic class conflicts has been the shadow of the Cold War and the self-appointed task of the Western powers, including the United States, to suppress what they regard as the faintest whispers of communism.[92] These have led to prolonged disasters and a complete collapse of the state – for example, Somalia or Afghanistan – and to new imperialist wars in Angola and Mozambique after their independence from Portugal, and in Iraq and the Balkans more recently. The contradictions emerging from this specific ensemble of conditions do not appear likely to be resolved in the near future. The social inequalities and economic inefficiencies that result from it are scandalous.

The development decades (as they came to be known) coincided with rapid population growth, which had begun in the 1920s, actually accelerated in the three decades or so from the 1950s and continued to the present, although one now sees significant regional variations. The most glaringly visible failures of the development decades are the growing numbers – if not percentage of the populations – of poor in both rural and urban areas in many countries, including ones that seemed to be tackling the challenges of development well in the immediate aftermath of their independence. In India – which has had a much harder time than countries in Southeast Asia, much less East Asia, in dealing with basic social issues – mass poverty is manifested in the desperate condition of the poor, visible even to a casual visitor, and the gender imbalances that have continued from the colonial period, and indeed have grown in recent years.[93]

While the issue of population growth and its relationship to poverty is susceptible to a Malthusian causal explanation, a better argument would identify an underlying structural issue whereby large sections of the rural economy are

---

91   Davidson 1992, p. 219; Lazarus 2011, pp. 4–5.

92   Parry 2002, p. 144.

93   'We conservatively estimate that prenatal sex determination and selective abortion accounts for 0.5 million missing girls yearly', according to Prabhat Jha, a public health professor at the University of Toronto, who headed a research team on sex-selective infanticide. 'If this practice has been common for most of the past two decades since access to ultrasound became widespread, then a figure of 10 million missing female births would not be unreasonable' (Gentleman 2006). Professor P.M. Kulkarni of Jawaharlal Nehru University points out that in the 0–6 age group, there were 962 girls to 1,000 boys in 1981, dropping to 945 in 1991, and further down to 927 in 2001. The most recent census figures indicate there are 914 girls to 1,000 boys in the 0–8 year group: <www.thehindu. com/news/states/tamil-nadu/article2074756.ece>.

locked into 'absolute surplus-value extraction' of which population growth and
mass immiseration are symptoms. Undoubtedly this would be one way to read
the 'subaltern split' – the subjection of the immediate producers in the rural
sector to the modern forces of technology and finance while they continue to
labour under social and economic constraints consistent with colonial or even
precolonial times. Technological progress *per se* does not appear adequate to
resolve that issue, since it often comes with the expropriation of the immediate producers and their relocation to cities, often to the teeming slums that
characterise the former colonial countries.

The Intensive Agricultural Development Programme's successor in India,
the Green Revolution, for instance, brought considerable growth in food output and may have contributed to ending the spectre of mass famine in India.
However, as a report of the International Food Policy Research Institute notes,
critics have claimed that Green Revolution practices – including the extensive resort to hybridised seed stock, inorganic fertiliser and pesticide use and
release into water sources, soil erosion resulting from intensive cultivation
and deforestation – have contributed to serious 'environmental degradation,
increased income inequality, inequitable asset distribution, and worsened
absolute poverty'. The Report concedes that some of these criticisms are valid
and will need to be addressed, but it also points to a tendency today to over-
state the problems and to ignore the 'appropriate counterfactual situation',
namely, what would have been 'the magnitude of hunger and poverty without the yield increases of the Green Revolution and with the same population growth?'[94] The assumption of such an 'appropriate counterfactual' in the
Report is almost certainly part of the problem of this line of reasoning. As for
the gender imbalance, that would seem to be much more than a function of
sedimented cultural structures and practices, and more a sign of the overall
failure of the state, not to mention social and political forces more generally,
to mobilise the necessary commitment for the virtually revolutionary change
that would be required to halt and reverse what is clearly a growing trend.

---

94   IFPRI 2002. The report goes on to note: 'In India, the percentage of the rural population
      living below the poverty line fluctuated between 50 and 65 percent before the mid-1960s
      but then declined steadily to about one-third of the rural population by 1993. Research
      studies show that much of this steady decline in poverty is attributable to agricultural
      growth and associated declines in food prices'. In response, it might be argued that the
      'poverty line' in India is exceedingly austere and has probably not shifted upwards since
      the 1930s, an unacceptable situation. If it had moved up as it should have, the percentage
      of those below the poverty line might still be as high as in the mid-1960s.

On this score, the blueprint set out by the Bombay Plan and its successors in the Five Year Plans have come up short. While postcolonial modernisation did represent a break with colonial-era policies, it has been plainly inadequate unless one accepts social inequalities and continued mass poverty as part of an unalterable inherited condition. Like its successors, the Bombay Plan aimed to raise per-capita income, but this is not inconsistent with widening social inequalities. Overall, the debate over the legacies of the development decades is unlikely to be resolved quickly one way or the other. Mainstream economists – like Jagdish Bhagwati at Columbia University – have judged them rather harshly as a 'bureaucratic control-infested straitjacket' that brought neither rapid growth nor social justice, leaving India with problems that it would take decades to solve.[95] Achin Vanaik, originally a Marxist trade unionist and now a professor at Delhi University, in his book, *The Painful Transition*, sees the development decades more charitably as having laid the indispensable groundwork for India's growth, but also for having achieved some political and social gains for untouchables and the poor.[96] With the usual caveats, this debate can be repeated in any number of Third World countries.

The end of the post-war boom has also meant, in effect, the end of the phase of postcolonial modernisation as 'autocentric' (or 'semi-autocentric') development. Throughout the ex-colonial world, the last quarter of the twentieth century has seen the virtual collapse of state-originated and introverted development projects – widely associated with the core principles of postcolonial modernisation. While those have not been entirely abandoned in a country like India, in the context of its somewhat managed version of structural adjustment and 'shock therapy', they now take a backseat to much more extraverted if not entirely export-led policies, and the outsourcing of key infrastructural and distributive projects to transnational corporations. A focus on issues of social justice – not least the redistribution of productive resources (most notably land), the use of a variety of state-backed initiatives including education and public health measures designed to ensure some level of enhanced socio-economic possibilities and opportunities to redress

---

95   Bhagwati 1993, p. 2. Published in 1993 – based on the Radhakrishnan Memorial lectures at the University of Oxford – after the launch of the so-called 'reform by storm' policies initiated by the government of Narasimha Rao and continued by Manmohan Singh, this book by a former member of the Indian Planning Commission has become something of a neoliberal guidebook for the study of the Indian economy.

96   Vanaik 1990 is no longer in print, but it provides perhaps the best explanation of political-economic trends in the years since independence. His second book is a far-reaching materialist analysis of the sociology of communalism in India; see Vanaik 1997.

inequalities inherited from an earlier epoch – and the rhetoric of socialism that accompanied it, has been replaced by a much more neoliberal market-first approach. Social expenditures, including price subsidies to poorer farmers have been systematically cut or eliminated from about the 1980s and accelerated in the 1990s, plunging many rural poor into severe crises of subsistence. Huge cuts in government spending were accompanied by the deregulation of all sectors, including finance, the removal of exchange controls, protective tariffs, and public ownership. Fire sales of government-owned enterprises became commonplace in many of the ex-colonial and Eastern European countries.[97] These changes, variously ascribed to some unstoppable dynamic built into capital – a kind of demiurge beyond any sort of social control – have been on the contrary, as Lazarus insists, a consciously framed set of policies designed to redress the falling rate of profits and to pass on the costs of recovery to workers and the poor in the ex-colonial world.[98]

The impact of these changes – prompted by the economic crisis manifested in a falling rate of profit after around the mid-1970s – has produced inflation without adequately stimulating the economy, 'provoking high levels of unemployment', aggravating chronic deficits in the balance of payments of the poorer countries by bringing down the price of their raw materials, while raising the price of oil and other imports. This has led to a huge expansion of the Third World international debt, which several countries were unable to repay, forcing them into default.[99] This was accompanied by a harsh new regime of debt collection and the imposition of the so-called Structural Adjustment Programmes as the precondition for new loans, which the recipient nations were in no position to refuse.[100] The new policies have generally but not exclusively followed the recommendations of multilateral agencies, most notably the IMF and the World Bank,[101] giving them a spuriously objective appearance. These changes have produced the odd spurt of jobless growth and made for feeble recoveries followed by long recessions, and since 2008 at least to what amounts to a global depression, in which many countries that had painfully

97 Saul 2001, p. 23; Lazarus 2011, p. 8.
98 Lazarus 2011, p. 8; Surin 1999, pp. 53–60. On the falling rate of profit, see Brenner 1999, pp. 64–5.
99 Larrain 2000, p. 133; Lazarus 2011, pp. 7–8.
100 Lazarus 2011, pp. 8–9.
101 For a good insider critique of the 'shock therapy' or structural-adjustment type policies, see Stiglitz 2002. For a far more excoriating study, which documents the return of massive famines or the ever-present threat of them, see Chossudovsky 1998.

bootstrapped their way out of chronic poverty have been returned to their former state.

But from our perspective, the most notable effect has been the restructuring of class relations: the breaking down of unions and organised labour, chronic unemployment for millions with no prospect of a job, draconian work regimes amounting to sleep deprivation in some factories – a form of torture, to be sure[102] – and a systematic overturning of the 'limited gains' made by working people in the post-war period,[103] a ferocious class war, in fact, but no longer fought on an exclusively national terrain.

In a country like India, where some form of input-output price protection for agriculture was considerable, their removal in part or full has led to the growing and painfully visible phenomenon of farmer suicides, not to mention levels of indebtedness that beggar the nineteenth-century levels that were condemned as cruel and undeserved punishment. Indeed, unpayable debt, often incurred to buy inputs at full market price against the backdrop of stagnant or falling prices of output for the immediate producers, is associated with those suicides. By a Government of India estimate, 200,000 farmers have committed suicide since 1987, sometimes by consuming the very pesticides that are supposed to protect their investment in genetically modified seeds and inorganic fertilisers. One might think of them as the collateral damage from 'neoliberal globalisation'.[104]

An explanation of the shift out of the development decades into neoliberal policies associated with 'globalisation' has to factor in the timing of it, for in India as in Russia, China, not to mention Southeast Asia, the initial movement

---

102 Marx argues that '[t]orture formed an organic institution in [Britain's] financial policy' in India (Marx 1968, p. 212). If so, we seem to have found our way back to mid-Victorian times, but now as a part of the labour process without apologies. Li Qiang, writing on FoxConn's labour practices in factories manufacturing for Apple computers, notes 'scheduling conflicts that disturb workers' sleep patterns'; see Qiang 2012. He also points to workers' suicides.

103 Wilkin 1997, p. 24; Lazarus 2011, p. 7.

104 The aforementioned Jagdish Bhagwati disagrees and notes that globalisation was not responsible for the surge of suicides among cotton farmers in the Indian states of Maharashtra and Andhra Pradesh: 'There are other states in India where cotton seeds have been absorbed and which are really prosperous. So you have to ask, why is it that these are breaking out? What's happening is very much like the subprime mortgages in the United States, where a whole bunch of salesmen went out and sold mortgages to people who couldn't afford them'; see <www.articles.cnn.com/2010-01-05/world/india.farmer.suicides_1_farmer-suicides-andhra-pradesh-vandana-shiva?_s=PM:WORLD>. The irony of the comparison seems lost on the admirable Bhagwati.

in this direction is usually dated to sometime in the late 1970s, with the full force of it becoming apparent in the late 1980s to early 1990s. In China, the post-1976 reforms associated with Deng Xiaoping reversed some crucial elements of the Maoist period and ushered in a period culminating in the neoliberal policies of 1992, almost exactly following the timeline of Indian developments.[105] Here again one sees the interaction of 'external' and 'internal' developments – as noted, the key developments followed the slowing of the economy in the North Atlantic countries and Japan.[106] These include the collapse of the Bretton Woods institutions, the so-called Nixon Shock, followed by attempts by the 'multilateral agencies' to impose a stricter regime of debt collection, structural-adjustment policies and finally the full blast of neoliberal globalisation closely following the epochal transformation of the political-economic landscape accompanying the collapse of actually existing communism in the Soviet Union and Eastern Europe or its adaptation in the case of China to an unfettered capitalism.

Capitalism undergoes periodic restructuring and the post-1989 moment appears to be only the latest, and if the world was not quite turned upside down, it still represented a massive tectonic shift in global economic balances.[107] These global forces reached countries whose internal evolutions had allowed for different degrees of cohesion and organised response to global forces. In the Indian case, impressive growth, which has made India the eleventh largest economy in the world, has kept company with massive levels of deprivation and poverty. As *The Hindu* reported on 15 July 2010:

> More than 410 million people live in poverty in [eight] Indian States, including Bihar, Uttar Pradesh and West Bengal, researchers at Oxford University, England, found. The 'intensity' of the poverty in parts of India is equal to, if not worse than, that in Africa. When the vast central Madhya Pradesh, which has a population of 70 million, was compared with the Democratic Republic of the Congo, the war-racked African state of 62 million inhabitants, the two were found to have near identical levels of poverty.[108]

---

105 A recent study that traces the history of economic policies in India from independence in 1947 to the present is Nayar 2007; see also Patnaik 1997, pp. 165–178.

106 For an in-depth study of the economic dynamic of the three leading economies of the post-war world up to around 2005 or so, see Brenner 2006.

107 The world turned upside down is, of course, the title of a famous book (Hill 1975).

108 <www.hindu.com/2010/07/15/stories/2010071564372200.htm>.

The shift from the so-called development decades to neoliberal globalisation coincides for all practical purposes with the dates attributed by Partha
Chatterjee to Subaltern Studies' becoming part of a postcolonial project. That
is, a momentous shift in global political economy is also when Subaltern Studies
'overlapped with and contributed to what has become known in the United
States and Britain as postcolonial studies', 'fed into' a growing literature on 'the
production of hybrid cultural forms in many different regions of the formerly
colonial world'.[109] Is this supposed to be the 'properly universalising' sense,
à la Stuart Hall, in which the 'postcolonial' can be said to be used nowadays,
marking a process that is, we are told, 'subverting' the old coloniser/colonised
binary in the new conjuncture?[110] If so, and based on the kinds of disavowals
to which Hall himself refers, perhaps we should think of the 'postcolonial' in its
uses in postcolonial studies not in terms of a properly theoretical and political
confrontation with new forms of social and global polarisation so much as a
strategy of containment, or even diversion; not so much a 'quickening' of the
political pulse as much as a slowing of it.

It should be evident from what has been said above that colonialism and
indeed the post-colonial experience of modernisation are central to a historical materialist perspective and are not regarded as some 'marginal or local'
subplot of a European transition narrative. Marx and Engels, no less than
their immediate successors like Lenin, Trotsky and Luxemburg, presented
colonialism as central to world history, and their successors in turn have done
the same for the experiences of postcolonial attempts at addressing the legacies of colonialism. In that sense, the perspective of postcolonial studies adds
nothing new, as Stuart Hall seems to imply. Colonialism can and should be
seen as indeed inaugural, the onset of a 'major, extended and ruptural world-
historical' moment,[111] with significant continuities and discontinuities in the
period after formal decolonisation. What makes it *ruptural*, however, is that
a new social form, associated with capital, becomes a worldwide reality. Its
internal dynamics, its secular cycles of growth and recession, its proneness to
crises, which give rise to periodic storms of major disruption, are inescapable,
even – and especially, one would think – for people on the peripheries of this
new social form.

If many of the central contradictions of the earlier period persist in new
forms, and indeed are 'internalised' in the decolonised society itself, this should
act as a call for a proper class analysis, bearing in mind the asymmetrical

---

109   Chatterjee 2010, p. 297.
110   Hall 1996, p. 246.
111   Hall 1996, p. 249.

power relations between the rich countries of the so-called 'global north' and
the poor countries of the so-called 'global south' that labour under the burdens
of mass poverty, hunger and deprivation, albeit in highly socio-economically
differentiated societies. It is the class issue and its roots in the capital social
form that appear to be missing from postcolonial studies. Indeed, attention
seems to have been shifted, almost deliberately, to other issues.[112] That is what
I mean by a strategy of containment, or even diversion.

2.3   Postcolonial Populism

The sense of 'uplift and regeneration' following political independence proved
to be relatively ephemeral. At most it coincided with the period of rapid economic growth in the advanced capitalist economies and in the Soviet bloc and
China, after the catastrophic destruction of the Second World War. When that
growth ground to a halt by the mid-1970s, many of the problems that the ex-
colonial countries had inherited from their recent past showed themselves to
be perduring and hard if not impossible to overcome within the parameters
of a modernisation-from-above agenda. The 'dependent and cruelly circum-
scribed positions' of the former colonial countries, or at least the vast majority
of them, were obvious to even the most superficial observer.[113] Writing in the
early 1990s, Basil Davidson diagnosed the problem in terms of the subordination of 'social imperatives', involving the redistribution of capital, resources
and services, to the class imperatives of 'elite entrenchment'.[114] The form in
which this issue is posed – that of a 'basic contradiction ... between an economic strategy of modernisation and industrialisation, and a political strategy of popular mobilisation and democracy'[115] – in effect sums up a critical
impasse in the development experience of most former colonies. Formal
decolonisation was accompanied by a class struggle in which bourgeois imperatives won out, something that the Leninist perspective of support for anti-
imperialist struggles – in effect, for Third World bourgeoisies that had often
placed themselves in the van of anti-colonial struggles – had not sufficiently
taken on board. Ironically, then, formal decolonisation created the conditions
for the consolidation of post-war capitalism worldwide and in the end prepared the grounds for today's globalisation.

112   See, for example, the discussion in Cusset 2008, pp. 131–7.
113   Lazarus 1999, p. 106
114   Davidson 1992, pp. 305ff; Lazarus 2011, p. 4.
115   Davidson 1992, p. 305.

Under the best of circumstances, modernisation theories developed in the advanced countries have operated under an overarching assumption that 'traditional' society in the former colonial countries not only survived colonialism, but has also stood in the way of a proper modernisation, and that overcoming its cultural resistance to modernisation would be a minimum precondition for self-sustaining growth. When internalised by Third World economists and development experts operating within the precincts of Planning Commissions and government bureaucracies, the need for rapid modernisation was seen not only as the unavoidable precondition for finding a proper place of respect vis-à-vis their former colonial rulers, but more generally as a requirement in a race among competitive nation states for the necessarily limited resources that would fuel development. The logic of the situation seemed inescapable. At a more subjective level, either a sort of cultural paternalism, an adversarial relationship, or 'benign neglect', has governed the relations of the ruling class to the working poor, but it has also seemed to be fuelled by some sort of a spirit of postcolonial shame at the backwardness, poverty, superstitions and general shabbiness of their countries.

All this has come in for some considerable criticism at the hands of a variety of populist thinkers. A critic of modernisation theories in India, Claude Alvares, has lambasted what he calls modernisation's 'lame hypotheses'.[116] He characterises its cardinal tenets as resting, variously, on the Harrod-Domar model in which 'saving and investment' are considered the critical element for growth (perhaps he means to suggest that these are euphemisms for exploitation in various forms), or the Arthur Lewis model to get backward economies to raise their rate of savings from five to 12–15 percent (presumably by turning the revenue screws on the working people, since tax avoidance among the wealthy is almost a religion in many countries), and the Clark Fisher hypothesis that equates economic advance with the movement of labour from primary to secondary and tertiary activity, all leavened by 'foreign aid' which was supposed to overcome bottlenecks posed by 'traditional' behaviour involving population growth and the like.[117] When these models ran aground of structural problems, the experts argued that what was needed was a change of values

---

116   Alvares 1994, p. 98.

117   Ibid. It is not clear what is meant by 'traditional behaviour' in this case. Eric Jones, for instance, equated population dynamics with rationality or the lack thereof. Europeans, he maintained, do not 'spend the gifts of their environment as rapidly as they got them in a mere insensate multiplication of the common life', which Asians supposedly did (Jones 1981, p. 3). John Hall makes a similar point via his notion of the 'relative continence of the European family' (Hall 1985, p. 131).

and attitudes. The 'most outrageous', in Alvares's opinion, was a psychologist, David McClelland, who ruled that people in the 'South' lacked 'achievement motivation';[118] in Gunder Frank's parody of this line of thinking, all that would be required for the South to become like the West was to inculcate in them the 'Protestant ethic'.[119]

Alvares suggests that development economics was nothing more than the 'mainstream economics' of the 'North' applied to the 'South' and 'though unwarranted' it took root because of the peculiar optimism of the time.[120] Its costs, although considerable at all times, seem to rise to the level of general consciousness at moments of major accidents and crises, such as the Union Carbide disaster in Bhopal. But even here mainstream economics seems to have a rationale to hand: as Adolf Jahn, the former president of the Swiss pharmaceutical company Hoffman La Roche, is reported to have said when asked about the dioxin spill from the Seveso plant in Italy in 1976: 'Capitalism means progress, and progress can lead sometimes to some inconvenience';[121] when asked about children crying in the hospitals he replied: 'It is normal: the children weep when they are subject to injections'.[122] Disasters like this will occur, Alvares argues, because the production involved is part of a schema of costs and benefits that is 'incomparable in its primitiveness', founded on a theory of man and nature that is 'an affront to human beings, particularly workers'.[123]

The charge sheet against modernisation is thus a formidable one. Modernisation is associated with 'displacement', for while it is possible to maintain

---

118 David McClelland was a prolific writer, with titles such as 1961's *The Achieving Society*, 1965's *Toward a Theory of Motivation Acquisition*, and the article of 1978 entitled 'Managing Motivation to Expand Human Freedom'.

119 Alvares 1994, p. 98. Andre Gunder Frank's own account of modernisation theories is given in his intellectual memoir, 'The Underdevelopment of Development', in which he characterises these theories as pursuing 'the neo-classical counter revolutionary, and even counter reformist, cold war ends'. This was published as chapter 2 of an eighteen-chapter festschrift for Frank; see Chew and Denemark 1996.

120 Alvares 1994, p. 98. The tendency now is to replace terms that have a political-economic resonance, such as First, Second and Third Worlds, with terms like North and South, which are said to be in civilisational opposition. The shift in the terminology reflects the moment and its use of the cardinal points is itself interesting, that is, North and South in place of West and East. North and South are as essential to a postcolonial geography as West and East were to a colonial geography, but the valences of the latter have often been quietly smuggled into the former.

121 This is quoted in Alvares 1994, p. 5.

122 For a fuller account of the disaster, see <www.varenya.hubpages.com/hub/Seveso-man-made-disaster>.

123 Alvares 1994, p. 3.

large numbers of people on the land on a relatively less intensively exploited resource base, simpler technology and a wide array of occupations and trades, this is not possible at all with the industrialisation project. The industrialisation project requiring ever-fresh resources to be brought to market has led to the appropriation of the free gifts of nature as private property: of forests, for instance, that were either 'no man's property before or were of use to millions'.[124] Of course, the entrepreneur does not create the value of the primary material, he simply appropriates it. Even the evolutionary capacities of plants, crystallised in their germplasm, is now appropriated by transnational corporations via patents.[125] Accordingly, development has become a kind of war, with governments in the South teaming up with international financial institutions to 'slaughter their own folk'. Weapons purchased by the government, ostensibly for defence, on closer inspection turn out to be intended for use in the 'development battles' that have broken out throughout the ex-colonial world. As far as consumption is concerned, the subsidies required to keep the prices of food grains within the reach of urban consumers do not help the rural consumers at all. Migration, corruption and abuse prevent the majority of the really poor even from utilising their own ration cards in countries like India.[126] Development, based as it is on 'uni-dimensional' ideas like productivity, profit and market, has produced its own pathology, commodities serving as markers of 'power, identity and meaning', filling up a kind of 'spiritual and emotional emptiness'.[127]

Indeed, the indictment does not stop at economics or the unequal struggles between small producers and giant corporations. Science itself is implicated in the violence. That is, the powers of modern science integrate property and technology to produce a scale of violence 'hitherto unknown', and this situation if continued can only increase the scale of violence and constitutes the 'most serious threat to human rights in our era'.[128]

---

124 Alvares 1994, p. 31.

125 Alvares 1994, p. 31.

126 Alvares 1994, pp. 8, 40.

127 Marglin 1981, p. 3, cited in Alvares 1994, p. 146. Marglin has contributed to a wide-ranging critique of mainstream economics from a communitarian position; see, for example, Marglin 2008.

128 Alvares 1994, p. 64. Alvares notes that his book was written as part of a project on *science and violence* carried out by Ashis Nandy on behalf of the Committee for Cultural Choices and Global Futures, Delhi, and the Peace and Global Transformation programme of the United Nations University, directed by Rajni Kothari and Giri Deshingkar. So the critique has powerful sponsors, often within the economics profession itself.

The countries of the 'global South', Alvares informs us, had gone from being 'colonised' to 'underdeveloped' (if a country registers a consistent growth pattern, as India or Brazil have done recently, then they can be seen as newly emergent or newly industrialised).[129] Their history before the age of colonialism is of no interest to development economics. They were given the option, during the Cold War years, of being either capitalist or socialist (communist), but there was not the option of being themselves. Alternatives, like the Gandhian vision, based on *'indigenous physical, spiritual, and mental resources'*, were distanced from the public debate by the imperial powers, and reflected locally by leaders like Nehru who, in Alvares's opinion, had utter contempt for their 'own peoples and *traditions'*.[130] This is the nub of much populist thought in the ex-colonial countries, whereby indigenous traditions and solutions exist that could help to develop authentic solutions to the challenges they face in a postcolonial world. However, it is in the interests of both the major powers and their dependent allies in those countries to suppress them. I would call this the spirit of postcolonial pride, rooted in the antiquity of non-European civilisations and their supposed achievements in a distant past, uncontaminated by foreign intrusion, when self-identical cultures flourished according to their own genius. This seems to be the postcolonial populist adaptation of the idea of a return to past indigenous 'sources of plenitude',[131] which were lost or partially lost when the West exploded into the East with its own designs of conquest and modernisation. Thus, it is no longer a living reality for most people, but is instead a body of thought kept alive in the writings of special people like Gandhi, and through oral traditions and the quotidian practices of the rural poor.

No recent writer has so fully embodied this traditionalist pride and indictment of postcolonial modernisation as Vandana Shiva. Rather like Alvares's, Shiva's argument traces a lineage back to Gandhi's early masterwork, *Hind Swaraj or Indian Home Rule*, written in 1909 as Gandhi prepared to return to India from South Africa.[132] Shiva has argued that Indian development has not only impoverished its rich natural and cultural legacies in favour of some notional gains in *per capita* income, but has also created a climate in which the often considerable expertise of the ordinary people, particularly in rural

---

129   However much China might fit with some of these descriptions, it is politically in a different league altogether, and as such, one would assume, it cannot be comfortably shoe-horned into the same category of the 'global South'.

130   Alvares 1994, p. 94, emphases added. So much for the Nehruvian consensus.

131   See the discussion of this topic in Jameson 1971, p. 128; Wegner 1988, pp. 58–73.

132   Gandhi 1997; see also Kaiwar 2007b, pp. 192–7.

settings, is sidelined by office-bound 'experts' and bureaucrats. The govern-ment, development economists and their fellow travellers, not to mention transnational corporations, have been charged with, among other things, bringing about the forbidding human consequences of their neglect, including the dislocation of people from the sources of their livelihood, massive injus-tices towards women, and environmental and ecological damage, all of which are implicitly understood to have been absent in traditional society.

Shiva develops her argument in a formidable series of books, from *Staying Alive, Ecology and the Politics of Survival, Biopiracy*, and *Soil Not Oil: Environmental Justice in an Era of Climate Change*, documenting conflicts over natural resources in India and the theft of India's (and other Third World coun-tries') biodiversity by transnational corporations, largely located in the West.[133] If the theft is undertaken nowadays by transnational corporations, it is nearly always facilitated by a compliant ruling class in the ex-colonial countries involved, when it is not also part of their own agenda. As the environmental and social problems associated with neoliberal globalisation have accumu-lated, Shiva's sharp and incisive critique of it has drawn praise and admira-tion both in India and abroad. Gender justice and ecological issues are now more than ever on the minds of an ever-growing constituency, and not only on the left.

Other major contributors to understanding the environmental implica-tions of development in India, both for the colonial and postcolonial period, include the ecologist Madhav Gadgil, and the social historian Ramachandra Guha. Their ecological history of India is a useful survey of the environmen-tal impact of colonial-era deforestation and policies that impoverished the natural basis of agricultural productiveness.[134] Both Gadgil and Guha have contributed more widely to a significant critique of development economics from an environmental perspective.[135] In their ecological history, they set out to explain both the preservation and loss of 'sacred groves', forests dedicated to nature deities in many parts of India. To do so, they develop a model in which rational-choice micro-foundationalism and the hold of religious ideol-ogy are combined to account for the coexistence of cultivated land and forests in a productive symbiosis in pre-colonial times. In the process, they advance two claims: peasants are rational in ways we can understand, but this reason

---

133   Shiva 1988, 1991, 1996 and 2008, respectively. Taken together, Shiva's works may be seen as laying out a manifesto of the need for autochthonous approaches to life rooted in the soil and the lives of the *volk*.

134   Gadgil and Guha 1992.

135   Guha 1994; Gadgil and Guha 1995; Gadgil and Vartak 1976, pp. 152–60; Guha 2000.

appears to operate according to a prudential rather than the devil-may-care profit-maximising logic associated with modern-day capitalists.

It would appear that religion must play a part in the operation of this prudential logic, although it is unclear if religion is simply part of a rationalisation mechanism given all sorts of resource constraints, or if it has some greater ideological priority. However, since the religious ideology appears to have a communitarian, prudential, nature-embracing tendency, we may also say that the reason of the peasantry is an ecologically informed one, as opposed to those of alienated modern beings whose reason is distanced from and in an antagonistic relationship to nature. In any case, by autonomising religion and making it part of a causal explanation, Gadgil and Guha attribute to it a degree of freedom from the social form; otherwise it could become a mere utilitarianism *avant la lettre*. In this model, reason operates at the social microcosm of the village, a small world of enclosed populations, while religion exercises an overarching metaphysical disciplinary function that is generalised over a larger space. The loss of this kind of overarching disciplinary function, brought on by modernity – specifically the kind of modernity that was brought to colonies like India from the West – then begins to unravel the homeostatic balance of humans and nature.

Taken together, these critiques of postcolonial modernisation declare the failure of the mainstream agendas of development. In this they are part of a broad global agreement. Indeed, from Japan to Mexico,[136] and not excluding the Western countries themselves, the idea of development as a defunct set of ideologies and practices is growing alongside neoliberal globalisation. Neoliberal policies – accompanied by 'austerity' for the working classes, now in force not only in the countries subject to recessionary downward spirals due to the draconian discipline of international financial agencies, but also in countries that have been undergoing fairly rapid growth since the early 1990s – may be seen as a decisive repudiation of the populist critique more so than the postcolonial modernisation outlined in the previous section, since the latter retained at least some notion of national autochthony and self-sufficiency and some commitment to a redistribution of wealth. In the language of 'posts', so

---

136   For examples, see Fukuoka 1978; Esteva 1987 and 1996. Fukuoka (1913–2008), a Japanese farmer and philosopher, advocated no-till agriculture 'traditional to many indigenous cultures'. Fukuoka's *One-Straw Revolution* is extensively cited in Colin Duncan's 1996 book, *The Centrality of Agriculture*. Esteva (born 1936) has been a prolific contributor to the critical literature on development, extolling the virtues of 'traditionalist' approaches to questions of land use, resource management, democracy from below, and so on. He founded the Universidad de la Tierra in the Mexican city of Oaxaca.

popular today, the stream of thought associated with postcolonial populism might qualify as 'post-development'.[137]

There is a lot in the indictment of the development experience that will ring true for many Marxists who see the manifold injustices of our times as not just a necessary price to be paid for 'progress', but as extracted by a system that piles on the wreckage. If Marx himself believed at one point in his life – perhaps in his 30s – that colonialism had a double mission, by the time he wrote *Capital* he had come to revise his views significantly, seeing it, at best, as a 'civilised barbarism'.[138] But there is something else to the 'post-development' populist tendency that would not be shared by Marxists. It is both excessively romantic about the pre-colonial past, and carries the autocentric impulses of postcolonial thought to an almost ethnocentric excess.

As the ever reliable Alvares puts it, for centuries the Chinese believed themselves both the measure of civilisation and the true measure of significance; people, ideas, technical inventions and commodities from outside the realm were of little consequence or import, and therefore kept at a distance. In India, likewise, up to about 1800, we are told, the society retained a similar notion of self-containment and sufficiency. By and large, traditional societies in Asia did not apparently feel the need to 'replace' their ideas and values with alien ones.[139] For centuries 'Indians were Indians, but now it seems wrong to be so', now they seem to have developed traits 'associated with the western personality'.[140] Alvares interprets Gandhi's *Hind Swaraj* as making a pitch for an urgent return to civilisational self-identity: 'All that comes from the West on this subject comes tarred with the brush of violence. I object to it because I have seen the wreckage that lies at the end of the road'.[141] Alvares also notes that Chatterjee interprets *Hind Swaraj* as a 'radical critique of bourgeois civil society and its institutions'.[142] Gandhi may have read or misread class as civilisation, the bourgeoisie as the 'west', for whatever polemical or political purpose was foremost in his thoughts at that moment.[143] Nowadays, it is simply another example of

---

137   Esteva, for example, styles himself as an advocate of 'post-development'!

138   Jani 2002, p. 91. This subject is discussed extensively in Jani 2002 and Nimtz 2002.

139   This will seem like so much nonsense to anyone familiar with the history of India or Southeast Asia, not to mention Ming and Qing China. See, for instance, Kosa Pan 2002; Jackson and Jaffer 2004; Golahny 2004; and in particular Elman 2004, pp. 37–49.

140   Alvares 1994, p. 107.

141   Gandhi 1934, cited in Alvares 1994, p. 131. A compilation of such essays written by Gandhi was published as a book in 1947 entitled *India of My Dreams*.

142   Chatterjee 1984, pp. 153–95.

143   Gandhi's article of 1934 in *Amrita Bazar Patrika*, cited above, suggests that he was concerned to contain and redirect the class struggles that he saw breaking out around

what Lazarus calls the 'fetish of the "West" ' in postcolonial theory, by which he means a transposition of categories whereby references to 'bourgeois civilisation' in Marx, for instance, are simply rewritten as the 'West'. Perhaps this is also what Chatterjee is doing, if by bourgeois we now understand, in addition to the West, the colonial-era compradors.

So what does it mean to be 'Indian' even before 'India' in any modern sense existed? Perhaps one can follow Shiva's tendency to posit some sort of ancient vital holistic force that she calls *prakriti*, whose source is Hindu cosmology, which she repeatedly refers to as 'Indian'[144] in a manner of generalisation familiar to readers of Subaltern Studies in its early and late forms. This vital force, which could act as the saviour of Indian society confronted with the alien forces of Western-style development, seems already to inform the worldview of Indian women, or at least those subaltern elements that live close to nature. The antidote to the reductionism of science and instrumentalisation of nature inherent in Western civilisation therefore lies ready-to-hand. Prakriti, in her view, can become the source of respect for nature as the 'creator and source of wealth' and opposition to Western science's treatment of nature as an exploitable resource. She is not above suggesting that the concept can also save the West from itself, in a gesture reminiscent of the romanticism of the Oriental Renaissance, or more particularly its nationalist variants. But as Meera Nanda notes, Shiva also seems to be in agreement with the spiritual turn in Western eco-feminism that finds in the goddess 'a metaphor for the re-enchantment of the world and liberation from the "tyranny of reason" '.[145]

In this view, the alternatives to Western science and the 'dissociated' Western personality are ancient, available and still valid for people in the East. All that it takes is some looking around. For Gandhi, a study of 'our Eastern institutions' is sufficient to 'evolve a truer socialism and a truer communism than the world has yet dreamed of'.[146] These would include, in the terms of his latter-day acolytes, reviving some of the virtues of the 'non-western human experience' for 'post-development'. Thus, Fukuoka's *One-Straw Revolution* is the alternative to modern agricultural science, a 'do-nothing' method of farming based on the values of Zen Buddhism, a vantage point for criticising economic

---

him. As he himself put it, 'I do not believe that the capitalists and the landlords are all exploiters by an inherent necessity, or that there is a basic or irreconcilable antagonism between their interests and those of the masses. All exploitation is based on co-operation, willing or forced, of the exploited'.

144   Shiva 1988, pp. 38–40.
145   Nanda 1991, p. 41.
146   Gandhi 1934, cited in Alvares 1994.

SITUATING POSTCOLONIAL STUDIES

development and progress. Fukuoka's recipe for the future consists of bringing about 'a movement not to bring about anything'.[147] And the greater the reliance on subsistence, the 'less dissociated the personality'.[148] As for illness and death, we are offered the lessons of 'herdity' (not heredity) developed by Manu Kothari and Lopa Mehta. This consists of arguing that the cause of disease is a function of the 'herd' we belong to: 'Out of every five people in the world, one must develop cancer: this is certain. Which one of the five will get it is uncertain and follows the law of probability', and every healthy individual carries with him an 'IOU card addressed to another individual not so privileged'.[149] Rather than the research and development of the medical sciences, the physician's task is simply to 'care', to ease people to their inevitable demise. This approach to the treatment of major diseases relies on the notion that what 'post-development' seeks to elaborate should be seen not so much in terms of an 'alternative' to interventionist science and medicine, designed to cure diseases, but as an 'introduction to an evaluation of lifestyles [sic], preoccupations, [and] social ideals that diverge from it or *remain uninfected* by it'.[150] The alternative to the restless energies of 'western science' and 'development' – capitalism presumably being simply an extrusion of the 'western personality' – is to counterpose to it heroic idleness (do-nothing) and fatalism in the face of the challenge of poverty, sickness and disease.[151] It is almost as if the spirit of the *Times* editorial writer of 1877 walks again, appearing now not as tragedy, but as farce.[152]

A similar set of challenges and failures have triggered comparable responses in other parts of the 'global South'. The Iranian Jalal al-e Ahmad's (1923–69) *Gharbzadegi [Plagued by the West]* of 1963 anticipates much of the later rhetoric of the Islamic revolution in Iran, and is even said to have been one of its inspirations.[153] For al-e Ahmad, the only thing that stood between Western capitalism and runaway disasters was indeed Islam. He warned that 'if not

---

147   Fukuoka 1978, p. 159.

148   Alvares 1994, p. 139.

149   Kothari and Mehta 1983, cited in Alvares 1994, p. 140.

150   Alvares 1994, p. 143, emphasis added.

151   Let us be sure that if either Kothari or Mehta fall ill, or anyone close to them should do so, they will avail themselves of the best that modern medical science offers; they will not visit a faith healer or a *hakim*, or try to persuade themselves of the value of resignationist care.

152   'Hegel remarks somewhere that all great world-historic facts and personages appear, so to speak, twice. He forgot to add: the first time as tragedy, the second time as farce' (Marx 1995 [1851–52], p. 5).

153   Afary and Anderson 2005, p. 59.

harnessed and put back into the bottle', the machine demon driven by science and materialism, 'will place a hydrogen bomb at the end of the road for mankind'.[154]

Gandhi and Khomeini make strange bedfellows, but for the likes of Alvares that is hardly a problem: after all, in the xenogeography of post-development being anti-western is *the* virtue. Thus, while Gandhi sought to liberate India (and the West itself) from modern civilisation, Khomeini sought to save Islamic civilisation from western culture. Both agreed, it seems, that the elaborate development effort to turn the people of 'post-colonial societies' into 'second or third-rate Europeans or Americans' was an 'unmitigated obscenity'.[155] The Islamic revolution in Iran is lauded for generating an either/or reaction to the institutions of the West, the conflict itself condensed to one between the forces of Islam and those of *kufr.* In Kalim Siddiqui's understanding, kufr includes the westernised elite who, rather like Nehru, are merely the local instruments of it. They may be nominally Muslim, but they pursue education, modernisation and development according to the meanings given to them by the west; they accept the 'philosophy' of the west, and it hardly matters that a 'fringe' of this elite calls itself leftist, socialist or even communist.[156] Kufr also includes nationalism, the nation state, capitalism, feudalism, modernism, and the 'western culture of nakedness, free will and liberal values'.[157] The answer to this capture by the west is to revitalise the resources of Islam, refounding science on the basis of Islamic concepts such as *tawheed* [unity], *khilafah* [trusteeship], *ibadah* [worship], *ilm* [knowledge], *halal* [praiseworthy] and *haram* [blameworthy], *adl* [social justice] and *zulm* [tyranny], *istislah* [public interest] and *dhiya* [waste]. And so '[s]cientific and technological activity that seeks to promote adl is halal, while that science and technology which promotes alienation and dehumanization, concentration of wealth in fewer and fewer hands, unemployment and environmental destruction is *zalim* (tyrannical) and therefore *haram*'.[158] Since the tenor of this critique of some of the effects of science and technology under capitalism has been a staple of the left, going back to Marx and Engels if not earlier, what Sardar has done is by now familiar. He has replaced socialism with Islam, while ridiculing socialists and communists for being stooges of the West, which stands for destructive development.

---

154   Al-e Ahmad 1982, p. 111.
155   Alvares 1994, p. 149.
156   Siddiqui 1985, p. 7.
157   Siddiqui 1985, p. 8.
158   Sardar 1984, p. 7.

For a 'leftist' like al-e Ahmad rediscovering the virtues of Islam, the problem was also internal and associated with the loss of the unity and élan of early Islam. Thus, he notes the weakening of the Muslim world by the Shi'i-Sunni divide, and the loss of vitality within the body of Shi'ite believers themselves once the 'discourses of jihad and martyrdom' were abandoned.[159] In his own colourful words, 'the day we gave up the possibility of martyrdom, and limited ourselves to paying homage to the martyrs, we were reduced to the role of door-men to the cemeteries'.[160] Perhaps it was this Islam of 'jihad and martyrdom' that Foucault imagined the Iranian revolution to be attempting to restore. As he saw it, the revolution was as much religious as it was political, and in confronting the Pahlavis, easily rendered as the pinnacle of an effete Westernised elite, the celebrated demonstrations themselves took on, in his eyes, the rhythm of 'religious ceremonies'. Foucault concludes that the 'drama caused a surprising superimposition to appear in the middle of the twentieth century', a movement that while strong enough to bring down a well-armed dictatorship nonetheless re-enacted 'old dreams that were once familiar to the West' when it too wanted to *inscribe the figures of spirituality on the ground of politics*.[161] The revolution, Foucault thought, was outside the 'Western paradigm' of revolution, embodying a timeless spirit of martyrdom, and indeed political spirituality, which the modern concept of revolution had 'vainly tried to supplant'.[162]

Modernisation in the ex-colonial world is subject to the most radical criticism via the attribution of the direst consequences to it. No good can come of an 'external' imposition that cannot square with indigenous culture, rooted in the blood and soil of the people. It is a deracinated and arbitrary way to proceed and indeed only benefits the West, the original exploiters of colonial wealth, and their native compradors. It is of some interest that populist strands of thought, while drawing on left-wing critiques of imperialism, employ predominantly bio-naturalistic arguments against modernity to which political-economic arguments against capital are assimilated, if capital even appears in the picture at all. Certainly, a historical materialist elucidation of the origins, tendencies and development of capital as a social form are anathema, since it would place them in proximity to Marxism, which they abhor as a foreign infection on the cultural body of the nation.

The only way ahead in the populist framework is to draw on the super-abundant riches of one's own culture that already contain the conceptual and

159 Afary and Anderson 2005, p. 59.
160 Al-e Ahmad 1982, p. 68, cited in Afary and Anderson 2005, p. 59.
161 Foucault, cited in Afary and Anderson 2005, p. 265, emphasis added.
162 Afary and Anderson 2005, p. 131.

practical guides to a properly oriented life, however that is defined, and to allow the ordinary *volk* in their wisdom to find the optimal pathways to securing their livelihood without the interventions of governments and bureaucracies and the whole phenomenon of irrational rationalisation with which they are associated.[163]

It would appear almost as if a notion of caste pollution has been taken to a new level of the self-identity of cultures rooted in age-old civilisations that then dictates what is authentically pure and what is inauthentic and contaminating. This is no doubt also a sign of the importance of a certain kind of organicist holism for populist thought, which then permits the articulation of the most apocalyptic scenarios based on threats to a bio-naturalistic cohesion by powerful outside forces (mostly, of course, the west).[164]

What can be said is that these views reflect and are to an extent derivative of a moral climate inherited from a time when Europe declared its independence from the rest of the world and stressed the autochthonous roots of its own civilisation, its immaculate conception scrubbed clean of an insertion within the geopolitical lines of force of the ancient Mediterranean.[165] Europe's subsequent development then could be seen as generated from within its own

---

163   In the broad agreement between the various forms of this type of cultural-populist postcolonial thinking, one can see a superficial resemblance to the 'doctrine of memory', or the notion of 'anamnesis', 'in which everything which in reality belongs to the future is attributed to the past, in which time is stood on its head conceptually' (Jameson 1971, p. 127). The future as such is blocked, if not abolished, unless one returns to the original sources of 'plenitude' found in the vital force of early Islam or early Hinduism or whatever religious variant. This is to be contrasted with Ernst Bloch's revolutionary 'doctrine of hope', a genuine opening to the future, 'an ontological pull of the future, of a tidal influence exerted upon us by that which lies out of sight below the horizon, an unconscious of what is yet to come' (Jameson 1971, p. 128; see also Bloch 1986).

164   This worldview is given free rein in Alvares 1994. 'India', Alvares declares at one point in his book, citing Nandy, 'is not non-West, it is India', an uncompromising formulation of civilisational self-identity that is the core of populist ideology (Alvares 1994, p. 143). The cover blurb, after describing Alvares as the editor of the Other India Press, a trustee of the Other India Bookstore, and the secretary of the Goa Foundation, goes on to say: 'in the time that remains he and his family look after rabbits, chickens, cows and trees', perhaps a sign of a wholesome life lived close to nature generating wholesome ideas.

165   The cultural pride through which Europe declared its independence from the rest of the world is discussed and criticised in Bernal 1987. Several of the responses to Bernal bear eloquent testimony to the continued salience of this notion for Eurocentric historiography; see Lefkowitz and Rogers 1996.

civilisational genius, the 'European miracle' in short.[166] In an imitative gesture, those subject to colonialism have often adopted the same posture, declaring that the search for the authentic and autarchic roots of their nation's cultural antiquity and independence must underpin their future trajectory,[167] and they have found within Europe a number of supporters who either believe civilisations have their own destinies or that the West can now learn, once again, from the East to avoid its own worst predilections.

In this post-development discourse, the themes of democratic self-determination and autocentrism have been represented as autarchy and finally xenophobia (expressed as anti-Westernism). Essentially, what is at stake is a 'clash of civilisations' now told from the perspective of the countries that have been generally at the receiving end of the discourses of the colonisers' and modernisers' civilising missions. Apparently, it matters little if in the process the interpretation of the past is forced or arbitrary, or if the end result is to create myths and delusions about societies 'uninfected' by the West, since the distance between myth and history has been all but obliterated. As Lévi-Strauss once observed, it mattered little 'if the thought processes of South American Indians take shape through the medium of my thought or whether mine takes place through theirs';[168] the post-development people, who no longer wish to be 'plagued by the West' have created a parody of Lévi-Strauss for their own polemical ends. The very notion of causality, a proper explanation for historical phenomena, comes to seem like the tyranny of the West.

At the most banal level, this requires resorting to a fairly stock Orientalist trope, that in the Orient (or, at any rate, non-Europe), for example, religion is the key to explaining social phenomena. As we have seen above, Gadgil and Guha resort to the disciplinary power of religion – presumably some variants of what later came to be understood as Hinduism – in explaining the preservation of sacred groves in pre-colonial times, whereas the deracinating touch of Western civilisation in the form of colonialism removed the restraints leading ultimately to the cutting down of the sacred groves and the disruption of long-preserved homeostatic balances between arable and forest. What is not explored is the way in which concrete circumstances (the social form of rural life in specific historical circumstances) affect thought and ideology (of which religion ought to be a constituent), rather than behaviour alone. If the 'reason' of the peasantry appears different from bourgeois 'reason', it is most likely to be

---

166   The clearest statement of this was in the original version of Jones 1981, although there
        have been any number of variants. For a full bibliography, see Blaut 1993.
167   For more detail on this, see Kaiwar 2003, pp. 13–61, particularly section VI, pp. 39–51.
168   Lévi-Strauss 1970, p. 15.

the result of the way in which information about complex realities or methods of analysing appearance forms are available in dramatically different ways to different social classes once the social-science disciplines, formal education and the institutions of modernity start to make their differential impact felt along class lines. In a social form like capitalism, scalar issues matter: on the time axis, the duration of an individual lifespan versus the secular trends of the mode of production,[169] and on the space axis, the spatial distanciation between sites of primary production, secondary manufacture and final consumption.[170] These are formative influences and to exoticise the social agency of the peasantry, based on an organicist view of culture, is rather lame.

In a more historically determinate perspective, alternative explanations come into view to account for the preservation of sacred groves: the near-constant warfare on a variety of scales endemic to pre-colonial times that had consequences for both fertility and mortality, with low population densities placing less pressure on natural resources; the agricultural taxation policies of those times; and the limited ambit of markets for agricultural products, all of which coincided to keep forests in place. Conversely, the cutting down of the sacred groves in colonial and postcolonial times can be explained in terms of changes in the working of the entire social formation: a rising demographic trend, following the establishment of colonial rule, combined with new taxation policies and indeed opportunities for sale of commercial crops on the world market that all conspired to put a premium on extending cultivation.

The Report of the Deccan Riots Commission of 1875 – set up to look into the causes of the riots in Poona and Ahmednagar districts of Bombay Presidency – cited among other things the land-settlement and revenue policies of the colonial government that acted in concert to create pressures to clear land for occupation and cultivation, even marginal land that might have been previously held as copses or scrub forests.[171] The introduction of private property in land during the course of the nineteenth century – eagerly seized on by immediate producers, not to mention landlords and merchants – appears to have broken communitarian constraints on the exploitation of the commons. Furthermore, there were two kinds of forest clearances: one, alluded to above as

---

169   For an exposition of the implications of the very different scales of human time and socio-economic time, see, for instance, Jameson 1993, p. 172.

170   I take the term 'spatial distanciation' from Giddens's 'time-space distanciation', discussed extensively in Giddens 1981, pp. 90–5.

171   See, Great Britain Parliamentary Papers (Commons), 1878, 'Report of the Deccan Riots Commission', Volume 58. This was originally published in India as the *Report of the Committee on the Riots in Poona and Ahmednagar* in 1876; see Kaiwar 1992a, pp. 255–300.

the clearing of village-level copses and groves – often marginal and secondary to the prime land held for cultivation, but still important for the maintenance and reproduction of livestock; and two, the clear-cutting of major old-growth stands of hardwood, thereby tapping India's supposedly 'inexhaustible forests' for infrastructure, public works and strategic military constructions.[172] The latter is an example of how financial incentives provided to contractors by the government, in conjunction with a growing market for timber associated with the expansion of the colonial infrastructure, proved inimical to the preservation of forests.

My argument is that rational but historically determinate explanations are preferable to the ahistorical rational-choice/religious ideology combination of Gadgil and Guha. While one does not want to discount altogether the possibility of religious ideology exercising some disciplinary (and dependent causal) agency,[173] the disappearance of sacred groves over the last two centuries or so would suggest either that the power of religion is waning – hardly credible in India – or that mundane explanations related to changing material constraints and incentives offer a better explanation. However, their very (near) extinction ironically leads to their rediscovery as the archaic, sacred, and so on, by social scientists if not the denizens of village India.[174] The remit of religion, in other words, is historically variable.

Attempts to found science on religious grounds – based on relegating 'Galilean' in favour 'civilisational' science[175] – are far more seriously flawed. The Vishwa Hindu Parishad (VHP) of the United Kingdom, in its 1996 book, *Explaining Hindu Dharma: A Guide for Teachers*, offers 'teaching suggestions for introducing Hindu ideas and topics in the classroom' at the middle- to high-school level in the British schools system, claiming that Hindu dharma is 'just another name' for the 'eternal laws of nature' first discovered by Vedic seers, and subsequently confirmed by modern physics and biological sciences![176] Pervez Hoodbhoy, for his part, gives examples of 'Islamic science' that are both hilarious and tragic: for instance, a Pakistani scientist, Chairman of the Holy Qur'an Research Foundation in Islamabad, advocated using fiery creatures called *jinns*, who presumably inhabit the heavens, to generate power, thus solving Pakistan's energy problem in an environmentally sound fashion.

---

172   Rangarajan 1994, pp. 147–67, esp. pp. 159ff.

173   Dependent, that is, on system-level pressures.

174   See, for example, Jameson's discussion of the archaic in the late modern or postmodern in 'The Antinomies of Postmodernism' (Jameson 1998, p. 67).

175   Alvares 1994, p. 144.

176   See, for instance, the detailed critique in Nanda 2004.

Similarly, others have used Einstein's theory to calculate the speed of heaven and the angle of god, and have provided other information beneficial to Pakistan's economic progress.[177] As for the effort to refound science on ten basic Islamic values, including *tawheed* [unity of God], *ibadah* [worship], and *khilafah* [trusteeship], and so on, Hoodbhoy concludes they are little more than platitudes.[178] What is so regrettable to a practising scientist like Hoodbhoy is that all this civilisational excess is such a complete negation of the phenomenal scientific advances of Muslim scientists over the centuries,[179] advances that fundamentally altered the intellectual landscape of the Middle Ages and indeed made possible modernity, as we understand it, in fields like medicine, mathematics, astronomy, chemistry, optics, and so on.

Something like a severe 'attenuation of truth' is at work in this discourse. As Anderson points out, the distinction between the true and the false is the 'ineliminable premise of any rational knowledge' and its 'central site' is evidence.[180] Once this premise is brought into disrepute, anything goes. A couple of examples should suffice. One such instance is brought to light curiously by Richard Lewontin in an interview that the Harvard biologist gave to Harry Kreisler at the Institute of International Relations at the University of California, Berkeley.[181] This relates to Shiva's indictment of the promotion of baby food based on genetically modified seeds in the poorer countries, part of her much broader critique of Western corporations. Lewontin refers to an argument that Shiva puts forward against the use of genetically modified foods and their dangers to health, in which she alleges that children who eat baby food processed from GM seeds are getting eight times the amount of oestrogen that a woman gets when she takes a contraceptive pill. That would be utterly shocking if true. On investigating the situation – in the first place because he took Shiva's credentials as a scientist seriously – Lewontin found that, yes, the children were getting 'eight times the dose of a thing', but it was a plant oestrogen whose physiological activity was one-thousandth that of the hormone oestrogen. Lewontin observes that Shiva must have 'known the truth of the

---

177 Hoodbhoy 1991, pp. 140–54; see also Kaiwar 1992b, pp. 39–56.
178 Hoodbhoy 1991, p. 75.
179 Hoodbhoy 1991, p. 90; von Grunebaum 1953, pp. 340–3.
180 Anderson 1983, p. 48.
181 Richard Lewontin is most certainly a person of the left. His classic works, with Richard Levins, explore 'the dual nature of science, on one hand a development of human knowledge with a millennial pedigree, and on the other an increasingly commoditised product of a capitalist knowledge industry for sale to the highest bidder and inaccessible to those who cannot pay'; see Lewontin and Levins 1987 and 2007.

matter' because she cited the paper from which she got the data, but concludes that she would probably regard it as a 'justifiable' distortion for the greater good. Lewontin's response to this bit of 'pseudo-science' is that it is likely to lead to cynicism and make a proper opposition to corporate agriculture nearly impossible.[182]

In a somewhat different vein, Fukuoka's 'one-straw revolution' is based on the most minute and arduous observation of nature and critically timed interventions in the natural cycle to optimise the output of food crops without arbitrary and destructive interventions. As Engels once argued vis-à-vis the relationship of science to nature:

> Let us not, however, flatter ourselves overmuch on account of our human conquest over nature. For each such conquest takes its revenge on us. Each of them, it is true, has in the first place the consequences on which we counted, but in the second and third places, it has quite different, unforeseen effects, which only too often cancel out the first ... At every step we are reminded that we by no means rule over nature like a conqueror over a foreign people, like someone standing outside nature – but that we, with flesh, blood, and brain, belong to nature, and exist in its midst, and that all our mastery of it consists in the fact that we have the advantage over all other beings of being able to know and correctly apply its laws.[183]

For Fukuoka to misinterpret his work, as if it were a call for a 'do-nothing' method rather than a call for a critical intervention in the direction of a more properly scientific approach to agriculture – knowing and correctly applying nature's laws – than the big corporations currently practise, is lamentable. It suggests that in this populist-civilisational discourse there is more than an element of self-deception, if not an outright deception of others.

Insofar as such a discourse – or a loose ensemble of discourses tending in the same direction – draws on issues first highlighted by the left, they have taken them in a conservative if not outright reactionary direction, aiming to preserve the few enclaves still remaining from a 'simpler era' or imagined to be such, or to recover some ostensible collective or communal forms of

---

182   Harry Kreisler interview with Richard Lewontin, <http://conversations.berkeley.edu/content/richard-c-lewontin>.

183   Engels 1940, pp. 291–2.

the past.[184] This is certainly the case with certain strands within postcolonial studies as well, especially the element that traces a lineage back to or that draws its inspiration from Subaltern Studies. On the issues that 'late' Subaltern Studies or Subaltern Studies in its postcolonial moment has written much about – for example, religious minorities, women and caste – what is distinctive now is not the positions they adopt, but a conceptual apparatus revolving around the politics of Being, biopower, anti-modernist modernism, and a metageography of East-West. Around this, there is some notion that solutions are being or could be fashioned from the ground up that are properly indigenous, on a human scale and vastly superior to anything proposed by deracinated modernisers, who rely on the crude power of the state to get the business done.[185]

Of course, that is also part of a much wider disavowal of the state in 'post'-theory, not least the 'post-development' tendency we have been examining in this section. 'As little state as possible' – or none at all – might be their motto, following Nietzsche whom Brennan declares the *'fons et origo* of radical theory over the last three decades'.[186] That there might be other ways to look at the state is now all but forgotten, but it is worth remembering that, as Gramsci noted, 'a revolution is a genuine revolution and not just empty, swollen rhetorical demagoguery, only when it is embodied in some type of State, only when it becomes an organised system of power'.[187] Like Lenin, Gramsci was not only positively invested in Fordist modernity,[188] but he like Marx might even have thought of the factory itself, under a new social system, no longer as the place of the 'terrifying...imprisonment' of industrial wage labour, but as a transformed space, a 'crystal palace of human development',[189] capable of producing 'fully developed human beings'.[190] But by now Lenin and Marx are figures of near-universal vilification among both the metropolitan postcolonialists

184   Jameson 2011, pp. 89–90. Only Marx, Jameson suggests, sought to combine a politics of revolt with the 'poetry of the future', and to recover that 'futurism' must be the 'fundamental task' of any left 'discursive struggle' today (Jameson 2011, p. 90). This takes us back, of course, to Bloch's Utopian impulse – more on that towards the end of Part V below.

185   See, for example, the discussion in Chatterjee 2010, pp. 299–301.

186   Brennan 2006, p. xiii. No doubt this has much wider resonances, not only in the works of Bobbio and Mouffe whom Brennan discusses in detail in this context, but also Foucault, Derrida and even some socialists like Holloway; see Derrida 1994; Holloway 2010.

187   Gramsci 1994a, p. 97, cited in Brennan 2006, p. 252.

188   Eagleton 2007, p. 56.

189   Jameson 2011, p. 118.

190   Marx 1977, p. 614.

and the post-developmentalists; less so is this the case with Gramsci, but only because he is read against the grain of his own views on a whole range of issues, including subalternity.

What late Subaltern Studies in its postcolonial moment brings to the mix, which is missing in the 'post-development' populists, is that alongside the civilisational xenology that acts as a backdrop to their academic endeavours – when it is not being mobilised as part of a critique of historicism seen from the vantage point of 'History II' – is the spirit of practicality and 'institutional realism',[191] and a quite straightforward decisionism, not to mention a certain kind of nescience about truth claims. Goddesses, like the Grihalakshmis of *Bhadralok* households, are to be understood as objects of postcolonial desire, and truth in that case might just be the capacity to articulate desire.

2.4   Subaltern Studies

Subaltern Studies emerged as part of a broad zone of engagement constituted by modernisation theory and practice, Marxist work on the 'mode of production' in agriculture and on working class movements, Maoism and the political uprisings it inspired in rural and urban India after independence, peasant studies, not to mention a complex of theories including structuralism and poststructuralism that developed in the wake of the 1968 uprisings in France, and the debates and polemics among them. Further, Ranajit Guha sought to situate the subalternist critique of historiography in a tradition reaching back to the nineteenth-century,[192] when a politically engaged scholarship emerged that subsequently articulated many of the themes of Indian nationalism. Of course, the term 'subaltern' has an immediate reference to Gramsci's work, but Subaltern Studies was also undertaken with critical attention to the writings of English Marxists like E.P. Thompson, Eric Hobsbawm, Christopher Hill, not to mention the 'transition to capitalism' debate that followed Robert Brenner's article in the pages of *Past and Present* in 1976.[193]

The influence of Susobhan Sarkar on Ranajit Guha has already been invoked. During the late 1950s, Chaturvedi points out, when most Marxists in the West were unfamiliar with Gramsci,[194] Sarkar began discussing Gramsci's work with

---

191   Chatterjee 2010, p. 297.
192   Guha 1997a, p. ix.
193   The debate has been published as a book: Ashton and Philpin 1985.
194   Presumably, Chaturvedi means to say that Gramsci was not very well known outside Italy. The next two paragraphs draw loosely on Chaturvedi 2000, pp. viii–ix.

his students at Jadavpur University, his ongoing interest in the Italian thinker resulting in publications in the late 1960s and early 1970s.[195] The availability of an English translation of *The Modern Prince and Other Essays* in 1957 had made some key writings of Gramsci available to intellectuals on the left who could read Sarkar's work with 'critical understanding'. Guha's first book, *A Rule of Property for Bengal*, was indeed dedicated to Susobhan Sarkar and attested to Gramsci's influence on the intellectual milieu in the circle around him.[196] All this in an environment in which mainstream left parties in India were 'lukewarm if not indifferent' to Gramsci, a situation that continues to this day.[197]

The idea for Subaltern Studies took shape in Britain, under Guha's leadership, in the late 1970s, at a time when Gramsci's work was influencing both historiographical work and the political culture of that country. From the early 1960s, Perry Anderson and Tom Nairn, among others, in the pages of *New Left Review* provided a comprehensive development and critique of Gramscian thought for an English-reading public.[198] In the 1970s, the influence of Gramsci extended into studies of popular culture in the works of Raymond Williams and Stuart Hall, for instance.[199] While Anderson and Nairn, Chaturvedi notes, were primarily interested in the 'uneven development of the European state form', the latter two focused on 'the authoritarian valences of popular culture and questions of hegemony'.[200] English Marxist historiography had already begun to develop the potentialities of a new social history based on the lives of ordinary people. By 1960, Hobsbawm's *Primitive Rebels*, and his 'For a History of Subaltern Classes', published in the Italian journal *Società*, employed Gramscian concepts to liberate the study of 'primitive' rebellions from the taint of crime and backwardness.[201] Thompson's work on the making of the English working class sought to depict the lives and voices of the working poor caught up in the swirling currents of radical movements, not to mention Protestant evangelism and the relentless pressures of industrialisation, in the process freeing

---

195   On Susobhan Sarkar's interest in Gramsci, see Datta Gupta 1994, pp. 18–21; Schwartz 1997, p. 130; Sarkar 1968 and Sarkar 1972.

196   Guha 1963; Chaturvedi 2000, p. viii.

197   Datta Gupta 1994, p. 18.

198   Anderson 1992, 'Foreword'; see also Anderson 1977 and Nairn 1977. In his more recent work, Nairn seems to have turned his back on Gramsci, and more broadly Marxism. For an assessment of this shift, see Davidson 1999.

199   Chaturvedi 2000, p. ix; see Williams 1977 and Hall 1988.

200   Chaturvedi 2000, p. ix. It should be noted that Anderson also provides an extended essay on Gramsci's notion of hegemony, tracing it back to the deliberations of the Comintern; see Anderson 1977.

201   Hobsbawm 1959.

them from what he called the 'enormous condescension of posterity'.[202] Hill's
study of Milton and the English revolution showed the influence of the radicals – the Levellers, the Diggers and the Ranters – on the poet's preoccupations
with free speech, divorce, regicide, and so on.[203] Chaturvedi rightly notes that
while Thompson's impact on Subaltern Studies has been acknowledged, most
amply by Sumit Sarkar, that of the others has not received the same attention.[204]
In any case, several of the key issues that were the subject of vital interventions in politics and historiography, from a broadly Marxist if not specifically
Gramscian perspective, were to find their way into Subaltern Studies in its
founding moment.

Closer to home, the emergence of Subaltern Studies in the early 1980s coincided with what Sumit Sarkar calls the development of a 'dissident' left-milieu
in which sharp criticisms of orthodox Marxist practice and theory – Stalinist
and Maoist, presumably – were combined with the retention of a broadly
socialist and Marxian political horizon. There were 'obvious affinities' with
the radical-populist moods of the 1960s and 70s, with peasant rebellions and
anti-imperialist revolutions, alongside a growing disillusionment with organised left parties, and the bureaucratic state structures of 'actually existing
socialism'.[205] The last was part of a much wider sphere of changes taking place
in the 1980s. Eurocommunism had originally been formulated in the mid-
1970s as a Western European alternative to the 'actually existing' variety of the
Soviet Union, which had come under sustained critical scrutiny since 1956.
Eurocommunism was partly based on an idiosyncratic reading of Gramsci as
having already anticipated 'theoretical modes of understanding' suitable to
the modern, media-saturated capitalist state.[206] Over time it became practically indistinguishable from the mildest form of reformist social democracy,[207]
whatever their original theoretical differences. Its subsequent disappearance
altogether, amid a global retrenchment of capitalism and a determined attack
on the bastions of organised labour, went hand-in-hand with a theoretical re-
evaluation of the revolutionary potential of the working class. After all, it was

---

202   Thompson 1966, p. 12.

203   Hill 1977.

204   Chaturvedi 2000, p. ix. This is not entirely true, as Hobsbawm is mentioned in the works
      of both Guha and Chakrabarty, although not in a particularly flattering way. Indeed,
      sometimes Hobsbawm is read in ways that seem antithetical to what might be considered
      reasonable, particularly his *Primitive Rebels*. There are several essays that examine
      Thompson's influence in great detail; see Sarkar 1997.

205   Sarkar 1997, p. 83.

206   Brennan 2006, p. 238.

207   Miliband 1978, pp. 158–71; Anderson 2009, p. 330, pp. 336–7.

in the 1980s when André Gorz's *Farewell to the Working Class*[208] summed up the feeling that had been growing on the left, namely, that the radical political potentialities of the working class were a thing of the past, if they had ever been true at all.

These were accompanied by the travails of revolutions from Vietnam and Nicaragua to Chile. Foucault's self-imposed silence on the Iranian revolution spoke for perhaps a larger silence in the aftermath of the defeats of the 1970s and 80s. The petering out of the 'mode of production' debate in India was simply a local manifestation of a world that was effectively disappearing, restructured out of existence by the political economy of 'late capitalism'. Ironically, it was in this world that the notion of peasant autonomy – the essential lines of the structure of peasant consciousness – came to be formulated as an integral part of the Subaltern Studies' project. Gramsci was reinterpreted as one whose work was applicable to the developing world, 'to feudal incrustations and religious backwardness, to weak and wavering bourgeoisies seeking ways to construct hegemony'. A Gramsci diametrically opposed to that of the Eurocommunists emerged, useful above all for an analysis of the *colonial* situation.[209] By the mid to late 1980s, however, the collision with reality would prove too strong: the search for a structure of peasant consciousness was then no longer acknowledged as valid, and with it – in a gesture imitative of so much that was already transpiring in Europe – Marxism itself came under a cloud, seen in this instance as much too limited a resource for a project that now claimed to contest Eurocentric, metropolitan and bureaucratic systems of knowledge.[210] The Orientalist Marx was henceforth a staple of Subaltern Studies and postcolonial polemics. The lukewarm reception accorded the original Subaltern Studies project in the US perhaps encouraged the transition; the lifeline thrown to it by Spivak (and less so by Said) no doubt helped make a transition towards US-style postcolonialism both relatively painless and, for some, quite profitable.

But for our present purposes, it is important to note that even before the formal launch of the Subaltern Studies project in 1982, the ground had been prepared by the coming together of a wide array of political, theoretical and scholarly developments across the world. As noted, since 1982 Subaltern Studies has mapped out the widest terrain of investigation of the rural world; there have been collections of essays published under the title *Subaltern*

---

208   Gorz 1982.
209   Brennan 2006, p. 238. For an extensive treatment of the uncertainties of bourgeois hegemony in the colonial world, see Guha 1997a.
210   Chaturvedi 2000, p. xi.

Studies, articles in journals, and full-length monographs.[211] 1983 saw the publication of Ranajit Guha's critically important *Elementary Aspects of Peasant Insurgency in Colonial India*.[212] A concern for writing the histories of the subaltern people, especially as they emerge from the shadows in the archives of the ruling classes, say, during times of rebellion, however fragmentary the evidence, underlay the original project. Guha wrote in the preface to the first volume of the *Subaltern Studies* series:

> The aim of the present collection of essays ... is to promote a systematic and informed discussion of subaltern themes in the field of South Asian studies, and thus help to rectify the elitist bias characteristic of much research and academic work in this particular area ... The dominant groups will therefore receive in these volumes the consideration they deserve without, however, being endowed with that spurious primacy assigned to them by the long-standing tradition of elitism in South Asian studies ...[213]

So the immediate concern of subalternist history was to correct the elitist bias of South Asian studies dominated, as Chatterjee argues, by a debate between two groups of historians, located in Cambridge and Delhi, the former maintaining that Indian nationalism was a 'bid for power' by a handful of Indian elites who used the traditional bonds of caste and community to mobilise the masses against the British, the latter arguing that colonial exploitation had created the material conditions for a cross-class alliance forged by a nationalist leadership who organised the masses in the struggle for independence.[214] The former could present the nationalist leadership as manipulative, while the latter could present them as idealistic or charismatic. The focus on leadership was accompanied by 'economistic assumptions',[215] and neither had any place for the independent political actions of the subaltern classes.

The elitist bias could certainly be extended to include the postcolonial modernisation that followed independence, a prime example of 'bourgeois-nationalist elitism' and its propensity to treat the countryside as a resource for largely urban designs. The main line of attack on postcolonial modernisation from the left has been that it was a continuation of policies begun under colonial rule.

---

211   Useful collections may be found in Chaturvedi 2000 and Ludden 2002.
212   Guha 1983a.
213   Guha 1982, p. vii.
214   Chatterjee 2010, pp. 290–1.
215   Sarkar 1997, p. 85.

This is a truism to the extent that colonial rule introduced the social form of production associated with capital – albeit at a very basic and stagnant level. Postcolonial modernisation sought to deepen the development of capitalism, not break with it – that is, concentrate on developing the productive forces in India which colonial rulers had no interest in doing – while aiming to do away with colonial-era impediments to that process. So it was a break to that modest extent, even if it has been widely castigated as a clumsily conceived and poorly executed one, a failure on its own terms, often instrumentalising the relationship of the state to the subaltern classes in the form of piecemeal intervention for very restrictive ends.[216] Be that as it may, Subaltern Studies was sharply critical of the nationalists' disposition to subsume the peasantry into a nationalist narrative in which they were subservient and backward, if not irrational, until they came into contact with nationalism's emancipatory potentialities.[217] The habit of seeing the countryside as a space of unrelieved backwardness, which it was the task of urban reformists to liberate, has been one of the constants of Indian modernising thought.[218] The key development, in the initial stage of the project, was thus to attack all forms of elitism and to accomplish this with great economy by unearthing the *structure of subaltern consciousness* at moments of rebellion. Doing so would expose the limitations of colonial elitism by showing that it completely failed to appreciate what subaltern rebellions were about when it branded them as a mere continuation of crime, a reaching for sticks and stones; it would also reveal the limitations of bourgeois elitism by showing the wrongheadedness of thinking that subalterns were only capable of pre-political actions until they encountered the bourgeois nationalists.

Arguably, the propensity to see the peasantry not so much as activists in their own cause, but rather as an appendage of more able social forces, was also a problem with the Indian Marxists, but this time with the industrial proletariat, not the bourgeoisie, in the role of the hegemonic class. To this end, from the late 1960s onwards, Indian Marxists launched wide-ranging studies of the countryside, and debates and polemics among themselves to develop a clear

---

216   This has been a consistent argument in Chatterjee's work. For an extended exposition of the forms that this takes, see Chatterjee 2004, pp. 27–78. However, insofar as Chatterjee analyses politics in present-day India, it does seem to revolve around the way bonds of caste and community are used by political elites to mobilise people for instrumental ends!

217   See, for example, Pandey 1978 and Hardiman 1981.

218   The tendency and its critique are quite well represented in the correspondence between Nehru and Gandhi, some of which can be found in Nehru 1958.

line of analysis. Their objectives were both historical and political: at one level, to ascertain the actual social form of rural relations – capitalist, 'semi-feudal' and variations on those combined and uneven forms of the capital relation, the directions of change in the decades after independence, internal differentiation within the peasantry, their relationships with other social classes, and ultimately their potentialities and limits as part of a revolutionary alliance with urban workers.[219] Insofar as the question of hegemony was debated it followed the classical Gramscian form of a relationship of forces within the oppressed and exploited classes, rather than the vexed issue of bourgeois hegemony over the exploited and oppressed classes as a whole.[220]

Absent in the 'mode-of-production' debate was any sense of the peasantry as historical actors, their culture, organisation, and consciousness. Some version of a 'middle-peasant' thesis was present in the work of Alavi, for instance, but it suffered from excessive formalism, if not a downright formulaic application of Mao's ideas on peasant revolution.[221] By and large, the Marxist debate offered a somewhat mechanical 'scientific' analysis from which the capabilities of each grouping of the peasantry for entering into revolutionary alliances was inferred. The debate reflected some larger weaknesses of left studies of peasant and labour movements that have tended to concentrate on economic conditions and political organisational work, if not ideological lineages.[222] While the debates mobilised 'data' in a sociological sense, there was no feel for the concerns of the actual working people or even their ability or willingness to enter into the kinds of alliances that were posited as necessary. In other words, Marxism notwithstanding, it was largely an academic debate.

Subaltern Studies supplied what was lacking in Indian Marxism, namely, a sense of the peasantry as rational-competent actors with their own goals,

---

219   A collection of these essays was published in Lahore in 1978; Alavi et al. 1978. At this remove of time, it is impossible to visualise any Indian writing – much less a collection of Indian Marxist essays – being published in Pakistan! This collection is hard to come by, but there is a more recent and readily available collection edited by Utsa Patnaik; see Patnaik 1990.

220   There is very little to suggest that the Indian Marxists who participated in the 'mode-of-production' debate had read Gramsci. Their ideas of hegemony were more likely derived from their familiarity with debates in the early Comintern. For some detail on the concept of hegemony in Lenin's writings, for example, see Boothman 2011, pp. 58–62. For an extended discussion of the different versions of hegemony in Gramsci's work, see Anderson 1977, pp. 5–78. A spirited response to Anderson's positions is developed by Thomas; see Thomas 2009.

221   Xaxa 2010, p. 92.

222   For more on this topic, see Sarkar 1997, pp. 85ff.

rather than a mere potentiality awaiting mobilisation by other social classes. Ranajit Guha and his colleagues in the self-styled Subaltern Studies collective were therefore concerned to show the self-organisation and self-activity of the peasantry long before they came into contact with and quite independently of either bourgeois nationalism or proletarian radicalism, their ability to understand the challenges confronting them and to formulate a course of action to overcome those challenges, the 'neglected dimension of subaltern autonomy in action, consciousness and culture',[223] the 'contribution made by the people *on their own*'.[224] Given the Marxist affiliations of a number of the early practitioners of Subaltern Studies, this was (at least in the climate of the late 1970s and early 1980s in India) an effort to rectify what they might have seen as a glaring defect in that body of thought.[225]

Subaltern Studies also evolved alongside populist strands of thought in India, incorporating their notions of the self-sufficiency and self-identity of the *volk*, uncontaminated by modernisation or its ideological assumptions and expressions in nationalism at least until the turn of the twentieth century. There is an ecological component to this mode of thought, which draws attention to the 'world' of the peasantry authentically immersed in an unreflected relationship with nature, of which the spirits that reside in it and intervene in human affairs are an expression. Their modes of life and work, consciousness, action, particularly rebellions, and so forth, are then extensions of that fundamental ecological substrate, and remain so for a while, even when the actors subsequently relocated to the cities or the cities began to engulf the countryside.[226] Perhaps this is traceable to a common inspiration, possibly in some of Gandhi's seminal writings, that surmised conventional assumptions about peasants, and not only in India. Gandhi's indebtedness to Tolstoy and the Narodniks in Russia, not to mention theosophy, is abundantly clear.[227] So what is represented in this mode of thought is a partial secularisation of all manner of spiritualist notions about cultural and civilisational difference, of

---

223 Sarkar 1997, p. 85.
224 Guha 1988, p. 39.
225 Dhanagare, however, has criticised Subaltern Studies for failing properly to engage with the literature on peasant rebellion in India going back to the 1940s; Dhanagare 1988, pp. 18–35. The same could be said of the mode-of-production debate in which one rarely finds references to pioneering studies of rural sociology and peasant rebellions, for example, the works of A.R. Desai; see the much reprinted Desai 1938.
226 Chakrabarty 1989.
227 Gandhi 1948; Gandhi 1997 [1919]; or see Lavrin 1960, pp. 132–9.

traditions rooted in the soil and bodies of the indigenes that became a power-ful inheritance of anti-colonial and postcolonial thought.

Sarkar posits that Guha used the term 'subaltern' rather in the way Thompson used the word 'plebeian' in the eighteenth-century English context,[228] the rationale for this lying in the fact that in the largely pre-capi-talist conditions of colonial India, class formation was 'likely to have remained inchoate'. 'Subaltern' then, Sarkar argues, would be of help in avoiding the 'pit-falls of economic reductionism', while at the same time retaining a necessary emphasis on 'domination and exploitation'.[229] But while there is no discount-ing Thompson's influence in this regard, it might also be that the cultural pecu-liarities of the English had an Indian counterpart, so to speak, bringing to the fore in due course alternative potentialities of a more problematic kind that were present all along in the Subaltern Studies usage of the term.

At any rate, Guha adopted as a programmatic guide the methodological cri-teria for a 'history of the subaltern classes' that Gramsci had developed earlier. These were:

1. objective formation of the subaltern social groups, by the *develop-ments and transformations occurring in the sphere of economic produc-tion*; their quantitative diffusion and their origins in pre-existing social groups whose mentality, ideology and aims they conserve *for a time*; 2. their active or passive affiliation to the dominant political formations, their attempts to influence the programmes of these formations in order to press claims of their own and the consequences of these attempts in *determining processes of decomposition, renovation or neo-formation*; 3. the birth of new parties of the dominant groups, intended to conserve the assent of the subaltern groups and to maintain control over them; 4. the formations which the subaltern groups themselves produce, in order to press claims of *a limited and partial character*; 5. those new formations which assert the autonomy of the subaltern groups, but within *the old framework*; 6. those formations which assert the integral autonomy ... etc.[230]

---

228   Sarkar notes that Guha frequently cited Thompson with approval, and the references, significantly, were to 1975's *Whigs and Hunters* and Thompson's 1975 essay in *Albion's Fatal Tree*.

229   Sarkar 1997, p. 83.

230   Gramsci 1971, p. 52, emphasis added.

This programme could not in itself yield anything as dramatic as an essential 'structure' of subaltern consciousness. In fact, Gramsci's formulation foregrounds the dynamic and dialectical relationship between economy (in this case, the developing capital form), politics and consciousness. Indeed, the very first item in the 'methodological criteria' Gramsci mentioned points to the primacy of *economic production*. What was needed was a foray into the 'language and methods' of French theory. Sarkar argues it was Lévi-Straussian structuralism that supplied the key to unravelling 'an underlying structure of insurgent peasant consciousness' extending across more than a century of colonial rule and over considerable variations of physical and social space. Guha, it seems, still confined his generalisations to Indian peasants under colonialism, and sought to preserve some linkages in his study of the many forms of resistance – 'from food riots to caste conflict' – with patterns of class exploitation.[231] But if Guha was literally trying to adapt Lévi-Strauss to the Indian case, he might have concluded, rather like Lévi-Strauss himself, that there was no essential difference between the 'concrete logic' of primitive societies and the 'abstract logic' of mathematised science in civilised societies,[232] no vital difference between the structure of the consciousness of the Trobriand Islanders and the modern-day denizens of Paris, with Indian peasants presumably sandwiched somewhere in-between. What one sees is, arguably, something else, more along the lines of a poststructuralist mode of positing completely different and irreconcilable paradigms at work, something in the vein of Foucault,[233] finding expression in this case in the essentialisation of the categories of 'subaltern' and 'autonomy', not only assigning them 'more or less absolute, fixed, decontextualised meanings and qualities',[234] but implicitly attaching them to some fundamental civilisational attribute.

All these tendencies come together in an exemplary work in the Subaltern Studies mode, Ranajit Guha's *Elementary Aspects of Peasant Insurgency*. Guha is not concerned to depict the class war in the countryside via a series of specific encounters, but instead is more interested in getting to its 'general form', elements of which derive from 'the long history of the peasants' subalternity and their striving to end it'.[235] Guha stresses, against the inclination prematurely and condescendingly to subsume peasant rebellions into either

---

231 Brennan 2006, p. 242; Sarkar 1997, p. 87.
232 Lévi-Strauss 1966, p. 269; Anderson 1983, p. 49.
233 Afary and Anderson 2005, p. 131. See also the development of the notion of two paradigms in Guha 1997a.
234 Sarkar 1997, p. 88.
235 Guha 1983a, p. 11.

a framework of inadequacy, misdirection or pre-politicalness – errors that he notes were made by no less a left-inclined historian than Eric Hobsbawm – that they were political, organised and revealed a will to transform the social relations in which the peasantry found themselves.[236] Nor is Guha concerned to paper over the limitations of the political dispensation the peasantry wanted to substitute for the one they were out to destroy, that their model did not conform to a 'secular and national state, … their concept of power failed to rise above localism, sectarianism and ethnicity' and their consciousness was 'inchoate and naïve'.[237] A similar assessment was also present in, for example, David Arnold's study of the *fituris* of the hill dwellers of Andhra. Here the seizing and burning of a police station, for example, was not the prelude to anything approaching a transformation of the oppressive social relations under which the subalterns lived, but rather a temporary 'inversion' in which the police had to beg their captors to spare their lives.[238] To the extent that studies like this represented an important theme in early Subaltern Studies, they reveal some of the frailties of 'spontaneous' peasant insurgency. Guha's motivation here seems to be – in opposition to nationalist and even socialist/communist attempts to write the history of peasant rebellions as if they were mere footnotes in some other history – to emphasise the 'sovereignty, consistency and logic' of peasant subaltern consciousness.[239] Guha was adamant that peasants were *autonomous* actors in the class war that raged in the countryside at least until 1900, after which externally originated frameworks – for example, nationalism – tended to 'invade' their world.[240] Despite this, he maintains that the elementary aspects of peasant insurgency continued to provide the *paradigm*

---

236   Guha 1983a, p. 5.

237   Guha 1983a, p. 11.

238   Arnold 1982, pp. 131–2.

239   Guha 1983a, p. 13.

240   I think this is too late a date for the onset of the intrusion of externally originated frameworks. Studies of the rural economy suggest that the impact of the world market in food grains and commercial crops, especially cotton, was considerable even by the 1860s. Merchant capital, originating as far afield as London, had 'intruded' into the smallest details of production and subsistence. The effects of these intrusions were widely felt, not least in the famines of the second half of the nineteenth-century. They have been well documented in the famine literature. For a synoptic overview of it, see, for example, Davis 2001. The forms in which these intrusions were registered, the methods employed to cope with them, including rural-urban migrations, must all have had an impact on the conceptual world of the peasantry; Satya 1997 demonstrates this very well. Nationalism, it is true, may have come later, but it should be seen as a relatively late stage in the 'intrusion' of externally originated frameworks.

for other struggles including those of urban rebels. Therefore, the centrepiece of Guha's work was a commitment to developing a critical body of knowledge about rural India based on the notion of peasant autonomy, and to argue the perdurance of a paradigm for struggles set down at a moment before political frameworks generated within other political-discursive modes 'invade' the world of the peasantry.

While stressing peasant autonomy might be seen as a necessary corrective, there are a number of difficulties for the claustrophobically enclosed model developed by Guha. In the first instance, as O'Hanlon points out, Guha seems to find the limits to the spread of peasant rebellions to be a function of the subalterns' 'habits of thinking and acting on a small scale',[241] rather than of the ways in which those habits interacted with the impediments set in place by colonial structures, which may have had the effect of deepening social rifts in an already deeply differentiated society. On a more general theoretical level, it is almost as if the 'independent organising principle of the insurgent's mind', grounded in 'a primordial and autonomous insurgent peasant tradition' directs if not determines the historical process.[242] Since Guha has elsewhere been so deeply critical of Hegel, this piece of unconscious Hegelian idealism seems quite ironic. In positing for the peasantry a consciousness marked by religiosity, existing in a pure state especially in the nineteenth century,[243] Guha seems to have fallen for a colonial representation of the peasant rebellion. British officials may have wished to represent peasant rebellion as if it had no causes outside the peasantry's own autonomous, religious consciousness, with no political, social, economic triggers, provocations, and so on, to that extent absolving themselves if not their compradors of any role in creating the oppressive conditions against which peasants rebelled.[244] In fact, this might be an ironic instance of colonial and bourgeois elitism making a covert inroad into Subaltern Studies. It shuts off the whole field of external structural interaction and determination – indeed, the search for causes that might originate outside the consciousness of the peasantry being dismissed as an elitist ploy, with cause seen as a 'phantom surrogate for Reason'[245] – so that 'the potentialities of a movement and its final limits are ... understood in terms of what the culture allows and not in terms of what the structure forecloses'.[246]

---

241   O'Hanlon 2002, p. 153; Gupta 1985, p. 13.

242   Gupta 1985, p. 9.

243   Guha 1983a, p. 13; Singh et al., 2002, p. 69.

244   Singh et al., 2002, p. 69.

245   Guha 1983b, p. 3.

246   Gupta 1985, p. 10.

Indeed, a sense of continuity based on 'primordial' community is a prominent element of early Subaltern Studies narratives of the forms of consciousness and actions, including studies of peasants-turned-workers at industrial plants. Despite offering a historically nuanced account of working-class conditions, Chakrabarty seems to see working-class consciousness as a function of 'primordial loyalties' of religion, community, kinship and language, which was the 'essence' of the pre-capitalist culture of the Calcutta jute-mill workers between 1890 and 1940.[247] There were, of course, greater continuities in a country like India that experienced very slow development through much of the nineteenth century than in the rapidly industrialising imperialist countries. Although the pace picked up in the twentieth century, many parts of India still remained largely agrarian in the mid-twentieth century and beyond. In the developed capitalist world, enclosures of land made a return to the countryside a virtual impossibility for people thrown onto the labour market. In India, such an enclosure movement did not and could not happen despite the interests of the odd British official in bringing plantation-style capitalism to India: the forces required to do this would have been prohibitive. In fact, the colonial government's legislation from 1875 onwards seems to have had the objective of 'protecting' peasant property rights even if the peasantry themselves were hopelessly locked into debt bondage with no prospect of escape. This set up the characteristic dynamics, either of regular circulation migration or a retirement to the village after a period of work in the cities. With the demographic situation of India from the late colonial period onwards, the working class *qua* strictly urban proletariat was always going to be a fraction of the total number who relied on wage work for a living.

Despite all of this, as Chandavarkar's work shows, there was widespread industrial action not only in Bombay, Ahmedabad, Kanpur and Madras, but also in Calcutta. Altogether between 1919 and 1940 there were eight general strikes, each lasting at least a month, some considerably longer.[248] Over the period, it has also been shown, there was a gradual shift from demands for religious holidays to demands for increased wages.[249] Being part of such mass industrial action implies a level of solidarity that goes beyond caste and religious lines, and it was bound to have a major impact on the class consciousness of those who participated in them.[250] Both for Indian workers and their

---

247 Chakrabarty 1983, p. 308.

248 Chandavarkar 1994, pp. 4–5.

249 Das Gupta 1994, pp. 322ff.

250 What Luxemburg says about the mass strikes taking place in Russia in 1905 could have been said, with modifications, of the strikes taking place in India in the aftermath of

English counterparts (the explicit point of contrast that Chakrabarty develops), class consciousness is not some constant, operating ahistorically across time. Bonds of local solidarity, embedded deep in local affective communities, worked very strongly among Welsh miners, as Raymond Williams has shown persuasively,[251] and the nature of class formation that allowed for a continued belonging in a rural community must have reinforced a sense of locational solidarity, regardless of considerations of caste and religion in colonial India.

No doubt, 'community consciousness', expressed through ritualistic relations to the means of production, and hiring dependent on ascriptive and place-of-origin criteria, did not disappear, and has yet to do so even if its forms have changed. But it has had to yield some ground to more impersonal methods, weakening the position of the Sardar,[252] and so on. In this case, the fact that the colonial government acted not as an administrator for capital-in-general, but often as a barrier to capital, is important. Just because the same government introduced limited capitalist social property forms in agriculture and brought about some spotty modernisation does not alter the general argument.

Over time, the notion of autonomy and its accompanying notion of a paradigm of thought and action based on culture have been applied to a larger field of actors, even if this extension has had to hide under a variety of guises, and the concepts themselves have been lost behind thickets of thick description. For instance, when Guha writes '[s]ince our access to the rebel consciousness lay, so to say, through enemy country, we had to seize on the evidence of elite consciousness and force it to show us the way to its Other',[253] the Other is the class enemy, and enemy country is the 'country' of landlords, and their collaborators, not to mention the bureaucracy that enforces class rule. This is the language of class war, even if a somewhat inchoate one. Its virtual disappearance in more recent works, in 'late' Subaltern Studies, brings a different kind of

---

World War I: 'here was the eight-hour day fought for, there piece-work was resisted, here were brutal foremen "driven off" in a sack on a handcar, at another place infamous systems of fines were fought against, everywhere better wages were striven for and here and there the abolition of homework. Backward, degraded occupations in large towns, small provincial towns, which had hitherto dreamed in an idyllic sleep, the village with its legacy from feudalism – all these, suddenly awakened by the January lightning, bethought themselves of their rights and now sought feverishly to make up for their previous neglect'; Luxemburg 1970, p. 175. For a useful introduction to Luxemburg's and Trotsky's views on the mass strike, see Thatcher 2007, pp. 34ff.

251   Williams 1989, pp. 105, 220.

252   This would include the hiring of scabs to break strikes. See, for instance, the discussion of the *badli* system in use in Bombay; Newman 1981.

253   Guha 1983a, p. 333.

polarity into view. This is the one that J.L. Mehta advances, quoted approvingly by Dipesh Chakrabarty in *Provincializing Europe:* '[T]here is no way open, to us *in the East,* but to go through this Europeanisation and to go through it. Only through this voyage into the *foreign and the strange* can *we* win back *our own self-hood*; here as elsewhere, the way to what is closest to us is the longest way back'.[254] The Other is no longer the class enemy; now, enemy territory is the quasi-friendly landscape of the foreigner/stranger. This is no longer a matter of class, but one of civilisational consciousness – part of an Orientalist geography of Asia-Europe, East-West. There seems to have been a hostile takeover of the idea of class contradiction by a class-free civilisational consciousness, a temptation to which Guha himself is not immune.

Even in *Elementary Aspects,* the consciousness of the peasantry seems to have been permeated by the 'Laws of Manu' through centuries of 'recursive practice',[255] which is a bit strained when one considers that it was the colonial policy makers who canonised such texts as representative of Hindu dharma. The substance of this argument runs through Guha's more recent *Dominance without Hegemony,* so one must conclude that this is not some new folly, but rather a 'recursive practice' originating with Subaltern Studies itself. The very idea of long continuities and the abolition of class differences and antagonisms in favour of organic communities of culture is closely affiliated, as noted, not only with a Gandhian legacy of *Hind Swaraj,* but also carries over into the populist thought of Vandana Shiva and others.

A similar logic of continuity appears to underlie the notion of 'paradigm' expounded in *Elementary Aspects.* The elementary aspects of peasant insurgency, informed by long recursive practice, provide the paradigm for later struggles, even for urban rebellions, strikes, insurgencies and the like. In some covert, untheorised way, the peasantry have left a legacy in India even in their collective death throes as a class that for all practical purposes is being extinguished by the relentless invasiveness of capital. They are seen not so much as a constituent element of a combined and potentially hegemonic force contributing to the kind of transformative action that Gramsci or for that matter the Indian Marxists may have envisaged once they had been objectively proletarianised, but one always subject to a precapitalist logic.[256] That is, the notion

---

254   Mehta 1976, p. 466. The quote is in Chakrabarty 2000, p. 298. I have added the emphases to underline the Orientalist categories of Mehta's thought, which are so naturally reproduced by Chakrabarty.

255   Guha 1983a, p. 37.

256   The idea of the endurance and longevity of the peasantry through a multiplicity of vicissitudes is based on an impressionistic notion of cultural continuity and 'existential

of paradigm – the grammar of the profoundly autonomous basis of peasant rebellion bequeathing its structures for subsequent challenges to established norms – now stripped of its radical dimension in class struggles of a particular time and place and immersed in a culturalist framework and agenda, can become the subtext of authenticity. It can inform the notion of an authentic form of self-identical culture, and cultural antiquity, that leaves its stamp on subsequent cultural expressions even – and perhaps especially – when subject to the pressures of actually existing globalisation and commoditisation in all its forms. It is as if resistance is built into the cultural DNA of India, however 'hybridised' and attenuated it might be now. This ties neatly in with the populist notion that only culturally deracinated bourgeois elitists will be permanently attracted to the foreign and the strange. The more authentic types will work their way through it and return to the native fold as Mehta hopes (speaking for a broader postcolonial constituency). India will always be India, in whatever original form it has been cast by populist thought. Since an authentic Indian culture is subterraneously linked with ancient Sanskritic norms and aesthetics, it is indeed the paradigm around which the contaminations of bourgeois elitism can be measured.

Chatterjee claims that Spivak's critique of the limits of representation [*darstellung*] in her famous 'Can the Subaltern Speak?'[257] was a critical moment in the project's evolution from inquiry into subaltern 'autonomy' at moments of rebellion through representations of the subaltern in the colonial archives and mainstream histories to a whole range of subjects connected to colonial governance, education, movements of religious and social reforms, the state and public institutions, modern ideas of rationality, science, regimes of power and related topics.[258] Chatterjee himself has explained the original thrust of the project in investigating 'moments of rebellion' by noting that only at such moments did the subaltern appear 'as the bearer of an independent personality'. That is, when the subaltern rebelled, the masters realised that the servant too has a 'consciousness', interests and objectives, methods and organisation. If one had to look for evidence of an 'autonomous subaltern consciousness' in the historical archives, then it would be found in the documents of revolt

---

form', rather than an understanding of their structural subordination to capital and attempts to limit and challenge, if not break free of, that subordination. In this latter perspective, notional continuities notwithstanding, the peasantry becomes in effect a proletarian labour force producing surplus value for capital, and its struggles form part of the larger arena of the class antagonisms generated by capital.

257   Spivak 1988, pp. 66–111; also in the same vein, Spivak 1985, pp. 338–63.
258   Chatterjee 2006, pp. 12–13.

and counter-insurgency.[259] This seems like an eminently reasonable historicising approach to peasant rebellion, their radical activism in their own cause, however limited and inchoate it was in terms of aims and goals. A critique like Spivak's – which pointed out that the subaltern cannot speak to us simply by a reading of the colonial archives against the grain, revealing, in the process, some deeper essence of subalternity, an essential 'structure' of subaltern consciousness, and so forth – could easily have led to a rethinking of the project of depicting and understanding subaltern rebellion and insurgency. Why it did not do so, but rather led to a scramble for the exits, a jettisoning for all practical purposes of the study of peasant insurgency in properly historical terms a scant five to seven years after the inception of the project, is at first sight somewhat obscure. One could still have examined the subaltern consciousness using a variety of documentary sources, rather in the way popular histories have been written by the likes of Thompson, or, for that matter, Carlo Ginzburg.[260] Or one could even have followed the subalterns into a period when they had learned to 'speak', although both of these approaches would have involved some loss of a (largely fictional) pristine essence and a proper insistence on context, the very 'opposite of the isolated contemplation of the fragmentary'.[261] It seems that one key to the abandonment might lie in the very austerity of the original project, its rejection of the idea that 'insurgency' might not be entirely a matter internal to the subaltern consciousness, and that Cause might not merely be a 'phantom surrogate for Reason', part of a bourgeois strategy of containment.

Guha's preface and introductory essay in the first volume, as Sarkar points out, had been full of references to 'subaltern classes', evocations of Gramsci, and the use of much Marxian terminology.[262] So there was always already a contradiction built into the original project, a tension, shall we say, between the subaltern as an 'active historical agent' on the one hand, and an 'ethically decisive being-in-the-world' on the other. The former evokes a political space of alliances and blocs, of 'leadership acting in the name of specific interests' and a 'collective subject' erupting into a transformative force. The latter evokes, by contrast, a subaltern whose existential being is separated off from an 'imposed and always arrogant rationalism' – indeed, a life 'privileged only insofar as it remains subaltern'.[263] Both versions are present in Guha's accounts of rebellion in an unreconciled tension, the first version, as Brennan notes, pointing

---

259   Chatterjee 2010, p. 292.

260   Of course, the classic is Ginzburg 1980.

261   Sarkar 1997, p. 94.

262   Sarkar 1997, p. 82.

263   Brennan 2006, p. 256.

the way to a condition to be overcome, the second a 'sacred refuge' from the disenchantments of bourgeois life, 'a dark secret space of revelation'.[264] Once the subalterns started behaving like proletarians everywhere, they had in effect lost some vital essence and could be forgotten when not reclassified as members of the dangerous classes.[265]

The repudiation of the 'essential structure' of subaltern consciousness was, as Chatterjee puts it, the arrival of the 'post-structuralist' moment.[266] Foucault, or rather Heidegger via Foucault,[267] would henceforth be quite prominent in the 'late' Subaltern Studies critique of the Enlightenment and western modernity. The shift in left focus that had already occurred with postcolonial studies in the US – from classes to identitarian groups, from class struggles to the new social movements, from material interests to 'immaterial desires and self-understandings' – was replicated[268] to a considerable degree in Subaltern Studies. Domination was conceptualised in cultural-discursive terms as the power-knowledge of the post-Enlightenment West. If at all embodied in institutions, it was identified with the modern 'bureaucratic nation-state'.[269] Chakrabarty summed it up as a shift from the attempt to 'write better Marxist histories' to an understanding that 'a critique of this nature could hardly afford

---

264   Ibid.

265   Chatterjee refers to the 'squalor, ugliness and violence of popular life', the violence and the danger posed to 'civil society' by the heterogeneous populations (political society) who float in and out of governmental programmes of reform in West Bengal see Chatterjee 2004, pp. 74, 129–130, 135, 142–147. In his own words: 'As I have frequently pointed out, political society is not like a gentleman's club; it can often be a nasty and dangerous place' (Chatterjee 2004, p. 130). The trope of violence, of course, extends back to the study of peasant rebellions in the early volumes of Subaltern Studies, but now that it is associated with an urban precariat, and no longer subject to patronage controls, there is a sense of a far more pervasive and present danger to the lives of the propertied classes. It is the closing of the space that might be a crucial dimension in the dire tone that Chatterjee occasionally adopts.

266   Chatterjee 1999, p. 416.

267   Schaub 1989, pp. 306–7. Schaub argues that Foucault conceals the influence of Heidegger's philosophy on his own thinking by never mentioning him. But as Erebon points out, Foucault conceded that his 'entire philosophical development was determined by [his] reading of Heidegger' (Erebon 1991, p. 30; see also Brennan 2006, p. 258). More to the point, the Romantic side of the Oriental Renaissance seemed to have a significant impact on Foucault's thinking. This becomes clear in reading Foucault's pronouncements on the Iranian revolution. The appendices in Afary and Anderson are very useful in collecting some of this material together; see Afary and Anderson 2005.

268   Brennan 2006, p. 245.

269   Sarkar 1997, p. 84.

to ignore the problem of universalism/Eurocentrism that was inherent in Marxist (or for that matter liberal) thought itself'.[270]

For a project now increasingly interested in a critique of the Western episteme, in a notion of the Eurocentric and economistic Marx, of difference posited along an East-West divide, the study of peasant rebellions – that are, for the most part, similar in form, structure and, sadly, outcomes as well – does not afford much room for the inventions of difference, especially along a culturalised axis. A study of peasant rebellions, over a significant span of time and space, should lead not towards an interest in fragments or culturalised difference, but towards a realisation of the socio-economic forces that produce class polarisation and an insurgent consciousness that informs class struggles. A strategic abandonment of that project would then point to something else. So perhaps Chatterjee might have included the pull of the 'something else' as a factor in abandoning the 'fragmentary, disconnected and incomplete' moment of peasant rebellions for the more salubrious regions of postcolonial understandings of governance, science, regimes of power and the like.[271]

It is surely an unintended irony that one of the cover blurbs of *Elementary Aspects* calls this book a 'classic in subaltern studies as well as in postcolonial studies'. This would be a sort of subsumption, or subduction, by which the concepts underlying the class concerns of Guha's earlier work have been swept under the civilisational concerns of postcolonial studies, by which a radical agenda aimed at illustrating how pre-literate rebellion was organised and fought has been quietly displaced by the agenda of a hyper-literate academic elite trying to find a respectable place at the banquet of multiculturalism. One does not get the impression that either the proponents of Subaltern Studies or postcolonial populism, who posit long-term continuities and global divisions, have made a deep study of either today's popular cultures or Sanskrit aesthetics, philosophy and related disciplines. So I assume that positing such continuities is simply a polemical device directed against those who would argue that ruptures and new beginnings are the stuff of history. This is especially the case as the autonomy and continuity of any acquired form of social life is under constant assault and imminent threat of dissolution with the further progression of the subsumption of hitherto autonomous social forms to capital.

In a March 1988 editorial, the *Social Scientist* – a journal with CPI(M) affiliations, which had paid close attention to the early volumes of Subaltern Studies – acknowledged the historiographical contributions of the project, but suggested nonetheless that '[s]ome may feel that . . . by now so much has

---

270   Chakrabarty 1993, p. 10.
271   Chatterjee 2006, p. 12.

been written on the "subaltern school" that the topic itself has become somewhat stale".[272] Coinciding as it did with the publication of *Selected Subaltern
Studies* in the US, with Ranajit Guha and Gayatri Chakravorty Spivak as editors
and with a Foreword by Edward Said, the fortunes of Subaltern Studies would
henceforth be tied to US-style postcolonial studies. While in the West, discussion and acclaim has proliferated since the late 1980s, within India by contrast
there has been a largely 'derivative adulation', but nothing remotely resembling the critical engagement of the early years.[273] For the American interlocutors of Subaltern Studies, it was the postcolonial-theoretical possibilities that
were attractive. As Said noted in a closing remark in his Foreword, 'All in all, the
first appearance of a selection from *Subaltern Studies* before a general Anglo-
American audience is a noteworthy event',[274] preceding that remark by noting:
'[s]o in reading this selection from *Subaltern Studies* one becomes aware that
this group of scholars is a self-conscious part of the vast post-colonial cultural
and critical effort' involving prominent poets, novelists, political theorists and
so on.[275] Even earlier, Ronald Inden had praised Subaltern Studies in terms
of 'Indians ... perhaps for the first time since colonization, showing sustained
signs of reappropriating the capacity to *represent* themselves'.[276]

So what was important was the capacity of Indians to represent themselves vis-à-vis the West, and for intellectuals from the former colonies to stake
a place in the spectrum of US-style identity politics and multiculturalism.
Neither Inden nor Said had much use for anything as exotic and barbarous
as the structure of subaltern consciousness, but found the Subaltern Studies'
critique of the Western episteme useful; for Said, it went along with his critique
of Orientalism. One can understand why an embattled Palestinian intellectual
in New York might wish to embrace – opportunistically, it must be said – a
contingent of intellectuals from India. They had their uses, but he would
have been less than enthused about their poststructuralist leanings. So for a
whole variety of historical reasons, the structure of subaltern consciousness
had to go – or go underground – and Spivak provided eloquent enough arguments. But one suspects that the postcolonial turn of Subaltern Studies may
have more to do with the reception in places like the United States, Britain,
Canada and Australia of French 'theory', and the whole complex of meanings
attachable to the notion of representation that it affords, than anything to do

---

272   Editorial Note 1988, *Social Scientist* 16(3), p. 1.
273   Sarkar 1997, p. 84.
274   Said 1988, p. x.
275   Said 1988, p. ix.
276   Inden 1986, p. 445, emphasis added.

with 'the realities of cultural decolonisation' or transformations of 'the international division of labour'.[277]

Perhaps 'French theory' itself was just a vehicle for a 'European' or (more
likely) German tradition, associated with Schopenhauer, Nietzsche, and on
to Heidegger, that Megill refers to as 'crisis-thought'.[278] All of them to varying
degrees had referred to the 'Orient', or any rate the Aryan Orient, in their philosophical texts, none more so than Nietzsche, who apparently called on the
Vedanta in his critique of European modernity.[279] Aryan India had been summoned to the great task of addressing the deficiencies of the West, and helping
it recover from the decline brought about by Christianity, the Enlightenment,
secularism, revolution, and all the other usual suspects. German 'crisis-thought'
suitably sanitised and deodorised in post-1968 Paris, a little helpful *pressing* taking the nihilism and the racism out of the equation, was now being summoned
for a similar task in another crisis. In its French manifestation, genealogy was
no longer about family in the extended sense or the 'genetic inevitabilities of
paternity';[280] it was about fragments, detotalisation and so on.

What was it about the integral structure of subaltern consciousness that
might have made it problematic in the American academic – particularly an
immigrant-academic – milieu? What exactly were the Subaltern Studies people foisting on the peasantry? Was it ultimately something to do with Aryanism
(the Aryan 'laws of Manu' for instance, with a little help from Nietzsche), a
once great civilisation reduced to subalternity and beggary? Perhaps it was
really a problem of the unconscious, an unacknowledged romanticism about
an ancient civilisation that had been passed through the phenomenological
guts of European crisis-thought and poststructuralism. Chakrabarty's reference to the culture of North Indian peasants, in his 'Conditions of Knowledge'
essay, is eloquent in this regard.[281] The North-South divide is paradigmatic in
Indian history – rural north India is the original Aryavarta,[282] and the north-
south pervasion of civilisation was, in Mortimer Wheeler's words, 'logical and
integral'.[283] So Subaltern Studies in its postcolonial turn had to leave the peasants of Aryavarta aside, put some distance between itself and the deep structure of an integral peasant consciousness *en route* to discovering a more global

277   Larsen 2002, pp. 204–5.
278   Megill 1985, p. 183.
279   Schaub 1989, p. 308.
280   Brennan 2002, pp. 186–7.
281   This is repeated in Chakrabarty 2000, pp. 76–7.
282   Moreland and Chatterjee 1953, p. 12.
283   Wheeler 1966, p. 136.

and salubrious destiny. Perhaps it was also a question of audibility: abandoning the residues of Marxism and adopting (or adapting) French theory would raise the immigrant intellectuals' voice above the threshold of inaudibility and let it take its place in a much wider movement of intellectuals coming to the US in the wake of the 1965 immigration reforms.

Insofar as Gramsci has survived the postcolonial turn, he has been assigned some light duties, transformed into a heterodox Marxist with an anticipatory foot in the politics of the new social movements with their ethics of 'dispersion, instability and displacement',[284] rather than in the Leninist project of a punctual overcoming of bourgeois civilisation involving, among other more political matters, a break with the stranglehold of organised religion, the Church, the reactionary clerisy, and so on. Chatterjee's injunction not to inject into 'popular life' a 'scientific form of thought springing from elsewhere', but to 'develop and make critical an activity that already exists in popular life',[285] might be read as a critique of elitism or bureaucratic centralism, but it hangs on to a residue of the old notion of a subaltern consciousness formed deep in the folds of a culture that remains inaccessible to outsiders. Representation then requires the authorised interpreter, someone armed with more than mere linguistic competence or some variant of now defunct vanguardist theory. In Chatterjee's more recent work, this 'making critical' has acquired a practical dimension – 'dirty[ing] one's hands in the complicated business of the politics of governmentality'[286] – a project of democracy in which the precariat can be assigned an acceptable place while it slowly develops out of its own cultural resources the behaviours and forms acceptable to civil society.

---

284 Brennan attributes the invention of the New Left, 68ist Gramsci to Norberto Bobbio and Chantal Mouffe; see Bobbio 1987, pp. 139–61; Mouffe 1979; Brennan 2006, p. 240.

285 Chatterjee 1993, p. 199.

286 Chatterjee 2004, p. 23.

Colonialism, Modernity, Postcolonialism

The following pages subject two of the keywords of the postcolonial lexicon – colonialism and modernity – to a close reading. They are simultaneously periodising concepts and structuring categories. They also inflect each other, as in the compound term 'colonial modernity', which is supposed to indicate the limits of a Eurocentric historical perspective that imagines modernity either to replicate the European pattern or to be considered inadequate, distorted or otherwise a corruption of the original. Colonial modernity is characterised in some versions, particularly the version made popular by some of the founding members of Subaltern Studies, through the spatial metaphor of Inside/Outside. The Outside is already a victory for the West in terms of its institutions of governance and its technologies of production and societal control. It is on the Inside that one looks for originality, and this is the domain of culture most generally portrayed in terms of fraternal affective bonds, gender relations, traditional social relations, and so on. The objective of the argument that follows is to illustrate that while postcolonial studies polemicises relentlessly against metanarratives, there are the makings of a culturalised and reified metanarrative within postcolonial studies. In analysing the constituent elements of this *grand récit*, the following pages also wish to make clear the limitations of organising a historical narrative around colonialism and modernity that fails in the first place to historicise them adequately.

3.1 Colonialism and Modernity in a Postcolonial Framing

Postcolonial studies seems to experience some considerable difficulty in foregrounding a critical study of capital as a centrepiece of its analysis of postcoloniality – capital smacks of political economy, and 'economism' as something to do with the economy is now a very bad word. Stuart Hall's judgement on what has followed the abandonment of 'deterministic economism' might stand as the definitive statement for now: not alternative ways of 'thinking about economic relations and their effects ... but a massive, gigantic, and eloquent disavowal'.[1] So what are the principal categories around which postcoloniality

---

1 Hall 1996, p. 258. There are some partial exceptions to this. Partha Chatterjee, for example, discusses the planning process in India with reference to the challenges of what he calls

is studied? Colonialism is one; modernity is another. Colonialism is perforce one of its principal categories. Otherwise, in the first instance, the very notion of postcolonialism would be abstract, ahistorical and vapid. It is not entirely unexpected, then, that with pre- and post-fixes colonialism becomes the foundation of historical transitions and transformations around which a virtual periodisation is achieved. Virtual because after all the postcolonial is said to originate in the first act of resistance to colonialism.[2] As for the 'pre' in this categorial organisation, it is as if:

> all that came before it becomes a prehistory of colonialism itself, so that literally thousands of years of contradiction, sociality and creativity come to be gathered up under the singular heading of 'precolonial', as if those diverse temporalities, those conflicts and principles of structuration, could now only be recalled in relation to the changes that the coming of the East India Company was to cause.[3]

There is no question that the changes brought about by the East India Company and its successor state constitute an indispensable part of the definition of colonialism, a historically determinate transition, a local manifestation of a wider phenomenon informed by an understanding of the structural economic subordination and subsumption of the autonomous pre-existing social forms of vast regions to the capitalism that had originally developed in parts of western Europe. The historical specificity of the colonialism that resulted, itself born of prior ruptures, transitions and so on, is not in question.

However, for postcolonial studies, as understood here, colonialism is more crucially the attempted erasure or submergence of a whole host of lifeworlds and 'unbroken traditions' that flourished in those regions until the arrival of modern Europe. Colonialism, then, is the colonisation of the lifeworlds of the various non-European peoples who came under European domination. What seems particularly important, in this definition, is that traditions kept alive through untold generations have by now been 'reduced' to history, are seen

---

'originary accumulation' of capital, although there is the characteristic postcolonial tic of seeing 'Europe' or the 'West' on one side, and 'India' on the other, as the categorial frame around which a globalised theory of difference can be constructed; Chatterjee 1993, pp. 208ff. I will return to this below.

2   This is pointed out by Ahmad 1995, p. 14.

3   Ahmad 1995, p. 30.

as 'dead',[4] or have simply assumed submerged forms in the consciousness and 'world' of the subalterns. The postcolonial denizen of any country should be able to identify the historical moment when something precious and definitive in the realm of the soul of their nation was lost, generally through the irruption of foreign and inauthentic elements. In the more progressive postcolonial circles, this is limited to the irruption of Western Enlightenment-inspired Europeans.[5] In less progressive (communalist) variants, the foreign, inauthentic element could be some other group, for example, the Muslims of Southwest Asia.[6]

To the extent that colonialism is the categorial focus, postcolonial studies, rather like the nationalism it likes to criticise, revolves around the colonisation of incipiently national territories and, more so perhaps, the minds of the original denizens of those territories, and their subjection henceforth to European norms. Generally, for reasons of education and linguistic competence, postcolonial historians focus on 'their' nation – the nation they have been educated to believe existed even before colonial rule burst in on it – if, that is, they are part of an immigrant intelligentsia.[7] The role of colonialism, then, is believed to lie in the foisting of an inauthentic geo-body on the cultural nation,[8] whose origins stretch back before historic time.

The colonisation of land and territory, in a formal sense, has ended, but an implicit argument is that the minds of the formerly colonised and their descendants are still somehow incompletely decolonised. Postcolonialism steps in to demonstrate the extent to which the post-Enlightenment project of modernisation is still and always was a continuation of the colonial project, and to demonstrate that there was an autonomous inner domain that was beyond the grasp of the colonisers and that was perfected to the requirements

---

4   See, for example, the following statement: '[T]he intellectual traditions once unbroken and alive in Sanskrit or Persian or Arabic are now only matters of historical research for most ... They treat these traditions as dead, as history' (Chakrabarty 2000, pp. 5–6).

5   The extent to which the colonial enterprise was inspired by Enlightenment ideals is anybody's guess. Mostly, it seems European colonies were run by the sorts of louts about which George Orwell writes, based on his experience in Burma in the 1920s; Orwell 1997 [1934].

6   This is the sort of discourse that the Shiv Sena, for instance, purveys, but it is anticipated by perfectly respectable Hindu nationalists of an earlier day; see, for example, Savarkar 1969, pp. 135ff.

7   Area-studies training is the other method by which historians with no 'ethnic' claim to belong to a former colony establish their competence, and perhaps even their belonging. On the overall continuities and discontinuities between area-studies and postcolonial studies, see Harootunian 1999 and Young 2001.

8   The concept of the geo-body is explored in depth by Thongchai Winichakul 1997.

of a cultural, often religiously infused, nationalism even prior to the 'battle' against political colonialism. If the latter was waged outside the home, the former was 'waged in the home...outside the arena of political agitation'.[9] Generally, the women's question looms large in such considerations, and the argument of an Inside/Outside dichotomy is sustained by the 'evidence' of the supposed absence of 'any autonomous struggle by women themselves for equality and freedom'.[10]

It is on the Inside that the originality of colonial modernity is revealed, whereas on the Outside European domination is conceded and political nationalism proceeds, as it were, in derivative and even imitative forms. It is in the former domain that the colonised and former colonised are more than 'mere consumers of modernity', and it is here that 'an anti-colonial nationalism uncontaminated by the force of a colonising presence' takes shape.[11] Henceforth, it is free to take, as required, anything on offer from Europe, since it is inoculated against Westoxication in the crucial domain of culture. However, such victories are by their nature fragile, and in Ashis Nandy's strictures on much nationalism in India today, one encounters the old themes of postcolonial nation states that have lost touch with their 'pre-modern pasts'.[12] The colonisation of minds by the post-Enlightenment project of European colonialism used to be a favourite taunt of the Gandhians and all manner of populist discourses, and it remains a popular theme, with suitable exemptions for the extraordinary abilities of a few great men to overcome the overwhelming grip of post-Enlightenment colonial power-knowledge, and leave a larger and more valuable legacy for the formerly colonised.[13]

An unspoken, unacknowledged condition of acceptability may be involved for postcolonial studies, ironically set largely by metropolitan interlocutors, which decides the initial conditions of entry and a subsequent broader reception. Postcolonial thought that had to do with the challenges of economic modernisation, or the more radical, politically charged liberation ideologies, never acquired the kind of acceptance that postcolonial studies of the poststructuralist variety has done in the Anglophone metropolitan academy.

---

9   Chatterjee 1993, p. 133.
10 Chatterjee 2010, pp. 133–4.
11 Harootunian 1999, p. 130.
12 Nandy 1994, p. 86.
13 A few great, generally male, thinkers are able to overcome the limitations imposed by the colonial inheritance; in Nandy's exposition, Tagore and Gandhi being the prime exemplars. On the originality of Gandhi and Tagore, respectively, in this regard, see Chatterjee 1986 and Guha 2002.

Does the latter somehow pose deeper and more important questions? Or is it the case that even Western modernisation thought thrived on the terrain of cultural difference and civilisational otherness, such that what the metropolitan interlocutors wanted to hear from their 'postcolonial' colleagues was not a universalising, much less totalising, discourse grounded in a close analysis of capital and its colonial forms? And by extension, were they almost certainly not expecting an analysis of the systematically polarising tendencies of capital that made a mockery of modernisation, but something else rooted in culture? The career of one of the keywords of postcolonial thought, 'difference', is instructive in this regard. When it enters the postcolonial lexicon, it quickly acquires connotations of exoticism, untranscendable otherness, and the like, which immediately links it with a long-standing tradition of Orientalism. Without a grand narrative of colonialism, and its *total* impact on 'pre-colonial' societies, postcolonialism would simply be a time-marked descriptive term. That it is not so indicates an exorbitation of the term beyond anything that Marxists, who are frequently accused of totalising and determinist schema, would consider. In the process, we get the reified, ahistorical categories of Europe/India (or China, or Senegal) that are the staples of culturalised metanarratives ('meta' in its proper etymological sense). However, since postcolonial studies generally, and Subaltern Studies in its postcolonial turn specifically, have aligned themselves with poststructuralist thought – Marxism being declared a dead dog – then it also needs to embrace the entire business of a suspicion of grand narratives, and so on.

Postcolonialism finds itself tracing, in a subaltern register, the tendency of poststructuralist thought to ground itself in a suspicion of totalities, totalisation – sometimes casually linked with totalitarianism,[14] no doubt following the dubious lead of Heidegger and Arendt in the use of the term[15] – and, of course, the grand narrative. The result is a paradox: if an encompassing and universalising narrative of the impact of colonialism and its enduring and seemingly ineradicable effects are indispensable to postcolonial studies, then we do indeed have a grand narrative. But postcolonialism must reject that description. This, I suppose, we could call a post-foundationalist move, a grand narrative undertaken in a spirit of absent-mindedness. Depending on how one looks at it, the motivation for this move will vary: (a) it is the unconscious lie

---

14   Dews 1987, p. 201; Thompson 2004, p. 15.
15   For example, Heidegger's idea of modernity's culmination in a 'totalitarian world technology', whether in its American, Soviet or Nazi versions, even though Heidegger was not unsympathetic to the last; Afary and Anderson 2005, p. 17; Steiner 1987, p. 28; Gillespie 1984, pp. 127–8. See also Arendt 1976.

that can never be examined, so postcolonial studies needs to do an end run around a properly historicising analysis of imperialism and its manifestations in colonialism; (b) the response to an urgent need to cover up the social form of the economic, thus naturalising inequalities under ascriptive titles; (c) the further naturalising effects of the displacement of categories like 'hybridity' from animal breeding to cultural identities; (d) the price to be paid for getting a hearing in the first place.

At the critique-of-metanarrative level, the *colonial* relationship between the coloniser and the colonised that is the lynchpin of postcolonialism becomes a redundancy, if not a liability. Epistemological uncertainty and the ensuing rejection of all efforts at causal explanation, or even contextual analysis, should certainly point to such a conclusion. After all, pain and pleasure, emotions of various kinds, confrontations, loss and gain, are all simply so many turns of the wheel associated with human life, as it were. So too the innocence that Nandy wishes to defend in his *The Intimate Enemy*.[16] The Foucauldian genealogical approach that seems to inform many of the micro-narratives of the Subaltern Studies variety is not interested in the big questions of the 'destiny of a peo- ple', certainly not with causal or contextual explanations, which all give rise to bad universal histories, but rather with 'accidents' and 'minute deviations', and even with 'errors' that somehow conspire to produce the modern axis of power and knowledge.[17] Since modernity is not just a European monopoly, and the colonised people are also 'producers' of modernity, the logical conclusion is that the 'colonial' in postcolonial can be dispensed with and postcolonial studies can take its place alongside poststructuralism or post-modernism as just another post-marked discourse interested in fragments that may come with names and places, but which all seem sufficiently homogenised as to be interchangeable. The reinsertion of this discourse of fragments into the world of colonialism – with its supposed post-Enlightenment epistemic violence and subjugating propensities (the demiurgic if not metanarrativist end of postco- lonialism) – strikes one as arbitrary, and theoretically incoherent.

This would be the case even if one were to reintroduce some context. So, for instance, in Pandey's studies of communal violence that take their stand against the 'economism' of secular intellectuals, which leaves 'little room for the emotions of people, for feelings and perceptions' through their emphasis on 'land and property'.[18] Merely to argue, as Sarkar does, that people can get emotional (experience pain and loss) over issues of land and property, and

---

16   Nandy 1983, p. ix.
17   Foucault 1984a, p. 81.
18   Pandey 1991, p. 566; Pandey 1994, pp. 188–221.

that therefore socio-economic and emotional issues are sometimes intimately interconnected is insufficient.[19] What is more likely to be at issue here is that an anti-causal argument seeking to avoid a grand narrative covertly assumes something about the nature of the protagonists: that they are somehow emotional creatures who do not respond to materialist notions and conform to a type. That is, there is the assumption – covert, to be sure – that transformations of social-property relations cannot help ground larger patterns of violence in, for example, colonial India, and indeed cannot account, to some extent, for the emotional investments made in certain types of (communal) politics and certain types of geographies of belonging and alienation (for example, the notion that Muslims are permanent aliens in the subcontinent). In itself, this is not inconsistent with administrative Orientalism and its rather generalised and homogenised assumptions about colonised populations being different from that of the colonisers. Possibly against his better political judgement, since he has elsewhere shown the socio-economic elements involved in communal riots,[20] Pandey has to conclude with some trite 'philosophical' comments about how historians depict pain and how difficult it is to do so. This suggests a demarche of the kind that Thompson and Jameson, writing about postmodernism, indicate: either towards 'a kind of metaphysical full stop',[21] or towards 'quite unphilosophical empirical and anti-systemic positivist attitudes and opinions' in supposed 'opposition to metaphysics'.[22]

In Nandy's case, the depiction of the pre-colonial condition contains an attack on 'modernity'. He contrasts the innate plurality and tolerance of 'religion as faith' of pre-modern times with the situation that came to prevail under the auspices of the Enlightenment-informed project that created the conditions for a less tolerant and monolithic 'religion as ideology', based on a fundamental secularising of the grounds of religious practice.[23] This, of course, reduces Indians to passive recipients of modernity generated elsewhere. The relationship of such developments to colonialism *per se* is rather adventitious and secondary. In either case, attempts to avoid a narrative – grand or otherwise – based on a properly historical grasp of causes and contexts that would necessarily include their relationship to a local development of a global mode of production, and that would in turn ground a critical historical materialist

---

19   Sarkar 1997, p. 102.

20   A number of such cases are discussed in Pandey 1990.

21   Thompson 1993, p. 188.

22   Jameson 1993, p. 184.

23   Nandy 1998, pp. 322–3.

understanding of colonialism and modernity, end up producing arbitrary and poorly conceptualised results.

The assumption that colonial rule brought about an absolute break in pre-colonial society – long-lived traditions now reduced to 'history' – is a crucial one for postcolonial studies. Colonial 'cultural' domination devoid of all 'complexities and variations' confronts an indigenous domain similarly homogenised.[24] To the extent that colonial anthropology worked with the notion of a non-contradictory hierarchy in pre-colonial society, it did not record the instances of exploitation, oppression and so on, indigenous to that society, or at any rate not in ways that would suggest the possibility of some, superficial at least, continuation into colonial times. The tradition-modernity dualism required clear geographic referents. The rupture that occurred was primarily in the cultural domain, and in the introduction of the categories of modernisation including capital and labour to a population to which they were alien.

The implicit Marxist critique of this method of thinking has required seeing all societies, including capitalism, as exploitative, albeit in historically determinate ways. Pre-colonial societies themselves, like pre-modern societies in Europe, were the sites of major social contradictions between immediate producers and those who extracted unpaid labour in kind and in services, which then interacted with the socio-economic imperatives of the emergent new form of capitalism, including its colonial variations, to produce singular outcomes that cannot be adequately expressed in the vocabulary of 'hybridity'.[25] This is especially so when the intended contrast posits Europe on one side and the colonised countries on the other. Culture in this case can be thought of both as the ideological 'dominant', intended to hold a contradictory social form together, and as a form of struggle against the dominant. The ideological dominant is unlikely to stress the social contradictions. The plebeian element of culture as a struggle against the dominant can be occluded either by positing a subaltern consciousness not open to 'causal' imperatives located in the larger social formation, or by turning it into an existential trope that works as a standing rebuke of Enlightenment-inspired modernity.

Postcolonial studies quietly adopts, or more likely adapts, some of the ideas of colonial anthropology, whereby pre-colonial societies have a non-exploitative, non-contradictory hierarchy until modernity comes along. The latter position was part of a very rich tradition of anti-modernist anthropology and sociology in Europe that applied this argument as much to Europe itself as to

---

24   Sarkar 1994, pp. 205–24.

25   Some of the methodological implications of this line of thinking are nicely anticipated in rather different contexts by Hilton 1990 and Kosambi 2009; see also Habib 1995.

the colonies. Thus, Louis Dumont's work can be considered a 'retranslation' into the post World War II universe of social anthropology, of philosophical and sociological questions previously expressed by the advocates of a conservative Catholic and nationalist culture in France. Among their ranks we find Charles Maurras and René Guénon, who 'denigrated reason while strongly supporting the concepts of social order and hierarchy'.[26] That is, the mid-1930s 'crisis' of an integral Catholicism with its nostalgia for an imagined organic community of non-contradictory hierarchy, ritual and continuity prompted some searching for a place where such things might have obtained until recently. 'Aryan' India – an inexhaustible resource for Europe – was found to be one such place. Dumont writes to reveal the 'hierarchical principle' that frames Indian society in terms of a 'Universal Totality', and argues that it teaches us something about *the structure of common, non-modern, I'm tempted to say, normal values*.[27] This privileging of traditional social orders over modern ones, for holding to properly universal values, including a non-contradictory (and presumably non-exploitative) hierarchy was a very powerful resource for certain 'traditional', or more likely reactionary, strands of Indian nationalism, and Gandhi's writings are replete with this theme.

In different forms, the privileging of the pre-modern, or in the European case the medieval over the modern, has also come via a certain strand of poststructuralism. Foucault's critique of Western modernity not only posited an Oriental difference but also an ancient and medieval one. In some odd way, Foucault even blurred the two, assimilating for instance the Graeco-Roman world to the East.[28] Rather like Dumont and earlier the intellectuals of Catholic intégrisme and German Romantics like Friedrich Schlegel, Foucault drew a dividing line between pre-modern and modern European societies. This tradition is of critical significance to Subaltern Studies, more so in its postcolonial turn. A variety of tributary streams have flowed into a broad river. Whereas Dumont and the Catholic intellectuals spoke in the name of a universal traditionalism that has been interrupted autochthonously only in the West, postcolonialists speak as if such traditionalism is a sign of difference. Catholic anti-modernists and agnostic or atheist post-modernists seem to be walking arm-in-arm. Implicitly, Europe is held to be always predisposed to modernity, even before modernity existed (always already modern, so to speak), and endowed with some sort of demiurgic desire to impose it on others.

---

26   Lardinois 1996, pp. 30–1.
27   Dumont 1983, p. 248, cited in Lardinois 1996, p. 33, emphasis added.
28   Afary and Anderson 2005, pp. 19–20.

In that case, the overwhelming nature of post-Enlightenment (colonial) power-knowledge is indigenous to Europe and is brought to bear on non-European indigenes in such a way as virtually to rob them of any original expression, to make them at best capable of 'derivative discourses', unless, of course, they were or are 'traditional' intellectuals who remain immune to the pressure, despite in some cases being fully exposed to Western discourses, as undoubtedly Gandhi and Tagore were. The socio-economic divide between the class of 'traditional intellectuals', overwhelmingly bound up with structures of landlord and bureaucratic domination, and peasant communities apparently do not matter;[29] hierarchies are non-contradictory as long as they are not modern ones. When Gandhi asks: 'What is the system of Varnashrama but a means of harmonising the difference between high and low, as well as between capital and labour?',[30] he gives expression to this view. The division that does matter is between the West and, in this case, India, or between a Westernised intelligentsia and 'traditionalists' in touch with their pre-modern pasts. Of course, the 'discourses' of the colonial bourgeoisie could have been both derivative and expressive of their class interests. On the one hand, they hoped to inherit the colonial structures as the new ruling class; they did not have to create anything through a 'bourgeois revolution'. On the other, they had no intention of going much beyond the structural limits of colonial capitalism.

For the moment, however, it is important to note that postmodern/postcolonial histories cannot consistently avoid connections to larger causal fields as part of any historical explanation: in looking for silences, ambiguities, and so on, even the most rigid sceptics are forced to dig deeper, beyond what is said to how it is said, how it is historically possible to say whatever was said, the historical forms of rhetoric, historically determinate silences, and so on. The whole pretension that history is just another literary narrative gives way to something else: a going beyond sheer micro-narrative and surface forms to investigate a deeper content. The content may be unstable – when has it been otherwise in history; after all, not even the most impeccable Rankean historian of today would interpret the French Revolution the way its contemporaries did – but that does not prevent the actual investigation of a reality that is not simply revealed to common sense or a superficial gaze. Something else is needed: a feel for time and place, for cultural nuances, for what might have been *meant*, and so on.[31] When postcolonial theorists, for example, come to considerations of the past, they are not above utilising not merely their linguistic competence,

---

29   Sarkar 1997, p. 92; see also Chatterjee 1986, p. 100; Chatterjee 1984, p. 176.

30   Gandhi 1947, ch. 8.

31   Thompson 2004, p. 40.

nuances of social and cultural practices, the special significance of the categories in use in specific circumstances, but also their sense of the history of the region they study, knowledge of longer term economic and political trends, not to mention abstract categories like capital and labour. In other words, they seek to locate a particular moment of a local history in longer term continuities and interruptions caused by a variety of historical forces.[32]

In many respects, there seem to be two layers in operation in postcolonial histories: claims about history as a text with all sorts of interpretative latitude, slapdash attacks on 'good history' as evolutionist and universalising,[33] but frequently enough accompanied by attempts to practice the same denigrated good history to understand longer term trends encompassing a larger arena than their micro-histories might involve. So perhaps this is the return of a repressed sense of history, not as mere textualisation, but a longer term unfolding of dynamics contained in the capitalist mode of production, conceived in its larger (dare one say, totalising) sense. If there is a grain of truth in this, then we might identify a dominant register within which postcolonial theory works to exoticise the regions it studies, while perhaps unintentionally naturalising by amnesia the commodity economy and putting forward an agenda suggesting an end to history's pretensions if not history itself. Furthermore, there is a subordinate register, which undertakes good historical analysis, even as it keeps alive some kind of hope of change for the better, even if it eschews a proper theorisation of the issues raised thereby.[34]

The implications of the foregoing raise an important question: if the colonisation of the lifeworlds of the subalterns is the critical defining moment, then why the need for the Europe-Other aspect of the definition? We must assume this submersion of the 'world' of the subalterns happened in Europe as well, much more comprehensively than elsewhere, since it seems now that this lost world of the subaltern in European societies is only recoverable through painstaking archival research into a fairly distant past, except perhaps on Europe's peripheries, for example, in the Orkney Islands or Sardinia. Whereas if we are

---

32   Sarkar 1987 cites Ranajit Guha's essay, 'Chandra's Death', in Subaltern Studies V, but there is more than a sense of this in Guha's more recent *Dominance without Hegemony*. This work is much overlaid with stock postcolonial themes, but frequently escapes their grasp. This is evident to a lesser extent in Chatterjee's and Chakrabarty's work, and even in Gyan Prakash's earlier work which will be examined below.

33   This is analysed in Kaiwar 2005b, pp. 136–50.

34   Thompson makes similar points about a postmodern historian of England like Patrick Joyce, suggesting these positions are not intrinsic to postcolonial historians; Thompson 2004, pp. 52–4.

to believe Ranajit Guha, exemplars of that older 'world' were walking relatively unscathed around rural Bengal within a stone's throw of Calcutta until about 1900, after which their world was only gradually 'invaded'. In that case we might argue, with some degree of logical consistency if not historical plausibility, that Europe colonised itself thoroughly before attempting a much weaker, and more compromised, version on the rest of the world!

One might be tempted to conclude that this kind of postcolonial categorial framing must include its own forms of suppression, objectification, condescension and aestheticisation. For a project that sought inspiration in Gramsci's writings, the tendency to pass lightly over the toll taken by 'traditional' religious practices on the subaltern population is puzzling. The type of subordination to which women of lower-ranked castes were subject within and outside temple precincts, the uses of Hindu dharma to naturalise inequalities, and indeed to justify untouchability, might have drawn inspiration from Gramsci's scathing portrayal of the reactionary nostalgia of what he calls 'Father Bresciani's progeny',[35] whom Brennan refers to as 'lowbrow literary popularisers of the superstitions of Catholic dogma',[36] and whose equivalents were and remain very much part of the Indian cultural scene. A study of the manner in which the so-called 'traditional' elite, itself tightly integrated into colonial rule via the structures of landlordism, waged its end of a class struggle in the countryside in pursuit of rack rents and taxes could have mobilised a critical understanding of their supposed immunity to Western Enlightenment norms. It would also have exposed the mechanisms of exploitation and oppression in the countryside.

As for the struggle over the 'women question' in the emerging urban society of nineteenth-century Calcutta, its structuring by certain strands of cultural nationalism around 'male nationalist anxieties' over the issues of 'cultural identity and colonial subjection' would have benefitted from something approaching a Jamesonian study of an ideological strategy of containment and redirection. Its portrayal by Chatterjee, for instance, as a 'resolution' that propelled nationalism forward seems almost apologetic by contrast.[37] At the

---

35   Gramsci 1985, pp. 298–341.

36   Brennan 2006, p. 260; see also Holub p. 211.

37   See, for example, Gopal's comments on Chatterjee's depiction of the 'ideological framework within which nationalism answered the women's question' (Gopal 2002, p. 163). It is unclear if Chatterjee proposes a causal link between the 'resolution' of the 'women's question' in the 'inner' domain and the subsequent development of an overtly male-dominated political nationalism in the 'outer' domain, or if this is simply a question of adjacency or sequentiality. He has certainly little evidence for a convincing causal argument.

same time, postcolonial studies cannot seem to include those in the Third World who find modernisation attractive,[38] or at any rate it needs to caricature them in culturalist terms as a deracinated lot even if they are of the popular classes. In Gramsci's way of thinking, the traditional intelligentsia 'strategically enlisted backwardness as a new *epistemology of otherness* to be preserved against metropolitan encroachments'.[39] For their part, the postcolonial critics of post-Enlightenment power-knowledge nowadays do not counterpose to it so much an 'indigenous philosophy' as a 'romantic nihilism', borrowed from the anti-Enlightenment wing of European thought, 'Heidegger as the liberatory voice of the Third World subject'.[40]

It is arguable that in our day class struggles from below can be most effectively conducted with the weapons prepared by the Enlightenment, rather than with those of Birsa Munda and his fellow insurrectionaries. The 'subaltern-split' – which, as noted above, could have a very useful socio-economic dimension if mobilised as part of an interpretation of the forms of exploitation perpetrated by the 'colonial mode of production' and their often catastrophic consequences – now stands in as a demonstration of the limits of Enlightenment categories and forms of thought, with the 'subaltern', in the sociological sense, providing the exemplary figure to make the demonstration. Subalternity, cast as 'resistant presence',[41] as a 'mode of being',[42] comes in handy in the service of quietism if not nihilism.

Perhaps it is the ulterior recognition of those inconvenient aspects of defining colonialism with very limited historically significant socio-economic referents, which must include capital as a social form, that then leads postcolonial theorists to focus on 'modernity', a term whose elasticity has acquired a new lease of life with the use of qualifiers like alternative, plural and hybrid. In their writings, Chatterjee informs us, postcolonial theorists have resisted the tendency to construct the 'story of modernity as an actualisation of the modernity imagined by the great theorists of the Western world'.[43] The unruly facts of subaltern politics will not, in the first place, oblige those who adhere blindly to the 'rationalist grid' of Enlightenment-derived 'elite consciousness'.[44] The next step in the argument is to suggest that when aspects of Western modernity

---

38   Dirlik 1994, p. 339.
39   Brennan 2006, pp. 260–1, emphasis added.
40   Brennan 2006, p. 264.
41   O'Hanlon 2002, pp. 203–5; Brennan 2006, p. 242.
42   Brennan 2006, p. 260.
43   Chatterjee 2010, p. 294.
44   Chatterjee 2006, p. 12; Chatterjee 2010, p. 292.

are 'domesticated' in non-European societies they will assume new forms, and those cannot be considered 'corruptions of the original'. Those different, multiple modernities are supposedly alternative and hybrid forms that have no evolutionary content, that is to say, they will not 'transition' into some close approximation of the European original. Or, as Sudipto Kaviraj puts it, 'transition narratives create the increasingly untenable illusion that, given all the right conditions, Calcutta would turn into London'.[45] This resistance to a convergence model was visible, so Chatterjee says, even in the Subaltern Studies days, but it has acquired greater force with the postcolonial turn expressed in arguments about 'other modernities'.[46]

This rather begs the question of whether European modernity conforms to that imagined by the great theorists of the Western world and their Enlightenment-derived consciousness. The answer to the question would turn on what one understands by 'modernity'. Using the image of base/superstructure, Jameson argues that modernisation is something that happens to the base (that is, the economy) as capital progressively colonises different aspects of pre-existing social formations. Modernism is the form the superstructure takes in response to that 'ambivalent development'.[47] Modernism, for Jameson as for Perry Anderson, is to be defined by its historic location, rather than with reference to some normative qualities one might assign to it.[48] This is in contrast to Zygmunt Bauman, for instance, who sees the contrast between modernism and postmodernism in modernism's commitment to design, order and planning, and postmodernism's more freewheeling, spontaneous, 'liquid' qualities.[49] Jameson locates modernism at the crossroads: temporally, at the moment when modernisation – the development of capital as a generalising social form that governs the ways in which things are produced and exchanged – had bit into people's lives and consciousness without totally obliterating the artisanal elements, and spatially, when an emerging social form has had to coexist with an older established one, within easy reach of individuals, that is, one's personal life-experience could encompass both.[50]

---

45   Kaviraj 1997, p. 113. Since every Marxist 'transition narrative' assumes prior difference and
      a singular course of development for each case, never to be replicated, the convergence
      model seems to be a fiction of Kaviraj's imagination.

46   Chatterjee 2010, p. 294.

47   Jameson 1991, p. 310.

48   Anderson 1988, pp. 317–38, esp. pp. 321–2, 329.

49   Bauman 1992. More recently, Bauman has resorted to the use of the term 'liquid' modernity
      in place of postmodernity, but it seems more a change of terminology than of substantive
      content; see Bauman 1999.

50   Jameson 1991, p. 307.

Modernity, in this definition, characterises the attempt to make something coherent out of their relationship. Modernity would describe the way 'modern' people feel about themselves. Modernity then is not so much about the products (industrial or cultural) as it is the producers and consumers and how they feel either producing the products or living among them.[51] If this materialist historicisation of modernity is better than a normative definition, then Chatterjee's position above is doubtful. Modernity would have its plebeian everyday forms of trying to make sense of the world, relatively unscathed, one imagines, by what the great theorists were thinking. So, Europe too would have had its multiple modernities, combinations of elite and popular forms, and so on. For a description of those aspects of European modernity one might turn to the historical studies that enrich the otherwise theoretical considerations of Gramsci's incomparable *Prison Notebooks*,[52] and his study of the Southern Question.[53]

So the reality of European modernity must be some distance from the idealised imagination of it and therefore the latter represents in itself no useful historically informed point of contrast with colonial modernity. It does need pointing out that seen in a properly historical perspective, not only did aspects of the 'old regime' persist well into the inter-war years in Europe,[54] but that modernity itself took shape, as it were, 'in the space between a still usable classical past, a still indeterminate technical present, and a still unpredictable political future'.[55] At a more general level, modernity is definable only with reference to the coexistence of old and new forms, of the 'archaic and the avant-garde', the 'complete interpenetration of technological and primitive modes of life',[56] history itself a 'stack of non-synchronous time-streams', rather than a unified stratum through which one might slice a neat cross-section, '*chronos* becom[ing] *kairos*',[57] and so on.

In that case, one would expect to find 'misplaced ideas', 'experiences of incongruity', and so on, as integral elements of modernity. This is in contrast to Roberto Schwarz's claim – expounded at some length by Cleary – that such ideas and experiences define something essential about the postcolonial condition.[58] For Schwarz, an idea is in place when it is an abstraction of social

---

51   Jameson 1991, p. 310.

52   Gramsci 1971.

53   Gramsci 1995.

54   Mayer 1981.

55   Anderson 1988, p. 326.

56   Benjamin 1985, p. 190.

57   Eagleton 2007, pp. 51–3.

58   Cleary 2002, p. 106.

processes to which it refers. While in Europe, liberal ideology constituted an 'abstraction of industrial capitalism', in Brazil, the 'imported liberal ideas' were elaborated in a social order of a very different kind, one based in fact on slavery, economic dependency, and a political system based on clientelism. The sense of 'ill-assortedness, dissonance and distortion' has obsessed commentators on Brazilian life ever since, or so Schwarz informs us.[59] The incongruity stems from the fact that 'dependent' cultures are always interpreting their own realities with intellectual methodologies created 'somewhere else', a characteristic 'typical' of postcolonial societies.[60]

This argument would lose its force if it could be shown to be typical of societies that were neither 'colonial' nor 'postcolonial' in some meaningful structural sense. As Marshall Berman demonstrates, feelings of incongruity, rather similar to those experienced in Brazil, were felt very strongly in Tsarist Russia, and indeed something of the postcolonial notion of authenticity was anticipated in the portrayal of St. Petersburg as representative of 'all that was foreign and cosmopolitan, pollution and miscegenation, secularism (even atheism)'; and Moscow representing Russia's 'heart', and all the accumulated indigenous and insular traditions of the Russian *narod* (the Russian subaltern), anti-Enlightenment, purity of blood and soil, sacredness.[61]

One can see where Cleary is coming from, but unless one is prepared to say something as absurd as the claim that all 'dependency' is a sign of postcoloniality, the Russian case illustrates one limit of Schwarz's ideas, as well as Cleary's misplaced use of them. If one thinks of where ideas originate from and where they find an enduring home in a somewhat broader and less dogmatic perspective, surely the picture is hugely complicated. In our day, Marxism, for example, has been adopted and transformed, vastly enriched by its encounter with peasant societies in poor countries as part of their project of emancipation; indeed the very terms 'Leninism' and 'Maoism' signify such a process of adaptation and enrichment, and one can point to numerous other efforts at 'translation' of Marxism into a variety of 'local dialects'. Indeed, Marx himself was enthusiastic about backward Russia's prospects for an original reinterpretation of the possibilities of his political theses.[62] Many of Marx's works, not least his political writings about France and India, and *Capital* itself, can be read as a text about time out of joint, when the most unlikely combinations are

59   Schwarz 1992, p. 25.

60   Cleary 2002, p. 107.

61   Berman 1988, p. 176.

62   Shanin 1983; Hudis 1983; and more recently Anderson 2010, pp. 196–236.

likely to fuel original thought and transformative action.[63] Ascendant societies in the past have often taken ideas from long-moribund ones to interpret their understanding of the world: for example, Greek philosophy and the science of Classical Antiquity as read, interpreted and indeed advanced by the medieval Arab scientists.[64] Closer to our day, the encounter with ancient Asian philosophy and religion has been followed by their partial adoption and acculturation within European thought.[65] Unless one is prepared to define colonialism, preposterously, as the colonisation of one society's ideas by those of another – a gesture one finds troublingly frequently in today's nativist 'blood and soil' versions of anti-Westernism – the potentialities for reinterpretation of ideas, and their reworking into new contexts, represents one of the more exciting developments associated with modernity. As both Losurdo and Mehta demonstrate, liberalism has frequently enough been associated with imperialism and conquest.[66] In that case, it is not the out-of-placeness of European liberalism in slave-labour based societies like Brazil that is critical to understand, so much as its ideological support for colonising ventures.[67]

Writing in 1988, Anderson argued that in the Third World a kind of shadowy configuration of what once – during the nineteenth century and the first two to three decades of the twentieth-century – prevailed in the First World still existed: precapitalist oligarchies of various, mostly landowning, types still hung on.[68] San Juan notes that amid a lack of cumulative growth, and a backward agriculture with a limited internal market, the accumulation of money capital was directed largely into speculative activities in real estate, usury and hoarding.[69] Where it did occur, capitalist development was more rapid than in the metropolitan countries, but much less 'consolidated or stabilised'; socialist revolution 'haunted' these societies as a permanent

---

63   Bensaïd 2002, p. 3.

64   This is beautifully expounded in al-Khalili 2012.

65   I suppose this is the gist of the 'Oriental Renaissance'; see Schwab 1984.

66   Mehta 1999; Losurdo 2011.

67   This is not to say that liberal ideas of equality before the law, for instance, have not fuelled popular mobilisation and could not have had revolutionary consequences in a slave-holding society. Overall, Schwarz's notion of 'misplaced ideas' is a conservative, possibly even reactionary, one. The notion of 'misplaced ideas' seems to have become an integral part of the ideology of a propertied class, which has lately discovered the virtues of intellectual nativism – which might also refer to some tendencies in postcolonial studies. I am surprised that Cleary should imagine that Schwarz's ideas could be mobilised for a critical historical materialist notion of postcolonialism.

68   Anderson 1988, p. 329.

69   San Juan 2002, p. 232.

possibility.[70] These 'unsynchronised and asymmetrical formations' were the natural habitat for 'magic realism and wild absurdist fantasies', as well as those cultural expressions described as 'hybrid, creolised, syncretic, ambivalent, multiplicitous', and so on,[71] the conditions that produced genuine masterpieces like Gabriel García Márquez's *One Hundred Years of Solitude* or Salman Rushdie's *Midnight's Children*.[72]

However, these are not timeless expressions of an ever-expanding process of modernisation, but instead emerge in quite delimited constellations, in societies still at a definite crossroads. The Third World furnishes no fountain of eternal youth to modernism.[73] In the 25 years since Anderson's essay on modernity and revolution, vast changes have come to the 'Third World'. In many places precapitalist oligarchies have mostly either transformed themselves into capitalists or given way to transnational corporations; capitalist development has undergone dizzying rates of expansion across the social landscape and socialist revolution no longer haunts those societies.

Trying to grasp the outlines of modernity without that element of historical dynamism, and its often unpredictable consequences, is a piece of theoretical nonsense. By accepting the idea of European modernity as a reflection of the ideas of the great theorists of the Enlightenment, postcolonial thought of the variety being discussed above lends strength to the idea of a hyperreal Europe as the normative, universal referent, while the others conform, Caliban-like, to a host of 'local specificities'.[74] Mired in their historical actuality, the latter may be alternatives, but rather poor ones, very much in the spirit of postcolonial shame. And in the context of the vast transformations that India – along with a host of other ex-colonial countries – is undergoing, to maintain, as Chatterjee does, that postcolonial studies has rejected the framework of 'modernisation as the necessary plot of history' can only be maintained by a wilful blindness to the unmissable realities of the day. For however adventitious the origins of capital as a social form in England might have been – and Brenner's interventions in the 'transition debate', by insisting on the role of localised variations in social-property relations and the quite uncertain outcomes of class struggles, logically underscores that position[75] – once established as a social form, it displays a powerful drive to consolidate the commodity form globally.

---

70   Anderson 1988, p. 329.
71   San Juan 1998, p. 140.
72   Anderson 1988, p. 329.
73   Ibid.
74   Jameson 1998, p. 105.
75   Perhaps the most exhaustive description of this remains Brenner 1982, pp. 16–113.

A universal process with 'an immanent logic of development' comes about, but it is 'historically determinate, not transhistorical'.[76] Indeed, breaking the spell of this 'logic of development' may be said to be Marx's central contribution to political theory.

It has been necessary for postcolonial theorists to polemicise against the use of capital as a central category of analysis. Prakash has been the most explicit and notorious instance of this, but it affects even those like Chatterjee who acknowledge the centrality of capital in our time. When the latter brings up capital it is often as a backdrop to a critique of central planning, or nowadays to issues of 'governmentality', the spirit of molecular reforms, or at best to rather formulaic pronouncements about 'globalisation'.[77] The claim to an 'adversarial relationship to the dominant structure of scholarship' is not, in these instances, particularly convincing.[78]

It is, of course, conceivable that having abdicated the responsibility for a close analysis of capital, postcolonialism is left with a rather idealised view of modernisation. In that case, postcolonial studies should acknowledge its affiliations with modernisation theory if only in the negative register. That is not as far fetched as it might seem at first glance. The strategy of postcolonial studies appears to be to focus critical attention on a normatively defined process with putative possibilities of imitative and secondary development following the path of the original, and the distance between that ideal and the actual situation of the regions or countries they study in detail, rather than on the uncertainties, flows and counterflows of capital. In the space afforded by the contrast between the ideal and the actual, the postcolonial appears as an arena for study, polemics, advocacy, alliance-building, and so on. However, I would maintain that the categorial transpositions that occur in the journey from a Marxist-informed critique of political economy to modernisation-theory-informed cultural studies take a considerable toll on postcolonial studies. In a critical Marxist perspective, each path to capitalism is singular by definition,[79]

---

76 Postone 1996, p. 258.
77 See, for example, the near-complete silence on the subject of the neoliberal 'reforms' being put into place in India in the late 1980s and early 1990s; Chatterjee 1993, pp. 200–19. See also the very schematic remarks in 'The World after the Great Peace'; Chatterjee 2004, pp. 81–106. But even these represent a great advance over what is available for the most part in the field of postcolonial studies.
78 Chatterjee 1993, p. 156.
79 This is Brenner's argument even with reference to the big three of global capitalism – the US, Japan and Germany. A fortiori, this would have been the case if China had been included in Brenner 2006. Jameson makes the point about the singularity of each 'path' to capitalism; Jameson 2002, p. 183.

none replicates an earlier form, indeed it can be expected not to do so, and each takes its hostages and victims *en route* to establishing its domination over an earlier social formation. De-modernisation – through 'the epidemic of over-production', 'extensive and destructive crises', the flight of capital and the moment of barbarism entirely internal to capital as a social form – is implicit in Marx and Marxist theories of all variants.[80] Modernisation theory takes a more benign view that once obstacles to modernisation are removed, it is a matter of a smooth self-perpetuating process with desirable results.[81] Postcolonialism posits the unremovability of those obstacles rather like some variants of modernisation theory, their perdurance and integrality to social formations outside Europe; hence modernisation on European lines cannot be the script of history.

That said, postcolonial studies cannot but fail to invoke capitalism often enough, but without a proper categorial or historical grounding and a fairly firm rejection of the framework of a 'transition' to capitalism – dismissed, ironically, on the grounds of historicism in the Popperian sense[82] – it is never properly analysed or periodised. The sort of commitment that led an earlier generation of theorists to inquire into the specificities of colonial capitalism – even to posit, as noted, a specifically colonial mode of production – is notably absent here, as is any broader impulse to periodise the career of colonial capitalism itself. Now one is more likely to encounter the 'world of the colonial labourer',[83] a world rich in gods and spirits, symbols of difference to the presumably disenchanted social world of Europe, rather than forms of labour subsumed (either formally or really) to capital, within specific historically determinate (colonial) relations in which consciousness and class action might unfold.

Postcolonial theory champions the fragments that are supposedly produced by the totalising projects of Enlightenment-inspired modernity. But in the

---

80   Marx and Engels 1980, pp. 21–2.

81   Rostow 1960.

82   A far more adequate understanding of historicism would be, of course, based on the notion of a wholly exotic past, in the Foucauldian sense; see Perry 2002, p. 164. In this sense, postcolonial studies inadvertently perpetuates a form of historicism, since the consciousness of the subalterns, which expresses the submerged traditions, seems so exotic to the modern world, despite their contemporaneity. I would characterise this as a kind of anti-historicist historicism, for those who like Sartrean paradoxes.

83   The title of an edited volume by Prakash 1992a. See also Chakrabarty, who makes all sorts of weighty claims about the 'consciousness' of Bengali jute workers, based on rich, if misleading, descriptions of what separates Bengali working-class consciousness from its ideal-typical metropolitan 'bourgeois' counterpart, as if this is a meaningful comparison; Chakrabarty 1989, especially pp. 217–8 and the conclusion.

absence of a proper analysis of capitalism and its structural properties, crises (breakdown points) and polarising social and geographical impacts, the fragments too often appear – in anecdotal micronarrative form – as 'exotic inventories of unrelated diversity',[84] detritus of a 'Third World' left behind by those projects. Consistent with this view is a sort of categorial exoticism, which begs the question of *why* people are constrained to live as they do and *why* their resistance or rebellion against their conditions of life assume certain historically determinate forms.[85] Respect for 'difference' should not lead to amnesia about the processes that entrench and intensify socio-economic differences.[86] Neither should it be overlooked that the notion of difference has sometimes been articulated from a metropolitan Utilitarian Orientalist vantage point – in effect from a universalist perspective.[87] To the extent that postcolonial studies does not theorise these possibilities, it unwittingly enters into a collusive relationship with the imperialists' 'antinomies of essential oppositions',[88] forgoes the opportunity to analyse the historic specificities of colonialism in the modern period, and abdicates the responsibility to grasp the nature of both anti-colonial and class struggles.

In light of all this, it would not be a very good idea to 'privilege' the scepticism of anti-foundational thinking in postcolonial studies over the 'truth' of the represented postcolonial experiences in the texts, the 'authenticity of what's different' (this 'truth' then being in some cases further reified by the

---

84 A phrase used by Fredric Jameson in his discussion of Althusser's notion of 'determination by structural totality'. Difference, Jameson notes, is to be understood as a 'relational concept' rather than as a 'mere inert inventory of unrelated diversity' (Jameson 1981, p. 41).

85 I have developed the argument about categorial exoticism in detail in Kaiwar 2005a, pp. 3732–8. Note in this regard, a work by Amin 1995, which begins with a preliminary 'Narrative of the Event' in which the socio-economic co-ordinates of the nationalist movement are mentioned and therefore too is a hint of the class anxieties that lay behind the early attempts at a cross-class mobilisation. But the potentialities of this line of thinking to reveal the specificities of colonial capitalism, Gandhian strategies of containment and redirection of popular rebellion, and the relationship of subaltern groups to the overall construction of a propertied-class bloc that Gandhi was instrumental in constructing – all are quickly replaced by the standard postcolonial invocation of colonial difference, a multiplication of exotic details including spectres and visions, rumours about Gandhi, and so on, from which we are expected to extract an understanding of peasant rebellion and 'peasant nationalism'! For substantial insights on the latter topics, we would have to go to old-fashioned 'good' history, as in Pouchepadass 1999.

86 For an illuminating discussion of how discourses about difference are 'far from innocent in the reproduction of capitalism', see Harvey 1996, pp. 172–5.

87 Wallerstein 1991, p. 173.

88 Chrisman 1994, p. 500.

sentimentality of US-dominated multiculturalism).[89] If the latter represents the phenomenological and Heideggerian turn in postcolonial studies, one is actually faced with a body of thought that seems to move restlessly and errati-cally between two rather dubious poles – 'cultural essentialism' on the one hand, and an 'indeterminate social system'[90] on the other – the movement itself signifying the impasse of postcolonial studies.

3.2   History's Ironic Reversals

We are now in a position to consider some of the further implications of the claims about intellectual migration and its critical contributions to postcolo-nial studies. There is no question that the migration of Indian intellectuals, for instance, has led to significant transformations in the study of India not only in the USA, where arguably the greatest impact has been felt, but also in other Anglophone countries. It was a significant part of the move away from the traditional emphasis on Sanskrit philosophy, philology, ancient history, reli-gion, and the like, to modern history, international relations, rural-urban and trans-border migrations, ecology, feminism, and a host of related fields.[91] To a substantial extent, the arrival of an important and highly productive group of political economists, anthropologists, sociologists, historians, not to men-tion a host of creative writers, by routes direct and indirect as graduate stu-dents or college professors, has been a catalyst in the transformation of South Asian studies, as it is institutionally known. One is unlikely to visit any major US university and not find Indian intellectuals in prominent positions, a situ-ation that is replicated in other Anglophone metropolitan countries, albeit on a lesser scale.

The shift from a largely elitist Orientalist emphasis, based in philological concerns, to historical and anthropological ones,[92] had begun earlier, even by the late 1950s. But the study of India in Western universities was mostly a mat-ter for experts in the field who spoke to each other at length, but probably had a minimal influence beyond. This was unlike the period that Raymond Schwab calls the 'Oriental Renaissance',[93] when the philological study of ancient India was considered crucial to global intellectual and political currents. Schwab

---

89   Boehmer 1998, p. 18.

90   Harootunian 1999, p. 145.

91   See, for example, the contributions to Assayag and Bénéï 2003.

92   Appadurai 2003, pp. 28–43.

93   Schwab 1984.

goes on to describe trends in European scholarship of the period from 1785 to 1850 or so, when the study of the furthest antiquity of the roots of the West in an 'Aryan' Orient was deemed vital to a range of European concerns with revolution and its containment. As theories of civilisational decline took on increasingly racial overtones in the nineteenth century, it fell to the likes of the above-cited Chamberlain to summon 'Aryan India' to Europe's rescue, and 'Indology' became part of an Aryan-Semitic dialectic around which the narrative of civilisation revolved well into the twentieth century.[94] This scholarship, steeped in a 'profound knowledge' of Hebrew and Sanskrit, not to mention the European classical languages, 'fortified by comparative study of linguistic data, mythology, and religion and shaped by efforts to relate linguistic structures, forms of thought, and features of civilisation', gave rise in fact to a 'tissue of scholarly myths... fantasies of the social imagination at every level'.[95] Indeed, in the words of one of its present-day commentators, the German Indological tradition produced 'knowledge rooted in itself', which barely needed India.[96] In the age of revolutions, counter-revolutions, competitive nation-building and, ironically, colonialism, India had come to serve quintessentially European purposes.[97]

I will return to the question of 'needing India' a little later, but for the moment it might be said, with not a little irony, that Indian intellectuals of the postcolonial migration have played a role – with the different emphases noted above – not dissimilar to their earlier counterparts of the Oriental Renaissance, returning the study of India to global significance, no longer entirely a matter for closeted specialists. The proponents of the 'Cambridge School' of Indian studies, and their counterparts in the US, might disagree with the above proposition, but it is unlikely that more than a very small number of academics in the US or Continental Europe, or for that matter Britain, have heard of it, and even fewer would contend that the efforts of scholars who might be associated with it could have given Indian concerns, particularly postcolonial ones, the worldwide prominence they have now acquired in the wake of the postcolonial turn in Subaltern Studies.[98]

94   On the development of Aryan model via the 'expulsion' of the Semitic influences on European civilisations, see Bernal 1987, pp. 317–66.
95   Olender 1992, pp. ix–x.
96   Dalmia 2003, pp. 66–75.
97   For more on this, see Kaiwar 2003, pp. 13–61.
98   Indeed, arguably, the scholars of the Cambridge School are better known now in the US, for example, for their trenchant reviews and debates with postcolonial scholars of India. See the debate between O'Hanlon and Washbrook on one side, and Gyan Prakash on the other; O'Hanlon and Washbrook 1992, pp. 141–67; Prakash 1992d, pp. 168–84.

The point Dirlik makes about the 'arrival' of Third World intellectuals with regards to when the 'postcolonial' began – involving either circulation migration of intellectuals or their permanent relocation to metropolitan centres of teaching and research – might have had some level of persuasiveness in the first instance, as perhaps an originary point, but it has become less so over time. For instance, we know that this relocation, or translocation, itself took place in the midst of an overwhelming reception of French theory (the poststructuralist moment of Foucault and Derrida, not to mention Deleuze and Lacan among others),[99] the end of the Vietnam war, the containment and institutionalisation of the civil rights movement that had originally both drawn some inspiration from anti-colonial struggles in Africa and the Caribbean and re-inspired them, not to mention the worldwide collapse of actually existing communism and the retreat of Marxism in its twin capacities as analysis of capital and an 'anticipatory expression of a future society'[100] – all subsequently recuperable as 'postcolonial' moments in a homogenised world history. If there is a widely acceptable metanarrative nowadays, postcolonialism would have to be one of its narrative categories.

To a substantial extent, it is metropolitan postcolonialism that has contained and redirected Third World arrivals,[101] and the transformation of Subaltern Studies in its postcolonial turn offers an instructive example, compactly stated in Chakrabarty's idea of the abandonment of the ambition 'to write "better" Marxist histories' in favour of a critique of Eurocentrism,[102] and the like. The precise 'national' or even local conditions that gave rise to the original Subaltern Studies is hardly a matter of concern to its metropolitan readers, nor its subsequent reckoning with poststructuralism as read in the US and other Anglophone countries. Sarkar suggests that metropolitan interlocutors of 'late Subaltern Studies' are, for the most part, satisfied with a simplified version of colonial history in which colonisers and colonised confront each other across a chasm constituted by Enlightenment power-knowledge.[103] Never mind that critics like Aijaz Ahmad have pointed to a much more complex reality, in which the valences of texts are entirely transformed in their passages from India to the US, for example, their caste-class dimensions lost

---

99   Cusset 2008. The subtitle of the book, 'How Foucault, Derrida, Deleuze and Co. Transformed the Intellectual Life of the United States', is no exaggeration. Intellectuals from the Third World were not immune to this transformation.

100   Jameson 1988, Volume II, pp. 175–7.

101   Ahmad 1996, pp. 399–418.

102   Chakrabarty 1993, pp. 10–17.

103   Sarkar 1997, p. 85, 92.

in their reading as 'postcolonial' texts.[104] To an extent, then, the postcolonial would encompass a situation in which events that transpire in the formerly colonised world are interpreted, analysed and presented as if to be read by a metropolitan audience, or if not anything so explicit, then certainly by an audience with an attentive ear to the requirements of the latter. Whether this also means that such postcolonial scholarship functions as an 'intellectual extension of global capital' or runs the danger of reflecting the globalisation of capital flows – a charge levelled variously by Dirlik, Young and Boehmer – is open to debate.[105] Of course, much less so is the sense that postcolonial studies describes a vast arc of reverse offshoring, its generative ideas developed in the context of *longue-durée* ideological and political ferment in the Third World, inextricably linked to geopolitical lines of gravitational force, but now mass produced in the academic centres of the metropolitan countries.

Subaltern Studies' preoccupation with an essential structure of 'subaltern consciousness' that found expression in one-off rebellions, insurrections, and so on, has no place in this new intellectual formation. Instead the fragmentary nature of that consciousness has acquired a substantive form: the fragments constituted by the all-too solid bodies of numerous ethnic, racial, caste and gendered communities living alongside each other and perhaps distantly recognising some political kinship with each other, but with nothing much in common, no common grounding, as it were, in the workings of late twentieth- and twenty-first-century capitalism. While Subaltern Studies carries on in name, in actuality it has had to be supplanted by a much more totalising ambition, signifying the transformation of a particular kind of closure into an equally particular kind of opening, marking a quite unprecedented moment that has engulfed the entire planetary political and intellectual landscape. This has required – indirectly now, through the mediations of Foucault and Derrida, and their intellectual forbears Nietzsche and Heidegger – a profound postcolonial revitalisation of an interest in the conceptual inheritance of the Oriental Renaissance, or more broadly Romantic Orientalism, or its equivalents; a development not confined, it seems, to any one country or region.[106]

If the original Oriental Renaissance posited a second Renaissance of Europe with the discovery of its cultural ancestry in the Aryan Orient of Sanskrit and

---

104   Ahmad 1992, pp. 184ff.
105   Dirlik 1994; Young 1998, p. 7; Boehmer 1998, p. 18.
106   Mazumdar 2009, pp. 43–81. I stress the conceptual inheritance rather than a literal
       Orientalism, in that it is the legacy of 'uncontaminated' indigenism that has come to the
       fore, a repository of alternatives free of the taint of Enlightenment rationalism.

Persian, an idea put forth by Friedrich Schlegel among others,[107] subsequent versions developed in India, for instance, during the colonial period stressed the Renaissance of Indian society, culture and religion with the rediscovery of its own ancient inheritance. Whether consciously or not, populist strains of postcolonial thought have reclaimed some of the issues of the Oriental Renaissance, albeit in a *volkisch* rather than elitist refrain, and not as issues intrinsic to Indian 'civilisation' alone as in the case of the neo-Hinduism that Wilhelm Halbfass writes about,[108] but as significant in thinking about events of world-historical significance.

In the postcolonial moment, this Orientalist undercurrent finds expression in a negative vein, as a loss of continuity and authenticity, in the process ironically recuperating the most constant element of Orientalist thought: the spiritual nature of the Orient that contrasts it with the more materialist West.[109] So if the first iteration had Europeans rediscovering their *Urheimat*, bypassing the perils of modernity that the age of revolutions had opened up, the second iteration offers us the aftermath from the other side: when multiple modernities have evolved that resist evolutionary schema, but exist now only as shards and fragments, underlying which, nevertheless, one can discern some final essences. The most notable of those is, of course, the tacit transformation in postcolonialism of the 'panurgic will' to power pulsing through all social-psychic structures – the ontological foundation of Foucault's genealogical methodological prescriptions of chance, serial, unpredictable outcomes[110] – into a characteristic of Western modernity. Colonialism is then a mere outward form of that panurgic will to domination. Insofar as a manifestation of it has survived colonial rule, it finds a secondary and bastardised expression in the

---

107   Léon Poliakov calls Friedrich Schlegel 'the real founder of the Aryan myth' (Poliakov 1974, p. 327).

108   Halbfass 1988, pp. 217–46.

109   Pouchepadass 2002, pp. 381–91. Foucault's writings on Iran develop the idea of 'political spirituality' lost to the West, but preserved intact in Iran; see Foucault, 'Is it Useless to Revolt', in Afary and Anderson 2005, pp. 131–2.

110   Anderson makes the following point regarding the link between chance and power: 'Their common derivation from Nietzsche indicates the linkage between chance and power, so interpreted, in Foucault's thought. Once hypostatised as a new First Principle, Zarathustra-style, power loses any historical determination: there are no longer specific holders of power, nor any specific goals which its exercise serves. As sheer *will*, its exercise is its own satisfaction' (Anderson 1983, p. 51). One sometimes gets the impression when reading postcolonial texts that colonialism was something that Europeans were driven to by an obscure force secreted deep within their culture and forming an invariant characteristic of the Western personality.

modern nation state, the most durable legacy of colonialism in the ex-colonial world. Where necessary, one accommodates to this reality in a decisionist or practical spirit, and where possible one retreats to an Inside, 'the unassailable domain of native interiority',[111] or to an ancient past.

Anderson's point regarding the split between the apparently unrelated registers of determinism and contingency in poststructuralism finds a derivative expression in postcolonial studies, transported now from the realm of language to that of history: a total initial determinism paradoxically ending in an 'absolute final contingency'.[112] Perhaps the paradox has been sharpened and given its unintended metageographic point by the additional influence of Derrida, in whose work the entire history of Western philosophy is amalgamated into a 'single homogeneous metaphysics', defined by the ubiquitous identity of its 'quest for "presence" '. On the other hand, any individual sentence or paragraph within that metaphysic is 'seamed and undermined by the irreducible heterogeneity of différance'. As Anderson notes, writing is, for Derrida, thus at once '*implacable* and *undecidable*, inescapably the same in its general structure and inexplicably *differing* and *deferring* in its particular textualisations'.[113]

Foucault, for his part, unable to explain the sudden mutations between the successive epistemes of his early work, each of which is treated as a 'homogeneous unity', later resorted to increasing celebration of the 'role of chance as the governor of events', which he argued in *L'ordre du discours*,[114] should no longer be seen in terms of cause and effect, but of the serial and the unpredictable.[115] The popularity of the 'metaphysics of presence' and *différance*, not to mention the genealogical method, were undoubtedly a function of and reinforced by the seemingly rapid and unpredictable changes that confronted post-World War II Europe and its former colonial peripheries. The application of such concepts and methods may have had locally persuasive effects, especially in the short term, but they also led to an abdication, for reasons already alluded to, of a properly causal historical explanation. The genealogical method, for example, gave up on the important dialectic of structure and subject for explaining the transformation of deeply-rooted structures via the unintended outcomes of collective efforts either to preserve or overcome positions held within them. One of the most protracted and compelling attempts of the latter kind

---

111   Harootunian 1999, p. 131.

112   Anderson 1983, p. 50.

113   Ibid., emphasis added.

114   Foucault's 1971 *L'ordre du discours* was rendered into English as 'The Discourse on Language', published as an appendix to Foucault 1972.

115   Anderson 1983, pp. 50–1.

has been, of course, Robert Brenner's efforts to theorise the transition from feudalism to capitalism, its huge impact on the entire historical field testifying to its importance.[116] The impact even reached Subaltern Studies through Chatterjee's work on modes of power and the peasantry, an attempt to combine Brenner and Foucault. If this was initially a welcome effort at historical explanation, which took into account precisely the 'dialectic' of structure and subject, the end result has been far from a happy one. In the postcolonial turn of Subaltern Studies, this has only had the effect of ridiculing transition theories as a whole. In the event too historical accounts have either turned on the force of personalities, sheer localised voluntarism, or a helpless drift in the face of a system that remains nameless and untheorised. Explanations dissipate into description, or rather description is made to stand in for explanation.[117]

The sum total of this demarche has been something of a collapse of history itself: the initial determinism – more often implied than stated or repeated in forms that suggest a common understanding – is expressed in the idea of cultures extruding essences that are relatively unchangeable in history, but which are curiously inconsequential inasmuch as actual outcomes are the result of chance encounters, resulting in endlessly changing 'hybridisations', liminality, and so forth. So while there are material outcomes for people, the outcomes themselves merely position them at a 'tangent' to 'European trajectories', as Prakash puts it.[118] But the European trajectories themselves, as Foucault might have insisted, are subject to chance events and dicey evolutions, which do not admit of any grand schematisation. The end result is a world of randomly colliding particles – fragments, shards, detritus – that might produce a descriptive panorama, but little else of significance. But this is where the initial determinism returns, indeed *must* return, in the form of the collision of great primordial structures, Europe invariably the universal pole around which the collisions with the many Others occur. That is, the panurgic will to domination must take form as Europe, or most likely in today's postcolonialism as modern Europe expressed in the Enlightenment. Behind the random outcomes, the primordial

---

116   Most important of these are: Brenner 1977; Brenner 1982; Brenner 1986.

117   All this has been succinctly captured by Harootunian as characteristics of what he calls 'cultural studies', but which for our purposes also inform postcolonial studies: a concentration on 'micro-technologies of power', displacement of the 'state and capital to *indeterminate loci of power* and its *local inflections*', an emphasis on '*discourses of power and their slippage*, splitting subjectivities and charting their subsequent dissemination, as if the movement constituted a natural function of an *unnamed conception of social order* that already exists, though *its proponents disavow totalities*'; Harootunian 1999, pp. 140–1, emphases added.

118   Prakash 1992b, p. 8.

structures exert their unseen force, the source of an overarching indictment, in postcolonial studies from the vantage point of the (Oriental) Other, whose mere existence is enough to point to the violence of Western colonialism. Western colonialism – or, more to the point, its writing machinery – is the articulate instance of the attempted repression and supersession of social orders beyond the reach and subversive of all the successive modes of 'Western Reason'. It is through the eyes of those social orders that Western Reason's common nature as 'repressive structures' stands revealed.[119] The subaltern in postcolonial studies can take the place of the originary Other in Foucault – whether it be the 'pure alterity' of madness in his earlier work or 'the innocence of the body and its pleasures' in his later work[120] – as the embodiment of the innocence that confronted Western colonialism.[121]

It is against this background that the claims of the subalternist historians writing for a metropolitan audience in a postcolonial vein must be assessed. After all, the arrival itself is a complex affair. To sum up, it had been prepared, so to speak, by numerous prior 'migrations'. In the first instance of British cultural studies, with its emphasis on proletarian culture and dissidence, to France, where the work of someone like Raymond Williams influenced Althusser,[122] who in turn had some initial impact on younger scholars like Foucault and Derrida. In due course, the work of the latter two migrated to the US where it took hold of the academic (and extra-academic) imagination at a moment when multiculturalism and a post-civil rights US were in the process of formation. This was a moment when not only American minorities, but also immigrants of the post-1965 wave were in the process of helping remake academic and, more broadly, public life in the US.[123] Progressively stripped of its immersion in class politics by a variety of converging processes during the journey from British cultural studies to American postcolonialism, with stops in Paris and Calcutta, and detours to Australia and so on, the long postcolonial way home took on board the reinvention of Gramsci by Eurocommunism alongside its own equally imaginative reading of his work against the grain

---

119   Anderson's discussion of Foucault in *In the Tracks of Historical Materialism* is suggestive of the possible ways in which Foucauldian genealogy was transfigured into postcolonialist history; see Anderson 1983, pp. 46ff.

120   Anderson 1983, p. 53.

121   Nandy 1983, p. ix. Of course, this depiction of the subaltern is also present in colonial documents, with a twist: the innocent peasant taken advantage of by cruel landlords and wily moneylenders. The duty of protecting the innocent peasant then devolves on the colonial officials themselves!

122   Turner 2003, pp. 65–6.

123   Cusset 2008, pp. 133–8.

of his own unrepentant Communist militancy. The end result is to reinforce Larsen's point, noted earlier, that postcolonialism has a great deal more to do with the reception of 'French theory' in metropolitan centres than it does with the realities of decolonisation.[124] Or in his own words:

> the real, genealogical order of determinations is turned upside down if we think of postcolonialism or the 'subaltern' as the 'theoretical' emissaries of the third world to the court of Western theory, whether poststructuralist or Marxist. Postcolonialism's origins are, at base, those of secular poststructuralism as a whole. The 'colonial' is here a variation on a 'post' theme, which travels from about as far East or South as a line traced by the lecture circuits and book distribution networks of French poststructuralist theory.[125]

In his sombre assessment of the elements that went into the formation of a conservative American academy in the post-1965 period, Brennan elaborates several developments that speak to the case in point: the popularisation of right-wing philosophies from interwar Europe and a fundamental confusion between conservative and radical rejections of capitalism, accompanied by a 'hyper-professionalism' that placed the humanities in competition with a 'post-literate media and entertainment sector' in a climate of privatisation, including that of the university. In addition, political belonging was ejected from the idea of identity,[126] now reduced to the ethnic and other communities that gathered around the so-called new social movements in endless flux,[127] and the flight of many left intellectuals from politics that sought to enter or 'make claims on the state'. These two gestures, in Brennan's opinion, are perhaps the only unambiguous political legacies of what was then beginning to be called 'theory'.[128] In this climate, Brennan writes, 'deans, talk-show hosts, and think tanks were dubbing "Marxist" anything outside an uncritical embrace of the American free market', and indeed the term 'Marxism' was attached even to a poststructuralist theory that in fact wanted to dismantle it, as though opinion-makers had found a way 'instinctively to create a buffer between the establishment and its dangerous other by inventing a proxy'. It was this academic-political milieu into which Third World intellectuals walked, already primed it seems to

---

124   Larsen 2002, pp. 204–5.
125   Larsen 2002, p. 215.
126   Brennan 2006, p. x.
127   Cusset 2008, p. 134.
128   Brennan 2006, pp. x–xi.

fit in, and here they 'automatically registered as the oppressed' even when that was seldom the case.[129]

With this as background, one can evaluate a couple of claims made by Chatterjee: (i) that despite the overlaps between Subaltern Studies and post-colonial studies, and the 'reorientation' under the influence of the latter of the original set of theoretical problems of the former, a 'crucial difference' continues to exist in the choice of problems and topics in the 'two strands of history writing'; and (ii) that the historical and polemical focus of (late) Subaltern Studies remains in the contemporary political debates of the countries of South Asia.[130] For a start, one wonders if he is not protesting too much. In any particular instance – and he gives the examples of the work of subalternist historians on the rewriting of communal conflicts in colonial India, the history of the partition of India, and the extension of those debates to neighbouring countries like Sri Lanka[131] – the contributions may be distinct especially when there are no parallels with metropolitan experiences. However, there is equally no question that the gravitational pull of American debates and American-style identity politics have queered the pitch significantly. For instance, the 'serious critique' of the nation state, as well as the ideology of nationalism that Chatterjee sees as a distinct contribution of subalternist historians, has been around a lot longer in the US than he seems to recognise, and while aspects of both need to be subject to critique, the tone and direction of it in the US have had seriously debilitating political and economic effects that are clearly visible. There is reason to believe that the same tone and direction, and the resultant confusion, are being replicated by the subalternist historians and their fellow travellers.[132] Brennan's point about the loss of distinction between 'conservative and radical' positions on issues is very much to the point here.

---

129 Brennan 2006, p. xi.

130 Chatterjee 2010, p. 298.

131 Chatterjee 2010, p. 298–9.

132 For instance, the tendency to use religious affiliations as a primary marker of 'community' has become something of a cliché in both the US and India, indeed in the works of Subalternist historians themselves. In the US, it was very much part of the neoliberal turn in politics: the community of money on the one hand, and the communities of faith on the other. In the case of the latter, this kind of demarcation has been tied in with piecemeal reforms that can easily be (and indeed have been) overturned, all the more so as communities themselves have become internally riven and fragmented. So Chatterjee's advocacy of 'broadening and deepening the practices of democracy', absent any further transformative politics at the national level, seems suspiciously like the politics of containment of precisely democratic demands brought to a high pitch of managerial perfection in the United States.

At the same time, while the Subaltern Studies attack on elitist historiography brought fresh vitality to Indian history writing, and the shortcomings of the development agendas of nationalism have been criticised for good reason, there is also little doubt that when the attack on elitism is extended to the domain of the cultural alienation of the elite from the people, they restate some stock themes of cultural *intégrisme*, with the English-educated deracinated cosmopolitan intellectual as prime exhibit. Both *Elementary Aspects* and *Provincializing Europe* are *tours de force*,[133] each in their own way. But perhaps they also unintentionally impart a sense that some salutary lessons are being given on what it means to be Indian in a properly authentic way. This sense is further reinforced in Guha's *Dominance without Hegemony*.[134] Astonishingly, Heidegger is the presiding philosopher in this exercise, the quietist philosopher after the end of the Nazi storm, not the militant of earlier decades.[135]

In whatever bowdlerised form, Heidegger has replaced Marx as a critical inspiration for postcolonial studies of Indian society and culture. Guha, for example, is clearly inspired by a range of Heideggerian concepts including 'aesthetic being', while Chakrabarty pronounces Heidegger as his 'icon'.[136] This is the philosopher who presented himself as a 'seer but not properly an intellectual',[137] lived contentedly in the provinces, a craftsman of thought who idealised the peasant, revelled in the mystificatory cult of the soil and a village craftsman's ideal of counter-technology, and combined all of that, appropriately enough in this context, with his 'orientalist borrowings from Eastern philosophy late in his career'.[138] Indeed, Guha seems to have worked out a connection between the Aristotelian concept of *thaumazein*, the Heideggerian *Befindlichkeit* and the Sanskrit *Adbhutarasa*, the essence of wonder, which knows 'how to contemplate the world and by contemplating understand it'. Understood thus, he concludes, certain aspects of a 'long lost European tradition show up in the light of an unmistakable affinity with the ancient Indian concept of wonder'.[139] The real wonder is that these Orientalist Aryanisms that were once all the rage in royalist and reactionary circles in late eighteenth- and

---

133   Guha 1983a and Chakrabarty 2000, respectively.
134   Guha 1997a.
135   Wolin 1990, pp. 137–46.
136   Guha 2002; Chakrabarty 2000, pp. 143–4. Chakrabarty claims that the last four chapters of *Provincializing Europe* were written under the sign of Heidegger, but it seems as if the whole book was written under such an influence. Marx is only present as a foil, and a rather inadequate one at that.
137   Brennan 2006, p. 259.
138   Brennan 2002, p. 187.
139   Guha 2002, pp. 48, 65.

early nineteenth-century Europe, and that managed to connect the Classical Antiquity of Greece to Vedic India via Germany, should be making a comeback through postcolonial studies.[140]

For its part, the concept of autonomy – going well beyond its original remit for understanding the structure of subaltern consciousness where it had already acquired some *volkisch* potentialities – can open the way for the conservative, even reactionary, agendas of the Oriental Renaissance to be redeployed as some sort of radical rethinking about decolonisation, dependency, and so on. This type of thinking – with its inevitable quota of nativism, still somewhat latent in the Subaltern Studies phase – has become acceptable in some quarters as a way of thinking about culture, community and political self-governance. What was once deployed on the global scale of the collision of civilisations will now do for the articulation of community autonomy.[141] This then would be the counterpart of metropolitan postcolonialism's multiculturalism, restated for an Indian context.

Both the administrative Orientalism of the colonial civil servant and the Romantic Orientalism of European philosophers postulated an authentic/ideal non-Western subject, a son of the soil, emphatically not an intellectual who had become deracinated by being exposed to Western thought.[142] The place of the Romantic philosopher, if not the colonial civil servant, is now occupied by the Subaltern Studies type of postcolonial intellectual, ensconced in a study in Chicago, London or Canberra, thinking long and hard about the survival of fragments and remnants of once sturdy, self-identical and independent social and cultural formations. Of course, the irony of the comparison lies in the fact that the postcolonial populists of all stripes – like Gandhi earlier – may be said to be far more informed by the West's archive of knowledge (and indeed seem

---

140   For the self-styled Baron Ferdinand von Eckstein, India could be claimed along with Persia and Greece as the precursors of the German Gothic, that is, the Germanic Middle Ages: 'Homer was the base, India and Persia the two lateral sides of the pyramid whose peak was the German Middle Ages'. Elsewhere he wrote: 'all Europe, which was formerly Latin, is now Germanic, for the peoples of the North established all the southern empires'. Von Eckstein was a royalist, whose ambition seemed to be to 'liquidate' the eighteenth century; see Schwab 1984, p. 262; also Stunkel 1975, pp. 228–39; Sonenscher 2008, pp. 145–6.

141   See, for instance, Menon 2010, p. 18, referring to Chatterjee's 1994 essay 'Secularism and Toleration', reprinted in Chatterjee 2010.

142   This was quite a staple of colonial-era fiction: see, for examples, E.M. Forster's *A Passage to India*, Paul Scott's *The Raj Quartet*, and George Orwell's *Burmese Days*. Such characters are, however, presented with a degree of sympathy by the novelists. For an extended discussion of the ambivalence, even hatred, of colonial officials towards the western-educated Indian, see Metcalf 1997.

to derive their understanding of authenticity from it) than by some clerical worker in a remote post in India who might nonetheless, if given the opportunity, find the Enlightenment and modernisation attractive. A kind of perverse populism has developed in India whereby the old colonial master's rhetoric is redeployed with reversed signs to denote the appropriate cultural virtues.

It is only to be expected, in this general climate, that from 1987–9 and beyond, more so perhaps after 1992, the critique of bourgeois elitism itself and its collusion with the Western powers have been significantly toned down in some quarters and recast in a more neutral tone of difference. The focus is now less, if at all, on the peasantry, and more on the bourgeoisie and the petit-bourgeoisie; less on class wars over land, labour and the overcoming of landlord power, and more on culture wars over Eurocentrism, the Enlightenment, science and power-knowledge. There are some continuities as well: an emphasis on communities of local belonging, a hermeneutic of authenticity and, as noted, a critique of history itself as some master code that does violence to the fabric of people's lives. In the new circumstances, the overall expressions and forms have had to readjust to speak in the register of quiet protest and realist reformism. The subalternist historians working within the new spirit of institutional realism give voice to a different set of aspirations – the largely rural subalterns have gone silent, but the more educated and reform-minded bourgeoisie has become more voluble and articulate. Such a happy coincidence was too good an opportunity to waste, the welcome news had to be brought to the metropolis and where better than the Ivy League and other elite universities, where an eager audience of multiculturalists was in search of difference and likeness at the same time.[143] It is almost as if now there are different registers at work simultaneously – the tug of the West and the repulsion from it informing them variously.

The Subaltern Studies project from its inception to the present has gone through several mutations and transfigurations: from a project that originally wished to develop the rich legacies of Marx and Gramsci, if not the British Marxist historians, to one that embraced French theory, albeit not in its most Dionysian moods, to one that combines a fascination with German phenomenological existentialism and through it the revival of themes familiar from the

---

143   One of the better examples of this is Chatterjee 2004: the usual observations about the limitations and singularity of Western trajectories, the need for India to develop its own indigenous solutions to its problems aside, the book reads remarkably like an old-fashioned liberal Tory reformist tract with 'enlightened' people leading the way on urban reform, working conditions and sundry issues of interest to the proper functioning of civil society.

period of the Oriental Renaissance with all manner of practical and quietist accommodations to the present order of things. Perhaps this should be read as one of history's many grisly and ironic reversals of an original intention.[144]

3.3 Who is the 'Subaltern' in Postcolonial Studies?

The consolidation of postcolonial studies on a planetary scale at the moment of the collapse of the Soviet Union must be referenced to a very large field of forces, well beyond the experience of any one country and its colonial legacies, or even a process informed by a Third-Worldist logic, but one that acknowledges the centrality and universal significance of events located in the leading metropolitan countries and their spiralling global effects. It could not be otherwise. One of the consequences of the collapse of the political landscape of the post-1917 era was the rise of a turgid triumphalism in the West, founded on the notion that a really existing pole of attraction – at least for some of the ex-colonial countries – had disappeared.[145] Francis Fukuyama's *The End of History* is much cited in this regard,[146] but the so-called neo-conservatives are perhaps a better example, with their obsession with full-spectrum dominance, the American century, and so on.[147] A further consequence was that systemic forms of thought that sought the outlines of an alternative social organisation in some really existing system took a beating, in some quarters a pretty severe one. This was acutely felt in many of the former colonial countries, as a defeat by some and a liberation by others.

Sections of the academic left predictably enough trimmed their sails to fit the wind – if the best that could be achieved was some form of representative democracy, why not settle in and accommodate oneself to the new reality? These events ought to have underlined the inadequacy of thinking about 'postcolonialism' without capital as a central referent. The terms 'colonial' and 'colonialism' have never been exhaustively explanatory in themselves.

---

144   Jameson 1981, p. 102.

145   The Soviet Union was most certainly a pole of repulsion rather than attraction for most progressive Eastern Europeans, and it had begun to lose its charms in Western Europe going back at least to 1956 and certainly with the formation of Eurocommunism. For wide-ranging studies of the politics of this period, see Judt 2011 and Anderson 2010, pp. 59–91.

146   Fukuyama 1992.

147   On full-spectrum dominance, <www.en.wikipedia.org/wiki/Full-spectrum_dominance>; for a critical perspective on the American century, <www.news.illinois.edu/news/08/0508superpower.html>.

Those terms work at best as periodising concepts to indicate that something had changed, namely, the economic structures of countries that came to be occupied and ruled directly by one or the other European power, or came to be ruled indirectly by them, were no longer autonomous of an external determinant, a metropolitan power through which the economic circuits were completed. This could only happen – as I argued in Part I – if the external determinant was capitalist. Under that external determinant, the local economies all underwent a significant degree of integration and subordination to capital, and subsequent transformation. The only way to make 'colonial' into a decisive moment is to bring capital into the analytical framework, not occasionally and *en passant* to make a point about modernity or secularism or what have you, but as a central structuring and anchoring concept, in which case the 'postcolonial' merely indicates a punctual transition within that mode of production.

This is all the more so since after 1989, liberated of the slightest pretension that it had to prove its moral superiority over another social form, capital has pushed past any restraint that might have operated earlier. One of its strengths in recent decades has been to invade every nook and cranny of the world, not only the conventionally understood possibilities of commodity production, but the very core of culture itself. When one is asked to find 'room for enjoyment' in the 'seduction of the commodity', the implicit understanding is that there is no 'outside' to capital – even difference has become a commodity; it gives us at least the illusion of multiple ways of living in a completely commoditised world.[148]

It is possible to see the Heideggerian moment of postcolonial studies as symptomatic: not only of the position of intellectuals in the formerly colonised countries and in their several migrations, but perhaps more significantly also of the deep changes in the world itself that have made the earlier focus on class struggles, whether peasant rebellion or working class revolution seem untenable, archaic or simply irrelevant to the world as it has been reconstituted in the last twenty to thirty years.[149] For the most part, postcolonial intellectuals from the Third World make little common cause with the working classes of the metropolitan countries in which they live or make their living, whose lives pass by without any reference to the issues the former seem interested in. When Chakrabarty polemicises against modern-day historical narratives that serve to

---

148   Of course, this is not how Chakrabarty presents 'the politics of human belonging and diversity' (Chakrabarty 2000, pp. 66–67). But now it is an unavoidable conclusion.

149   Dirlik 2000a, pp. 1–18.

suppress human solidarities other than those demanded by the modern state,[150] he must also be suppressing – if only unintentionally and somewhat absent-mindedly – those histories of working class solidarity, even revolutions, that emerged in the wake of the spread of industrial capitalism and the modern state.

What then of the histories that are not under the influence, so to speak, of the demands of the modern state? Are they also somehow secretly co-opted into the projects of the modern state? If so, history itself could be construed as fatally damaged from the start. No doubt, some such gesture is implicit in postcolonial studies, which might explain the polemic against history that seems so central to it and the ensuing drift towards literary studies and idealist philosophies of ideas that ironically recapitulate the sort of hostility to the Enlightenment that characterised French neo-Catholicism or ultramontanism,[151] and their latter-day secularised equivalents. To the extent that these latter were, in their different ways, coded ways of speaking about anxieties that came in the wake of capitalist crises – the inter-war economic depression would be a case in point – and working class rebellion, perhaps postcolonial studies traces those anxieties in the context of a new moment in capital's erratic and crisis-prone history. Lazarus's idea of the 'postcolonial unconscious' points to both the repression of the need for rethinking genuine projects of emancipation after the 1989–91 conjuncture, and the return of the repressed in the wake of the nightmare of a Western episteme that chokes off the possibilities of so doing.[152] This is the moment of a new politics of Being, which finds expression in numerous postcolonial tracts.

In a change of tone, more so than of particular content or political orientation, Chatterjee makes the point that in order to rescue politics from those 'fraternal enemies', the politico-religious communalists on the one hand, and the secularists on the other[153] – the moral equivalence of the two might find acceptance in some multiculturalist quarters, but is surely most likely to provoke offense among secular-minded readers and is probably intended to do so – 'subalternist critics' have been forced to deal with a range of issues to do with democracy, governance, and civil and political society in their countries of origin. They do so not from the vantage point of the 'considerable creative freedom' afforded by the relative marginality of postcolonial studies in the United States and Britain, but instead from the 'realist confines of national

---

150   Chakrabarty 2000, p. 45.
151   Lardinois 1996, pp. 27–40; Stunkel 1975, pp. 228–39; Vermeil 1940, p. 134.
152   Lazarus 2011, pp. 9–14.
153   Vermeil characterised Roman Catholicism and the Enlightenment as fraternal enemies.

politics'. That is, they have had to assume the full responsibility demanded by considerations of practicality and institutional realism.[154] But this political homecoming has been accomplished not via a long march through enemy (class) territory, but through the 'foreign' if no longer 'strange' domains of French (poststructuralist) theory, German (existentialist) philosophy and US (multiculturalist) politics, as we have seen just above.

In fact, what has occurred is that at some global level there has been a confluence of theory and practice, and these have converged to inform an anti-secular 'subalternist' politics informed by practical realism. Whether or not this is an example of what Chatterjee generally advocates – of not injecting into popular life a 'scientific' form of thought springing from somewhere else, but of developing and making critical an activity that already exists in popular life, a process that Gramsci is believed to have pioneered,[155] and presumably an effective antidote to elitism – is a moot point. After all, the same Chatterjee also seems alarmed by the fact that popular life characterised by 'squalor, ugliness and violence' is now invading the sanitised precincts of bourgeois life.[156] But from Chatterjee's perspective, the postcolonial theorist needs to get involved in politics, perhaps to make sure, in the process, that those who are governed learn the limits of reformism and work within them, or acquire the proper methods for bumping themselves up from 'political' society into the more respectable 'civil' society. Institutional realism may be understood as a strategy for dealing with the inescapable systemic features of capitalism through the methods of indirection, a preference instead for speaking about modernity and its multiple forms. Labour, for its part, is a categorial imposition that, like the unmarked bourgeois individual, is manufactured by colonialism in the first instance, from which point it materialises itself in a variety of postcolonial forms. Since non-corporate (indigenous?) capital is said to be governed by livelihood needs, unlike corporate capital that goes after profit-maximisation,[157] we can also dispense with the exploitation that produces surplus value.

---

154 Chatterjee 2010, p. 298.
155 Chatterjee 1993, p. 199. Chatterjee's latest position seems to split the difference between assigning subalternity an existential value (perhaps that is now confined to those who have stepped up to assume the symbolic place of the subaltern!) and 'exploding subalternity' in the manner of Leninist and Gramscian politics – Brennan notes that when the latter position is acknowledged as being Gramsci's he is also taken to task for it (Brennan 2006, p. 257).
156 Chatterjee 2004, pp. 104–5.
157 Chatterjee 2008, p. 58.

COLONIALISM, MODERNITY, POSTCOLONIALISM

Faced with the rival elitist (secular and religio-communalist) strategies of consolidating the regime of the nation state, subaltern groups in India, Chatterjee argues, are devising independent strategies of coping, particularly as they are convinced about the inadequacy of the nation-state form for dealing with ethnic violence and authoritarian politics.[158] Chatterjee's position is for communities to have adequate autonomy and self-determination, as it were, so that in some contexts they may do 'things differently' as long as they explain themselves adequately to their own chosen forum. This will involve processes, Chatterjee notes, by which 'each religious group', for example, 'will publicly seek and obtain consent for its practices insofar as those practices have regulative power over its members'.[159] The issues of who is to decide what constitute those contexts, and who indeed will ensure that the religious groups in question are in fact democratically governed, are left hanging. This would especially be the case involving groups that are communalist and might even believe themselves to represent a majority, and will probably never ask their poorer members and women for consent. Perhaps this is where the state comes back in, no longer adequately theorised but invoked *ad hoc* as the case may be.

In any case, the theory that informs Chatterjee's practice seems less Gramscian than Foucauldian, and possibly even Deleuzian, detotalised, fragmented and informed by questions of bio-power, if not quite the phenomenological existentialism that has taken hold of 'subalternist critics' who have no actual interest in investigating social questions. The suspicion of secularism that Chatterjee articulates sits rather badly with Gramsci, who advocated 'the *absolute* secularisation and earthliness of thought'.[160] And at a time when even a conservative thinker like Brzezinski wonders if a 'pre-revolutionary situation' may be taking shape in late capitalism, community self-determination seems like pretty thin gruel. To the extent that capital is mainly invoked as planning, 'globalisation', modernity, and so on, in various descriptive registers, it seems that 'subalternist critics' have abdicated developing a proper response on an adequate scale. It is almost as if French theory has made its postcolonial appearance mediated through American-style libertarianism, and this at a time when the state has withdrawn from its 'development obligations' and abandoned people to the tender mercies of an ever more unstable capitalism.

The resistance to a systemic analysis rooted in the capital social form and its class contradictions is, in the current postcolonial circles, generalised and widespread, going well beyond any sort of 'internalist' narrative that explains a

---

158   Chatterjee 2010, p. 299.
159   Chatterjee 1994, p. 1775.
160   Gramsci 1971, p. 465.

local reaction emerging out of specific experiences of the bureaucratic degeneration of left-wing parties, factionalisation, sectarianism, bourgeois elitism, and so on. A work that sums up the *fin de siècle* positions on these issues is a 1997 edited volume by Lowe and Lloyd, wherein the editors set out to displace class analysis and political mobilisation from their implied prominence in elitist anti-colonialism. They express the by now standard objections to politics that might make demands on the state, instead advocating a respect for dispersed resistances among the 'alternative rationalities' of cultural, feminist and anti-racist opposition, which have been apparently sidelined by elitists as 'feminine' and 'racialised' spaces.[161] That 'dispersed' resistances might accord with elite interests and be welcomed by capital seems no longer to be a subject of critical self-reflection. The idea of opposing, 'without violence', popular customs that have negative effects on the oppressed population, and organising dispersed resistances and sporadic rebellions into a 'coordinated, participatory, and revolutionary activity',[162] directed towards overcoming a 'coercive state apparatus', and ultimately the mode of production it upholds, might be construed in the present circumstances as hopelessly elitist.

Elitism seems to have become a catch-all term that now most likely includes what in earlier times, when great revolutionary movements were afoot, would have been the role played by a revolutionary leadership. That such a leadership functioned as an organisational and political vanguard that sometimes hardened into an elite, with revolutionaries becoming bureaucrats or dictators and even assuming the functions of a ruling class,[163] revolutions degenerating into a historical dead-end,[164] and indeed exploiting and consuming their own,[165] are all well-known. For some, this is reason enough to dismiss all revolutionary movements as sanguinary excesses that are best avoided. But the point is that such movements do not arise by voluntarist fiat, but only when existing reformist alternatives have demonstrated their futility in addressing even the basic needs of the vast majority.

---

161   Lowe and Lloyd 1997, p. 6.
162   Parry discusses the ideas of a number of African and Caribbean socialists who wrote and spoke on the subject. Many of them, like Fanon and Cabral, are nowadays part of the postcolonial canon, but their commitment to a cultural revolution based on a transformation of old cultural forms that they believed were simply inadequate to transformative politics, or that had become degenerate under colonial rule, seems to get lost. For example, Fanon 1968, pp. 316ff; Parry 2002, pp. 139–41.
163   Djilas 1957; Djilas 1998.
164   Trotsky 1991 [1937].
165   Deutscher 1984.

The postcolonial intellectuals who speak about and advocate marginal and dispersed resistances might consider that they too have assumed some sort of leadership role, certainly representing – even if uneasily and with reservations – the underlying dynamics and tendencies of the 'alternative rationalities' they perceive among the movements about which they write. It is undeniable that life for many billions of people is lived precisely on the borderline of starvation, brought about by low-wage, scandalously exploitative work, a liminal existence on the constant verge of unemployment, sickness and misery, all of which are unavoidable, structural tendencies – almost laws – in capitalism: as Jameson notes, this is the lesson Marx wanted us to take away from *Capital* – 'a form of "naked life" far more deeply rooted in the economic system itself than Agamben's hopeless inhabitants of the concentration camps'.[166] If the now dispersed and fragmented resistances should ever begin to coalesce into a movement, *no longer a resistance to but a movement against the present order*, one can be sure that they will produce a revolutionary vanguard that will have the task of organising and leading the movement.[167] That such vanguards may not all possess personally attractive qualities is almost an occupational hazard. As Brecht put it in his poem 'To Those Born After': 'Oh we, who wished to lay the foundations for peace and friendliness, Could never be friendly ourselves'.[168] Or as a socialist in Raymond Williams's novel *Second Generation* remarks: 'We'd be the worst people, the worst possible people, in any good society. And we're like this because we've exposed ourselves and we've hardened'.[169] What marks out Williams's thought on this question, as Eagleton points out, is that he regarded the conflict between the struggle for socialism and socialism itself not just as a regrettable necessity that history will find it in its heart to forgive, but as tragic.[170]

One sometimes gets the impression that lurking behind the notion of 'alternative rationalities' is a rather paternalistic outlook on politics and culture: the peasants and working class do not quite experience things in the same way

---

166 Jameson 2011, p. 125.
167 As Eagleton rightly points out, such vanguards often arise out of the ranks of the oppressed population themselves, and have no interest in prolonging their subaltern condition (Eagleton 2007, p. 47).
168 The stanza goes: 'Even so we realised / Hatred of oppression still distorts the features, / Anger at injustice still makes voices raised and ugly. / Oh we, who wished to lay for the foundations for peace and friendliness, / Could never be friendly ourselves'; Brecht wrote three poems collectively entitled *An die Nachgeborenen*, or 'To Those Born After', probably in 1939 while in exile from Nazi Germany.
169 Williams 1964, cited in Eagleton 2007, p. 48.
170 Eagleton 2007, p. 48.

as the bourgeoisie. Anti-elitism consists of upholding 'subalternity' as a way of Being-in-the-world lost to a deracinated and cosmopolitan bourgeoisie, the subalterns as a 'standing reserve' of cultural values worth preserving in their difference. Both the Tory elitism of paternalist reformism, and the 'romantic nihilism' of the anti-Enlightenment wing of European thought, existed in colonial Orientalism – on both sides of colonial rule as it were.[171] In the post-colonial moment, the former tendency expresses itself in small-scale interventions in everyday life among postcolonial theorists who have maintained a connection with their countries of origin and feel the need to do something; the latter tendency is the subject of theoretical and polemical interventions among postcolonialists-at-large.

Be that as it may, as expressions of the post-1989 moment, and the diminished political perspective it offers, the 'post' in postcolonialism no longer refers exclusively to colonialism as a historical phenomenon, but to revolution as a punctual rupture with actually existing capitalism. At least in the heady years after World War II, the radical wing of the postcolonial project had envisaged, at a programmatic level, vast transformations of the socio-economic terrain, the revolution that Marx had prophesied for the 'social state of Asia' with European takeover, but which the subsequent career of colonialism had betrayed.[172]

All this can be construed as the abandonment of an unfinished project, and arguably not only by the postcolonial intellectuals who ought, in this context, to be seen as a symptom of a much wider problem. In the process of focussing attention on Eurocentrism, Enlightenment-inspired designs and symbolic issues of identity at the expense of a concern for political economic issues, postcolonial studies tends to ignore, in Dirlik's view, a rather bleak situation in much of the ex-colonial world and prefers instead to celebrate a victory over Eurocentric universalism – a victory largely manifested, it might be said, within select sections of the liberal Anglophone academe in the form of curricular changes. It goes without saying that the intellectuals who complain about their lost traditions have no use for them: if they do get around to reconstructing their supposed indigenous intellectual heritage, it sometimes comes across as an anticipation of Graeco-German thought, or worse a racial kinship of the *herrenvolk* that somehow history has sought to suppress.

So what is actually being celebrated, Dirlik claims, is the 'newfound power' of postcolonial intellectuals within some particular academic niches, rather

---

171   On the forms this tendency has taken in postcolonial studies, see Brennan 2006, p. 236, p. 264.
172   Marx 1974, p. 307.

than any transformation in the larger sphere of class or regional inequalities.[173] It might be added that this new found power, such as it is, would in itself have not been possible without the prior victories of the civil rights, feminist and anti-colonial movements that fought their struggles on behalf of a basic idea of human equality and the need to overcome ascribed places in a traditional social hierarchy, deepening not rejecting aspects of the 'great revolutionary bourgeois tradition, along with its material developments'.[174] The extent to which that 'revolutionary tradition' is written off in a fit of moralistic self-righteousness, and correspondingly, cultural 'traditions' are recuperated minus their manifold cruelties and exploitation, suggests the kinds of occlusion and forgetfulness of history that accompanies the trajectory of postcolonialism. Of course, the 'post' in postcolonialism might also, more generally, stand for an 'age that has forgotten to think historically in the first place',[175] but then that forgetting would seem to be a politically motivated one. For people used to seeing triumphalism coming from the ranks of the ex-Cold Warriors, this kind of celebration of 'newfound power' must be somewhat mysterious and easy to misrecognise.

It is within this amnesiac moment that one might place three key developments that characterise this moment of postcolonialism. The classical history from below in Europe, Chatterjee has argued, enriched but did not essentially disturb the solidity and triumph of European modernity. History from below was essentially about a 'lost history'.[176] Not so in India, for instance, where no such narrative of modernity is possible. Rejecting the framework of modernisation as the 'necessary narrative of history', and 'sceptical about the established orthodoxies of both liberal-nationalist and Marxist historiographies', Subaltern Studies affirmed the autonomy of subaltern consciousness and later the alternative and hybrid modernities that prevailed elsewhere. As we know by now, the fiction of an 'autonomous' subaltern consciousness was one of the first casualties of the postcolonial turn of Subaltern Studies, and the issue of different modernities has become a largely empiricist exercise in description, with *ad hoc* invocations of 'theory'. Either the progress of real history – the rapid modernisation of India, in this case, in the late 1980s and 1990s, and more so in the present century – was making the original claims look a bit silly, that is, modernisation was indeed the 'plot of history' once one took into account

---

173   Dirlik 1994, p. 339. See also Dirlik 2000a; Dirlik 2000b, pp. 25–47.
174   Eagleton 2007, p. 58; Sarkar 1997, p. 107.
175   Jameson 1991, p. ix.
176   Chatterjee 2010, p. 294.

the rather complex global dynamics of capital over a proper span of time,[177] or history from below was not really about 'lost' histories of the past as about a history of the present, a connection to the actually existing forms of class struggle that might in the present circumstances express themselves in forms not easily recognisable and lead to a misidentification of them as fragments, or multitudes, or whatever.

Regarding the three issues on which late Subaltern Studies has apparently made a 'productive intervention' – caste, religious minorities, and women – opening up the way to 'rethinking the political formation of the nation as well as the political process of democracy',[178] the central questions posed seem perfectly obvious from a mildly reformist perspective. Rethinking the political formation of the nation state is well-known and extensively written about, frequently enough either from a neoliberal sociological standpoint or from a libertarian-communitarian one, identifying the limitations of the nation state and its supersession in due course by all manner of communitarian formations.[179] Of course, the question of capital – particularly its most abstract form of finance capital and all its derivatives – remains a matter of sporadic and at most descriptive appraisal.

The spirit of practicality and institutional realism that informs these inquiries raise some obvious questions. If 'practicality', then practical from whose perspective? The religious leaders of the 'community' – since now the tendency is to define such communities principally in terms of religious identities[180] – in an echo of Thatcherite and Blairite politics? If institutional realism, which institution, principally? The state, presumably? And by extension, shall we say, what is acceptable within the present configuration in which the *nation* is coming to be defined principally in terms of ethno-religious identifications, in Europe as elsewhere, and the *state* which is increasingly becoming the bankers' state, outside the nation and positioned at a 'tangent' to it? So, once again, we have the community of money and the communities of faith alongside each other, one reinforcing the other. Around this unconfessable impasse there is some notion within institutional-realist postcolonialism that people

177   Without a proper theoretical foundation, it is impossible to discern *the more fundamental dynamics of history* that play out over much longer periods than a single human life span. Naturally, anti-foundationalist polemics have the secondary effect of occluding precisely those dynamics. For a discussion of this, see Jameson 1993, p. 172.
178   Chatterjee 2010, p. 299.
179   Van Creveld sums this up very nicely; van Creveld 1999; see also van Creveld 1996, pp. 4–18; Giddens 1994; Giddens 1999.
180   Sarkar 1997, p. 82.

will somehow find solutions to their manifold problems of subsistence and existence outside the project of the modern nation state, although they might need its help and access to resources occasionally. As noted, what is distinctive about late Subaltern Studies is not so much the positions they adopt as the supporting conceptual apparatus, which no longer needs Gramscian (let alone Marxist) concepts and categories, their methods of analysis or their political outlook.

This might well be one of the faces of the 'materialist turn' in postcolonial theory: institutional-realism combined with a postcolonial politics of Being, staged within a metageography of East-West couched either in culturalist terms,[181] or in terms of a revival of the grand existential drama of the Oriental Renaissance.[182] The general thrust of the post-1989 restructuring of social thought has been to eschew the issue of state power and advocate the formation of some sort of local collectivity (or collectivities) to resolve local problems. This is entirely consistent with the argument that Jameson advances, that socialism is now thought of as some sort of reaching for a more human scale,[183] eschewing the pitfalls of modernity, a sort of Narodnism with a post-structuralist touch, rather than the vision that Marx offered in which a politics of revolt is combined with the 'poetry of the future', in which socialism will be 'more modern than capitalism and more productive',[184] and more properly global in its reach and appeal.

Quite surreptitiously, then, a history from below has been replaced by a history from the margins in postcolonial studies. A history of class struggles to overcome the legacies of colonialism has been replaced by a pseudo-history of civilisations, taking its place in a quite respectable genealogy of histories from the margins that go back in the US at least to Jefferson's dabbling in Orientalia. The ethnic or national identities of postcolonial critics in metropolitan academic settings have simply stood in for entire regions of the 'authentic' Third World, even as its beneficiaries dismissed authenticity as a 'humanist fiction', denouncing nationalism while promoting cultural nationalism.[185]

It is significant that this has occurred in the context of what I would call a 'political selection' that has been taking place within social movements with complex internal dynamics and contradictory potentials. The Civil Rights

181 As is the case with Chakrabarty, for instance.

182 Guha's latest foray into the history of ideas, courtesy of Nietzsche and Heidegger.

183 Jameson 2011, p. 90.

184 Jameson continues: 'To recover that futurism and that excitement is surely the fundamental task of any left "discursive struggle" today' (Jameson 2011, p. 90).

185 Brennan 2006, p. 68.

movement, for example, had both a civic-universalist side and an ethnic-particularist one. In the former register, the active principals stepped forth as the representatives of suffering humanity with no divisions in the ranks; in the latter as the voice of a particular ethnic group that could be represented as having suffered more, and more singularly, than any other group, a logic of competitive bidding. To the extent that this side has come to represent African American Studies on campuses across the US, it was part of a ruling class strategy, part of the class struggle. That which survives and comes to represent the whole is the ethnic-particularism. That is, the more conservative, fragmenting, separating, ethnicising moments of social movements are selected (by the state and private agencies) for funding, support, publicity and ultimately co-optation. The ethnically-particularising moment of a struggle becomes its ultimate legacy and representative, while the more radical, universalising tendency is remembered only as 'history', and a nightmare of violence and chaos at that. Multiculturalism as the outcome of this class struggle by other means signals not the vitality of a struggle, but its debility. With every new wave of immigration, multiculturalism has expanded its portfolio, as it were, adding further layers of difference and separation. This is where postcolonial studies meets ethnicity and nation in the presence of French theory and German phenomenological existentialism. The upshot in the US itself has been to provide an additional reinforcement for the ethnic-particularist components of US multiculturalist theories.

Presiding over this debacle is the mangled and deformed body of Gramsci's work. If the Gramsci that postcolonial studies inherited was not quite the 'harmless gadfly' that Peter Thomas has said was made of him by Eurocommunist theorists,[186] his work has undergone a fairly thorough makeover so as to yield a 'heterodox' Marxism.[187] Three issues were critical to this reading: one, that Gramsci, in contrast to his predecessors in the Communist movement, was the theorist of the war of position; two, that he had built a 'conceptual wall' between state and civil society, locating all effective political work within civil society; and three, that he privileged the superstructure over the economy.[188] These positions were supposed to be a logical corollary of the

---

186   As Thomas puts it, the 'conversion of an unrepentant communist militant into a harmless gadfly is surely among the most bizarre and distasteful episodes of recent intellectual fashion' (Thomas 2009, p. 57).

187   This is the contention of Chaturvedi, and it is more or less in accord with one of ways in which Gramsci has been read in the postcolonial literature (Chaturvedi 2000, p. vii). Let us call this the 'postcolonial Gramsci'.

188   Brennan 2006, p. 239.

kind of oppositional movements possible in advanced capitalist countries, but were effortlessly transported to the ex-colonial world, where they informed the sort of reformist and 'situational politics' about which Chatterjee writes. Thus, Gramsci, mobilised against himself, emerged rather in the spirit of Derrida as an alternative *both* to Marxism and conservatism,[189] closer to the latter perhaps than the former, at least in the alternation between the existential and instrumental invocations of the 'subaltern'. The patient political work needed to overcome subalternity, the construction of a 'proletarian antithesis' to bourgeois dominance, had to go.[190]

Gestures like provincialising Europe develop a list of negative attributes of modernity, tacitly presenting the pre-modern as an abstract of toleration, communal well-being, non-work, and so on, and make use of this vision to advocate (without really advocating, that is, by slyly implying) some authentic nationalism achievable by the people on their own, a nation-coming-into-its-own, the nation as the earthly container for people's collective soul, and so on. This, if properly enunciated, would resemble some form of agrarian fascism, so it is best left merely implied. When Chatterjee says that the idea of subaltern history, having travelled from Italy to India, has now produced a 'generally available methodological and stylistic' approach to modern historiography that can be used anywhere,[191] he might in fact be suggesting some sort of modular transportable method: a few changes of name and place and perhaps even a slight adjustment of focus to fit the local situation. But as we learn from Vieira, 'oriental imports' are not always welcome, particularly in Latin America,[192] which prefers to get its theory directly from Europe. However, to the extent that subaltern history, influenced by Subaltern Studies, has in fact limped around the world devoid of anything resembling Gramsci's unrepentant communist militancy, it is mostly about indigenism and the mysterious properties of the 'resistant presence' of the indigenes among the civilised and

---

189   Ahmad notes with regard to this observation: 'Suffice it to say simply that the influence that deconstruction came to command in sections of the non-communist (often anti-communist) academic Left in American and European universities was certainly facilitated by the fact that it was *not* a discourse of the Right – even though many Marxists [including Ahmad himself] have argued that in its *unconditional war against political Marxism*, in its *antipathy toward working-class organisations* and against *organised* politics of the Left, and in its advocacy of *a global hermeneutics of suspicion*, it unwittingly *contributed* to openings for the resurgence of a fully fledged right-wing intelligentsia' (Ahmad 1999, p. 98, emphases added).

190   Thomas 2009, p. 223.

191   Chatterjee 2010, p. 301.

192   Vieira 1999, p. 290.

Europeanised, if thereby deracinated, bourgeoisie.[193] In its global moment, we may also see this de-Gramscianised history as part of an elaborate attempt at ideological closure, an avoidance of the ultimate consequences of the confrontation of capital and labour on the world scale.

Stripped of its immersion in and emergence out of the history of capitalism with its political eddies and flows, cross currents, not to mention intellectual structural adjustments, postcolonial studies can represent itself as a self-identical body of thought that explicates hybridity, difference, heterogeneity and a whole host of concepts that are of history yet unhistoricisable, conceived at some distance from the blood and gore of that history, requiring an authentic accounting of itself by itself. Hence the frequent repetition of the cliché regarding the scrupulousness of its practitioners. When one speaks of postcolonialism in the US nowadays, the main point of reference is not to the historic colonialism, which is poorly understood, but rather to some quite abstruse concerns with the breakdown of organic cultural communities under the onslaught of the West, the imposition of Enlightenment-inspired categories (including capital and labour!) on a population that had to resist the violence of such categorial impositions,[194] the development of a body of theory that apparently draws inspiration from the 'world' of the subaltern, and carries forward this resistance to the Western academic setting.

Bhabha's 'postcolonial criticism' that focuses on 'social pathologies – "loss of meaning, conditions of anomie" – that no longer simply cluster around class antagonism, [but] break up into widely scattered historical contingencies',[195] dispenses with even that bit of pietism. He makes it clear that the 'colonial' in postcolonial is a mere convenience, perhaps to suggest that the 'postcolonial' has some non-Western referents. For, as Lazarus notes, Bhabha's statement gives no reason as to why the 'colonial' should be implicated in the 'putative obsolescence' of class analysis.[196] Indeed, since Bhabha is also concerned to dispute the continued salience of 'the ideological discourses of modernity' that are said to 'flatten out complexity, to simplify the sheer heterogeneity'

193 On the spread of Subaltern-Studies'-inspired historiography to Latin America, see the extensive bibliography in Chaturvedi 2000; see, in particular, Mallon 1994, pp. 1491–1515; Latin American Subaltern Studies Group 1993, pp. 110–21; Mignolo 2000. Of course, theories of deracination do not work in the Latin American case, but elsewhere in Asia and Africa they do their disorienting work with persistent effect. More on this in part IV.

194 While Prakash develops the position regarding labour explicitly, it is part of a wider postcolonial polemic regarding Western categorial impositions; see Prakash 1992a, pp. 1–46.

195 Bhabha 2005, p. 171.

196 Lazarus 2011, p. 12.

of real conditions, reducing them to a binary structure of opposition, post-colonial criticism could be more appropriately called either 'post-Marxist' or 'post-modern'.[197]

With the replacement of class antagonism by 'cultural difference', 'ambiva-lence', the more 'complex cultural and political boundaries' that exist 'on the cusp of those often opposed political spheres',[198] Bhabha signals what post-colonialism is about these days: both anti-Marxist and postmodern, since postmodernism is in fact a repudiation of Marxist 'grand narratives', although not necessarily of all grand narratives; those that have a grounding in long-surviving spiritual traditions are deemed acceptable. So are civilisational narratives – the history of Western philosophy since its inception, the meta-physics of presence, the political spirituality of Orientals, two paradigms that have existed since time immemorial and still survive as vestiges, fragments, and so on. Somehow, Bhabha notwithstanding, an oppositional pole to Europe, in longstanding civilisational traditions, seems to be an occupational necessity for postcolonialism. As such, the fragments tend to gather around the powerful gravitational field of an implicit metanarrative.

Postcolonial intellectuals have become adept at playing the field: on the one hand, vis-à-vis their metropolitan host society they are specular, border intel-lectuals, with all the characteristic postmodern gestures in which Bhabha (and Prakash) engage. On the other hand, as authorised interpreters of their societ-ies of origins, their greater linguistic competence, not to mention their privi-leged access to Authentic Being, comes into play. In this guise they can write certain ways of Being-in-the-World of their societies of origin, of 'practices, aesthetic and spiritual, sedimented into language itself and not referring to concepts that the mind elaborates or that contain experiential truths' into an idiom that their Western counterparts might understand.[199]

In the multiplicity of these convergences, divergences, struggles, and so forth, the colonies – and more generally the former colonies – are a sort of gambit to clear the ground for various kinds of representation (of both variet-ies). The history of the colonies and their specific struggles – leading to, among other things, decolonisation – are merely incidental, and are of no detailed interest to postcolonialism's metropolitan interlocutors. The more abstract and generalised the form in which those actual histories can be represented, the better: a certain kind of formulaic presentation goes down very well, and

---

197 Ibid.
198 Bhabha 2005, p. 173.
199 Chakrabarty 2000, pp. 176–7.

ultimately names and places are interchangeable and serially dispensable, rather like the World Bank country reports.

Indeed, postcolonialism is now more or less completely detached from the study of the political economy of colonialism, and is attached instead to cultural studies of the postmodern variety, mainly but not exclusively of the former colonies. In the 'postcolonial' moment, we are all somehow still under the epistemic sway of the 'colonial' even as we resist under the sign of something 'post'. But since this is understood to have been true when the colonial powers ruled their extra-European colonies, and possibly in the future as well, the postcolonial is not related to the departure of colonial powers from their colonies. The 'postcolonial' is not primarily about time, it would seem: a moment when colonialism as understood within a mode of production paradigm comes to an end. It is really more about space, a virtual location across the barrier of the Enlightenment. Given the global ambition of postcolonial theory, the postcolonial – if not the colonial – is presented as the concurrent condition of humanity on both sides of the old colonial divide(s). This opens the way to a metropolitan postcolonialism and the promise of a postcolonial metanarrative, even if it is composed of fragments of other theories, combining a nostalgist and sometimes organicist vision of ex-colonial societies and cultures, elements of a critique of Enlightenment-inspired projects of modernity drawn from the Frankfurt School, anticolonial nationalism, poststructuralism, postmodernism, and Maoism.[200]

Ironically, of course, the significance of all these gestures might emerge more fully in the light of an enlarged narrative of capital. Whereas in the nineteenth-century, colonialism was a necessary moment, so to speak, in the initial articulation of pre-modern forms to capital, the rise of postcolonialism coincides with the moment when capital finally overcomes the barriers imposed by both the pre-modern social forms and by colonialism itself. This is when capital completes its 'conquest' of the entire world, including those regions that were once colonies of the Western powers. If so, postcolonialism is a record of the world fully colonised by capital, after the lapse of a generation or so following formal independence from the former colonisers, when the archaic forms of political colonial rule were finally rendered obsolete and completely consigned to a dusty corner of historical memory by capital's Promethean inventiveness and global reach. Postcolonialism – although a record of a fully capitalist world with no outside, no reserves of natural productivity à la Luxemburg (and Žižek) left to conquer,[201] no free gifts from outside its own

---

200 I have developed this argument at greater length elsewhere; Kaiwar 2007c, pp. 48–71.
201 Luxemburg 2003, pp. 348–74; Žižek 2000a, p. 358.

realm of surplus value – nonetheless incorporates in its name the claim that the object of analysis is colonialism. Or rather that it is directed towards the resistance offered by the colonised people and their descendants – not to mention all the migrating and criss-crossing fragments that reflect the unevenness of the world today – to Europe's pretentious universalism, to history's 'repressive strategies and practices'.[202] But reading Bhabha's postcolonial manifesto makes one wonder whether there might be something more along the lines of a strategy of containment, of 'structural limitation and ideological closure',[203] a concerted attempt in fact to close off the implications of a growingly unmediated confrontation of capital and labour on the planetary scale.

So, is there a subaltern in postcolonial studies apart from the empirical subalterns that are occasionally dusted off and pressed into the service of 'subaltern history'? Does social standing actually matter in a diasporic context? In a different context – of colonial India – Ranajit Guha pointed to the 'fluidity' of the dichotomy between elite and subaltern, especially in relation to uneven regional development, class formation, and in specific institutional relations involving the colonisers.[204] Guha noted that some members of the local elite could in certain circumstances take on 'the air of subalterns'. In a diasporic context, Brennan notes in response that racialised or ethnicised subjects – including the postcolonial intellectuals – could assume a rather different role: if not that of an elite, then at any rate that of a subaltern in a somewhat problematic sense of 'dominating and constraining' political (or certainly theoretical) alternatives. They do so through a displaced 'Southernist' strategy: political quietism under the guise of authenticity.[205] Postcolonial theorists have had to jump through some hoops to get heard: neither American minorities nor the dominant Euro-American ruling class are interested in grubby illiterate peasants who cannot read or write, and whose idea of which country they live in is as vague as Marx's working class students.[206] The subaltern has had to become an abstraction around which a Third World can be written for a metropolitan readership. In the process, there has also been a somewhat untheorised

---

202   Chakrabarty 2000, p. 45.
203   Jameson 1981, pp. 52–53.
204   Guha 1988, p. 44.
205   Brennan 2006, p. 261.
206   Testimony taken by the *Children's Employment Commission, Fifth Report, 1866*, p. 55, cited in Marx 1977, p. 370, n. 66: Jeremiah Haynes, aged 12 – 'Four times four is eight; four fours are sixteen. A king is him that has all the money and gold. We have a King (told it is a Queen), they call her the Princess Alexandra. Told that she married the Queen's son. The Queen's son is the Princess Alexandra. A Princess is a man'. William Turner, aged 12 – 'Don't live in England. Think it *is* a country, but didn't know before'. And so on.

reaching for Orientalist symbols and tropes, hastily reworked or excused as something like a 'strategic essentialism'.

The substitute for the subaltern in the postcolonial project must now be the intellectual who implements the totalising projects implicit in the post-colonial metanarrative on behalf of all those disappeared and disappearing fragments, which can no longer – if ever they could – speak for themselves, and also the one who resists the sway of Enlightenment-inspired categories and worldviews, and the whole secularising, rationalising drive of modernity. If that seems far-fetched, a reading of Chapter 3 of *Provincializing Europe* will disabuse the reader.[207] This is where Chakrabarty more or less tears apart the idea that 'subaltern' refers to any particular social group or groups.

We must assume that anyone who 'worlds' the earth, experiences time, and so on, in ways that challenge the imperious code of historicism, can fill in for the absent subaltern. Social position itself is virtual; it is the tyranny of homogeneous, empty time that is the target of theoretical underlabouring. The practice of subaltern history is to take history, the code, to its limits in order to make its 'unworking' visible.[208] And in this mode, the subalterns are those who stoutly resist the call to 'Always historicize ... the one absolute and we may even say "transhistorical" imperative of all dialectical thought'.[209] The goal of postcolonial critique, as Brennan notes, must be to preserve the 'essential resistance of the voiceless' as a 'jumbled, useless, noble suffering, revelatory excess'.[210]

The form and structure of postcolonial studies have to be placed squarely within the force-field created by the intersections of geopolitics, the econom-ics of global capitalism, and the increasingly otiose resurrections of difference that draw on an old conceptual inheritance of the West and the Rest that has been a constant companion of all manner of Orientalist thought. To the extent that the old Orientalist construct of Occident-Orient (Europe-Asia) has been part of the conceptual inheritance around which difference has been con-structed, its revitalisation in a postmodernist idiom is not entirely unexpected. And to the extent that the metropolitan Anglophone academy, especially the American university system – perhaps because of its early and comprehensive involvement with the worlds of government and corporations, not to mention the global study of the world's cultures – captures these trends, it reflects what

---

207   This is the chapter entitled 'Translating Life-Worlds into Labour and History' (Chakrabarty 2000, pp. 72–96).

208   Chakrabarty 2000, p. 96.

209   Jameson 1981, p. 9.

210   Brennan 2006, p. 260.

appear to be contrary currents: on the one hand towards a flattening out of any sense of the local, and on the other to an occlusion of what is in fact common to the experiences of working people everywhere. But this appearance is deceptive. The latter (the occlusion) is, as this book argues, the ideological accompaniment to, *not* the contradiction of, the former (the flattening-out). However inchoately realised, it is perhaps this ideological feature of postcolonial studies that has made it attractive to a metropolitan Anglophone academy. And that it seems is the interesting and obscurely understood part of the 'arrival' with which this book began.

CHAPTER 4

Provincialising Europe or Exoticising India? Towards a Historical and Categorial Critique of Postcolonial Studies

The following pages will closely analyse two major texts, namely, Dipesh Chakrabarty's *Provincializing Europe* and Ranajit Guha's *Domination without Hegemony*, for the insights they provide into what has been called late Subaltern Studies, or perhaps more accurately the postcolonial turn of Subaltern Studies. They illustrate a distinctive aspect of Subaltern Studies in their continuing engagement with major historical themes, exemplified by their detailed readings of the colonial archive and fundamental vernacular texts, their critiques of imperialist and colonialist historiography, and withal a willingness to engage in vigorous debate and polemics around the issues of modernity, historicism, hegemony, power and representation, which continue to define the vital terrain of postcolonial history.

To grasp the key contentions of *Provincializing Europe*, one almost has to turn to the end, where after over 250-odd pages Chakrabarty summarises his argument. As he puts it, 'this book is not committed to either Marx or Heidegger in any doctrinaire or dogmatic sense, the spirit of their thinking and their guiding concepts preside over the two poles of thought [the analytic and the hermeneutic, as Chakrabarty presents them] that direct the movements of this book'.[1] The analytic heritage, the practice of abstraction helps us to universalise and we do need universals, Chakrabarty argues, to produce critical readings of social justice. Yet, he maintains, this critical analytic tradition 'evacuate[s] the place of the local' and tends to 'sever the relationship between thought and modes of human belonging'. To restore the latter, Chakrabarty has recourse to the works of Heidegger, reinstituting in the process the relationship 'within thought itself between thought and dwelling'.[2] It is 'under the sign of Heidegger' that the crucial chapters in the book describe the distinctive features of a colonial modernity that neither replicates that of Europe nor should, for that reason, be regarded as a failure. It is about people making themselves at home in capitalism, even as that home appears to be tossed about in the

---

1 Chakrabarty 2000, p. 254.
2 Chakrabarty 2000, p. 255.

'furious oscillations of modern times'. It is also under the sign of Heidegger that the key concluding section ('Beyond Historicism') is developed.

Dominance without Hegemony expounds at great length, and via an examination of the categories that define and compose it, the distinctive features of colonial modernity in India, a result of 'the braiding, collapsing, echoing, and blending' of two idioms – the British and the Indian – in such a way as to baffle all descriptions of this process as either a dynamic modernity overwhelming an inert tradition, or 'the mechanical stapling of a progressive Western liberalism to an unchanging Eastern feudal culture'.[3] A distinctive feature of *Dominance without Hegemony* is its emphasis on an 'Indian historiography of India', with a critique of 'colonialist elitism and bourgeois-nationalist elitism'[4] as a necessary if extended preamble. That this 'Indian historiography' turns out to have some reactionary and regrettable features is a point that becomes the subject of lengthy apologia, rather than a forthright engagement of its limitations, but more on that below.

4.1   Marx and Difference in Provincializing Europe

Three aspects of the larger agenda developed in Chakrabarty's work are important to note right away: (1) the apparent neutrality between Marx and Heidegger is misleading; nowhere is the critique of Marxist thought for evacuating the local and the many ways of being-in-the-world paralleled in the book by an exploration of the limits of Heideggerian thought for developing a project of social justice adequate to the challenges of our time;[5] (2) the act of 'writing some very particular ways of being-in-the-world [Chakrabarty's vignettes of Bengali life, which I shall examine below] into some of the universal, abstract and European categories of capitalist/political modernity'[6] has no counterpart in 'writing' the abstract categories of Enlightenment thought in ways that might have a meaning for a subaltern facing injustice; (3) the invocation of a capitalist/political modernity – and its implicit and problematic equation with Europe – remains curiously disembodied, despite its evident centrality to

---

3   Guha 1997a, p. 61.

4   Guha 1988, p. 37, para 1.

5   Incidentally, the limits of Heidegger's thought are well explored by both Pierre Bourdieu and Richard Wolin in their otherwise very different books: Bourdieu 1991 and Wolin 1990.

6   Chakrabarty 2000, p. 255.

constituting the very fabric of life in colonial India.[7] The ways in which some colonial subjects themselves shaped colonial capitalism and profited at the expense of those most proximate to them is the subject of considerable amnesia in Chakrabarty's tale.

Chakrabarty appears to engage Marx mainly as a negative example of post-Enlightenment thinking that forces the 'many ways of being in the world'[8] into abstractions, not the least of which is abstract labour. To claim difference and resist the translation of difference into common terms via abstractions are, in this view, emancipatory gestures in a world grown tired of pretentious Eurocentric universalism.[9]

Provincializing Europe, however, is not devoid of politics. By emphasising the non-goal-oriented nature of much middle-class Bengali social life and by articulating a kind of nostalgic desire of a diasporic intellectual for that social life, Chakrabarty seems to be suggesting that the older Subaltern Studies emphasis on struggles for social justice, however inchoate, were a bad dream from which a mature version has woken up. To defuse the charge that he has replaced struggle with a kind of existentialist conservatism, Chakrabarty strives mightily to argue that the real roots of oppression in modern Bengal (or India, or the 'Third World' by extension) lie in a rampant Eurocentrism and historicism,[10] not in income inequalities, mass poverty, patriarchy, the exploitation of labour, or the manifold oppressions of the state. The struggle is displaced on to the level of discourse. The postcolonial radical now has no desire to seize the means of production and socialise them on behalf of the immediate producers. Mainly, in a diasporic reincarnation, he (in this case) wishes to seize the academic curriculum and rid it of Eurocentric diffusionist elements.

The starting point for Chakrabarty's attack on historicism is, of course, to define the term itself. Drawing on Ian Hacking's view that 'historicism is the theory that social and cultural phenomena are historically determined and that each period has its own values not directly applicable to other epochs', and Maurice Mandelbaum's notion that 'an adequate understanding of any phenomenon and an adequate assessment of its value are to be gained through considering it in terms of the place it occupied and the role . . . it played in the

---

7   The best that the rest of the world can aspire to is, as noted, an alternative, different, hybrid (and similar) modernity.

8   Chakrabarty 2000, p. 33.

9   As Chakrabarty puts it, the place of the universal is but a placeholder into which steps a proxy that usurps its position in a gesture of 'pretension and domination' (Chakrabarty 2000, pp. 70–1).

10   Chakrabarty 2000, p. 7.

process of development',[11] Chakrabarty notes two prime characteristics of historicism: (1) the notion of development and the elapse of homogeneous, empty time as the medium of development; (2) a pre-posited internal unity of the object that undergoes development.

Historicism, in this sense, Chakrabarty suggests, is common to Marxist, liberal and similar histories of capitalism, industrialisation and nationalism, and is premised on a variety of strategies. In dealing with capital as a mode of production, for instance, historicist accounts either suggest that it is a world-historical process that will eventually sublate differences, producing a more or less smooth terrain of development, or one that is not only not committed to overcoming differences, but positively produces and proliferates them. Both accounts are historicist in sharing a view of capital as arising in one part of the world and diffusing out to others, or if 'global' nonetheless operating as a 'totalizing unity'.[12] The only history that counts in this regard is the history that can be retrospectively constructed as the history of the 'becoming of capital, when it is not yet fully hegemonic or dominant', that is, the past as 'posited by capital itself' (Chakrabarty calls this History I), the staple of transition narratives and historicism. Arguably, however, this is not the sum total of histories, even of capitalism, and to do justice to the complexity of the reality, not to mention the practice of historians, another history has to be brought into the picture. This is History II, that is to say, history not 'as antecedents established by itself [i.e. capital], not as forms of its own life-process'; capital may seek to subjugate those antecedent forms, but, citing Marx, Chakrabarty notes that all sorts of remnants of 'vanished social formations ... still partially unconquered' survive those efforts.[13] No simple metanarrative of capital will suffice to unravel the complexity of modernity. Chakrabarty wants us to resist thinking of the future simply in terms of the unfolding of some potentiality inherent in capital, History I marching on to the end of history, and to consider the 'pasts that live in the present', which resist yielding some simple agenda to make that happen.[14] The 'pasts that live in the present' will take Chakrabarty into an exploration of the Bengali pasts that contributed to the making of colonial modernity. *Provincializing Europe* is thus an attempt to 'produce a reading' in which the very category 'capital' becomes a site where both the 'universal

---

11   Hacking 1995, p. 298; Mandelbaum 1971, p. 42; both cited in Chakrabarty 2000, p. 22.

12   Chakrabarty 2000, pp. 23, 47.

13   Chakrabarty 2000, p. 65.

14   Chakrabarty 2000, pp. 250–1.

history of capital' and the 'politics of human belonging' are allowed to interrupt each other.[15]

To do so with any amount of success involves confronting a number of
issues. First is the acknowledgement that European colonial rule in India
marks a definite caesura. Intellectual traditions, Chakrabarty asserts, 'once
unbroken and alive in Sanskrit or Persian or Arabic are now only matters of
historical research for most'; categories once subject to 'detailed theoretical contemplation and inquiry now exist as practical concepts, bereft of any
theoretical lineage, embedded [merely] in quotidian practices in South Asia'.[16]
When South Asians wish to theorise, they have recourse to European 'traditions', some of indisputably greater antiquity than the 'dead traditions' of
South Asia. Second, and allied to the first, is the near universal attraction to
Enlightenment-inspired notions among the colonised and ex-colonised globally. He cites Hichem Djait, a Tunisian philosopher, who accused imperialist
Europe of 'denying its own vision of man', and Frantz Fanon, who struggled
to hold on to the Enlightenment idea of the human, even when he knew that
European imperialism had reduced that figure to the male white settler. The
attraction of the Enlightenment stems from the fact that there is no easy way of
dispensing with the abstract figure of the rights-bearing individual or Reason
in its revolutionary guise in the conditions of political modernity, or for developing a social science that 'addresses the issues of modern social justice'.[17]

Chakrabarty's response to historicism (in this view, the global unfolding of
capital as a self-identical entity) and the idea of the political (the abstract figure of the human and Reason as the agency of history) develops a complex
notion of time and place within which to disrupt their implicit triumphalism. That requires acknowledging both the indispensability and inadequacy
of European thought. Indispensable not only in articulating a programme
of social justice precisely in terms of Enlightenment abstractions, but also
because in its radical register as Marxism it plays a role in demystifying the
ever-present tendency in the West to see capitalist expansion as a case of altruism; inadequate because it occludes questions of belonging and diversity. This
is something of a central challenge, from Chakrabarty's point of view, since in
fact the indispensable elements of European thought contain a powerful dose
of anachronism, which he explains as the desire of modern humans to 'reduce
the past to a null point' outside oneself and one's time, so as to be free of it and

---

15   Chakrabarty 2000, p. 70.
16   Chakrabarty 2000, pp. 5–6.
17   Chakrabarty 2000, p. 5.

to liberate oneself for the project of social justice.[18] Historicism of one variety or another, it seems, is central to the project of social justice.

However, this kind of reductionism is also problematic for Chakrabarty since he wants to interrupt this narrative with those unvanquished elements of History II. To do this, he must assert not only that 'difference' – a key term that will recur throughout *Provincializing Europe* – is not external to capital, but that it lives on in 'intimate and plural relationships to capital, ranging from opposition to neutrality'.[19] Why opposition to capital must come from History II and not History I, that is, from antecedents (for example, labour) reduced to moments of capital's self-expanding circuit, is a mystery that Chakrabarty does not clear up.[20] He insists that the issue is not about the resistance of this or that group to the spread of capitalism; it is not outside in place, but in a time that includes the category of capital, that is, it violates that category's internal coherence, in effect disrupting History I with History II, counterposing other forms of temporality to the homogeneous, empty time of post-Enlightenment modernity.[21] On this account, subaltern history cannot give up either Marx or difference.

Marx and difference are supposedly exemplified in two intellectual traditions (both European), seemingly at radical odds with each other: the analytical and the hermeneutic. The analytic tradition, Chakrabarty tells us, seems to evacuate the local by assimilating it to some abstract universal; it seeks to 'demystify' ideology by looking forward to a 'more just social order'. Marx is held up as one of the progenitors of this tradition. The hermeneutic tradition, on the other hand, with Heidegger as its chief icon, finds 'thought intimately tied to places and to particular forms of life' and is 'innately critical of the nihilism of that which is purely analytic'.[22] The polemic against Enlightenment universalism that Chakrabarty launches here maintains that the universal is but a placeholder into which steps a proxy, which usurps its position in a 'gesture of pretension and domination'. Let us say that Eurocentric diffusionism, or the coloniser's model of the world,[23] is one such gesture of pretension and

---

18   Chakrabarty 2000, p. 244.

19   Chakrabarty 2000, p. 66.

20   After all, one of Marx's most celebrated axioms is that the barrier to capital is capital itself, not the remnants of vanquished social forms that live on in the present (Marx 1981, pp. 349–50). See also my contribution to the Symposium on Robert Brenner's *Economics of Global Turbulence*, held at Duke University, 27 March 1999 (Kaiwar 1999, pp. 47–52, esp. p. 48).

21   Chakrabarty 2000, p. 95.

22   Chakrabarty 2000, p. 18.

23   The title of James Blaut's thought-provoking book; see Blaut 1993.

domination. Histories from the margins attempt to challenge that pretension and domination by giving us other life histories.

We will ignore for the moment why a 'critique that looks forward to a more just social order' should be considered nihilistic *per se*, or why 'thought intimately tied to places' should not be implicated in injustices and tyrannies of all kinds, or the larger question of why a programme for a just social order must evacuate the local, or why life histories from the margins must eschew a programme for social justice. These questions are never seriously broached in *Provincializing Europe*, remaining merely implicit, and that constitutes perhaps a political failing. Nor does Chakrabarty come to grips with the dialectical unfolding of the local and the global, the universal and the particular. This appears to be a significant methodological limitation.

4.2   The Not-Yet of Historicism

Historicism is what allowed European domination of the world, Chakrabarty asserts, thereby correcting one's naïve assumption that it must have been the heavy artillery of imperialism. It does so by making modernity or capitalism look not simply global, but global over time, by originating in one place and spreading to others.[24] Historicism posits historical time as the measure of the cultural distance assumed to exist between the West and the non-West; in the colonies it legitimated the idea of civilisation. Historicism assumes we are all heading in the same direction, but some have got there first and must direct the traffic for later arrivals. This is what he calls the 'not-yet' of colonial rule whereby the colonised – whether Indians, Africans or Irish for that matter – must wait and learn the codes of modernity and citizenship from the coloniser. Up to a point, nationalist thought goes along with this historicist approach to questions of modernity, but at others it balks at the limits it places on the mass mobilisation of peasants and others not yet drawn into the vortex of modernity for the eminently modern project of nationalism. The 'not-yet' of colonial rule is then replaced by the 'now' of anti-colonial thought, as those 'not yet' schooled in the 'doctrinal and conceptual' responsibilities of a secular civil society explode on to the historic stage.[25]

---

24   Chakrabarty 2000, p. 7. Of course, he has elsewhere asserted, on page 47 of the same book, that the latter position would still yield to capital the role of 'totalising unity', making it no less historicist than a diffusionist position.

25   Chakrabarty 2000, pp. 8–9.

Chakrabarty's criticism is not limited to colonial pretensions on this issue (the civilising mission), but also takes to task the English Marxist historian Eric Hobsbawm for describing peasant rebels as 'primitive' and 'pre-political', admitting non-secular, non-rational elements into their thought.[26] This kind of historiography, Chakrabarty states, is echoed in India where the peasantry, under 'world-historical notice of extinction', has survived and remains a sign of India's particular, not incomplete, transition to modernity. Chakrabarty describes the peasant as no less a part of Indian modernity than the secular-rational bourgeoisie and argues that the primitive (peasant) rebel's reading of the relations of power was 'by no means unrealistic or backward-looking'.[27] Indeed, Chakrabarty states, there is no need to translate – as part of a secular-rational civilising mission – the practices of the rebels who called upon gods and spirits, and attributed much agency to them, into some acceptable and 'more real' secular equivalent.

To the extent that nationalist narratives are trapped within the 'not-yet' of historicism and the signs of inadequacy and primitiveness of the subaltern classes, they presuppose that the subaltern classes needed to be educated out of 'their ignorance, parochialism', or depending on your preference, 'false consciousness'. In trying to subsume a variety of narratives not written from a modern 'subject position' into narratives that bear approximation to that of a private citizen, nationalist narratives essentially tried to make Indian history look like a chapter in European history, adding only that it happened later and was perhaps an inferior copy of that original. This deprives modern Indian history of its multiple and 'contradictory themes', reproducing Indian moder-nity as a project of 'positive unoriginality'.[28] In a show of even-handedness, Chakrabarty is intent on implicating even Subaltern Studies, at its inception, in this project of studying 'the historic failure of the nation to come into its own, a failure due to the inadequacy of the bourgeoisie as well as the working class to lead it into a decisive victory over colonialism and a bourgeois-democratic revolution of the classic nineteenth-century type'.[29]

---

26   Hobsbawm 1959, is the cited work. It is widely credited with having launched the 'new social history' that brought the methods of critical-comparative historiography to the subaltern classes. Chakrabarty seems to attribute some sort of political judgement in the way the term 'primitive' is used, but the OED notes that 'primitive' refers to 'ancestor' or 'progenitor', and in that sense Hobsbawm's use of 'primitive' might connote some sense of time or history, rather than an ahistorical judgement.

27   Chakrabarty 2000, pp. 11–13.

28   Chakrabarty 2000, pp. 33, 38–9. The term 'positive unoriginality' is taken by Chakrabarty from Morris 1990, p. 10.

29   Chakrabarty 2000, pp. 30–31, quoting Guha 1988, p. 43.

Arguably, Chakrabarty is right to distance himself from this form of historicism – which as we shall see has not entirely died out among the founding principals of Subaltern Studies – but his arguments do raise some thorny theoretical, methodological and political issues that cannot be easily discarded. For instance, when he notes that the presence of gods and spirits in the manifestoes of peasant rebels is not symbolic of some 'deeper, "more real" secular reality', he is in fact avoiding dealing with the problem of the symbolic in human thought. To attribute some crude literalism to peasant thought avoids the question of what the gods and spirits may symbolise even if they do not stand in for something 'more real'. Equally, Chakrabarty seems to imply that in the thought of 'disenchanted' workers in their struggles for social justice there is, in effect, a straight equivalence between thought, action and description. This kind of literalism is no help in sorting through the multiple and instantaneous translations that take place not only in the sphere of everyday politics, but also in the upheavals that take place in more exceptional times, and is probably why his questions of how do 'we' (presumably narrators, interpreters of subaltern consciousness) handle the issue of the presence of the divine or the supernatural in the history of labour, and whether the project of social justice requires the use of some sort of 'disenchanted' universalist language, remain largely rhetorical.[30] As for the red herring of the untranslatability of experiences into a common currency, we might only note that while Indian and British workers labour in different 'life-worlds', they have been no more or less attentive to the radical calls of democracy and socialism, although they might very well interpret those terms quite differently. Any suggestion that disenchanted workers will hear the call to secular social justice, while workers for whom gods and spirits are an everyday reality will not be able to do so, is belied by working class history itself.

As for the 'not-yet', and the lack or inadequacy that it appears to imply and that informs the drive to develop programmes for social justice, why should this be interpreted merely as an example of the imperialism of post-Enlightenment thought? Every programme of reform or revolution, even in the disenchanted West, implicitly acknowledges some inadequacies in the present state of things, and to the extent that it succeeds in mobilising people to the cause perhaps even convinces them of the importance of addressing those inadequacies. If all we could come up with as an alternative were the 'many

---

30   Sumit Sarkar notes that in what he calls 'late' Subaltern Studies, texts were 'still' being read in a 'flat and obvious manner, as straightforward indicators of authorial intention' (Sarkar 1997, p. 103). Perhaps this is a limitation in the interpretive strategies adopted by what I have been calling postcolonial studies.

ways of being in the world' there would be no need for a programme of social justice, since at least some if not most could happily adjust to the manifest injustices of their time. Altogether Chakrabarty's Platonic questions about gods, spirits, not to mention Reason – 'Can we give Reason the same mission the world over?'; 'In what do we ground the "reason" that unavoidably marks the social sciences, if not in a historicist understanding of history?'[31] – may only convince the reader of the need for a more sophisticated sociology and hermeneutics than *Provincializing Europe* seems able to muster. One would also need to go beyond repeated references to translation, agency, historicism and universals, and get down to some serious comparative history and ethnography.

It is in light of the above that we must assess Chakrabarty's claims about provincialising Europe, which he explains to be a way of exploring how European thought – both indispensable for and inadequate to thinking about the thorny problems of colonial and postcolonial modernity – may be renewed 'from and for the margins'. For Chakrabarty, this involves dispensing with the by-now archaic concern with the transition to modernity/capitalism, resisting the translation of different life-worlds into a common currency, instead looking for 'conjoint and disjunctive genealogies for European categories of modernity'.[32] It also involves the possibility of an alliance between the dominant metropolitan histories and subaltern peripheral pasts whose task must be to expose the collaboration of European imperialism and Third World nationalism in making Europe universal and to formulate a 'radical critique and transcendence of liberalism', most notably bureaucratic constructions of citizenship, the modern state, and bourgeois privacy.[33] If successful, provincialising Europe should result in a recognition of the many roads to a many-sided modernity in which Enlightenment-inspired liberalism is only one discourse and a provincial one at that. And what would be the end result of that, apart from (ironically) a liberal tolerance if not celebration of diversity? While the latter might suffice in an elite private-university setting in the West, one wonders how it would address the real, material deprivations of the world's poor and oppressed. Respecting the beggar's right to sleep under a bridge or on the sidewalk, and his or her invocation of gods and spirits in a cruel world, while avoiding such historicist issues as income redistribution is in fact to give the game away. One might be led to ask if the project of provincialising Europe

---

31   Chakrabarty 2000, p. 236.
32   Chakrabarty 2000, pp. 16, 255.
33   Chakrabarty 2000, pp. 42, 76–7, 239.

is a sophisticated apology for global and class polarisation, an aestheticisation of poverty and human misery.

I would like to suggest, for the moment, that we should consider an alternative approach to provincialising Europe, which takes its cue from what Jameson calls the 'growing contradiction between lived experience and structure', or between 'a phenomenological description of the life of an individual and a more properly structural model of the conditions of existence of that experience'. While in older societies, or even in the early stages of capitalism, the immediate and limited experience of individuals might still have been able to encompass and coincide with the economic and social form that governed that experience, at a later moment these two levels drift ever further apart and 'really begin to constitute themselves into an opposition', '*Wesen* and *Erscheinung*, essence and appearance, structure and lived experience'.[34] In advanced capitalism, the phenomenological experience of an individual becomes limited to a tiny corner of the socio-economic world, while the 'truth of that experience' no longer coincides with it. The truth of the 'limited, daily experience' of someone in London may lie, as Jameson points out, in India, Jamaica or Hong Kong, bound up with the whole colonial system of the British empire. In the same way, the 'truth' of the limited experiences of someone living in Calcutta might lie not only in London, or the metropolitan countries, but also in that of the other colonies, say, Jamaica or Hong Kong. The colonial system determines the very quality of the individual's '*subjective life*', and yet the 'structural coordinates are no longer accessible to the individual's lived experience and are often not even conceptualisable for most people'.[35] The experience of the metropolis can no longer serve as a universal referent. *A fortiori* this is the case in post-colonial times. Global capitalism scrambles the hitherto relatively stable geographies of metropolis and colony, core and periphery. A stage theory of politics loses all meaning.

While the above addresses the spatial co-ordinate of modernity, there is also a temporal co-ordinate that needs to be factored into an understanding of the challenges of theorising modernity. And this is what Jameson calls a fundamental peculiarity of human history, namely, that 'human time, individual time is out of synch with socio-economic time, with the rhythms or cycles ... of the mode of production'.[36] He goes on to say that as 'biological organisms of a certain lifespan, we are poorly placed to witness *the more fundamental dynamics of history*, glimpsing only this or that incomplete moment'. The space-time

---

34   Jameson 1991, pp. 410–1.

35   Jameson 1991, p. 411.

36   Jameson 1993, p. 172.

distanciations of advanced capitalism raise the problem of the true and the authentic, and it is the task of theory to 'deduce the absent totality that makes a mockery of us, without relinquishing the fragile value of our own personal experience',[37] a process that becomes especially urgent as capital on the global scale unleashes its vast cycles of growth, recession, crises, its interminable miseries, as well as its sanguinary euphoria. It is this very materiality of capital that affords the objective basis of provincialising Europe, while keeping in full view the need for a universalist discourse of rights and justice, and for bringing into the foreground the 'structural coordinates' that are no longer conceptualisable in terms of the lived experiences of most people, either among the former colonisers or the colonised. That is, it underscores the need for a large conceptual framework that does not pre-empt historical inquiry by recourse to arbitrary divisions, and the importance of not allowing a concern for difference to precipitate forgetfulness about the processes that create difference. It may, of course, be historicist in one of the ways in which Chakrabarty defines historicism, but it is a much more promising line of inquiry, not only to explain the contours of modernity, but also to create a politics adequate to countering capital's relentless drive to planetary dominance.

4.3   Why Historicise?

Historicism, for Chakrabarty, is part of the attempt by proponents of post-Enlightenment thought to universalise the notion of homogeneous, empty, disenchanted time. There are other ways of experiencing time than as a relentless sequence of secular cause and effect, other ways of worlding the earth, as it were. To think of European modernity, he says, is to think of modern industry, technology, medicine, legal systems, and so on,[38] into which are coded not only a transition narrative, but also the above mentioned homogeneous, empty, disenchanted time. Subaltern historians cannot accept this imperium of the European experience as a universal referent.[39]

But is the matter so simply resolved? Chakrabarty himself comes close to arguing that modern history and historical consciousness are material necessities, since bureaucracies and other instruments of governmentality can only hear particular types of argument coded with the ubiquity of the commodity economy and its categories, in which abstract time and labour are key

---

37   Ibid., emphasis added.
38   Chakrabarty 2000, p. 34.
39   Chakrabarty 2000, pp. 93–4.

categories. Subaltern classes will need this knowledge in their struggle for social justice. But one might argue that this is a somewhat crudely 'decisionist' approach to history. To think of modern industry, technology, medicine, and other innovations, is in fact to come face to face with the question, posed in *The Communist Manifesto*: '[W]hat earlier century had even a presentiment that such productive powers slumbered in the lap of social labour'?[40] It is the real, visible and experienced material difference that opened up in the course of the nineteenth century between industrial and non-industrial societies, which continues to sustain the 'transition narrative' in its global form, not just some imperious code of post-Enlightenment modernity.

The history of lack, deficiency, and other cognate terms, the ulterior leit-motiv of much of the historiography of the former European colonies, locates itself in an obscure realisation that what unleashes the powers of social labour lies not in the economic sphere – powers that can be released by mere changes of policy – but in the course and aftermath of sweeping social transforma-tions, that is, in the disturbing (for some) sphere of radically undecidable class struggles. The modernity that Chakrabarty attacks is the modernity of liberal theorists like John Stuart Mill, and of their latter-day modernisation counter-parts, in which 'traditional' societies are transformed into 'modern' ones by the diffusion of Western institutions and practices.

Chakrabarty makes much of the fact that Indian historians are expected to know the works of their European counterparts, that is, European history is part of the archive of Indian history, but the reverse is not true. In fact, the 'Third World', when it is of interest at all to European historians is as a living fossil of social forms long ago consigned to the museum of history in Europe itself. The point is well taken, but the issue is how effectively does he (or Guha, for that matter) use the European archive *to write history*. The Europe that Chakrabarty invokes is by his own admission hyperreal; Europe's modernity appears as some mythical Protestant ideal filtered through Locke and Hume. Huge chunks of counterhegemonic thought in Europe, much less the radical critique of political economy developed by Marx and successive generations of radical thinkers, are simply ignored. What emerges is a caricature, one that is likely to be greeted with derision by anyone who knows European history.

There is another concept of modernity, and in the plotting of its co-ordinates Perry Anderson notes the coexistence of significant elements of *ancien-régime* culture and economy at a time when Europe was recognisably modern in the common sense of that term. There is no law that dictates an inevitable and inexorable movement away from those *ancien-régime* mores. If

---

40   Marx and Engels 1998, p. 21.

that has come to pass, it has been by an act (or many acts) of political will and organisation, many of which at any rate originated not among the so-called revolutionary bourgeoisie, but among workers and peasants whose vision of an alternative to *ancien-régime* bondage was not the unfettered reign of capital, but something far more radical, articulated by, for example, the Levellers and Diggers in the English Revolution.[41] *It is by suppressing this radical dimension that modern Europe emerges* fully self-identical and armed with a retrospective, seamless and elitist genealogy from ancient Greece to modern England. Freed from the constraint of recognising radical impulses from below, and premised on their suppression, bourgeois rule emerged triumphant with a limited offering of rights, self-determination and democracy. Concessions have had to be won at the cost of considerable struggle throughout Europe, and have been and are being rolled back at every opportunity. The history of those radical-popular interventions appears in Chakrabarty's narrative to be the subject of considerable postcolonialist amnesia. The Europe that predominates in his narrative – and, as we shall see, in Ranajit Guha's as well – is one that traces a lineage from Aristotle to John Stuart Mill, via Locke and the apologists of colonialism. Here perhaps there is an unintended collaboration between those 'fraternal enemies', that is, the metropolitan elite intellectuals and the postcolonial 'subaltern' historians, in defining the scope of the Europe to be provincialised by the latter.

Chakrabarty seems able at best to give us vignettes of Bengali life that I shall address below, constituted around terms such as 'difference', 'excess' and 'plenitude'.[42] Under these terms lies an 'Indian' tradition, alive and unbroken in both theoretical and practical registers before the colonial encounter, but

---

41 For an exploration of the radical ideas of the Levellers and Diggers, not only on issues of property and work, but also on sexuality and its relationship to economic equality, see Hill 1975, p. 257. See also the following: 'The English revolution of the mid-seventeenth century was the dawn of women's liberation. The revolution brought peasant and working women on to the arena of history, and raised many fundamental questions about the structure of society, including women's place in it. The religious and political sects that mushroomed at the time of the revolution and civil war had a special appeal for women. Some sects gave them equal rights. A new morality, including a new sexual morality, blossomed. Sadly, the blooms withered fairly quickly – when the revolution stopped in its tracks, when a new unity was achieved between the victorious bourgeoisie and the old aristocracy which led to the restoration of the monarchy, the lords and bishops. The new ideas about women's equality and sexual morality came to life among the radicals of the revolutionary camp. It was among such people that the Levellers, Diggers and Ranters emerged'; Cliff 1984, <www.marxists.org/archive/cliff/works/1984/women/01-birth.htm#n8>.

42 Chakrabarty 2000, pp. 58–60.

which now sustains itself in quotidian practice and to some extent in literature and art, without the benefit of theoretical reasoning. It is the survival of this tradition, in however attenuated if not debased forms, that Chakrabarty is at pains to recuperate. All those other things that social historians have been and remain interested in – political, economic and social struggles – which utilise Enlightenment and Enlightenment-derived, not to mention a variety of 'indigenous', forms of thought and action, in this account become background noise. The ways in which modernity is constructed in each dynamic context, shaped by a variety of political tendencies, responding to, articulating or obfuscating the understanding of a world buffeted by capital and colonial rule, are at best faintly visible.

There is, of course, a more interesting way to come to grips with modernity, consistent with the idea developed above that the truth of any limited phenomenological experience is actually tied in to a much larger sphere, a global one in fact. Here again, we have recourse to an idea developed by Jameson:

> When one is immersed in the immediate ... the abrupt distance afforded by an abstract concept, a more global characterization of the secret affinities between those apparently autonomous and unrelated domains, and of the rhythms and hidden sequences of things we normally remember only in isolation and one by one, is a unique resource ... Historical reconstruction, then, the positing of *global characterizations and hypotheses, the abstraction from the 'blooming, buzzing confusion' of immediacy, was always a radical intervention in the here-and-now and the promise of resistance to its blind fatalities.*[43]

This capacity to think in large, conceptual, systemic terms – arguably made possible by the 'in-between, or both together' character of the modern – is seemingly lost to our age, the postmodern moment of capitalism, a 'purer and more homogeneous expression of classical capitalism', in which, as Perry Anderson argues, '[t]he possibility of other social orders' has all but vanished.[44] The resistance in postmodern and postcolonial theory to 'globalising or totalising concepts' like the mode of production (or the dreaded transition narrative) are a function of precisely the globalisation of capitalism that began in the post-World War II period but has accelerated tremendously in the last quarter of a century. As Jameson puts it, '[w]here everything is henceforth systemic the very notion of system seems to lose its reason for being, returning only by way

---

43   Jameson 1991, p. 400, emphasis added.
44   Anderson 1998, p. 92.

PROVINCIALISING EUROPE OR EXOTICISING INDIA?

of a "return of the repressed" in the more nightmarish form of the "total system" fantasized by Weber or Foucault or the *1984* people'.[45] The rejection of the 'pernicious categories of a totalising Western Marxism' – not limited to but finding its most active use in the arsenal of the postcolonial theorist – and the preference for the 'discrete genealogies of, say, Michel Foucault',[46] emerge as much from this historical context as from any desire to achieve a sense of identity 'uncontaminated by universalist Eurocentric concepts and images'.[47]

Those aversions and preferences emerge too at a moment when the ideologies of progress and modernisation, whose human and ecological costs have often been fearful and whose results have frequently been dubious to say the least, have gone into a terminal crisis. Furthermore, terms like conservatism and revolution seemingly no longer mean what they did previously, and indeed have no clear referents. The spatial economy of global capitalism is now so 'jumbled up' that regions in the pathways of global capitalism undergo development, growth, commoditisation; others find it virtually impossible to do so. Some in the erstwhile Third World participate in a new global culture, while others turn to finding solace in 'cultural havens as far apart from one another as they were at the origins of modernity, even though they may be watching the same TV shows'.[48]

Ironically, then, postcolonial theory – and no better exemplar can be found than Chakrabarty – has 'rearranged [this] global situation, objectively quite pessimistic, into a celebration of the end of colonialism', and the necessary tasks for the near future as 'the abolition of its ideological and cultural legacy'.[49] However, it is difficult to understand how this ideological and cultural legacy (Eurocentrism, as some prefer to call it) comes to have a special significance absent capitalism's foundational status. Without it, as Dirlik cogently points out, Eurocentrism would have been simply another ethnocentrism comparable to the Chinese, the Indian or for that matter 'the most trivial tribal solipsism'.

---

45 Jameson 1991, pp. 405–6. Adorno and Horkheimer argued that the Enlightenment represents Western culture's attempt to utilise a 'controlling rationality' to dominate sensuous existence, a process which found its fullest expression in the eighteenth century. Far from ensuring the progress of reason and emancipation, Enlightenment reason has resulted in the 'return of the repressed' in the form of fascism and other barbarisms of the twentieth century; see Schott 1996, p. 471. Ironically, perhaps, Jameson uses the phrase – return of the repressed – to refer to the capitalist system itself, amnesia about which seems to characterise so much poststructuralist thinking.

46 Anderson 1998, p. 119.

47 During 1987, p. 33.

48 Dirlik 1994, p. 353.

49 Dirlik 1994, p. 343.

An exclusive focus on Eurocentrism as a cultural, ideological or discursive factor 'blurs the power relationship that dynamized it' and 'endowed it with hegemonic persuasiveness'.[50] Postcolonial theory fails to explain why Eurocentrism,
in contrast to local and regional ethnocentrisms, was able to define modern
global history and 'define itself as the universal aspiration and end of history'.
It merely 'throws the cover of culture over material relationships, as if one had
little to do with the other ... and diverts attention from the criticism of capitalism to the criticism of Eurocentric ideology'.[51]

    How does Chakrabarty put his agenda of provincialising Europe into
motion? Like other postcolonial critics who claim to be influenced by Marxism
while resisting its imperious code, Chakrabarty has an odd way of doing so.
Insofar as anything of Marxism survives the 'anti-colonial spirit of gratitude'[52]
with which he embraces Heidegger – Fascist warts and all – it is translated
into a poststructuralist language, in which the universalist ambitions of
Marxism are deconstructed, decentred, and so on. Unlike earlier Marxists
who had perforce to render Marxism into a local vernacular – Dirlik gives the
example of Mao Zedong; one can think of a host of other equally important
translations – the repudiation of practical transformative challenges in postcolonial thought leads 'not to its dispersion into local vernaculars but a return to
another First World language with universalist epistemological pretensions'.[53]
Anti-universalist universalism appears no less foundational than its predecessor Eurocentric form and probably more imperious, we might imagine, from
the sheer lack of any need to render it intelligible to those who have been
on the wrong side of imperialism and its supposedly Enlightenment-derived
ideologies.[54]

    Why historicise? Because 'difference', 'excess' and 'plenitude' turn out to be
misdirected slogans after all, because 'a system that constitutively produces differences remains [still] a system', and because knowledge of the system might
be an indispensable ally to overcome the 'seemingly blind and natural laws of
socio-economic fatality'. If the Third World theorist objects that 'something

---

50   Dirlik 1994, pp. 346–7.
51   Ibid.
52   Chakrabarty 2000, p. 255.
53   Dirlik 1994, p. 342; see also Jameson 1991, pp. 255–6.
54   As Cusset puts it, 'Marx's *Communist Manifesto* was available to the German (and other
      European) workers when first formulated but now postcolonial theory is no longer
      available to the subalterns, for example' (Cusset 2008, p. 158). Of course, he might have
      noted that Marxism of a sort that goes now by the name of Maoism (a variety of anarcho-
      communism) is very much part of the mass struggles over land and resources in many
      parts of India, and is equally prominent in Latin America.

precious and existential, something fragile and unique about [their] singularity, will be lost irretrievably when [they] find out that [they] are just like
everybody else ... so be it; we might as well know the worst'. That objection,
Jameson notes, is 'the primal form of existentialism (and phenomenology),
and it is rather *the emergence of such anxieties that needs first to be explained*'.[55]

In view of the preceding considerations, it is perhaps not so unexpected that
Chakrabarty should write about other social orders, while adopting a theoretical stance appropriate to a moment of world history when the possibility of
other social orders besides or beyond the planetary hegemony of capital seems
to many if not most simply unimaginable. The social order that Chakrabarty
offers as the Other of Western modernity is at best a reactionary one, even on
the terms of the founding ideas of Subaltern Studies. His theory and polemics implicitly rule out a progressive, indeed revolutionary, alternative to really
existing capitalism.

4.4   Tattooed by the Exotic

As noted, Chakrabarty rejects the notion that modernity requires us to think
exclusively in terms of a secular, disenchanted time in which history unfolds.
He cannot accept the notion that gods and spirits are social facts, and that the
social somehow exists prior to or apart from them. Although the god of mono-
theism may have taken a few knocks, and was perhaps even declared dead in
the nineteenth century, the gods and spirits of 'superstition' (in India and presumably many parts of the Third World) are, he assures us, alive and well.
Chakrabarty claims to take gods and spirits as 'existentially coeval' with the
human, and thinks from the assumption that the question of being human
involves the question of being with gods and spirits. Being human means –
quoting Ramachandra Gandhi – discovering the possibility of 'calling upon
God without first being under an obligation to establish his reality'.[56] The
Santal rebel, facing death, could offer in his defence the plea 'I did as my god
told me to', which Chakrabarty concludes is about the consciousness of the
Santal and about the Santal as our 'immediate contemporary', a figure illuminating a life possibility for the present.[57] This existential coevalness of gods
and spirits allows Indians to mobilise anti-historical notions of the past that
are fully integrated into their modernity. In other words, there is no way to

---

55   Jameson 1991, pp. 342–3, emphasis added.
56   Gandhi 1976, p. 9, cited in Chakrabarty 2000, p. 16.
57   Chakrabarty 2000, p. 108.

consign the Santal's consciousness to the museum of history, while privileging the secular consciousness of disenchanted rebels for the present and future. They both coexist as facets of modernity.

By themselves, these claims are quite uninteresting. People who invoke god in everyday life do so without having to prove his or her prior reality. This is a fairly ordinary definition of faith. As for modernity, one of its 'essential horizons' is precisely the coexistence of different social and imaginative orders.[58] It is the further claims that Chakrabarty makes on behalf of the supposed existential coevalness of the secular and the spiritual world that begin to unravel his claims on behalf of the difference underlying Indian modernity. For example, he distinguishes between 'good' history and 'subversive' history. A good history – trying to assimilate the Santal's explanation of what made him rebel – would recast his explanation into a causal mode in which his *thakur* [god] would be given a materialist reading to the ends of privileging a purely secular, perhaps socio-economic, account of the rebellion itself. If we see the causality attributed to *thakur* as massive self-estrangement, then we have merely done 'good history'.

A subversive history, on the other hand, would take the Santal's account literally and leave open the possibility of loose ends that will not need to be tied into a neat secular knot, thus giving us a peek into a very different form of thinking about causality than the relentless secular cause-and-effect sequence of much modern historiography.[59] Subversive history, it turns out, is nothing more than a proxy for what Chakrabarty elsewhere calls the time of the gods. It is unclear what has been subverted, and in favour of what? If the end of this kind of history is causal and political agnosticism, what happens to the project of social justice? If it is epistemic charity, then why is it not patronising and Orientalist? One is left with the suspicion that the time of the gods becomes in this type of account a mere placeholder, which can be replaced by whatever scraps of Orientalism are ready at hand.

We must remind ourselves that modernity is defined by the conjunction of two sets of circumstances: the legacy of a still living pre-industrial past and a situation in which a global (capitalist/colonial) system inscribes its imperatives at the very heart of human experience, with those circumstances in turn affecting artistic and political endeavours. This context, in which both European and Indian modernism emerged, enabled the creation of 'remarkable new languages and forms', 'haunted by the exotic' and 'tattooed with foreign

58   Anderson 1998, p. 92.
59   Chakrabarty 2000, pp. 105–6.

place names'.[60] Perhaps what the historian of colonial modernity needs to understand is that the foreign and the exotic lie not on the other side of the globe, as it were, but in the intimate proximity of the colony itself. Chakrabarty betrays a misunderstanding of colonial – in his case, Bengali – modernity when he suggests that 'subaltern pasts act as a supplement to the historian's pasts', that they remind us of a 'shared, unhistoricizable and ontological now'. This is to turn the subaltern into an exemplary character who illustrates the contemporaneity of the non-contemporaneous, an inhabitant of the psychic basement of bourgeois consciousness.[61]

Let us suppose, for the moment, that we were confronted not with a subaltern rebel, but with a fundamentalist Zionist who rationalised his role in the occupation of the West Bank by saying that God had given that land to Israel. Would we extend to him the same epistemic charity, the same causal and political agnosticism as Chakrabarty wants us to in the case of the Santal? Both statements seem identical in their structure, abdicating responsibility, partaking of the logic of extreme authoritarianism, utter absolutism. On what grounds would we differentiate the statement of the land-grabbing Zionist supported by his government and the world's superpower from that of the oppressed and exploited Santal rebel, since this particular brand of 'subversive' history gives no basis for such comparative judgement, since all is difference, excess and plenitude?

In point of fact, neither the existential coevalness of the time of the gods and the spirits, nor calling upon god without having to establish his or her reality, form any part of Chakrabarty's methodology in *Provincializing Europe*; they are merely empty gestures. Despite his disclaimers, he does offer a fairly straightforward anthropology of faith, if not of religion, of the forms in which gods and the ineffable are invoked, the occasions when they are, and what those invocations signify, written by a metropolitan historian with an outsider's point of view. A political 'translation' might help avoid the *cul-de-sac* to which Chakrabarty's argument leads: in the conditions of subaltern struggles against an armed and hostile opposition, some ideological armour might have been necessary before entering the fray. Attributing a causal role to the

---

60   Jameson 1991, p. 411; see also Anderson 1998, pp. 55ff.

61   Perhaps Chakrabarty has all along been discussing 'Indians' – presumably including middle-class urban ones – rather than Santals in particular. The Santal serves as a demonstration figure of Indians' anti-historical versions of modernity, unless the Indians in question had become culturally deracinated by over-exposure to the West. This is one of the characteristics of the version of postcolonialism that derives from Subaltern Studies.

gods – and alienating responsibility to them – would have been part of the strategy of class warfare. In that case, we might see the Zionist argument differently: not as an invocation born of the fear of imminent liquidation, but as ideological manipulation.[62] The Santal's case would be different, and acquire a more complete secular reality.

4.5   Under the Sign of Heidegger, I: The Woman's Question

Not surprisingly, in the last four chapters of *Provincializing Europe*, supposedly written under the sign of Heidegger, we find neither the kind of insight into Bengali urban life that a 'good' historical approach might provide, nor even an inkling of what projects of social justice might have been developed out of nineteenth-century Bengali urbanism. There is no discussion of how Indian political, economic and cultural ideas were, or could have been, mobilised for such projects. Those concerns are replaced by the more familiar trope of 'Indian exceptionalism'. The endless spinning around on the notions of 'difference' and 'excess' seem mainly designed to spirit economic and social inequalities, injustice and oppression out of sight (and on the occasions when these are brought into view, they are quickly aestheticised and rendered unusable for any project of social justice). Indeed, Chakrabarty's positive reading of hierarchy, images of worship, the thoroughgoing relativisation of patriarchy – all contribute to making modern city life in Bengal part of an exotic moral economy and the site of an apolitical difference and excess.

Chapter 5, 'Domestic Cruelty and the Birth of the Subject', traces the emergence of the caste Hindu widow both as the object of much solicitude in Bengali writings of the colonial period and as a person with a complex emotional life, whose sufferings she herself could write about and about whom articles and books were written. How was the condition of the suffering Hindu widow presented in this newly emerging literature? Much of it seems to have been through fairly straightforward calls for social reforms to ameliorate the condition of the widow, often accompanied by analyses of the problems posed by Hindu customs and joint-family life. For Chakrabarty, however, the need to go beyond 'good' history is so insistent that he proceeds to set aside these

---

62   The Israeli occupation of the West Bank may be a done deal in the United States, especially in academia, but elsewhere the occupation has altogether other political implications, the unease being caused by its resemblance, in some ways, to the white-settler colonialism of the nineteenth century, or more appropriately to the apartheid regime of twentieth-century South Africa.

concerns, or the voices of the widows themselves, except for the odd paragraph here and there.[63] Perhaps the widows have been rendered mute by
the workings of an all-encompassing and powerful nationalist patriarchy
that could command, alongside the 'traditional' resources, those of Western
'reason' as well?

Chakrabarty is much more concerned to show that the plight of the Hindu
widow came to be articulated within a field constituted by two spheres of
thought: one, the Enlightenment sphere of natural sentiments, in which
reason plays an important part in regulating 'blind custom', thus releasing a
human capacity to experience sorrow for the plight of those who have been
subject to especially poor treatment; the other, the sphere of 'Indian aesthetics', which asserts that only the particularly large-hearted could feel the pain
of others. The point is that the Enlightenment field of interpretation did not
swamp the Indian counterpart, but coexisted with it, and that the suffering of
widows – undeniable in both traditions – generated alternative and incompatible readings of human capabilities, endowments, and so on.[64] If we assume
Chakrabarty's reading of the situation to be correct, are we then to conclude
that somehow the life of the Hindu widow was enriched, and her suffering
lessened, by the coexistence of these traditions? If not, are we permitted to
entertain a sneaking suspicion that Chakrabarty is more interested in aestheti-
cising the sufferings of the widow than in understanding the actual dynamics
of social-reform movements that grew up in engagement with and in the inter-
stices of the two traditions?

Are we also to assume from this that the Enlightenment view was the generally accepted one in, say, eighteenth- or nineteenth-century Europe, that similar antinomies were not present in European modernity? If not, the best that
one can say is that in the unprecedented conditions created under colonial rule
in Bengal, social spaces may have opened up that 'Indian aesthetics' could not
theorise and explain, so that some form of Enlightenment philosophy would
become an important theoretical, political and social resource. Enlightenment
philosophy was available to urban Bengalis and could be pressed into service;
otherwise, undoubtedly, modes of thought existing in India would have been
wrestled with in order to generate a new conceptual order adequate to the new
situation. The appropriation and invention of traditions is very much a part

63   Chakrabarty 2000, p. 139.
64   Chakrabarty 2000, pp. 127–9.

of every modernity, with the Enlightenment itself, reinterpreted to suit, being one pole of it.[65]

Chapter 8, 'Family, Fraternity, and Salaried Labour', is an example of what Chakrabarty has in mind when he writes about the inextricably conjoined but disjunctive nature of colonial modernity that calls into dispute historicist (evolutionist) notions of modernity. Among other things, this chapter deals with the idealisation by the nineteenth-century Bengali middle-class of the *grihalakshmi* figure (the idealised housewife, member of a clan and indeed its saviour, so to speak, against the ravages of modern life) and *grihakarma* (the disinterested work of maintaining the familial collective) versus the denigration of office work as routinised, soul-killing stuff (and perhaps also as individualistic and utilitarian?). Along the way, Chakrabarty also examines differences in the ways conceptions and practices of fraternity were developed in Europe versus Bengal. The history of Bengali nationalism, he informs us, gives us a glimpse into a colonial modernity intimately tied to European modernity, but one that avoided reproducing the latter's autonomous individual as a figure of its own desire. This problematises, for Chakrabarty, the place of liberalism in Bengali modernity, while avoiding the temptation to think of the more collective (familial) fraternal bonds that accompanied Bengali modernity as somehow incomplete, compensatory or as an ideological cover for the grosser forms of exploitation of women and younger siblings.

Citing an 1823 text (*Kalikata kamalalaya* [Calcutta the abode of Kamala]) to make the point about difference, Chakrabarty argues that the author displayed a steadfast desire to maintain a critical symbolic boundary between the realms of gods and ancestors on the one hand, and that of the public secular domain on the other, and resisted disciplining the time of the household to that of 'civil society', which is conceived of as the site of compulsion, unfreedom, a forced interruption of higher duties to one's gods and ancestors. However, and this is the point Chakrabarty wishes to emphasise, the author himself was a member of a voluntary association that followed European rules and was dedicated to 'improvement'.[66] If the story were to end there, perhaps it would neatly illustrate Chakrabarty's point, although it is very doubtful that office work as such was ever the subject of sustained poetic rapture by a salariat anywhere! However, within a few pages, another story starts to emerge. For instance, he

---

65   Undoubtedly, for postcolonial theorists, the Enlightenment would be one of those 'misplaced ideas' producing a besetting 'experience of incongruity' (Schwarz 1992, p. 25). In fact, it was not misplaced at all since it served as a powerful weapon in the struggle against colonial rule and its native (and nativist) allies.

66   Chakrabarty 2000, pp. 220–2.

notes that by the late nineteenth-century, in contrast to the world of *Kalikata kamalalaya*, 'Victorian fetishes of discipline, routine, and order had become some of the most privileged and desired elements in Bengali imaginings of domestic and personal arrangements'. Time it seems had become the essence of this reconfigured Bengali bourgeois life.[67] There is certainly the making of a transition narrative here, but Chakrabarty neither follows this through, nor does he inquire into its material co-ordinates with the level of historical detail that he devotes to 'difference'. Instead, we are offered a rather lame conclusion, following Sudipto Kaviraj, to the effect that 'the more modernity unfolds it seems to appear inescapably plural [sic] ... Transition narratives create the untenable illusion that given all the right conditions ... the Bengali rich and poor would "understand" the principles of being private and public in the right ways'[68] – an extremely platitudinous statement in this context, to put it mildly. Chakrabarty asks, 'How do we find a home for reason, even as we acknowledge the plural ways of being human that we ourselves posit'? Of course, it goes without saying that modernity is inescapably plural, but can it be subjected to good historical analysis or do we take refuge in vague generalisations, verging on essentialisation, of an East-West dichotomy?

One certainly ought to be able to track the development of notions of time and space in colonial modernity without necessarily giving into hard notions of transition, whereby every society is bound to follow a rigid sequence of social and economic forms and arrive at more or less the same end point. This would be more the approach of a rigidly bureaucratised and Stalinist version of Marxism, captured or recuperated for neoclassical economics in the Cold War period by people like W.W. Rostow and latterly at least in claims about the end point by Francis Fukuyama – impeccably bourgeois thinkers – than of any critical school of Marxist theory.[69] In this context, an interesting question might be: what were the ways in which older themes survived and how were they modified as a new regime of time and space emerged in the urban culture of Calcutta during the colonial period? One might reasonably posit three overlapping moments:

---

67   Chakrabarty 2000, pp. 224–5.

68   Kaviraj 1997, p. 113, cited in Chakrabarty 2000, p. 235.

69   Rostow 1960 and Fukuyama 1992. Much recent Marxist theorisation has been critical of Stalinist stage theory and has thereby rendered the notion of transition from one social form to another altogether more complex; see, for example, Mészáros 1995; or Jameson 1988, Volume II, p. 155.

one   in which ritual, religion and economy are inextricably imbricated; indeed, perhaps it would have been impossible for people in such a social formation to separate and autonomise aspects of social life that we casually describe as if they were autonomous and separate, a not uncommon situation in many social formations that precede the development of capitalism;

two   a moment of genuine tension, when the 'economy' is being pulled apart from other aspects of social life, in this case largely through the initiatives of a self-consciously 'superior' and alien power, a moment in which ritual and religion achieve significant autonomy and become associated with an agenda of purity and authenticity over against the foreign rulers; let us call this *the moment of tradition*, when 'tradition' is constructed as an oppositional pole to modernity;

three   the moment when the cleavage is far advanced and the economy begins to exert its gravitational power over the symbolic arenas of identity and culture; let us call this *the moment of 'neo-traditionalism'*, when the capital form subsumes culture (including religion and ritual) and gives it the characteristically commoditised existence widely recognisable today in India as elsewhere.

The antinomies generated in the process and the contradictions they signal would tell us something significant about the ways Bengalis themselves mobilised old and new ideas for their projects, and take us beyond a substantialised aesthetic agency acting behind the backs and seemingly above the control of social agents. This is not a trivial consideration, especially when examining the issue of patriarchy, which recurs on several registers in chapters 5–8 in considering, for example, the idealised figure of the housewife [*grihalakshmi*], the Hindu widow, and even *adda*, a supposedly non-end-oriented practice of orality that Bengalis came to prize as part of their adaptation to the exigencies of urban living. How does Chakrabarty's brand of subversive history cope with patriarchy?

Chakrabarty is uneasy about a purely historicised explanation of the emergence of the idealisation and romance around the figure of grihalakshmi and grihakarma, dismissing the tendency in Indian historiography to see this as the particular way in which a middle class constructed new patriarchal norms in the face of colonial exclusions and racism, and the shock of being subjected to 'foreign' norms in the public domain and the anxieties accompanying this situation. There are two major shortcomings to this approach, according to Chakrabarty: *one*, that it effectively reduces the aesthetic to its mere ideological functions; *two*, that it foreshortens historical inquiry. To reduce the categories of a nationalist aesthetic to its ideological function alone would be to miss out on the histories of contesting desires contained in them. Imagination and desire are 'always more than rationalisations of interests and power'.[70] From Chakrabarty's point of view, it is crucial that we investigate the proposition that Bengali modernity might have imagined lifeworlds in ways that never aimed to replicate the political or domestic ideals of modern European thought, that instead of the contractual individualism of European fraternity, a conception of fraternity based on the solidarity of brothers in an extended family developed in which *bhakti* was mobilised as a 'modern political sentiment'.[71] And in keeping with the emphasis on difference, one ought to resist the temptation to see this as a lack, a deficiency among middle-class Bengalis.[72]

However, as we well know, there was a ferocious amount of litigation between family members, including brothers, over inheritance matters, and occasional instances of solidarity were massively undercut by a near-constant sense of grievance and mutual suspicion. If nothing else, this suggests that individualistic tendencies existed in tension with, perhaps even in contradiction to, the familial solidarities that normative ideology, fostered within specific historic co-ordinates, emphasised. Chakrabarty might respond by saying that one must not confuse the actual situation on the ground for the idealisations involved in this aesthetic practice, but if we were to follow this approach, we could do little more than a side-by-side narration of how different civilisations, moved by high-textual aesthetic and philosophical prescriptions, gave voice to those 'traditions' – resulting in a civilisational narrative resembling in form that of Samuel Huntington's, for example, even if the valence of the universal was diametrically opposed.[73] 'Difference' could be spun out to the nth degree and description would displace explanation altogether. This could easily lead to a variety of historicism that Chakrabarty would not wish to deal with.

Lest we see this patriarchal culture as singularly oppressive of women, Chakrabarty assures us that women did not necessarily view it as an 'iron cage of unfreedom'. He cites the example of a book entitled *Patibrata Dharma* (English subtitle: 'A Treatise on Female Chastity') by Dayamayi Das, which goes on to celebrate the land blessed with women devoted to their husbands, which should celebrate women as goddesses. The book also gave its author an opportunity to celebrate her eroticism and individuality, and express her

---

70   Chakrabarty 2000, pp. 216–8.
71   This argument, as we shall see, is also a key component of Ranajit Guha's construction of Indian modernity.
72   Chakrabarty 2000, pp. 217, 235.
73   Huntington 1996.

exhilaration at becoming literate.[74] Depending on what the baseline is, this might indeed be construed as bringing out the 'creative side' of this nonliberal patriarchy. But is it any way unusual? After all, bourgeois women are given some space – as patriarchy becomes less private and more civic-national – to exercise a degree of power over proletarian women and to develop a social role. As we know, the sense of power and the exhilaration that goes with it – confined to a very few women, even of the dominant classes – is something that women of the Hindu Right now experience. After all, they can participate (if only vicariously) in the blood rites of Hindutva.[75] Fascism offered 'Aryan' women some sense of mission and accomplishment.[76] This may be creative, but it is hardly something to celebrate.

What is the idealisation of housewife and housework, *grihalakshmi* and *grihakarma*, but a local statement of the widespread tendency to develop and institutionalise a cult of domesticity, to build in sanctions against those women who would stray from rather narrowly stated norms of behaviour, and to accompany the idealisation of the female figure of virtue with a denigration of the male world of work and sordid compromise? The inversion of the symbolic and the economic hierarchies involved here is typical of patriarchal discourses everywhere. Bengali patriarchy may have idealised the extended family as the unit of solidarity, but even so, it did not violate the wider norms of controlling female sexuality, branding and punishing those women whose personal desires may have driven them to violate those norms. The figure of Alakshmi, the malevolent counterpart of Lakshmi, has its likeness in other cultures.

What larger solidarities and anxieties were being expressed in this dialectical counterpositioning of Lakshmi/Alakshmi? On the one hand, the mobilisation of an indigenous idiom is one way of limiting the assimilation of the Bengali bourgeois woman to alien (read: European) norms, even if that alien figure was also bound by the limits of Victorian patriarchy. On the other, there is the anxiety of upper-caste, not necessarily upper-class, men thrown into the maelstrom of capital and into an indifferent public sphere by a foreign power that professed contempt for their religion and social arrangements. Conceivably, then, there could have been a levelling down of the pretensions of upper-caste men to those of people below them in the caste hierarchy, whose values in matters of sexuality might have been heretofore more distinctly

---

74   Chakrabarty 2000, pp. 232–4.
75   Mazumdar 1995, pp. 1–28.
76   Koonz 1987.

liberated. If the role of *grihalakshmi* was to maintain the 'integrity of the kula',[77] this may well have been because that integrity was always fragile, under threat from within as from without.

In this situation, one would have to reconsider Chakrabarty's contention that Bengali modernity rejected the agonistic individualism of modern Europe in favour of a 'natural solidarity'. In the first place, rejection implies active consideration before a decision is made. Arguably, colonial rule itself – for reasons of economical governance, among others – may not have encouraged, and indeed may actually have actively restrained, the emergence of agonistic individualism, not that it could contain all countervailing tendencies in that regard. Overall, colonial rule, and not only in India, was decidedly conservative. The historical conditions may have played a significant – if undiscussed in *Provincializing Europe* – part in the ways in which an older aesthetic and philosophical tradition gained the effectivity it did, if only in a limited temporal conjuncture. Aesthetics and high-textual traditions cannot be made into self-moving forces in history; this is precisely how a civilisation-narrative model short-circuits historical investigation.

But it is the larger – in this case, nationalist – significance of solidarities based on kinship or pseudo-kinship through which we must sift. Whatever the actualities of family solidarities on the ground, it is clear that ethno-nationalism in India mobilised religious solidarities even as they were being crafted.[78] Nationalism operates simultaneously in the civic-universal and ethnic-particularist registers, and membership of the imagined community of a nation modifies and qualifies unmarked universal individualism; individuality is historically conditional on membership of the group.[79] Chakrabarty deals with this rather complex development of nationalism using his by now formulaic invocation of the idioms of family solidarity that mark a crucial difference with Europe. He informs us that an assumed fraternal compact underlay the tendency – pervasive in *Bengali* and *Indian* nationalism – to think of the country as Mother. *Hindu* nationalists portrayed themselves as children of the mother. Popular nationalist songs captured the affective side of the brotherly unity on which this 'patriarchal nationalism' was based, and the myth of fraternity was 'one crucial difference between the patriarchal assumptions of nationalist politics in Bengal and the classical themes of European political

---

77 Chakrabarty 2000, pp. 227–8.
78 For a critical study of this topic, see Kaiwar 2003; and Kaiwar and Mazumdar 2003, pp. 261–87.
79 Kaiwar and Mazumdar 2003, pp. 278–85.

thought'.[80] The politics underlying this assumed fraternity is no great secret, and perhaps in this case 'difference' ought to take into account the historical-conjunctural factors in the evolution of anti-colonial and, indeed, communalist versions of nationalism. Absent that type of investigation, no essentialised difference between Europe and Bengal (or India) is likely to be persuasive.[81]

4.6   Under the Sign of Heidegger, II: Imagined Communities

Chapter 6 ('Nation and Imagination') takes up the question of the nation as imagined community and the specific connotations of imagination. Chakrabarty is keen to show that India was not imagined according to some European conception alone, but owed a lot to the animation, in new circumstances, of an 'ancient' Indian tradition. One component of modern Indian imagination about the nation is informed by incorporating European thought in which it is seen as a 'mentalist' construct with an active, thinking historicising subject participating in the formation of the imagined community; the other is the Indian component, *darshan*, a 'subjectless practice', which implies the cessation of the world – the ordinary historical world, *samsara* – and its sudden replacement by a new dimension of reality. The enjoyment of the *rasa* [essence] of nationalism requires, in modern India, the coming together of both traditions. Chakrabarty insists that 'plural and heterogeneous ways of seeing ... raise questions about the analytical reach of the European category "imagination"'.[82] This is an arguable assertion; one might suggest that Indian bourgeois thought of the nineteenth century is actively inventing a tradition or creating multiple and ever-more complicated examples of sophistry, rather than simply recapitulating some ancient tradition.

Chakrabarty is further interested in linking the peasant mode of imagining and seeing with the ancient (elite) tradition of Sanskrit aesthetics. Thus, he asserts, the 'Bharat Mata' of the peasants – as opposed to the 'India' of the intel-

---

80   Chakrabarty 2000, p. 229.
81   The fate of Hindu widows, no longer *grihalakshmis*, separated from their children, packed off to widows' colonies in Varanasi or Vrindavan, where they were supposed to devote the rest of their lives to the memories of their deceased husbands, is the counterpart of this kind of male solidarity. For some graphic reading on this, see: <www.womennewsnetwork .net/2007/11/05/nothing-to-go-back-to-the-fate-of-the-widows-of-vrindavan-india/>. Perhaps a properly subversive history would have devoted some time to discussing this issue.
82   Chakrabarty 2000, p. 174.

ligentsia – is imbued with this age-old practice of *darshan*, and refers to 'practices, aesthetic and spiritual, sedimented into language itself and not referring
to concepts that the mind elaborates or that contain experiential truths', and
that such practices were the 'legitimate ground of peasant nationalism'.[83] We
are being asked to believe that an ancient Indian tradition, shared by elite and
peasants alike, distinguished not only Indians from Europeans, but surely by
implication Hindus from Muslims, and that this was true for all the subcontinent's authentic Hindu denizens through time. Despite Chakrabarty's earlier
polemic against historicism, this is a sheerly dogmatic statement of conservative historicism and Orientalism, wrapped up in the kind of organicist fantasy
to which Subaltern Studies-inspired postcolonial thought seems to be increasingly drawn. One wonders about the price to pay for setting aside a secular
causal account of the national imagination.

For a start, the '*Bharat Mata*' of the peasants could be the earth beneath
one's feet or the whole world. Why should we call this nationalism, since
nationalism carries the charge of belonging in a community constituted precisely by shared notions of the past, vicariously experienced commonality
with people one will never meet, and some notion of boundaries? Educated
nationalists like Tagore, Nehru and others might use *darshan* self-consciously
to indicate an equivalence or difference – both should be possible – with
other, Enlightenment-influenced theories of nationalism. But short of systematic investigation, one cannot summarily suggest that there is some organic,
class-indifferent tradition that binds all Hindus together. Furthermore, what
notion of 'imagination' corresponds to the realist mode even if we know what
corresponds to the poetic? In fact, the nationalist imagination, à la Benedict
Anderson, contains both the notion of origins and time, therefore history in
some sense, and the suspension of time itself.[84] In the latter mode, the nationalist imagination dwells in an unhistorical present that connects individuals
into a community regardless of subjective will; or it manifests itself as the
consciousness of a timeless collective Being that suspends the very notion of
origins. Via its poets, and secular priests, the nation becomes an almost sacred
entity experienced in moments of devotion, when the rational, critical facul-
ties are suspended and one submits to fancy.[85] These facets of the nationalist
imagination might suggest that the imagination is itself a multifaceted thing
to be investigated in each historical context for what it can reveal about the
poetry and pathos of nationalism. But Chakrabarty wants so much to wring

---

83   Chakrabarty 2000, pp. 176–7.
84   Anderson 1983.
85   Smith 1995, pp. 160ff.

the maximum mileage out of difference and excess that he must ransack every bit of Sanskrit aesthetics he can muster to press his case, even if that involves, ironically, arguing within precisely the enclosures of the Orientalism and nativism bequeathed by the colonial legacy he otherwise wishes to challenge.

Chapter 7 on '*Adda*: A History of Sociality' – the longest in the book – begins with Marshall Berman's question: 'How can one become a subject as well as object of modernisation', 'get a grip on the modern world and make oneself at home in it?'[86] The cultural location of *adda* – a form of sociality that is not end- or result-oriented, and which is peculiar, so Chakrabarty will conclude, to colonial Calcutta – has something to do with a history in which the institution came to symbolise a particular way of dwelling in modernity, almost a comfort zone in capitalism. The passing of *adda* as a social practice over the last several decades in postcolonial Calcutta seems then to have become the occasion for a great deal of nostalgia and mourning, as if its passage carried away with it an exciting if problematic period in the history of modern Bengali urbanism. In Chakrabarty's view, an unresolved question 'remains buried' in the current nostalgia for adda: 'how to be at home in a globalized capitalism?'[87] The requiem for *adda*, then, brings with it a deeper anxiety: how to cope with a fast-changing world, in which 'uninterrupted disturbance of all social relations, everlasting uncertainty and agitation' seem to be the order of the day.[88]

Chakrabarty concedes at the outset that what is peculiar is the Bengali claim that the practice of *adda* is peculiarly Bengali. He quotes Nripendrakrishna Chattopadhyay, somewhat ironically, to the effect that: 'No other race has been able to build up such an institution as adda that stands above all ideas of need and utility. To enjoy adda is a primordial and perennial practice of life – no other people have succeeded in acknowledging this in life as Bengalis have'.[89] He also cites Nirad Chaudhuri,[90] an iconic figure of Bengali letters, who argued that *adda* signified a lack or deficiency in Calcutta's natives, whom he likened to Galton's oxen, which were hardly conscious of each other when in a herd, but showed extreme distress when separated from each other.[91] For Chakrabarty, *adda* cannot be seen as a carryover of a 'feudal' culture, 'surviving

---

86   Berman 1988, p. 5, cited in Chakrabarty 2000, p. 180.
87   Chakrabarty 2000, p. 215.
88   Marx and Engels 1980, p. 19.
89   Chakrabarty 2000, pp. 182–3.
90   Nirad Chaudhuri (1897–1999), prolific writer in both English and Bengali, acerbic critic of Bengali culture, and an apologist for right-wing Hindu nationalism, is probably best known in the West for his *Autobiography of an Unknown Indian*, and *Continent of Circe*.
91   Chakrabarty 2000, p. 215.

as an obstacle to Bengali modernity'; it would be a mistake to see it as defending a 'precapitalist sense of time and sociality', and equally wrong to hear the ghosts of Luther and Weber in Nirad Chaudhuri's strictures against it. The participants in *adda* were, as he points out, the people who helped form a Bengali literary public in Calcutta and who contributed to a distinctly modern sense of nationality.

These must be the key ideas, one would think, and an apt subject for an extended meditation on the transitions that are inevitable for any society drawn into the gravitational field of capital, and perhaps even the occasion for a stab at a comparative history of sociality in the transition to a capitalist urbanism, especially when the space that was created (as in Calcutta) did not pre-exist colonial rule, and the city itself was quite consciously modelled on London. But predictably, Chakrabarty has another agenda: to show that the history of sociality in Calcutta does not follow metropolitan precedents. *Adda* is not the salon, the coffee-house, the party; it does not replicate Western ideas of sociality. Nor is he interested in a historical comparison with societies making similar colonially driven transitions from older social forms (Cairo, for example). And other Indian cities, of a similar recent vintage (like Bombay or Madras) are outside his ambition. Perhaps he does not consider them important enough – the point of comparison is always the metropolitan other.

The ambit of Chakrabarty's historical curiosity seems remarkably narrow, with rich descriptions on one side (Calcutta) and rather stark schematic outlines on the other (Europe). To make the point about difference, Chakrabarty has recourse to the 'tension' between the ideals of *adda* and those of modern civil society; they are, he informs us, 'mutually antithetical organisations of time and space'. Civil society, in its '*ideal* construction, builds into the very idea of human activity the telos of a result', and structures its practice on obtaining a product and a result informed by a 'developmentalist and utilitarian logic'.[92] *Adda*, by contrast, is opposed to achieving such definite outcomes, and the idea is for the participants to enjoy 'a sense of time and space' that is not subject to the constraints of any explicit purpose. To do so would kill the very spirit of *adda*, or to quote his favourite source, Buddhadev Bose, drive one 'from the heaven of adda to the barren land of duty'. So *adda* would seem to be a practice that defines a key element of Bengali modernity, singular to be sure and not comparable to anything else. If the chapter began with some ironic reflection on Bengali claims to *adda*'s uniqueness, Chakrabarty quickly retreats to his favourite method, namely, comparing an ideal Western construction – be it of civil society or modernity – to the actual experiences of modernity that

---

92   Chakrabarty 2000, p. 204.

characterised Calcutta, from which he draws his conclusion that there were crucial differences between European and Indian conceptions of modernity.

The model could, of course, be vastly enriched by considering the complexities of Western modernity itself, and the actual existence within it of many different ways of being or becoming modern. A similar procedure for a range of societies making their transitions from older ('feudal') social forms to capitalism under conditions imposed by conquest and occupation would, in the end, illustrate two rather important points: that each instance of modernity is indeed singular, and yet they all have something to do with the incursions of capital into everyday life and culture, not to mention family life and gender relations. For difference to be a properly historical concept in relation to modernity, it requires an understanding of the workings of historically developed social formations and the structural force of capital, and their relationship over time.[93]

But this is not the place to go into an extended exegesis on the importance of maintaining historically determinate comparative points of view on phenomena that range across wide expanses of time and space, rather than an ideal on one side (which is nonetheless implicitly posited as the actual practice of particular societies in Europe) and the really existing forms on the other (in each society that serves as an oppositional pole to Europe). How such a project can manage to provincialise Europe is a mystery, since everyone who is not European is comparing their Caliban-like peculiarities to Europe's invariable universalism. Of course, it goes without saying that this is the method that pervades Orientalist thought, both in its Utilitarian and Romantic modes. As for avoiding historicism, we might note that using descriptions to establish 'historical difference' is hardly avoiding it. Indeed, it is a surreptitious way of establishing at the same time the self-identical evolution of a civilisation over time until it comes up against, in this instance, an exogenous impact that renders its past 'dead', mere history to be studied for whatever salutary lessons one might wish to draw from it.

---

93   Berman's study of St. Petersburg from its origins as the westward-facing modern capital of Russia to its role in the 1905 revolution and beyond is a richly documented example of a city caught up in the 'modernism of underdevelopment' (Berman 1988, pp. 173–286). While St. Petersburg was not a city born of colonial conditions, Berman's study will have much to say to people interested in colonial-era urbanism. The richness of Berman's study stems in part from the wide ambit of his historical interests, its comparative nature and willingness to draw global conclusions about the relationship between modernisation, modernity and modernism. His case studies of Paris, New York and St. Petersburg capture the singularity of each city, but they are not dominated by the monotonous drum-beat of difference.

The irony of this situation is that there were plenty of universalist Utopian impulses in the culture of colonial Calcutta, which could have been the focus of Chakrabarty's study of urbanism. He himself cites the case of the Four Arts Club founded by two men of modest background: one, Dineshranjan Das, who worked at a pharmacy, and the other, Gokulchandra Nag, who worked at a florist's. A considerable idealism informed their outlook on the 'redemptive role of art': 'I imagine a resting-house where people tired by the burden of their lives can come and rest, where *nationality, sex and position* will not be barriers, [where] men will make their own work joyful and by freely mixing with others will find themselves fulfilled in the easy working out of their own desires'.[94] Further, the same chapter quotes Nripendrakrishna Chattopadhyay, who points out that the import of books to Calcutta's burgeoning reading culture had acquainted young Bengalis with 'trends in world literature and thinking'. It also quotes an anonymous source to the effect that behind all the seeming disorder of metre and rhyme in the poetry being published in Europe of the late 1910s and 1920s, there is 'a very big tragedy. The Great War came and destroyed all the old-world beliefs in the minds of their young, their restless minds are seeking a new refuge'.[95]

What does Chakrabarty make of this? That the market and the taste in the consumption of literature are all mediated by the conversation of the *adda*, whose non-end-orientation, we have already been told, was a distinctive feature of Bengali modernism! Chakrabarty's 'subversive' move here is unfortunately also quite banal if not conservative. He does not explore what might have provided an impetus among working class intellectuals to the kind of Utopian impulses behind the founding of the Four Arts Club, and their interest in the radical new forms assumed by world literature in the interwar period. An exploration of this kind would have been particularly apposite given the quotation from Marshall Berman that began the chapter, and Berman's own understanding of modernism as a 'flaring up of the most radical hopes in the midst of their radical negations' and people's desire to 'explode [their world] from within', even if at another level they were at home or tried to make themselves at home, in it.[96] How did the churning of the world by war, revolution and emergent fascism generate, at the same time, a deep desire to transform it? The question then arises as to which Europe is being provincialised by Chakrabarty, and to what ends? What does it mean when a global circulation of books and news media – not then as subject to corporate control as they now

94   Chakrabarty 2000, pp. 198–9, emphasis added.
95   Chakrabarty 2000, p. 200.
96   Berman 1988, pp. 19, 121.

are – carried radical impulses across different domains? What relationships developed between print media and orality in the construction of movements against fascism and colonial rule? The mediations are, one would imagine, too complex to be contained in Chakrabarty's superficial formula of difference.

Is it a sign of some profound difference that people adapted world events to their local place-bound lives? In the modern period, the universal not only arises out of the most singular experiences, but also in turn creates new senses of locality. Did the range of responses to war, colonialism and imperialism vary significantly between the radical reading public of London and Calcutta? Did the great events of the early decades of the twentieth century create solidarities across the colonial divide? Can all that be subject to good historical (materialist) analysis? I can only say that the term *adda* itself – used variously to refer to conversations about tigers in zoos and to more momentous concerns with war and revolution – is too indiscriminate at one level, and too homogenising at another, to be of any great use. In Chakrabarty's usage it is also much too self-exoticising to yield insights about the contours of the urban culture of colonial Calcutta.

The challenge now is to think about difference without falling over into exoticism, and to think about identity without concluding that it refers to sameness. After all, the history of capital in its planetary extension gives us the opportunity to do just that, to see beneath all the most 'astonishing mutations and expansions' the operation of some basic, persistent structure.[97] Perhaps too some hypertrophied concern with historicism – as implying an evolutionary scale of cultures – ought not to prod us into a historicism-in-reverse, whereby cultures are but extrusions of some putatively indigenous theology or aesthetics, ultimately linked to some deeper ecological exchange between socialised humans and the life of the land, a kind of ecologised racism in fact. We could end up reconstructing Orientalism, Negritude minus all its radical potentialities,[98] and a host of related ideologies.

---

97   Jameson 1998, p. 171.

98   C.L.R. James, according to Benita Parry, was not averse to the making of an oppositional, insurgent black identity, arguing that where racism was integral to capitalism, the category of class required re-examination. 'Negritude', James wrote, 'is what one race brings to the common rendezvous where all will strive for the new world of the poet's vision' (James 1992, p. 303, cited in Parry 2002, p. 134). It is possible, of course, to reinterpret this to suit the cultural turn, and thereby drain James's proposal of all radical potentialities. Such slippages are not only possible, but seem to be bearing rich fruit in postcolonial circles.

To go beyond the antinomies of East and West, Europe and India (or whatever the poles of the antinomy, but always with Europe or the West at one end), we might begin to work at a different level, whereby we recognise that Difference becomes the keyword of a period in which the easy promises of development and social justice through economic growth – and the other aspirations that found expression in the immediate aftermath of decolonisation – no longer obtain. It is all the more important then for social theorists to probe the question of what the 'many ways of being-in-the-world' actually mean in a world of profound socio-economic and regional inequalities, and the politics implicit in forms of sociality that evolve among people trying to make themselves at home among the increasing detritus being left in the wake of the operations of capital. We could, I expect, read texts for the buried and repressed histories of class struggles, look beyond the ideological antinomies for the social and historical contradictions. We could also, as Jameson suggests, recognise the simultaneously ideological and Utopian functions of literary texts and evaluate their potentialities for a radical political praxis.[99]

4.7   Lack/Inadequacy or Plenitude/Creativity

Too many readers of *Provincializing Europe* might be tempted to skip chapters 5–8 and all the cultural exotica presented there. However, that would be a mistake, for it is here that the project of provincialising Europe meets its methodological, theoretical and, dare one say, political limits.

Chakrabarty's desire to invert the terms of the 'transition' narrative, and for lack/inadequacy to substitute plenitude/creativity, may have a soothing sound for a Western audience steeped in the clichés of multiculturalism. For sidewalk-dwellers in Calcutta, this would simply be a cruel joke at their expense. Despite his disclaimers, Chakrabarty's book is about translating the Bengali middle-class world for its Western counterparts. Conveniently, *Provincializing Europe* glosses over the elitist, patriarchal, anti-minority, anti-Untouchable sentiments of that world, and emphasises the dreamy, non-end-oriented activities like *adda*. This is an Orient that an Occidental could learn to like, patronise and perhaps even exploit in the age of globalisation, without fear of backlash. The occasional mention of poverty, filth and cruelty is curiously disembodied; this is a world in which poetry can 'reconstitute' harsh realities,[100]

---

99   Jameson 1981, pp. 20, 229.
100   Chakrabarty 2000, pp. 171–2.

in which poverty is mere deprivation – one supposes that the rich have an *excess* of wealth and there is some *difference* between them and the poor.

Provincializing Europe appears to have seamlessly incorporated some aspects of American academic and political life that are quite seriously disabling for any kind of project of social justice, or, for that matter, even the more limited stated objective of provincialising Europe. In the wake of a series of recent political disasters, not to mention the hammering of the poor in Asia, Africa, Europe, Latin America, and the United States, projects for social justice need to do more than engage in polite chatter about provincialising Europe or rescuing from oblivion 'different ways of being-in-the-world'.[101] Celebrating difference would have some meaning in a world in which the basic needs of all humans were met and where really democratic institutions were able to safeguard precisely different ways of being-in-the-world without pushing many of those into dire poverty and catastrophic crises, and in which difference was not tied to primordialised ascriptive identities that the many who suffer under them did not choose and would not perpetuate. Oddly, for a historian of the subaltern, Chakrabarty's project appears to be a somewhat top-down history, unable to develop even a rudimentary agenda of what needs redress in this world. To do so calls for a militant universalism, in which, for all its attendant risks, the tasks of transformation will be paramount, even if some of the hypothetically many ways of being-in-the-world will be lost in the process.[102] Some are, in any case, being lost now – even as others are being generated – under the iron discipline of neoliberalism, structural adjustment, new-age crusades of the imperialist powers, and so on.

It is deeply ironic that Subaltern Studies at its inception was informed by concerns specific to Marxist thought, even as it challenged the bureaucratised, mechanical and brutal aspects of what one used to call 'really existing communism' and its weak replicas in India. This distinguished and, in the work of Dipesh Chakrabarty, continues to distinguish, to a very small extent, Subaltern Studies from other varieties of postcolonial thought, which are indifferent if not actually quite hostile to Marxism. Since many postcolonial theorists have known Marxism only in its Stalinist version, and can be dismissive if not contemptuous of it, I suppose one must be somewhat grateful that Chakrabarty

---

101   Chakrabarty 2000, p. 255.

102   This is hardly the place to discuss in detail the kinds of challenges that come up in the context of finding common ground amongst the numerous militant particularist movements against the dominance of capital in the world today. A very important intervention that does not try to cut through the complications and problems involved is Harvey 1996.

is still able to present the indispensable if, in his view, limited ('decisionist') value of Marx to his enterprise of keeping alive some notion of projects for social justice.

That said, provincialising Europe cannot, *pace* Chakrabarty, just be a matter of elaborating difference as it reveals itself in middle-class Bengali (or Chinese or Senegalese, for that matter) writing. If the Europe to be subjected to critique is the Europe of imperialism and colonialism, then the task needs to incorporate the spirit of Marx, draw on the rich legacy of Marxist writings on the subject, and base itself on a politics that creates the grounds for a new universalism that will go well beyond the limited and Eurocentric universalism of our day. This requires thinking and writing in an altogether more militant register. The task of theory is to map the terrain that needs to be transformed and the struggles that contribute, however inchoately, to this process. Perhaps only when the present unjust world order is transformed will its gestures of pretension and domination die with it. *Provincializing Europe* does not have much to say about this need, the injustices of the current world, or even the injustices of the world about which Chakrabarty writes with great familiarity – the world of colonial middle-class Bengal.

Provincializing Europe is also Orientalist in a fairly obvious sense. As noted in Chapter I, the text that seems to inspire Chakrabarty's work is Jarava Lal Mehta's book on Heidegger that speaks of a 'homecoming' by way of a journey through the *'foreign and the strange'*, except that the latter refers to Europe![103] From an Indian bourgeois-intellectual point of view, the characterisation of European philosophical (much less political-economic) thought as 'foreign' and 'strange' is frivolous; for the poor, the journey through Europeanisation is a non-starter. Either way, it offers a clue to the impasse in which this project of provincialising Europe finds itself. Of course, the 'homecoming' may simply be part of a moral parable whereby those who have hitherto led a deracinated and inauthentic life will somehow work through it, before returning to a more authentic life grounded in the age-old verities of India, or if that is indeed impossible then to engage in a bit of postcolonial handwringing.

What is so unproblematically assumed here, and in the vignettes that Chakrabarty offers us, is the truth of the spatial geography and categories of Orientalism that now seem so central to the kind of postcolonial thought that we are being treated to in the safe spaces of the Euro-American academy. But lurking beneath this surface is something of greater political significance. Postcolonial gestures aside, Chakrabarty's neo-Orientalism is perhaps a decoy, drawing us into the unspoken logic of a post-McCarthyite academy. We are

103   Mehta 1976, p. 466.

allowed to invoke Marx if at the same time we safely quarantine the political dimension of his analysis of capital to the realm of 'decisionism', and limit ourselves to petitions to the state for ameliorative action, and the like. Otherwise, under the sign of Heidegger, we are offered anodyne formulae about different ways of being-in-the-world as a cover for the immense suffering, cruelty and injustices so casually and thoughtlessly inflicted on the lives of the exploited and oppressed poor. If one can – apparently with a considerable level of acceptance in some academic quarters – point to the use of abstractions, transition narratives or something else, anything but capital, as the source of the inequalities and distress from which the many actually existing ways of being-in-the-world must be rescued, then the project of social justice is already a quixotic enterprise.

4.8   'Dominance without Hegemony': Historicism by Another Name?

As noted above, one of Ranajit Guha's main aims in *Dominance without Hegemony* is to study the emergence of an autonomous 'Indian historiography of India', whose objective is not to write a history of empire or a history of India as merely an 'interesting' chapter of British history, but to give expression to a range of nationalist concerns. Guha's work presents two visions: one of a historical compromise between the modern and what he calls the 'semi-feudal' in modern Indian society, in which the latter progressively swamped the former with economic, political and cultural results that he finds clearly regrettable; on the other, an Indian historiography of India, which by naming colonialism as the antagonist, and organising a struggle against it, might be expected to try to break this compromise in a revolutionary direction. But in what seems like a paradox, if not a contradiction, the version of Indian historiography that Guha singles out as 'authentic' carried with it significant elements of conservatism, if not nativism, xenophobia and communalism, that would undercut any such progressive mission. These two elements of his work are plainly at odds with one another. A willingness to consider models of a more liberating historiography of India that foregrounded the original concerns of Subaltern Studies with class struggle, storming the class-enemy country, as it were, seems to have become something of a casualty of this later enterprise.

Interestingly enough, in light of where the book ends, its point of departure is to illustrate the limitations of any historiography produced within a particular social formation to develop a radical critique of it. Guha is concerned to demonstrate the blind spots that historiography develops, precisely in regard to distributions of power, the loci where power is produced and reproduced, and the characteristic lacunae that result. In outlining his argument Guha does not hesitate to use elements of a mode-of-production narrative. He locates historiography within the co-ordinates of the social form that gives rise to it and the ideology that represents both the limits of the worldviews generated within that mode and the ways in which the ruling classes articulate their interests, while attempting to occlude from plain view their domination over other classes. In other words, *Dominance without Hegemony* might be read as a corrective to Chakrabarty's rather sweeping critique of a materialist analysis of ideology including religion.

Guha follows his analysis of the limited capacity of historically evolved ideologies, and the accompanying historiography for a critique of the dominant mode of production, with an argument about the necessity to locate a radical critique outside the parameters of that mode of production. As we shall see, Guha does not hesitate to suggest a lack or inadequacy not merely in the historiography itself, but also in the social formation that it seeks to describe and rationalise. Insofar as he draws on philosophy, it is the classical philosophy of Locke, Hobbes, Montesquieu and Hegel, not to mention Marx, none of whom can be said to be reticent about locating their historiography in relation to a doctrine of progress.[104] On this issue at least, Guha does not appear to be tempted by a blandly multiculturalist version of postcolonialism and its apology for many ways of being-in-the-world. This might be a function of primary location and political interests.

Guha starts with a tripartite division of historical development: slavery, feudalism, and capitalism, with historiographies corresponding to each of those divisions, each expressing, as it were, specific class interests in what they would claim were universally defensible propositions. Thus, both Classical Greece and Imperial Rome not merely tolerated but positively supported slavery by naturalising it to the condition of certain people and advocating it as a positive social good, as in the cases of Aristotle and Xenophon, for example. Aristotle, seen by some as the progenitor of Western philosophy, saw slavery as natural and justified: 'by nature, some are free, others slaves, and that for these it is both right and expedient that they should serve as slaves'.[105] Xenophon, a fellow Athenian, wanted to set up a state fund of public slaves to provide every Athenian citizen with at least three slaves.[106]

However, Enlightenment philosophers like Montesquieu and Hegel had no difficulty seeing through the apologetic nature of those arguments by counter-

---

104   Guha 1997a, p. xiii.
105   Aristotle 1974, p. 34, cited in Guha 1997a, p. 7.
106   Anderson 1975, p. 23, cited in Guha 1997a, p. 8.

posing the radical notion that 'all men are born equal', that helotry was 'contrary to the nature of things' (Montesquieu), or that Greek freedom was 'only a fortuitous, undeveloped, transient, and limited efflorescence, and ... a harsh servitude of all that is humane and proper to man' (Hegel).[107] Guha argues from this example that intellectuals, by and large, had no critical distance from the ruling order in their understanding of the basic power relations of, in this instance, a slave society, historiography itself being 'an instance of the ideological correlate of the material prosperity of the master class, unable to break away from its moorings in slavery and deal critically with it'.[108]

A similar case can be seen in Kalhana's account of the civil wars in twelfth-century Kashmir, which Guha takes as an example of the limitations of the feudal intellectual. Kalhana's account exhorts the nobles and kings to get their house in order but falls short, as his modern critics R.C. Majumdar and A.L. Basham point out, by attributing causal efficacy to gods, spirits, not to mention *karma* and transmigration. Majumdar, for instance, although admiring Kalhana for his critical attitudes to kings and nobles, faults him for his tendency to explain events by fate and divine will, rather than 'any rational cause'; and Basham provides a secular-humanist and disenchanted critique of Kalhana for not acknowledging that humans are 'makers of their own history and masters of their own destiny', and for attributing to 'superhuman forces or beings ... the biggest part in the destiny of man'.[109] All of these points no doubt ought to be important in mobilising not only a critique of colonial historiography, but also an 'Indian historiography of India'.

So where does criticism of a social formation originate? The unambiguous answer for Guha is: from outside the 'universe of dominance which provides the critique with its object', indeed 'from another and antagonistic universe'. From this vantage point, Montesquieu and Hegel, for instance, were able to see through Aristotle's hollow pretences about natural slavery. People captive to the gravitational field of ruling-class ideology of any particular historical epoch, on the other hand, have a 'necessary [and] congenital blindness' to the paradoxes of their times. The lesson for our times is that liberal historiography, operating within the cramped imaginative space of 'bourgeois consciousness', can never shine a light powerful enough to 'penetrate and scan some of the strategic areas of [that consciousness] where dominance [a structural component of any system of class rule] stores the spiritual gear it needs to justify

107   For a brilliant study of Hegel's politics and philosophy that situates Hegel vis-à-vis the more reactionary political currents of his time, see Losurdo 2004.

108   Guha 1997a, pp. 7–8, 11.

109   Majumdar 1961 and Basham 1961, cited in Guha 1997a, p. 12.

and sustain itself'.[110] Liberal historiography in its colonial and postcolonial guises, as Guha notes, is congenitally blind to the paradoxes of colonial and postcolonial rule in South Asia. The critique must again come from outside, from an ideology 'antagonistic towards the dominant culture [and which] declares war on it even before the class for which it speaks comes to rule'.[111]

Undeterred by the possibility that all this might be construed as hopelessly historicist, Guha plunges on to develop an outline of British historiography of India that not only relates history to ruling class ideology, but also traces its evolution to the internal transformations of power relations. The point of departure is the recognition that colonial capitalism and colonial modernity were not merely a replica of their European counterparts, but were something *sui generis*, an 'original alloy' composed of the historic failure of capital to realise its universalising tendency under colonial conditions and a corresponding failure of the metropolitan bourgeois culture to dissolve or assimilate fully the indigenous culture of India in the power relations of the colonial period.

The colonial state in India was fundamentally unlike the metropolitan bourgeois state in England. The chief difference between the two was that while the metropolitan state was hegemonic in character 'with its claim to dominance ... based on a power relation in which *the moment of persuasion outweighed the moment of coercion*',[112] the colonial state was, by comparison, non-hegemonic with persuasion outweighed by coercion in its structure of dominance.[113] At home, champions of the right of nations to self-determination, the metropolitan ruling elite, denied the same right to their Indian subjects, and their antagonism to feudal values in their own society made little difference to their 'vast tolerance' of pre-modern values and institutions in Indian society,[114] despite what Guha considers their much publicised albeit rather ineffective campaigns against *sati*, child marriage, and so on. The 'contemporary element [that is, the British/European political culture] so vigorous in its metropolitan soil' failed to strike root as a graft and remained 'shallow and restricted in its new site'. As an upshot, bourgeois notions of rights remained weak. By and large coercion won out over persuasion. Guha concludes that any

---

110   Guha 1997a, pp. 7–8.

111   Guha 1997a, p. 13.

112   Guha 1997a, p. xii, emphasis added.

113   This is, of course, reminiscent of the way in which Gramsci elaborated the notion of bourgeois hegemony; see Gramsci 1977. For a more detailed exposition of the notion of bourgeois hegemony in Gramsci, and far greater complication than Guha's account presupposes, see Anderson 1977, pp. 20ff.

114   Guha 1997a, pp. 4–5.

universalising design one might attribute to post-Enlightenment capitalism is false. Colonialism stands not only for the 'the historical progeny of industrial and finance capital, but also for its historic Other'.[115]

Even such a staple of bourgeois hegemony as individual rights was unavailable, it seems, to colonial subjects. As Gandhi is said to have stated while in South Africa: 'I discovered that as a man and as an Indian, I had no rights. More correctly, I discovered I had no rights as a man because I was an Indian'.[116] To be fair, Guha does acknowledge that what he calls 'dominance without hegemony' had a nationalist aspect as well, a result of the failed universalising mission of colonial rule, which in turn saw a corresponding failure of the Indian bourgeoisie to dissolve the indigenous culture of India. Vast areas of the life and consciousness of the people were never integrated into bourgeois hegemony, and over such areas the bourgeoisie could only exercise a largely coercive dominance.[117] The limitation of much liberal historiography lies, in Guha's opinion, precisely in not recognising that the discrepancy between metropolitan and colonial social formations was not a mere 'exceptional and aberrant instance of malfunctioning' or 'local difficulties' destined to be overcome, presumably by modernisation, but a 'structural fault' in the project of colonialism.

Guha's quarrel with colonial historiography lies in its failure even to recognise this problem. In its origins and development, he argues, colonial historiography was concerned with statist priorities and projects. He cites Hegel to make the point: 'It is the state which first supplies a content which not only lends itself to the prose of history but actually helps to produce it'.[118]

The philosophy underlying the first school of colonial historiography, developed during the mercantilist period, is memorably captured in Alexander Dow's statement: 'The success of your Majesty's arms has laid open the East to the researches of the curious'. This school – intended for the education of the East India Company's officers – aimed to elucidate the relations of state power and landed property in India so as to extract an efficient surplus.[119] *Itihasa* [history], as Guha puts it, had become a component of *Arthashastra* [Treatise on material gain].[120] A second school – corresponding to a more mature phase

---

115   Guha 1997a, pp. 67–68.

116   Guha 1997a, pp. 65ff, quote on p. 69.

117   Guha 1997a, p. xii.

118   Hegel 1890, p. 136, cited in Guha 1997a, p. 73.

119   Guha 1997a, p. 74.

120   D.D. Kosambi translated *Arthashastra* as 'Science of material gain', but 'shastra' is closer to 'treatise' than 'science'. A.L. Basham translates it as 'Treatise on polity', but that does not

of colonial rule in which the coloniser spoke not merely as a merchant or tax-collector, but as a legislator as well – produced the knowledge of the past that would serve as a guide to the future. Here the idiom of Improvement took its place alongside that of Order, and Indian history found itself reduced to merely a 'highly interesting portion of British history', with James Mill's *History of British India* as prototype.[121] The civilising mission was the operative concept for this school.

Why was a historiography of India necessary in the first place? Guha argues that the colonial idiom of Order and Improvement both required a knowledge not merely of contemporary custom, but also of the past, to ascertain with authority issues of ownership, rights of owners and the government, not to mention a whole host of social issues. But more importantly, it was the result of an ethnographic encounter in which colonial officials suspected that specialised local knowledge, and even general knowledge of statecraft and political economy, was being withheld from them by local officials. History was 'ethnology's surrogate' and in the end a more 'scientific' one as well,[122] in which the higgledy-piggledy of local arrangements was more scientifically reclassified in line with modern statecraft. To Guha this is not the basis of an Indian historiography of India so much as a history of the British in India, their concerns, priorities, and so on.

Nor apparently does this type of historiography end with colonial rule; a good example of the carryover of colonial-period paradigms, if not specific issues, into the present is the 'Cambridge historiography', particularly of the 1960s and 1970s.[123] Continuing with the notion of the civilising mission of British rule, government is seen in this historiography as supplying the stimulus, either directly to a class of people (collaborators) to perform according to proper ('modern') rules of conduct, or indirectly via the formation of various associations that replicate the rules and modalities of governmental organisations. Either way, colonial rule works as a school of liberal modernisation, using market mechanisms to create collaborators out of subjects. Guha is quite scathing in his assessment of this liberal-modern characterisation of collaboration, and points to the limited monopoly-like character of the benefits distributed by the British, more like 'feudal jousting' than 'free bargaining in an open market'.

---

capture the meaning of 'artha'. I am grateful to Sucheta Mazumdar for pointing this out to me. The various renderings of the meaning of *Arthashastra* can be found at <www.en .wikipedia.org/wiki/Arthashastra>.

121   Guha 1997a, p. 79.

122   Guha 1997a, pp. 160–4.

123   Guha 1997a, p. 83.

More to the point, the focus on collaboration hides the rather large social arena in which resistance to colonial rule developed. By definition, resistance is consigned in the earlier instalments of the Cambridge historiography to the realm of the prepolitical, a mere reaching for sticks and stones.[124] Of more recent instalments of Cambridge historiography, Guha is no less caustic, seeing them as doing nothing more than replacing some worn-out fittings, while keeping the basic foundations and structures intact. Thus Guha responds to David Washbrook's claim that the non-Brahman movement was a result of the 'novel processes [including the creation of a public sphere] of early twentieth-century Madras', a movement supposedly without a political existence prior to that period, by noting that the emergence of the colonial state and the substantial effects it had on caste conflicts did not amount to transforming an apolitical movement into a political one, but rather signalled a shift from one kind of politics to another.[125] Guha's conclusion is that this school of historiography – for all its 'coherence and lucidity' – remains an act of 'bad faith', not concerned with the history of India at all, but like James Mill writing it as 'portion of British history'. As such, it constitutes 'a misappropriation, a violence'.[126]

The central point is the degree to which *Dominance without Hegemony* still occupies ground from which others in the postcolonial camp seem to have distanced themselves, namely, the issue of a transition or, more exactly, a *failed transition*, and the limitations and handicaps introduced into Indian society as a result. Additionally, Guha seems entirely unrepentant about relating religion to politics, and ideology to praxis in a secular-materialist mode, that is, translating the world of religious ideas into a 'more real' secular explanatory scheme. Recall now Chakrabarty's opposition to treating the presence of gods and spirits in subaltern politics as 'merely symbolic' of 'some deeper and "more real" secular reality'.[127] But on this reading of *Dominance without Hegemony*,

---

124   Guha 1997a, pp. 86–7.

125   Guha 1997a, pp. 93–4.

126   Guha 1997a, pp. 84–5.

127   Chakrabarty 2000, p. 14. Ironically, a footnote cites Ranajit Guha's *Elementary Aspects*, and goes on to argue that Marxist historians 'typically emptied religion of all its specific content by assigning to its core a secular rationality' (Chakrabarty 2000, p. 262, n. 44). It seems that there is a real tension at work here: when convenient, some underlying 'real' secular content can be assigned to ideological practices, including religion, while at other moments, a polemic is directed against such an approach. Clearly, Guha prefers the former approach, at least in *Dominance without Hegemony*. Chakrabarty is more consistently against a secularising reading, except in a 'decisionist' mode when petitions have to be presented to the government, when implicitly some secular content has to be attached to non-secular expressions. At such times, the gods can be relegated to the

Subaltern Studies and its postcolonial successor cannot do without a principled sociology and politics of religion. This will become apparent in the next
section as we delve into Guha's more detailed account of the historic compromises of colonial modernity.

4.9   The Constituent Elements of Colonial Modernity

To explain more fully the combined nature of Indian modernity, Guha has
recourse to a schematic of power around the concepts of Domination [D] and
Subordination [S], which are structural components of any relation of power
in a class-divided society. Each of those terms in turn is overdetermined by a
pair of interacting elements, D by Coercion [C] and Persuasion [P], and S by
Collaboration [C*] and Resistance [R]. Schematically, this can be represented
as follows:

Schematic of Domination/Subordination

POWER			
Domination [D]		Subordination [S]	
Coercion [C]	*Persuasion* [P]	*Collaboration* [C*]	*Resistance* [R]
Order and Danda	Improvement and Dharma	Obedience and Bhakti	Rightful Dissent and Dharmic Protest

The first item in each pairing in the last row represents, for Guha, the European element, the
second the Indic element.[128]

While D and S imply each other 'logically' and are intrinsic to all 'structural,
modal and discursive aspects' where an authority structure can be discerned,
this is not true of other pairs of concepts, which imply each other

background. No doubt, violations of civil rights, imprisonment on trumped-up charges,
expropriation of landholdings, gross police violence, and so forth, would all come under
the 'decisionist' banner. One wonders if the real subalterns themselves would agree to
such a 'decisionist' approach.

128   Guha 1997a, p. 21.

'contingently'.[129] Drawing on the Marxian notion of the 'organic composition of capital', Guha develops a framework around the 'organic composition of power' in which C, P, C*, and R, in various combinations and permutations, constitute 'the warp and the weft in the fabric of world history'.[130]

Guha further breaks down each constituent part of D/S into European and Indic elements, the former associated with the modernising drive of English bourgeois rule, and the latter the recasting and reconfiguring of India's 'feudal' culture in the context of colonial modernity. Thus C is broken down into Order and *Danda*, P into Improvement and *Dharma*, C* into Obedience and *Bhakti*, and R into Rightful Dissent and *Dharmic Protest.* The failure of a 'bourgeois revolution' in the Indian context is signalled, for Guha, by the extent to which the latter term in each dyad survives and indeed constitutes a determining element in Indian life up to the present, a fact that an Indian historiography of India has to deal with. Politics, no less than culture, is constituted by such coexistence, which in another context has been described as the uneven and combined development of an 'existential and psychic kind',[131] alongside the uneven and combined development of the economy.

Order, for example, represents an impersonal rule-governed system designed to curb the extra-economic coercive powers of institutions and ideologies in order to win the consent of the governed. The realm of Order in India extended well beyond the normal sphere of governance in Europe to embrace public health, sanitation, municipalisation, labour mobilisation for plantations, and recruitment to the army. In all of these areas, the idiom of Order interacted with that of *Danda*, 'central to all indigenous notions of dominance' and defined as the manifestation of the 'divine will in the affairs of the state'. *Danda* extended to the creation and use of private armies, levies, caste and territorial panchayats, caste sanctions, bonded labour and *begar*, the jurisdictional powers of landlords over tenants, punitive measures against women for disobeying patriarchal codes, and so on. Danda operated in 'every walk of life outside the jealously guarded realm of official Order' and was employed to uphold in every little kingdom 'every putative king's authority' constituted by D and S in all relationships of gender, age, caste and class.[132] Notwithstanding the inconsistencies of the exposition – for example, Danda infiltrates the idiom of Order, exists alongside and outside the realm of Order – Guha's argument stresses the reactionary quality of colonial rule.

---

129   Guha 1997a, pp. 20–1.
130   Guha 1997a, p. 21.
131   Jameson 1991, p. 366.
132   Guha 1997a, pp. 25–30.

Similarly, Improvement coexisted with Dharma. Improvement refers to the long list of reforms including Western education, Orientalist projects of exploring, interpreting and preserving India's ancient and medieval culture, not to mention more mundane enactments of labour law, the abolition of sati, Hindu polygamy, infanticide, and laws to improve working conditions. All of those reforms were signs, Guha avers, of 'an optimistic and ascendant bourgeoisie' intent on proving itself adequate to its 'own historic project'. But true to form, Improvement had to share and, one suspects, concede considerable ground to *Dharma*, the 'indigenous ... organic societal doctrine of Hinduism'. What *Dharma* brought to the mix of P was in fact a pre-rights paternalistic notion of the government as 'protector, trustee, and friend of the people', not to mention caste-based exclusivism. The hierarchical, Hindu components built into the notion of *Dharma*, when deployed during the Swadeshi movement, for example, succeeded in dividing Muslims from Hindus, upper castes from Namasudras, and landlords from tenants. Its subsequent adoption by the Gandhian Congress had much to do with 'saving' the country and landlords, in particular, from socialism. As Gandhi himself put it: 'I enunciated this theory [of trusteeship associated with *Dharma*] when the socialist theory was placed before the country in respect to the possessions held by zamindars and ruling chiefs'.[133] Guha thinks that *Dharma*, like *Danda*, was an accommodation to the old and moribund order, rather than a vigorous challenge to it, embraced alike by Gandhi and Ghanshyamdas Birla.[134]

Similarly with C* and R, Guha unfolds his theory by juxtapositioning Obedience with *Bhakti*, and Rightful Dissent with Dharmic Protest. According to Guha, Obedience was developed to a fine-tuned doctrine by Samuel Smiles, and not only urged 'obedience to the parent, to the master, to the officer', but upheld the soldier as the epitome of the virtues of obedience and duty, especially in holding the empire together.[135] Smiles, in effect, advocated a form of guardianship based on sympathy between employers and employees, rather

---

133   Gandhi 1960, p. 5, cited in Guha 1997a, p. 37.

134   Ghanshyamdas Birla (1894–1983) was a pioneering industrialist and a friend of Mohandas Gandhi. He not only set up a jute firm in Calcutta, thereby challenging a British monopoly, but also the Birla Engineering College in Pilani.

135   Guha 1997a, pp. 41–42. Samuel Smiles (1812–1904), was the author of several books including: *Self-Help* (1859), *Character* (1871), *Thrift* (1875), *Duty* (1880), *Life and Labour* (1887). Smiles may have begun his political life as a working-class radical liberal, but seems to have ended up retreating quite far to the right after the 1850s. Guha goes on to point out that Smiles's works, produced within the two decades following the Mutiny of 1857, exude the 'heavy and – for his chauvinistic working-class and petit-bourgeois readership – endearing smell of gunpowder' (Guha 1997a, p. 42).

than class militancy.[136] Nonetheless, Guha insists that while bearing some superficial resemblance to *Bhakti*, Obedience is still distinguishable from it in that it had a countervailing notion of rights and just rebellion if authority should fail to live up to its commitments. *Bhakti*, for Guha, has no such redeeming features. With the *Bhagvad Gita* as its ur-text, it linked all the collaborationist movements of subordination in Indian thinking and practice during the colonial movement to an 'inert mass of feudal culture which had been generating loyalism and depositing it in every kind of power relations for centuries before the British conquest'.[137] *Bhakti*, unlike Obedience, operated basically in a servile mode, *dasya*, and there was no 'notion of equality' even in its erotic expression, which merely spiritualises and aestheticises male dominance of gender relations. Guha is at pains to show that *bhakti* is an ideology of superordination *par excellence*, with its stark binaries of protector/subject, master/servant, superior relative/inferior relative. Many 'feudal' cults addressed to the lower strata of Hindu society had it as their function to try to endear the dominant to the subordinate and thereby assuage the rigour of *dasya*.[138] In this sense, *bhakti* might be an analogue for feudal cults that had no idea of rights except as those of the superordinate to the subordinate – its exceptionalism, in Guha's narrative, lies in the extent to which it became so central to Indian modernity. And here, critically, Guha argues that *bhakti*, as it operated in colonial India, was not simply a carryover of the force of traditional religiosity among the subaltern masses. Bankimchandra – who will resurface later in Guha's book as an architect of an 'Indian historiography of India' – was one among many eminent intellectuals who stepped forward to adapt *Bhakti* to colonial rule: 'Whoever is superior to us and benefits us by his superiority is an object of Bhakti...Unless the inferior follows the superior, there cannot be any unity...or cohesion...in society nor can it achieve any

---

136   Smiles rejected the class analysis, which identified a naturally hostile relationship between labour and capital: 'I maintain that the interests of capitalists and labourers are identical' (Smiles 1839, cited in Morris 1981, p. 100). Class militancy resulted, for Smiles, in the 'mad riot in human life...among the Nihilists in Germany and Russia, and the fire and destruction of the Communists' war in Paris' (Smiles, 1880, cited in Guha 1997a, p. 41). Guha avers that this is a 'remarkable though by no means solitary instance of a sentiment once so supportive of Chartism pulling up sharply as it comes face to face with the enduring force of class struggle' (Ibid).
137   Kosambi 1972, pp. 208–9, cited in Guha 1997a, p. 47.
138   Guha 1997a, p. 48.

Improvement'.[139] The allusion to the 'superior' in this case might very well have been to the colonial state as a proxy for the West.

Bankimchandra laments the loss of *bhakti* in Indian society, Indians having failed to grasp the true significance of the western doctrine of egalitarianism and perverted it to mean that 'people are equal everywhere in every sense and nobody owes bhakti to anyone else'. Guha argues that Bankimchandra was influenced by the 'religion of Comte', more worthy in his opinion than the 'religion of the Hindus',[140] but that this attempt to draw the Indian element into the orbital sphere of Comtean sociology had no real impact on the 'subaltern masses', who were so far removed from Western-style education and liberal values that they could hardly be receptive to the 'positivist-liberal modifications of their cherished beliefs'. However, it is the nature of the Indian bourgeoisie's compromises with the old order that Guha is keen to stress, citing Bankimchandra's casting of the relationship of husband and wife as one in which theoretically *Bhakti* was supposed to be mutual, but in practice remained strictly patriarchal, *Bhakti* towards the husband being 'the first step . . . towards Bhakti for God'.[141] As with the family, the patriarchal character of the state in Bankimchandra's writings virtually dissolved all constitutionalist and republican sentiments into a plea for submission to absolutism. All attest to the weak hold of Western positivism, egalitarianism, and humanism, in favour of the terms of a culture and politics of a precapitalist kind.[142]

Finally, Guha makes the point that the notion of Rightful Dissent – which drew on an important current of English liberalism going back to John Locke, and which later informed the Indian Civil Disobedience movement – coexisted with the notion of Dharmic Protest, which was manifested in subaltern uprisings of all kinds. These uprisings – such as the ones studied by Guha in *Elementary Aspects of Peasant Insurgency* – were premised not on the notion of citizens' rights, but on the defence of *Dharma*, and founded in values such as *vichara*, a providential justice having nothing to do with the English law courts,

---

139 Guha 1997a, p. 51, quoting Bankimchandra Chattopadhyay's *Dharmatattva*. Bankimchandra Chattopadhyay (1838–1894) served as deputy magistrate and deputy collector in the Government of British India from 1858 until his retirement in 1891. He is best known as one of the pioneers of the modern novel in India, but he was also a highly imaginative satirist and political commentator. He composed the hymn, *Vande Mataram*, which the Indian National Congress adopted as its anthem. Vande Mataram, with its overtly Hindu imagery, is widely thought to have alienated Muslim members of the Congress.

140 Guha 1997a, pp. 50–2.

141 Cited in Guha 1997a, p. 53.

142 Guha 1997a, p. 53.

and *nyaya*, legitimacy conferred by the ethics of *Dharma* far removed from secular political morality in any modern sense. Gandhi attempted to link the two by grafting the Western notions of liberty and citizens' rights to Dharmic Protest, the result being a 'hybrid' category called *satya*.[143] Mass protest in colonial India, whether the swadeshi movement or the later Civil Disobedience movements, used mechanisms associated with the dharmic order, including social boycott. Indian liberals – such as Surendranath Bannerji and Aurobindo Ghosh – involved in the swadeshi movement not just condoned but actively promoted this kind of boycott. While Gandhi set his face firmly against it, he nonetheless indirectly winked at its practice. Guha's overall point is that 'Indian liberalism, thanks to the rather peculiar conditions of its development within colonial power relations ... belonged to an ideological and cultural category altogether distinct from its Western prototype'.[144]

In this sense, Guha concludes, colonial political culture represents an accumulation of paradoxes: whatever is indigenous is borrowed from the past, whatever is foreign is mostly contemporary; the element of the past (Indian) is moribund but not defunct, the contemporary element (British/European) so vigorous in its metropolitan soil, finds difficulty in striking roots as a graft and remains shallow and restricted in its penetration in its new site. The originality of Indian politics, for Guha, is revealed by the following: on the colonial side, for example, a Mother of Parliament presiding over a state without citizenship; on the side of the indigenous elite, an emergent capitalist class keen on masking its role as buyer and seller; and on the subaltern side, a working-class struggle carried on as a campaign for Truth.[145]

Why, Guha asks, did this peculiar socio-political formation take shape and prove so durable? 'Why two paradigms not just one? Why did the establishment of British paramountcy in South Asia fail to overcome the resistance of its indigenous culture to the point of being forced into a symbiosis?' Why did the universalising drive of the world's 'most advanced capitalist culture' fail to match the strength and fullness of its political dominion by 'assimilating, if not abolishing, the precapitalist culture of its subject people'? After all, it is that drive to abolish, rather than settling in amongst other or older forms of culture, which gave the bourgeoisie its hegemonic power.[146] Guha's explanation rests on the idea that colonialism could only continue in power in the subcontinent on condition of failing to live up to the bourgeoisie's universalising mission.

---

143   Guha 1997a, pp. 55–9.
144   For an extended discussion of this point, see Guha 1997a, pp. 100–14.
145   Guha 1997a, p. 62.
146   Guha 1997a, p. 63.

Emerging as it did not by 'internal process', but as an 'external force', it was doubly alienated from the local culture, both in its becoming and in its being. As an 'absolute externality', colonial rule was structured like a despotism, with no 'mediating depths', no space for transactions between the will of the rulers and the ruled. This produced what Guha calls a *décalage*, the insertion of the world's most dynamic power of the contemporary world into the power relations of a world 'still living in the past'. The colonial state was an anachronism embodying the paradox of an advanced bourgeois culture 'regressing' from its universalist impulse to compromise with 'precapitalist particularism *under colonial conditions of its own making*'.[147]

The end result was an immensely complex social formation that acquired its specificity from 'the braiding, collapsing, echoing, and blending of these idioms' in such a way as to baffle all descriptions of this process as either a dynamic modernity overwhelming an inert tradition, or 'the mechanical stapling of a progressive Western liberalism to an unchanging Eastern feudal culture'.[148] The Indian bourgeoisie, for its part, had no wish (nor, one would assume, any capability) to destroy this social formation, whatever the private unease of some. In this 'mediocre liberalism', the watchwords were 'compromise and accommodation'.[149]

4.10   Modernity as Class Struggle

The issue of autochthonous emergence versus external imposition has been at the heart of debates about the development of capitalism. In a modernisation framework, it is the persistence of old social forms and their resistance to the new that constitute the main barrier to modernisation. In parts of Europe, the old social forms were said to have given way through molecular processes over a period of time that then created the basis of autochthonous modernisation. Depending on the account, capitalism either arose in the cities and spread to the countryside, or in the countryside and spread from there to the cities and beyond, through the initial subsumption and ultimate overcoming of older social forms. Elsewhere, when modernisation was imposed from the outside, it encountered a variety of obstacles – not least the ability or willingness of the colonisers themselves to undertake the arduous labour of uprooting older forms in societies to which they were outsiders and which they understood

147   Guha 1997a, pp. 63–5, emphasis added.
148   Guha 1997a, p. 61.
149   Guha 1997a, p. 5.

rather poorly. The upshot was often a set of compromises that decomposed some elements of the old and introduced some elements of the new, the resulting entity having neither the cohesion of the older social form nor resembling in any way the capitalism of the metropolitan ruling power. Within these broad outlines, variations exist: there are cases of older polities successfully transforming themselves under pressure from the outside, Japan being the paradigm example, while others (the hard cases) resisted and were often colonised, becoming over time 'underdeveloped' or 'maldeveloped'. In this model, India would have been one of the harder cases. Guha's argument follows this script rather closely, the details and the bravura with which he expounds them hardly masking what is a fairly classic account of failed modernisation.

The issue for us here is not whether Guha's characterisation of colonial rule and the colonial social formation is an accurate one. At any rate, it is not incompatible with some Indian Marxist descriptions of Indian society as 'semi-feudal',[150] although some scholars might quibble with the use of the term 'feudal' to describe the *ancien régime* in India. We might simply note that Guha's counterpositioning of colonial rule as a dominance without hegemony, with contemporary Europe as the hegemonic rule of the bourgeoisie, is much too stark. The rhetoric of *The Communist Manifesto* – a sombrely triumphalist account of European capital and its agents sweeping all obstacles before them – masks a much less heroic reality. As some commentators on the manifesto have maintained, Marx was probably not describing the realities of his day so much as projecting a reality that is closer to ours.[151] In late nineteenth-century France, for example, 'feudal' prejudices and aspirations of every kind had firm roots – so feudalism survived even in that most Enlightenment-influenced and republican of countries.[152] Historians like Arno Mayer have pointed to the survival of all manner of 'feudal habits', not to mention historic compromises with feudalism across Europe even after the devastation of the First World War.[153]

The difference between the autochthonous transitions to capitalism and the colonially engineered ones could have been, *pace* Guha, more a matter of degree than of kind. Indeed, the Gramscian notion of 'passive revolution' can be read in terms of 'the mutual military invasions of the European powers' in the nineteenth century in order to effect the social and economic changes the home country itself failed to achieve on its own.[154] One might think of autoch-

150   Bhaduri 1973, pp. 120–37.
151   Harman 2010, p. 3; Callinicos 2010, p. 8.
152   Hussey 2008.
153   Mayer 1981.
154   Brennan 2006, p. 234.

thonous transitions to capitalism, even in Western Europe, as possibly more an exception than a rule.

Furthermore, Guha's method seems to imply that the secular freedoms associated with the West were a free gift from the bourgeoisie to the people in the various parts of Europe, rather than hard won if only partially realised rights. Between the highly compromised intent of the European bourgeoisie to sweep away feudal powers, institutions and habits on the one hand, and the institution of a modern secular polity embodying real rights for citizens on the other, lies a trail of broken bodies caused by war, revolution and counter-revolution. Revolution and counter-revolution battled each other almost to a standstill, and barring the massive shocks of the two world wars, we might still be living in that world.

It is therefore quite unclear under what conditions the universalising impulses of the bourgeoisie might have had the amount of play they did in Western Europe, at least in Guha's description. How deep did the 'internal process' have to be and how far did it have to extend? Eurocentric historians have tended to posit the rational rights-bearing individual, ostensibly a uniquely European phenomenon, as the heroic subject of their history.[155] Guha's statement that 'an uncoercive state is a liberal absurdity',[156] and the extent to which such coercion at the ideological level mobilises the old – moribund but not defunct – elements, could be developed as a useful tool of comparative analysis, and a caution against getting carried away by an unqualified Europe-Other contrast.

Unfortunately, Guha seems to have taken on the bad habit one sees in postcolonial critiques of European universalism of counterposing an ideal and hyperreal Europe on one side to actually existing colonial (and postcolonial) social formations on the other. That method affords little insight into the specific compromises with the old order within Europe itself, a function of the uneven spatio-temporal rhythms of national unification, capitalist development and modernisation, not to mention geopolitical lines of force, and the further implications of those distinctive national trajectories on the very particular types of political dispensations developed in the various extra-European regions that the European states colonised. Add to this the 'vagaries of precolonial social orders' and the 'differentials of anticolonial resistance', and we get a sense of the real differences that defined colonial situations.[157] And while colonialism was an integral moment in the structuring of a global

---

155   MacFarlane 1987.
156   Guha 1997a, p. 23.
157   Cleary 2002, p. 111.

capitalist order, postcolonial histories should be able to take into account difference on this scale so as to develop a 'good' comparative rendering of real historical dynamics, while keeping in mind the more general and invariant features of the colonial mode of production.

As it was, the British ruling class could barely be seen as the agents of a surging industrial capital,[158] or forward-looking representatives of the most advanced ideals of the French Revolution. Indeed, they stepped forward during the nineteenth century as the firm bulwark of a counter-revolutionary vanguard.[159] Either way, empire was hardly the place to send their most advanced minds; those who did go to India were often firmly wedded to all manner of moribund but not defunct aspects of British hierarchy, and attempted to reproduce them in a country whose elite seemed quite attached to its own versions of hierarchy and inequalities.[160] Overall, Guha's analysis reveals some rather important lacunae in a historian who would draw his inspiration from an historical-materialist methodology. The concrete analysis of concrete situations has to work on both sides of the colonial divide.

The issue of historical difference in Guha's model is fully addressable as a political problem and might inadvertently strengthen the hand of a revamped modernisation theory. For if one pays close attention to his argument, the triad of categories deployed – power, modernity and tradition (older cultural forms) – is precisely that used by modernisation theory. Traditional society, more or less abetted by the colonial state, appears to have held back the tide of modern ideas that came in the wake of the world's leading metropolitan power by maintaining all kinds of backward-looking communitarian features in place of a more strictly modernising (individualist-utilitarian?) calculus. Guha's analysis is thus entirely compatible with nineteenth-century sociological theory – the operational terms of which constitute an opposition between 'community' or *Gemeinschaft* and 'society' or *Gesellschaft*, with the former injecting considerable inertia into the emergence and dynamic functioning of the latter. There is a scant *soupçon* of Marxist rhetoric thrown in, but the essential lines of Guha's argument are clear. 'Modern' comes to stand implicitly for a 'democratic', 'rational and secular' society; 'traditional' stands for the very opposite of that – the entire socio-cultural bastions of a world that pre-existed colonialism and was reinforced by it.[161] The twist to the more ordinary tale of

---

158   Cain and Hopkins 1986, pp. 501–25.

159   See, for instance, Losurdo 2004, pp. 305–10; see also Mori 2000 and Philp 2004.

160   Metcalf 1997; Gilmour 2007.

161   See, for example, Wolf 1984, pp. 11–13.

modernisation comes, as noted, in the form of a colonial state that betrays the revolutionary avocation of its metropolitan parent.

Guha's rendition of the causes and conditions of the failure of (bourgeois) hegemony – that is, the inability or unwillingness of colonial rulers and the Indian bourgeoisie to bring about a situation in which the moment of persuasion outweighed the moment of coercion, especially vis-à-vis the working people in rural areas – and the resulting absence of liberal modernisation in India along British lines, contrast rather markedly with Gramsci's more radical version of the issue. As the founder of *Subaltern Studies* one might be tempted to assume that Guha would have been interested in carrying forward Gramsci's insights to the Indian context. In *The Southern Question*, as in his later *Prison Notebooks*, Gramsci excoriates the way in which class alliances between the north and south of Italy (northern industrialists and southern landlords) had sacrificed the interests of the peasantry of the south in favour of the needs of the northern industrialists.[162] Gramsci calls for an alternative hegemony based on the northern proletariat providing a radical leadership to the southern peasantry, in the process resisting what the translator of *The Southern Question* characterises as Southernist – that is, culturalist – readings of the question of the role of the southern peasantry in Italian development.[163] This issue of hegemony within a working people's coalition had also been a concern of the Marxist 'mode-of-production' debate in India. Both drew on a long history of interest in the concept and its history within the Communist International.

The distance between deploring a failed bourgeois hegemony from above and a call for a radical hegemony from below (to be built in the face of the challenges of fascism and ruling class intransigence) should be fairly obvious. Indeed, in some very real ways, Guha's reading of the Indian situation converges quite nicely with Italian-style southernism.[164] Guha's contribution to a more radical understanding of hegemony seems to have been his notion of a peasant 'paradigm' that continued to inform even working class actions in India. In the first instance – that is, when studying the 'world' of a newly

---

162   If one were to overlook the north-south references here, the class alliances in colonial and post-independence India would appear to be rather similar to the Italian case.

163   Gramsci 1995.

164   As Gramsci characterises it, Southernism adopted the position that 'the [Italian] South is the ball-and-chain', a backward region that inhibits national progress largely through its internal social characteristics (Gramsci 1995, p. 20). Guha's position, namely, that the capitulation of the British colonisers to Indian society's cultural characteristics (which would undoubtedly include those of the peasantry themselves) prevented the full force of advanced British ideas from bearing fruit in India, is not dissimilar in form.

relocated working population from the countryside to the cities – this would have been an acceptable formulation, but as implying something enduring it seems far-fetched. It is almost as if the patterns of work, industrial discipline, the experience of life in large urban agglomerations and being drawn into capital's orbit as productive labour are powerless in the face of a deeply rooted peasant culture and ethos. If this is in fact the case, it rather undermines Guha's own explanation of colonial inadequacies. After all, how revolutionary would the interventions of the metropolitan bourgeoisie in the affairs of its colony have had to have been to uproot forms of social life that appear so sturdy in their ability to survive massive dislocations and relocations?

Even if one accepts Guha's analysis of the problem of colonial modernity, there should be no reason to foreclose the possibility that in different historical conditions, let us say a different period in the history of a particular colony, the overcoming of difficulties posed by the issue of indigenous cultural forms can be attempted by the very descendants of the earlier nationalist bourgeoisie. This might be a plausible reading of what is happening in India today, attended by all the harsh calculations of such a project. Modernity – to modify Lenin – is not the pavement of the Nevsky Prospekt.[165] Modernity, both in its revolutionary and post-revolutionary moments, has been a matter of serious uprooting and upheaval in the interest of capital accumulation, not simply a matter of temporal marking. That is to say, it is a matter of class struggles carried on now, as in the nineteenth century, under the banner of progress and civilisation, even if ideological softeners were and still are mobilised to offset the bleakness and violence of the proceedings.[166] This line of thinking runs up against a conviction in postcolonial intellectual circles that somehow the moment of emergence permanently marks off colonial modernity from its metropolitan counterpart, that difference is attributable to profound cultural roots, and that hybridity – and the alternative-different modernities that result from it – defines the 'postcolonial'. My argument has been that the last characteristic – let's call it uneven-combined development, rather than hybridity – is a defining feature of modernity if one sees it along the axis of time (as well as space).

---

165   'Revolution is not the pavement of the Nevsky Prospekt'; Lenin 1965, pp. 62–75. The Nevsky Prospekt was, of course, the main thoroughfare of St. Petersburg, later renamed Proletkult Street [Ulitsa Proletkul'ta], 'a name that remained long after the organisation's demise' (Mally 1990, p. 44).

166   On the issue of periodic resort to direct methods of redistributing productive resources – call it shock therapy, slum clearance, enclosure, primitive or original accumulation – see Harvey 2003. Chapter 4, 'Accumulation by Dispossession', should perhaps be necessary reading for all concerned about the issue of modernity.

In that case, 'colonial modernity' and all its adjectival qualifiers are merely descriptive; they have no analytical or theoretical value.

4.11   Orientalism and Nativism

Recall that in analysing the condition of colonial modernity in India, Guha employs four pairs of concepts, each with a European and an Indic element, which together constitute the elements of D/S: Order and *Danda*, Improvement and *Dharma*, Obedience and *Bhakti*, Rightful Dissent and Dharmic Protest. In doing so, Guha tries to show the peculiar qualities of colonial Indian modernity, a function of the arrival and social implantation of a foreign and secular idiom in a land that, by his argument, had not known any autochthonous movement in the direction of a secular modernity. It is unclear, from Guha's account, what precise weight should be assigned to the possible ways in which this type of modernity came about: was the incorporation of Indic elements, for example, a strategic move on the part of the colonial rulers to utilise Indian idioms familiar to their subjects so as better to control them, or was it an attempt by the Indian upper classes to assert an autonomous domain by refurbishing parts of their own tradition? To what extent was the 'tradition' itself a function of the arrival of colonial rulers from Britain, and their ethnographic reconstruction of the Indian past? How should this issue figure in an 'Indian historiography of India'?

Insofar as Guha discusses the Indic elements in colonial modernity, he seems to be flirting with some stock Orientalist themes. Apparently, the Indian elements trace an unbroken lineage back to the laws of Manu; they can be referred exclusively to a 'Hindu' (Brahmanic?) tradition, and contribute via 'the braiding, collapsing, echoing, and blending of these [Indic and European] idioms' to the immense complexity of colonial modernity in India.[167] Even more problematically, this 'Indian tradition' seems to have rooted itself in popular culture so seamlessly and thoroughly that we can understand many aspects of peasant insurgency by recourse to the 'theoretical' insights revealed by a mastery of what is arguably an elite tradition of thought. Furthermore, the reach and symbolic power of this elite tradition of thought in the aeons of the subcontinent's history preceding the onset of the East India Company's

---

167   Guha 1997a, p. 61. Is colonial modernity more complex than European modernity, which undergoes a transition from feudalism to capitalism, shedding the ancien regime values along the way? This seems more like rhetoric than analysis, since such statements can only be made in a proper comparative framework.

rule is held to be axiomatic. This is historically dubious. Guha's misreading of the hold of the 'Laws of Manu' constitutes a particularly egregious example. Translated by William Jones, a judge in the employ of the East India Company, they were ritual texts, misconstrued by the British as legal texts in their zeal to found an Indian legal code on what they saw as an authentic 'Hindu' basis, an alternative to the complex skein of the Indo-Islamic legal structure they found in place. As Burjor Avari puts it:

> The text was never universally followed or acclaimed by the vast majority of Indians in their history; it came to the world's attention through a late eighteenth-century translation by Sir William Jones, who mistakenly exaggerated both its antiquity and its importance. Today many of its ideas are popularised as the golden norm of classical Hindu law by Hindu universalists.[168]

All this Orientalist enthusiasm on Guha's part sits awkwardly with his more straightforward use of a transition narrative and with his unabashed insinuation of a lack/inadequacy in the Indian social formation. It also ignores the implications of the consciously developed anachronisms of colonial modernity, and comes uncomfortably close to the organicist fantasies of the right about 'tradition'.

Guha traces the evolution of both modern Bengali fiction and historiography – replacing the structure of epic and myth with a secular, rational account of events in 'homogeneous, empty time' – to 'a decisive victory in that struggle to free the Indian past from the coils of epic time which had begun with the pandits of Fort William College'.[169] It was from the English that Bengali intellectuals learnt to rethink their own past according to a post-Enlightenment rationalist view of history; and it was from the influence of the same source that a modern Bengali prose began. Once that happened, however, Guha is convinced that a Bengali historiography of Bengal – which he insists on refer-

---

168   Avari 2007, p. 142; see also Thapar 2002. The exaggeration of the significance of the Manusmriti may also have come down to Indian thinkers through Nietzsche, who deemed it 'an incomparably spiritual and superior work' to the Christian Bible, '[h]ow wretched is the New Testament compared to Manu, how foul it smells' (Nietzsche 1895). Nietzsche's pose was part of the enthusiasm for a pagan Aryan Orient among a certain class of German philosophers that fuelled the Oriental Renaissance. Nietzsche is now also an inspiration, though indirect for the most part, for postcolonial theory; see Brennan 2006, p. xiii.

169   Guha 1997a, pp. 184–7.

ring to as an Indian historiography of India – is likely to be 'more sensitive, and interesting, than anything a foreigner' could turn out, not only due to the 'superior linguistic capabilities' of native speakers, but also because the latter have a variety of other factors going in their favour, for example, extra-linguistic beliefs, cognitive structures, and a myriad of other factors that 'interact with underlying competence to determine actual performance'.[170] Presumably, Bengalis writing about non-Bengali, but still Indian, history would have no such advantage, and presumably some of this advantage would be lost when Bengali historians of Bengal wrote in English, and all this without even asking where the boundaries of Bengal, let alone India, begin and end.

By this token, Indians will never be able to claim to write a competent history of England. The racism of the coloniser will meet the cultural chauvinism of the colonised. History will become segmented by nationality, religion, gender, caste, down to the most trivial ascriptive identity. This will never happen, of course, but is this an ideal to uphold? Or if a position historically taken by certain individuals or groups, is it not one that should be subject to the same level of critique that Guha undertakes in relation to Cambridge historiography? As for 'underlying competence', one must wonder exactly what this consists of: is this something imbibed with mother's milk or something acquired by writing a doctoral dissertation at one of the leading Western universities?

Be that as it may, Guha proposes to drive this theme home, citing the introduction to Nilmani Basak's 1857–8 *Bharatbarsher Itihas*, to the effect that Indian history written in English is not only prejudiced and ill-informed about the Hindu past, that students who read them at school were led to believe that 'the religions and customs of this country were all based on falsehood and that the ancient Hindus were a stupid lot', but also that such writings utterly lacked aesthetic quality.[171] In the second half of the nineteenth-century, Bankimchandra Chattopadhyay carried Basak's concerns forward: 'There is no history of Bengal...There has to be a history of Bengal...Who is to write it?...Anyone who is a Bengali has to write it', suggesting that the need to establish an autonomous historiography was also a sign of 'an urgent, insistent, though incipient nationalism'.[172] This seems to be an astonishing about-face, for Bankimchandra was presented in the earlier part of Guha's work as a political quietist and arch-reactionary who tried to refurbish patriarchy and

---

170 Guha 1997a, pp. 192–3. Guha cites Chomsky on several instances on these pages (Guha 1997a, p. 230, n. 66–9). However, it seems unlikely that Chomsky would find it comforting to have such a nativist interpretation placed on his writings.

171 Guha 1997a, pp. 187–8.

172 Guha 1997a, p. 201.

political submission with a re-reading of *bhakti* for modern times, but who now re-emerges as the hero of an autonomous Bengali historiography fully equipped with the principles of armed struggle.[173]

Guha claims that colonial education as 'a code of culture' and 'a code of power', coming together in the English-educated Indian, opens up a chasm between the latter and those educated in Bengali, even translation from one to the other unable to render their ideas mutually compatible. English education, we are told, cut off the English-educated Indians from their 'own tradition', and by the same token made *'their own past inaccessible to them as history'*.[174] Far from promoting the development of a distinctively Indian historiography of India, Anglophone education ended up as a vehicle of ideologies that hindered it. Whether Guha intends this to be taken in an ironic or critical spirit is not clear. The standard slander of the colonisers about deracinated Indians has now been made respectable by being pressed into the service of a subaltern history or an Indian historiography of India. A case of anti-racist racism perhaps?

Writing novels and histories in Bengali was tantamount to the making of a nation, a potentially transformative if as yet inchoate use of fiction and history to challenge colonialist attempts at dominance. Guha continues: 'A movement, with its springs rooted deeply in that relation which man as species being has with his [sic] natural language, it was no more than a reflex action of the will. The passions it inspired and the metaphors of motherhood used to describe it, were all evidence of its rootedness in such a primordial connection'.[175] Stripped of any mention of its class content and somewhat questionable political ambitions, Guha's attempt to theorise the nineteenth-century creation of a standardised literary Bengali out of numerous dialect forms[176] – the vehicle, one might say, of the *bhadralok*'s own feeble and incomplete attempt at hegemony, a failure Guha himself admits in so many words earlier in the book[177] – in idealist and organicist language brings Guha's narrative within shouting distance of the nativism of blood and soil, so popular among the petit-bourgeois right

173   See part IV, section XII, below.

174   Guha 1997a, pp. 174–5, emphasis added.

175   Guha 1997a, p. 190. Recall Chakrabarty's reference to metaphors of motherhood that dominated Hindu notions of fraternity. Now, in Guha's account this theme is referred back to some unspecified primordial level. On the face of it, there seems to be an unresolved Oedipal tension in postcolonial studies that might require deeper investigation.

176   Bhattacharyya 1987, pp. 56–63.

177   Guha 1997a, p. 151.

in India (and, incidentally, among their class counterparts in Europe) from the late nineteenth century onwards.

Guha's exegesis of the role of the *matribasha* [mother language] in the proj-ect of nation-building bears an uncanny resemblance to Sadik Al-Azm's notion of 'Orientalism-in-Reverse'. Quoting Edward Said, Al-Azm notes: 'The exagger-ated value heaped upon Arabic as a language permits the Orientalist to make the language equivalent to mind, society, history and nature. For the Orien-talist *the language speaks the Arab Oriental, not vice versa*'.[178] In Orientalist thought, the primordial – 'mind,' 'psyche,' 'essence' – shines through the events, circumstances and accidents forming the history of Oriental peoples. The primordial reveals its 'potency, genius and distinguishing characteristics through the flux of historical events and the accidents of time, without either history or time ever biting into its intrinsic nature'. Conversely, one can work backward through history and time to the unchanging Arab 'mind,' 'psyche' or 'essence'.[179] Substitute 'Bengali' for 'Arab/Arabic' and we can see how, in post-colonial times, as earlier, Orientalism is a theory that seems to travel well and inhabit different bodies of thought.

So determined is Guha in these pages to portray the foreigner as the expro-priator in need of expropriation as a precondition for the efflorescence of a nationalist historiography that he does not pause to examine the implications of the dominant (upper-caste) Hindu motifs in Basak's and Bankimchandra's writings. To say the least, this is a curious lapse of memory for one who had earlier chastised nationalism for employing the idiom of *Dharma*, which effectively drove a wedge between Hindus and Muslims, upper castes and Namasudras, and so on.[180] The foreigner – supposedly as alien to the histori-ography of India as s/he was to the process of nation formation – could quite as easily be the Muslim (in a Hindu nationalist rendering of Indian history) as the British. Bankimchandra's equation of former glory to the glory of our forefathers could simply be the prototype of one of the stock images inherited by right-wing Hindutva-inspired nationalism. At least in this form, an incipient Indian historiography of India turns out to be the short road to communalism.

Orientalism-in-reverse, xenophobic nativism (unable to separate the *for-eigner* from the *coloniser*), Bengal standing in for India (as empty a 'gesture of pretension and domination' as any white-supremacist universalism), become the components of an Indian historiography of India. Those are, to say the least,

---

178   Said 1978, p. 321, cited in Al-Azm 1981, p. 20.
179   Al-Azm 1981, p. 20.
180   Guha 1997a, p. 37.

somewhat Pyrrhic victories to be celebrating. Guha's concept of an Indian historiography of India seems to be off to a rather sorry start.

4.12   Bahubol and the Muslim Question

It is perhaps some ulterior discomfort with this romantic and idealist foray into nationalist historiography that causes Guha to draw attention to *bahubol* (literally, 'muscle power', used in this case to signify the power of armed struggle) as an important ingredient of Bankimchandra's historiography and thence to an 'Indian historiography of India'. In Bankimchandra's thought, the concept of *bahubol* stood for 'that rat-hole which allowed history to flood into what would have been a banked-up and interiorised nationalism'. Bahubol was predicated on an object and the power of arms was power only 'in the sense and to the extent that it had an object for its exercise'. The object, Guha wishes to persuade us, was none other than colonial rule, and the power of arms was an essential condition for a critique of the necessity of colonialism. Guha's point seems to be that a historiography of colonial India would 'qualify as genuinely Indian and autonomous only if it allowed *bahubol* to operate as a decisive element of that critique [of colonialism]'.[181] He continues by noting that, in doing so, Bankimchandra problematised Indian historiography at a higher level of politics than had been the case so far in the liberal tendencies of Indian historiography. Above all, it 'armed Indian historiography with a principle that would allow it to expropriate the expropriators by making the Indian people, constituted as a nation, the subject of their own history'. A genuinely national history – *prakrita itihas* – would address the 'slander against Indians' by setting the record straight on *bahubol*.[182]

Ignoring the bizarre logic of this argument, what is of significance for us is that Guha is forced to acknowledge, although he does not seriously come to grips with, the implications of a 'slippage' in the object of bahubol. He obsessively debates why Bankimchandra hardly deals with armed conflict against the British, while mentioning many instances of it against Muslims. The direct and sufficient answer might be that he thought British rule was providential and good for India. But Guha's apologetic response on behalf of Bankimchandra is to say that 'the force of ideology [had] brought about a series of displacements to make the Musulman rather than the British the object of bahubol and the remote pre-colonial past rather than the recent colonial past its tem-

---

181   Guha 1997a, p. 205.
182   Guha 1997a, pp. 205–6.

poral site'. Putting *bahubol* in the wrong place denied it a role in the process of *jatipratishtha* (nationality formation). Without correctly placing *bahubol*, 'the formation of nationhood, hence the writing of history, would not be possible in the era of imperialism'. Nationhood, and indeed nationalist historiography, cannot assert their autonomy without a recourse to arms. Guha concludes by noting that what was absent in Bankimchandra's writing was overcome by the later development of a kind of *samizdat* literature in the early twentieth century.[183] He does not discuss precisely how such a samizdat literature actually contributed to an autonomous historiography of India, whether a Marxist historiography of India owes much to the theme of recourse to arms, or even the political orientation of the various attempts to cut history's Gordian knots through *bahubol*. It is only worth pointing out that mere recourse to arms is insufficient to do the radically remedial work assigned to *bahubol* by Guha.

Given the history of communalism in colonial Bengal – and its spectacular eruptions in the form of riots and pogroms from time to time – Bankimchandra's argument about *bahubol* can be plausibly construed to mean precisely the deployment of force against Muslims as the eternal foreign incubus in Hindu India, as opposed to the British, who could be seen as a passing presence and who in their brief sojourn as rulers had brought some good to the subcontinent. In that case, does *bahubol* take on the characteristics of Savarkar's later call, in the 1920s, to 'Hinduise all politics and militarise Hindudom'?[184] Or perhaps it has the aspect of a durable political 'philosophy', as in Golwalkar, who describes a nation as 'a hereditary society of common spirit, feeling, and race bound together especially by *a language and customs* in a common civilisation', and who derided as 'amazing' a theory that the Nation was composed of 'all those who, for one reason or another happen to live at the time in the country'.[185] Such blood-and-soil ideas, of course, had a long pedigree among European reactionaries, going back to Edmund Burke's *Reflections on the Revolution in France*.[186] Indeed, Golwalkar almost exactly mirrors the ideas of Adam Müller, the German translator of Burke's *Reflections*, who expressed the sentiment that 'people' are not 'a bundle [Bundel] of ephemeral beings with

183   Guha 1997a, p. 212.

184   Savarkar (1883–1966) maintained: 'Thirty crores of people, with India for the basis of their operation, for their Fatherland and Holyland, with such a history behind them can dictate terms to the whole world. *A day will come when mankind will have to face the force*' (Savarkar 1969, p. 141).

185   Golwalkar 1939, p. 19.

186   There are, of course, any number of editions of this famous text. A recent version is Burke 2001. An online version of the text can be found at <www.constitution.org/eb/rev_fran.htm>.

a head, two hands, and two feet', who happen to live together at a particular place and time, but rather a 'beautiful, immortal community', 'the sublime community ... of a long series of past generations, living and future, united through life and death by great, intimate ties'.[187] Müller credits Burke for discovering what he defines as a 'spiritual India', the idea that the 'social contract' involves not only the living, but also 'past and future generations'. According to this idea, society is to be considered an 'alliance' that includes those who are tied to each other by a shared space, those who are born in the course of time on the same native soil.[188] The concordance of these ideas with those of Hindu nationalists is unambiguous.[189]

Golwalkar's ultimatum to the Muslims characterised them, predictably enough, as a 'foreign race' who 'must either adopt the Hindu culture and language, must learn to respect and hold in reverence Hindu religion, must entertain no idea but those of glorification of the Hindu race and culture, i.e., of the Hindu nation'. Failing this, they would have to forfeit all rights, claim nothing, 'not even citizen's rights'. Golwalkar urged his readers to deal 'as old nations ought to and do deal, with the *foreign* races, who have chosen to live in our country'.[190] In October 1938, following the Munich Agreement, Savarkar approved the Nazi occupation of the Sudetenland, a predominantly German-speaking province in Czechoslovakia, on the grounds that its inhabitants shared with Germans 'common blood and language'.[191]

Is it possible to read *bahubol* – armed with the language of 'blood-and-soil' nationalism – in this instance as part of a reactionary, if not proto-fascist, ideal developing simultaneously in Europe and India? While armed struggle against colonial rule, and any other unjust system, can be justified, it has minimally to be a principled recourse for socially transformative ends, not some cult of violence à la Savarkar, Golwalkar and the RSS goon squads that regularly terrorised minorities in colonial India and indeed continue to do so in the name of correcting imagined historical wrongs.

---

187   Müller, cited in Losurdo 2004, p. 294.

188   Losurdo 2004, p. 294.

189   It also reflects the ideas of postcolonial populists of all stripes.

190   Golwalkar 1939, pp. 47–8, emphasis added.

191   In 1938 and 1939, both the *Hindu Outlook* and the *Mahratta*, an English-language journal founded by B.G. Tilak in 1881, wrote editorials praising Franco, Mussolini and Hitler. Savarkar's piece was in the *Hindu Outlook*, 12 October 1938. The editorials were in the *Hindu Outlook*, 2 November and 30 November 1938, and in *Mahratta*, 6 November 1939; cited in Jaffrelot 1996, pp. 51–2, n. 174.

An Indian consciousness expressed in political and creative writings speaks in two registers simultaneously: a romantic-rejectionist register, whereby the symbols of Western modernity themselves become the target of distancing India from the West, and a civic-universalist register, in which the absence or negation of the principles underlying those symbols in the political life of the colony become the subject of a critique of colonialism.[192] In the writings of Tagore, this latter position is expressed as disillusionment: 'The idea is fast gaining ground in India as well as in England that European principles are meant for Europe alone. Indians are so very different that the principles of civilisation are not suited for their needs'.[193] Difference was, of course, a stock theme of the administrative Orientalism of colonial rulers. A bourgeois nationalism that aspired to and, to some extent, succeeded in leading a mass movement against colonialism addressed the question of rights ('European principles') in a very partial and incomplete way. As Guha himself notes, it often tended to substitute discipline (both external and self-discipline) for the seemingly intractable problem of developing an agenda radical enough to mobilise the masses to obtain those rights, tolerating in the meantime all sorts of carryovers of inequalities and inequities from 'feudal culture'.[194] As such, 'it was a bumpy road which the elite had to negotiate in its ride to hegemony. It never arrived'. *Bahubol*, we might imagine, could have helped it to do so, but then again what kind of force of arms, organised by whom, directed at what and whom, behind what ideology and programme? Arrival would have implied, at the very least, a radical transformation of society.

The implicit contrast to the Indian bourgeoisie that 'never arrived', namely a progressive European bourgeoisie that did so, is debatable. Guha himself concedes that even in Europe the capitalist mode of production did not triumph without 'encountering, combating, overcoming, and yet in a certain sense yielding to the feudal mode'.[195] And even so, we must further qualify the relationship between capitalism as a mode of production and bourgeois hegemony as the moment when persuasion outweighs coercion. It is this last characteristic that requires serious analysis, not at the level of Europe-wide generalisation, but in the kind of detailed historiography that Guha demands for India. Surely

---

192 For an extended discussion of those two registers in which anti-colonial nationalism speaks, see Kaiwar and Mazumdar 2003, Ch. 9.

193 Cited in Guha 1997a, pp. 71–2. In the civic-universal register, in which Tagore seems to be writing, difference would not have the same valence as that found in *Provincializing Europe*, nor in the kind of postcolonial studies about which Chatterjee writes.

194 Guha 1997a, p. 47.

195 Guha 1997a, p. 178.

a comparable history of Europe would illustrate the numerous failures of bourgeois hegemony, not only in the period 1789–99, but more conspicuously in
1848, 1871, not to mention 1914–18 and through the entire inter-war period in
Central and Eastern Europe. Workers, peasants and women in many parts of
Europe may have felt, rather like Tagore and Gandhi, that 'universal' rights were
not intended for them. If, after many false starts, detours, and some partially
successful and many failed revolutions, they achieved some measure of formal
rights, it was not due to the kindness of the bourgeoisie, but their own resolute
autonomous mobilisation.[196] It is in the realm of social movements and class
struggles that the proper sphere of comparative historiography lies. The place
of *bahubol* in this sphere needs systematic investigation, and its potentialities
and limitations demand a more rigorous methodology than Guha supplies.
Guha's failure to engage this issue in full makes *Dominance without Hegemony*
incomplete and the discussion of *bahubol* merely rhetorical when it is not
problematic.

---

196   Marx's articles on France document the ways in which the 'bourgeois revolution' was
       pretty much a work in progress, with numerous halts, retreats and spectacular blow-ups
       in the course of the first seven decades or so of the nineteenth-century; see, in particular,
       'The Civil War in France', <www.marxists.org/archive/marx/works/1871/civil-war-france/
       index.htm>. Parts III and IV of this piece, along with Engels's 1891 introduction, are
       reprinted in Tucker 1978, pp. 618–52. For graphic accounts of what followed the final
       defeat of the Paris Commune, see 'After the defeat of the Commune', 8–12 June 1871,
       <www.marxists.org/archive/marx/works/1871/civil-war-france/news.htm>.

Uses and Abuses of Marx

The works of Marx, and aspects of Marxist theory, were important at the inception of Subaltern Studies. Although less so now, Marx remains an important reference point for Chakrabarty and Guha – if only as a foil for postcolonialism – in addressing a range of historical, historiographical and political concerns arising out of the experience of colonialism, decolonisation, political independence and the ongoing struggles within India and now in a global world that perforce has to deal with the powerful legacies of colonial and 'Western' archives of theory and knowledge production. In *Provincializing Europe*, this takes the form of evaluating the potentialities and limitations of the Marxist use of abstractions, powerfully illustrated in Marx's discussion of abstract labour in a number of his major texts from *Capital* to the *Grundrisse* to *The Theories of Surplus-Value*, as a sign of the way in which abstractions can strategically be used for political ends and the risks that such uses carry for a history of different ways of being-in-the-world and stories of affective belonging. A critique of abstraction, then, would be vital for a history that avoids triumphalism and inevitability in favour of one that stresses the role of the vital force of life itself in resisting abstractions. In Guha, Marxist theory supplies – via the more politically direct notions of expropriation and hegemony – theoretical instruments for a critique of historiography. This constitutes an interesting attempt at the deployment of a concept in Marx that organises his understanding of the inescapable originary moment of the capital social form, what Marx himself was to call 'original' or 'primitive' accumulation – that is, the transfer of (landed/productive) property from the generally usufructuary domain within which the peasantry held it, in freehold or tenancy relations, to a form of property used to generate profits via the reorganisation of production. In Guha's usage of the term, the capture of an autonomous 'Indian' domain by the British is followed by their writing of Indian history as simply an interesting chapter of British history. Guha's subsequent discussion of the Gramscian concept of 'hegemony' reveals the extent to which Indian modernity under colonial conditions is distinct from its metropolitan counterpart(s), and generates in turn an Indian historiography of India, whose task is to remedy the shortcomings of the colonial construction of the Indian past. In both cases, history and historiography are subject to critical scrutiny for traces of historical evolutionism that contains its own political agendas, including, for example, the 'civilising

mission' of colonialism. The language of the mainstream social sciences is particularly implicated in this type of practice.

The pages that follow will be concerned to debate the range and adequacy
of Chakrabarty's and Guha's engagement with Marx and Marxist theory via
three topics of historical and political interest. These relate to abstract labour
and its corollaries productive/unproductive, not to mention socially necessary
labour; hegemony, including the related issues of coercive dominance, persuasion and leadership, as well as the question of the determinants of hegemony
in colonial and non-colonial social formations; and finally the question of the
place of historicism in Marxist theory, and more generally in a historiography
of colonial modernity. The following pages will also discuss issues of relevance
to what one might call the 'politics of knowledge' that a critical engagement
with postcolonial thought raises.

5.1   Abstract Labour, Difference, History I and II

Chakrabarty argues the centrality of the concept of abstract labour in Marx's
thought and the need to rescue this concept from its reductionist uses that
would limit history to History I, the 'self-expanding process of capital itself',
whereas in fact much of the history of people, he contends, is outside capital's
'life process'. Chakrabarty wishes to use the latter history (History II) to show
how Marx's thought may be made to resist the idea that the logic of capital
'sublates difference to itself'.[1] Abstract labour, Chakrabarty holds, is the key to
understanding 'how capital can encounter difference and still extract surplus
value from labour', while abstracting it from 'all the social tissues in which it is
embedded and which make any particular labour, even the labour of abstracting, concrete'. In a hypothetical 'barbarian' society, labourers might evince a
practical 'indifference to specific labour', but this would not be visible to an
analyst; in capitalist society, by contrast, the particular work of abstracting
(from the specific qualitative aspects of each labour process and its output)
would itself 'become an element of most or all other kinds of concrete labour
and would thus become visible to an observer'. Abstract labour, Chakrabarty
maintains, is to be understood as a practical, performative category, rather
than the result of a 'large-scale mental operation'.[2] He quotes Marx to the effect
that 'men do not bring the products of their labour into relation with each
other as values because they see these objects merely as material integuments

---

1   Chakrabarty 2000, pp. 49–50.
2   Chakrabarty 2000, pp. 53–5.

of homogeneous human labour. The reverse is true: by equating their different products to each other in exchange as values, they equate their different kinds of labour as human labour. They do this without being aware of it'.[3] Given this practical, performative character of the abstraction – that is, equalisation of different kinds of labour by abstracting from their particular useful qualities and qualitative differences in the conditions of their production – Chakrabarty concludes that Marx 'decodes abstract labour as a key to the hermeneutic grid through which capital requires us to read the world'.[4]

For Marx, in his polemical engagement with political economy, abstract labour was the key to understanding the historicity of the capital social form. Instead of making the value form – and from it exchange value and surplus value – a transhistorical reality, Marx argues it is characteristic of a particular historical epoch, in which all aspects of the production process have become commoditised. This includes, of course, the workers' labour power, which they are constrained to sell in return for a wage because they have been separated, by one process or another, from direct access to their means of subsistence – that is, they no longer have non-market access to their means of subsistence. The precise manner in which Marx phrases this is important: 'the possessor of labour-power, instead of being able to *sell commodities in which his labour-power has been objectified, must rather be compelled to offer for sale as a commodity that very labour-power which exists only in his living body'*.[5] In return for the performance of a concrete work process over a period of time, workers receive a definite quantity of money – a wage.

It is out of this historical situation in which the commodity form is generalised that the role of money, not only as means of exchange but as store of value, undergoes a vast expansion, and indeed it is out of this situation that quantification and abstraction emerge at a socially general level. With reference to labour, for example, this involves the determination of value by abstracting from concrete work processes often with ascriptive characteristics

---

3 Marx 1977, pp. 166–7, cited in Chakrabarty 2000, p. 55.

4 Chakrabarty 2000, p. 55.

5 Marx 1977, p. 272. As we will see below, this is important in historical terms. Formal freedom and compulsion can coexist; what is important is that some people be compelled to sell their (abstract) capacity to work to others who possess the means of production. The exact process by which this comes into existence, the range of intermediate forms, even the prolonged coexistence of juridically free and unfree labourers is, in itself, the subject of much debate and discussion in Marxism, including the aforementioned mode-of-production debate in India. It does not alter the insight that some degree of economic compulsion to sell labour power is the crux of the capital relation – the foundation of the development of the sort of historically determinate abstraction being discussed here.

attached to them.[6] As Sohn-Rethel points out in his 'critique of epistemology' –
drawing undoubtedly on Marx's critique of political economy – commodity
exchange is the original source of abstraction. He argues further that there is
a formal identity between the social form of exchange in a situation of generalised commodity production and 'bourgeois epistemology', in that both
involve an abstraction, and he attempts to demonstrate that Kant's *a priori*
categories were grounded not in a timeless 'transcendental subject', but in the
historical development of the abstractions of exchange involving the commodity form.[7]

Jameson makes a cognate point that the tendency towards abstraction is
a function of the world itself having 'become abstract',[8] that is, in a world in
which abstractions are routinely performed at the very heart of the material
reproduction of human life, they tend to take on a life of their own. However,
both Sohn-Rethel and Jameson point to the 'real' character of abstraction – its
emergence out of a particular historical reality. In the case of abstract labour,
we may say that it is a historically determinate abstraction – a 'practical, performative' act that remains anchored to the realities out of which it emerges,
and does not require theorisation by those who perform such acts, but which
runs the risk in the hands of some theorists of being hypostatised into a historically indeterminate form.

All this points to the need for some initial caution: that rather than see
abstract labour as a 'transhistorical and affirmative category' as with political
economy we should see it as 'historically specific and critical, grasping *what
is essential to capitalism*'.[9] This is perhaps the best or the most charitable way
to read Chakrabarty's statement about Marx decoding 'abstract labour as
a key to the hermeneutic grid through which capital requires us to read the
world'.[10] Capital as social form becomes intelligible to the extent that we read
the abstraction involved in 'abstract labour' as a historically limited and critical
category, but then abstractions do have a way of becoming an ideological reflex
of the extent to which the world has 'become abstract'. Indeed, as noted, in the
hands of political economists (not to mention marginalists), abstractions tend
to be used – whether in the classical form of the former, pertaining to value
as labour embodied in a commodity, or in the neo-classical form of the lat-

6   Marx 1977, pp. 274–5.
7   Sohn-Rethel 1978, pp. 64–5. Sohn-Rethel's examples embrace ancient Egypt and Greece,
      but clearly the force of his arguments would be greater in fully-fledged capitalism.
8   Jameson 1981, p. 66.
9   Postone 1996, p. 356.
10   Chakrabarty 2000, p. 55.

ter, pertaining to marginal value and subjective human valuation – with little reference to the historical conditions of emergence. But such a historicising reading of Chakrabarty's statement turns out to be a mistake.

For Chakrabarty, abstract labour is a problematic idea not only because of its homogenising effects, obliterating difference and subjecting many different entities and processes to a common substance, but also because the abstracting tendency gives us analytical histories that render supreme and perhaps unquestionable the universalising language of the social sciences. This is to ignore the 'affective narratives of human belonging' where life-forms 'though porous to one another do not seem exchangeable through a third term of equivalence', such as abstract labour.[11] The universalising language of the social sciences follows too closely the logic of a capitalist economy. Chakrabarty would prefer to give us the other histories – of difference, of affective belonging, and so on – which resist homogenisation to a third term. Although capital may discipline workers in their capacity as workers, and subject them to the full force of abstraction, Chakrabarty suggests that the real limits to capital's dominance lie in some vital human quality that capital needs but cannot fully subjugate. Life itself, in its biological, conscious capacity for wilful activity (the 'many-sided play of muscles') is the 'excess that capital, for all its disciplinary procedures, always needs but can never quite control or domesticate'.[12] Life, Chakrabarty declares, is a 'standing fight' against processes of abstraction, which are likened to death threatening the unity of the living body with dismemberment.[13] Chakrabarty does make an important point here, striking a note of defiance in relation to the tendency to create an apolitical language of abstract signs and then assign it a supremacy over human affairs – a form of fetishism, to be sure. The elevation of a certain type of social-scientific abstraction into a timeless expression of unalterable realities is not only pseudo-scientific, but also desocialising and demoralising. It is, one might say, the mother of all variants of the TINA ('There-is-no-alternative') doctrine.[14]

Ultimately, however, according to Chakrabarty, this is precisely where Marx founders. Acute as Marx's insights into the violence implicit in the abstracting process may have been, his commitment to the 'idea of productive labour' is such that he overlooks the rich possibilities of the standing fight, difference, History II. Chakrabarty finds objectionable the distinction between productive

---

11   Chakrabarty 2000, p. 71.

12   Chakrabarty 2000, pp. 58–60.

13   Chakrabarty 2000, p. 61.

14   See Mészáros 1995, pp. xvii, 118–26, for a scathing assessment where this doctrine actually originates and where it leads.

and unproductive labour that Marx develops in his parable of the piano maker whose labour is productive and the pianist whose labour is not. In a passage in the *Grundrisse*, Marx indeed goes so far as to say that the pianist's labour, important though it may be to the formation of the aesthetic sensibilities of an audience, is no more productive than the 'madman's delusions'.[15] This baleful equation is a sure sign of just how weak was Marx's capacity to deal with the Histories II that punctuate and interrupt capital's dominance. For Chakrabarty, the pianist is the quintessential figure of difference, of worlding the earth, whereas the 'mad man' is 'world poor'.[16] It is clear that Chakrabarty has limited patience for Marx's failures in this regard. He concludes his discussion of Marx's notion of abstract labour by noting that while Marx uses his vision of the abstract human embedded in the capitalist practice of abstract labour to generate a radical critique of capital itself, historical difference remains 'sublated and suspended' in this particular form of critique.[17] Marx may have recognised that the limits to capital are 'constantly overcome but just as constantly posited',[18] and may have registered too the survival of unvanquished remnants of older social formations in the social order of capital, but for him (or so we gather from Chakrabarty) the 'not-yet' triumphed over the 'never'. Difference, on the other hand, Chakrabarty states, is 'not external to capital, nor is it subsumed into capital, [but] lives in intimate and plural relations to capital, ranging from opposition to neutrality'.[19] This is where Heidegger presumably can help address the limits of Marx. In Chakrabarty's terms, subaltern studies can give up neither Marx nor difference.

Thus, History I and History II, taken together, destroy the usual topological distinction between the outside and the inside that mark debates about whether the whole world has come under the sway of capital. History II is not about a programme of writing histories that are alternatives to the narratives of capital, not 'the dialectical Other of the necessary logic of History I'; nor is it subsumed to History I. History II is charged with the 'function of constantly interrupting the totalizing thrusts of History I'.[20] History II is not necessarily precapitalist or feudal, or even inherently incompatible with capital. If that were the case, Chakrabarty declares, capital would truly be a case of unrelieved and absolute unfreedom. History II gives us insights into how humans 'can be

---

15   Marx 1973, p. 305.
16   Chakrabarty 2000, p. 68.
17   Chakrabarty 2000, p. 62.
18   Marx 1973, p. 410.
19   Chakrabarty 2000, pp. 65–6.
20   Chakrabarty 2000, p. 66.

at home – dwell – in the rule of capital, create room for enjoyment, the play of desires, or the seduction of the commodity', and makes space, in 'Marx's analytic of capital, for the politics of human belonging and diversity'. It 'gives us grounds on which to situate our thoughts about multiple ways of being human and our relationship to the global logic of capital'.[21] From this vantage point, Chakrabarty takes on the hollow universalist pretensions of History I's totalising thrusts. The universal is a placeholder, visible only when some particular takes it over in a gesture of pretension and domination. The globalisation of capital is not the same as capital's universalisation; globalisation does not mean that the 'universal and necessary logic of capital' has been realised. Various Histories II always modify and interrupt History I and thus 'act as our grounds for claiming historical difference'.[22]

I will return to the 'not-yet' and the 'never' in a while, but here two issues need to be considered before we embark on an investigation of productive and unproductive labour and its significance for Marx. It would be difficult to deny the grain of truth in Chakrabarty's attack on the hollow universalism of capital's apologists, but why implicate Marx in the same attack? The notion that globalisation does not equal universalisation would have been news to Milton Friedman and his acolytes of the Chicago School, not to mention a host of erstwhile Cold Warriors lost in the mists of their own triumphalist rhetoric, and perhaps some present and past members of the Planning Commission in India. However, it will most certainly not be news to Marxists who have for the longest time now been pointing to the partial, limited and often destructive nature of the globalisation brought about by capital. Certainly if universalisation implies an 'end of history' scenario – that is to say, a thorough capture by the operational logic of capital and its ideological hegemony, and a denial of alternatives based on overcoming the operational logic and ideological hegemony – we are as far from it now as in Marx's day.

Marx's stinging criticism of colonial rule, not to mention his growing interest in the 'unvanquished' remnants of past epochs of social-economic life, has served as a prototype of many such accounts.[23] His essays on European society (whether *The Class Struggles in France – 1848–50, The Eighteenth Brumaire of Louis Bonaparte, The Civil War in France*, or the prospects for revolution further

21   Chakrabarty 2000, pp. 66–7.
22   Chakrabarty 2000, pp. 70–1.
23   Marx 1972; Marx and Engels 1972; Hudis 1983, pp. 38–52. The *Ethnological Notebooks* and Peter Hudis's brilliant analysis of Marx's late writings on colonialism are a must-read, given the sweeping, totalising and ignorant generalisations that are being made about Marx's capture by Orientalist discourse.

east) reveal a keen interest and insights into the limits to capital, whether internal, that is, those generated by its own 'laws of motion' or more often by resistance from communities facing subsumption to capital's onward march.[24] Much Marxist historiography has followed in this vein. Gramsci's historical studies explored the enormously complex social formation of Italy,[25] and go much further than the generalisations involved in Chakrabarty's 'mutual interruptions' of History I and II, as does E.P. Thompson's magisterial work on the making of the English working class, in the Preface to which the author declared: 'I am seeking to rescue the poor stockinger, the Luddite cropper, the "obsolete" hand-loom weaver, the "utopian" artisan, and even the deluded follower of Joanna Southcott, from the enormous condescension of posterity'.[26]

On the other hand, Jameson argues that globalisation may be understood as the final phase of a long 'bourgeois revolution' – involving an element of accommodation or surrender to the realities of a thoroughly generalised commodity economy – and that in this mode we are 'programmed' and made 'increasingly at home' for life in what would otherwise be a 'distressingly alienating reality'.[27] In that case, we must see the globalised phase of the 'bourgeois revolution' as a final and very specialised moment of that 'immense process of superstructural transformation' whereby the inhabitants of older social formations are 'culturally and psychologically retrained' for life in the commodity system.[28] Globalisation, then, is precisely the kind of universalisation we might associate with capital – its class nature clearly revealed in the ways in which it conquers new terrain, while its older presuppositions have all but vanished. Of course, we would also have to accept that capital's universalisation is always truncated, limited and productive of no small amount of misery. My argument does not hinge on the acceptance of this proposition, but it must be considered.

The career of Subaltern Studies inspired postcolonialism and Chakrabarty's limited ambitions for History II would be an indirect manifestation of the foregoing argument about reprogramming for life in a generalised commodity economy. What are the supposed mutual interruptions of History I and II? If difference is unthinkable outside History I, no less than History II, then clearly difference is as much a part of capital's drive to subsume a variety of autonomous social formations to itself as it is a matter of 'unvanquished' remnants

---

24   Shanin 1983.
25   Gramsci 1971.
26   Thompson 1966, p. 12.
27   Jameson 1981, p. 236.
28   Ibid.

of the past. Chakrabarty may recognise this in the abstract, but his historiography cannot cope with the problems this poses for the issue of capital's commodity-determined and truncated universalism. From the perspective I have developed, it is arguable that subsumption of hitherto autonomous social formations does involve sublation – in the sense of preservation and cancellation; preservation of some similarities of external form and aspects of the superstructure, which are nonetheless subtly altered, while cancelling more or less entirely their ability to function independently of capital's overall cycle of reproduction. This is the real historical ground for claiming difference, one might even say the moment when 'tradition' is born. Outside this sublative process, 'difference' hardly qualifies as anything more than mere empiricism.

As for issues of human belonging, it is undeniable that Marx did not produce anything on the subject approximating the scale and depth of his analysis of capital's 'laws' of tendencies that the three volumes of *Capital*, for instance, give us. He never lived to finish his volume on labour, for example. His remarks on the conditions of working people do have a deeply felt quality to them, particularly the images of absolute exhaustion, pauperisation, even the approach of life's premature end as a result of overwork and starvation.[29]

Even so, two preliminary qualifications are necessary: (1) Marx set out to anatomise the mystifications of exploitation under capital, an indispensable undertaking given the apologist nature of political economy and the sheer confusion expressed by such slogans as 'a fair day's wage for a fair day's labour'; (2) he called upon workers to solidarise and fight together against numerous other mystifications involving the manipulation of ascriptive identities manifested not only in racial arguments, ethnicity and so on, but also in wage differences. His remark that 'labour in a white skin cannot emancipate itself where it is branded in a black skin', was paralleled by Engels's pioneering study of the use of wage differentials to drive a wedge between Irish immigrant workers and their English counterparts.[30] Many of Marx's addresses to working class audiences had a practical-political element to them, which incorporated and

---

29   See, for instance, Marx 1977, pp. 359, 364–7, 593, 824–5.

30   The quote from Marx occurs in *Capital*, Volume I; Marx 1977, p. 414. Engels's remarks on
      Irish workers in England occur in his *The Condition of the Working Class in England*, 1844,
      in the chapter on Irish immigration, where he quotes Thomas Carlyle's *Chartism* on the
      supposed shortcomings of the Irish character; see Engels 1844, <www.marxists.org/
      archive/marx/works/1845/condition-working-class/cho6.htm#[5]>.

popularised hard won theoretical insights, and these remain as true in the age of globalisation as they were in his day, perhaps even more so.[31]

But does a closer look at the issue of abstract labour and the closely related notions of productive and unproductive labour in Marx tell us something about Marx's politics, and help to clarify the political implications of Chakrabarty's intervention?

5.2   The Piano Maker and the Piano Player: Productive and Unproductive Labour

We have seen that, for Chakrabarty, the issue of abstract labour connects through History I and History II to issues of human belonging and diversity. In some senses, this is a fairly standard argument, namely, that labour under capital's rule is so unremitting, empty and abstracted of all meaningful social ties that humans seek diversity, community and meaning outside the labouring nexus with capital. It remains to ask specifically why Marx insists that the labour of the piano maker is productive while that of the pianist is not. As Marx explains: 'What is productive labour and what is not ... has to emerge from the dissection of the various aspects of capital itself. Productive labour is only that which produces *capital*'. 'The piano-maker', Marx insists, 'reproduces capital; the piano-player only exchanges his labour for revenue'.[32] The cycle of capital and the cycle of revenue remain distinct in Marx's analyses, even if over time revenue itself becomes a function of the profits of capital. Labour, for Marx, becomes productive only insofar as it produces its opposite, and the productive labourer is one that 'directly augments capital'.[33]

Marx is clearly developing the notion of productive labour here as a relation of production, that is, a relational category linking living labour to the augmentation of capital via its exploitation in the process of production.[34] 'The *transformation of labour* (as living, purposive activity) into *capital* is, *in itself,*

---

31   The polemic engagement of Chakrabarty's *Provincializing Europe* would have gained added depth if he had laid out the achievements and, dare one say, the limitations of Marx's own writings and Marxist historiography on the subject of labour under capitalism in the requisite detail.

32   Marx 1973, p. 305.

33   Marx 1973, p. 305.

34   Exploitation should be understood here as productive utilisation without, of course, excluding the moral charge it carries of an unequal exchange. That is, labour must be made to produce surplus value if the capital system is to reproduce itself.

the result of the exchange between capital and labour, in so far as it gives the capitalist the title of ownership to the product of labour (and command over the same)'. Labour is productive, Marx insists, 'only if absorbed into capital, where capital forms the basis of production, and where the capitalist himself is in command of production', the productivity of labour thus becoming the 'productive force of capital'. Labour 'in its *immediate being*, separated from capital, is not productive'.[35] It should be clear by now that productive labour is not a 'natural' relationship between the worker and his or her activity, but a specific economic relationship.[36] Marx is recasting a commonly used category (productive labour) from something that could be used to describe a type of activity involving the transformation of 'raw materials' (wood, metal, glue, and so on) into a tangible final product (say, a piano) in terms of a social form that might involve any activity that augments capital. This becomes abundantly clear in Marx's discussion of Richard Jones, in the *Theories of Surplus-Value*, where he states:

> Jones quite correctly reduces Smith's productive and unproductive labour to its essence – capitalist and non-capitalist labour – by correctly apply-ing the distinction made by Smith between labourers paid by capital and those paid out of revenue ... The distinction made between the labourers who live on capital and those who live on revenue is concerned with the *form of labour* ... This difference must be kept in mind and the fact that all other sorts of activity influence material production and vice versa in no way affects the necessity for making this distinction.[37]

Now, the pianist can also become a productive labourer if she is hired by a com-pany to play concerts, make recordings, and so on, while on a salary. In that case, the product of her labour is alienated, objectified and commoditised – say, in the form of compact discs or online downloads – and she becomes quite clearly a productive worker in the Marxian sense. The relationship can con-tinue as long as the wage labourer, in our case the pianist, continues to produce a profit for her employers. It should not be altogether unexpected that since Marx's day pianists have become productive labourers no less than piano makers, that culture itself has become progressively commoditised. Perhaps History II is now more completely subsumed to History I than Chakrabarty allows.

---

35   Marx 1973, p. 308, emphasis added.
36   Marx 1973, p. 310.
37   Marx 1971, Volume III, pp. 431–2, emphasis added.

From this transformation of what was a 'transhistorical' category in political economy into one that is 'historical', Marx develops what he sees as characteristics of the capitalist system of production that account for the role of living labour in its ongoing valorisation, its economic dynamism and the need ultimately to overcome the condition of productive labour by transforming the basis of production itself. Productive labour is the direct means of capital's valorisation, that is, to its 'self-expansion'. Production in capitalism is necessarily quantitatively oriented, towards ever-increasing amounts of surplus value. As Postone notes in his study of Marx's theory of labour, this is the basis of Marx's analysis of production in capitalism as production for the sake of production. This means that production is no longer a means to a substantive end, but 'a means to an end that is in itself a means, a moment in a never-ending chain of expansion'. Production in capitalism becomes 'a means to a means',[38] in which productive labour is the indispensable mediation.[39] The goal of production in capitalism – ever-increasing amounts of surplus value, a function of the competition of capitals – exerts a 'form of necessity on the producers'; it is neither given by social tradition nor decided upon consciously, but rather confronts people as 'an external necessity'. Producers can only decide which products would likely maximise surplus value.[40] It is out of this situation that, historically, the richest possible concrete development (the lavish explosion of commodity production) emerges, so much so that Marx begins the first volume of *Capital* by saying: 'The wealth of societies in which the capitalist mode of production prevails appears as an immense collection of commodities'.[41] And it is precisely as a reflex of this, and labour's mediating role (objects as 'material integuments of homogeneous human labour'),[42] that the very 'abstraction of labour' arises. As Marx explains:

> Indifference towards any specific kind of labour presupposes a very developed totality of real kinds of labour, of which no single one is any longer predominant. As a rule, *the most general abstractions arise only in the midst of the richest possible concrete development, where one thing appears as common to many, to all.* Then it ceases to be thinkable in a particular form alone. On the other side, this abstraction of labour as

38   Postone 1996, p. 181; see also Marx 1977, pp. 742, 1037–8.
39   This is why Marx insists that the question of whether capital is productive or not is an absurd one; Marx 1973, p. 308.
40   Postone 1996, p. 182.
41   Marx 1977, p. 125.
42   Marx 1977, pp. 166–7.

such is not merely the mental product of a concrete totality of labours … Not only the category, labour, but labour in reality has here become the means of creating wealth in general, and has ceased to be organically linked with particular individuals in any specific form … The simplest abstraction, which expresses an immeasurably ancient relation … nevertheless achieves practical truth as an abstraction only as a category of the most modern society.[43]

The indifference to 'any specific kind of labour' does not in the least imply that the labour process in capitalism is anything but brutally specific and burdensome, but that is one aspect of labour. It is the other, more abstract element that often escapes characterisation, and here it is worth remembering Marx's utilisation of the terminology of spectres ('phantom-like objectivity') and vampires, not to mention the vocabulary of chemical changes – latency, transformation, crystallisation – to describe the process by which the specificity of actually performed labour is transformed into the abstractions of the circuit of value,[44] a form that does not appear to contain an iota of materiality.

The abstraction of labour corresponds to the abstraction of time. With the establishment of capitalism, homogeneous, empty (that is, abstract) time, 'free to pass by independently of man and events', establishes its tyranny to which people are 'constrained to submit'.[45] The concept of 'socially necessary labour time', so central to Marx's analysis of generalised commodity production, is not simply a measure of the time employed in the production of a commodity, but a socially constrained amount of time within which the production of a commodity must take place if producers are to receive the full value of expended labour time, that is, if the commodity is not to become devalorised in exchange. As a result of the socially mediating role of labour under capitalism – that is, value understood not as a 'subjective category', but as an objectified social mediation constituted by labour and measured by socially necessary labour time – 'labour time expenditure is transformed into a temporal norm', not only abstracted from but standing above and determining individual action,[46] operating with an implacable law-like regularity. In the capitalist mode of production, the 'definite, particular labours' of individuals must manifest themselves as their opposite, as 'equal, necessary, general

43   Marx 1973, pp. 104–5.
44   Marx 1977, p. 128; Bensaïd 2002, p. 323; Elson 1979, pp. 134–6.
45   Gurevich 1976, p. 242.
46   Postone 1996, p. 214.

labour, and in this form [as] social labour'.[47] Individual labours thus become 'cellular components of a large, complex and dynamic alienated system that encompasses men and machines'.[48]

The historical development of capitalism involves two quite diametrically different processes: (i) the ongoing transformation of social and economic life as a function of the continual appropriation of science and technology into the production and circulation of commodities – all the astonishing mutations and transformations visible in everyday life under capitalism; (ii) the reconstitution of the fundamental structural opposition of capital and labour in the production process – *the capital relation* – as an 'unchanging feature of social life', and with it the reproduction of the socially mediating role of labour.[49] Even as humans proceed, with the development of capitalism, to overcome personalised forms of social domination (of the kind that obtained under tributary modes of production, for instance), and liberate themselves from their overwhelming dependence on nature's vagaries, they do so by a 'non-conscious and unintentional creation of a quasi-natural form of social domination' constituted by labour, a sort of 'second nature', as Postone refers to it, following Lukács.[50] The concept of a second nature is expressed in some detail in Lukács's *History and Class Consciousness*. There Lukács develops the idea that feudal society was far too unorganised and had far too little control over the totality of relations between producers for the reality of 'man as social being' to appear to consciousness as the reality of humans. It is only under capitalism – with the overcoming of 'the spatio-temporal barriers between different lands and territories' and 'the legal partitions between the different "estates" (Stände)' – that humans become, in the true sense of the word, social beings, or in Lukács's words, 'society becomes the reality for man'. Thus, the recognition that society is reality becomes possible only under capitalism. But the class that carried out this revolution did so without consciousness of its function and the social forces it unleashed. The *'very forces that carried it to supremacy seemed to be opposed to it like a second nature*, but a more soulless, impenetrable nature than feudalism ever was'.[51] Lukács further grounds this idea in Marx's understanding that:

---

47   Marx 1971, Volume III, p. 130.
48   Postone 1996, p. 270.
49   Postone 1996, p. 300.
50   Postone 1996, p. 381.
51   Lukács 1971, p. 19.

The mysterious nature of the commodity-form consists therefore simply in the fact that the commodity reflects the social characteristics of men's own labour as objective characteristics of the products of labour themselves, as the socio-natural properties of these things. Hence it also reflects the social relation of the producers to the sum total of labour as a social relation between objects, a relation which exists *apart from and outside the producers*.[52]

Lukács refers to this as the 'basic phenomenon of reification',[53] and it sets the condition in which a system based on productive, abstract, socially necessary labour (in the Marxian sense) underpins social relations that are 'blind, processual, and quasi-organic'.[54]

The core of the capital relation is thus constituted by the two-fold character of labour: (i) as an active if progressively minor force in creating material wealth, much of which is now contributed by the awesome powers of science, technology, and in general by the harnessing of the powers of nature;[55] (ii) as the source of value (socially necessary labour time) and surplus value. In Marx's analysis, the working class remains important, indeed indispensable, as the source of value, but no longer of material wealth. Value does not, from Marx's point of view, express human relations with nature, but is constituted by abstract labour alone, a function solely of socially necessary labour time. Although increased productivity does result in more material wealth, it does not necessarily result in more value.[56] However, it is not material wealth but *value* that is expressive of the general form of wealth under the productive system of capital. As Marx puts it sardonically, '[n]o scientist to date has yet discovered what natural qualities make definite proportions of snuff tobacco and paintings "equivalents" for one another'.[57] To explain the general nature of profits, 'you must start from the theorem that, on an average, commodities are sold at their real values, and that *profits are derived from selling them at their real values*, that is, in proportion to the quantity of labour *realised* in them'.[58]

---

52 Marx 1977, pp. 164–5, emphasis added.
53 Lukács 1971, p. 86.
54 Postone 1996, p. 270.
55 Marx 1975ff., p. 480; Marx 1971, Volume I, p. 391.
56 Postone 1996, p. 195.
57 Marx 1971, Volume III, p. 130.
58 Marx 1975, p. 42.

Labour in capitalism, far from being the standpoint of Marx's critique, is its *object*.[59] Fundamental to it, in Postone's judgement, is the 'constituting central-ity of labour in capitalism as the ultimate ground' of the abstract structures of domination; the increasing fragmentation of individual labour and individual existence involving paradoxically the subsumption of individuals as 'mere organs of the whole';[60] the progressive hollowing out of social relations; the domination exercised over humans by the non-human side (commodities, money, capital);[61] the blind runaway logic of capitalist society necessitating the ever-increasing exploitation of nature;[62] and the ever-larger scale of organ-isations that subsume humans. Marx's analysis of capital sees the working class as an 'integral element of capitalism rather than as the embodiment of its negation'.[63] The working class remains structurally important to capitalism as the indispensable source of value, but over the course of its history becomes a minor component of material wealth. Postone contends that far from con-stituting 'the socialized productive forces that come into contradiction with the capitalist social relations and thereby point to the possibility of a post-capitalist future', Marx argued that the working class was the 'essential consti-tuting element of those relations themselves'. Both the capitalists and workers are bound to capital, but the latter is more so. The working class, rather than embodying the socialist future, is the necessary basis of the present under which it suffers.[64]

Therefore, insofar as the working class represents 'capital-constituting rather than capital-transcending forms of action and consciousness', overcom-ing capital must be understood in terms of abolishing proletarian labour rather than realising it more adequately.[65] For Marx, it was far more important for the working class to abolish itself in its capacity as an aspect of capital (variable capital), and thereby to free human life from the abstract, quasi-natural form of domination by production, than for it merely to seize the means of pro-duction and continue 'capital-determined production' even if under workers' control.[66] Only then would humans be able to appropriate the 'socially general

---

59   Postone 1996, pp. 357, 388.
60   Marx 1970, p. 30.
61   Smith 1990, p. 62.
62   Burkett 1999b, p. 161.
63   Postone 1996, p. 389.
64   Postone 1996, p. 357.
65   Postone 1996, pp. 370–1.
66   For a discussion of this, see Postone 1996, pp. 364–5. Of course, militant workers might choose to abolish a system of which their labour is the constituting factor, rather than

knowledge and capacities' – produced by harnessing nature and natural laws via science and technology – that had hitherto been constituted as the alienated power of capital and thereby open up the possibility that 'people might begin to control what they create rather than being controlled by it'.[67] For Marx, 'the realm of freedom' really begins where labour determined by necessity and external expediency ends:

> Freedom, in this sphere, can consist only in this, that socialised man, the associated producers, govern the human metabolism with nature in a rational way, bringing it under their collective control instead of being dominated by it as a blind power; accomplishing it with the least expenditure of energy and in conditions most worthy and appropriate for their human nature.[68]

It is not too much of a stretch at this point to see that Marx – committed as he was to a historical analysis of the idea of productive labour and to a future in which humans would live in intentional communities in which the 'realm of freedom' would be vastly expanded – could have had no commitment to some transhistorical idea of productive labour and certainly not to productive labour in its capitalist guise. Indeed, Marx argued that labour's historical role as the key mediation in the value form – productive, abstract, socially necessary labour under capitalism – produced a massive waste of 'the worker's life and health'.[69] He likened capital to a vampire sucking the blood of living labour in order to reproduce itself,[70] and deplored the way in which 'socio-economic relations are uncoupled from social considerations and made in terms of independent objective factors'.[71] Being a productive labourer, Marx concluded, was '*not* a piece of luck but a misfortune'.[72]

In light of the above, Chakrabarty's idea that 'historical difference would remain sublated and suspended in this particular [Marxist] form of critique' is not only beside the point, but trivial and obfuscatory.[73] Historical difference

---

merely act as a corporative force that perpetuates their captivity to the value-positing, value-producing form of labour.

67   Postone 1996, pp. 372–3.
68   Marx 1981, pp. 958–9.
69   Marx 1981, p. 182; see also Burkett 1999b, p. 99.
70   'Capital is dead labour, that, vampire-like, lives only by sucking living labour, and lives the more, the more labour it sucks' (Marx 1977, p. 342).
71   Smith 1990, pp. 93–4.
72   Marx 1977, p. 644.
73   Chakrabarty 2000, p. 62.

is one of the keys to Marx's critique of capital. It is really up to Chakrabarty to say why the kinds of human difference that are possible under the dominance of capital are so important *per se* as to override Marx's point that it is only in overcoming capital – in the sense of the specific social relations of production of our epoch – that humans can experience the full flowering of their creative powers, implicitly establishing the conditions for the expression of human difference in creative, non-antagonistic ways. What are the mutual interruptions of History I and History II supposed to achieve? If they merely create some space for the seduction of the commodity, the play of desires, and so on, while leaving value-positing, value-producing labour well alone, then one must conclude that History II remains captive to the logic of History I. In the end, this particular hermeneutic strategy has the main function of spiriting the possibility of an epochal transformation of the social form of capital out of sight. After all, while Marx may not have produced a detailed transition narrative – in the sense of a transition from feudalism to capitalism – much of his work was concerned to point to the absolute historical necessity of the other transition, namely, one that would have as its point of departure an overcoming of the rule of capital.

Chakrabarty seems unwilling to confront and draw out the implications of a rather important distinction, namely, that a respect for different life worlds in a hierarchical world order should not imply any respect for the processes that created those hierarchies, including the uneven geography of world capitalism, and that any understanding of the significance of resistance to absorption into capital's processes should also ask when *a resistance to* becomes *a struggle against*. That particular distinction, and the question of resistance and struggle, requires one to work under the sign of Marx, not Heidegger. Otherwise we end up with a sentimental, postmodernist Third-Worldism, no better than its discredited positivist-historicist predecessor.

5.3   Millennial Toil as the 'Nightmare of History'

Chakrabarty's excursus on the category of abstract labour in Marx is part of a wider postcolonial critique. Gyan Prakash, a leading proponent of Subaltern Studies-inspired postcolonialism in the United States, claims that the colonial categories of 'capital' and 'labour' were a sign of how distant the colonial government was from the 'world' of its indigenous subjects. As categories, they were alien impositions, inappropriate to describe the lives people led or to help them organise their relationships to each other and their past. In the world of subaltern indigenous subjects, Prakash notes, mundane matters –

such as caste hierarchy, ritual notions of purity and pollution, and patriarchal domination – were all mediated through interactions between humans and the spirit world.[74] He proclaims the main virtue of postcolonialism as being precisely its abandonment, along with 'nationalist ideas' of history and reason, of the modes-of-production narratives of Marxism.[75] A focus on production would be tantamount to 'economism', which would effectively ignore people's many-sided creativity in favour of an obsessional reduction to detailed function and maximum productivity, or, worse, by reinforcing 'a near-exclusive concern with the economic', would end up with 'the bourgeois "naturalisation" of the economy as the foundation of all societies at all times'.[76]

Prakash maintains that the administrative departments of the colonial state did precisely that, instituting the economy as the 'foundation' of society, while simultaneously using the decennial Census to place numerous groups of people in the discursive field of labour, thus making them available for scholarly study.[77] Prakash goes on to assert that British rule 'created' a class of agricultural labourers by 'rendering Indian society knowable as a collection of economic groups'.[78] It would appear that the colonisers created a *class of labourers* by manipulating language and through discursive bad faith, rather than by transforming Indian society via the introduction of the capital social form at however basic a level, in the process subsuming a variety of modes of work into the circuit of value on the global level. One would have to conclude from Prakash's argument that if people were not placed in the 'discursive field' of labour then they would not be available for scholarly study. Given the relative paucity of studies of the Indian working class during the period of colonial rule, this might come as a surprise to many. Mere placement of people in a discursive field does not guarantee that they are 'available' for study. To the extent that the situation has changed since then, it is a function of the vast transformation of the global economy as capitalism deepens its hold on many of the peripheral economies of the world, and labour relations acquire a clarity they did not possess in the colonial period, rather than being the result of a top-down manipulation of categories.[79] A massive irony of the situation is that

---

74   Prakash 1992a, pp. 1–46.

75   Prakash 1992b, pp. 8–20.

76   Prakash 1992a, p. 2; see also Chakrabarty 2000, pp. 58–71.

77   Prakash 1992a, pp. 9–10.

78   Prakash 1992a, p. 19.

79   There are a number of recent studies of the working class in India. A central contribution has been the work of Rajnarayan Chandavarkar; see Chandavarkar 1994 and 1998. Other notable contributions include: Bahl 1995; Basu 1993; Bear 2007; Breman 2005; Das Gupta

even as capital proceeds to proletarianise the last reserves of the peasantry worldwide, the reality for many millions of those so rendered propertyless is not a lifetime of work, but instead what Sarkar calls 'worklessness',[80] and what economists dub 'jobless growth'. The prospect of permanent unemployment has become a nightmare weighing on the brains of the living.[81]

But to return to our main line of thought here, it almost seems, from Prakash's account, that 'labour' was extruded from the category-making socio-logical imagination of colonial officials. It might be useful to remind ourselves here that Marx himself was at great pains to underscore the 'objective and historical' preconditions for his discovery of the 'labour theory of value' – or perhaps more accurately the 'value theory of labour'[82] – at a moment in which for the first time land and labour were becoming commodities. Marx's discovery of this 'scientific truth', which had not only eluded Aristotle, but also his immediate predecessors and contemporaries among the political economists, was premised thus on two coinciding determinations. *One*, the *historical situation* in which for the first time, 'labour-power takes in the eyes of the labourer himself the form of a commodity which is his property', that is, in which it assumes the form of wage labour. It is only from this moment that 'the produce of labour universally becomes a commodity'.[83] *Two, the categorial system* that Marx himself developed, by which the ahistorical category of value in political economy was historicised, as discussed above. It is not only the objective originality of the historical situation, but also the subjective transformation

1994; Holmström 1984; Joshi 2005; Heller 1999; Kerr 1995; Kude 1986; Nair 1994; Simeon 1995. Of course, there is also Chakrabarty's 1989 *Rethinking Working-Class History*, written in a Subaltern Studies mode, which implicitly treats Indian working class consciousness as somehow distinct from that prevailing in the West (Chakrabarty 1989, pp. 217–8). Chandavarkar's work, on the other hand, may be seen as a direct rejection of this sort of culturalist model of working class history, and reasserts not only a non-exceptionalist model, but also the critical role of the working classes in the development of Indian capitalism. For more on working class history in India, and its recent prominence, although attended 'with much less fanfare and attention internationally or even within the country' than the earlier interest in the rural subalterns, see Sarkar 2004, pp. 285–313.

80   Sarkar 2004, p. 310.
81   See, for instance, Larsen 2002, p. 218, on some of the unanticipated consequences of chronic, even permanent, unemployment, on what he calls the 'secondary barbarism' and 'the trend to pathological forms of rebellion such as religious fundamentalisms and ethnic particularisms (for these, too, are historical forms of the "subaltern")', and the prospects for emancipation from the margins.
82   Elson 1979, pp. 144–74.
83   Marx 1977, p. 170, n. 1.

in which the workers themselves can see their labour as a commodity, which then brings forth the category of 'labour' as a scientific category, which can then be retroactively used to 'recover the truth of even the millennia of pre-capitalist human history'.[84]

If so, labour as a category 'emerges' twice: as *a social reality* sufficiently autonomous of its customary integument to be visible as a key component of production relations under capital; and as *a category of analysis* that reveals the nature of exploitation and alienation of a whole host of preceding histori-cal epochs, even if that particular aspect of the relationship was of no great moment to the normal view of contemporaries. Or, put differently, to those who lived in older social forms, the methods of surplus extraction were so transparent that, unlike in the epoch of capital, they received no specific 'theo-retical' thought; the latter instead being directed towards more cosmological and mysterious matters that must have seemed a matter of urgency to people who lived at the far greater mercy of nature. In other words, the ideological dominant and the economic determinant did not coincide.

In a colonial context, value-positing, value-producing labour emerges as a productive force through the so-called 'land-and-labour settlements' that par-tially or fully commoditise land and labour. Even if the English progenitors of those settlements had not come to India, for example, with the vocabulary of political economy ready-to-hand, in transplanting the social-property rela-tions of their home country, they would have introduced into India the real categories corresponding to the relations of production under those new con-ditions. They might have had to resort to neologisms. Labour too in those cir-cumstances would have acquired indigenous names unrecognisable to colonial rulers, but a perduring categorial dissonance seems untenable.[85] A close look

---

84   Jameson 1988, Volume II, p. 164.

85   The question of whether the class of labourers in colonial India was formally free or not seems to be a particularly juicy red herring, leading to the notion that 'pure free wage labour' in the 'double Marxian sense' is an ideal type to be distinguished from the real existence of bondage and various degrees of unfreedom in colonial conditions; see Amin and van der Linden 1997, p. 3. Marx's statement that 'labour in a white skin cannot emancipate itself where it is branded in a black skin', suggests that chattel slaves on plantations were part of the worldwide spectrum of productive labour in the capitalist sense explicated above (Marx 1977, p. 414). This recognition of something other than 'pure free wage labour' is part of a long Marxist tradition of analysis. Lenin, for example, in *The Development of Capitalism in Russia*, notes the existence of 'semi-patriarchal, semi-bonded forms of hired labour one so frequently meets in the central black-earth belt', and notes in general the tendency of migrant labour to borrow money 'from priests, landlords and local kulaks' to be repaid in labour (Lenin 1974, pp. 245, 247). These relations are

at the ways in which spirits and gods were mobilised by rural people in India – and possibly elsewhere – shows a clustering around questions of the owner-ship of the means of production, and around the control and distribution of the product of labour. Arguably, a variety of ideological formations – whether informed by categories derived from spirit cults or neoclassical economics – have had a role to play in generating descriptions of social-productive rela-tions. The categories themselves develop in relation to the enforcement of social discipline and methods of extraction of the product of labour, whether by depressing the immediate producers' share of the total social product, lengthening or intensifying the working day, segmenting it spatially, or sub-jecting workers to the pace and intensity of machines. Generally, the densest thicket of symbolic categories develops in close proximity to some aspect or other of production, either:

> (i) the 'natural' component of production relations, including the pas-sage of seasons in an agricultural social-economy;
> (ii) the 'social' component – relations of dependency, direct and indirect forms of social domination;
> Or (iii) in combinations of 'i' and 'ii' that might have the effect of promot-ing the naturalisation of social relations.

At transitional moments, this naturalisation starts to break down and has to be reinstituted by resort to reworking and revitalising all manner of symbolic resources. And through their resistance, workers also enrich this discursive field, creating or reinvigorating symbolic categories of resistance. Customary class balances may be 'alienated' to the spirit world, and invoking it may be a way for immediate producers to resist new demands, consistent with a new socio-political dispensation – for example, colonialism.[86] The historicity of forms of exploitation and oppression becomes more transparent to the subor-dinated groups, fuelling further resistance. The very intensity with which tradi-tions were invented during the colonial period is a sure sign of heightened

---

reminiscent of Indian conditions in which smallholders and landless labourers migrated annually to agricultural and small and large industrial sites for work where they encountered a variety of working conditions, some verging on bondage; see Breman 2007, p. 59, for a further elaboration of the relationship between what he calls 'neo-bondage' and capitalist production. The issue of freedom in the Marxian double sense is a matter of both the development of the productive forces and class struggles over working conditions.

86   See Wallerstein 1991, pp. 193–5, for a discussion of organised and planned resistance using cultural symbols familiar to the people using them.

struggle at a time when new realities had come into existence.[87] In such junctures, the discourses of exploiters and exploited enter into a more or less sharp dissension, and allow for the imagination of alternative horizons of possibility, including a reworking of the past through an idealised recuperation of its best elements,[88] and the prospect of organising new forms of collective resistance. In the modern epoch of capital, this also means the clarification to some extent of the very category of class.

Marx's method demonstrates both the historical character of the realities that thought analyses, and the equally historical character of the concepts such thought constructs to explain those realities.[89] Undoubtedly, this is unacceptable to some, both on the left and the right. Althusser, as Jameson notes, rejected this 'absolute historicism' because he feared it would relativise science.[90] For postcolonial theorists, this is a variety of pretentious historicism that attempts to render the life-world of subaltern people knowable in terms of a 'more real' secular reality. But there are other perspectives from which to grasp both the importance and limits of this type of historicisation. Gramsci, for instance, did not hesitate to emphasise the historical limits of Marxism, but also acknowledged the legitimacy of Marxist science within those limits,[91] and sought to go beyond the science-ideology distinction in order to 'determine every thought by means of the immanent recognition of its historical conditions of realisation'.[92]

---

87 Prakash himself, in more sensible moments, discusses the ever-changing field of the spirit world *in response to* transformations in the social-property relations under colonial rule. But he seems unwilling to follow through on the ways in which capitalist social-property relations effectively subsume the 'subaltern' world of the peasantry to the new order of colonial capitalism. This should not be surprising, as after all, in his view, capital and labour are merely colonial sociological conventions, alien to the real symbolic and material world of rural Indians; see Prakesh 1992c, pp. 282–304.

88 See, for example, Jameson's discussion of 'the place of quality in an increasingly quantified world, the place of the archaic and of feeling amid the desacralisation of the market system' (Jameson 1981, pp. 236–7).

89 Godelier 1973, p. 303; Jameson 1988, Volume II, p. 164.

90 Jameson 1988, Volume II, p. 164.

91 The emergence of an insight applicable, with the qualifications made above, to a wide range of social formations out of a contingent history, the conjunction of an 'absolute scientific truth' and its quite contingent conditions of formation, goes to the heart of a Marxist historicism; therefore, it is neither a universalism that elides difference nor a historical relativism that denies the scientific nature of its historic insights.

92 Spiegel 1983 and Tosel 1995, cited in Thomas 2007, p. 255.

If Prakash among others should still object to placing people in the 'category of labour' – an unfortunate phrase, but one we will work with for the moment – as if that would somehow equate to the 'bourgeois naturalisation of the economy', a response might include the following four points: (1) an understanding of the role of value-positing, value-producing labour can yield critical insights into the workings of capital, its differential economic impact on various social formations in which it has taken root, or in which it has been implanted under 'colonial conditions', indispensable, one would have thought, precisely for organising, from below, principled resistance and subversion – two of the favourite buzzwords of postcolonial thought; (2) as political sociology, an anatomisation of the conditions of labour – ranks and privileges, wage differentials, racism and segmentation (all of which must also count as difference) – would serve to highlight the ways in which capitalists seek advantages in the field of struggle that is already so weighted in their favour; (3) a study of the deadening routines imposed on workers, their social and psychological effects, and an organisation of struggles around their alleviation – if not abolition – might help to address the fatalism of accepting existing conditions as some sort of primordial human condition, that is, seeing punishing labour as a timeless and unalterable fact of existence; (4) an analysis of the trajectory of the capitalist system over time, its constant crises of overproduction and overcapacity, the deleterious impact of those in-built tendencies on the physical and social environment of which working people often experience the worst; this is true not only under colonial conditions but more so in today's actually existing globalisation. All of this would combine to undermine, not promote, the 'bourgeois naturalisation of the economy'.[93] Avoidance of this topic might be a form of reactionary political theology, but it is not subversive in the slightest.[94]

Difference must be understood as taking shape against the background of some more general identity, without entirely losing the autonomy of the elements that constitute it. This is to suggest that capital does not swallow everything in its path whole, but that its actions on a wide range of already existing

---

93   A very important study in this regard is Brenner 2006.

94   An example of truly subversive work in these regards is, of course, Engels 2009 [1844]. Harold Mann, an official in the Agricultural Department of the Bombay Presidency, undertook a study of two villages in the Bombay Deccan between 1916 and 1921, following up in one case with a study some years later, in something of the Engelsian spirit, revealing the worsening plight of tenants, agricultural labourers and the peasantry under colonialism. Indeed, he also points to the horrendous levels of indebtedness of the peasants, often to local moneylenders. What Mann develops is a valuable internal critique of the social consequences of colonial capitalism; see Mann 1917 and 1921.

social formations transform their constituent elements, not into identical clones of some master instance replicating the same motion, but in a mode of 'structural difference and determinate contradiction'. There is no great inconsistency in respecting both the 'methodological imperative' implicit in the concept of totality or totalisation, while paying attention to 'discontinuities, rifts, actions at a distance, and so on'.[95] To think in categories like (abstract) capital and (abstract) labour (the capital relation) is not to obliterate or do violence to categories generated within other fields of self-understanding, but to acknowledge that such categories are only relatively autonomous. There may be many culturally specific names for work, but over time, under the dominion of capital, they come down to different names for socially abstract labour.

Difference is thus conceptualisable within a field constituted not only by the advance of capital as a force invading the lives of people living and working in numerous social formations that are its historical antecedents, but also by the eruptions of revolts, revolutions and class struggles of all varieties engendered by this advance. Given a world in which capital threatens to dissolve all fixed signposts before they have had a chance to be firmly erected, it will not do to treat difference as if it had either secure cultural or geographical coordinates that moreover appear to define some arena of authenticity. Capital as dynamic social form does not allow some static replay of the past. This is not just a methodological issue, but a political one. The challenge of capital's universalism – however truncated, pretentious and hollow – requires a suitable riposte in theoretical, political and scalar terms.

When Chakrabarty confronts the issue of the potential terrain of capital's dominance – if not hegemony – maintaining that History II is not necessarily precapitalist or feudal, he opens up a line of reasoning that reveals tellingly (if quite unknowingly) the political underpinnings of *Provincializing Europe.* Thus, if History II were reckoned to be antecedent to or outside of History I, there would be no way for humans to be '*at home – dwell – in the rule of capital*'; capital would be 'truly a case of unrelieved and absolute unfreedom', obliterating 'human belonging and diversity'.[96] In fact, being at home in the rule of capital, that is, somehow accommodating oneself in a subaltern position to capital, is a rather poor example to choose to make a point about human belonging and diversity. For much of the world, massive and continuous deprivation has become the norm under the rule of capital. People do make themselves at home under bridges, on sidewalks and parks, not to mention refugee

---

95   Jameson 1981, pp. 56–7.
96   Chakrabarty 2000, p. 67, emphasis added to the first quote.

camps, but celebrating being at home in these situations is macabre.[97] As for
the seduction of the commodity and the play of desires, the proper analysis is
to note the co-extensiveness in our times of economy and culture – economic
life 'pervaded by the symbolic systems of information and persuasion' and
culture thoroughly informed by the logic of commoditisation – that making
oneself at home in the rule of capital is very much part of the totalising thrust
of History I.[98]

Might Prakash and Chakrabarty be arguing that rather than focusing on
labour and economy, one might as well focus on human creativity and difference? It is unclear as to why this needs to be a choice. Indeed, one should look
at the manner in which class struggles call forth human creativity, sacrifice,
solidarity, betrayal, not to mention difference as overcoming. So a focus on
the primal struggle at the heart of capital has much to recommend it. Labour
qua labour in the work process of capital – or, for that matter, in any other
antecedent mode of production – has had limited possibilities for expressing
humanity's many-sided creativity. But workers in their attempts to overcome
that situation have been the fount of social creativity. Indeed, the ultimate in
creativity will have to be mobilised to overcome the 'labour-determined' social
form we call capital. Little wonder then that for Marx the 'not-yet' should trump
the 'never'. But what was the 'not-yet' of Marx? Was it the still unrealised potentialities inherent in the capital social form? Was that what he sought to praise
and encourage? Or was it the 'not-yet' of the search for intentional community:
of humans living in dignity as free associations of producers, 'bequeath[ing]
[the earth] in an improved state to succeeding generations as *boni patres famil-
ias* [good heads of household]'.[99] If it is the latter, the 'not-yet' should super-
sede the 'never'; the 'never', then, is a sign of the pessimism and defeatism of
'post'-marked theories of which postcolonialism is only one.

---

97   According to the 2011 Census there were 70,000 homeless in Kolkata, up from 55,000 in
     2001. NGOs feel the actual numbers are much higher, pointing out that states suppress the
     numbers to improve their credit rating; see <http://articles.timesofindia.indiatimes
     .com/2012-09-12/kolkata/33788485_1_poverty-line-beautification-drive-bpl>.

98   Anderson 1998, p. 73.

99   Marx 1981, p. 911. As Marx declared of capital's treatment of nature: 'nature becomes
     purely an object for humankind, purely a matter of utility; ceases to be recognised for
     itself; and the theoretical discovery of its autonomous laws appears merely as a ruse so as
     to subjugate it under human needs, whether as an object of consumption or as a means
     of production' (Marx 1973, p. 410). By contrast, Marx stresses the need for 'conscious and
     rational treatment of the land as *permanent communal property... the inalienable
     condition for the existence and reproduction of the chain of human generations*' (Marx 1981,
     p. 949).

What are the implications of this type of postcolonial critique of the category of labour? In part, of course, it might be a recognition that there are any number of conditions in which working people do not necessarily adopt identities coinciding with their place in the capital relation, especially when it is still inchoate or unfamiliar, or when they are constantly on the move in ways that prevent the consolidation of their working lives. This is true, for example, of migrant labour when it is on the move between farm and factory, subject to the sorts of 'semi-patriarchal, semi-bonded' methods of control in the former that are quite familiar in India and elsewhere, and insecure employment in the latter. But it could also dovetail quite nicely with a broader drive – along a wide spectrum of political persuasions – to effect a wholesale evisceration of working class solidarity. This has been part of a push back against the gains workers had won in the immediate aftermath of the Second World War and during the long boom, becoming particularly acute in the Thatcher-Reagan strategies that have spawned so many imitators elsewhere.

At this political moment, therefore, it is worth reminding ourselves that categories themselves carry a political charge, and that for Marxism the categories of power are not the ultimate ones. The trajectory of contemporary social theory from Weber to Foucault that appeals to it 'is often strategic and involves a systematic displacement of the Marxist problematic'.[100] 'The ultimate "nightmare of history"', Jameson declares, 'is rather the fact of labour itself, and the intolerable spectacle of the backbreaking millennial toil of millions of people from the earliest moments of human history', an 'ultimately scandalous fact of mindless alienated work, and of the irremediable loss and waste of human energies, a scandal to which no metaphysical categories can give a meaning'.[101] The entry of Subaltern Studies and postcolonialism into the discursive sphere informed by the categories of Weber and Foucault is indicative. This particular 'nightmare of history' cannot be conjured away by the aestheticisation of the commodity from which all traces of 'dead' labour have somehow been abstracted.

5.4   'Bourgeois Hegemony' and Colonial Rule

While abstract labour represents, for Marx, a window into the exploitation of workers and the drive towards limitlessness under capitalism, he always maintained that the capital system's universalistic pretensions were rife with

---

100   Jameson 1988, Volume II, p. 162.
101   Ibid.

contradictions and internal limits. At first sight, capital's universalism appears to find its objective resonance in the development of a world market and in the massive transformations in the social and cultural fabric of the *ancien régimes* of Europe. However, ironically, this very development proceeds in a contradictory fashion – creating, overcoming and recreating obstacles to itself, thus leaving in its wake not only a highly uneven and polarised world geography, but also highly localised social formations that appear to share very little in common with one another. Much of this is attributable to a dynamic interaction between *capital as social form and economic system*, driving to subsume and discipline pre-existing forms of production, making them adequate to capital accumulation when not supplanting them altogether with new production processes, and *the class divisions within this new form*. The latter is signified, on the one hand, by the still considerable presence of dominant classes of the old regimes. It is also signified by the masses of working populations, including, in the course of the nineteenth century, significant concentrations of proletarians in the great industrial conurbations of Western Europe, subject to new methods of control and discipline. These are no longer based on extra-economic coercion, but on forms of economic compulsion and gradual co-optation into the institutional structures of parliamentary democracy that emerge in the course of the nineteenth century. The concept of bourgeois hegemony emerges within this new constellation of forces and was the subject of considerable theorisation in the early decades of the twentieth century.

This concept is revived for the study of colonialism by Ranajit Guha in his *Dominance without Hegemony*. Guha begins his attack on the problems of the specificity of the Indian social formation under colonialism and the limits of bourgeois hegemony therein by locating it in a global framework embracing capital's revolutionising of society from the mid seventeenth century onwards. He notes that both in the *Communist Manifesto* and the *Grundrisse*, Marx opens up a 'vista of receding horizons over an endless cultural space'.[102] Compared to the epoch of capital, all earlier social formations were, quoting Marx, 'mere local developments of humanity' and 'nature idolatry'. Capital as a revolutionary force tears down barriers that hem in the development of the material (and scientific) forces of society. But, as Guha notes, this is where the ideal and the reality differ. Capital may posit every limit signified by 'national barriers and prejudices', 'nature worship', 'traditional, confined, complacent, encrusted satisfactions of present needs', as a hindrance and 'get *ideally* beyond it, but that does not mean that it has *really* overcome it'.[103]

---

102   Guha 1997a, pp. 14–15.
103   Marx 1973, p. 410; Guha 1997a, pp. 14–15.

In reality, each 'bourgeois revolution' that had transformed the societies of Western Europe and North America exhibited specific national characteristics based on its ability to transcend the limits imposed by its *ancien régime*. Marx himself ranged Germany, England, France and the United States in an ascending order in terms of the extent and the manner of their adequacy 'with regard to the universalist ideal'. By this reckoning, both 1648 in England and 1789 in France were victories not only for the bourgeoisie, but 'the victory of a new social order, the victory of bourgeois ownership over feudal ownership, of nationality over provincialism, of competition over the guild,...of Enlightenment over superstition...of industry over heroic idleness, of bourgeois law over mediaeval privileges'. By contrast, 1848 in Germany was not 'a question of establishing a new society', but a way of betraying the people and compromising with 'the crowned representatives of the old society...refurbished interests within an obsolete society', in other words, a mere parody of 1789.[104] Guha wishes to locate Indian history under British colonial rule in this regression. Colonial rule in India represented, according to him, an even more egregious compromise with the old order than the German case, as described above. British rule in India, liberal dogma to the contrary, did not represent the expansion of the universalising mission of the Enlightenment or the revolutionary bourgeoisie.

Almost as a reflex of this, the nationalist movement too, Guha argues, did not represent the energies of a revolutionary bourgeoisie able to assimilate the class interests of the peasants and workers into 'a bourgeois hegemony'. Rather, the Indian National Congress, as the voice of the leading sectors of the Indian bourgeoisie, found itself flanked both by communalism and autonomous peasant and working class politics, never being able in that regard to become the 'representative of the whole society'. 'Nothing testifies', Guha adds, 'more clearly to the predicament of a bourgeoisie nurtured under colonial conditions and its difference from its opposite numbers in Western Europe'.[105] Therefore, not only did colonial rule fail to bring to India the universalistic *élan* of the English and French bourgeoisie in their respective revolutionary moments, but the historiography of India produced by the colonial rulers represented merely the particular interests of the colonisers in their portrayal of Indian history as an interesting chapter in British history. That is, they denied any autonomous creative role to social and cultural forces in the subcontinent itself. Guha likens

---

104   Marx, 'The Bourgeoisie and the Counter-Revolution', *Neue Rheinische Zeitung No. 169*, December 1848, <www.marxists.org/archive/marx/works/1848/12/15.htm>. Both passages are cited in Guha 1997a, p. 18, but Guha renders 'refurbished' as 'renewed'.

105   Guha 1997a, pp. 130–3.

this to a form of appropriation, or expropriation. British dominance (without hegemony) in India was registered and objectified in the appropriation of the Indian past, ousting Indians from the 'site of an autochthonous occupancy, violating the traditions of a pre-existing right of use'.[106] In this way, Guha links the contradictory, historically compromised, universalising mission of capital with the nature of colonial rule in India and the subsequent failures of the Indian bourgeoisie to go beyond their particular interests to represent their hegemony over the entire society. The political point, of course, is to show that only an autochthonous Indian historiography of India could begin to point the way out of this impasse, presumably to recover some sort of autonomous space in which such a role might be articulated.

I have argued in Part IV that the 'Indian historiography of India' Guha singles out for elaboration hardly makes much headway in this direction – producing at best a very limited and qualified version of the universalism of its English or French counterparts. In reflecting on Guha's phrase – the 'site of an autochthonous occupancy' – the identity of the occupants is a key issue. Had not expropriations of the so-called tribal groups already occurred prior to colonial rule, and was that not the settled reality of the India that the British came to control? And were not the expropriators the ones who worked with the British to set in place key components of the colonial social order? The price of this type of historical amnesia – in answering the question of who was to write a history of Bengal ('anyone who is a Bengali' writing in *bhadralok* Bengali) – is indeed to reduce the Indian past to a *tabula rasa*, a null-point, accepting (to all practical purposes) the colonisers' view that the history of the colony begins with their arrival.

But the uncertainties revealed by Guha's argument lie deeper, in his schematic discussion of the concept of bourgeois hegemony, the mechanical counterposing of dominance and hegemony, and a historiography that fails to reckon with the burning out of the bourgeoisie's revolutionary *élan* in the heartlands of the 'bourgeois revolution' in Western Europe. The last, in particular, not only spurred some of the comparative enquiries of Marx and Engels, but also Gramsci's investigations of Italian politics and his working out of the concepts of hegemony, passive revolution and transformism in his *Prison Notebooks*. The following pages will turn to an examination of these issues.

---

106   Guha 1997a, pp. 194–5.

5.5 Modernity in the 'Fullest Sense'

The term hegemony itself, as Perry Anderson reminds us, was not coined by Gramsci. It had a long 'prehistory' in debates and discussions within the ranks of the Russian Social Democrats, and later the Comintern following the Russian Revolution of October 1917. The slogan of the hegemony of the proletariat in a Russian bourgeois revolution was a common political inheritance for Bolsheviks and Mensheviks of the Russian Social Democracy from 1901 onwards.[107] At the Fourth Congress of the Comintern, in 1922, the term hegemony was extended, perhaps for the first time, to the domination of the bourgeoisie over the proletariat, referring to a situation in which the former succeeded in confining the latter to a 'corporative' role: 'The bourgeoisie always seeks to separate politics from economics, because it understands very well that if it succeeds in keeping the working class within a corporative framework, no serious danger can threaten its hegemony'.[108] In this formulation, the economic-corporative, domination and hegemony are combined in a tightly integrated set of concepts. Gramsci's studies of the history of bourgeois hegemony in Western Europe evidently drew on this conceptual inheritance, vastly enriching it in the process, and it was further premised on what he saw as the need to construct the 'proletarian antithesis' of bourgeois hegemony in countries where the bourgeoisie had created a much more elaborate political-cultural structure than had historically existed.[109] He took his cue from Lenin, who had said as early as 1918:

[T]he world socialist revolution cannot begin so easily in the advanced countries as the revolution began in Russia – in the land of Nicholas and Rasputin, the land in which an enormous part of the population was absolutely indifferent as to what peoples were living in the outlying regions, or what was happening there. [T]o start without preparation a revolution in a country in which capitalism is developed and has given democratic culture and organisation to everybody, down to the last man – to do so would be wrong, absurd.[110]

---

107 Anderson 1977, pp. 15–16.

108 *Manifestes, Thèses et Résolutions des Quatre Premiers Congrès Mondiaux de l'Internationale Communiste 1919–23* (Paris 1969 reprint), p. 171, cited in Anderson 1977, p. 18.

109 Thomas 2009, p. 223.

110 Lenin, 'Report on War and Peace', dating from 7 March 1918, published in 1923, cited in Thomas 2009, p. 205.

According to Gramsci, the period from the French Revolution of 1789 to about the revolutions of 1848, and perhaps up to about the time of Paris Commune of 1870, was a period of expansion in which the new state of a victorious bourgeoisie – with the ever-present threat of popular rebellion – undertook a 'programme of social and political "education" and elevation'.[111] During this period, the bourgeoisie was able to present itself as possessing all the 'intellectual and moral forces necessary and sufficient for organising a complete and perfect society'.[112] In arguing thus, as Thomas notes, Gramsci was supplying a political counterpart to *The Communist Manifesto's* praise of the bourgeoisie's economic transformations, the two seen in a 'complex relation of dialectical interaction', wherein the bourgeoisie presented itself as an 'organism' in continuous movement, capable of absorbing the entire society, assimilating it to its 'own cultural and economic level'.[113] Unlike the previous ruling classes, which were essentially conservative, in the sense that they did not 'tend to construct an organic passage from the other classes into their own' – in effect, being a 'closed caste' – the bourgeoisie had an expansive notion of their role; the State had become 'an educator'.[114] Gramsci saw this as a genuinely revolutionary project, the 'Rubicon beyond which lay modernity in the fullest sense' – which, for Gramsci, signalled the victory of a 'relation between classes', supplanting a 'castal logic'.[115]

For the first half of the nineteenth century at least, the bourgeoisie – or certain sections of it – was confident in its universal claims to produce real historical progress and institutionalise it in a new state form, and if at this stage it had not yet constructed the sophisticated apparatuses penetrating into the 'innermost depths of civil society', which Gramsci calls the 'integral state', it had at least established an 'irrevocable' principle of modern life. Instead of sporadic and largely coercive appearances in public life, the state undertook through its presence in civil society a 'capillary and permanent direction of an entire social fabric'.[116] It is one of the ironies then of the very concept of 'bourgeois hegemony' that the institutional structures of this 'capillary and permanent

---

111   According to Ghosh, Gramsci constructed his historical narrative around the French and
        Italian experiences. The dates and events referred to by Gramsci would seem to bear this
        out, although one might note that some of these developments were not national *per se*,
        but represented at the level of Western Europe, a sort of 'uneven and combined'
        modernity; see Ghosh 2001.
112   Gramsci 1971, p. 271.
113   Thomas 2009, p. 142.
114   Gramsci 1971, p. 260.
115   Burgio 2002, p. 25, cited in Thomas 2009, p. 142.
116   Burgio 2002, p. 29, cited in Thomas 2009, p. 143.

direction' of society were constructed generally in the aftermath of the waning of the bourgeoisie's most revolutionary period. As Gramsci noted, the period after 1848, and more so 1870, ushered in a new phase of historical development.

The 'progressive expansivity' of the bourgeois project encountered an 'organic crisis', signifying not a momentary interruption or internal conflict among the ruling coalition, but rather something more profound: the moment when, as Peter Thomas puts it, the bourgeoisie's claims to universality, to advance the common good, were shown to be in the service of 'particularist interests', namely, the accumulation of capital in the hands of the ruling class.[117] 'Optimistic magnanimity soured into cantankerous parasitism', while consent was redefined to include coercion, or in Gramsci's words, 'the conception of the State as pure force is returned to'.[118]

It is within this complex and contradictory historical development, signified not only by the economic ascent and political consolidation of the bourgeoisie, but also a realignment of class forces, that the construction of a maze of trenches – the array of institutions and associations of the integral state – commenced. It is in the period after 1870 – with the colonial expansion of Europe – that Gramsci sees the full development of this process, whereby the 'internal and international organisational relations of the State become more complex and massive'.[119] The massive structures of the modern democracies, both as state organisations and associations in civil society, are 'for the art of politics what "trenches" and permanent fortifications of the front are for the war of position'.[120]

It is also within this constellation of forces that the modern European states come into existence 'by successive small waves of reform rather than by revolutionary explosions like the original French one', the successive waves made up of a 'combination of social struggles, interventions from above of the enlightened monarchy type, and national wars'.[121] Gramsci saw the Risorgimento, for instance, as being shaped by 'a complex and contradictory historical development which achieves wholeness from all its antithetical elements: their struggles and the reciprocal modifications ... the function of latent and passive forces like the great peasant masses, and above all, naturally the function of international relations', and ultimately directed as much against the (Italian)

---

117   Thomas 2009, p. 145.
118   Gramsci 1971, p. 260.
119   Thomas 2009, p. 148.
120   Gramsci 1971, p. 243; Thomas 2009, p. 149.
121   Gramsci 1971, p. 115.

South and the peasantry as against the old order of the church, the aristocracy and the Austrian alliance.[122]

It would appear, then, that the greatest period of political manoeuvre for the plebeian masses came before the 1870s – and that it was concentrated over a couple of generations at most – between the overthrow of feudal privileges and the onset of the process of full institutionalisation of the integral state of the bourgeoisie. The trenches and permanent fortifications that were being erected as part of bourgeois consolidation were constructed not so much against the old feudal elites as against the workers, whose participation had been vital to the 'bourgeois revolution' in the first place. The discovery of the importance of civil society – the crux of a political definition of modernity – seems to have been largely negated by the obstacles to institutional innovations within it as the state apparatus expanded to encompass civil society.[123]

Part of the realignment of forces in the second half of the nineteenth century was what Gramsci calls 'transformism', the winning over of elements of the opposition, including intellectuals, to the side of the now-chastened and more cautious upper reaches of the bourgeoisie. Gramsci sees two periods of transformism: the first from 1860 to 1900, which he calls 'molecular' transformism, the incorporation of individual political figures formed by the democratic opposition parties into the conservative-moderate 'political class', whose prime characteristic seems to have been its aversion to any intervention by the popular masses in state life; the second from 1900 onwards, involving transformism of entire groups of leftists who pass over to the 'moderate camp'.[124] Transformism, for Gramsci, was part of an 'overarching logic of disintegration' – transformation, absorption and incorporation – an integral part of what he called the passive revolution,[125] dedicated to the goal of preventing the 'cathartic moment' when the subaltern classes cross the line separating an 'economic-

---

122   Gramsci, *Quaderni del Carcere*, cited in Adamson 1980, p. 189.

123   Adamson 1980, p. 221.

124   Thomas 2009, p. 151. Gramsci's study of intellectuals – Benedetto Croce and Piero Gobetti, among others – expresses his understanding of the formation and function of intellectuals in this type of historical milieu; see Gramsci 1995, p. 44.

125   Gramsci touches on the issue of 'passive revolution' at a number of points in his *Prison Notebooks*. He refers to the Risorgimento, for instance, as a 'revolution without a revolution or a "passive revolution"', crediting Vincenzo Cuoco (1770–1823) with the expression. Cuoco, a Neapolitan conservative, had argued in 1799 that Italy could avert its own version of the French Revolution only by an active campaign of social and political reform; Gramsci 1971, p. 59; Adamson 1980, p. 186. However, Gramsci also points to the 'danger of this thesis ... of historical defeatism, i.e. of indifferentism, since the whole way of posing the question may induce a belief in some kind of fatalism, etc.' (Gramsci 1971, p. 114).

corporative' phase from a truly 'hegemonic' one in which they become the genuine 'architect and *faber* of a historical epoch'.[126]

Across much of Europe, the First World War may have destroyed the formal control of the *ancien régimes* of Austria-Hungary, Germany and Russia, but this only modified rather than destroyed the historical accommodations that had been reached between them and the captains of industry and finance. Advanced industrial organisations and mass consumption were as yet confined to the United States of America, while revolution and counter-revolution 'battled [each other] from the Vistula to the Ebro'.[127]

The failure of revolution in Western Europe, in the immediate aftermath of the First World War, also dramatised the extent to which the 'political classes' of the bourgeoisie and its allies could mobilise political common sense in an anti-progressive, anti-revolutionary direction.[128] And even when a fresh surge of the forgotten classes burst forth in a storm of mass movements across interwar Europe, which sought, in Adamson's words, 'to free the political system from the inertia of half a century of transformism',[129] they could be contained, directed against the more militant sections of the working class and the 'foreigners' in their midst, while the top levels of the leadership of those movements made their peace with the various sections of the ruling classes, including the landlords and industrialists. Modernity was caught in an 'Arnoldian twilight',[130] or as Gramsci famously put it: 'the old is dying, and the new cannot be born; in this interregnum a great variety of morbid symptoms appear'.[131]

The triumphant bourgeois project may have suffered setbacks in these historical cross-currents, but it still seems to have been able to endure, and in some senses deliver real progress. In the period between the wars, and more so after 1945, the modern integral state was fully developed, a remarkable achievement, one might think, for a social order faced with chronic political and economic challenges and crises. It was within these constraints that the bourgeoisie found a way to advance its own, now contradictory, form of modernisation – a massive increase in the forces of production through new forms of collective work, the division of labour, and the deployment of the forces of science and technology in factories and farms, the defence of private property, and limitations on the political power of the popular classes.

---

126   Thomas 2009, pp. 151–2.
127   Anderson 1998, p. 81. Some of this is vividly captured in the case of France; see Brown 2011.
128   Adamson 1980, p. 216.
129   Adamson 1980, p. 198.
130   Thomas 2009, p. 148.
131   Gramsci 1971, p. 276.

It was also structurally committed to mystifying the true nature of its project, by 'manufacturing' consent. In the words of Valentino Gerratana:

> a class that manages to lead, and not only to dominate, in a society based economically on class exploitation, and in which the continuance of such exploitation is desired, is constrained to use forms of hegemony that obscure this situation and mystify this exploitation; it therefore needs forms of hegemony designed to give rise to a manipulated consent, a consent of subaltern allies.[132]

The climax and hub of the institutionalisation of the 'capillary and permanent direction' of society, the forms of hegemony that 'obscure' the limits on the working class's room for manoeuvre within advanced capitalism, is indeed the Western parliamentary state that took shape during the course of the second half of the nineteenth century, with significant variations across Western Europe, and further consolidated itself in the inter-war and post-Second World War years. Parliamentary democracy, which Anderson dubs the 'objective structure of a once great – still potent – achievement', is where bourgeois hegemony has been really secured. In his opinion, the highly elaborated 'cultural control systems', including mass education and the mass media, within civil society play at best a critical complementary role, as does the 'distorting prism' of market relations and the numbing structure of the labour process.[133]

The subjective side of this development – the novelty of consent under advanced capitalism – is rooted in the structural separation of the economic and the political, and the sense emerging from universal suffrage and regular elections that the parliamentary state represents the juridical sum of its citizenry, reflecting 'the fictive unity of the nation back to the masses as if it were their own self-government'.[134] The working class – confined to an economic-corporative role undertaken through the proper representative channels – may conclude that they exercise an ultimate self-determination within the existing social order and tolerate their impotence because there is a belief that there is really no ruling class, and that bourgeois democracy offers real freedom. Or as Lenin was to put it: 'Whereas the Russian Tsars ruled by force, the British and French bourgeoisie had developed another method, the method of deception,

---

132   Gerratana, 1997, cited in Thomas 2009, p. 227.
133   Anderson 1977, p. 29.
134   Anderson 1977, p. 28.

flattery, fine phrases, promises by the million, petty sops, and concessions of the inessential while retaining the essential'.[135]

Of course, bourgeois hegemony does not simply rest there: a more careful scrutiny of the matter would also highlight a structural difference between the rule of the Russian tsars and Western parliamentarians. The normal conditions of the ideological subordination of the masses – the day-to-day routines of parliamentary democracy and the operation of the variety of cultural-institutional 'trenches' of the integral state – are themselves backed up by a 'silent, absent force', which gives them their currency: the state's monopoly of violence.[136] Deprived of this monopoly, Anderson maintains, the system of cultural control would be instantly fragile, since the limits of possible action against it would disappear. With the backing of this force, the state is immensely powerful. In the normal course of life, violence may not appear within the 'bounds of the system'. The normal structure, then, of capitalist political power in the democratic states is simultaneously and indivisibly '*dominated* by culture and *determined* by force'.[137] Anderson maintains that a 'non-additive and non-transitive' relationship exists between ideology and repression, consent and coercion. The Western parliamentary-democratic state was stronger than the Tsarist state because it rested not only on the 'consent' of the masses, but also on a '*superior repressive apparatus*'.[138]

Gramsci, Anderson suggests, had underestimated the structural underpinnings of bourgeois hegemony in a 'superior' repressive apparatus, and the latter's functional relationship to the representative machinery of 'suffrage and parliament'. But that appears now to be a misreading. As Thomas reminds us, Gramsci maintained that coercion was not eclipsed by consent, nor was their 'combination' a merely external relation, a sum of distinct parts. Rather, coercion and consent 'counterbalance' one another in a unity that requires the maintenance of a precise 'unbalanced' equilibrium between its poles. In parliamentary regimes, coercion is the 'ultimate guarantee' of consent, 'coercion by consent', as it were. Domination, including the silent, absent force of coercion, is conceived as including hegemony as one of its necessary moments.[139] Undoubtedly, this type of coexistence and co-determination of coercion and persuasion, repression and co-optation is only conceivable within the very specific historical form of the capital relation, wherein a class of juridically free

135   Lenin, cited in Anderson 1977, pp. 26–7.
136   Anderson 1977, pp. 42–3.
137   Anderson 1977, pp. 42–3, emphasis added.
138   Anderson 1977, p. 52, emphasis added.
139   Gramsci 1971, cited in Thomas 2009, pp. 164–5.

workers separated from their means of subsistence confronts a class of people with a monopoly of the means of production. A juridically free exchange of labour power for wages mediates the exploitation of workers in the production process. Outside the production process lies 'the very Eden of the innate rights of man'.[140] If these are historical rather than innate rights, they are not thereby an illusion.

Anderson is right to stress the novelty of consent under capitalism – a purely secular, non-ascriptive, universal form of legitimisation, resting on a free if unequal exchange between capitalists on the one side and workers on the other, which is the source of surplus value, the basis of profit, the very lifeblood of the entire system and a perennial mystery. *Pace* Gerratana, the bourgeoisie is not required to mystify it. Workers are apparently quite able to manage the mystification without help. The resistance to Marx's exposition of the roots of the unequal exchange between labour and capitalists is grounded in its profoundly counter-intuitive form, its expositional challenges formidable enough to have required three dense volumes of an unfinished opus. If modernity in the fullest sense lies on this side of the Rubicon, and it is, in Gramsci's terms, a relationship of classes, then on the other side must lie something else whose imagination requires going beyond modernity.[141]

5.6   Beyond the Bourgeois Revolution? Hegemony Revisited

In thinking about these issues, and particularly about the ways in which the advanced capitalist system has worked to confine the working classes to an economic-corporative framework, a critical understanding has to reach beyond the policies of transformism, co-optation into the integral state of political and civil society, or, for that matter, bourgeois ideology in whatever historical sense one uses the term. Other, more objective mechanisms operate:

---

140   Marx 1977, p. 280.
141   It goes without saying that there are other definitions of modernity, which obscure the relationship of classes that is integral to Gramsci's. For instance, Jameson writes of Marx applying himself 'to demonstrate that socialism was more modern than capitalism and more productive' (Jameson 2011, p. 90). In other texts, Jameson's understanding of modernity also appears to have a class-relational component to it. For a variety of reasons, it seems preferable to foreground the centrality of class relations to an understanding of modernity. In which case, socialism will have to be something else, based on overcoming the most developed form of class relations obtaining under capitalism. This is consistent with Postone's understanding of the mediating role of labour in the production of surplus value under capitalism.

for example, the effective repressive powers of the state, the politics of the par-liamentary form, not to mention the multiple lures of the commodity econ-omy at large and the possibility of social mobility in an expanding and highly innovative system of production.

Within the parameters of the ever-present possibilities of crisis and peri-odic contractions of the economy (recessions, depressions), capitalism none-theless has had a hugely transformative effect on the lives of people subjected to its disciplinary powers. In countries where these have not operated, and still do not operate with any widespread degree of effectivity, the order of the day appears to be a combination of long-running insurrections – often lumped together under the rubric of 'Maoism' – and brutal repression from above.[142] A map of the worldwide distribution of overt violence from above and insur-rections from below ought to give us some approximation of the limits to the operation of hegemonic political-cultural forms. The latter should be under-stood as systems of effective containment of the tendencies mentioned above with some real social gains to sustain their legitimacy, held together, as it were, by the buoyancy provided by the system of capitalist production.

In any case, the issue of bourgeois hegemony brings together the political and the economic: the political, as we have seen, involving the development of the integral state within a process of the 'passive revolution', not to men-tion the interpenetration of 'political society' (the state) and 'civil society'; the economic involves the development of capitalism as a socio-economic sys-tem, premised upon the effective separation of the immediate producers from their means of subsistence who then have no option but to sell their labour power for a living wage,[143] the monopolisation of the means of production by a class of capitalists, the very special economic dynamism associated with

---

142   For an excellent analysis of the vast rural rebellion in the so-called tribal regions of central and eastern India, distinguishing the aims of the peasant uprisings there from the aims of the CPI (Maoist), see the interview with Jairus Banaji in *Platypus Review*: <www .platypus1917.org/2010/08/06/the-maoist-insurgency-in-india-end-of-the-road-for-indian-stalinism/>.

143   Just to make my point here very clear, effective separation does not imply physical removal from the property in question. As the prior references to Lenin's work on the development of capitalism in Russia and the Indian mode of production debate should indicate, history yields any number of examples of actual situations in which apparent continuities with prior tributary-style modes of production last well into the twentieth century, and even to this day. However, it also seems to be the case that some examples of the purer form of the capital relation are a requirement on the global level for the other, more 'archaic' forms to continue under the worldwide domination of the capitalist mode of production. That is, the continuation of seemingly archaic forms provides examples of

the resulting recombination of the means of production and the labour power of the now propertyless workers in collective labour processes of increasing scale and sophistication. This is hardly the place to trace in any degree of detail either the emergence of a bourgeoisie out of the decay of the feudal system, or the co-evolution of base and superstructures and the expansionary pressures they exerted over the centuries that have seen capital as a social form emerge as a worldwide phenomenon.

A useful point of departure for a more summary exposition is Ellen Wood's caution against identifying 'bourgeois' with 'capitalist' and both with 'modernity'.[144] All of these are tied into some hypertrophied claims about the Enlightenment – whether favourable or, now in postcolonial circles, largely unfavourable – being the source of rationalism and rationalisation. In this view, the Enlightenment is supposedly the major turning point in the evolution of modernity, and by conflating modernity with capitalism, the Enlightenment is made the parent of the latter as well. Economic rationalisation, a feature of capitalist production, is then assimilated to Enlightenment reason as the informing principle that gave us science, democracy, and so on. Ergo, capitalism, science and democracy co-evolve out of a single overarching eighteenth-century development. To unravel this line of reasoning, Wood argues that much of the Enlightenment project belongs to a 'distinctly *non*-capitalist – not just *pre*-capitalist – society',[145] emerging at a time of royal absolutism in France, associated with an overwhelmingly rural society and fragmented markets of commercial profit-taking. That is, it was based on profits of alienation, rather than profits generated via the production of surplus value in a labour process that brought together capitalists and proletarians. Now, we must remember, of course, that for Marx, no less than for Wood, commercial capital was not the origins of modern capitalism. The elements of a precapitalist system – for example, commerce or merchant capital – are not evolutionary predecessors of modern-day capital.[146] This non- or anti-teleological reading of merchant capital is a useful way of addressing the tendency to simply conflate all forms of capital together via the resort to prefixes like 'proto' or adjectives like 'incipient'.

The bourgeoisie in this absolutist social formation was not a capitalist class; the main bourgeois actors in the French Revolution were professionals, office-

---

the uneven-combined nature that capital assumes on the world stage. For a detailed examination of one such case, see Kaiwar 1989, and Kaiwar 1994, pp. 793–832.

144   Wood 2002, p. 182.
145   Wood 2002, p. 183.
146   See Marx 1981, pp. 379ff (Part 4); Jameson 1981, p. 139; Jameson 1988, Volume II, p. 155.

holders and intellectuals. 'Their quarrel with the aristocracy', as Wood cogently notes, 'had little to do with liberating capitalism from the fetters of feudalism'.[147] The Enlightenment idea of universalism arose from an aversion to feudal particularism and privilege. As for the bourgeois attitude to the absolutist state, Wood points out that as long as the bourgeoisie had lucrative careers as functionaries of the state, they had no problem with it; indeed, far from repudiating absolutist principles, they 'simply extended them'.[148] As Hobsbawm notes, many of the more politically cautious and moderate continental champions of the Enlightenment put their faith in enlightened absolute monarchy.[149] Paradoxically, however, the Enlightenment also stood for general human emancipation – in which case, it could be read as an emancipatory universalism and an abolition of the prevailing social and economic order of royal absolutism, which would explain its attraction for radical thinkers and revolutionaries.[150]

To underline the full complexity of the situation, Wood draws on the contemporary example of England, a country that had developed a national market for everyday mass consumer goods (especially food and textiles), with an agricultural economy that already operated on capitalist principles by the eighteenth century, and that was well on the way to launching the first Industrial Revolution. Here the characteristic ideology was not Cartesian rationalism and rational planning, but the 'invisible hand' of classical political economy and the philosophy of British empiricism. Even the English state, as Wood notes, was far less 'rational' than the bureaucratic French state, and English Common Law, based on a tangled skein of precedent, far less so than the Roman Law-based French codes.[151] English improvement consisted of improvements to property, not to humanity *per se*.

The Brenner debate – in particular Brenner's own contributions to it – underline the extent to which merchants were not the agents of a revolutionary transformation of production, which was largely carried forward in the seventeenth century and the first half of the eighteenth century by members of the English aristocracy and gentry in collaboration with their yeoman

---

147   Wood 2002, p. 184.
148   Wood 2002, p. 186.
149   Hobsbawm 1996a, p. 22.
150   Ibid.; Wood 2002, p. 187.
151   Wood 2002, p. 188. Wood offers some qualifications to show that there were English thinkers interested in Enlightenment values and French thinkers interested in English-style improvements, but the contrast she offers is compelling for the period from about the mid-eighteenth- to mid-nineteenth century.

tenantry, in quite specific historical circumstances.[152] Indeed, Brenner's argument sees the early instances of agrarian capitalist development as unintended and, in the first instance, highly localised breakthroughs brought about by class struggles over traditional usufructuary rights to land, or unintended consequences of demographic growth or parcellisation of peasant property in areas where peasant property was individually held, rather than any visionary idea of new and untested possibilities undertaken by a revolutionary bourgeoisie.[153] Or, as Brenner concludes, pre-capitalist economies have 'an internal logic and solidity which should not be underestimated', and capitalist development in the early historical instances is 'more limited, surprising and peculiar' than is often appreciated.[154] Brenner's argument seems to suggest that a transformation of the very basic level of agricultural production was a necessary moment in the initial development of capitalism. Subsequent cases would be less dependent on localised breakthroughs in the agrarian sector in order to detonate a process of economic development, being able to draw on the accumulated experiences of the pioneers and a variety of actions undertaken by the state.

Early industrial development in England rested on the innovations of 'small men' like Robert Owen, an ex-draper's assistant, who in 1780 borrowed £100 in what were localised circuits of lending to start a cotton mill. By 1809, he had bought out his partners in the New Lanark Mills for £84,000 in cash.[155] As late as the 1830s, Hobsbawm points out, cotton manufacturing was the only British industry in which the factory or the 'mill' predominated.[156] Factory production was slow to develop in other branches of textile production. The machinery that drove the first industrial revolution in cotton manufacturing in England was based on simple innovations carried out by craftsmen and artisans. Even

---

152   Ashton and Philpin 1985. The Brenner debate, as it came to be called, was launched by a *Past and Present* article by Robert Brenner in 1976, and was concluded by Brenner's response to his critics in the same journal in 1982; Brenner 1976; Brenner 1982.

153   Brenner distinguishes three variations on conditions in Europe itself: the English, the French, and the Eastern European, all of which produced quite radically different economic outcomes from political struggles over landed property rights and extra-economic coercive powers. Thus, any notion of a precocious Europe-wide breakthrough to capitalism is simply false; see Brenner 1976, pp. 30–75; Brenner 1986, pp. 23–53, in particular pp. 52–3.

154   Brenner 1986, p. 53. McLennan also notes: 'material and social relations can be long-term, effective real structures that set firm limits to the nature and degree of practical effect that accident and agency can have' (McLennan 1981, p. 234).

155   Hobsbawm 1996a, p. 36.

156   Hobsbawm 1996a, p. 37.

the critical innovations of the so-called second industrial revolution – the steam-engine, mining, and the railways – were driven by men like George Stephenson, the self-made colliery mechanic, or people like Matthew Boulton and James Watt who despite their slightly more genteel background were, what Hobsbawm terms, products of an intellectual climate in which practical tinkering rather than technological education was the norm.[157]

In these circumstances, clearly the development of capitalism did not require, in the first instance, bourgeois hegemony at all. Neither did the positions of a radical bourgeoisie in the ideological sphere guarantee the development of capitalism. France remained in the eighteenth and nineteenth centuries far behind England in that regard. By the late nineteenth century, it had been economically outstripped by a newly unified and rapidly industrialising Germany, hardly a place one associates with a radical Enlightenment-inspired class of capitalists. If, indeed, over time, capital and the bourgeoisie did converge to the point that later thinkers like Weber could conflate Enlightenment rationalism with English rationalisation (improvement), this was the result of a long historical process. This involved a de-radicalisation of Enlightenment ideas, consistent with the end of the more revolutionary aspirations of the bourgeoisie in the period after 1830 or so, and long-term trends in capitalism. The latter were the consequence of further rationalisations of production as it moved from farming and small-scale family firms to larger-scale production based on factories, together with the mobilisation of sciences like chemistry and physics and the applied arts like engineering.[158]

The 'bourgeois revolution' is thus a historically variable convergence – not the outcome of the actions of a promethean group fired by revolutionary zeal. The best that one can say is that the bourgeois revolution – that might finally be resumed as a combination of the radical principles of the Enlightenment,

---

157   Hobsbawm 1996a, p. 187.
158   See, for instance, the work of Alexander Gerschenkron, who proposed the idea of 'latecoming' development that does not replicate the stages of development of earlier developing capitalism, but indeed leapfrogs to the latest technologies and takes advantage of the development of technical and theoretical education in the physical sciences, not to mention banking and related methods of concentrated mobilisation of finance. His paradigm case of the latter methods was post-unification Germany; see Gerschenkron 1962. Once the social form associated with capital had established itself in one country, or parts thereof, and that country could exert wider influence through economically and politically expansionary policies, it could serve to kick-start subsequent transformations, except under certain colonial circumstances where such development was blocked. But Amsden examines the varying recent experiences of a number of former colonial countries, which suggests that colonial-era obstacles are no longer decisive; see Amsden 2001.

the development of an integral state with its hub in parliamentary democracy, and the development of an unprecedentedly dynamic economic form – is a somewhat summary term for a whole series of historical evolutions. The latter might take in, over a long epoch, a diverse spectrum of autonomous developments that we name the Renaissance, the Reformation, the Enlightenment, not to mention struggles over land and property, a range of civil rights, the working day, and so on – all of which contributed, in a non-teleological and contingent fashion, to an outcome that now seems a *fait accompli*.

This last idea is reinforced by the observation, made by Anderson and others, that the development of the complex of state, economy and civil society, which we associate with the 'bourgeois revolution', had little to do with the outright revolutionary victories of the bourgeoisie over the *ancien régime*. Abstractly designating a 'bourgeoisie' as the agents of a far-reaching transformation might serve as part of a simplistic class-analysis mode of writing history, but then what we have is a *deus ex machina*, a demiurge driven to remake the world. In this formulation the very historicity of the 'bourgeois revolution' – however inexact the phrase itself may be – will be lost. Arguably, the hegemony of a dominant social order could signal a situation in which the universe of all classes is more or less fully contained in an elaborate set of constraints constituted by the normal workings of a system. The bourgeois revolution has to be understood not so much in class terms, even retrospectively, but as a complex historical effect. It is worth being reminded that if the initial thrust towards modern capitalism was driven by members of the aristocracy and gentry, then 'the civic freedoms and suffrages of bourgeois democracy' as a regular, taken-for-granted aspect of our lives, 'whose loss would be a momentous defeat for the working class', were historically put on the agenda by grass roots revolutionary movements and consolidated in part by the labour movement.[159]

In view of the above, any simplistic notion of 'bourgeois revolution' must give way to a complex series of innovations, interventions and mediations, by which a particular socio-economic order, associated with capitalism and bourgeois democracy, was constructed in Europe. Bourgeois hegemony might be seen as a moment of historically determinate consolidation, rather than the origination of the process. This is not to deny that the cumulative result was anything other than a transformation of life in Europe, signalling the arrival of

---

159　Anderson 1977, p. 28. The examples of the 1848 revolutions and the Chartist movement comes to mind here. By the late 1850s, Chartism, as an independent movement of the working classes, had died away and even its most persistent champions like Ernest Jones (1819–69) had reorganised themselves as a 'pressure group' on the 'radical' left of liberalism; see Hobsbawm 1996b, p. 31.

modernity as we understand it. And it is in this context that Thomas's point about Gramsci's theory of hegemony – that is, as not simply a generic set of maxims about the manner in which consensus was achieved in 'governance', a technical act, but instead as a continued commitment to revolution – strikes an important corrective note.[160] In other words, his *Prison Notebooks* project was a politically informed theoretical effort, following Lenin's maxim, that in countries where advanced capitalism and democracy had developed, the call for a revolution to overcome capital would be a much more difficult and protracted endeavour. Perhaps it was also motivated by a sense that the sort of 'deterministic' confidence that had propelled revolutionary thought of an earlier generation[161] was no longer sufficient after the defeats of workers' uprisings in Germany and Italy, and the subsequent rise of fascism.[162]

Thomas argues that Gramsci made a conscious theoretical effort to 'reconstruct' the history of the bourgeois integral state from the perspective of a 'truth revealed' during an attempt to overcome it. The guiding thread of Gramsci's carceral research was the search for 'an adequate theory of proletarian hegemony in the epoch of the "organic crisis" . . . of the "integral State" '.[163] Insofar as the proletariat was constrained to develop its hegemonic project from a subaltern position, its 'theoretical comprehension' had to proceed from the theoretical dissection of the solidified integral state as an expression of the culmination of 'bourgeois hegemony' to its practical dismantling in reality. If the conditions in which the project was undertaken were 'necessarily national', the perspective from which they were viewed was equally *'necessarily internationalist'*.[164] Gramsci's great merit was to resist seeking 'general laws' of historical development in favour of developing a view that linked theory and practice by identifying concretely and historically how people came to constitute – and could therefore reconstitute – their worlds,[165] an arduous method and, one would think, worthy of further effort in our times.

Gramsci's argument about the bourgeoisie having an expansive understanding of its role as 'educator', forging an 'organic passage from the other classes into their own', classes it sought to lead (and dominate) via the interpenetration of political and civil society, has probably encountered a sort of historical terminus in our day. Not only has capital implanted itself in a number of

---

160   Thomas 2009, pp. 220–1.

161   See, for example, Engels 1989 [1892].

162   Gramsci 1968, pp. 69–70; see also Engels 1989 and Suvin 1976, pp. 66–7.

163   Thomas 2009, pp. 136–7.

164   Thomas 2009, p. 223, emphasis added.

165   Adamson 1980, p. 235.

countries that appeared not to be tracing their own autochthonous path to capitalism, but the very historicity of the uneven and combined development that resulted has had an impact on the Western, erstwhile colonial powers. Here, one might say, following Perry Anderson, that the bourgeoisie itself – as known to 'Baudelaire or Marx, Ibsen or Rimbaud, Grosz or Brecht' or, for that matter, Gramsci – has all but vanished in a world in which capital has thrust its way past all remnants of the hitherto 'unvanquished' older social formations. For as Anderson argues, following Schumpeter, capitalism as an 'intrinsically amoral economic system', driven by profit-maximising and dissolvent of all barriers to the cold cash-nexus, 'depended critically on pre-capitalist – in essence, nobiliary – values and manners to hold it together'. As those have failed in the postmodern moment of capital, a symptomatic feature has been, indeed, the disappearance of the 'substantial figures ... grandees from a seigniorial past'.[166] In the new constellation of a globe-encircling capitalism, what we have instead of that solid amphitheatre is an 'aquarium of floating, evanescent forms – the projectors and managers ... administrators and speculators' of global capital, functions of a 'monetary [financial?] universe that knows no social fixities or stable identities'.[167] This intensifies the paradox noted earlier, namely, that when the bourgeoisie seemed to be at its most developed, it was culturally and politically, to an extent, in partnership when not dominated by the aristocracy and its camp followers across much of the Continent, while capitalism itself was in a somewhat rudimentary state. But as capital has established itself as a dominance *par excellence*, the bourgeoisie itself, in its classical sense, has vanished in all but name.

The working class, or more narrowly its supposed representatives in the Social Democratic and Labour parties, has historically played a crucial role not in trying to overcome capital, but in managing its contradictions, as the capitalist system has lurched from one crisis to the next. And here we might go further to propose that in recent decades even this role has eluded it, as the formerly working-class parties have gradually distanced themselves from the class they were supposed to represent.[168] The working class itself – as a solid amphitheatre of organised forces with stable careers and a pathway into organised politics – has gone with the bourgeoisie. To speak now of 'bourgeois hegemony' is absurd; what we have are unstable formations operating massive surveillance and coercion, under the appearance of continuities of constitutions, laws and

---

166   Anderson 1998, p. 85.

167   Ibid.

168   Driver and Martell 1998; Driver and Martell 2001, p. 48; and the debate with Rubenstein 2000.

precedents. The dominant has emerged more visibly from behind the screen of the determinant in the age of the dictatorship of the bankers. The absence of an organised response to the present crisis is a function of determined union-busting, disorganisation and fragmentation, workplace bullying even of the most abstractly computerised and impersonal variety,[169] rather than of ruling-class persuasion. Socio-economic polarisation has once again acquired a nakedness and divisiveness reminiscent of the early industrial period.

The question that Lenin and Gramsci suppressed was why the proletariat of the advanced countries should want a revolution in the first place. Was it simply to fulfil a prediction that Marx made, or to help out Third World countries that had launched a successful blow against imperialism? If capitalism could provide democratic culture and economic advances down to the last person, then perhaps for the workers themselves the current management into which they had been co-opted was doing its job. If not, they could change the management through elections, rather than take over the shop altogether. By comparison, we now have a rather different moment: there is a need, objectively considered, to take over the shop, but it seems that the forces for it no longer exist. If in the age of imperialism, hegemony took on the form of 'trenches' and 'fortifications' that slowed the progress of the proletarian forces, then what form does 'hegemony' – if, indeed, this concept is still valid – take now, after decolonisation and post-1989? This might signal the need for a great effort to parallel Gramsci's over what sort of transformative agenda to set, and what might be needed in preparation for it, especially in conditions in which many of the classical features of capitalism on which earlier generations of Marxists relied seem to be irrevocably lost. What is certain, of course, is that postcolonialism with its theory of alternative, different and hybrid modernities is singularly unfit for the task.

5.7   The Historic Moment of Colonial Dominance in India

The progressive, revolutionary moment of bourgeois hegemony in Europe was past its prime by the time the mature colonial state came into existence in India. Generally, 1857 is seen as a watershed, the massive uprising of that year in north India coinciding with the terminus of one of the more aggressive phases of territorial expansion post-1818. The uprising of 1857 has been widely interpreted as having been triggered by an accumulation of a whole slew of discontents that finally burst forth in a series of rebellions embracing sections

---

169   Labica 2009, pp. 177–205.

of the army and civilian society.[170] When the dust had settled on the reprisals that came with its suppression in 1858,[171] so the argument goes, the British decided not only to transfer power formally from the East India Company to Parliament, but the more in-your-face, Utilitarian reforms of the earlier phase also came to an abrupt halt. Henceforth, the British were to set up an administrative structure in which not only was policy-making more tightly connected to Whitehall, but also the emphasis became a more sustainable level of surplus extraction in the form of Home Charges, profits to British banks that operated via a host of intermediaries, regular salaries and pensions on a properly regulated scale for civilian functionaries and military officers.

At the same time, with the more secure and rapid transportation and communication made possible by steamships, telegraphs and subsequently the Suez Canal,[172] the very structure of British residence in India changed, and the individual exit option premised upon the development of a rigidly bureaucratic apparatus became more regularly structured and available. The political conjuncture, coinciding with the so-called second Industrial Revolution, and the rise of the United States and Latin America as arenas for capital investment in industrial development, changed the position of India in the total scheme of British imperialism.[173] It is within this overall global context that the localised development of Indian history in the second half of the nineteenth century and the early twentieth century has to be understood. The British would henceforth have no interest in transforming India, leaving it to local propertied classes to run their affairs subject to the continued subordination of India within the parameters of a 'colonial mode of production'. The consequences of this would be ghastly for many in the subcontinent, but quite profitable for some, especially those with access to capital, whether it originated in the metropolis or the colony itself.[174]

For a generation or two after 1857, the consent of the Indian bourgeoisie – a product of British rule, for such a class had no independent existence under the earlier regimes in India – was secured by the spectre of the massive uprising

170   See, for example, Mukherjee 2002.
171   The reprisals are documented in gripping detail by Dalrymple 2008.
172   Headrick 1988.
173   Stone 1968, pp. 311–39.
174   According to George Wingate, one of the architects of the revised revenue settlements in the Deccan, following the riots of 1875 in the Poona and Ahmednagar districts, it was British laws and policies that helped the moneylenders to profit from the misery of the peasantry, setting up the conditions for pauperisation and immiseration on a vast scale, the legacies of which are still with us.

and the undoubted gains offered to them in the form of placement in the lower, provincial reaches of a colonial civil service, jobs in urban administration, and over time within the professional ranks of lawyers, school teachers, college lecturers, and the like. And while many of the more prominent ones were or became critics of British administration,[175] and despite the rhetoric of nationalism, some degree of bourgeois consent was a constant thereafter, fluctuating with the impact of wars, famines, recessions and, more trivially, with the political persuasion of the Viceroys, Prime Ministers, and Secretaries of State for India. Some such sentiment is surely implied in Tilak's statement that the 'Extremists of today will be Moderates tomorrow, just as the Moderates of today were Extremists yesterday'.[176] A process of transformism was working its molecular way through the ranks of radical nationalism. As for the remnants of the old warrior elite, in the decades after 1858 they were slowly turned into a loyal 'aristocracy' with secure titles, an English education, privy purses and so on. Parasitism, rentierism and bureaucracy at all levels came to prevail. India was beginning to look like a proper caricature of England.

For people in those positions, perhaps the nightmare haunting their dreams was popular jacqueries and uprisings, which over time British rule seemed to make more likely, with its sloppy and often callous handling of economic and social issues, especially in relation to rural India. In the first instance, it is arguable, indeed, that the animus of writers like Dutt had more to do with British

---

175 Fierce critics of colonial rule often came from within the ranks of this bourgeoisie. To take but two examples: Romesh Chunder Dutt (1848–1909) and Bal Gangadhar Tilak (1856–1920). Dutt was a graduate of Presidency College, Calcutta, and University College London, and was also a member of the Indian Civil Service, whose brilliant polemical economic tracts made his reputation. He is best known now for his economic history and polemical interventions in the famines debate; see Dutt 1902 and Dutt 1900. But he also wrote prolifically on ancient history and culture, often in an Orientalist mode; see, for example, Dutt 1936. Tilak, a graduate of Deccan College, Poona (Pune), a schoolteacher and journalist, founded journals in both Marathi and English, and while denouncing Western education did not hesitate to ransack the Classicist and Orientalist archives for his studies of race and nation; see, for example, Tilak 1955 [1893] and Tilak 1956 [1903]. Of course, he could not even have conceptualised his case in global racial terms if it had not been for the power and reach of those archives. Tilak was especially drawn to the works of F. Max Müller; see, for example, Max Müller 1883.

176 Excerpts from B.G. Tilak's address to the Indian National Congress of 1907, cited in Tilak 1919, p. 55.

misrule than with any developed nationalist ambition as such. They might have welcomed a partnership in empire, had it been offered.[177]

In the Indian case, the failure of the colonisers thoroughly to renovate the economy and social order follows a common colonial script. They lacked the forces to do so, especially against the resistance of the classes they depended on, who were also the creations of their own rule. At the same time, the situation in Europe itself had settled into its 'Arnoldian twilight' – gains there certainly were, some emanating from the colonial expansion of Europe, but no revolutionary transformations of the socio-political order. One could barely expect colonisers to exceed the logic of the domestic situation that drove them to seek colonies abroad. But this diagnosis needs to be set against their undoubted success – discernible in the longer historical view – in establishing a socio-economic order in which capital and its accessory institutions would establish themselves, however crudely, as the horizon of possibility and desire of most people.[178] In that sense, colonial dominance was an interlude to secure the hegemony of the global capitalist order in India, which in turn has reduced the possibility of a purely autochthonous mode of politics or culture. If modernity in the 'fullest sense' implies the supersession of a 'castal logic' with the 'logic of classes', then certainly what prevailed in India throughout the colonial period and until now (albeit to a lesser extent) was *modernity not in the fullest sense*, where castal logic has pulled against the logic of classes, dominating in some arenas, while giving way in others, and in which a definitive subsumption of the former to the latter was not fully accomplished. Such a situation was clearly unstable, as witnessed by the violent methods often used to secure the domination of a castal logic, but its dissolution is a slow if certain process. In matters like this, the appropriate comparison is not between India and the United States, but between India and the more traditionalist social formations of Europe, which have only begun to unravel completely in the last two generations or so.[179]

---

177   The presence of significant Indian populations in Southeast Asia and East Africa is an example – some of them made considerable fortunes while others toiled in the mines and plantations. For a fine study of this in the case of South Africa, see Bhana and Vahed 2005. See also my review of this book: Kaiwar 2007b, pp. 192–7.

178   A quick visit to India today, a scant two generations after the departure of the British, ought to settle the issue.

179   Apart from the work of Arno Mayer, previously cited, a classic work in this regard is Weber 1976. The process of the modernisation of rural France may have begun in the 1870s, following the Commune, but over half of the population still lived in the countryside as late as 1930, and it was only in the post-Second World War generation that the process was really completed. Richard Wolin believes that some of the dislocations associated with

As Part II of this book argues, a significant shift of initiative occurred in the inter-war years from the colonisers to the Indian bourgeoisie. However weak their hold over the countryside, a partnership with the upper-ranked caste/ economic groups there allowed the Indian bourgeoisie to exercise power, often indirectly via the considerable survival of personalised forms of domination exercised by their rural partners, although here again the direction of change is unarguable – the assertiveness of the lower-ranked caste groups forming, as it were, the red thread of rebellion against the prevalence of an archaic logic of power. The much maligned parliamentary democracy of India does imply a sort of hegemony of the propertied classes, a reaching into and transforma- tion (if only in the mode of a passive revolution) of the lives of people, behind which significant changes have come to India. That much is undeniable, even if the changes have not gone far enough or fast enough. If colonial rule did little to enable the development of civil society to reach down into the lives of the plebeian masses, which would have allowed them to whittle away at the bas- tions of oligarchic power, post-1947 there has been a definite emergence of civil society, a less oligarchic vision of life and a greater challenge to settled privi- lege. Popular politics does express a political dynamic of historic proportions.[180]

In his *Dominance without Hegemony*, Guha maintains that the moment of coercion vastly outweighed the moment of persuasion in colonial rule, but then he argues that the colonial regime utilised many of the indigenous idi- oms to fasten its leadership over the propertied classes of India. Along with this, one might consider the import of the construction, under colonial aus- pices, of racialised models of Indian history, the racialisation of caste, the powerful inducements of Brahmanisation (or Sanskritisation) that have had such perduring effects on the thought and action – and therefore the politics – of substantial ruling sections of the Indian population.[181] This would have

---

the process may have been one of the triggers of the 1968 moment in France; see the interview on WKNO: <www.publicbroadcasting.net/wkno/news.newsmain/article/9088/ 0/1848768/Counterpoint/Interview.with.Richard.Wolin>.

180   Jaffrelot 1998, pp. 35–52; Jaffrelot 2003.

181   Trautmann 1997, pp. 208–11; Kaiwar 2003, pp. 46–51. Ironically, when Bhim Rao Ambedkar sought to organise the Dalits around an autonomist doctrine of politics, he had recourse to the same Aryan model of history that served the upper castes so well, but he employed it as an indictment of race war, carried out by invading 'white' Aryans against the indigenous 'black' people, the so-called *dasyu*, their native opponents and later subjects; see Ambedkar 1970. Ambedkar's argument owes much to Vincent Smith, a colonial civil servant whose book became standard reading for incoming civil servants; see Smith 1958 [1919], p. 32. It is ironic, of course, that the substance of Smith's argument later became part of the historical sociology of Dalit resistance.

allowed the British to extract some degree of 'coercive consent' from those whose collaboration was required for colonial rule to persist. The British presence would then have been the indispensable condition for the emergent nationalist bloc to develop their own version of coercive consent, at least until they were able to shake off their dependence on the colonisers' structures of domination. The political realities of dependence could in turn become the ground on which a discourse of tradition, autonomy and independence was constructed. Nationalism comes in many guises – it is a deceptive ideology whose rhetoric is best not taken at face value.

In this longer time frame, hegemony does not have to imply something progressive or transformative. It simply implies the capacity to lead and co-opt. In the mode of a passive revolution, it involves sufficient reform to head off more radical demands, while buying off the antagonists piecemeal. It could also imply a version of the transformism of intellectuals. So if coercive persuasion is the very core of hegemony, the British version of it appears to have acted well enough to have secured their presence in the subcontinent for almost two hundred years with a very small deployment of civil servants, and an army the bulk of whose rank-and-file and some of the officer corps were recruited from among the populations of the subcontinent. Perhaps there was more persuasion than Guha allows, or at any rate the 'coercive consent' that operated contemporaneously in Europe had its colonial counterpart.[182] And when finally the colonisers left India – after the considerable blood-bath of the partition – what remained to India was a structure sturdy enough to head off insurrectionary solutions to socio-economic grievances, or confine them, by and large, to rural areas in the more backward parts of the country. These are the areas where archaic forms of landlordism and tenancy still prevail – many of them coinciding with the formerly *zamindari* land settlements of the colonial era. Others are in the so-called tribal belt of the east and southeast of the country, often in areas of rich mineral deposits (coal and uranium among them), where state and central governments are pushing to expropriate the people who live there on behalf of large corporations.[183]

---

182   Amitav Ghosh's *The Glass Palace* provides a much better sense of the texture of colonial rule in South and Southeast Asia, and the psychological and social elements that comprised bourgeois and petit-bourgeois worldviews, than either Guha's or Chakrabarty's texts; see Ghosh 2002.

183   Over the last several years, the Indian government has begun a large-scale campaign to combat an armed insurrection led by the Naxals (CPI-Maoist), who now have a presence in 180 of India's 671 districts.

In the end, no stark contrast between metropolis and colony will do – the distinctions call for a more subtle anatomisation. From the vantage point afforded by Gramsci's study of hegemony, we can return to the question of *bahubol* – the force of arms, as Guha defines it. Does Guha mean to suggest that the Bengali historians who sought to develop 'an Indian historiography of India' were in the trenches constructing an alternative historiography as a way towards a counter-hegemony in relation to colonial dominance, even if we accept, for the sake of argument, this disposition of concepts? If so, how successful were they vis-à-vis the Bengali bourgeoisie, peasantry, working class? On the face of it, one presumes, very little. By and large, they seem not to have been able to construct a symbolism and culture of sufficient weight and momentum to function as an alternative code to the colonial capitalist order. One wonders if that was indeed even their aim. After all, the colonial code encapsulated in the way in which caste Hindus were seen as the authentic, autochthonous denizens of the subcontinent, and its natural leaders, served them very well and gave them access to relatively privileged positions in the colonial hierarchy. They were subaltern in the very precise meaning of the term. Even if the colonial rulers did not otherwise develop a successful method of renovating a society in dire need of it, they did develop the institutional and ideological structures that provided the emergent nationalist movement with its grammar and syntax. In this context, an Indian (Bengali?) historiography of India (Bengal?) that advocated a recourse to arms might have been operating not within a revolutionary frame, but, *pace* Guha, within an archaic and limited horizon, a reactionary force rather than a liberating one, more comfortable directing the force of arms against religious minorities and the rural poor than against the colonisers, except via the pseudo-anarchist methods of the assassination of individual representatives of the ruling order.

What was the status of a 'war of manoeuvre' vis-à-vis colonial rule, and why was it largely outstripped by the 'war of position' (in compressed form, Gandhism, as Gramsci called it)?[184] An interesting analysis of the Bengali historiography of Bengal – or more so an Indian historiography of India – would have sought to focus on the ways in which tensions between these strategies revealed themselves, and the pressure of circumstances in which the protagonists moved from one position to the other. Clearly, the answer to those questions must take us well beyond the terrain explored in *Dominance without Hegemony*. A more mature historiography would perhaps have sought precisely ways to address what a war of position would have looked like, not only in textual presentations or in the political exegeses of individual representatives of

---

184   Gramsci 1971, p. 107; Adamson 1980, p. 186.

a nationalist movement, but also at the level of popular struggles, where surely the tensions between those strategic moments must have been most keenly felt. One would expect a historiography dealing with such momentous issues to register, if only in muted accents, the contradictions of colonialism, not least of all the ways in which the hegemony of a social order established itself even as Indian nationalism moved vocally, and sometimes militantly, against its more superficial aspects. The historian's task is to perceive the contradictions where only antinomies are thematisable, especially in a situation in which 'castal logic' appeared to be locked in battle with the logic of classes.

The latter part of the preceding sentence most nearly defines *modernity not in the fullest sense*, and is also the most adequate definition of 'alternative modernity'. In light of that fact, if indeed 'modernisation' is not the script of Indian history as Chatterjee assures us, then is that tantamount to saying that India is forever stuck between a 'castal logic' and the 'logic of classes', and that neither will prevail? One can see how the Guhas, the Chakrabartys, the Chatterjees and the Kavirajs – and the postcolonial intellectual progeny of 1989 – who in their global peregrinations move comfortably from a dominant position in the former to a very cosy position in the latter, might find this situation agreeable. But it is a statement about themselves, and says nothing about authenticity and autonomy or the situation of the working classes, who would undoubtedly prefer modernity in the fullest sense and 'the freedom of moderns' that accompanies it.[185]

If the alternative modernities that do not lead to a replication of the situation in the more advanced countries of the world is the 'forever' situation of India, we must indeed deplore this, and argue the need for a revolution, now no longer a bourgeois revolution whose moment has been historically surpassed. Resistance – mostly by those whom a castal logic favours – involves holding fast to a situation that is to their advantage. What sort of making oneself at home is this? What sort of home? And subversion of what? The linguistic chauvinism by which the Bengali of the *bhadralok* is posited as the vehicle of an Indian

---

185   The phrase in quotes is part of the title of Losurdo's 2004 book. Losurdo cites an intriguing passage in Hegel's *Vorlesungen über die Philosophie der Weltgeschichte* [Lectures on the Philosophy of World History] as follows: 'From France, the Enlightenment moved to Germany, where it gave birth to a new world of ideas. Its principles were interpreted more deeply. Yet, these new notions were not so often distinguished publicly from dogma; rather, sacrifices and distortions were made in order to maintain at least the appearance of the recognition of religion, something which is done, after all, even nowadays' (Hegel, cited in Losurdo 2004, p. 4). The principles of the Enlightenment have most certainly not been deeply interpreted by postcolonial studies, but the 'sacrifices and distortions' to maintain the recognition of difference, of which religion becomes symbolic, remain.

historiography of India, and class struggles have been superseded by a kind of militant nativism, is surely a caricature of Gramsci. Gramsci's exposition of hegemony signals not a political paralysis, nor even a passive reflection of the antinomies of the age, but a sharp registry of the contradictions of his epoch and an attempt to wrest from them the political key to transformative action. From a Gramscian perspective, *Dominance without Hegemony* turns out to be a red herring, promising much but offering little in the way of insight into Indian historiography.

5.8 A 'Liberation from Blinding Bondage', or the Question of Historicism

Chakrabarty's critique of historicism is premised on three positions. The first relates to attempts to write Indian history as if the coming of the British and the undoubted effects it had on Indian culture can be described as a 'liberation of the mind from a blinding bondage to the superstition and customs of the middle ages'[186] – in this case, to struggle against historicism is to tell a different history of reason. The second questions the Eurocentric notion of modernity as a narrative of the arrival of John Locke's 'autonomous, sovereign and propertied individual', supposedly the supreme embodiment of modernity, and in the process gives us other, more communal or familial understandings.[187] The third involves the tendency of historicist narratives to reduce the past to a null-point outside the present from one which charts a course towards a desirable future. While such a periodisation may have played a part in radical programmes of social justice, it may also create a sense that historical time is a measure of the distance assumed to exist between the West and the non-West, which legitimised in the colonies the 'idea of civilisation'.[188] Over time, Chakrabarty states, Locke's theological positions became secularised into the common assumptions and protocols of 'Marxism, liberalism, and similar histories of capitalism, industrialisation, nationalism', and so on.[189] The culmination of Chakrabarty's critique of historicism calls on readers to resist the idea that 'everything can be historicized and that one must always historicize',[190] and therefore to turn away from Jameson's call to 'Always historicize . . . the one

186 Chakrabarty 2000, p. 295.
187 Chakrabarty 2000, p. 236.
188 Guha 1988, p. 43; Chakrabarty 2000, p. 7.
189 Chakrabarty 2000, pp. 22–3.
190 Chakrabarty 2000, pp. 112–3.

absolute and we may even say "transhistorical" imperative of all dialectical thought'.[191]

Chakrabarty's rather casual tossing together of 'Marxism, liberalism, and similar' is hardly a confidence-inducing categorisation of the histories of capitalism, industrialisation and nationalism. The notion that Marxism represents a leftward extension and culmination of liberalism may be one of the instrumentalist myths of postcolonial studies.[192] This can be read in two ways: either that liberalism is the healthy product and Marxism its unhealthy progeny, or that liberalism might be damned by association with Marxism. Both positions will find takers in the contemporary political spread. Indeed, given the rightward drift of US politics, even the mildest forms of reformism might come to be damned by being thrown together into a hopper with a liberalism tainted by Marxism.

However, my main purpose in the following pages is to show that historicism is a much more complex phenomenon than Chakrabarty allows, and that a Marxist historicism sets out precisely to rescue history from metaphysical and speculative formulations. In addition, it carries a radical political charge that involves a future beyond the futures that already exist, to a radically different social order that calls for something other than the rather quietist Heideggerian turn of recent postcolonial studies. The latter is now perhaps mediated, as Said implied, through a Foucauldian theory of power, which 'captivated not only Foucault himself but many of his readers who wish to go beyond Left optimism and Right pessimism so as to justify political quietism with sophisticated intellectualism', while wishing 'to appear realistic, in touch with the world of power and reality'.[193]

The first corrective, of course, is to restate for the purpose of clarification that the attraction for many on the Indian left of studying the 'historic failure of the nation to come into its own',[194] a concern shared by their counterparts in other ex-colonial countries, has a material basis: such failures – both in the immediate context of decolonisation, and more so in the all-encompassing capitalist development of today – carry forbidding social consequences. These include mass poverty, famines, and epidemics, in addition to the chronic grinding down and demoralisation that affect millions of people. Simply to dismiss this as an example of historicism – on the grounds that Indian modernity, for

---

191   Jameson 1981, p. 9.
192   The nonsense involved in this kind of thinking is given a most forensic treatment in
        Losurdo 2004 and Losurdo 2007; see also Mehta 1999.
193   Said 1983, p. 245; Brennan 2006, p. 112.
194   Guha 1988, p. 43; Chakrabarty 2000, pp. 30–1.

instance, does not have the developmental potentiality of its metropolitan counterpart – shows a grievous loss of political perspective.

The battle between 'reason' and 'superstition' is not merely the invidious rhetoric of a colonial power imposing an alien order on pre-existing indigenous forms, but rather constitutes part of a war of position within the bourgeoisie itself: between those conservative elements that united behind a nostalgist ideology, and those that gravitated to more progressive positions. Within the polemics of emergent nationalism, unsurprisingly it took the form of authenticity versus deracination, religion versus secularism, Indian versus Western, tradition versus modernity, and so on. The different history of reason that Chakrabarty wishes to tell us is entirely familiar from other examples, for these polemics are neither uniquely Indian nor, for that matter, colonial, but occurred in every European society – German Romanticism and Russian Narodnism being two examples of cognate instances within Europe.[195] At determinate historical moments, when political-economic transformations threaten to sweep away an established social order, political debate takes on those familiar forms.

As for John Locke and Christianity, the latter is not, in the first place, a 'European' religion, nor is it still confined to Europe. Did Christianity in Anatolia, Egypt, the Balkans, or, for that matter, Kerala, retrace the same connection between the individual and reason? If not, then the Lockean philosophical conception of the autonomous individual is not strictly a matter of Christianity alone, but a more complex outcome of Church-State struggles, the Reformation and Counter-Reformation, the Thirty Years War and so on, deeply embedded in a singular history in which the secular and the theological intersected, or perhaps the secular was informed by a dominant theological idiom that over time gave way under the pressure of events.[196] Was the 'unmarked individual', for instance, more prominent originally in the Protestant Reformation than in the Catholic Counter-Reformation? Chakrabarty's stark Europe-Other binary is in fact an erasure of history – a hypertrophied concern with historicism tending to homogenise vast territories behind unified conceptions of Self and Other. The call to resist historicising the forms taken by cultural and political expression is a conservative, possibly even reactionary, political gesture.

In the same vein, it can be pointed out that a narrative of steady progress is not the *leitmotiv* of Marxist historiography in general. Althusser rightly noted

---

195   Berman 1988, pp. 175–6.
196   See the discussion of the vanishing mediator in Part VI, section III below.

the debilitating effects of this kind of historicism,[197] and Daniel Bensaïd has highlighted that the three volumes of *Capital* offer an organisation of time that involves 'cycles and turnovers, rhythms and crises, strategic moments and contretemps'. Time is layered, fragmented, fractured, and so on, hardly an example of homogeneous unfolding. The 'old philosophy of history' fades into 'a critique of commodity fetishism on the one hand and political subversion of the existing order on the other'.[198] Marx's theory captured the contradictions of the period by insisting that '[m]achinery, gifted with the power of shortening and fructifying human labour, we behold starving and overworking it ... All our invention and progress seem to result in endowing material forces with intellectual life and in stultifying human life into a material force'.[199] Of the sheer wanton destruction of the natural basis of life, Marx said that 'there exist symptoms of decay, far surpassing the horrors recorded of the latter times of the Roman empire', and cautioned that progress is not to be regarded with the 'usual abstractness'.[200]

Rejection of progress in the abstract is also central to Marx's critique of political economy. For as he explains in the third volume of *Capital*, the fetishism that characterises the value form reaches its highest pitch with the further development and elaboration of capital, in particular the attribution to interest-bearing capital – 'the mother of every insane form' – of mystical creative powers apart from any connection to the exploitation of labour.[201] Indeed, this form of fetishism intensifies as the instability of the overall system reaches its apogee in the process occluding the structural antagonisms that were apparent in earlier times. Even Gramsci's argument that colonial domination consigned the colonised populations to the 'past times' of the colonisers can be read in a non-evolutionary manner, rather than as an expression of a 'normative and progressivist' notion of capitalist development.[202] It can be seen as reflecting the extent to which relations of domination impose a structural unity on the disparity of historical experiences – difference then emerges against the backdrop of the structural unity imposed by imperialist expansion. It is only if capitalism is accepted as the final horizon of human possibilities that this

---

197   See Thomas 2009, pp. 29–30 For an extended discussion of Althusser's concerns about historicism, see Thomas 2009, pp. 29–30. For the original expression of Althusser's concerns, see Althusser and Balibar 1970, pp. 119–44 in particular.

198   Bensaïd 2002, p. 3.

199   Marx 1974, p. 298.

200   Marx 1974, p. 298; Marx 1973, p. 109.

201   Marx 1981, p. 596.

202   Thomas 2009, p. 285.

becomes an evolutionist position, otherwise it is a sign of the fractured times of modernity on the world scale.

Marxist transition narratives have been prompted by the understanding that historic ruptures and structural transformations have occurred in the past inaugurating a new epoch associated with capitalism, and are occurring in the present, holding open the possibility of a future that involves the overcoming of capital. A very substantial historiography has developed to understand the nature of these breaks, what they imply for an understanding of the present and the potentialities for a future transformation, which must by the very nature of the existing mode of production present challenges of an altogether different order than the prior transitions.[203]

Somewhat schematically, Marxist accounts of the transition from feudalism to capitalism begin with two fully constituted terms in which the first (feudalism) is not an 'ur-stage' of the second (capitalism). As Jameson notes, what is being investigated in such accounts is a structural transformation. Marx's *Capital*, for instance, does not argue that the elements of a feudal system – say, commerce or merchant capital – are the evolutionary predecessors of modern-day capital.[204] Rather, it offers a 'synchronic' model in which once the capital form is fully constituted, merchant capital or commerce, or, for that matter, the 'original' accumulation of land – the transfer of property by coercive mechanisms, debt bondage and the like – which in feudalism were not anticipatory of anything, can be rewritten as capital's 'preparatory requirements'.[205] The implication of this is that feudalism does not evolve into capitalism; it is finally overcome by its antagonists. In retrospect, the punctual breaks that occurred along the way, and the long-term transformations of a mode of production in its entirety, might be summed up by the word 'revolution'. But this in itself is a protracted process, historically comprising, as Blackbourn and Eley point out, 'two levels of determination and significance':

> the revolution as a specific crisis of the state, involving widespread popular mobilisation and a reconstitution of political relationships, and ... the deeper processes of structural change, involving the increasing predominance of the capitalist mode of production, the potential obsolescence of

---

203   A major intervention in these debates is Callinicos 1989.
204   This has also been shown quite exhaustively by Brenner 1993, with reference to the merchants of the East India Company.
205   Jameson 1988, Volume II, p. 155.

many existing practices and institutions, and the uneven transformation of social relations.[206]

In Bensaïd's words, Marx 'definitively rejects any supra-historical general schema clamped on to the determinate unpredictability of actual historical development'.[207] The four-centuries-long transition involved in the genesis of capital, which was 'sporadic and uneven', was not accomplished solely on some evolutionary potential built into economic forces or production relations, but by way of 'wars, conquests, state intervention, religious conflicts and legal reforms',[208] not to mention struggles over access to the means of subsistence. The full range of consequences of all of the above could not have been foreseen, nor can they serve as a template for predicting the outcome of all the inchoate struggles underway at present. However, once established, a mode of production has definite properties that can be analysed, tendencies that cannot be avoided – for example, towards crises of falling productivity in feudalism or overproduction in capitalism. It is in the wider social and political fall-out of these crises, and the ultimate form of their 'resolution' or overcoming, that the realm of uncertainty begins.

In the meantime, some of the cultural practices associated with an *ancien régime* may be reproduced in everyday life, often via an adaptation of them to the life of the social classes that come to the fore in the new order, but the old social relations of production that underpinned them are superseded. At the same time, powerful institutions may survive revolutions and upheavals – for example, the Church – and constitute within the new order a point of attraction for all manner of disaffected social groups. Marxist narratives are not about simple linear transitions. This has not prevented, it should be said, the construction (whether by Stalinists, Maoists or others) of a mechanical four- or five-stage succession of modes of production, a model of supra-historical development that has had its advocates in India, and was part of the catechism imparted to the faithful in orthodox Communist Party circles. In the teleology built into this model, history progresses from backward to more advanced forms, from 'superstition' to 'reason', if you like, and here a debt to the more mechanical forms of Enlightenment thought sustains the postcolonial critique. Perhaps it is this teleological notion of progress culminating in 'modernity' to which Chakrabarty and others, like Kaviraj, are objecting. But perhaps also implied in their reservations about transition narratives is the

---

206   Blackbourn and Eley, pp. 82–3.
207   Bensaïd 2002, p. 28.
208   Bensaïd 2002, p. 29, citing Godelier 1991.

concern that the vision of the future described by such models – and for which people were expected to make sacrifices – was really a totalitarian nightmare, or had become so in its Stalinist version. But as Jameson notes, while it may be desirable to rid oneself of bourgeois or Stalinist images of progress and the future, to nervously abandon in the process any Marxian vision of the future altogether ('an operation in which Marxism itself is generally abandoned in the process') is much less desirable.[209]

Indeed, as Peter Thomas explains, there was in Gramsci's work both the notion of a 'time of duration' – implying a sort of degenerate progress, 'mere quantity adequately measured in chronological terms', rather like the 'homogeneous, empty time' of Benjamin – and the notion of 'constituting an epoch', among the 'cardinal concepts of the Gramscian theory of history'.[210] If the former implied the persistence of a historical form, 'reproducing itself consistently in the force of the equilibrium between its own capacity of innovation and the progressive development of its own powers of "viscosity"', the latter implied a rupturing of the continuum of the time of duration, 'shatter[ing] its linearity – already in the womb of the preceding social formation...to break into a new historical form'.[211] It is therefore quite odd that a project like Subaltern Studies, which began its work under the sign of Gramsci, should now abandon one of his cardinal concepts. This abandonment makes an unobtrusive appearance in the new 'institutional-realist' spirit of postcoloniality expressed by Chatterjee when he says that 'the postcolonial theorist...is born only when the mythical time-space of epic modernity has been lost forever'.[212] While it might seem that Chatterjee is addressing himself to the question of nationalism, one suspects that riding just below this bourgeois Utopianism is the rejection of the potentiality of a breakthrough into a new historical form. It is also in this light that one tries to decipher the political implications of a statement like the following:

> It is possible to cite many examples from the postcolonial world that suggest the presence of a dense and heterogeneous time. In those places, one could show industrial capitalists delaying the closing of a business deal because they hadn't yet heard from their respective astrologers, or industrial workers who would not touch a new machine until it had been consecrated with appropriate religious rites, or voters who would set fire to

---

209   Jameson 1988, Volume II, p. 154.
210   Burgio 2002, p. 18, cited in Thomas 2009, p. 152.
211   Burgio 2002, pp. 19–20, cited in Thomas 2009, pp. 152–3.
212   Chatterjee 2004, p. 23.

themselves to mourn the defeat of their favourite leader, or ministers who openly boast of having secured more jobs for people from their own clan and having kept the others out. To call this the co-presence of several times – the time of the modern and the times of the pre-modern – is only to endorse the utopianism of Western modernity.[213]

The 'nation' and the 'West' have acquired all manner of valences in postcolonial theories, not least those that are alluded to under Chakrabarty's critique of historicism (described at the outset of this section).

However, in the process of consistently foregrounding the 'postcolonial world' and the West as the prime categories of analysis, we are left with the notion that 'the real space of modern life consists of heterotopia'.[214] This is a world in which industrial capitalists (together with their astrologers and ministers) exist alongside industrial workers (and presumably the masses of marginally employed and unemployed) in a dense and heterogeneous temporal configuration that does not have to take into account the relationship of exploitation that necessarily obtains between capitalists and workers. And perhaps more to the point, one is not supposed to inquire too closely into attempts to occlude the relationship of exploitation via the mobilisation of all manner of ideological resources (astrology, prayer, magic, not to mention the all-consuming power of fire). Whether or not these avoidances work, Chatterjee's heterogeneity seems to be a function of enforced, ascriptive, inherited inequalities that it is now the task of the postcolonial critic to reconcile if not perpetuate.

From this vantage point, a properly historical explanation will recognise the existence in Chakrabarty's work, for instance, of an implicit stages narrative, and will attempt to locate it in its time-space, political-economic co-ordinates. For after all, colonialism is said to have interrupted the continuity of old and unbroken intellectual traditions, reducing them to practical concepts, 'bereft of any theoretical lineage, embedded [merely] in quotidian practices in South Asia'.[215] Colonialism thus marked a break from the plenitude and creativity of a pre-colonial past, and inaugurated a new historic moment, with which postcolonial studies in all its forms is trying to come to terms. Jameson's identification of a 'genetic trope' in historicism might be useful here. In his explanation, what 'teleological thought' reads as a 'narrative progression from a fallen present to a fully constituted future', is displaced in 'genetic thought' to the past, so as

213   Chatterjee 2004, p. 7.
214   Chatterjee 2004, p. 7.
215   Chakrabarty 2000, pp. 5–6.

to encompass 'origin, development and ultimate fate'.[216] Modifying Jameson's description and leaving aside the question of ultimate fate, which is rigorously excluded in postcolonial studies, of interest is the identification of a fall from an original state of plenitude to the somewhat degenerate present. It ought to be clear, of course, that we are not dealing with an evolutionary scheme, but with a rupture, a break, except that it cannot be represented in the manner of the old Communist stages theory as portending the ultimate emancipation of human beings from exploitation and oppression.

Jameson suggests that the original emergence of this trope may have been characteristic of a brief moment of history – that of the rapidly transforming nations of nineteenth-century capitalism – and that it provided a 'conceptual narrative mechanism', which allowed people to make sense of a very particular situation.[217] This was one in which a single lifetime could span both the experiences of collective, face-to-face village communities and the great industrial cities, and here it may have provided a way of thinking the vastly different terms of rural and urban experiences together, and thus resolving some of the lived consequences of the uprooting and relocation. The uprooting from rural communities and relocation to urban centres was part of a vast economic and cultural revolution that is now referred to euphemistically as 'modernisation'.[218] The narratives of the Bengali intellectuals in Chakrabarty's portraits of colonial Calcutta – now rewritten mainly it seems for a metropolitan audience – capture very well the sense of loss, and the acknowledgement of it by conceding the 'outside' material domain to the 'West' while preserving the autonomy of the inner spiritual domain that represents 'one's inner spiritual self, one's true identity'.[219]

If the intellectuals of the colonial period were trying to make sense of the economic and cultural revolution they experienced in terms of a fall from original plenitude, a different set of imperatives comes into view in postcolonial studies. Of course, these include other ways of being-in-the-world, the unanticipated potentialities of European phenomenological theories once read through a postcolonial perspective, provincialising Europe by showing it the limits of its universalism, perhaps even reviving some of the pretensions of the Oriental Renaissance, all the while avoiding that which is of the most pressing concern to the 'postcolonial world': the question of socialism. Combining

---

216   Jameson 1988, Volume II, p. 154.

217   Jameson 1988, Volume II, p. 156.

218   Ibid.

219   Like Chakrabarty, Chatterjee also draws out the patriarchal aspects of this particular division of the home and the world; see Chatterjee 1993, p. 120.

a historical understanding of the 'genetic trope' with the political implications of the notion of 'dense and heterogeneous times' gives us a clear indication of the absolutely apologist nature of postcolonial studies as practiced by Chakrabarty, Chatterjee and their epigones.

It is something of a tribute then to the great Marxist 'transition' theorists that they captured the historic transformations without abolishing the future, all the while avoiding the teleological or genetic tropes in their theories.[220] And, if anything, later transition narratives – such as those of Dobb and Brenner – have gone further in introducing a non-evolutionary orientation to transition narratives.[221] In this sense, transition narratives are strictly non-predictive, founded on a recognition that a social formation contains within it contradictions and tensions whose outcomes are radically undecidable in advance. The Marxist concept of social totality is qualitatively distinct from theories founded on the 'unification of contradictory elements' and 'a self-reinforcing and (potentially) self-transparent moment of pacific totalisation'.[222] Indeed, recent Asia-centric theories may be a good example of the latter, to the extent that they accept no contradictions – merely heterogeneity – in their societies, or if they do accept them, the contradictions are not of the sort that would produce anything of the order of class conflicts. Those are reserved for the 'West'. At any rate, the conflicts indigenous to non-Western societies cannot disturb the self-identity of those societies preceding or even coinciding with the period of European colonialism.[223]

---

220   Of course, Marx is the pre-eminent example, but Jameson calls for a similar recognition for Darwin, 'the whole scandalous force of the synchronic mechanism of natural selection' being 'a rigorously "meaningless" and non-teleological process' (Jameson 1988, Volume II, p. 155).

221   Dobb 1947.

222   Thomas 2009, pp. 29–30.

223   Needless to say, there are more muscular discourses that have also come into existence recently – the second rise of Asia, the revival of 'Asian values', Asia-centric narratives of globalisation, and so on. Some Asia-centric critiques of Eurocentrism nowadays tend to combine the critique of Eurocentrism with the notion that the old Asian empires had already developed incipient forms of capitalism based on trade that were then interrupted by colonial rule. Decolonisation has allowed the Asian countries to resume their historical trajectory. This is to suggest that Asia was pre-emptively capitalist before Europe, or that a non-capitalist market economy peculiar to Asia, prefigured before colonialism, is now coming into its own, for example, in China. Indeed, it is arguable that some such economic foundation is central and necessary to postcolonial thought that seeks to go beyond identity politics. For an exposition of tendencies in this regard, see, for instance, Frank 1998; Arrighi 2002; Arrighi 2009. For a critique, see Wood 2002, pp. 29–30. In light of all

In postcolonial studies, 'community consciousness' may be the key to this sort of self-reinforcing and self-transparent unification. Thus Chatterjee maintains that while the peasant community was by no means 'an egalitarian and harmonious' one, 'free from internal dissension and struggle', it was nonetheless the site of a unity based on recognising 'differential rights ... entailing differential duties and privileges'.[224] With this as a conclusion, we are invited to work back to a study of 'an Indian history of peasant struggles', rather than a 'history of peasant struggles in India', to ground 'one's historical consciousness in the immanent forms of social development that run through Indian history'. Once confronted in its 'sheer vastness and intricacy', Chatterjee is confident that this material will prove incomparably richer than that contained in the received histories of Europe, a fact that the efflorescence of modern anthropology in the period after the Second World War has brought home to the 'European consciousness'! If properly received, this Indian material will achieve 'a fundamental restructuring of the edifice of European social philosophy as it exists today'.[225]

Will the reverse apply? That is to say, will a proper confrontation with the realities of European history, rather than the garbled versions with which postcolonial theorists seem to work, effect a fundamental restructuring of the edifice of postcolonial thought? Somehow one doubts very much that this is likely to happen any time soon. Suffice it to say that this type of postcolonial narrative mechanism – influenced by the 'new [sic] sciences of anthropology and linguistics'[226] – seems to be part of a revival of cultural historicisms grounded in civilisational archives, even if the latter have been partially submerged by the onslaught of capitalism. Not surprisingly then, Chakrabarty's aversion to transition narratives, as implying an evolutionary historicism, seems on the face of

---

this, I think it would be premature simply to hail a 'materialist turn' in postcolonialism. That it may represent a further turn to the right needs to be borne in mind.

224   The key to unraveling Chatterjee's argument may lie in the status of the word 'recognising'. Who does the recognising? Is this assumed to be an unspoken understanding, immanent to 'Indian' peasant community, the function of a consciousness alien to the understanding of the West, something that can be seized on only by the authentic denizens of a particular cultural formation?

225   Chatterjee 2000, pp. 17–20.

226   Chatterjee 2000, p. 19. The 'efflorescence of modern anthropology' to which Chatterjee refers on the same page seems to have a close affinity to the one associated with Louis Dumont. To the extent that Dumont himself wrote against the backdrop of a social crisis confronting right-wing intellectuals in 1930s France, this is perhaps the return of the repressed with a vengeance. See the discussion of the political lineages of Dumontian anthropology in Lardinois 1996.

it to contain a serious misreading of *Capital*, and more broadly of the Marxist tradition. In the present context of postcolonial studies, this may, of course, afford him a strategic opening to reground his account of nineteenth-century histories, which saw numerous transitions to capitalism within and outside colonial conditions, in a more congenial narrative of self-identical civilisations facing each other as radically different formations, each with its own immanent logic of unfolding until the fatal collisions of the colonial period.

Chakrabarty's account has at least the merit of getting down to developing a narrative replete with all manner of details based on an underlying civilisational geography. What it does very well in the process, and perhaps unintentionally, is to capture the dilemma of a cultural historicism, as it alternates between identity and difference, as a narrative of decline, loss, nostalgia. It affirms the difference between India and Europe – two fairly arbitrary categories – and posits the existence of ancient traditions, unbroken and alive in Sanskrit or Persian or Arabic until the colonisers sundered them, and introduced a split that the colonised were forced to endure, and make themselves at home in, while resisting the imposed forms of modernity. Thus, clearly an element of his narrative – or that of Ranajit Guha – is that traditions deeply embedded in the Indian cultural soil are not only the ancient and authentic elements of Indian life, but continue to constitute, via the native languages and cultural competence 'sedimented into language itself and not referring to concepts that the mind elaborates or that contain experiential truths', the only legitimate ground of nationalism.[227] In the polemical field it corresponds to authenticity, religion, Indian tradition, and the like. Conversely, those in modern India who wish to establish a critical distance between themselves and those so-called sedimented traditions might be labelled secular, deracinated and Westernised. It is hard not to see in this case a certain form of historical narrative underpinning the taking of positions in the *Kulturkampf* of Indian politics. This rather more modest political *position-taking*, rather than the grandiose and delusional goal of rocking 'the edifice of European social philosophy as it exists today', may be the key to understanding the postcolonial critique of (Marxist) historicism.[228]

---

227   Chakrabarty 2000, pp. 176–7.
228   The former applies to the national context of the country of origin from which a postcolonial theorist hails. The latter has become part of the postcolonial rhetoric in its more diasporic or metropolitan manifestation.

5.9   Marxism and Historicism

In the case of a very common expression, Gramsci remarked, one should put
the accent on the first term – 'historical' – and not on the second, 'which is of
metaphysical origin'. The philosophy of praxis – Gramsci's name for 'historical
materialism' – is 'absolute "historicism", the absolute secularisation and earthliness of thought, an absolute humanism of history'.[229] He continues: '[m]atter
as such ... is not our subject but how it is socially and historically organised for
production' and 'natural science should be seen correspondingly as essentially
an historical category, a human relation'.[230] Peter Thomas explains that, in
Gramsci's perspective, historical materialism is 'neither identified with any of
the preceding cultural and philosophical formations, nor is it seen as descending from any particular formation or combination of them';[231] rather, it is 'a
moment in a movement of renovation' that reveals, 'possible, sometimes hidden, affinities between phenomena that otherwise appear as discrete and dis-
parate', and a dialectic between the initiatives and experience of the 'subaltern
classes ... and the established order'.[232] Its status in relation to them is heuris-
tic, in the sense of permitting a 're-organised narrative of modernity', rather
than synthetic, in the sense of permitting a 'final annulment of contradictions
between elements in a teleological progression'.[233]

Jameson offers a related insight: each mode of production, seen as a synchronic form (slavery, feudalism, capitalism), designates – in a Marxian framework – not merely a specific type of 'economic production', labour process
or technology, but also a 'specific and original form of cultural and linguistic
production' along with the determinate place of the other traditional Marxist
superstructures – the political, the juridical, the ideological, and so on.[234]
Contemporary Marxism, exposed as it is to the fragmentation of life in our day,
would not wish to exclude, for example, the psychoanalytic (the construction
of a historically specific 'psychoanalytic' subject) or the phenomenological
(the organisation of daily life) in a given social formation, but would insist that
all those various 'instances' are dialectically modified according to the structural place assigned to them within the organisation of the various 'modes
of production'. Thus, the concept of 'production' – or, for that matter, the

---

229   Gramsci 1971, p. 465.
230   Gramsci 1971, pp. 465–6.
231   Thomas 2009, p. 248.
232   Thomas 2009, pp. 248–9.
233   Thomas 2009, p. 249.
234   Jameson 1988, Volume II, pp. 172–3.

'economic', 'labour', and so forth – cannot be retrojected to a prior epoch based on the place it occupies in capitalism. Neither, for that matter, would it be possible to do so with respect to the centred bourgeois subject, the Unconscious, and the like – theorised from modern psychic experiences.[235]

In this view, Marxism's 'absolute historicism' rests not just on the historically determinate form of material production, economics or even class struggles, but, as Jameson insists, on a very different category called the 'mode of production', which projects a total synchronic structure in terms of which a variety of phenomena theorised by a number of different methods of analysis and interpretation find their 'appropriately subordinate structural position'.[236] The 'mode of production' understood synchronically would thus resemble a hub-and-spoke pattern in which the position of the various instances along a hypothetical rim would change according to the mode of production being represented, and none would necessarily occupy a privileged place throughout history.[237]

The Althusserian distinction between structural domination and structural determination is used to explain the difference between the social form of capitalism and the earlier ones.[238] The determination of all these social formations is economic, in the sense of the type of production current in each. Yet each has its own distinctive version of a unifying ideology (the dominant): various forms of religion, or the ethos of the polis or ancient city-state in Classical Antiquity, or else power relations exercised through an elaborate hierarchy of superordination and subordination in feudalism, and so on. In these cases, the ideological or religious dominant is distinct from its determinant in the type of production involved. But as Marx remarked, 'the Middle Ages could not live on Catholicism, nor could the ancient world on politics'; it is the manner in which they 'gained their livelihood' that explains why in one case politics and in the other religion played the chief part.[239]

Only in capitalism is the economic determinant also the secular dominant, that is, the latter is structured by the money form.[240] The various pre-capitalist societies, whatever their technical production, were all organised collectively – although it should be pointed out that in the cases where slave or serf labour predominated, this was a coerced collectivity. Only capitalism constitutes a

---

235   Jameson 1988, Volume II, p. 173.
236   Jameson 1988, Volume II, p. 149.
237   For a diagram representing a 'mode of production or structure', see Jameson 1981, p. 36.
238   Jameson 2011, p. 15, n. 15. For an exposition of the Althusserian distinction, see Terray 1972.
239   Marx 1977, p. 128, n. 26.
240   Jameson 2011, p. 16.

social formation united by the absence of collective organisation, by 'separation and by individuality'. The identity of dominant and determinant in capitalism in principle constitutes it as the first 'transparent society', that is to say, the first social formation in which the 'secret of production' is revealed – a knowledge of society becoming possible when commoditisation has become 'tendentially universal', that is, when wage labour has largely superseded all other forms of class relationship.[241] Yet this possibility of 'truth' in capitalism is immediately 'occulted' by ideology in the narrower sense of what ideologists produce and invent to conceal that truth.[242]

To argue, as postcolonialist historians do, that community was the basis of social existence in colonial India, for instance, is just another way of saying that capital had not fully separated and individuated people yet, that is to say, their pre-capitalist social forms (still) had a degree of collective socioeconomic vitality. On the other hand, this notion of community has degenerated in the later postcolonial thinking because in fact the 'real' community has given way under pressure from capital. And what exists now is in fact the pseudo-communities or virtual communities of people with self-consciously similar if not identical identitarian positions based on religion, race, ethnicity, and so on, most of which are instrumentally conceived to pursue either political ends (seats in elected bodies) or economic ends (competitive pots of money) and the like. Communitarian mobilisation nowadays – rather like mainstream economics – seems to be a form of politics organised to deflect attention from the possibility of following through on the implications of a knowledge of the 'secret of production'. Indeed, postcolonialism's disavowal of the possibility of pursuing the 'secret of production' into all its hidden abodes is a fairly telling indictment.

As I have tried to suggest, the 'transition' from one mode of production to another would be a matter of both deep structural transformation and punctual ruptures, in the end the overcoming of older forms rather than merely a matter of evolution from one to the other in a straightforward non-contradictory manner. If now the threads of the foregoing argument are drawn together – for example, the mode of production as a 'synchronic' totality, the structural dominant and determinant, together with the imperative towards totalisation implicit in Marxism – it might begin to explain the latter's ability to 'transcend' more specialist disciplines. It does so by showing that specialised objects of study, and the codes they generate, are not self-enclosed entities, but 'conceal a seam' that closes them off from the social totality. It might also reveal the

---

241 Ibid.
242 Ibid.

extent to which arguments about not seeking a 'more real' secular reality are really about occulting the possibility of social knowledge. Thus, for example, the apparently self-enclosed practices of 'mediaeval' religious rituals and theological doctrines, can only be revealed – retrospectively historicised – as a symbolic representation of the 'natural' order of hierarchies on earth once secular thought has emerged as an autonomous domain of human activity, that is, with what we call modernity. In a positive register, then, Marxism does not seek to exclude or repudiate specialised objects of study, but rather serves to 'demystify' the various frameworks that operate as strategies of containment by which they claim the status of self-sufficient systems of explanation.[243]

In a different context, Eric Wolf points to the practical emergence of specialised and completely secular social science disciplines in the aftermath of 1848, largely as a reaction to the revolutions of that year and to the potential threat posed by Marxism in alliance with them, and the implications of the 'strategies of containment' represented by the disciplines.[244] The minute division of the overall totality of capitalist society into the economic, social, cultural, political, and so on, gave the impression of overall coherence to the descriptions generated by the disciplines, allowed them to categorise post-1848 Europe in certain ways, and were designed to develop methods of specialist control over what was seen as the rising threat posed by the dangerous classes. At the same time, these disciplines also excluded from view the fears and anxieties that underlay the disciplinary developments, and pushed the repressive methods of control into the domain of practical everyday forms of governmentality – into the domains of institutional realism and practical reforms in fact.

In trying to work through the issue of absolute historicism from a Marxian perspective, it is important, as Jameson advises, not to yield to the cultural relativism of seeing one's relation to the past in purely contemplative terms as that which obtains between an individual and a cultural formation in the past, to which the theorist may relate either in the mode of identity or difference, but rather to think in terms of the quite different relationship of an *objective situation* in the present with an *objective situation* in the past.[245] In the process, we enter a mode of relating to the past in which each individual reading, every local interpretive practice, is then grasped as the 'privileged vehicle' through which two distinct 'modes of production confront and interrogate each other'.[246] An individual reading thus becomes 'an allegorical figure' for a col-

---

243   Jameson 1988, Volume II, p. 149.

244   Wolf 1984, pp. 8–23.

245   Jameson 1988, Volume II, p. 164.

246   Jameson 1988, Volume II, pp. 173–4.

lective confrontation of this kind. In this mode, encounters with the past are no longer a matter of mere aesthetic experience, but constitute a much more political act, in which the past speaks to us – in the register of difference – about the structure and habits of our life: its ubiquitous commoditisation, monadisation, instrumentalisation, and so on.[247]

Jameson suggests that among the conditions of possibility of Marxism as this new type of dialectical thought was the commoditisation of land and labour completed by the development of capitalism. Marxism's 'absolute historicism' may be said to originate with the understanding that only in the capitalist epoch does 'labour-power, in the eyes of the worker himself', take on the form of a commodity which is his property; his labour consequently [taking] on 'the form of wage labour'; it is from this moment that the commodity form of the products of labour 'becomes universal'.[248] It is the universal commoditisation of labour power and the universalisation of wage labour that also defines the moment of emergence of the world market and globalisation, which is not to be conflated with the mere existence or extension of trade routes, but rather understood by the transformation of 'older modes of exploitation' in agriculture and the crafts into wage labour.[249] But if that were its only precondition, Marxism would be 'merely a theoretical reflection' of that mode of production. However, it is also the 'anticipatory expression' of a future society, a 'partisan commitment' to a future mode of production that seeks to emerge from the hegemonic mode of production of our present.[250] So it is not only the past that is brought into a relationship with the present. Jameson insists that in the act of confronting the past, we also face the future. This necessary rectification of political perspective then creates an aperture to the future, to what Ernst Bloch called the Utopian impulse.[251]

It is with this 'partisan commitment' in mind that one views Marx's own reservations about Utopian thought and later Marxist readings of its possibilities. In the meantime, it is unclear how the 'new' sciences of linguistics and anthropology (are there other candidate sciences for the job?) are supposed to achieve the grandiose transformations that Chatterjee hopes for, but what is reasonably apparent is the manner in which the genetic trope is being

247   Jameson 1988, Volume II, pp. 175–6.
248   Marx 1977, p. 274, n. 4.
249   Jameson 2011, pp. 16–17, n. 16. This contrasts with the more conventional descriptions of globalisation in terms of financialisation, speculative flows of casino capital, commodities and futures trading on the 24-hour stock markets, and so on.
250   Jameson 1988, Volume II, p. 176.
251   Jameson 1988, Volume II, p. 176.

employed to project the future and frame the rejection of 'dangerous' Utopian propositions.

For the most part, as David Harvey points out, the most effusive propositions about the future have been proffered by the thinkers of a right-wing persuasion and they have primarily espoused what he calls a 'Utopianism of process'. The odd thing here has been that the negative connotations of 'Utopia' and 'tele-ology' have not been attached to the right-wing assault on the social order.[252] This is very much in the spirit of the post-1989 period, in which the right holds forth its Utopia of a 'free-market' capitalism as being simultaneously anchored in an eternal human nature and holding the promise of the 'most advanced form of future productivity and innovation'.[253] But it is apparent as actually existing globalisation unfolds that some of this productivity and innovation has come at the expense of intensifying inequalities, partly a function of the operations of a supposedly free-market across a variegated geographic terrain of resource endowments, communications, cultural histories, labour quanti-ties and qualities, and so on, which is, as Harvey rightly points out, in itself a function of prior capitalist development.

The limitations of the presentation of this process as a deterritorialised and 'geographically anonymous behemoth', or as a tidal wave of 'technology and irresistible market forces' sweeping aside all the old boundaries erected by archaic social formations, not to mention the earlier moments of capitalism itself, are being addressed by its radical critics, Marxists among them. Indeed, actually existing globalisation has been shown to rest not merely on the 'equal treatment of unequals', but on a deliberately framed political project whose aim has been a 'savage restructuring of class and social relations worldwide'.[254] Rather than a smooth progression towards 'homogeneity and equality', the neoliberal capitalist Utopia has been attacked for multiplying both regional and class inequalities.[255]

The broad rejection of Utopianism by the left in the post-1989 period, a process that certainly began much earlier, should be understood in the first place in terms of the collapse of specific Utopian projects. The end-of-history scenarios that accompanied the definitive collapse of the Soviet Union and its satellites is beginning to take on the air of a prolonged nightmare with no

---

252   Harvey 2000, pp. 176–7. Harvey cites Frankel 1987 to make the point.
253   Jameson 2011, p. 90.
254   Lazarus 2011, p. 7. Additional useful interventions have been made: see Tabb 1997; Gowan 1999; Bourdieu 2003; Saad-Filho 2003. A more complete bibliography can be found in Lazarus 2011, p. 206.
255   Harvey 2000, p. 178.

end in sight.[256] The lack of attention given to the future, which Jameson suggests might be based on the notion that it might be construed as essentially
frivolous when so much exists already,[257] might have other causes: that of a
closure of alternative horizons of hope in the face of what seems like a gar-
gantuan machine, which seems frequently enough to break down but which
recovers only by growing larger and more all encompassing, and, to a very
significant proportion of humanity, more menacing. The ideological 'occultation' in response to the frequent breakdowns of the capitalist machinery of
production – crises of overproduction and so on – has been to shift attention
to the market, which is supposed to endow capitalism with a 'unifying principle and a natural form of collectivity', and moreover represent it as an expression of 'a permanent feature of human nature'.[258] As a collectivity, the market
is endowed with a will and an agency denied individuals who are supposed to
make themselves available to its moods and its caprices. Thus, the occultation
of the secret of production revealed by the capitalist mode of production. We
will need to return from the noisy sphere of circulation to the secret abode of
production to take stock of the situation.

This might turn out to be one of the better reasons for not consigning
Capital to the 'archival cemetery'. For all the mutations that have occurred in
economy, social and political institutions, culture, not to mention the texture
and pace of everyday life, each new stage of capitalism – shaped by crises of
accumulation and recoveries therefrom – has remained true to the original
'essence and structure' of capital first laid out in exhaustive detail in the three
volumes of Marx: 'the profit motive, accumulation, expansion, exploitation of
wage labour'.[259] This is where the true originality of *Capital* resides, informing its 'ambitious dimensions and structural intricacy'.[260] Indeed, Marxists like
Mandel, writing in the late 1970s, could argue that as the 'archaic or residual'
elements still present in the earlier stages of capitalism were eliminated, the
'purer and more functional abstraction of the system' built by Marx became
'ever more true, ever more relevant to contemporary conditions'.[261] In the
late 1970s, and more so in the 1980s, as renewed and more persistent crises
of overproduction and overcapacity have settled over global capitalism, one

---

256 Harvey notes that the Utopianism of process has been coming under attack by
     conservative thinkers as well: see, for example, Gray 1998, p. 207.
257 Jameson 1971, p. 125.
258 Jameson 2011, pp. 16–7.
259 Jameson 2011, p. 9.
260 Ibid.
261 Mandel 1977, p. 82.

has witnessed opposing tendencies at work: on the one hand, the increasing abstraction of capital and the ever-increasing scale of production and velocity of circulation of credit; on the other, a return to almost Victorian conditions of work: sweatshops, child labour, extra-economic coercion, the maintenance of reserve armies of labour in countrysides that now produce no agricultural products, and so on.[262] Nonetheless, the tendencies Marx projected in *Capital* have held true, by and large: 'heightened polarisation, increasing unemployment, the ever more desperate search for new investments and new markets'.[263]

If the limitations of the Utopianism of process are becoming apparent with the passage of the years, it should be noted that Marx in his day opposed the Utopianism of spatial form, or rather its underlying philosophical and ideological formation.[264] In *The Communist Manifesto*, for instance, Marx and Engels declared that the oppositional forces to capital were in such an undeveloped state that 'fantastic pictures of future society' come to represent 'the first instinctive yearnings' for a general reconstruction of society. The 'practical measures' suggested by Utopian socialists such as:

> the abolition of the distinction between town and country, of the family, of the carrying on of industries for the account of private individuals, and of the wage system, the proclamation of social harmony, the conversion of the function of the state into a mere superintendence of production – all these proposals point solely to the disappearance of class antagonisms which were, at that time, only just cropping up, and which, in these publications, are recognised in their earliest indistinct and undefined forms only.[265]

Marx and Engels also noted that the revolutionary literature had 'necessarily' a reactionary character, inculcating 'universal asceticism and social levelling in its crudest form', and that the proletariat existed for them only from the point of view of being the 'most suffering class'.[266] As for the dream of an experimental realisation of the social Utopias of its founding principals – Saint-Simon, Fourier, Owen – a dream based on establishing isolated 'phalansteres', 'Home Colonies', or a 'Little Icaria', these were 'castles in the air' for whose realisation they had to appeal to the 'feelings and purses of the bourgeois'. The result was

---

262   For an overview of these tendencies in late capitalism, see Hobsbawm 2011.

263   Jameson 2011, p. 9; see also Harman 2010, p. 3; Callinicos 2010, p. 8.

264   Harvey 2000, p. 195.

265   Marx and Engels 1980, p. 42.

266   Marx and Engels 1980, p. 41.

merely to 'deaden the class struggle and to reconcile class antagonisms', and so on.[267] In his open letter to the Icarians, Marx also pointed out: 'For communists – and surely Icarians – who realise the principle of personal freedom, a community of communal property without a transition period, actually a democratic transition where personal property is slowly transformed into social property, is as impossible as is harvesting grain without having planted'.[268] But even so, Marx and Engels concluded that in attacking 'every principle of existing society', the Critical-Utopian socialists and communists provided the most valuable materials for the 'enlightenment of the working class'.[269]

Whatever optimism Marx and Engels may have had – with regard to the progress of proletarian consciousness to the point of being able to act collectively to abolish capital and usher in the future – seems to have retreated if not disappeared in more recent times. The period between the two world wars in western Europe may be viewed as a decisive repudiation of the proletariat's revolutionary potentials. So much so that Lenin was moved to ask in 'Imperialism and the Split in Socialism' in October 1916: 'Is there any connection between imperialism and the monstrous and disgusting victory opportunism (in the form of social-chauvinism) has gained over the labour movement in Europe?' This he regarded as 'the fundamental question of modern socialism'. Lenin noted that neither Marx nor Engels lived to see the imperialist epoch of world capitalism, which began not before 1898–1900, but they were already aware that England had revealed at least two major distinguishing features of imperialism – vast colonies and monopoly profit. Lenin cites a letter from Engels to Marx, dated 7 October 1858, which states: 'The English proletariat is actually becoming more and more bourgeois, so that this most bourgeois of all nations is apparently aiming ultimately at the possession of a bourgeois aristocracy and a bourgeois proletariat alongside the bourgeoisie. For a nation which exploits the whole world this is of course to a certain extent justifiable'.[270] Lenin thinks that such a proletariat cannot be mollycoddled: 'The bourgeoisie of an imperialist "Great" Power can economically bribe the upper strata of its workers by spending on them a hundred million or so francs a year, for its super profits most likely amount to about a thousand million. And how this little sop is divided among the labour ministers, "labour representatives" ... labour members of War Industries Committees, labour officials,

---

267   Marx and Engels 1980, p. 42.

268   Harvey 2000, p. 30.

269   Marx and Engels 1980, p. 42.

270   Engels to Marx, 7 October 1858: <www.marxists.org/archive/marx/works/cw/index.htm>.

workers belonging to the narrow craft unions, office employees, etc., etc., is a secondary question'.[271]

But then again, the capitalist wheels do move forward relentlessly, and inevitably this must open up once again the possibility of new revolutionary conjunctures. Profits – let alone monopoly profits – may not be drying out in our day, but they are extracted against the backdrop of prolonged and apparently insoluble crises. There are fewer sops to be handed out to workers, and the pretensions of a labour aristocracy have been levelled out quite decisively. Lenin may not have spoken the last word on the subject.

To conclude this section with a few observations: as Suvin points out when discussing Engels's *Socialism: Utopian and Scientific*,[272] 'once the propagandistic role of deterministic optimism is exhausted,...the cognitive role of the "scientific" definitions in *SUS* [Socialism: Utopian and Scientific], while undoubtedly a very valuable contribution in a historical perspective, is revealed as insufficient'.[273] He concedes that it was a 'great cognitive step' to have stressed that 'an unclear future ideal' or 'will' (of socialising the productive forces) must also become possible through 'concrete economic conditions'. However, that possibility is not defined precisely enough simply by speaking of 'historical necessity'. Historical necessity is only one – 'strong but potential' – force, which can be actualised or repressed by other forces. In such a dialectic, determinisms work (or do not work) through voluntary actions; in other words, 'scientific' preconditions must be in their turn fused with 'utopian' *élan* and projects. The so-called Utopian socialists, Suvin concludes, are to be rightly criticised for not taking both the inertia and the potential real forces of material history into account. Theirs is 'a picture of society designed as though there were no other factors at work than conscious human will'.[274] On the other hand, scientistic so-called historical materialists are also to be criticised for stressing economic determinism. Surely, the dialectically mature use of these somewhat one-sided oppositions, the only use liable to be a good guide to action, is a synthesis of what he calls the 'bold, vertical Utopian will to revolution and the careful, horizontal knowledge of preconditions for revolution'. Marx's criticism of the Utopian socialists and communists was that they saw in 'poverty only poverty, without noticing its revolutionary and subversive aspects, which will overthrow the old society',[275] and to their 'doctrinaire'

---

271   <www.columbia.edu/~lnp3/mydocs/origins/brenner_thesis.htm>.
272   Engels 1989.
273   Suvin 1976, p. 67.
274   Buber 1950, p. 8, cited in Suvin 1976, p. 67.
275   Marx, cited in Bottomore and Rubel 1974, p. 81.

science was to be opposed a 'revolutionary science' associated with the historical movement of the working class.[276]

In this mode of encountering past and future Marxism signals its originality
and the politics of its absolute historicism. If we recognise, in the process, that
Capital is a 'systematic reconstruction' of a historical phenomenon, not a 'historical account of the genesis of that phenomenon',[277] and that even part VIII of
the first volume of *Capital*, which describes capital 'dripping from head to foot,
from every pore, with blood and dirt',[278] is a dramatisation of a specific process
of uprooting and upheaval that occurred in England as opposed to some generalised transition narrative, then we might also arrive at the recognition that
the transition Marx cared about was something that would be premised on
the overcoming of capital. And while his references to it were spotty and omit-
ted concrete details – he was not a Utopian in that sense – it is clear that his
analysis of capital had an alternative horizon, in which the labour-determined
mode of production could be superseded by life in intentional communities,
in which the non-human side (commodities, money, capital) would no longer
dominate humans, as it does in the present of capital.[279] There is no doubt that
in his detailed exposition of capital's tendencies he saw a direct relationship
between 'the techniques and the degree of combination of the social process
of production' and the simultaneous 'undermining [of] the basic sources of
all wealth – the earth and the worker'.[280] Capitalism was ultimately unreform-
able; its structural tendencies could not be abolished without overcoming the
mode of production itself.

By the same token, it should not be imagined that revolution was to be
'simplemindedly' opposed to reform, of which Eagleton informs us Marx

---

276   Thus, the development from Proudhon, Owen, et al., to Marxism, Suvin declares, was not
    a development from 'utopia' to 'science', but from a 'doctrinaire' to a 'revolutionary'
    science; see Suvin 1976, p. 68.

277   Smith 1990, p. 95.

278   Marx 1977, p. 712.

279   Smith 1990, p. 62. The problems involved in imagining, let alone working towards, this sort
    of future have been admirably debated; see Harvey 2000. Particularly noteworthy is
    chapter 9 ('Dialectical utopianism') in which, by way of an engagement with the work of
    Roberto Unger, Harvey lays out the potentialities of going beyond Utopia as 'pure signifier
    without any meaningful referent in the material world' (Harvey 2000, p. 189). Unger
    himself articulates the dilemma: 'Nothing worth fighting for seems practicable, and the
    changes that can be readily imagined often hardly seem to deserve the sacrifice of
    programmatic campaigns whose time chart so often disrespects the dimensions of an
    individual lifetime' (Unger 1987, p. 443).

280   Marx 1977, p. 638.

himself was a 'persistent champion',[281] while being fully aware of the processes by which sections of the working class were being co-opted by the capitalists in his own lifetime. His harrowing descriptions of overwork, fatigue, extreme exhaustion, all of which have such a contemporary ring to them, were produced against the known limits of reform and barely imaginable potentialities of revolution.

For his part, in perceiving the fractures of present time, the apertures they opened on to new political vistas, Gramsci demonstrated that the notion of a unified present is not objectively given in its sheer immediacy, but rather is a function of the social and political hegemony of the dominant social group. The latter seeks to impose its 'present' as an unsurpassable horizon for all other social groups, an 'absolute horizon' not simply of knowing but also praxis. Insofar then as we can talk about a unified present or contemporaneity in Gramsci, it only emerges as the hegemonic present of a dominant class. The ongoing struggle to unify the present, to produce a 'coincidence of times', denies in the process the actuality of the present as a *Kampfplatz* of contradictions'.[282] For Subaltern Studies, and more so its 'postcolonial' successor, the contemporaneity of the non-contemporaneous seems to be a maxim. The Santal is our contemporary. For Gramsci, as for Marx, the non-contemporaneity of the contemporaneous – time out of joint – is vital, the need to emphasise once again that different classes have different horizons and different time-frames for their projects. It is, as Gramsci notes, the non-contemporaneity of the present that is a function of and symptomatic index of the struggle between classes. In this perspective, 'difference rather than unity is primary'.[283]

It is this view of difference – times of class struggles, the aperture to a radically different future, time out of joint – rather than the one opened up by the postcolonialist view of alternative and hybrid modernities existing alongside each other apparently without contradiction, which is important to capture. It is in fact an insight given expression by the absolute historicism of Marxism. So perhaps there is something other than the hollow comfort of various ways of being different in a world dominated by capital. One can even imagine humanly enriching ways of being different opening up when the realm of freedom is vastly expanded beyond anything that any sort of relations between classes – modernity even in the fullest sense, in Gramsci's definition – of whatever kind can offer.

---

281   Eagleton 2011, pp. 13–4.
282   Thomas 2009, p. 285.
283   Thomas 2009, pp. 285–6.

The Postcolonial Orient

The final chapter of this book explores the politics of difference and the limits of a 'postfoundational' approach to explaining such issues as fragmentation, dispersion, atomisation and heterogeneity, locating them instead in the very seams of the current moment of the historical evolution of capital. The 'post-foundational' spirit in which postcolonialism embraces and even celebrates fragments and heterogeneity is an indication of the wider disorientation and disillusionment experienced in the metropolitan countries and the ex-colonies, reflecting to an extent the workings of molecular and institutionalised 'transformism' in the Gramscian sense and the subsequent loss of a political will to grasp the workings of the capitalist system in its totality. The concluding pages argue for a revitalisation of the irreplaceable Marxist will to grasp history understood as a condition born of a systemic rather than anecdotal curiosity about the fate and destiny of the capitalist system and its constituent parts. Fragments may be no more than the detritus of a system that pulverises social solidarities and eviscerates collective life, in which case resisting 'decomposition' into heterogeneity is probably the best way to rebuild what capital is in the process of destroying and effect a totalising grasp of the directional dynamics of the system. The postcolonial Orient – conceptualised as an arena in which cultural claims, political debate and polemical exchanges of the theoretical kind converge, rather than as a geographic space – emerges in this context as a crystallisation of aspects of the post-1989 development of postcolonial thought.

6.1 The Play of Difference, the Merchandising of the Exotic, Tradition and Neo-Traditionalism

The social order of capital, not only now but back in the colonial period (although admittedly in a more embryonic fashion then), operates simultaneously at two levels: the uniformitisation implicit in large-scale political and economic projects on the one hand, and the play of difference, the seduction of the commodity, the merchandising of the exotic and so on, on the other. The latter is now an integral part of the cultural lexicon and ideological hegemony of a far more encompassing capital than any colonial-era example can convey. One of the roots of difference lies in the drive of capitalism to go beyond the forms of commoditisation familiar to us from the classical period of the

CHAPTER 6

industrial revolution. Now, as capital colonises culture, the lavish multiplication of commodities that characterises the commodity economy takes over the logic of culture itself. The evil genius of postmodern capitalism is to present the play of difference and, more covertly, the merchandising of the exotic as a form of emancipation. There is no shortage of pretentious universalising gestures in the world of a more total and all-colonising capital. But these gestures are of the anti-totalising kind: that one can live in different worlds, move freely and inhabit different cultural skins, and make room for enjoyment of the world's wares. The notion of culturalised difference underpinning it is a political gesture. It traces at the ideological level the prometheanism of late capitalism. In this case, the notion of different ways of being-in-the-world is no longer part of some phenomenological-existentialist project. It is inscribed in the very DNA of postmodern capital. The postcolonial historians' most signal shortcoming may be their failure to convey this, and their futile attempts to make a virtue out of the deeply capsized political perspective that comes in its wake.

These contentions can be illustrated by considering Prakash's argument linking the postcolonial, foundationalism, essentialism, heterogeneity and capital. Prakash states that 'the postcolonial exists as an *aftermath*, as an after – after being worked over by colonialism'.[1] He also calls on us to reject 'foundationalism' in history, defining it as the assumption 'that history is ultimately founded in and representable through some identity – individual, class or structure – which resists further decomposition into heterogeneity'.[2] Prakash's rejection of capitalism as a foundational category on the grounds that 'we cannot thematise Indian history in terms of the development of capitalism and simultaneously contest capitalism's homogenisation of the contemporary world',[3] does appear to be arbitrary, a 'self-defeating refusal', a 'deliberate closing down' of interpretative or analytical options.[4] With a little patience, reintroducing capital as precisely a foundational category allows one to explain a great deal of both colonial and postcolonial history, as the following pages will try to show. However, this is not to suggest that the entirety of 'Indian' history, or any other

---

1   Prakash 1992a, p. 8, emphasis added.
2   Prakash 1990b, p. 397.
3   Prakash 1992b, p. 13.
4   Williams 1999, p. 283.

302

history, is thematisable in this way, or that historians have generally done so or even advocated it.[5]

After all, Prakash's point about 'decomposition into heterogeneity' goes to the heart of Jameson's definition of difference in the postmodern moment of capitalism as 'variety and infinity, metonymy, and – to reach some more influential and seemingly definitive and all-encompassing version – heterogeneity'.[6] Heterogeneity, then, can also be seen as a culmination of an all-encompassing process of the evisceration of social solidarities, collective life, even organised resistance, that capital seeks to impose on all forms of hitherto existing collectivities and solidarities, with mixed success.

When it comes to defining the Third World, Prakash says: 'rather than appearing as a fixed and essential object, the third world emerges as a series of historical positions, including those that enunciate essentialisms'.[7] So now, even essentialism can be part of heterogeneity. But then it is worth noting that essentialist arguments shift ground over time. Orientalism and racism are both essentialist ideologies wedded to the notion of difference, but over time the criteria (ontological, biological, cultural) by which such difference was to be understood have changed.[8] Structure and movement are part of any dynamic understanding of capitalism, and the psychological states engendered by the operations of the system itself. Thus, the same system can spin out a vast heterogeneity in the levels of economic development, experiences of modernity, consciousness, and the like, while subjecting all to the homogenisation implied by the value form. As Jameson notes, heterogeneity hardly 'means anything suitably subversive until homogeneity has historically emerged, to confer upon it the value and force of a specifically oppositional tactic'.[9] Homogeneity here is nothing other than the operation of the structural force that we call capital. In this sense, one can say the same about fragments as about heterogeneity. That is, fragments can only be perceived as fragments of something whole. By the time one perceives them as fragments, there is in operation already the structural force that designates them as such. In the absence of the structural

---

5 Prakash is setting up a straw man for demolition, but it is a useful one for our purposes here as it does illustrate something of the characteristic procedures and ideological closures of postcolonialism.

6 Jameson 1998, p. 63

7 Prakash 1990b, p. 384.

8 See, for example, George Mosse's discussion of racism: Mosse 1985, pp. 234ff.

9 Jameson 1998, p. 65.

force, a 'fragment' does not designate difference in any meaningful sense. It is *sui generis*, its own thing, with no value for posing an alternative of any kind.

So, in order to grasp difference as heterogeneity, it is important not to lose sight of capital as the homogenising force that gradually colonises the world. That is to say, heterogeneity is itself evidence of capital's directional dynamic, which while subsuming everything to itself in its onward path also separates, fragments, autonomises and dissociates what were once bound together in symbolic respects that no longer operate.[10] The capitalist mode of production might thus be characterised as the *moment of difference* in a purely historical sense – of fragmentation, alienation, exploitation, societal crises of all kinds,[11] 'infinite divisibility of social relations',[12] and just as importantly a crisis in the relationship of humans to nature.[13] It is useful to remind ourselves of Perry Anderson's remark in a different context of 'pulverisation beyond measure or order' that is so characteristic of our time.[14] Indeed, difference manifesting itself as heterogeneity can be seen as a self-propelling process without end in late capitalism. In the process, difference itself can become commoditised, and heterogeneity a source of surplus value.

If, in this context, difference has become the 'providential ally' of advanced capitalism, one of the very components of the 'new spirit of capitalism' able to co-opt critics and absorb alternatives to its logic,[15] the principal instrument of the 'management of biopower', a 'partitioning of bodies', a 'renaturalisation of social types',[16] this is not to be understood as simply an 'obliterating absorption' of something that already existed as difference that is now subject to the core capitalist logic of the production of surplus value.[17] Rather, it is a process of making or remaking all manner of empirical and lived differences into various appearance forms of the capital relation. The very space for the proliferation of forms of mobilisation nowadays – beyond the standard struggles for democracy and social justice – in the new social movements clustered around ecology, environment, gay rights, feminism, ethnicity, and so on, is sustained by the recent stage in the development of capitalism, by what Žižek calls its 'reflexive

---

10   Jameson 2002, p. 91.

11   Smith 1990, p. 64.

12   Jameson, 'Interview with Leonard Green, Jonathan Culler, and Richard Klein', in Buchanan 2007, p. 36.

13   See the work of Paul Burkett in this regard: Burkett 1999a, pp. 89–110; Burkett 1999b.

14   Anderson 1983, p. 55.

15   Boltanski and Chiapello 2005, cited Cusset 2008, p. 333.

16   Cusset 2008, p. 333.

17   Cusset 2008, p. 160.

colonisation' of the last vestiges of 'privacy and substantial immediacy'.[18] This
reflexive colonisation constitutes the condition in which family and sexual life,
for instance, can be experienced as belonging to the sphere of free choices,
that is, as an analogue to the realm of circulation of commodities, 'the very
Eden of the innate rights of man'.[19] Similarly, the colonisation of culture by
capital gives cultural identity, and the 'politics' attached to it, the semblance of
a free if still somewhat constrained choice, although the constraints seem to
be dropping off with the passage of time, as capital's pulverisation of social life
proceeds apace. That is, you elect to enter the political domain as a representative of a 'community' defined by culture, religion, language, sexual orientation,
and so on, in a field in which that community jostles with other communities
for the attention of the Big Other.

It is not the economic *per se* that is being privileged in Žižek's analysis,
although he seems to think so;[20] rather, it is the social form of capital that is
driving the economy and inexorably informing the fragmentation and fluidity,
with groups forming and dissolving all the time.[21] Capital has now, more than
ever, and certainly more so than in Marx's time, invested the domain of culture
and identity, bringing them within the purview of the commodity form, of production and circulation at ever greater velocity. The abusive extension of the
term 'economism' to encompass any explanation that attempts to grasp the
workings of such a process is perhaps the neurotic response to this situation,
especially so if the objective of postcolonial studies is to 'understand, critique
and enable opposition' to the globalised operations of capitalism. Even at the
local level, to achieve limited aims, as Patrick Williams points out following
Lukács, an oppressed group – in Lukács's case the working class, but this could
apply *a fortiori* to the various social movements – needs to understand the
'totality' of the system that it confronts.[22] An interest in totality in no way contradicts a commitment to the local, the aleatory, the 'fragile value of different
individual and social experiences',[23] and the like, but it does require something
more than a simple retailing of a series of shifting positions. It is worth emphasising that 'totality' by no means implies something complete (and completed),
which one invokes as an object. Rather, as with Lukács, it is the imperative to
totalise that is at stake, rather than a dogmatic or 'positive' conception of the

---

18   Žižek 2000a, p. 395, n. 35.
19   Marx 1977, p. 280.
20   Žižek 2000a, p. 395 n. 35.
21   Žižek 2000a, p. 394.
22   Williams 1999, p. 284.
23   Jameson 1993, p. 172.

system. The imperative to totalise is always a dialectical process with no premature closure involved.[24] That is, it will have to pay careful attention not only to the historic moment of capitalist development, but also the state of the class struggle, the potentialities for popular oppositional mobilisation, and so on.

Prakash's characterisation of 'essentialism' as one of a series of shifting positions in postcolonialism brings up another issue for consideration, namely, the normally fierce hostility towards 'essentialism' in some postcolonial criticism. Eagleton argues that this signifies, among other things, the rejection of the notion of a 'general common humanity' or 'human nature' as a liberal humanist stratagem for suppressing cultural difference.[25] However, if one assumes that the qualities that postcolonial critics find attractive – cultural 'hybridity', fluidity, and so on – constitute a desirable condition for some, then short of either stereotyping others as not being able to possess those qualities, being innately 'Other' so to speak, or denying them the possibility of realising those qualities for whatever reason, which could be regarded as tyrannical, postcolonial critics will have to acknowledge a common humanity. As Eagleton insists, it is 'sheer humbug or evasion' to pretend otherwise.[26] The same with people subject to oppression for being 'different'; if the argument is that this is undesirable in some cases, then it will have to be so in most others involving at minimum some notion of universal human rights.

At the same time, not all political difference is equally tolerable. Prakash himself would find the essentialism of Hindutva offensive and might like to place real constraints on its free operations especially in Muslim-dominated areas of India. On the other hand, the moral equivalence that Chatterjee seems to draw between the Hindu chauvinists' and the secularists' projects, both supposedly involved in 'consolidating the regime of the modern nation-state',[27] as opposed to 'subalternist critics' who are doing something else (undermining the regime of the nation state, or consolidating it differently?), can be seen as misplaced and unquestionably offensive.

The difference summoned in postcolonial studies emerges both in the macro context of civilisational meta-spatialisations and in the micro context, in the latter case taking the form of the most minute differences associated with style, orientation, semi-private associational life, and so on. Oddly,

---

24   In this spirit, Jameson insists that the 'various historical forms of Marxism can themselves equally effectively be submitted to just such a critique of their own local ideological limits or strategies of containment' (Jameson 1981, pp. 52–3; Jameson 2011, pp. 5–6).
25   Eagleton 1998, p. 25.
26   Ibid.
27   Chatterjee 2010, p. 299.

postcolonial invocations of Europe generally posit a unitary totality operating within some relatively unchanging civilisational imperatives, while the fragmentariness is mostly associated with colonial and postcolonial subjects. Chatterjee's description of heterogeneous populations in postcolonial India, who are incompletely integrated into civil society and figure in piecemeal top-down reformist attempts by the state, has no counterpart in his delineation of the contemporary West. In the latter, 'civil society' seems to encompass everyone (except perhaps immigrants from the former colonies).[28] The plight of African Americans and Native Americans, the Roma in Europe, and the millions of others excluded by the erratic workings of the state, discriminatory rules, not to mention the desperate daily grind of survival, vanish into thin air.

If the macro context of civilisational meta-spatialisations authorises the production of the kind of postcolonialist historiography this book has discussed, the micro context has become part of a postcolonial politics of hybridity, multiplicity, transgressiveness, and so on.[29] This is not only associated with the 'spheres of affinity' and the 'intimacy of small or invisible differences', but is almost certainly reflective of a 'fine-grained segmentation of the market place',[30] and an extension of capital into the very pores of social life at every level. The Inside/Outside model of colonial modernity apparently has its postcolonial counterpart. That is to say, at one level a historiography that slyly leans on essentialisation, at another a politics that draws on fluidity, flux, and so on. The two may be in contradiction, but they are part of the heterogeneous whole of postcolonialism.

It is entirely conceivable therefore that heterogeneity marks a world in which capital has become thoroughly global and abstract at one pole, and thoroughly imbricated within communities-of-local-belonging at the other,[31] and ubiquitous in all human relations. Thus, communities subsumed to the ever-expanding drive of capital enact all the concrete experiences of dislocation, separation, the evisceration of all manner of solidarities, and the ensuing pulverisation of society. I would further maintain that an analysis of the tighter subsumption of labour to capital, the ensuing (partial or complete) decomposition of older social forms, and the disjuncture between the concrete experience of modernisation and the increasingly abstract domination of capital, would constitute precisely the best line of challenge to the 'bourgeois naturalisation of the economy'. Prakash's post-foundational notion of difference

28 Chatterjee 2004, pp. 104–5.
29 Eagleton 1998, p. 25.
30 Cusset 2008, p. 333.
31 Brown 2000.

signals the tacit victory of capital. In the end, any politically oppositional stance must place heterogeneity within its proper historical co-ordinates. Contra Prakash, a proper foundation is necessary for social inquiry, without immediately descending into polemics about foundationalism. A celebration of heterogeneity in this context may be premature if not ill-judged, not so much subversive as entirely in conformity with the new 'spirit' of capital. On the other hand, resisting 'decomposition into heterogeneity', or at minimum historicising it properly, may turn out to be an important and necessary political stance.

On the question of 'essentialism', to what could Prakash be referring? What is the relationship of essentialism to the Third World? In his much debated 1986 article in *Social Text,* Jameson argued that he took the point of criticisms of the use of the expression 'Third World', in particular those that stressed the way in which it obliterated 'profound differences' between a whole range of non-western countries and situations. But he goes on to say, he saw no comparable expression that articulated the 'fundamental breaks' between the capitalist first world, the socialist bloc of the second world, and a 'range of other countries which have suffered the experiences of colonialism and imperialism'.[32] In Jameson's description there is already a considerable theoretical component, for as Georges Labica notes with reference to Lenin's 'Report on the Party Programme' of 19 March 1915, there could be no imperialism without prior capitalism, indeed an 'immense lower layer' of it that had developed in relationship to imperialism.[33] In other words, the very concept of a Third World is incomprehensible without both metropolitan capital and the 'immense lower layer' that had developed in the colonies in relationship to it. And the tensions and contradictions stemming from that relationship, not to mention the political struggles it unleashed, are integrally a part of nation-formation and nationalism in the Third World itself. As Aijaz Ahmad puts it: '[f]or human collectivities in the backward zones of capital ... all relationships with imperialism pass through their own nation-states, and there is simply no way of breaking out of that imperial dominance without struggling for different kinds of national projects and for a revolutionary restructuring of one's own nation-state'.[34] The very articulation of a nationalist project – insofar as it was exposed to the fire of value-positing, value-producing labour and subject to the domination of capital – has involved class struggles, not only vis-à-vis metropolitan capital, but also with regard to its local 'lower layers' of capital.

32   Jameson 1986, p. 67.
33   Labica 2007, p. 227.
34   Ahmad 1992, p. 11.

Once colonised by the more 'advanced' nation states, there was no way back
for the people who had been colonised. Their private fantasies of going back
to a smaller scale of life, to a more 'human' scale of attachments and affinities
had to pass through the nation state. To a very substantial extent, this is what
populist versions of nationalist ideology expressed, the nostalgia, the sense of
loss undergirded, in its more bourgeois variation, by the looming fears of a
class struggle that might become something more than a mere sporadic local
eruption. In some inchoate way, uncovering these layers of complexity was
what Subaltern Studies set out to do, although it is clear by now that this facet
has been substantially overlooked.

However, none of this is to argue that 'First World' nationalism was just
a matter for captains of industry, lords and bishops. It too contained an element of radicalism from below. After all, what was 1789 if not a revolutionary
attempt to define the basis of a national-popular idea founded on the Rights
of Man and Citizen? And what of 1648 and the Levellers, Diggers, and Ranters?
Needless to say, there is a historicity to the concept of the Third World, but to
insist prematurely and one-sidedly on difference is to overlook the fact that
capital is no kinder to peasants and workers in Europe than it is to people
abroad who have been subject to colonial rule. The sun may not have set on the
British Empire, but it almost certainly never rose on the slums of East London.[35]

It is useful in this instance to have some sense of history, to think historically, and not just adopt shifting positions. After all, the 'traditions' that define
the essence and antiquity of a nation are part of every nationalist mythogra-
phy and became integral to the history of a whole spectrum of struggles to
define community and representation. This was emphatically so in the various socio-political formations that came to be included in the Third World.
When they first encountered the West in the form of colonisers and modernisers, not only were they brought under the domination of the latter, but in a
counter-move something like an inchoate 'traditionalism' emerged, often generating compact sets of beliefs affirming the authenticity, originality and antiquity of 'national' traditions, and emphasising that they were a bulwark against
Westernisation and in many ways preferable to it. The fact that such inchoate ideas were generally systematised by Western rulers themselves and their
'native' interlocutors would in time generate the tradition/modernity binary

---

35   This is a statement attributed to Will Crooks (1851–1921), Labour Member of Parliament in
     the early twentieth century. Crooks spent part of his childhood in a workhouse and was
     educated in a Poor Law school.

in which the West came to stand for modernity and the East for tradition,[36] underlining an absolutised cultural or religious difference. Orientalism, in this sense, was born at the moment of the colonial encounter.[37]

Of course, the claims of originality and authenticity made on behalf of 'tradition' must have had a material basis in the very nature of colonial rule, which appears to have left significant areas of life in the colonies relatively autonomous, attempting to preserve or, more to the point, *creating* a traditional order replete with ranks, hierarchies, endogamous relationships and ascriptive identities, which would have unravelled had the full force of modernisation been unleashed on it.[38] These then became the original ground for claiming difference. My argument is that the Third World needs to be given a historical form.

Once given this form, it is not a transhistorical term, but one that is, like 'modernity', historically delimited. It is associated with a certain moment of capitalist history that coincided with the immediate aftermath of a period of forcible occupation and restructuring of a number of polities, large and small, which in our geography of continents we associate with Asia and Africa, although a case can be made that some parts of the Americas also fit this description. The Third World excludes cases where the local populations were more or less wiped out and replaced by European settlers, the ensuing social formation coming to resemble quite closely the metropolitan originals they sought to emulate. It includes places where pre-colonial populations and socio-cultural forms were neither wiped out nor completely marginalised, although they were transformed in subtle and not so subtle ways. This left social formations in which there appeared to be significant vestiges of older social formations, which in each case served as a pole of attraction to indigenous populations badly treated by colonialism, and therefore as a standing reproof of the violence and mayhem created by the imperialist powers.[39] The Third World took shape within this constellation of forces; it included ex-colonies that adopted capitalism or socialism (after a fashion). It is much too drastic to

---

36   This would sum up Ranajit Guha's rendering of the two paradigms – that of the coloniser (modernity) and that of the colonised (tradition). His two paradigms seem quite similar to Foucault's and may have a common ancestry in German Orientalism.

37   In his chapter, 'Orientalism's Genesis Amnesia', Mohamad Tavakoli-Targhi argues that Orientalism was the outcome of a 'dialogical' process involving coloniser and colonised (Tavakoli-Targhi 2003, pp. 98–125). A more adequate description might be to call it an outcome of 'symbiotic antagonism'. I believe this phrase was coined by Moore 1993.

38   On this latter point, Metcalf 1997.

39   Probably the violence and mayhem was just as great if not greater in the white-settler colonies; see, for example, Hughes 1988.

reduce the Third World merely to 'the name of a political desire (as in: Cuba "very much identifies itself with the third-world")'.[40]

The sentiments associated with traditionalism were not limited to the Third World by any means. A nostalgia for authenticity and cultural autonomy was as much a metropolitan issue as it was one for the colonies and ex-colonies. The Catholic Right in France, for instance, also bemoaned the loss of both in the wake of the French Revolution. If we expand that view slightly to include the imputed effects of the post-Enlightenment project beyond Europe, we find a rather similar argument in the colonies and ex-colonies, except now it is supplemented by a politico-cultural geography of Inner–Outer, Europe–Other, and so on. The two sides are tied together by certain strands of Orientalist anthropology. When Guénon, Dumont *et al.* made their interventions in the interwar and post-World War II cultural wars in Europe, they did so on the side of a 'universal traditionalism' that had been interrupted only in the West. In the Indian context, for example, the colonial rupture took on a slightly different valence: Europe – always already predisposed to modernity – had foisted its agenda on older civilisations that had until then enjoyed their traditions uninterrupted,[41] and so it became a sign of difference.

Prakash may wish to dismiss these issues, claiming that the 'effect of colonial power [can be seen as] *the production of hybridisation* rather than the noisy command of colonial authority or the silent repression of native traditions',[42] almost certainly intended as a critique of some of the themes of early Subaltern Studies from the vantage point of American postcolonialism. Keya Ganguly, no doubt partly in response, counterposes to postcolonialism's 'decentred, textual, anti-essentialist' moves and gestures of 'performativity, semiotic play, and indeterminacy' that are supposed to provide us with our 'preferred coordinates for all criticism', the 'spectre of Marxist thought with its reliance on the hoary concepts of class, determination, exploitation, and Utopia',[43] that would open a window on something other than the production of hybridisation. She concludes that while in the present climate the 'burden of vulgarity' weighs heavily on Marxist concepts, they remain indispensable to an attempt to think concretely about the lived realities of colonial and post-colonial existence, which cannot be waved off as 'naïveté about the real'. Her argument draws on Adorno's struggles to 'adequate' concept and object, truth and knowledge, around which to reckon with the concreteness of experience

---

40   Lazarus 2011, p. 106.

41   Chakrabarty 2000, pp. 5–6.

42   Prakash 1992b, p. 12, emphasis added.

43   Ganguly 2002, p. 242.

or the necessity of determination, which she concludes are not at all similar to 'theoretical frameworks in which questions of truth, objectivity, and meaning are taken to be the effects of various discursive productions'.[44]

Indeed so, but where does this leave the question of authenticity? Postcolonial theorists, by and large, have no problem with authenticity, but it is one that is surreptitiously located, in the diasporic context at any rate, in the 'ethnic or national identities of postcolonial critics in the metropole' standing in for entire regions of the authentic Third World, even as they decry authenticity as a 'humanist fiction'.[45] But behind this gesture lies something else, and this holds for the 'national' contexts of immigrant intellectuals: the nation state as a secularised business enterprise might be damned as inauthentic. But there subsists another nation – defined by age-old traditions – that is best understood, to take the case of India, through a concept like 'darshan', the indispensable means to grasp the *rasa* [essence] of nationalism,[46] rather than through the 'hoary' concepts of Marxism! For postcolonial critics in this second guise, the limits of the reach of 'European' concepts are also the starting points for discovering authentic concepts that can help reground 'nationalism' and, one assumes, a form of authenticity that it must be difficult if not impossible for people inadequately attuned to the culture to grasp. It is not difficult to see the pitfalls of authenticity in either register.

Marx and Engels, in *The Communist Manifesto*, wrote about 'uninterrupted disturbance of all social relations, everlasting uncertainty and agitation' as the inevitable fall-out of the helter-skelter way in which capital established its worldwide dominance.[47] They sought to place the disturbances, uncertainty and agitation within a picture of an overall huge growth of output, a promethean optimism about remaking the world, a demolition of all obstacles posed by the obdurate civilisations of old. All these tendencies, amplified and reworked, have come down to us. In this sense, Marxism ought to be able to locate historically the characteristic gestures and moves of postcolonial studies, placing them within the dialectical alternations of Dionysian optimism and profound pessimism and despair, the furious oscillations of modern times, the loss of any concrete sense of being anchored in a stable reality, and explain them rather than leaving them to the mystificatory dissipation of 'idealist versions of theory'.[48] In those historical-materialist terms, authenticity may also

---

44   Ibid.
45   Brennan 2006, p. 68.
46   Chakrabarty 2000, p. 174.
47   Marx and Engels 1980, p. 19.
48   Ganguly 2002, p. 242.

be interpreted as registering life's historical disasters, with all its 'traumatic contradictions', rather than a retreat to an allegedly 'prior state of plenitudinous wholeness' before the fall into alienation.[49] That is, to amplify a point made earlier, the 'genetic trope' itself is susceptible to a historical-materialist interpretation.

And so, when we leave the colonial period and fast-forward to the present, we see that traditionalism of the older variety has, to all intents and purposes, disappeared in most places with the onward rush of capitalism (modernisation). In most countries, it is the *aftermath of colonialism* that has made capital ubiquitous and chained the ex-colonial world more firmly to capital, rather than the rule of the ersatz aristocracies of the nineteenth century that sought to recreate elements of an archaic social order in the colonies that was rapidly vanishing at home. With the immediately preceding considerations in mind, we return to Prakash's contention that the postcolonial exists as an aftermath only to realise that this implies a further – *from formal to real* – subsumption of the ex-colonies to the planetary domination of capital, and the greater socio-economic polarisation that follows.[50] *It is not economism to insist on a proper economic foundation for postcolonialism.*

It is in this world that the place of tradition has been taken over by what might be called *neo-traditionalism*: a wholesale recasting of older traditions, the invention of new traditions, identities, and politics fashioned around those identities, sustained by mass public rituals, political theatre on the grand scale, television plays, and computer images, all dependent on the technologies of the (dis-)information age.[51] That is, neo-traditionalism is what takes the place of tradition when the material conditions that sustained the former are no longer available. The material conditions would include the formal departure of the colonisers (post-colonialism as an 'after' in the chronological sense), but also the structural transformations outlined above (post-colonialism as an ideological effect of the structural-economic dynamic of capital's onward movement).

It is a characteristic of the economic and political conditions accompanying a far more globally encompassing capitalism that issues once considered settled are no longer so. If, for instance, the national question was once, in colonial times, 'resolved' after a fashion on the minds and bodies of middle-class women defining and controlling their mobility and sexuality, and containing

---

49   Jay 2006, p. 29.

50   A point repeatedly stressed by Samir Amin; see Amin 1985 and Amin 2003.

51   This description would aptly fit the political theatre of right-wing mass politics in India of the Shiv Sena and BJP variety; see, for example, Heuzé 1996.

when not excluding minorities and lower-ranked castes, recent conditions have unravelled the earlier resolution. The inner/outer and similar binaries, around which the resolution is supposed to have occurred in colonial times, failed to forge a passage from the minorities and the other excluded populations to the ruling class, thus undermining itself when the historical conditions were transformed beyond anything the earlier generations could have imagined. With all the necessary caveats, sweeping changes have also come to Europe and the US, where the national question was also once resolved by framing the issue in terms of the control of women and exclusion of minorities, especially African Americans and Jews, on the basis of race if not primarily religion.[52]

Recent developments have seen the mass entry of women and minorities into public life, and no longer as subalterns, crossing earlier boundaries not simply as assertions of 'autonomous subjectivity', but as architects and participants in deep historical processes of change.[53] By doing so, they have entered, as it were, the 'external domain' of political conflict.[54] The democracy project, such as it is, no longer needs a postcolonial perspective. It might, however, benefit from a popular internationalism grounded in an understanding of the co-ordinates of late capitalism, including crucially the workings of finance capitalism and its impact on state formation, and the limits henceforth to the creation and maintenance of anything like the welfare state of earlier times.[55]

There is a third sense in which one can speak of the postcolonial as an after, and here a comparison with Terry Eagleton's witty description of postmodernism is relevant:

> The power of capital is now so drearily familiar, so sublimely omnipotent and omnipresent that even large sectors of the left have succeeded in naturalising it, taking it for granted as such an unbudgeable structure that it is as though they hardly have the heart to speak of it. One would need, for an apt analogy, to imagine a defeated right-wing eagerly embroiled in discussions of the monarchy, the family, the death of chivalry, and the possibility of reclaiming India while maintaining a coy silence on what engages them most viscerally – the rights of property,

---

52 For some important points on this subject, see Weiss 1996, pp. 97–111.

53 Gopal 2002, pp. 164–5.

54 Chatterjee claims that women's 'autonomous subjectivity', during the colonial period, is to be found in the domestic archives of home, rather than 'the external domain of political conflict' (Chatterjee 1993, p. 137). Both Gopal and Sarkar demur; see Gopal 2002, p. 165 and Sarkar 1997, p. 96.

55 Svallfors and Taylor-Gooby 1999.

since these had been so thoroughly expropriated that it seemed merely academic to speak of it.

He continues:

> With Darwinian conformity, much of the cultural left has taken on the colours of its historical environs: if we live in an epoch in which capitalism cannot be successfully challenged, then to all intents and purposes it does not exist.[56]

In an era in which neoliberal economics has taken on such unprecedented political importance, the 'New Left', as Žižek calls Eagleton's 'cultural left', has been directing the focus of 'progressives' away from what really matters in shaping public life. As soon as the prospect of any far-reaching change affecting the economy is raised, as Žižek notes, an 'unwritten *Denkverbot*' [prohibition against thinking] kicks in to suppress the questioning of global capitalism.[57] The blanket application of the term 'economism' serves precisely such a purpose. Whereas earlier it might have referred to a project that limited itself to economic-corporative goals in the Gramscian sense, it now applies to any form of critical thought that addresses the economy as the site of class struggles. Despite the fashionable 'anti-hegemonic' rhetoric, this sort of suppression happens, in Žižek's opinion, as much in the postmodern academy as in the mainstream media. Philosophers as different as Jacques Derrida and Jürgen Habermas adopt the same 'left-of-centre' liberal stance, and one should not be fooled, Žižek suggests, by the outrage on the right at their 'relativism', 'permissiveness' and 'adversarial culture'.[58] Even a minimal sign of engaging in political projects that aim seriously to change the existing order elicits a response along the following lines: 'benevolent as it is, this will necessarily end in a new gulag'. The 'return of ethics' in today's political philosophy shamefully exploits the horrors of the gulag or holocaust as the ultimate bogey for 'blackmailing us into renouncing all serious radical engagement'.[59] Indeed, the conclusion seems inescapable: the postmodernists' celebration of difference, 'becoming', otherness and the new plurality of lifestyles is 'radical' only from the perspective of the cultural conservatives they oppose.[60] Of course,

---

56   Eagleton 1996, p. 23.
57   Žižek 2000b, pp. 127–8.
58   Sharpe and Boucher 2010, p. 33.
59   Žižek 2000b, p. 127.
60   Sharpe and Boucher 2010, p. 33.

Eagleton and Žižek could also have been speaking about postcolonialism. This may well be the most important register in which we understand postcolonialism: the political, not having the heart to speak of it (capital), and making a virtue of it by resort to all manner of concepts and notions drawing on the intellectual heritage of Orientalism, some lost 'plenitudinous wholeness'.

The resurgence of religio-civilisational meta-spatialisations – for example, Christian Europe, the Muslim Middle East, Hindu India, Confucian China, to name but the most common – accompanied by an intense geographic fragmentation, and an advocacy on behalf of regional formations on a smaller scale, can be seen as symptomatic of this moment. This is already visible in the ex-colonial countries, but also in the Europe of regions and in the so-called 'four-nations' history that appears to be gaining ground in Britain.[61] Each is associated with a distinct territorial quality in a world that appears otherwise to have lost distinctness.

This brings us back to Jameson's point about the place of quality in a world dominated by quantity, but in the case of postcolonialism this is within the confines of the reactionary spirit of Orientalism or its functional equivalents. Postcolonial intellectuals have a complex relationship to 'tradition' and neo-traditionalism. Tradition appears as the proper domain of the postcolonial intellectuals, while neo-traditionalism is relegated to the domains of vulgarisation, mass culture, mass politics, and the like. But, of course, tradition as such has disappeared in any meaningful sense. Therefore, it must be the case that postcolonialism is in fact part of a neo-traditionalist reaction to the demise of historical projects of transformation, albeit invoking the grounds on which tradition rested (authenticity, originality, difference). It is part of a latter-day worldwide Thermidor, or at least its passive accompaniment.[62]

Undoubtedly, while neo-traditionalism claims continuity with the earlier traditions, it is more accurate to see it as a fall-out of the collapse of the latter, and the form that authenticity can achieve in a world of simulacra. And even those who bring an incredulity towards neo-traditionalism seem quite captivated by traditionalism, as if it were not as invented or as inventive as the former.[63] Indeed, the issue of authenticity that pits nativism against the West

---

61   See, for example, Samuel 1998, pp. 21–40.
62   As already pointed out, there are more muscular (and militant) versions of this Thermidorian moment in Asia. It would be worthwhile tracing the connections, open and clandestine, between the quietist postcolonialism and the militant Asian-values tendency.
63   A key point made by Pouchepadass 2002.

has a subordinate register in the opposition of tradition to neo-traditionalism.[64] In light of the foregoing, if I were to hazard a definition of postcolonialism, *it would have to include a triangulation of postmodernism, traditionalism and neo-traditionalism.* But since a perduring fascination with the Orient – not as a geographic entity, although this cannot be discounted entirely, but as a symbolic-discursive space of authenticity, difference, tradition, a vital categorial underpinning for postcolonial Third-Worldism – is so much a part of the political and academic culture of our times, one could with some adjustment of sights call this *postcolonial Orientalism*, a form of self-exoticisation, in which the binary of East-West, Europe-Other, is as integral as in any classically European Orientalist text.

A major constituency of neo-traditionalism is, not accidentally, the large immigrant communities from Asia who now live in dense concentrations in parts of most major US cities and whose children attend the top universities in that country.[65] A notable fact of the present moment is that the ever-shifting boundary between 'East' and 'West' that formerly was said to run somewhere to the east of the Ural mountains runs now through every city of the Euro-American world, or so Niall Ferguson informs us.[66] Given Ferguson's political orientation, and his bellicose rhetoric, he no doubt intends this as a provocation, the Oriental immigrant as a permanent incubus on the body of Europe and North America, a point that is perfectly familiar to the right in both regions. I suspect, at least in the USA, that Ferguson and his comrades-in-arms

---

64   This opposition is a constant presence in Ashis Nandy's writings; see, for example, Nandy 1983.

65   Across the United States, at elite private and public universities, Asian enrolment is near an all-time high. Asian-Americans make up less than five percent of the population, but typically make up 10 to 30 percent of students at the nation's best colleges: In 2005, the last year with across-the-board numbers, Asians made up 24 percent of the undergraduate population at Carnegie Mellon and at Stanford, 27 percent at the Massachusetts Institute of Technology, 14 percent at Yale, and 13 percent at Princeton; Timothy Egan, 'Asian Americans Challenge Ideas of Race in U.S. universities', *International Herald Tribune*, 7 January 2007, <www.iht.com/articles/2007/01/07/news/asians.php?page=1>. Asian-American enrolment in higher education surpassed one million students in 2001 and continues to increase each year. The trends also underscore the fact that Asian-Americans are benefitting from civil rights gains made in higher education over the last several decades; Higher Education Research Institute March 2007 report, 'Beyond Myths: The Growth and Diversity of Asian American College Freshmen: 1971–2005' <www.gseis.ucla .edu/heri/PDFs/pubs/briefs/AsianTrendsResearchBrief.pdf>.

66   Ferguson 2006, p. 645.

Samuel Huntington and Pat Buchanan[67] are in a minority. A majority of the post-1965 immigrants from Asia, and their American interlocutors, are from comfortable middle-class backgrounds. The former have attained the status of a 'model minority', causing little trouble and generally espousing positions conforming to the broad spectrum of middle America. These immigrants are touted for their work ethic and adherence to tradition, which might turn out on closer scrutiny to be some form of neo-traditionalism. It is in this milieu that postcolonial theories find a safe and acceptable ground.

6.2 The Non-Commissioned Officers

To continue with Prakash's claims on behalf of 'postcolonial criticism', as he calls it:

> [I]t seeks to undo the Eurocentrism produced by the institution of the west's trajectory, its appropriation of the other as History... Criticism formed in this process of the enunciation of discourses of domination occupies a space that is neither inside nor outside the history of western domination but in a tangential relation to it. This is what Homi Bhabha calls an in-between, hybrid position of practice and negotiation, or what Gayatri Chakravorty Spivak terms catachresis; 'reversing, displacing, and seizing the apparatus of value-coding'.[68]

These statements occur in the same passage as the one quoted earlier, in which Prakash claims that the postcolonial exists as an 'aftermath', after having been worked over by colonialism. Obviously, the postcolonial exists as an aftermath, but what is it about postcolonialism of the poststructuralist variety that Prakash finds so special? That it resists appropriation of the 'other as history', and that this is the ground on which fellow postcolonialists like Chakrabarty claim difference?

A response to these claims might begin by noting that the appropriation of the 'other' is a continual process under capitalism. That is, it is part of the continuous subsumption of a variety of previously autonomous social formations to the sway of capital. To the extent that this is also the process by which the 'other' is drawn into modern historical narratives, the 'other' is constantly appropriated and the postcolonial critic's resistance to this appropriation is

---

67   Huntington 1996; Buchanan 2006.
68   Prakash 1992b, p. 8.

quixotic to the extent that it is voluntaristic, academic and fundamentally apolitical, even reactionary. There is no particular institution of the 'west's trajectory' that is not at one and the same time associated with the specific geography of capitalism and imperialism, resting ultimately on the worldwide spread of generalised commodity production. In this sense, the invention of a binary geography of East-West (à la Hegel's beginning and end of history)[69] must also include an effort to mask the grounding of the west's trajectory in the contingent origins of capitalism in parts of Western Europe and its outward spread via the mechanisms of colonialism. This geography must also count as part of a huge ideological effort to mark Europe's singularity scrubbed clean of historical contingency. To the extent that the 'west's trajectory' – or the Eurocentric reading of it as a 'European miracle' – is not itself the subject of challenge, which would include the genesis of capital in localised and (at least in the early instances) unintended outcomes of wide-ranging class struggles not limited to the 'west', the work of 'undoing' has hardly been started let alone achieved. In this case, the 'west' can begin to function as the category that buries the contingent. What then remains is an essentialised West, the home of capital, modernity and the ultimate destination of Hegel's westward moving train of civilisation.

As for claiming 'difference' as part of the process of 'undoing', difference is already something bestowed on the colonised by the coloniser (or in the metageography of Orientalism on the 'East' by the 'West'). Thus, to claim 'difference' as part of the process of 'undoing' is a Caliban-like response to Prospero's magic. It effectively cancels any conceptual distinction between difference and 'otherness', and is part of a self-exoticising strategy, claiming some always already liberated zone from which to conduct 'practice and negotiation' à la Homi Bhabha. Difference makes better sense if the historical specificity (singularity) of the subsumption of social formations in a variety of historical locations to capital is foregrounded with a keen understanding of the limits to the process.

From this perspective, the 'futures that already "are"' might serve as a ready-made apology for capital, a case for giving unto Caesar the things that are Caesar's, and giving unto God the things that are God's. The postcolonial critic might be a social theologian in disguise. As a case in point, one might take Kaviraj's statement that modernity becomes increasingly plural over time. It is tempting to read this as an argument that modernity leads over time to widening divergences between classes and between regions of the world. Perhaps we

---

69   '[T]he History of the World travels from East to West, for Europe is absolutely the end of History, Asia is the beginning' (Hegel 1890, p. 109).

should ask why this is so? What do the widening divergences signify? Are they a consequence of some original cultural 'difference' whose operations over time and space produce these results, in which case it must surely count as a defect given its dire social consequences? Or are they a result of active initiatives and political programmes to halt and reverse income distribution from the top down? So, then, is 'increasingly plural' a sign of widening social and economic divergences brought about by a class struggle in which the people at the top have successfully imposed their priorities on the rest? Simply to accept an implicitly culturalist argument with more than a hint of cultural *intégrisme* built into it – that is, Bengalis, for example, just do not (will never?) know the 'right' (read: 'Western') way to be modern – is not only question begging, but also politically reactionary.[70] Bengalis may not know the 'right' way to be modern, but it is sheerly appalling to explain what exists in India (50 percent of the world's indigent and more than half the world's illiterate population, and one of the worst gender imbalances in the world) as part not only of culturalised difference, but also as something that is likely to remain or worsen with time. One might conclude that the retreat of a prominent postcolonial theorist like Chakrabarty into Heidegger's post-war quietist (and dare one say, self-mystifying) posture is over-determined by the inescapable social realities of India. The surging demands of the lower castes for more power and a larger share of social wealth, not for an alternative modernity based on the 'time of the gods', seems to have put the frighteners on a whole host of social theologians.

Prakash's claim that postcolonial criticism has put some distance between itself and Marxism ('the universal mode-of-production narrative'), not to mention nationalism ('Reason and Progress'), is open to qualification.[71] Undoubtedly, modes-of-production narratives are not in favour among postcolonial critics, nor apparently are 'Reason' and 'Progress' (if nationalism can be reduced to those, then nationalism is also out). But it is really the state, in the nation state compound – and the project of consolidating its regime – at which postcolonial thought of the kind represented by Prakash targets its polemic barbs. Inspiration derives, no doubt, from Nietzsche – '[a]s little state as possible' – whom Brennan characterises as the *fons et origo* of 'radical theory' over the last three decades, but we might be forgiven for seeing parallels with

---

70   In his response to Foucault's reading of the Iranian revolution, Rodinson uses the term
      intégrisme in both its descriptive and activist aspects. The idea that an integral culture,
      whether grounded in religion or not, governed all aspects of people's existence until the
      colonial rupture or even to this day is certainly still widespread; see Rodinson, 'Islam
      Resurgent', in the Appendix to Afary and Anderson 2005, pp. 223–38.
71   Prakash 1992b, p. 8.

the libertarian right in the US for whom the 'State' as a 'monolithic ghost rather than a variable political form' is not only dishonest and corrupt, but is 'rife with a sinister compulsion to survey, spy, moralize, and suppress'.[72] But there is reason to question whether the 'nation' is similarly in disfavour. After reading Chakrabarty's *Provincializing Europe*, Guha's *Dominance without Hegemony*, and Chatterjee's *Politics of the Governed*, the best conclusion seems to be that what they express is an alienation from the nation state as a sheerly civic-secular entity, the product of all manner of political horse-trading, but not the 'authentic' nation which acquires a terrestrial body in the nineteenth century, an imperfect container for the national spirit, and so on. Nationalism in this version originates in a struggle against colonialism, declaring '*the domain of the spiritual* [the inner] its sovereign territory' and refused to allow the colonial power to intervene in it.[73] The nation, in other words, was imagined into being in the spiritual domain before it went to work in the political.

One might wonder if Chatterjee intends this inner/outer dialectic to work for others, for example, the Dalits. In that case, perhaps the nation the Dalits might have imagined into being would have probably been much less hierarchical, less unequal, certainly less Brahmanical than the one the caste elite put together as part of their political strategy with, one imagines *pace* Chatterjee, the very considerable help of their colonial rulers. For the Brahmanical patriarchal nation imagined by Chatterjee's *bhadralok* was one that colonial disciplines from archaeology to philology and anthropology conjured up for them. Louis Dumont captured the more romantic side of those colonial disciplines when he wrote: 'One would rather see the vocation of anthropology, as well as *fundamental science*, in an inverse and complementary relationship to that of (*classical*) *science* and to modern ideology in general: re/unite, com/prehend, re/constitute that which one has separated, distinguished, decomposed'.[74] Anthropology would thus accomplish 'its redeeming mission': to 'transcend' the modern world, 'or rather to reintegrate it within the more human world which societies once had in common'.[75] One cannot but see in statements like these something of the programmatic dimension of postcolonial thought, although frequently it is only implied and easily lost sight of. The inner/outer

---

72 Brennan continues: '[a]t the risk of overstating the case, I would argue that the humanities have played a large and influential part in the descending spiral of political options after 1980. Or rather a corporate university administration found in the cultural-studies' crowd partisans of other positions willing to do their work' (Brennan 2006, p. xiii).

73 Chatterjee 2010, p. 27.

74 Dumont 1983, cited in Lardinois 1996, p. 34, emphasis added.

75 Ibid.

dialectic may have found its dominant expression in its anti-colonialism; however, it has its subordinate expressions in anti-Westernism, and in the anxieties it displays towards the class divisions of modern society.

In that case, the position of postcolonialism vis-à-vis the class struggle is probably informed by a patrician disdain for the whole sordid matter of plebeian priorities, or some involvement in a practical decisionist spirit to keep the social lines more or less intact. What postcolonial thinkers like Chatterjee and Chakrabarty, not to mention Kaviraj and Prakash, may be trying to accomplish in the field of theory (postcolonial 'criticism') is to abstract from what is clearly a class struggle, even if carried out within the distinct idioms of caste and the iconography that accompanies it. Far better if people would retreat to their separate spheres, live in their own alternative modernities, their own sense of time and place, and not encroach on what was an upper-caste space of privilege.

It would appear that the 'subaltern split' is itself split between two readings: (i) it can claim to be about class, that is, the split is a sign of the 'world' imposed on the working, exploited populations (their millennial toil as the nightmare of history), in which case no geographic commonsense can encompass it;[76] or (ii) it can claim to be part of an East-West (Orient-Occident) divide developed as part of colonial rule, in which the salient categories are not those of class but of civilisation and its derivative forms. If the subaltern-split incorporates the geographic commonsense of the second reading – however mediated and slyly hidden it is by all sorts of qualifications required by a sophisticated academic discourse – then we have a situation in which History I and II are haunted by the spectre of Hegel's *Philosophy of History*, in which to all intents and purposes History I stands for the fully realised historicity of the 'West' and History II for the 'mere presuppositions of elements' of historicity prevalent in the 'East' whose combination into history would require the agency of the West.

Perhaps this is what Bhabha's 'in-between, hybrid position of practice and negotiation' seeks to encompass. Bhabha's position is not too distant from Prakash's, for whom the principal effect of colonial power is 'the production of hybridisation',[77] presumably in the domain of the 'outer' public culture, rather than in the inner 'spiritual' domain. These positions are supported by a wider stream of thought ably captured by Stuart Hall, for whom the move from difference to *différance* [read: from colonialism to postcolonialism] requires that the oppositional form in which colonial struggle has been depicted must be

---

76   For a discussion of geographic commonsense, see Mazumdar, Kaiwar and Labica 2009, pp. 2–4.

77   Prakash 1992b, p. 12.

reread in terms of negotiation. It must be reread as 'forms of transculturation, destined to trouble the here/there cultural binaries for ever'.[78] Neither Hall nor Bhabha would have much use for the class dimension of the 'subaltern-split', but it seems that even civilisational difference is now to be massaged away by the practice of in-betweenness and negotiation. Parry's comment on positions like this – namely, that they 'serenely defy' the logic of colonialism's theory and practice, and more so, one might add, the logic of capitalism then and now – is most likely what stimulates more militant positions in the spectrum of postcolonial thought. Spivak's idea of seizing (as in expropriating?) the apparatus of value-coding supplies precisely the element of militancy in place of Bhabha's postcolonial mendicancy of negotiation.[79] This is a paraphrase, of course, of the phrase 'militancy not mendicancy', attributed to the so-called Extremist faction of the Indian National Congress, led by Bal Gangadhar Tilak, except that the slogan referred to seizing power from the colonisers on behalf of the Indian bourgeoisie or at any rate on behalf of those fractions of it that rejected the Enlightenment and its associations. Undoubtedly, the idea of seizing the apparatus of value-coding is meant to chime with the punctual, revolutionary overthrow of a moribund order, but this time in the academic domain. It is, however, a mere diversion. Value-coding is not value in the Marxian sense. Value (surplus value, exchange value) has a foundation in the capital social form. It is that *foundation* that is to be overcome in seizing the apparatus of state power and transforming the social-property relations in which production is organised. Overcoming the value form would be revolutionary in the proper sense of ushering in a new epoch of socialised humanity. Nothing equivalent is achieved in Spivak's post-foundational 'seizing' of the apparatus of value-coding. What is of interest, of course, is that even in this degenerate form – a discourse of values – the value form asserts its presence in 'theory'.

Postcolonialism in its post-Subaltern Studies moment may indeed have abandoned all the things Prakash claims it has, although they surely sneak in through the side doors, windows and cracks in the foundation. What this means is not that the postcolonial theorist's ambition is not global or totalising. Indeed, the argument of this book is that this is precisely what characterises postcolonial studies in its current metropolitan manifestation. Postcolonial theorists are not averse to the employment of universalising notions and their accompanying claims of explanatory primacy, or offering totalising explanations and the like, but these gestures are often quite reactionary in their

---

78   Hall 1996, p. 247. See, for example, Parry's comment on this approach as 'serenely defying the logic of colonialism's theory and practice' (Parry 2002, p. 144).

79   Bhabha 1989, pp. 112–31; Spivak 1990, p. 228, both cited in Prakash 1992b.

political implications when advanced through such notions as autochthonous ways of being-in-the-world, authenticity (Authentic Being) and autonomy, while excluding capital from a critical understanding of how such notions come to hold sway at a time when social life is so thoroughly within the gravitational field of the value form. The significance of what has been abandoned has to be considered.

Insofar as there are theorists around for whom Bloch's 'synchronicity of the non-synchronous' – the coexistence of realities from radically different moments of history, handicrafts alongside the great cartels, 'peasant fields with the Krupp factories or the Ford plant in the distance'[80] – is a lived reality, they would have to be from the ex-colonies, although even here the presence of capital in the countryside is a reality and has been for a century or more. But let us say that for them the 'corrosive unevenness' of the process would be more of a lived reality than for most people living in the fully industrialised societies. What this means in reality is that capital in its most developed forms now invades and occupies the lives of working people who will certainly not be aware of the full range of capital's operations even as the most basic subsistence needs and subsistence production are subordinated to it. For many millions this will mean a loss of access to a livelihood, chronic unemployment, unsanitary living conditions, massive exposure to dangerous chemicals, and so on. To turn this 'corrosive unevenness' into some variation of a postmodern gesture, of 'negotiation of incommensurable differences creat[ing] a tension peculiar to borderline existences',[81] seems like wilful blindness. To speak in terms that reflect the peculiar end-of-history perspective 'characteristic of the bourgeois economists',[82] who famously believe that 'there has been history, but there is no longer any',[83] as if class struggles and projects of economic and social transformation have lost their salience, is itself an oddity of the uneven and combined development of ideology. The obverse of the arrival of the Third World in the First, is the arrival of the First World in the Third.[84] This may well be an additional dimension of postcolonialism, and in the end its most durable one.

---

80   Jameson 1991, p. 307
81   Bhabha 2005, p. 218.
82   Jameson 2011, p. 105.
83   Marx 1977, p. 175, n. 35.
84   I should note that the use of these terms no longer requires the adoption of a Wallersteinian 'centre-periphery' model; see Appadurai 1996, p. 32. The world economy may be all jumbled up, but as someone might insist, Calcutta will never become London!

It is arguable that, on its terms, postcolonialism is unable to supply a methodology for provincialising Europe, much less come to grips with important issues like social justice. Indeed, the notion of the 'social' as implying an identity not decomposable into monadic fragments is inadmissible, if Prakash is to be taken at his word. As Margaret Thatcher famously said, 'There is no such thing as society. There are individual men and women, and there are families',[85] and postcolonial theorists may be inclined to agree. Similarly, 'justice' as implying anything not open to a primordialist cultural appeal is suspect for its entanglement with the Enlightenment. Of course, the latter (cultural primordialism) contradicts the former (monadism), but it is precisely contradictions like this that give one an inkling of the significance of 'what does not compute' in postcolonial studies.

It is then of some *historical* significance that postcolonialism of the variety Prakash extols arrived in the metropolitan academy at a particular temporal conjuncture in the larger cultural world that encompasses it. This is a conjuncture in which one can talk endlessly about freedom, so long as it is freedom to aspire to be different in the arena of consumption, freedom from the oppression of Eurocentrism, rather than freedom from the truly obscene oppression of hunger and privation, about *choice* so long as it is trivial, about *class* so long as it is 'middle', and one admits that social transformations are a bad dream of the past, now safely quarantined behind the wall of 1989. All mixed in with profound ambiguity about whether one should be 'for or against consumer pleasures, national sovereignty, tribal loyalties, or ambiguous non-places whose jurisdiction is in flux or indefinable'.[86] The castigation of 'economism' can be seen in the same terms as Eagleton's example of the expropriated members of the ruling class engaging in polite chatter about culture ('the death of chivalry', and so on). Rather like Žižek's cultural left, postcolonialists 'silently accept that capitalism is here to stay', such that the 'very mention of *capitalism as world system* elicits the accusation of essentialism, fundamentalism and other crimes'.[87] The many ways of being-in-the-world is what is left to celebrate when overcoming an oppressive economy is no longer on the agenda.

Jameson's idea of 'transcoding' is useful here. As he puts it, '[w]hat is blurred, left out, what does not compute or is "inexpressible," in this or that theoretical language may ... be a more damaging indictment of the "theory" in question than traditional ontological or metaphysical critiques'. He also suggests that

---

85   <www.margaretthatcher.org/document/106689>.

86   Brennan 2006, p. xiii.

87   Žižek 1997, p. 46. Ironically, of course, it is quite okay to essentialise Europe, or the Enlightenment, but not okay to speak of capital or a capitalist world system.

'whatever its own (very considerable) truth claims, Marxism must also take its chances on this polemic level and ... measure its range, by way of the trans-coding operation, against its various methodological rivals or alternatives'.[88] If this is indeed the situation, then polemic engagement rather than anodyne 'readings' or insipid attempts at synthesising will be the requirement of the day, a view not alien to Marx, Lenin or Gramsci. As Gramsci wrote in a letter from prison, 'My entire intellectual formation has been of a polemical order; even thinking "disinterestedly" is difficult for me, that is, studying for study's sake ... Ordinarily, I need to set out from a dialogical or dialectical standpoint, otherwise I don't experience any intellectual stimulation ... I want to feel a concrete interlocutor or adversary'.[89] Indeed, the idea of doing a fundamental critique without engaging in polemics seems like some sort of post-sectarian withdrawal symptom of those who once engaged in sectarianism too freely and promiscuously.

In this polemical mode, I would maintain that something like a postcolo-nial transformism has taken place, with entire groups of (ex)-leftists passing over to the 'moderate camp'.[90] Ahmad does not quite say so, but in a sense the 'unconditional war against political Marxism', 'antipathy toward working-class organisations' and against organised politics of the Left, and the 'advocacy of a global hermeneutics of suspicion',[91] characteristic of this formation, is today's version of transformism, that is, the passing over of a large number of former intellectuals of the left not so much to the right as to a floating intermedi-ate position from which both left and right can be attacked. But with the pro-viso that the incline of contemporary politics is such as to make it entirely likely that those groups will fall into a field dominated by right-wing maxims, such as the TINA doctrine.[92] The latter functions as a compact shorthand for a wholesale attack on 'metanarratives' that includes any attempt at an enlarged narrative of capital involving 'culture' within the dynamics of the produc-tion and realisation of surplus value, and on a range of other exclusions of which a categoric line drawn between class and community seems to be a key. A comprehensive definition of transformism can no longer be limited to the convergence of 'historic' left and right parties in terms of their programme[93] – although this has surely happened to any number of left parties moving to the

---

88   Jameson 1988, Volume II, p. x.

89   Gramsci 1994, cited in Brennan 2006, p. 266.

90   Thomas 2009, p. 151.

91   Ahmad 1999, p. 98.

92   TINA stands for 'There is no alternative'.

93   Gramsci 1971, p. 58.

right and adopting right-wing positions on crucial economic and social issues. However, it must certainly include the 'inexorable logic of progressive groups imperceptibly and unselfconsciously adopting conservative positions'.[94]

How does this transformism occur in late capitalism? It is virtually impossible now to think of it as a function of the cultural prestige exercised by a national bourgeoisie by its ability to deliver democratic culture and economic advances down to the last person. The more likely form these days is the negative force exercised by momentous historic reversals and the vast if mostly invisible power of multinational capital securely invested in the culture industries and the corporate university system against the backdrop of the closures of the post-1989 moment. In that case, the 'arrival' of postcolonial intellectuals from the Third World must be seen as an expression of complex tectonic shifts in global capitalism – the abandonment of some postcolonial (in the properly historical sense) goals, and the embracing of others. Gramsci's suggestion about intellectuals operating not only in 'civil society' but also in political society, in an 'organising role' that traverses the boundary between political society and civil society,[95] is important here and quite appropriate for the postcolonial intellectuals under consideration.[96]

With suitable modifications, to take account of the changed historical circumstances and roles, Gramsci's description of elite southern intellectuals may be extended to their postcolonial counterparts operating in 'the in-between, hybrid position of practice and negotiation'. As the 'non-commissioned officers' of more 'fundamental' social groups or classes, they function in their practical 'hybrid' position as 'mediating moments' of transmitting a class's hegemonic project from one 'attribute' of the integral state to another, the agents of condensation of social forces into political power.[97] They function not simply as constructors of the 'trenches' that characterise the complexity of a fully developed modern state. In their seemingly 'non-political' organisation in civil society, they function 'as points of prestige and attraction' for a class's hegemonic project, and embody those trenches themselves.[98] In the more

---

94   Brennan 2006, p. 271.

95   Thomas 2009, p. 413.

96   It is not a little ironic that the principal categories Chatterjee employs in his 'realist' political writings are 'civil' and 'political' society, defined in his own somewhat eccentric manner; see, for example, Chatterjee 2004, ch. 2 ('Populations and Political Society'). However, there is no question that Gramsci's notion of transformism is shown at work in Chatterjee's thought process and in the tenor of his political advocacy.

97   Thomas 2009, p. 413.

98   Ibid.

developed capitalism of our day, perhaps the two functions have been split up. The constructors of trenches (the activist, political intellectuals) and the constructors of ideology (the 'passive' academic intellectuals) nowadays rarely communicate directly, it seems, but nevertheless they often enough effectively get the business done. Dirlik's comment that what postcolonial intellectuals in the First World academe are celebrating is their 'new-found' power takes on a quite significant political meaning, even if the intellectuals under discussion here are a relatively minor if highly visible component of it.

The role of diasporic intellectuals, often arriving from the peripheral regions of imperial formations, formed an important part of Gramsci's thinking on the subject. In the Roman Empire, for instance, Gramsci argued that 'freed men of Greek or Oriental origin' formed a key stratum of 'traditional intellectuals', whose presence in Rome promoted 'centralisation on a massive scale' and whose role in the social organisation of empire was largely a pacifying one.[99] In the United States, Gramsci found another adaptation for the diasporic intellectual. There, he noted:

> The necessity of an equilibrium is determined . . . by the need to fuse together in a single national crucible with a unitary culture the different forms of culture imported by immigrants of differing national origins. The lack of a vast sedimentation of traditional intellectuals such as one finds in countries of ancient civilisation explains, at least in part, both the existence of only two major parties which could easily be reduced to one only . . . and at the opposite extreme the enormous proliferation of religious sects.[100]

The American 'Negro' intellectual, Gramsci wrote, would have a key role to play in the 'extension of American civilisation' and the 'conquest of the African market'.[101] Diasporic intellectuals have played all the roles Gramsci assigns to them in various historical junctures. It is hardly disputable that their arrival in large numbers in the US after 1965 has been an element in the prolongation of American dominance via the extension of 'American civilisation' into a variety of national arenas that might otherwise have remained indifferent or hostile to it. For the 'Southern intellectuals' of postcolonial studies – after their brief flirtation with subaltern consciousness and subaltern autonomy – there was little to hold their attention in the 'permanent stasis of tradition, the

99   Gramsci 1971, p. 17.
100   Gramsci 1971, pp. 20–1.
101   Gramsci 1971, p. 21.

endless obeisance, the tired re-enactments of hierarchy' in their own country of origin.[102] Their turn to the great ideas of European phenomenological existentialism, and its detotalisation in French poststructuralism, was probably to be expected once Marxism was consigned, ironically enough, to the scrap heap of Eurocentrism, a doctrine defeated it seems by history's inexorable progress. Prestige, we must conclude, no longer attaches to historical materialism and its categories and forms of thought. Insofar as Marxism breaks the surface of postcolonial studies nowadays, it is seen as practically continuous with those versions of European, or Eurocentric, thought, which imposed on the non-West its technological and epistemic violence, and was antagonistic to 'non-Western forms of emergence'.[103]

That said, postcolonial intellectuals differ from Gramsci's Southern intellectuals inasmuch as they are not products of the old classical, elitist *Bildung*. For the most part, they are principally educated in modern history and the social sciences, if not English literature and psychology, and many of them (in their early careers at least) had a real interest in Marx and the 'radical' formations descended from Leninism if not from anarchism and Maoism.[104] And they have played a more troubled role in the anti-intellectual atmosphere of the US academy.[105] However, as we have seen, in the case of Indian intellectuals of the Subaltern Studies variety, they are not above claiming some knowledge of their national classics and linking them to Classical European Antiquity in a manner reminiscent of the most elitist, textual version of Orientalist thought. This sort of pseudo-classicism seems to have become a requirement for prestige and position in the New Rome.

Perhaps there is some underexplored resemblance between the self-image of Gramsci's transformed intellectuals and Max Weber, and between Max Weber and the postcolonial intellectuals. Of course, postcolonial studies is unlikely to acknowledge the connection because Weber's scientific attitude to the study of religion and society apparently has little to do with the more overtly Heideggerian views of theorists like Chakrabarty. Still, Weber's frustration at the inability of the second Reich to resolve the contradictions of the German *Sonderweg*, and realise its true 'world-historical nature' and his uncertainty over the position of his class and their hegemony in Germany,[106] bears

102   Brennan 2006, p. 270. Readers are referred to Brennan's stimulating discussion of 'Southernism' and transformism; see Brennan 2006, pp. 262–71.

103   Brennan 2002, p. 188; see also Nandy 1995, p. 82; Prakash 1992b, pp. 8–9.

104   Sarkar 1997, p. 85.

105   Brennan 2006, p. 271.

106   Thomas 2006, pp. 147–58.

an interesting comparison with some of the dilemmas of the postcolonial intellectuals. On the one hand, the frustration of the German intellectual with the Reich's failure might indeed find its echo in the themes that are outlined in Guha's 'Indian historiography of India' culminating in *'the historic failure of the nation to come into its own'*.[107] As for the uncertainty about class position, *a fortiori* now more than even in post-unification late nineteenth century Germany, faced with the ruptures of colonialism, the vulgar ostentation and the new wealth of the postcolonial dispensation, the place of a genteel, learned bourgeoisie is marginal at best. Beneath the narrative of a different (alternative, hybrid) modernity one senses a certain nostalgia for traditions lost, and for a Brahmanical exegetical tradition rendered defunct by the circumstances of the times. Max Weber, reinvented after the War of 1914–18 as an intellectual who 'transcended politics' and found consolation in personal and mystical life,[108] would fit well with the postcolonial intellectuals in their metropolitan home, safely insulated from political conflict, free to meditate in an aestheticised fashion on conflicts happening elsewhere.

The irony of the situation is that there is an immense repression and forgetting of the close association between the communist mobilisations and movements of the twentieth century and anti-colonial and later postcolonial struggles. As Robert Young has pointed out, communism was the first and only political programme to recognise the interrelationship of the 'different forms of domination and exploitation' and the necessity of 'abolishing all of them as the *fundamental basis* for the successful realisation of the liberation of each'.[109] The uprising that was to topple the tsar began with demonstrations on International Women's Day in 1917, and the Bolsheviks made equality for women an urgent political priority, a principle that was extended to the colonial peoples and their struggles, a 'commitment unmatched by any party then or since'.[110] Eagleton is right to insist that at its heart anti-colonial and postcolonial struggles were and ought to be seen as class politics.[111]

The impetus for much of this radical thinking emerged from what we might identify as the classical tradition of Marxism, which found expression in a number of initiatives in Europe itself. Brennan lists a number of them: in France, for example, *Le Paria*, the organ of the 'Union Intercoloniale', the branch of the French Communist Party founded in the early 1920s to support insurgency in

107   Guha 1988, p. 43.
108   A reinvention that could apply to Heidegger almost three decades later.
109   Young 2001, p. 142, emphasis added.
110   Young 2001, p. 143; Eagleton 2007, pp. 54–5.
111   Eagleton 2007, p. 54.

the colonies.[112] There was also the *Comité de Défense de la Race Nègre* founded in Paris in 1926 by Lamine Senghor (1889–1927), a Senegalese politician, who also launched *La Voix des Nègres* in January 1927 and participated in February of that year in the *Congrès constitutif de la Ligue contre l'impérialisme et l'oppression coloniale*, organised in Brussels by Willi Munzenberg, one of the members of the Communist International.[113] In England, the Communist Party of Great Britain sponsored a number of anti-colonial organisations including the League Against Imperialism, the Negro Welfare Association, the League of Coloured Peoples, and the India League. The party also published journals such as *Inprecor*,[114] *Communist International*, and *Labour Monthly*, which were read not only in England, but in the colonies, carrying essays by the likes of Caribbean activist George Padmore, and future independence leader Jomo Kenyatta on 'The Revolt in Haiti', 'Forced Labour in Africa', and 'Labour Imperialism in East Africa'.[115]

These interventions were not limited to organisational or journalistic work alone; they informed the arts in ways perhaps unrecognisable now. Raymond Williams, as Brennan points out, was persuaded that the enabling condition of avant-garde cultural practice in Europe was the 'sudden proximity of intellectuals from distinct national traditions'.[116] In their turn, the Surrealists, for example, collaborating with the Communist Party of France (PCF), organised a counter-exhibit to the 1931 Colonial Exhibition in Paris entitled 'The Truth about the Colonies'. Recent research has begun to reassert some interest in the 'quite overwhelming evidence of anti-colonialism's communist currents'.[117]

---

112 Ho Chi Minh and Hadj Ali were among those involved; Brennan 2002, p. 191.

113 <www.fr.wikipedia.org/wiki/Lamine_Senghor>.

114 Originally founded by the Third International to allow communists to read the documents and thoughts of their comrades around the world, it continued after World War II under the Fourth International and was published in four editions: in French *Inprecor*, German *Inprekorr*, Spanish *Punto de Vista Internacional*, and English *International Viewpoint*; see <www.en.wikipedia.org/wiki/Inprecor>.

115 Callaghan 1997–8, p. 518, p. 522, cited in Brennan 2002, p. 191.

116 Williams 1989, pp. 43–7; Brennan 2002, p. 195.

117 Brennan 2002, p. 193, p. 195, noting the work of Edwards 1998 and Richardson 1996. More typical of the garbled writing available today is Kelley 1999, pp. 1–21, which makes the truly staggering assertion that Aimé Césaire's 1950 work, *Discours sur le colonialisme*, was trying to 'revise Marx' by suggesting that the 'anticolonial struggle supersedes the proletarian revolution' as the fundamental historical movement of the post-Second World War period. Marx, however, had considered this possibility as early as 1867 in relation to the English proletariat and the question of Irish independence from British rule! See Nimtz 2002, pp. 73–4; Cleary 2002, p. 120; Kevin Anderson 2010, p. 151.

All this by way of showing that there were radical alternatives to the view of the colonies presented by colonial administrators, missionaries, anthropologists, and so on. So when the PCF leader Maurice Thorez wrote that 'France, like Algeria, is but a mélange of twenty races', or when Gramsci claimed that the 'indigenous peoples of Algeria were not even left their eyes for weeping...For several years we Europeans have lived at the expense of the death of the coloured peoples; unconscious vampires that we are, we have fed off their innocent blood',[118] they were not expressing heterodox views, but in fact the 'collective wisdom' of the Third International on the colonial question. The influence of Marxism in the interwar years was such that Brennan concludes as follows:

> Marxism produced a particular constellation of thought that achieved mass density in regard to its colonial object, became a source of inspiration on a continental basis, knit together systematic investigations in several disciplines simultaneously, and lay behind the compulsive turning toward colonial motifs – often highly mediated ones – in writers who never consciously adduced Marxism, who were hostile to it, or who flirted with it briefly before heading off in new directions.[119]

One will search in vain for an acknowledgement of this parentage in today's postcolonial studies. If in colonial times history was ethnology's surrogate, as Ranajit Guha informs us, in postcolonial times a vastly exorbitated ethnology has become history's winding sheet.

Sarkar argues towards the end of his 'Decline of the Subaltern in Subaltern Studies' that 'culturalism' has in fact fed into an amnesia about class and class struggles.[120] In India, however, a significant left presence still allows for the study of historically determinate socio-economic factors as causal elements in popular struggles, and makes room for significant left-wing interventions in the political domain. But such scholarship is poorly known and basically unrecognised in the United States. There is room for the American-born Marxist in the US, but for the foreign-born Marxists – especially those born in the ex-colonies – there is very little room or interest. Even American critics of

---

118   Gramsci 1990, p. 19 cited in Brennan 2002, p. 198.
119   Brennan 2002, p. 192.
120   Sarkar 1997, p. 89. He contrasts this to E.P. Thompson's approach, which never gave up the attempt to situate plebeian culture 'within a particular equilibrium of social relations, a working environment of exploitation and resistance to exploitation – its proper material mode' (Thompson 1991, p. 7).

postcolonial studies generally seem to cite an older generation of the anti-colonial left: Fanon, Césaire, Lumumba, *et al.* Aijaz Ahmad and Arif Dirlik have made it into that rarefied pantheon, Ahmad generally through his *In Theory* rather than his Indian publications. For the rest, there is not much patience: Sarkar gets a brief nod here and there. The Indian postcolonialists themselves in their major publications – Chakrabarty, Chatterjee, Guha, Prakash, Spivak – basically ignore them. However, three ranks of postcolonial intellectuals are welcome:

1. Postcolonial populist writers like Vandana Shiva, whose positions on authenticity are quite close to Nandy's and latterly Chakrabarty's, and who might fulminate against corporate greed, but do so in the name of a properly authentic politics of Being;
2. Ex-Marxists like Chakrabarty himself, who while citing Marx and even discussing his work at length, have decided to find in Marxism a left outlier of Eurocentrism;
3. Foucauldians, or pseudo-Foucauldians, like Chatterjee, who manage to combine Foucault's championing of the 'specific' intellectual as opposed to the 'universal' intellectual'[121] with a newly discovered spirit of practicality and institutional realism, while availing themselves of the 'considerable theoretical freedoms' afforded by the metropolitan academy on postcolonial issues of hybridity and the like.

While area studies might have anticipated many of these tendencies,[122] postcolonial studies has been far more effective and totalising in its approach. A blanketing strategy would involve supplementing area studies' specialists, who can only 'stand in the place of the native', with authentic representatives from different parts of the world,[123] the 'freed' persons of the empire, so to speak. And it is best in that case to bring in people who can speak and write with the weight of personal experience, while steering the argument in directions that ultimately compound confusion with debility, and adding the weight of their 'national' traditions to metropolitan 'theory'.

Is the reception of postcolonialism a causal or symptomatic feature of the present impasse? One should not exaggerate the causal factor. While, of course, some form of leftish critique is never absent in the academy, its forms are important. If it contributes to the confusion, alienation and disorientation

---

121   Foucault 1984b, p. 68.
122   This is the burden of the argument in Harootunian 1999.
123   Harootunian 1999, p. 145.

that is already widespread with the rapid restructurings of capitalism in the post-Second World War period and particularly over the last twenty or so years, so much the better, especially if it also sounds radical. In some ways, postcolonial studies typifies this situation, with its critiques of economism and historicism (read: political economy and history, respectively), critique of metanarratives (read: mainly Marxism), and general orientation in a cultural-ist direction (adapting German aesthetic nihilism 'with its fear of civilisational decline and its ponderous explanations of world history in terms of racial classifications',[124] via French theory, to today's rainbow consumer culture). My argument is that the prominence of postcolonial studies is explicable in terms of what reaches the level of audibility in the current academic setup. The lat-ter's connections to capitalist restructuring is a matter of sophisticated and mediated articulations, rather than a simple causal link. So, in some ways, it is closer to symptomatic, that is, of all the possibilities offered by Third World intellectuals, it is neither the grotesquely militant political right, nor the activ-ist and historical materialist left that reaches this threshold. A small group of postcolonial intellectuals meet and exceed the level of what can be heard.

The intellectuals in question must have a critique of imperialism, now refocused on the Enlightenment legacy that is not well defended in the West, either for being Eurocentric or for having contributed to colonialism, or now for wreaking violence on non-European ways of being-in-the-world. Since glo-balisation claims to have ended the epoch of imperialism, this line of think-ing serves many purposes. They must also have some knowledge of Marxism and political economy, but must be able to point to its defects: having sup-posedly failed in 1989, a properly 'sophisticated' account of Marxism's limits and failures coming from the ranks of those it was supposed to have helped is very useful. Once a threshold of audibility is reached by the critique of imperialism directed towards the Enlightenment, and a critique of Marxism as a quintessential expression of it, through plausible inferences rather than systematic and serious reading of Marxist texts, all manner of Third-Worldist interests and concerns can be slipped in. This will involve, for the Indian intel-lectuals, for example – and they are a prominent contingent of postcolonial studies – attaching themselves to the romantic-idealist strain in Indology. This is a venerable stream of thought, pioneered by Schlegel and his fellow German Romantics, picked up and developed during the inter-war period by Guénon and Dumont, among other French intellectuals, who adapted some of the favoured theses of the Catholic Right regarding the dangers of secularism, and

---

124   Brennan 2006, p. 236.

were given an institutional form in the US by the likes of Mircea Eliade[125] and others who helped popularise the study of South Asian religions and civilisation in the United States.[126] All this can then be resumed under the banner of a phenomenological existentialism linked to Heidegger, and a poststructuralism linked to the likes of Foucault and Derrida, if not Deleuze and company. Some of the old political issues and cultural neuroses of a once-colonised country like India are nicely reinforced by recourse to the above-mentioned strands of a philosophical and theoretical organon. This combination is hard to crack in a purely textualist mode. And here the non-commissioned officers await the future: either a demobilisation as the present phase of intellectual production inevitably winds down, or a reassignment for which they might not be ready, especially if it involves a further sharp right turn.

6.3   The Orient as 'Vanishing Mediator'

The notion of a bedrock of the authentic, beyond the vicissitudes of history, seems to exert a central categorial and interpretive force in postcolonial history. In the case of postcolonial theorists from countries that are seen as the cradles of 'ancient civilisations', an 'Orient' in all but name is often conjured up to play this role, especially in today's diasporic manifestations of postcoloniality. The Orient mediates the disorientation produced by 'colonial modernity', while the rediscovery of elite and plebeian forms of authenticity – grounded in traditions that while sadly diminished and rendered into 'history', or 'hybridised'

---

125   Mircea Eliade (1907–86) was a Romanian historian of religion, philosopher, and eventually professor of religion at the University of Chicago. His flirtation with the Romanian Right is well known, although after his arrival at the University of Chicago his biography seems to have been thoroughly cleaned up by his pupils, stripped of its quasi-Fascist flirtation and re-presented in a more philosophical mode. Of course, it helped that he was staunchly anti-Communist. As Thomas notes of Weber's habilitation in the US, the re-presentation of politics as philosophy has historically been part of the 'customary qualifications that have been used for the integration of some of the least democratic' of modern European thinkers into 'the transatlantic liberal conscience' (Thomas, 2006, p. 157). For a typically sanitised version of Eliade's life and work, see Ellwood 1999.

126   There is a connection here between area studies and postcolonialism, which Harootunian's essay does not fully investigate, but which bears close scrutiny, that is, the ways in which the inter-war European right structured a series of concepts and a narrative of civilisations that have become rich grounds for the manoeuvres of both area-studies and postcolonialism.

by contact with the coloniser's culture (the West in this polemic mode)[127] –
nonetheless offer psychic consolations of various kinds. As this is a continuing
condition, albeit under new (postcolonial) conditions, the Orient persists and
plays an enduring role, albeit in elaborate guises, recovered through a rediscovery for postcolonialism of a Nietzschean-Heideggerian genealogy. No doubt
Brennan is correct in insisting that Heidegger is not a 'pronounced source' in
all postcolonial theory, yet there is equally no question that the turn to Being is
a philosophical gesture that has 'proven irresistible'. In part, this is because 'it
elevates the overly pragmatic discourse of identity politics to a more dramatic
plane without changing its substance'.[128] Needless to say that both Heidegger
and Nietzsche have found their way on to the reading lists of important postcolonial theorists like Ranajit Guha and Dipesh Chakrabarty, from whose work
their influence can flow downwards into second- and third-order theorising.
The Orient – explicitly in the founding philosophies of Being, and implicitly in
derivative versions – anchors the politics of postcolonial studies.

What about Latin America or Africa in that case? Functional substitutes for
the Orient have always existed – repositories of timeless tradition, authenticity and similar keywords supposedly with their roots in pre-colonial times – in
Latin America and Africa, revived for our times in indigenism or Afrocentric
reworkings of African history.[129] In the Euro-American world, mainly still the
Anglophone countries, the discovery of postcolonialism provides a fertile way
of addressing the disruptions produced by late capitalism – the debt crises,
national disintegration, the collapse of the welfare state, the massive disenchantment of a life determined by quantity with no alternative in sight, global
warming, immigration, ageing, and so on – at an ideological-discursive level.
The audience for postcolonialism is in this case a section of the 'left', both left
liberals and repentant Marxists. Neo-traditionalist postcolonialism may be a
version of anti-colonial authenticity for the global age. But it must be said that
for a properly metropolitan audience the Orient has no enduring significance.
The metropolitan audience will discover its own sources of authenticity, if
need be, in traditional Christianity, or in secularised hermeneutic readings of

---

127   I have already indicated that my uses of the term 'West' take into account its employment
         in postcolonial studies as both a reified entity and social agency – characteristics it
         acquired during the eighteenth century and onwards through the Cold War, in each case
         serving as a central axis around which difference and, indeed, inferiorisation could be
         constructed.

128   Brennan 2006, pp. 259–60.

129   Coronado 2009, pp. 1–24; Barnes 2003, pp. 62–92; Martin and West, 1999.

Christian texts, alongside the pleasures of an unspoiled rural life, not to mention fantasies about feudalism minus its brutal realities.

In Jameson's explication of the logic of the vanishing mediator, originally opposing moments of an emerging social form are mediated by the evolution of one of them to serve as a necessary link at the level of the ideological superstructure to facilitate the adequate development of the social form. That is, the mediator serves an indispensable function at a transitional moment when a new social form is taking shape,[130] serving to normalise or make acceptable an unfamiliar way of conducting a familiar activity. Thus, the emergence of a particular form of Protestantism – in Jameson's example, the Calvinist form of it, rather than the Lutheran – facilitates the moral-ethical universe of religion to inform the domain of economic activity, giving the latter a prestige altogether lacking in medieval times. After a while, the religious mediation is no longer vital to the development of new forms of economic activity and retreats, as it were, to a purely or largely spiritual domain. Having given its all, the Calvinist form of justification of economic activity for its own sake, as an end worthy in itself, can vanish from the economic domain, leaving the new economic form in its adequate self-sufficiency. Historically, the (vanishing) mediator ushers in a new epoch when the prestige attendant on economic activity in the new social dispensation actually leads to a whole new dynamic, transforming it from a purely ends-oriented activity to a means-oriented one (for example, capitalist economic production as a 'means to a means').[131] That is, it opens the way for the identity of dominant and determinant with which we are familiar in the developed capitalism of our day. Diagrammatically, Jameson represents the relationship in the following way:[132]

	Medieval	Luther	Calvin	Modern
RELIGIOUS ENDS	+	+	+	−
RATIONAL MEANS	−	−	+	+

Since the countries that colonised large parts of Asia and Africa, in addition to the European-settler ex-colonies like the USA, Australia, Canada and New

---

130   Jameson 1988, Volume II, pp. 3–34.
131   Postone 1996, p. 181.
132   Jameson 1988, Volume II, p. 24.

Zealand, are all now considered postcolonial (perhaps even more properly postcolonial than India, for example), it is worth asking whether the postcolonial is simply a discursive position, rather than a structural one?[133] If, indeed, the West, including its settler offshoots, is more properly postcolonial than the rest, it is quite arguable that the element of nostalgia for an Orient as it was (or is imagined to have been), before the irruption of the Occident in the form of Enlightenment-inspired colonial projects, must fade away from metropolitan postcolonialism. Even among the small section of the Western intelligentsia with an interest in the East, however the latter might be construed, there appears to be a preference for material presented without too much detail or complexity, and in a way that fits into the 'slots of [an] anti-Western cultural nationalism' or a 'post-structuralist play' with fragments.[134] Of course, the two are not the same, with the former relying on the plenitude of wholeness violently interrupted by colonialism, while the latter is committed to a notion of 'hybridity' that acknowledges no such hard knocks. That the latter view is gaining ground at the expense of the former is perhaps an important sign of things to come. In discussing Chatterjee's *The Nation and Its Fragments* in this light, Sarkar notes that this book tells us nothing about the powerful anti-caste movements associated with Phule, Periyar or Ambedkar, all of whom ought to have been of keen interest in a history of social thought and mobilisation emerging from the social margins of Hindu society in India. No book can be expected to do everything, Sarkar writes, but 'silences of this magnitude' are 'dangerous' in a book that appears comprehensive enough to serve as a 'standard introduction' to colonial India for non-specialists and newcomers, especially abroad.[135] However, there is a logic to Chatterjee's presentation. Plebeian attraction towards secularism (Periyar), or towards modernisation (Ambedkar), cannot be allowed to interrupt a narrative in which subalternity, by and large, has come to represent the occult layer of bourgeois consciousness, a resistant presence that signifies postcolonialism's indispensable foundation.

Similar observations can be made about Chakrabarty's *Provincializing Europe*, whose stresses and omissions signify a definitive moment of the production of knowledge: in this case, pressing into service a range of Orientalist keys to compose an elitist, Brahmanical worldview as something authentic, indigenous and unproblematic in a properly nationalist context. In this case, a Western audience is being asked to assent to a native interlocutor's superior command – going beyond mere linguistic competence – of source materials,

---

133   Dirlik 1994, p. 332.
134   Sarkar 1997, p. 95.
135   Sarkar 1997, p. 96.

the cultural nuances of a class of which he is a member, and the like. Of course, we can recognise here routines that have become familiar to us from the claims and counterclaims made in the writing of European history. In the new post-colonial regime, postcolonial theorists are being given the same rights, as it were, in the spirit of multiculturalism. Difference, in this context, also comes to signify interpretive exclusivity.

If, in this type of political-cultural milieu, an exotic element is to be found within Europe, it can easily be generated out of a neo-traditionalist reading of the *ancien régime*, the beauty and charm of country life, a recapture of the territorialisations of a Europe before nation states, even a sentimental regard for the old Church, all reworked into the specific terms of a postcolonial politics. The 'fully operative enchantment kit' that enabled the 'priests of science' to supplant the 'priests of god',[136] at the dawn of modernity, will have to be replaced if the secular hermeneutist successors of the 'priests of god' are to restore Old Europe to some proper civilisational standing. Provincialising Europe then is not just about showing the limits of Enlightenment reason; it has its own built-in version of a 'civilising mission', for Europe anyway, a 're-civilising' of Europe for postcolonial times. The work is well under way.

This could plausibly take the form in metropolitan postcolonialism of a Europe from which all traces of colonial histories have been erased. The objective of the 'four-nations' history, alluded to above, may be to take down an England-centred historiography, but the result is often an explicit postcolonial perspective fudging all the older, entirely valid distinctions of metropolis and colony that are key elements of a definition of colonialism,[137] not to mention the equally valid distinctions of class. The 'four-nation' postcolonialism appears to have little to do with colonialism as classically understood, as an exploitative socio-economic relationship between coloniser and colonised.[138] That perspective, given memorable expression by Marx in Volume I of *Capital*, in which modern colonialism and modern capitalism developed simultaneously – in part by *the capture of resources*, 'the discovery of gold and silver in America, the expatriation, enslavement, and entombment in mines of the indigenous population of that continent, the beginnings of the conquest and plunder of India, and the conversion of Africa into a preserve for the hunting of blackskins'; in part by the *capture of territory and markets* and their subsequent monopolisation by the 'mother country'; and finally by the

136 Bauman 1994, pp. 10–11.
137 See Part II, section I, 'Definitions: Colonialism, for example'.
138 Samuel 1998, pp. 21–40. Even more staggeringly, a 500-plus page book by the same title manages to say virtually nothing about colonialism, empire and the like; see Welsh 2011.

transformation of looted treasure into capital[139] – is in danger of disappearing. In its place, we have more pacific readings based on a civilisational predisposition, built into the 'West'.

As Huntington puts it, 'Western civilisation arose in the eighth and ninth centuries', developing its distinctive characteristics in the following centuries long before it began its modernisation in the seventeenth and eighteenth centuries, or to put it simply: 'the West was the West long before it was modern'.[140] Lazarus notes two further implications of this teleology of the West in Theodore von Laue's work. In essence, von Laue asserts that from the sixteenth century onwards, the world was brought together – for the first time in human history – into inescapably intimate and virtually instant interaction by the actions of a 'small minority commonly called the "West"'; and for the first time, this minority imposed its own accomplishments – including the 'arts of peace' (!) – as a universal standard to which all others, however reluctantly, had to submit.[141] The end result is that the global dispersal of capitalist modernity is presented in terms of the 'universalisation of the "West"'. Lazarus finds this tendency reproduced in the work of theorists as different from one another as Anthony Giddens, James Coleman and Francis Fukuyama – in which the West itself is constructed in a 'fundamental or primary sense' as a cultural disposition, a civilisation always already primed to dominate the lesser ones, but which in its essential Being can be understood without any such intervention of history.

In different ways, European and North American postcolonialisms could be finding their own regional paths towards such an amnesiac recharacterisation of their histories, a move made possible in part by the deployment of the categorial arsenal of 'authenticity', 'autonomy', and 'paradigm', which are also central to postcolonialism 'from the margins'. While Huntington, von Laue and their ilk purport to find in the West the highest development of reason, science, modernity, the only properly universalist civilisation, and the like, postcolonial critics see in these claims little more than a masking of the 'grimly functional instruments of the West's brutal rise to hegemony'.[142]

Of course, in any longer historical perspective, East and West seem to have been rather amorphous and expandable or collapsible entities. The 'earliest

---

139   Marx 1977, p. 915, p. 918, pp. 925–6.

140   Huntington 1996, p. 69.

141   von Laue 1987, pp. 3–4; Lazarus 2002, pp. 46–7.

142   Lazarus 2002, p. 60. Lazarus cites Chandra Talpade Mohanty's widely read essay, 'Under Western Eyes', as an example of the latter, but it is part of a much larger body of literature emerging from the former colonies; see Mohanty 1994, pp. 196–220, but for examples of the latter, see Chapter 2, section III above.

European form' of the West, according to Raymond Williams, originated in the division of the Roman Empire from the third century onwards, followed in the eleventh by the schisms and divisions within the Christian churches, both superseded in turn by the contrast between the West as a Christian civilisation and an 'East' defined either as Islam or as the civilisations beyond it from India to China.[143] Western and Eastern (or 'Oriental') worlds were commonly defined in this way from the sixteenth century.[144] During the Cold War, Lazarus refers to a further 're-functioning' that gave the binary opposition of 'West' and 'East' a new geopolitical significance, resting originally on the 'evident political divisions between Western and Eastern Europe', but subsequently generalised to be part of a 'universal contrast between political and economic systems of different types'.[145] Since the development of the East/Communist bloc could be represented in the West as 'a disease of the transition',[146] the diagnosis could be quietly extended to those other parts of the world that appeared to be suffering from identical symptoms.

Fernando Coronil argues that in postcolonial theory a cartographic term is used to represent the 'relatively intangible "historical relations among peoples" in terms of "the material, thinglike, tangible form of geographical entities"',[147] resulting in a fetishisation of the West or, more likely, its reification. Lazarus amplifies this to suggest that the West is used metonymically to refer not to a polity or a state (nor even a confederation of states), but to a civilisation, 'something altogether more amorphous and indeterminate'.[148] So amorphous and indeterminate in fact that Foucault was able to turn the tables on those who had constructed an imperial genealogy for Europe extending back to classical Greece and Rome. Foucault's 'Orient', as Afary and Anderson point out, seems to include the Graeco-Roman world as well as the more generally accepted 'Eastern one'.[149] Nietzsche's *Genealogy of Morals* includes in the category of 'noble races' at the bottom of which one cannot fail to see 'the beast of prey' – the 'splendid blond beast prowling about avidly in search of spoil of victory' – not only the Homeric heroes, the Roman, the Germanic and the Viking, but also the Arabian and Japanese nobility, all sharing in this

---

143 Williams 1983, pp. 200–1.

144 Lazarus 2002, p. 45.

145 Williams 1983, p. 200; Lazarus 2002, p. 45.

146 Rostow 1960, pp. 162–3.

147 Coronil 1996, p. 77, cited in Lazarus 2002, p. 44.

148 Lazarus 2002, p. 44.

149 Afary and Anderson 2005, p. 18.

'hidden core'.[150] Undoubtedly, some affinity for *bahubol* seems to be shared by all the members of the Aryan race, straddling the accepted divide of East and West, with the odd inclusion of the Semitic Arabs. What they all share is a nobility standing above the supine masses.

The contrast, for Nietzsche and Foucault, was between 'tradition' and 'modernity'. In this version of the Orient, there is no denunciation of upper-class (or caste) predation, spoliation, violence, and so on, since they all predated the decidedly effete and degenerate values of the Enlightenment and modernity. Some version of race solidarity and aristocratic virtue was part of the more romantic end of Orientalism – described in Vincent Smith's version of ancient India, as 'an essentially mobile society of a kind typical of the heroic age in other lands ... in Homeric Greece, for example, and in the Celtic West ... a warrior aristocracy, interested in feeding and fighting but little concerned with its humbler foot-slogging peasantry'.[151] Smith was doing nothing more than summarising a well-worn tradition of depictions of Aryan civilisation, and from that perspective neither Nietzsche nor Foucault was being particularly innovative. At most, they were perhaps being just a tad more inclusive in their idea of the Orient. Indeed, the Orient (or the 'East' in a more prosaic rendering) was part of a civilisational battle in which its traditional virtues were pitted against those of a modern Occident.

Depending on the values being promoted, this civilisational battle was no simple matter and has included, from the late eighteenth century to the present, the very definition of what constituted the 'West' in Europe itself, alongside the delineation of the essential lines distinguishing it from the East. When Edgar Quinet came to define the Western world in the mid nineteenth century, he included Russia, together with England and France, among the 'wise men' destined to carry the light of civilisation and Christianity to the Orient through colonisation.[152] Closer to our time, for altogether different reasons, Friedrich Hayek excluded not only Germany, which had since the time of Bismarck adopted positions 'antagonistic to "Western civilisation"', but also the 'French tradition', leaving just the 'Anglo-Saxon tradition', minus those who had shown some enthusiasm for the French Revolution (for example, William Godwin, Joseph Priestley, Richard Price, Thomas Paine and Thomas Jefferson, at least the Jefferson who had been 'fatally contaminated by his "stay in France"'!)[153] Hayek included Hegel and Marx among the 'disastrous Eastern imports', while

---

150   Nietzsche 1967, pp. 40–1.
151   Smith 1958, p. 2.
152   Quinet 1985, p. 148, cited in Losurdo 2004, p. 269.
153   Hayek 1973–79, p. 22; Losurdo 2004, p. 270.

Karl Popper, for his part, condemned Marx for his support of a 'collectivist and holistic' theory deriving from Hegel, along with Plato and Aristotle, whom he labelled 'totalitarians'.[154]

But Hayek and Popper disagreed on the centrality of Christian virtues to the West. Hayek viewed Christianity with suspicion when he claimed that 'a large section of the clergy of all Christian denominations' borrowed the aspiration to 'social justice' from socialism, and expressed grave doubts about saintly figures whose 'moral and religious beliefs can destroy a civilisation'. According to Losurdo, his words recall Nietzsche's view of Christianity, although he lacked the 'intellectual courage to proclaim his horror of Christianity'. Popper, on the other hand, praised the ideas of 1789, the synthesis of 'individualism' and 'altruism', which he celebrated as the 'basis of our Western civilisation' and a product of the 'central doctrine of Christianity'.[155] The fate of Immanuel Kant is instructive: Émile Boutroux included him among the other representatives of barbarism pouring in from the East,[156] but over time he has been fully rehabilitated by assimilation to the Anglo-Saxon world. Ralf Dahrendorf, for instance, claims that Kant 'discovered and developed the British tradition for Germany, or rather for Prussia'.[157] This notwithstanding Kant's own views of Britain as 'the most depraved of all nations', its tendency to regard other countries and peoples as 'mere appendices or instruments for its will to power', and the fact that he called William Pitt an 'enemy of mankind'.[158]

Hayek's condemnation of Hegel is interesting: branded as alien to the Western world and tied to the despotic and illiberal (if not barbaric) Orient for the 'extraordinary influence' he exerted, through Marx, 'on the East', this time via Leninism and Bolshevism.[159] Hayek, as Losurdo notes, is drawing on a motif that had spread through much of European culture after the October Revolution. Authors as far apart as Bernstein and Weber saw the cause of the Russian Revolution in Hegel's dialectics and philosophy, which for the most part was equated with the 'cult of success and force'.[160] Hegel was also subject to criticism by the Nazi ideologue Alfred Rosenberg,[161] who in his implicit

---

154 Popper 1945, Volume 2, p. 336, n. 15; Losurdo 2004, p. 270.
155 Popper 1945, Volume 2, p. 30; Losurdo 2004, p. 271.
156 Boutroux, cited in Losurdo 2004, p. 272.
157 Dahrendorf, cited in Losurdo 2004, p. 272.
158 Ibid.
159 Losurdo 2004, p. 280. For the extraordinary care with which Lenin read and noted Hegel, see Anderson 1995.
160 Losurdo 2004, p. 280; for Max Weber's position, see Beetham 1985.
161 Alfred Rosenberg (1893–1946) is considered one of the main authors of numerous key Nazi positions on racial theory, persecution of the Jews, Lebensraum, abrogation of the Treaty

attack on Hegel's philosophy of history expressed his complete revulsion by what he called 'materialist historicism' for being a philistine philosophy of life,[162] certainly not suitable, one would imagine, for a blond beast of prey.

However, Losurdo warns that to try to contrast German reactionism and Nazism on the basis of an 'exalted pathos of the Western world' would be a 'major mistake'.[163] In reality, the criticism of the West as an enemy of Germany in Nazi and Third Reich circles was strictly tied to a 'boundless celebration of the Western world, of which Germany [saw] itself as a bulwark and as an authentic interpreter'.[164] When Hayek passionately praised 'Western man' from ancient Greece onwards,[165] he was unaware – or so Losurdo maintains – that he was using an expression and a motif already 'largely present in the culture of the Third Reich'.[166] Losurdo concludes that 'the elimination of actual historical facts' was a necessary part of the construction of the West, the seemingly arbitrary inclusions and exclusions, but most absurdly of all its twentieth-century reduction to the 'image of England and the liberal Western world' of the nineteenth century as the standard for the 'Western' values of individualism, freedom and human rights.[167] England was the country not only of rotten boroughs, but also that of the political monopoly of property owners, whose system, according to Jeremy Bentham (hardly a revolutionary himself), perpetuated the 'all-embracing imposture' of British legal and cultural tradition that paved the way for all sorts of 'falsehood and deceit'.[168] His contemporary, John Stuart Mill, described the same system as 'a degrading idolatry which instead of perpetuating 'the perfection of reason' constituted 'a disgrace for [the] human intellect'.[169]

Since the 'elimination of actual historical facts', the randomisation of history and a contempt for 'materialist historicism' have all become naturalised in today's postcolonial world, one should not expect the construction of either the West or the East, the Occident or the Orient, to follow any decently rigorous criteria of definition, if that were even possible. With political reaction in full flow, perhaps it is time to wonder about Foucault's fascination with Iran, and its

---

of Versailles, opposition to 'degenerate' modern art, and the rejection of Christianity: <www.en.wikipedia.org/wiki/Alfred_Rosenberg>.

162   Rosenberg, cited in Losurdo 2004, p. 278.

163   Losurdo 2004, p. 279.

164   Ibid.

165   Hayek 1960, cited in Losurdo 2004, p. 279.

166   Losurdo 2004, p. 279; see also Losurdo 2001, pp. 226–8, 237–9.

167   Losurdo 2004, p. 282.

168   Bentham, cited in Losurdo 2004, p. 281.

169   Mill, cited in Losurdo 2004, p. 281.

larger ideological ramifications. Afary and Anderson pose the question about Foucault's interest in the Iranian revolution, while he showed no similar interest in the Nicaraguan revolution, which was unfolding at the same time, and only 'slightly greater concern' with the Solidarity movement in Poland.[170] The authors also wonder about the 'perplexing affinity' between this poststructuralist philosopher, this 'European critic of modernity', and the anti-modernist Islamist radicals who eventually hijacked the Iranian revolution for their own ends. Often construed as his 'error', this perplexing affinity may point instead to some of the implications of his Nietzschean-Heideggerian discourse, his attraction to 'Oriental forms of ascetic speculation' that went along with his fascination with monasticism, and the rituals and techniques that could be reinvented for a new (political) spirituality, a modern form of penitence, a Heideggerian 'freedom-towards-death', and a Nietzschean 'will to power'.[171] Afary and Anderson suggests that both the Islamic radicals and Foucault were searching for a form of political spirituality, both clung to idealised notions of pre-modern social orders, both admired individuals who risked death in attempts to reach a more 'authentic' existence.

Afary and Anderson maintain that an examination of Foucault's writings on Christian monastic literature, including lectures he gave before travelling to Iran and in preparation for writing the second and third volumes of *The History of Sexuality*, will show that Foucault, like Heidegger, was interested in a 'secular, hermeneutic reading of Christianity', especially of those rituals and techniques that could be reinvented for a new spirituality. Foucault also reworked the Heideggerian 'freedom-toward-death' as a 'liminal space for artistic and political creativity'. Khomeini's call to millions of Iranians to sacrifice their lives in the struggle against the Shah's regime seems to have become, for Foucault, an instance of Nietzsche's 'will to power'.[172] Heidegger's call of conscience and questioning of modernity have been likened to 'Oriental forms of meditation, including Japanese traditions', and linked to Foucault's preoccupation with various forms of Christian and Jewish mysticism, as well as 'magic, hermeticism and gnosticism'.[173] Uta Schaub further argues that the appropriation of 'Oriental lore' in Foucault nonetheless went along with the idea of an 'East that remained supposedly incomprehensible to the modern, rational European world'.[174] Indeed, like a passionate Romantic, Foucault may

---

170   Afary and Anderson 2005, p. 13.

171   Afary and Anderson 2005, pp. 13–4.

172   Afary and Anderson 2005, p. 14.

173   Afary and Anderson 2005, p. 17; Schaub 1989, p. 306.

174   Schaub 1989, p. 308.

have 'exoticised and admired' the East from afar, 'while remaining a Westerner in his own life'.[175]

Be that as it may, a 'dualism' emerges in which the pre-modern social order – assumed also to operate in many Middle Eastern, African and Asian societies of today – is privileged over the modern Western one. What Foucault admired about the pre-modern order is instructive. In an interview of 1982, Afary and Anderson note that Foucault combined an admiration for the Orient with 'a certain nostalgia for the aristocratic, ostensibly paternalistic system of taking care of one's subordinates',[176] which modernity had replaced with 'a callous form of individualism'.[177] This goes along with an admiration of silence, which Foucault believes to be a 'more interesting way of having a relationship with people'. What sort of people though? Foucault continues: 'Young Romans and Greeks were taught to keep silent . . . according to the people with whom they were interacting', and he goes on: 'I'm in favour of developing silence as a cultural ethos'.[178] As Afary and Anderson remark, there are echoes of Heidegger in this encomium to silence, for as Heidegger claimed, '[t]he discourse of conscience never comes to utterance'.[179] Alongside that, Foucault also regretted that 'we' – that is, the West – 'don't have a culture of suicide either'.[180]

Afary and Anderson seem to think that Foucault was 'blissfully unaware' in his encomium to silence of the hierarchical traditions that regulated relations between adults and youths, men and women, and upper and lower classes, in pre-modern societies.[181] But that is highly unlikely. It is much more likely that Foucault's invocation of innocence, authenticity, not to mention the organicity of the traditional community, is now part of a profound reorientation

---

175   Brinton 1967, p. 206; Afary and Anderson 2005, p. 17.

176   This should remind us of Chatterjee's admiration for the paternalism of the Indian peasant community, and Sarkar's sardonic comment on it. Chatterjee admits that the peasant community was never egalitarian, for 'a fifth or more of the population, belonging to the lowest castes, have never had any recognised rights in land'. Sarkar comments: 'No matter, however: this profoundly inegalitarian community can still be valorised, for its "unity . . . nevertheless established by recognising the rights of subsistence of all sections of the population, *albeit a differential right entailing differential duties and privileges*"' (Chatterjee 2000, p. 17, emphasis added; Sarkar 1997, pp. 97–8).

177   Carette 1999, cited in Afary and Anderson 2005, p. 18.

178   Ibid.

179   Heidegger 1962, cited in Afary and Anderson 2005, p. 19.

180   There is a lot of suicide about – poor farmers, for instance, or now Greeks and Spaniards subject to austerity and losing everything, ending their lives in despair – but alas, for the likes of Foucault, this is probably inadequate because it is not sufficiently aristocratic.

181   In this context, see the discussion in Matin-Asgari 2009, pp. 133–4, 149.

of political culture towards a respect for hierarchy, order, tradition, and the like. All the more so if it can be fused with authentic tradition and opposed to the unleashing of egalitarian and levelling forces associated with the radical Enlightenment and its nineteenth-century amplifications under the inspiration of Marxism. And just as important, although hardly admissible, so long as those who romanticise that 'traditional' order do not have to live under it. This is the magic of neo-traditionalism. The combination of Nietzsche-Heidegger-Foucault, Orientalism and cultural kitsch constitutes the powerful foundation on which postcolonialism builds.

Foucault's evocation of political spirituality may have been 'intended' to provoke controversy in France – and it certainly did in what Afary and Anderson call the 'most determinedly secular of any Western country'. But what is significant for my argument is the crucial point that, for Foucault, France itself had important lessons to learn from Iranian political spirituality. In a relatively unnoticed 1978 roundtable on *Discipline and Punish*, Foucault mentioned 'political spirituality' as an alternative to the hyper-rationality of the modern disciplinary apparatus.[182] Perhaps in this overall context, the earlier point that Dumont was 'translating' into the language of social anthropology a whole range of philosophical and sociological questioning about the direction of French modernity takes on a new significance.[183] A number of exogenous impacts – many originating with the Enlightenment and the Revolution of 1789 – had knocked the organic community of hierarchy, ritual and tradition sideways, and created a host of alienations, anomie, and so on, preventing *the French nation coming into its own.*

Sarkar wonders – in the historical context of colonial India – about the curious equation of the 'spiritual' with home, domesticity and femininity. How, he asks, 'did highly patriarchal religious traditions like Hinduism and Islam manage such an identification?'[184] The answer may lie in the politics of 'political spirituality' – the search for new bases of patriarchy, hierarchy, a gerontocratic and unequal system in all social dimensions, a return to core civilisational values of Hinduism, Islam, Christianity, and so on, reformulated in a secular hermeneutic manner. The very equation of community with religion points in that direction. How ironic it would be if the blond beast prowling avidly in search of spoil and victory should be temporarily refreshed by a postcolonial search for authenticity. Perhaps some neo-traditionalist will rediscover the Aryan roots of Bengali civilisation. Like Ranajit Guha, the Orientals may desperately want to

182 Anderson and Afary 2005, p. 287, n. 16.
183 Lardinois 1996, p. 31.
184 Sarkar 1997, p. 96, n. 36.

retain a 'long-lost' connection to Homeric heroes and Germanic tribes, but for the blood descendants of the blond beast in the West no such connection will be necessary or even desirable. The long way home for Europe – the 'home-coming' after a journey through the *foreign and the strange* – will almost certainly involve a forgetting.

One anticipates seeing the eventual recasting of the old literary trope of the Middle Ages as Europe's exotic-within, but perhaps now as the bedrock of European identities, or its postcolonial manifestations, Europe as rejuvenated Christendom, a new Holy Alliance, positioned against the Islamic Other, for example. Huntington sounds the militant note when he argues that the 'West's very survival is at stake', and Europeans and Americans must reaffirm their 'Western identity', accept their civilisation as unique and 'renew and preserve it against challenges from non-Western societies'.[185] These being postmodern or postcolonial times, a certain amount of cultural kitsch may be expected to come along for the ride in the form of neo-traditionalist popular culture, not to mention restaurants, boutiques, pilgrimage centres,[186] and tourist destinations, along with the postmodern commoditisation of terroir,[187] the Disneyfication of the medieval, and so on.[188] In the process, the Europe of the post-1989 period must yoke itself to its own properly European roots, a project aided by the 'incorporation' of the former Eastern bloc into 'Europe'. From these margins will arrive the latter-day Eliades, some no doubt claiming to be on the left.

The Orient works as a placeholder in the sense that it is the figure ultimately of self-identical authenticity in the postcolonialism that emerges from a former colony. To the extent that Europe must discover its own version of such

---

185   Huntington 1996, pp. 20–1.

186   The increase in pilgrim traffic to Lourdes or to Santiago de Compostela might be read as a sign of this already happening.

187   Jameson notes that in our time the 'terroir' itself has been commoditised and reckoned into the exchange value of the wine or its ingredients without a consciousness of the labour that went into its production. It is almost as if value is a function of nature; see Jameson 2011, p. 25.

188   On the place of the Middle Ages, see Kaiwar 2003. Karl Hillebrand attempted to fuse all the legends of India, Greece, Scandinavia and Persia into a universal religion that would 'regenerate a world distracted by rationalism'. As noted, for the royalist convert from Judaism to Protestantism and finally to Catholicism, von Eckstein, India along with Persia and Greece were precursors of the Germanic Middle Ages and 'all Europe, which was formerly Latin, is now Germanic, for the peoples of the North established all the southern empires' (Schwab 1984, pp. 221, 262). A bizarre version of the politics implicit in this last notion seems to be playing itself out in Europe in recent years.

self-identical authenticity, it must work through this placeholder, ultimately rejecting it, while substituting something equally durable in its place. The Orient, then, must vanish once Europe has supplied itself with its own version of self-identical authenticity. Diagrammatically, this can be represented as follows:

	Ex-colonial (Third World) postcolonial	Postcolonial (metropolitan arrival)	First World (metropolitan) postcolonial
ORIENT	+	+	–
OCCIDENT	–	+	+

The collective confrontation of two social forms, or historical epochs, that this sort of model stages is the reactionary counterpart of the framework Jameson has in mind when the past sits in judgement, as it were, on the present, informing us of the ubiquitous commoditisation, monadisation, instrumentalisation, and so on, of life in the age of capital.[189] This sitting-in-judgement is only productive for the other political rectification Jameson has in mind – the aperture to a future in which the capital social form is overcome – to the extent that the present that encounters the past as a different social form is *not* informed by the 'spirit' of postcolonialism.

6.4   The Unrenounceable Project

The logic of capital, as Jameson notes, is dispersive and atomistic, 'individualistic' – unlike the various forms of pre-capitalist modes of production that achieved 'their capacity to reproduce themselves through various forms of solidarity or collective cohesion' – an 'anti-society rather than society', its 'systematic structure . . . a mystery and a contradiction in terms'.[190] Even as capital homogenises the exploitation of human energies in pursuit of profit, 'constantly revolutionising' the instruments of production, 'the relations of

189   Jameson 1988, Volume II, pp. 175–6.
190   Jameson 1991, p. 343.

production, and with them the whole relations of society,[191] it creates massive disorders on the world scale, and psychic and emotional crises to match. The disenchantment experienced by people and expressed by social theorists as an inevitable feature of modern life is in fact a social effect of a historically unprecedented but rather perverse form of enchantment (the seduction of the commodity world, its play of difference, and so on), and the simultaneous giving up of hope of making sense of or even acknowledging the existence of an economic system, once sucked into the strange vortex of the value form. To the extent that people get subsumed under the strange, estranged, disorienting value form and its enchantments, they emerge disenchanted about overcoming its psychic and emotional disorders, naturalise them in their everyday life and appear to be chronically afflicted with uncertainty.

Moreover, to the extent that workers and working-class consciousness are brought into the desiccated fold of bourgeois disenchantment, the end result is business unionism undertaking to manage the contradictions of capitalism and contain the class struggle on behalf of corporate masters, seeking respectability in looking and behaving like poor imitations of their class superiors, and indeed even going to the extent of denying their membership of an exploited class. Cultural-identity politics steps in to address the situation, but it remains trapped within the very system of the reproduction of capital, merely responding to it by creating illusory escape hatches. Religion – and its secularised surrogates like psychology and philosophy – may step in to advise and pacify, but they largely transport people into the now commoditised domains of the unconscious, the ontological and the mysterious, which are all starting to sound alike in their mediation through money. Disenchantment, then, can be understood as an effect of the enchanted world of money that miraculously produces more money via its self-propelling velocity. The 'nightmare of history' – nothing less than the loss of countless generations of children, women and men sacrificed through a lifetime of back-breaking labour to produce the comforts of the ruling class and its hangers-on – has itself been displaced either on to some ontological or cultural level. It can be portrayed as a consequence of the abandonment of myth and acceptance of 'linear historical time',[192] or perversely now shifted on to that demiurge that we are told has brought so much misery to the non-West, namely, the Enlightenment. The latter appears to have a will of its own to suppress the time of the gods and spirits, replacing it with science, design, order, surveillance and control, to repress History II for the benefit of History I.

---

191   Marx and Engels 1980, p. 19.
192   Eliade 1954, ch. 4; Eliade 1959, pp. 231–45; see also Cronin 1982, pp. 435–48.

Marx and other radical thinkers acknowledged that we now inhabit a much larger world than our predecessors, in which a world literature and world history have emerged as almost unreflected realities of our lives, but they also noted that these have occurred mostly within forms admissible under capital's dominance.[193] The universalism we experience is seriously truncated, incomplete and, for many, crippling and 'incapable of resolving the problems engendered by [capital's] own expansion'.[194] The postcolonial attack on universalism, however, is grounded in a different line of thought: the idea that as modernity unfolds it becomes increasingly plural, untranslatable and even perhaps the subject of mutual incomprehension and non-communication across cultural divides. This is a rather outlandish suggestion when, as is usual with postcolonial studies nowadays, the dividing line is between Europe on the one side, and the many other, alternative and hybrid modernities on the other.

But this is also inevitably a consequence of the fact that postcolonialism is, as Eagleton suggests, or has become in my reading of its trajectory, like postmodernism inasmuch as it tends to inflate the significance of 'cultural factors' in human affairs. Eagleton maintains that this is a vice to which literary intellectuals are especially prone, but again, as this book has tried to show, it is a tendency if not a vice that has conquered the historical and social-scientific disciplines as well.[195] It would be comforting for them, Eagleton continues, if what was at stake 'between the north and south of the globe' were questions of 'value, signification, ... identity, cultural practice rather than arms, trade agreements, military alliances, drug trafficking', and the like. He concludes that the acknowledgement of 'difference, hybridity and multiplicity' is a drastically impoverished kind of political ethic in contrast to 'the affirmation of human solidarity and reciprocity'.[196] In our day, we may have to fight our way through the seductions of 'difference, hybridity and multiplicity' to develop the necessary 'solidarity and reciprocity', but this is a fight to which apparently postcolonialism is not willing to commit itself. There is too much at stake – including all manner of academic institutional inducements, not to mention the great historic reversals of a generation or more – to want to undertake it. We may have to look beyond its purview.

The operations of culture-based identity politics are far from being a purely 'verbal invention of idle academics'.[197] The perception of oneself as first and

193   Marx 1980, pp. 21–2.
194   Amin 1989, p. 10. For a review of this work, see Kaiwar 1991, pp. 69–78.
195   Eagleton 1998, p. 26.
196   Ibid.
197   Cusset 2008, p. 132.

foremost a member of an ethnic group, a religiously based community, a minority, and so on, alongside the expulsion of 'political belonging' from the sphere of identity,[198] especially one based on something as old fashioned as *human solidarity*, let alone class-based mobilisation, had spread throughout all levels of society, as Cusset notes in the context of the United States. In turn, those are integrally linked to several political-economic developments: the cultural repercussions of the struggle for civil rights (or, more likely in my opinion, the gravitation of those struggles away from a class-based internationalism towards ethnic-particularism under the pressure of repression and co-optation); the decline of the democratic left; identity-based clustering in an increasingly competitive economic climate (especially as the boom-bust cycles and their accompanying recessions deepened); and the segmentation of consumers into likeminded identity groups.[199]

However, in the age of globalisation, these tendencies have not been confined to the world's largest capitalist power. Similar tendencies were operating with some degree of punctual coincidence in other capitalist Anglophone countries, and with some time lag in other countries, including the ex-colonial ones as well. If one were to look for the source of the workings of a delirious 'otherness machine',[200] it would have to be traced to capital in search of profits in a climate in which the older methods that worked for a generation or so after the Second World War had ceased to be effective. That is, once the extensive job of rebuilding after the destruction of the war had more or less been completed, what was left was not only the conquest of nature and the unconscious, but the body itself. The body, segmented and parcelled out into the most minute differences, was now the final market to be conquered. This was a climate in which the strategic production of identity – not only race, but everything else that could count as 'difference' – operated in a manner in which a 'mobile, radically contingent and hierarchically organised lexicon of "oppressions" was beginning to displace more foundational schemas of domination and exploitation'.[201] By the same token, it can be argued that identity politics has had to cluster around the commoditised body *sans* a critique of capital.

---

198   Brennan 2006, p. x.

199   Cusset 2008, p. 132.

200   Appiah 1991, p. 356.

201   Lazarus 2011, pp. 100–1. Lazarus makes a good point here. A competitive notion of oppression, suffering and deprivation seems to be at the heart of ethnic politics and its academic counterpart, ethnic studies. To an extent, it reproduces the competitive surplus value seeking behaviour of capitalists.

The postcolonial critic effectively had to disavow those foundational schemas and write 'within theory', which given the historical moment of its emergence meant poststructuralist theory.[202] The postcolonial critic was authorised
to write about historical or textual matters with the assurance that 'such
commentary was always ultimately about the self', a 'hovering emphasis', as
Brennan puts it, would be on an epistemological divide based on national, ethnic, psychic being.[203] What identity politics needs to suppress – particularly in
university circles – is class. It might be necessary, of course, to mention class
(and that awful word, classism) in any course on Race, Class and Gender, or
some variation thereof, dependent on location, but it will be equally necessary
to quickly suppress class in favour of the others, not as a temporary strategic
device either for people to think through the contradictions of identity politics
or on the way to enriching a notion of class, but definitely as a form of erasure,
as a bad dream of yesteryear, a surrogate for all the crimes of what was once
called actually existing (now defunct) communism. This is fertile reactionary
ground, particularly well tended in the US academy and gaining ground elsewhere, a carnival that postcolonial studies has participated in, if not initiated.

From this vantage point, I find puzzling what appears *prima facie* to be a
reversal on Cusset's part, after he has shown his readers the liabilities of the
fragmentation of identity politics, and its operations in the academic world.
This is a world in which 'the mere enunciation' of cultural difference and thus
identity is made to appear as 'a political act of crowning importance', rather
than what it usually signifies, namely, 'the disappearance of politics, as such'.[204]
Cusset rightly points to its deleterious impact, especially on minorities outside the university. However, towards the end of his book, Cusset notes that
everywhere, except in France, Deleuze, Foucault, Lyotard and even Derrida
'hypercriticism' incarnate the possibility of continuing a 'radical social critique'
beyond Marx, a critique that relative to Marx was finally 'detotalised, refined,
diversified', but more so opened up to 'questions of desire and intensity, to flux
and signs of the multiple subject', to social movements confronting the crucial
question of difference.[205] Perhaps he has in mind a long journey through the
realms of desire, intensity and flux to arrive once again at an enriched and
expanded purview for Marxism? Then again, perhaps not. After all, for that
to happen we would need, once again, a movement based on the relationship
of exploitation that is fundamental to the capitalist mode of production, and

---

202   Brennan 2006, p. 115.
203   Ibid.
204   Cusset 2008, p. 140.
205   Cusset 2008, p. 330.

which would place all of the above into a framework in which difference itself could be seen as a moment of capital. But as we know, that has not been the case in the countries where French theory was welcomed and embraced, most notably in the United States. Separating politically debilitating forms of difference from politically energising and enabling ones will require a prolonged engagement with capital starting, dare one say, with *Capital.*

As Anderson concluded long ago, French theory itself appears not to provide the tools for concrete social investigation – witness not merely Levi-Strauss's 'fleeting field-work and fictive map of kinship systems', Lacan's 'ten-minute psychoanalytic sessions', Foucault's 'credulity' in the Ship of Fools and fable of the Great Confinement,[206] not to mention the altogether more deplorable consequences of his fatuous generalisations about the Iranian revolution; all not so much personal limitations or lapses of the practitioners concerned as the 'normal and natural licences in a play of signification beyond truth and falsehood'.[207]

When Žižek contends that today's post-politics cannot attain the properly 'political dimension of universality' because it 'silently precludes' the sphere of economy from politicisation, he is, of course, calling attention to something crucial. The domain of global capitalist (market) relations, he suggests, is the 'Other Scene' of the so-called repoliticisation of civil society advocated by the partisans of 'identity politics' and other postmodern forms of politicisation.[208] However, some clarifications are needed here: for one thing, the economy is far from being depoliticised in its entirety. The battles over taxes, the social welfare system, the imposition of 'austerity' on the working class, the looting of their pensions, and so on, all involve politicisation of the economy by other means and methods. They are part of a class war, conducted by capital and the state, a supranational state in the case of the European Union, against the workers in a time of crisis. It is conducted in a way that intensifies the crisis itself – policies leading to renewed recessions, and so on, which in turn have the effect of fragmenting the sphere of 'civil society' even more. What is completely excluded – and this is where Žižek's argument has the potential to become significant – is any possibility of changing the social basis of production, transforming, so to speak, the social relations of production. It is not the 'noisy' sphere of circulation – market relations where everything 'takes place

---

206   Anderson 1983, p. 48.
207   Ibid.
208   Žižek 2000a, pp. 353–4. Žižek tends to reduce capitalism to market relations sometimes, simply using the term 'capitalist market relations' as if there are no capitalist production relations that are anterior to the market relations.

on the surface' – but the 'hidden abode of production' that is at stake.[209] This is where the 'real trick' takes place, where the process of the exchange of equivalents turns into private profit for capitalists or, at any rate, where the process begins – a process in which the proletarian is merely a machine for the production of surplus value.[210] The noisy sphere is what we might call, following Žižek, the abode of 'post-politics'.

Every instance of modernity is, of course, singular, but the proper analytical approach is to reveal what they all have in common that makes singularity part of the larger movement of history. Terms like unhistoricisable, untranslatable and uncomprehending are the terms of a culpable abdication of a responsible politics of academic practice. They are at best self-exoticising propositions, designed to mystify. Calcutta may never become London, but then neither will Shanghai, Moscow or Paris, for that matter. A proper History II will recognise that Calcutta – or Shanghai, Moscow, Paris, and all the spaces around and between – has seen more than its share of dispossession, insurrection, class struggles and miseries. All of them house any number of 'secret abodes' where workers, no matter what their cultural or ethnic identity, are systematically exploited through a process by which the products of their labour appear as capital, as alien property and as an alien power that in effect they now seem powerless to confront.

Perhaps this recognition is one of the adequate grounds for universalism, albeit a negative universalism in the first instance. That is, it grounds universalism in expropriation and exploitation. There are two advantages to this approach: one, it locates a possibility for universalism in opposition to the dominant social form (capital) of our epoch, and makes a critical analysis of it possible; and two, it directs attention to labour, including 'productive labour', as the form that structurally underpins the virtually limitless multiplication of commodities and services that govern our lives. Instead of those possibilities being explored and enriched, what we get now is a certain 'displacement effect' whereby the structural aspects of the struggles of socio-economically 'marginal' populations are presented as secondary (if mentioned at all) to their religious, gender, ethnic and cultural identities and struggles for recognition. The ferocious and concerted attacks on unions and organised labour has coincided with the entry into the ranks of wage labour of many millions of people who were outside those ranks a generation or two ago – that is, the entry of marginalised peasants now fully proletarianised. These processes have rendered the very category of the 'marginal' an amorphous and expandable one.

---

209   Marx 1977, p. 279.
210   Marx 1977, p. 742; Jameson 2011, p. 67.

In the planet of slums we occupy, is it necessary to argue about what is happening when the 'ethnically' or otherwise marginalised people, who depend on wage labour, assert themselves – however fleetingly or inchoately – against their employers or against the state for simple resources (say, for water, electricity, housing, and suchlike), all of which should be counted as part of their wages? Is this not integrally a part of the class struggle even if fought under a variety of banners?

When Eagleton refers to certain forms of political conflict that are proving hard to crack, he might be referring either to the fact that ruling class domination has become more involved and complex, and less transparent certainly than it was previously (if not as hard to decipher as the workings of finance capital), or that surveillance and repression have become more all-encompassing and effective.[211] To speak in contingent, metonymic, aleatory terms seems better than to speak in terms of structural transformation. Either way it signals the possibility that 'post-politics', of which postcolonialism is a significant representative, begins with a tactical withdrawal, which after a period of time begins to acquire what seems like a strategic dimension. And when Žižek refers to the 'spectral presence of Capital' as the figure of the 'big Other', which inexorably compels the forms of our life that are seemingly dominated by fluidity and becoming, not to mention new forms of politics based on ethnic, gay, ecological, and other groupings, forming and dissolving all the time, I think he means to say that capital has now, more than ever, certainly more than in Marx's time for instance, invested the domains of culture and identity. In the process, it has brought them within the circumference of the operations of the value form. Since the 'depoliticised economy' is the 'disavowed fundamental fantasy' of post-politics, a properly political act would necessarily entail the 'repoliticisation of the economy', for, in Žižek's words, a 'gesture counts as an act only in so far as it disturbs ... its fundamental fantasy'.[212] And since there is no 'economy' that is not also the site of exploitation, a primal scene of classes in direct confrontation over such basic issues as wages and working conditions, repoliticisation is also another way of speaking of class issues and class struggles, whatever other layers of overdetermination and complexity one might wish to add to it.

The persistent desire, then, to deflect attention from that primal scene, a good deal of the urge to think away the 'unthinkable reality' of alienated labour, is at the root of the postcolonial attack on 'economism'. It is also at the root of the desire to see the deprived lives of working people in terms of

211   Eagleton 1998, p. 26.
212   Žižek 2000a, p. 355.

(cultural) plenitude, to romanticise the lives of peasants and artisans as symbols of autonomy and self-determination at a time when the real subsumption of their labour to capital makes a mockery of what little autonomy and self-determination they may have formerly possessed, and to conjure up the many-sided creativity of people who have few opportunities to exercise it.

In this world, historically determinate abstractions (capital, labour, socially necessary labour time, and cognate categories) have been declared signs and symptoms of the Enlightenment tyranny of homogeneous, empty time. What we are given instead are ahistorical abstractions: Authentic Being, Nothingness, Time of the Gods, and so on. Rhetorical flourishes aside, the field of postcolonial studies operates simultaneously in two modes: one, the theoretical mode, in which all sorts of poststructuralist flourishes are part of the rhetoric of hybridity, marginality, liminality, and so on; and two, a historicising mode, in which all manner of continuities are posited by native experts whose interpretation of texts is supposed to be adequate to settle the issue. The two are loosely linked by a critique of transition theories and economism, historicism and, astonishingly, nihilism, alongside the advocacy of populist decisionism. This toxic combination actually leaves untouched or even reinforces the universality of a certain segment of the ruling class – those whose ethnicity is encompassed by their Euro-American-ness or derived European-ness – who have placed themselves outside the domain of identity politics, a position from which they adjudicate claims and counter-claims of identity and authenticity. While identity politics is based on an inchoate sense of oppression, the machinery of difference production steps in to make sure that the actual, historically realised power structure is hardly shifted at all; it simply goes underground.

From the ahistorical abstractions come pseudo-concrete formulae: the many ways of being-in-the-world, the authenticity rooted in primordial cultural roots sedimented into language, and the paradigms bequeathed by dying generations of social life. It is in this world too that it becomes easier to contemplate the thoroughgoing deterioration of the earth and nature than the breakdown of late capitalism.[213] A triumph, one might conclude, of the bio-naturalistic over the political-economic, grounded in the idea of communities of soil-and-blood, a characteristic we earlier recognised in postcolonial populism,[214] and now in a somewhat more sophisticated and all-encompassing form in postcolonial studies.

So when in reference to a couple of essays by Gyanendra Pandey – in which the author engages in agonised contemplation of 'violence' and 'pain'

---

213   Jameson 1994, p. xi.
214   See Chapter 2, section III above.

as 'fragments',[215] the perception of which is implicitly assumed to be direct and certain – Sarkar quotes Jameson's comment about 'empirical and anti-systemic positivist attitudes and opinions' presented as 'heroic forms of resistance to metaphysics and Utopian tyranny',[216] he no doubt means to suggest precisely the triumph of ahistorical abstractions and pseudo-concrete formulae, all kept afloat by some version of postcolonial existentialism. This is reinforced by E.P. Thompson's observation regarding the fatuity of statements about the 'human condition', which unless further 'qualified and disclosed' – properly historicised, we might conclude – amount to nothing but a kind of 'metaphysical full stop', or worse, 'a bundle of solecisms about mortality and defeated aspiration'.[217]

Some such considerations need to be kept in view when confronted with claims on behalf of the new forms of politics emerging 'all over the world', incessant activity of 'fluid, shifting identities' focusing on particular issues, the construction of multiple *ad hoc* coalitions, and so on.[218] In the US, between 1980 and 1990, the number of Americans claiming 'Native American' status increased by 255 percent, while in the same decade twenty times more people called themselves Cajun, and three times more people affirmed their Francophone heritage.[219] Since these affirmations are part of an unfolding of ethnic politics, there is no way to assume that such identities will somehow settle into permanent formations, rather than yield ever-more fantastic combinations in the future. Cusset, who cites this evidence, notes that while outside the university these take the form of community rituals or are at most reflected in Census statistics – and some marginal funding for projects – in the university itself 'minorities' are encouraged 'piously [to] cultivate what Freud called the "narcissism of minor differences"'.[220] It is doubtful that similar levels of ethnic fragmentation and fluidity can be replicated elsewhere in the world, but within the postcolonial framework under analysis even the past is not safe from this sort of ethnic fragmentation. History itself has been taken captive by ethnology's imperatives. From the perspective of the state overseeing the vast upward distribution of wealth over the last thirty years or so, these are most welcome developments and are to be encouraged by any means whatsoever.

---

215   Pandey 1991, pp. 559–72; Pandey 1994.

216   Jameson 1993, p. 184.

217   Thompson 1993, p. 188, cited in Sarkar 1997, p. 102.

218   Žižek 2000a, p. 354.

219   The fact that there is no such stampede on the part of Euro-Americans to claim African-American status tells us something about the symbolism of these claims.

220   Cusset 2008, p. 132, draws these statistics from Gitlin 1995, p. 162.

More consequentially, while the 'postmodern politicisation' of domains hitherto considered outside the public domain of politics – Žižek cites feminism, gay and lesbian politics, ecology, ethnic and 'other so-called minority issues' – has had a 'liberating impact', and the point is not to return to some new version of 'so-called economic essentialism',[221] both the fragmentation and the depoliticisation of the economy have had the effect of conceding far too much ground to consolidated right-wing formations, which often have the state at their back. And that combination has today become, Žižek claims, the main obstacle to the realisation of the 'very (feminist, ecological ...) demands on which postmodern forms of political subjectivisation focus'.[222] The argument for a return to the 'primacy of the economy' then rests on precisely creating the conditions for the more effective realisation of the issues and demands raised by postmodern forms of politicisation.

Perhaps this is the best one can do at the moment – social democracy for the postmoderns – but it must also be weighed against the understanding that there is something 'inauthentic' about all this 'incessant activity of fluid, shifting identities ... multiple *ad hoc* coalitions', as well as, I might add, about the methods that emerge to formalise all those manner of social divisions, as if they originated outside a historically determinate set of conditions. Žižek's conclusion is well taken, namely, that ultimately there is a resemblance here to the behaviour of 'the obsessional neurotic who talks all the time and is otherwise frantically active precisely in order to ensure that something – what really *matters* – will not be disturbed, that it will remain immobilised'.[223] Eagleton's dispossessed right, eagerly chattering away about reclaiming India while avoiding the issue that most exercises them, namely, the rights of property, has its popular 'left' equivalent, or so we learn from Žižek.

Moreover, if the 'social turbulence' emerging from a variety of movements remains 'unsystematic and disorganised', but continues to grow under the pressure of events, the response will most likely be an intensified state repression, wherever piecemeal concessions were not possible, and perhaps even a strengthening of the right wing.[224] Historically, the social constituencies that today's identity-based movements encompass have tended to do well when intimately connected to large-scale liberation movements – whether these were national liberation movements, revolutions or civil-rights movements – when those were organised under a secular-universalist banner, rather than

---

221   Žižek 2000a, p. 356.
222   Ibid.
223   Žižek 2000a, p. 354.
224   Eagleton 1998, p. 26.

an ethnic-particularist one. At a time when there are so many battered, besieged economies around the world, and the contagion of recession and austerity seems to be spreading, and when, as noted, even a dyed-in-the-wool Cold Warrior like Zbigniew Brzezinski does not expect the reign of the 'indispensable nation' to last forever and is led to speculate if a 'pre-revolutionary' situation is not taking shape,[225] it is hard to summon much patience for the 'production of hybridisation' and other postcolonial gestures.

So, yes, it is time – as Keya Ganguly reminds us – to question the supposed superiority of relying on the constructionism of 'discourse' over the essentialism of 'reality'.[226] For after all, it is a system that is in question, and this system of capitalism, while registering the most astonishing mutations and changes during its historical course, also remains *essentially* the same in its fundamental structural properties and tendencies – the 'profit motive, accumulation, expansion, exploitation of wage labour', constantly breaking down and 'repairing itself not by solving its local problems but by mutation onto larger and larger scales',[227] using space to buy time.

And here, two further points need to be considered. The first is the point made by Žižek concerning Marx's metaphor of capital as a vampire-like entity, feeding on the blood of living beings.[228] That is, if the image is designed to tell us something essential about capital, it is that capital needs some form of 'pre-reflexive' natural productivity, outside itself, as it were, to feed upon – whether this be uncommoditised nature, the labour of peasants and artisans whose access to the means of subsistence still lies substantially outside market circuits, or the autonomous talents of scientists, artists, and so on, paid out of the circuit of revenue.[229] In Luxemburg's view, capital resolved its crises of profitability by helping itself, through extensive colonisation, to pre-capitalist areas, bringing them under its formal subjection in the first instance. But this is a self-extinguishing process, since each new conquest of natural or 'pre-reflexive' productivity limits the spaces outside capital. In its latest

225 Brzezinski 1998, pp. 196–7; Labica 2007, p. 234. Since Brzezinski wrote his book, there have been any number of movements with revolutionary potentials, not only in the Arab countries, but also in Southern Europe, Latin America, and increasingly now in parts of Asia. All of them have formulated programmes that are unsurprisingly similar and basic in their universalism, some version of bread, dignity and freedom, combined with mass mobilisation (peaceful where possible; armed where not).
226 Ganguly 2002, p. 241.
227 Jameson 2011, p. 6, 9.
228 Žižek 2000a, p. 358.
229 On the relationship between capital and 'natural productivity', see Foster 1998, p. 6; Marx 1977, pp. 637–8.

mutation, capital has turned to an intensive colonisation bringing into the circuit of surplus value all forms of labour, even those involved in the most marginal sorts of services,[230] activities associated with the production of art, science, culture, along with human relations and language itself,[231] not to mention the sale of body parts or their products including kidneys and ovaries, and so on,[232] remaking all of them into moments of the circulation of capital.

The second is Marx's insistence that the limit to capitalism is capital itself, a limit exposed by the 'eroding [of] the last resistant spheres of non-reflected substantial being, which has to end in some kind of implosion', when capital 'will no longer have any substantial content outside itself to feed on'.[233] If so, the implosion may take the form of prolonged crises with no immediate prospect of resolution, but also the form of a massive assault on acquired standards of living at the very heart of the capitalist world, a process that began slowly with some halts and resumptions after the mid-1970s, but has acquired an unmistakeable urgency and clarity after 2008. However, this is not the end of the story, or it would be a monstrous dystopia.

Capitalism began the world-historical process of developing the productive forces on a planetary scale, but, as Georges Labica puts it, globalisation as every internationalist has dreamed of it is 'still something to be won'.[234] In his view, quoting Luxemburg, it can only be won by 'the application of socialist principles'.[235] Capitalism's inherent contradictions prevent it from completing the task it began. But it is also worth reminding ourselves that many of the 'left' movements (of the 'post'-political variety) today are conservative, if not reactionary, in their implicit romance with the past of small-scale production and community. The free-market right seems to have captured the rhetoric of innovation and 'modernity', insisting both that their 'market ideal' is anchored in an eternal human nature, and that it is the most advanced form of future productivity and innovation.[236] Much 'post'-politics veers erratically between the romance of pre-capitalist community and a practical capitulation to the logic of neoliberal rhetoric of markets and commodities. The point is, as Jameson insists, that Marx alone sought to combine 'a politics of revolt with

---

230   See, for instance, the piece by Benanav 2010: <wwwendnotes.org.uk/articles/1>.
231   Labica 2009, pp. 190–1.
232   Lois Rogers and Jane Mulkerrins, 'Young Women Selling Their Eggs To Pay Off Student Loans': <www.rense.com/general10/youngwomenegg.htm>.
233   Žižek 2000a, p. 358.
234   Labica 2007, p. 234.
235   Luxemburg 2003, p. 447.
236   Jameson 2011, pp. 89–90.

the "poetry of the future"' and applied himself to demonstrate that socialism was both more modern and more productive than capitalism. To recover that 'futurism and that excitement' is surely the 'fundamental task of any left "discursive struggle" today'.[237]

And here we might remind ourselves that even after 'the end of history', a persistent historical curiosity asserts itself, as Jameson notes in *The Seeds of Time*, 'of a generally systemic – rather than a merely anecdotal – kind', an anxiety about the 'larger fate or destiny' of our system or mode of production as such.[238] A persistent curiosity that apparently can neither be fully contained nor vanquished, even if it can be misdirected. The irreplaceable will of the Marxist heritage is to 'master' history in whatever form that turns out to be possible, to find a way out of the nightmare of history via the conquest by human beings of the otherwise seemingly 'blind and natural "laws" of socio-economic fatality'.[239] This is a prospect that cannot be expected to hold much attraction for people uninterested in seizing control over their own destinies.[240] The nightmare of history, as this book argues, is indeed the 'millennial toil' of generations, the alienation from the workers of the product of their labour and its crystallisation in the form of capital that then confronts the workers as alien property endowed with mysterious properties of self-expansion. It is this process that grounds the phenomenon of 'reification' – as an attempt to efface from the commodity 'the traces of production', not so much the technical process that is the stuff of capital's triumphalism, but the social form of production, the presence within each commodity of the 'dizzying and culpabilising' store of the alien, exploited labour of other people.[241] It is the social form that also contains the secret of the 'systematic structure'.

Here a history grounded in the social form (capital) is potentially a resource against 'anti-society' and an ally in unravelling the mystery of the systematic structure. It might also be a way to think of the conditions in which an authentic form of autonomy and self-determination might emerge. At a historical moment like ours, when capital is intent on colonising every hitherto autonomous sphere of life, when it has all but obliterated the last vestiges of

---

237   Jameson 2011, p. 90.
238   Jameson 1994, pp. xi–xii. The 'seeds of time' is, of course, a reference to those famous lines in Shakespeare's *Macbeth* (Act I, scene III): 'If you can look into the seeds of time / And say which grain will grow and which will not / Speak then to me, who neither beg nor fear / Your favours nor your hate'.
239   Jameson 1998, p. 37.
240   Jameson 1998, p. 37.
241   Jameson 1988, Volume II, p. 163.

pre-capitalist social forms, harnessed every wilderness in a world 'abluted of nature', a world in which the economy has expanded to become 'virtually co-extensive' with culture itself, where every pore of the world is saturated in the 'serum of capital',[242] it is sheerly a form of class violence to neglect to unlock the mystery of the systematic structure and to instead venture off in the direction of celebrating autonomy, creativity and authenticity in the forms of culturalised difference. A celebration of the 'futures that already "are"'[243] seems to be nothing less than a ready-made apologia for capital.

The 'unrenounceable Marxist project' remains a totalising comprehension of an apparently unlimited capitalism. The collective agency required to confront the disorders of the present may be missing, but, as Perry Anderson remarks, 'a condition for its emergence [is] the ability to grasp [it] from within, as a system'.[244] The ambition to do so seems to have become a casualty of the postcolonial moment.

6.5 Provincialising Europe

The onward march of global capital may have succeeded in provincialising Europe in some respects, but this very process has also seen the rise of the United States as the apotheosis and safeguard of 'Western civilisation'.[245] As early as January–February of 1850, Marx and Engels had written in the *Neue Rheinische Zeitung*:

> Now we come to America. The most important thing which has occurred here, more important even than the February Revolution [of 1848], is the discovery of the Californian gold-mines ... The centre of gravity of world commerce, Italy in the Middle Ages, England in modern times, is now the southern half of the North American peninsula ... Thanks to California gold and the tireless energy of the Yankees ... [t]he Pacific Ocean will have the same role as the Atlantic has now and the Mediterranean had in antiquity and in the Middle Ages – that of the great water highway of world commerce and the Atlantic will decline to the status of an inland sea.[246]

---

242   Anderson 1998, p. 55.
243   Chakrabarty 2000, p. 251.
244   Anderson 1998, pp. 65–6.
245   Arrighi 1994.
246   Marx and Engels, cited in Davis 2000, p. 251, n. 74.

The years since have seen something more than the flowering of commerce. They have witnessed a concentration of industrial and military power on a scale unprecedented in world history.

This second coming of the West is a phenomenon of a different order to historic Europe, in that it has allowed for a regrouping of power relations in ways that make them quite impervious to what used to be thought of as the emancipatory potentials of anti-colonial nationalism and piecemeal detachments from the status quo. More so than any earlier 'dominant' social formation, the United States has also obfuscated the very nature of class power, reinforcing the notion that there is no ruling class as such. In addition, the United States is globally inclusive to a much greater degree than any European country, inasmuch as it draws continually on waves of immigrants, including, more specifically, waves of intellectual migration, whether or not the migrants actually settle here.[247] It is a far more osmotic and absorptive culture situated in a capitalism that has burst all bounds. Everyone is free to be different and find their private visions of emancipation.

All the potentialities opened up by those properties of the United States were vastly accentuated – if only for a brief moment – by the defeat of communism and the global triumph of capitalism, the dismantling of the left in countries in which they had exercised a significant role in the decades following the Second World War, and the crushing of organised labour movements across the world. As Ahmad makes clear, 'the Cold War did not just fade away; it was *won* by one side, *lost* by the other'.[248] He adds that it was precisely these interrelated developments that gave licence to the ideologues of capital to move to the far right and, we might add, to drag any number of intellectuals with them, at least part of the way. But the 'manic triumphalism', which accompanied the politics of the end of the Cold War, has not ushered in a new golden age of capitalism. On the contrary, the economic slow-down, stagnation and recessions visible at least since the mid-1970s have only intensified, and capital has become in the process 'more threatened and threatening' than ever. What we have before us is not a period of 'enhanced liberty, but one of far more brutal regimes of accumulation, and of resurgent racisms and Fascisms'.[249] Ironically, it is in this world that we are presented with culturalised 'difference' as the final frontier of human emancipation, and with pointless reproaches directed against 'economism' and its derivative 'economic determinism'.

---

247   See, for instance, the discussion of the impact of French intellectuals in the United States in Cusset 2008.

248   Ahmad 1999, p. 96.

249   Ibid.

However, it is precisely in this world that one has perforce to rethink the significance of the anti-colonial spirit of gratitude, especially when it manifests itself as the postcolonial spirit of surrender within co-ordinates that are consistent with archaic designations of the world.[250] Provincialising Europe is all well and good, but any attempt to overlook the global lines of power and force is sheer escapism. The world may not have followed Europe's path and is surely now unlikely to do so, but pointing out such a banal truism is neither a great historical insight nor particularly theoretically significant. If one is tempted to go in that direction, it will not do to claim that the mobilisation of the concept of 'Europe' is 'hyperreal'.[251] One is required to examine the historicity of the Europe that is to be provincialised, and the significance of the American location of postcolonial thought within the geopolitical lines of force of our world. The book began with this theme and the intervening pages have made the argument that it is more imperative than ever to refocus attention on close analyses of the social form to understand both colonialism and postcolonialism, and indeed to grasp the historicity of the theories that attempt to explain them.

If, in Cleary's words, colonialism is conceived as a historical process whereby societies of diverse kinds and location are 'differentially integrated' into a world capitalist system, then it is on what he calls a 'comparatist conjunctural analysis' of such processes that debate must be developed.[252] He also goes on to say that 'cultural analysis' has an important role in this conjunctural analysis, since this is the 'decisive area' where social conflicts are experienced, articulated and evaluated. But it is 'ultimately' the structural properties of the wider capitalist system that shape those conflicts, whether 'cultural, political or economic'.[253] In fact, as already indicated, this sort of materialist postcolonial studies – the kind advocated by Cleary – is no different from what one used to think of as Third World Marxism. But this is not where postcolonialism is nowadays, and while some postcolonial critics or theorists (or whatever they are calling themselves) invoke Marx, it is never in the spirit of a totalising understanding of the world, or even a Marxist analysis of capital, let alone the political implications that follow.

In response to Cleary, one might also point out that the novelty of colonialism, as we understand it, was that by the nineteenth century it had become completely a moment of capitalism itself. For the first time, we have a truly

---

250 I refer readers back to the discussion in Part IV, section IV above.
251 Chakrabarty 2000, p. 28.
252 Cleary 2002, p. 122; see also Larsen 1995, pp. 214–215.
253 Cleary 2002, p. 122.

planetary-scale system, meaning that, effectively, very many societies are integrated differentially into this system (and after a while the system itself is the totality of these differential moments). The economy under capitalism exerts a tremendous field of force over culture and politics that in other modes may have exerted their own force over activities governed by the need to produce the material necessities of life. However, while capitalism tries to swallow everything in its path, it sets in place more or less different forms everywhere, informed to a greater or lesser extent by antecedent modes of social production, a process that appears to generate greater differentiation even as its 'serum' permeates social life around the world more fully. Difference becomes meaningful in this structural context. The overall workings of capital are so opaque and counterintuitive that it is not easy to grasp its internal mechanisms, and more so its colonisation and commoditisation of culture.

Jameson argues, quite familiarly, that the objective of different forms of left political mobilisation has been either to reach for a more human scale, aiming to preserve the few enclaves still remaining from a simpler era, or to recover something of their collective or communal social life,[254] or in the case of social democracy to aim at reforms that will help the capital social form work better for a short period, to innovate and grow without becoming completely disruptive.[255] However, vis-à-vis factory legislation, for instance, Marx observed: 'as soon as capitalism is subjected to state control, even at a handful of points on the periphery of society, it seeks compensation all the more unrestrainedly at all other points'.[256] Such legislation, he also pointed out, hastens capitalist concentration, the demise of competitive small business, and the ultimate maturing of its in-built tendencies which bring the system to its breaking point. That is to say, neither the reactionary reaching for the small scale, nor social democracy's attempt to manage the contradictions of capital, do more than momentarily deflect capital's onward motion, which has the cumulative effect of revealing more sharply its underlying contradictions between growth and crisis, development and immiseration, its tendency to grow with differential effects in the core and peripheral countries, or increasingly now with hugely disruptive effects between town and country or between regions in individual countries, and to take the form of gross polarisation and unmanageable environmental dangers.

---

254   For an interesting discussion of the political implications of this sort of production of
       difference at the level of local social formations, see Jameson 2011, p. 89.

255   Jameson 2011, p. 146.

256   Marx 1977, p. 621.

In this broader scenario, there can be no farewell to work, unless it is the pink slip, the lay-off, enforced idleness when one is (sometimes) paid by capital not to work. For most people, a livelihood involves selling their labour power to capital in return for a wage, mostly to work in conditions that rob them of their health and well-being. A few, perhaps Negri's 'immaterial' workers,[257] might escape this fate, but for most this is hardly an option. If, indeed, *Capital* is a book about unemployment, then it must be that the fate of the unemployed was of some concern to Marx, and should be so to Marxists – at the very least to the extent it reveals the fundamental and inescapable nature of capitalism as such, by which an unemployed reserve of labour is 'structurally inseparable from the dynamic of accumulation and expansion'.[258]

Larsen argues, in anticipation of Jameson, that far from being in a productive relationship to capital, much potential labour is unemployed.[259] As the productive capacity of technology grows, fewer and fewer workers are needed to produce the commodities and services on which the system depends before overproduction, declining rates of profits, and so on, set in. So ironically, while working time is still the measure of value, it is no longer the measure of material wealth, as Postone convincingly argues;[260] moreover, it is no longer an everyday reality for a vast and growing number of workers or potential workers. All but a dwindling number of individual labourers are now or are *en route* to becoming 'superfluous', 'unexploitable' – a situation manifested in layoffs, lockouts, destitution and an upwelling of reactionary movements of all kinds.[261]

It is in this light that we might read the dialectic of globalisation – the coming to fruition of overwork and unemployment, overproduction and scarcity, overconsumption and starvation, simultaneously – and reckon with a form of 'naked life' more deeply rooted in the economic system than Agamben's 'hopeless inhabitants of the concentration camps'.[262] Jameson maintains that the 'destitution of unemployment' is the more fundamental and concrete form of 'naked life', for what is concrete is 'the social, the mode of production, what is humanly produced and historical'; metaphysical conceptions – such as those

---

257   Lazzarato 1996, pp. 133–46.
258   Jameson 2011, pp. 148–9.
259   Larsen 2002, p. 218.
260   Postone 1996, p. 195.
261   These are the working populations depicted in Chatterjee's *Politics of the Governed*, although he manages to avoid the structural implications of their forms of work and life in the emerging worldwide context of a massive 'reserve army' that will never find much beyond the most marginal kinds of work.
262   Jameson 2011, p. 125, referring to Agamben 1998.

involving nature and death – are 'ideological derivations of that more basic reality', and explains that Agamben's 'pseudo-biological' concept proves in reality, like those of Foucault, to draw on categories of domination. These considerations would also apply to Pandey's 'agonised contemplation of "violence" and "pain" as "fragments"'.[263] When one is prone to 'philosophise' on violence and pain, then we already know that these have been fully integrated into the workings of the political economy as a daily profitable aspect of it.

Jameson holds open the possibility of a 'productive change in theory and practice' by situating all the 'lost populations' – not only the unemployed, but also the homeless, the refugees, victims of ethnic wars and famines, and people who are 'prey to the incursions of warlords and charitable agencies alike' – in relation to exploitation rather than domination.[264] If this picture of immiseration were all, we would merely conclude with a moralising denunciation of capitalism and probably proceed from there to a regression to communities of soil-and-blood and all those backward-looking temptations, or alternatively to hopeless and agonised depictions of pain and loss. What is distinctive about Marxism is also the presentation of an immense development of the system, constant revolutionising of the means of production, constant innovation and turbulence, gales of creative destruction. Jameson suggests, following Karl Korsch,[265] that Marxism contains two codes, which could alternate with one another, be substituted for one another or translated into each other: that of value (and the development of the productive forces), and that of class struggle (exploitation and domination). The choice of which one to emphasise at any moment is political, not scientific or logical, and would depend on what could politically energise and mobilise people – the positive (hope) or the negative (anger). But, of course, under capitalism, and thus far only under capitalism, it should be said, does exploitation lead to economic development.

As Brenner once noted, the feudal social-property system produced the very opposite of economic development. In fact, it established certain distinctive mechanisms for distributing income and, in particular, certain limited methods for developing production, which led to 'economic stagnation and involution', doing so because it imposed upon the members of the major social classes – feudal lords and possessing peasants – 'strategies for reproducing

---

263   Pandey 1991, pp. 559–72; see also Pandey 1994.

264   Jameson concludes his work thus: 'To think of all [those populations] in terms of a kind of global unemployment rather than of this or that tragic pathos is . . . to be recommitted to the invention of a new kind of transformatory politics on a global scale' (Jameson 2011, p. 151).

265   Korsch 1963, pp. 228–9.

themselves which, when applied on an economy-wide basis, were incompatible with the requirements of growth'.[266] Capitalist exploitation is productive in that, as Marx notes, the workers themselves forged their own 'golden chains', and that through their own labour they produced 'capital and all its accumulation'. However, they have done so by being dispossessed of their means of subsistence and forced to sell their labour power to the (now) owners of the means of production. It is the competition among the latter for market shares and profits that henceforth drives the processes of innovation, and acceleration of the productive forces. This requires one to see the relationship of exploitation and domination rather differently. Both capitalists and workers are dominated by the abstract tyranny of a socially-necessary time of production established not by class collusion, but by the competition of capitals on an ever-increasing scale and by the concrete domination in the places of production of capitalists over propertyless workers.

The argument for socialism is not an either/or: not just anger or hope but both; not the mere realisation that capitalism is 'poisoning human survival'[267] – for that could lead to a despairing surrender to the present logic of development – but that the innovations, the development of the productive forces, indeed the unlimited sociality of capitalism has created the potentiality for a transformation from its now indirect, market-mediated form to a more direct social form.[268] The 'free association of associated producers' would be more transparent, not only in the collective choice of priorities, but also in the way that the priorities would be 'available for collective inspection'.[269] It would also be immensely more productive, not in the matter of forging or strengthening the 'golden chains' that bind labour, but in fulfilling some of the unfulfilled possibilities that capitalism first creates. Thus, '[m]achinery, gifted with the power of shortening and fructifying human labour' would actually do so instead of 'starving and overworking it' and all 'our invention and progress' would no longer 'result in endowing material forces with intellectual life and in stultifying human life into a material force'.[270] The only solution to the runaway logic of capitalist development and the immiseration of millions would have to be some version of the 'direct socialisation of the productive forces'.[271]

---

266   Brenner 1982, p. 17.
267   Ahmad 1999, p. 95.
268   Smith 1990, p. 64.
269   Jameson 2011, pp. 142–3.
270   Marx 1974, p. 298.
271   Žižek 2000a, p. 350.

A commitment to that elusive goal ought to be informed both by anger (at the present state of things) and hope (for the future).

When push comes to shove, there will be pitched battles on the streets, in town squares, factories, offices and elsewhere – there can be no peaceful accession to socialism. Even minimal demands for dignity and democracy seem to make the ruling classes of the world anxious beyond measure or order. That being so, some unity of the resistant forces will be necessary, whether this is in the first instance tactical, strategic, principled or whatever. People will have to find a way to recognise and deal with whatever imposed and ascriptive differences appear to govern them now. Difference is radically incomplete without class struggle. If one thinks in terms of Revolution I and II – in a faint doff of the hat to the History I and II of Chakrabarty – Revolution I, the mature version of the bourgeois revolution, was accomplished for a while anyway in the post-Second World War boom, in a limited corner of the world (the 'West', the First World, the developed world, the 'global North', or variations thereof). It is now rapidly unravelling – unevenly but consistently – across a broad front, spatially and socially. It was a long time coming, lasted a very short time, and seems to be ebbing very rapidly indeed. This might be the clinching argument for Revolution II – the one that will overcome capital and set up some self-transparent system of workers' power. Yes, workers' power. After all, no matter what 'identity' one dons, most people are also workers: employed, semi-employed, unemployed temporarily or permanently (structurally).

The argument for socialism (and a democratic socialism at that, unless democracy is already included in a definition of socialism) based on a free association of associated producers is that the cast-off are an intolerable indictment of the system as a whole, that their numbers are bound to grow and that anyone can find themselves in this position. Even the most productively employed and well-paid workers must be persuaded of the necessity of socialism, and for that we expect, minimally, that the system's powers of recovery (from its frequent crises) and growth must be fatally impaired in some ways (the closing-off of the possibilities of restarting growth within the old parameters), and that they must feel the pain of those who are its victims or feel its imminence, not see it as someone else's misfortune. In this regard, capitalism's very dynamic of blowing through every obstacle in its path clears the way for its overcoming.

Much of the drive to conceptualise the discordance of times, the 'not-yet' implicit in it, stems from an impulse to remember the millennial waste into which a large part of human life – that of exploited and alienated labour – has disappeared into silence and amnesia, and to ground the desire for an alternative on some properly historical and political understanding of the crucial

categories of capital and labour. The not-yet is not, as a certain strand of postcolonial thought imagines, a sign of the inadequacy of colonial social formations
and their postcolonial aftermath, a sign that some people are permanently consigned to the waiting-room of history. It is not about hanging around for events
to transpire during the quiet passage of 'homogeneous, empty time'. History, as
Walter Benjamin remarked, 'is the subject of a structure whose site is not homogeneous empty time, but time filled by the presence of the now'.[272] It implies
'rupturing the continuum' of a duration of degenerate progress, 'shattering its
linearity', ushering in a 'new epoch',[273] radicalising the elements of a crisis that
have been growing within the old social form, a dialectical leap into the 'open
air of history which is how Marx understood the revolution'.[274] The universal
too might, in those circumstances, acquire a valence altogether different from
that of a mere placeholder for pretentiously empty gestures, becoming instead
an antidote to capital's dispersive and atomistic tendencies, and perhaps even
a sign that 'a total subversion of the existing order' is possible.[275]

However, radicalising the elements of a crisis that have been growing
within the old social form hardly seems to be on the agenda. More typically,
one encounters something along the lines of Cusset's formulation that the
'real problem' and the one that 'all intellectuals' from the Third World have
faced since the end of the decolonising process' is that the battle cannot be
fought but with the 'arms of the adversary' itself. That is, the terms of a programme of 'postcolonial emancipation' have still to be taken directly from
the 'Enlightenment and rational progressivism': democracy, citizenship,
constitution, nation, socialism, and even culturalism.[276] This does seem like

---

272   Benjamin 1969, p. 261.

273   Burgio 2002, pp. 19–20, cited in Thomas 2009, pp. 152–3.

274   Benjamin 1969, p. 261. To quote the entirety of Thesis 14 of Benjamin's 'Theses on the
       Philosophy of History': 'History is the subject of a structure whose site is not homogenous,
       empty time, but time filled by the presence of the now. [*Jetztzeit*]. Thus, to Robespierre
       ancient Rome was a past charged with the time of the now which he blasted out of the
       continuum of history. The French Revolution viewed itself as Rome incarnate. It evoked
       ancient Rome the way fashion evokes costumes of the past. Fashion has a flair for the
       topical, no matter where it stirs in the thickets of long ago; it is a tiger's leap into the past.
       This jump, however, takes place in an arena where the ruling class give the commands. The
       same leap in the open air of history is the dialectical one, which is how Marx understood
       the revolution'.

275   The phrase is from Tocqueville, 1952, cited in Losurdo 2004, p. 291. Tocqueville wrote: 'great
       general ideas … announce that a total subversion of the existing order is approaching'.
       The suspicion directed at 'great general ideas' seems to be part of a broad political retreat.

276   Cusset 2008, p. 144.

a rather incoherent list, a kind of mish-mash of elements taken from a range of political positions from right to left as if all of them derive from the 'adversary'. Does 'rational progressivism' culminate in socialism? What does socialism have to do with culturalism? And who, finally, is this adversary? The West? If so, this statement is more or less a direct inversion of Huntington's view that there are adversary civilisations – culturalisms? – out there against which the West must unite. Now it seems the Third World must do likewise in reverse. In support of this view, he cites Gayatri Spivak to the effect that the task at hand – for which French theory (which remained 'Western') would hardly be useful – was to 'wrench [those] regulative political signifiers out of their represented field of reference'.[277] Spivak seems to have a penchant for 'seizing' (the apparatus of value-coding) and 'wrenching' (regulative political signifiers out of their represented field of reference). When this is cast into the terms of *de-Westernisation*, for example, that 'the large concepts of political change needed to be *de-Westernized* – a vast project that in more concrete terms came to inspire subaltern studies',[278] one must assume that Cusset is referring to a much larger field of criticism than subaltern studies. For the West is, as Lazarus makes clear, an indispensable fetish of postcolonial studies.

Two gestures proceed from this. The first, as Lazarus notes, is the desire to 'provincialise Europe' – to dismantle Eurocentrism by demonstrating that the enabling concepts on which it has been founded are not 'obvious', 'transparent' or 'universal', but rather are situated, contingent, and so on. The objective here is to demonstrate 'how – through what historical process – [Enlightenment] reason, which was not always self-evident to everyone has been made to look obvious far beyond the ground where it originated'.[279] The second consists in the contention that within the problematic of 'modernity', there is no space or act of utterance that is not Eurocentric. The argument that follows is that it is necessary to do away 'with all the traditions of modern thought in order to break with their Eurocentrism, for modern thought is constitutively Eurocentric'.[280] But as Lazarus rightly insists, the way in which 'Europe' has been conceptualised by the 'provincialisers' fatally undermines the efficacy of their critique, involving as it does the 'hypostatization of "modernity" and "the West" – [a] dematerialisation of capitalism, ... misrecognition of its world-historical significance, [and a] construal of it in civilizational terms, as "modernity"'.[281]

---

277   Spivak 1992, p. 57.
278   Cusset 2008, p. 144.
279   Chakrabarty 2000, p. 43, cited in Lazarus 2002, p. 59.
280   Lazarus 2002, p. 59.
281   Lazarus 2002, pp. 59–60.

The result is that 'the *structurality* of the global system [is rendered] either arbitrary or unintelligible'.[282]

De-Westernisation, in whatever form, seems to be the category within which postcolonial theory works; indeed, it is its constitutive form, as it were. It might be too much to require postcolonial theorists to ask what the 'west' might consist of, quite apart from the incoherence of the term itself,[283] an incoherence shared by Hayek, Popper, Huntington and their epigones. What if the concept of the 'west' itself is constituted by prior acts of repression, some of them undoubtedly of the most vile and violent kind, and if the 'west' can emerge as a sanitised category only once the repression is complete? What if 'de-Westernisation' is complicit in this repression, through a kind of unspoken elitist compact entered into by both Eurocentric intellectuals and their postcolonial counterparts from the former colonies? Finally, is there a 'de-Westernised' method of overcoming capital, or is this an unimportant consideration, part of the debris floating in the wake of 1989?

In any case, the whole issue of de-Westernisation has other historic valences that also speak to the contemporary project of provincialising Europe. For de-Westernisation has two moments in the anti-colonial struggles of the nineteenth and twentieth centuries that I will elucidate with reference to the Indian case. The first coincides with what we might call, following A.G. Hopkins, the moment of self-government, when an emergent ruling class – a bourgeoisie nurtured by colonial rule in fact – tries to establish its autonomy and difference from the colonial rulers, while making a pitch for a modest share of power, a junior partnership in the profits of empire. This claim was realised in small part by opening channels to emigration to British colonies in Africa and Southeast Asia, and by favouring forms of exploitation in India itself that allowed the local bourgeoisie to cream off a part of the profits of alienation in both town and country. But any larger scheme was frustrated not least because it coincided with a hardening of lines between coloniser and colonised, and because it overlapped with the economic downturn of the late nineteenth century (the so-called Depression of 1873–96, which may have actually begun earlier and certainly lasted down to the First World War). Racism had already emerged as the counter-ideology to partnership and was exemplified by Curzon's statement that the highest ideal of truth was a 'Western conception'.[284] The names of Naoroji, Dutt and Gokhale, and any number of minor regional equivalents, would be associated with this phase.

---

282   Lazarus 2002, p. 60.
283   See the discussion in Chapter 6, section III above.
284   Dallmayr 1989, p. 24.

The second we might call the moment of independence, when some measure of power sharing had already been instituted and the indigenous ruling
class had acquired a degree of self-definition and self-confidence – in the immediate aftermath of the often reactionary and patriarchal 'settlement' of social,
mainly gender and class, issues to which Chatterjee refers. But this was also the
moment when it had fully recognised that empire itself had become a moribund structure, and that the main lines of colonial investment and innovations
flowed either to the white-settler colonies or indeed to the informal empire in
Latin America when not to the United States.[285] Recognising the need to construct their own dominance within a postcolonial nation, and the requirements
of conducting class struggles and class repression without the aid of the colonial state, this moment of de-Westernisation would require more than the usual
claims of cultural autonomism. This was a period associated with the names of
Tilak, Lajpat Rai, Savarkar, Golwalkar and the rest of their hangers-on, when
vis-à-vis the colonial rulers they presented an ideal of independence and
self-determination, which they were fully prepared to deny to those lower down
the social order. This was the moment when, under the banner of democratic
opposition to the continued rule of the coloniser, the brutal repression of even
the most modest claims on the national income could be mounted. The ruling
class of the colony now implicitly took on board what was learnt during the
period of colonial rule, prefiguring in the political domain what postcolonialism admits in the discursive one: the spirit of indebtedness to Europe as the
indispensable mediation for their own trip into modernity.[286]

De-Westernisation had therefore a historic-strategic dimension, but to
acquire any sort of moral-ethical cachet it had to be recast in terms of a
cultural-transhistorical set of imperatives. This type of recasting also serves
as a definition of culturalism *tout court*. Postcolonialism inherits the tertiary
aspect of culturalism – the need to wipe the historic dimension clean in order to
represent class-specific tasks as culturally transcendent ones. Postcolonialism
from the margins is a form of nationalism, but one that is easily misrecognised,
especially as it becomes overlaid with all sorts of poststructuralist flourishes in
its metropolitan location. The 'wrenching' of political signifiers is an altogether
more dubious matter than Cusset seems to recognise.

In its postcolonial context, de-Westernisation involves the covert appropriation of the more conservative technical aspects of the strategic class-specific
political dimension (for example, the practical spirit of realism when it comes

---

285   This has been demonstrated by Davis and Huttenback 1988; Cain and Hopkins 1993; Cain
         and Hopkins 2002.
286   See, for instance, Chakrabarty 2000, p. 6, pp. 16ff.

to containment and repression of the dangerous urban classes). It also involves the presentation of the essential tasks facing the ex-colonies, the Third World, or what have you, in terms of cultural and moral-ethical self-governance, now that globalisation has made true economic independence (semi-autocentric development) a virtual impossibility. It is in fact politics in counterflow. If in the first iteration, in late colonial times, it was mostly enacted in the form of tragedy – the instrumental suppression of even the most basic requirements of the people for land and subsistence – in the second iteration it is mostly farcical, involving some piecemeal reformism and a separation of the moral-ethical tasks of cultural reconstruction from the political-economic tasks of governmentality.[287]

If one now thinks of the project of provincialising Europe in the context of de-Westernisation, it assumes a properly historical dimension. In the latter, a consistent repression of class issues is required for provincialising Europe as the commonsense of postcolonial studies to take root. This consistent repression has needed a vital mediator. The United States has here fulfilled its appointed role to the ex-colonial world: not only in facilitating the development of area (civilisational) studies, the cultural geography of which allows postcolonial people to orient themselves vis-à-vis their ex-colonisers and vis-à-vis each other, but also in providing a home for its global-diasporic (transnational) supplement, which goes by the name of postcolonial studies. It is now well understood that transnational studies can never replace area studies, but can serve as its necessary supplement, and it is equally well accepted that without a cultural and more so civilisational dimension transnationalism is mere corporate ideology masquerading as the production of critical knowledge of the world.

Provincialising Europe is not really about the non-universalism of European development. This has been all along the mantra of Eurocentric theories of the European miracle – one of the most conservative and doctrinaire ideological formulations of all time. Huntington puts it very clearly when he writes that European civilisation is unique, not universal.[288] So postcolonialism adds nothing new to this idea; it just writes the same script from the margins. What is essential to postcolonialism's 'de-Westernised' agenda of provincialising Europe is precisely the suppression of vital elements of both European and ex-colonial histories. In this, they might be taken as part of a broad stream of historiography of the past thirty years or more, and a necessary moment of the global consolidation of right-wing ideologies for the twenty-first century.

---

287   This is the political subtext of the literature on alternative, hybrid, plural modernities, or variations thereof.

288   Huntington 1998, pp. 20–1.

References

Adamson, Walter 1980, *Hegemony and Revolution*, Berkeley and Los Angeles, CA: University of California Press.

Afary, Janet and Kevin Anderson 2005, *Foucault and the Iranian Revolution: Gender and the Seductions of Islamism*, Chicago, IL: University of Chicago Press.

Agamben, Giorgio 1998, *Homo Sacer: Sovereign Power and Bare Life*, Stanford, CA: Stanford University Press.

Ahmad, Aijaz 1992, *In Theory: Classes, Nations, Literatures*, London: Verso.

—— 1995, 'Postcolonialism: What's in a Name?', in *Late Imperial Culture*, edited by R. de la Campa, E. Ann Kaplan and M. Sprinker, London: Verso.

—— 1996, *Lineages of the Present: Political Essays*, Delhi: Tulika.

—— 1999, 'Reconciling Derrida: "Spectres of Marx" and Deconstructive Politics', in *Ghostly Demarcations: A Symposium on Jacques Derrida's Spectres of Marx*, edited by M. Sprinker, London and New York: Verso.

Alavi, Hamza 1975, 'India and the Colonial Mode of Production,' *Economic and Political Weekly*, 10: 33–5.

—— 1981, 'Structure of Colonial Formations', *Economic and Political Weekly*, 16: 10–12.

Alavi, Hamza et al. 1978, *Studies in the Development of Capitalism in India*, Lahore: Vanguard Publishers.

Al-Azm, Sadik Jalal 1981, 'Orientalism and Orientalism in Reverse', *Khamsin: Journal of the Revolutionary Socialists of the Middle East*, 8: 5–26.

Al-e Ahmad, Jalal 1982 [1963], *Plagued by the West (Gharbzadegi)*, translated by Paul Sprachman, Delmor, NY: Center for Iranian Studies, Columbia University.

Al-Khalili, Jim 2012, *The House of Wisdom: How Arabic Science Saved Ancient Knowledge and Gave Us the Renaissance*, Harmondsworth: Penguin Books.

Althusser, Louis and Étienne Balibar 1970, *Reading Capital*, translated by Ben Brewster, London: New Left Books.

Alvares, Claude 1994, *Science, Development and Violence: The Revolt against Modernity*, Delhi: Oxford University Press.

Ambedkar, Bhim Rao 1945, *What Congress and Gandhi Have Done to the Untouchables*, Bombay: Thacker.

—— 1970, *Who were the Shudras? How They Came to be the Fourth Varna in Indo-Aryan Society*, Bombay: Thackers.

Amin, Samir 1978, *The Law of Value and Historical Materialism*, translated by Brian Pearce, New York and London: Monthly Review Press.

—— 1985, *Delinking: Towards a Polycentric World*, London: Zed Books.

—— 1989, *Eurocentrism*, translated by R. Moore, New York: Monthly Review Press.

—— 1990, *Maldevelopment: Anatomy of a Global Failure*, London: Zed Books.

—— 2003, *Obsolescent Capitalism: Contemporary Politics and Global Disorder*, London: Zed Books.

Amin, Shahid 1995, *Event, Metaphor, Memory. Chauri-Chaura: 1922–92*, Berkeley, CA: University of California Press.

Amin, Shahid and Marcel van der Linden 1997, *Peripheral Labour: Studies in the History of Partial Proletarianization*, Cambridge: Cambridge University Press.

Amsden, Alice 2001, *The Rise of 'the Rest': Challenges to the West from Late-Industrializing Economies*, London: Oxford University Press.

Anderson, Benedict 1983, *Imagined Communities*, revised edition, London: Verso.

Anderson, Kevin 1995, *Lenin, Hegel and Western Marxism: A Critical Study*, Urbana, IL: University of Illinois Press.

—— 2010, *Marx at the Margins: On Nationalism, Ethnicity and Non-Western Societies*, Chicago, IL: University of Chicago Press.

Anderson, Perry 1974, *Lineages of the Absolutist State*, London: New Left Books.

—— 1975, *Passages from Antiquity to Feudalism*, London: New Left Books.

—— 1977, 'The Antinomies of Antonio Gramsci', *New Left Review*, 100: 5–78.

—— 1983, *In the Tracks of Historical Materialism*, London: Verso.

—— 1988, 'Modernity and Revolution', in *Marxism and the Interpretations of Culture*, edited by C. Nelson and L. Grossberg, Chicago, IL: University of Illinois Press.

—— 1992, *English Questions*, London: Verso.

—— 1998, *The Origins of Postmodernity*, London: Verso.

—— 2009, *The New Old World*, London: Verso.

—— 2010, 'Two Revolutions', *New Left Review*, 61 (Jan.–Feb.): 59–91.

Apffel-Marglin, Frédérique and Stephen A. Marglin (eds) 1996, *Decolonizing Knowledge: From Development to Dialogue*, Oxford: Clarendon Press.

Appadurai, Arjun 1996, *Modernity at Large: Cultural Dimensions of Globalization*, Minneapolis, MN: University of Minnesota Press.

—— 2003, 'Knowledge, Circulation and Collective Biography', in *At Home in Diaspora: South Asian Scholars and the West*, edited by J. Assayag and V. Bénéï, Bloomington, IN: Indiana University Press.

Appiah, Kwame Anthony 1991, 'Is the Post- in Postmodernism the Post- in Postcolonial', *Critical Inquiry*, 17, 2: 336–357.

Arendt, Hannah 1976, *The Origins of Totalitarianism*, New York: Harcourt, Brace, Jovanovich.

Aristotle 1974, *The Politics*, Harmondsworth: Penguin.

Arnold, David 1982, 'Rebellious Hillmen: the Gudem-Rampa Risings, 1839–1924', in *Subaltern Studies I, Writings on South Asian History & Society*, edited by R. Guha, Delhi: Oxford University Press.

Arnold, David and David Hardiman (eds) 1994, *Subaltern Studies VIII: Essays in Honour of Ranajit Guha*, Delhi: Oxford University Press.

Arnold, David and Ramachandra Guha (eds) 1995, *Nature, Culture, Imperialism: Essays on the Environmental History of*

South Asia, Delhi: Oxford University Press.

Arrighi, Giovanni 1994, *The Long Twentieth Century: Money, Power and the Origins of Our Time*, London: Verso.

—— 2002, 'The Rise of East Asia and the Withering Away of the Interstate System', in *Marxism, Modernity and Postcolonial Studies*, edited by C. Bartolovich and N. Lazarus, Cambridge: Cambridge University Press.

—— 2009, *Adam Smith in Beijing: Lineages of the 21st Century*, London and New York: Verso.

Ashton, T.H. and C.H.E. Philpin (eds) 1985, *The Brenner Debate: Agrarian Class Structure and Economic Development in Pre-Industrial Europe*, Cambridge: Cambridge University Press.

Assayag, Jackie and Véronique Bénéï (eds) 2003, *At Home in Diaspora: South Asian Scholars and the West*, Bloomington, IN: Indiana University Press.

Augier, Marie 1842, *Du crédit public et de son histoire*, Paris: Guillaumin.

Avari, Burjor 2007, *India, the Ancient Past: A History of the Indian Subcontinent from c. 7000 BC to AD 1200*, New York: Routledge.

Aydin, Cemil 2009, 'The Question of Orientalism in Pan-Islamic Thought: The Origins, Content and Legacy of Transnational Muslim Identities', in *From Orientalism to Postcolonialism: Asia, Europe and the Lineages of Difference*, edited by S. Mazumdar, V. Kaiwar and T. Labica, London: Routledge.

Bagchi, Amiya Kumar 1982, *The Political Economy of Underdevelopment*, Cambridge: Cambridge University Press.

Bahl, Vinay 1995, *The Making of the Indian Working Class: The Case of the Tata Iron and Steel Co., 1880–1946*, New Delhi: Sage Publications.

Balibar, Étienne 2004, *We, The People of Europe? Reflections on Transnational Citizenship*, Princeton: Princeton University Press.

Banaji, Jairus 1977, 'Modes of Production in a Materialist Conception of History', *Capital and Class*, 3: 1–44.

—— 1978, 'Capitalist Domination and the Small Peasantry in the Deccan Districts', *Studies in the Development of Capitalism*, Lahore: Progress Publishers.

Banerjee, Sumanta 1984, *The Simmering Revolution: The Naxalite Uprising*, London: Zed Books.

Bardhan, Pranab 1999, *The Political Economy of Development in India*, expanded edition, New Delhi: Oxford University Press.

Barnes, Andrew E. 2003, 'Aryanizing Projects, African "Collaborators", and Colonial Transcripts', in *Antinomies of Modernity: Essays on Race, Orient, Nation*, edited by V. Kaiwar and S. Mazumdar, Durham, NC: Duke University Press.

Bartolovich, Crystal 2002, 'Introduction: Marxism, modernity and postcolonial studies', in *Marxism, Modernity and Postcolonial Studies*, edited by C. Bartolovich and N. Lazarus, Cambridge: Cambridge University Press.

Bartolovich, Crystal and Neil Lazarus (eds) 2002, *Marxism, Modernity and*

Postcolonial Studies, Cambridge: Cambridge University Press.

Basham, A.L. 1961, 'The Kashmir Chronicle', in *Historians of India, Pakistan and Ceylon*, edited by C.H. Philips, London: Oxford University Press.

Basu, Deepika 1993, *The Working Class in Bengal: Formative Years*, Calcutta: K.P. Bagchi and Co.

Bauman, Zygmunt 1992, *Intimations of Postmodernity*, London: Routledge.

—— 1994, 'Morality without Ethics', *Theory, Culture, Society*, 11: 1–34.

—— 1999, *In Search of Politics*, Stanford, CA: Stanford University Press.

Bayoumi, Moustafa and Andrew N. Rubin (eds) 2000, *The Edward Said Reader*, London: Granta.

Bear, Laura 2007, *Lines of the Nation: Indian Railway Workers, Bureaucracy, and the Intimate Historical Self*, New York: Columbia University Press.

Beetham, David 1985, *Max Weber and the Theory of Modern Politics*, Cambridge: Polity Press.

Bellamy, Richard (ed.) 1987, *Which Socialism? Marxism, Socialism and Democracy*, Minneapolis, MN: University of Minnesota Press.

Benanav, Aaron 2010, 'Misery and Debt: On the Logic and History of Surplus Populations and Surplus Capital', *Endnotes*, 2, <www.endnotes.org.uk/articles/1>.

Benjamin, Walter 1969, *Illuminations: Essays and Reflections*, edited and with an introduction by H. Arendt, translated by H. Zohn, New York: Schocken Books.

—— 1985, *One-Way Street and Other Essays*, translated by E. Jephcott and K. Shorter, London: Verso.

Bensaïd, Daniel 2002, *Marx for Our Times: Adventures and Misadventures of a Critique*, translated by G. Elliott, London: Verso.

Berger, Mark T. 2003, 'Decolonisation, Modernisation and Nation-Building: Political Development Theory and the Appeal of Communism in Southeast Asia, 1945–1975', *Journal of Southeast Asian Studies*, 34, 3: 421–448.

Berman, Marshall 1988, *All That is Solid Melts into Air*, New York: Penguin.

Bernal, Martin 1987, *Black Athena: The Afroasiatic Roots of Classical Civilization. Volume I: The Fabrication of Ancient Greece 1785–1985*, New Brunswick, NJ: Rutgers University Press.

Bhabha, Homi K. 1989, 'The Commitment to Theory', in *Questions of the Third Cinema*, edited by J. Pines and P. Willemen, London: BFI Publishing.

—— (ed.) 1990, *Nation and Narration*, Oxford: Routledge.

—— 1992, 'Postcolonial Criticism', in *Redrawing the Boundaries: The Transformation of English and American Literary Studies*, edited by S. Greenblatt and G. Gunn, New York: MLA.

—— 2005, *The Location of Culture*, Oxford: Routledge.

Bhaduri, Amit 1973, 'A Study in Agricultural Backwardness Under Semi-feudalism', *Economic Journal*, 83, 1: 120–137.

Bhagwati, Jagdish 1993, *India in Transition*, New York: Oxford University Press.

Bhana, Surendra and Goolam Vahed 2005, *The Making of a Political Reformer: Gandhi in South Africa, 1893–1914*, New Delhi: Manohar.

Bhargava, Rajeev (ed.) 1998, *Secularism and Its Critics*, Delhi: Oxford University Press.

Bhattacharyya, Jnanabrata 1987, 'Language, Class and Community in Bengal', *South Asia Bulletin*, 7, 1 and 2: 56–63.

Bidet, Jacques and Jacques Texier (eds) 1991, *Fin du communisme? Actualité du marxisme*, Paris: Presses Universitaires de France.

Blackbourn, David and Geoff Eley 1984, *The Peculiarities of German History: Bourgeois Society and Politics in Nineteenth-Century Germany*, Oxford: Oxford University Press.

Blackburn, Robin (ed.) 1991, *After the Fall: The Failure of Communism and the Future of Socialism*, London: Verso.

Blaut, James 1993, *The Colonizer's Model of the World*, New York: The Guilford Press.

Bloch, Ernst 1986, *The Principle of Hope*, translated by N. Plaice, S. Plaice and P. Knight, Oxford: Blackwell.

Blyn, George 1966, *Agricultural Trends in India, 1891–1947: Output, Availability, and Productivity*, Philadelphia, PA: University of Pennsylvania Press.

Bobbio, Norberto 1987, 'Gramsci and the Conception of Civil Society', in *Which Socialism? Marxism, Socialism and Democracy*, edited by R. Bellamy, Minneapolis, MN: University of Minnesota Press.

Boehmer, Elleke 1998, 'Questions of Neo-Orientalism', *Interventions: International Journal of Postcolonial Studies*, 1, 1: 18–21.

Boltanski, Luc and Eve Chiapello, *The New Spirit of Capitalism*, translated by Gregory Elliott, London: Verso.

Boothman, Derek 2011, 'The Sources of Gramsci's Concept of Hegemony', in *Rethinking Gramsci*, edited by M.E. Green, Oxford: Routledge.

Bose, Sugata and Ayesha Jalal 1998, *Modern South Asia*, New York: Routledge.

Bottomore, Tom (ed.) 1983, *A Dictionary of Marxist Thought*, Cambridge, MA: Harvard University Press.

Bottomore, T.B. and Maximilien Rubel (eds) 1974, *Karl Marx: Selected Writings in Sociology and Social Philosophy*, Harmondsworth: Penguin Books.

Bourdieu, Pierre 1991, *The Political Ontology of Martin Heidegger*, Stanford, CA: Stanford University Press.

—— 2003, *Firing Back: Against the Tyranny of the Market*, translated by Loïc Wacquant, London: Verso.

Boutroux, Émile 1926, 'L'Allemagne et la guerre: Lettre à M. le Directeur de la "Revue des Deux-Mondes"', 15 October 1914, in *Études d'histoire de la philosophie allemande*, Paris: Librairie Philosophique J. Vrin.

Breckenridge, Carol and Peter van der Veer (eds) 1993, *Orientalism and the Postcolonial Predicament*, Philadelphia, PA: University of Pennsylvania Press.

Breman, Jan 2005, *The Making and Unmaking of an Industrial Working Class: Sliding Down to the Bottom of the Labour Hierarchy in Ahmedabad, India*, Amsterdam: Amsterdam University Press.

—— 2007, *Labour Bondage in West India: From Past to Present*, New Delhi: Oxford University Press.

Brennan, Timothy 1997, *At Home in the World: Cosmopolitanism Now*, Cambridge, MA: Harvard University Press.

—— 2002, 'Postcolonial Studies Between the Two European Wars: An Intellectual History', in *Marxism, Modernity and Postcolonial Studies*, edited by C. Bartolovich and N. Lazarus, Cambridge: Cambridge University Press.

—— 2006, *Wars of Position: The Cultural Politics of Left and Right*, New York: Columbia University Press.

Brenner, Robert 1976, 'Agrarian Class Structure and Economic Development in Pre-Industrial Europe', *Past and Present*, 70, 1: 30–75.

—— 1977, 'The Origins of Capitalist Development: A Critique of Neo-Smithian Marxism', *New Left Review*, I/104: 25–92.

—— 1982, 'The Agrarian Roots of European Capitalism', *Past and Present*, 97, 1: 16–113.

—— 1986, 'The Social Basis of Economic Development', in *Analytical Marxism*, edited by J. Roemer, Cambridge: Cambridge University Press.

—— 1993, *Merchants and Revolution: Commercial Change, Political Conflict, and London's Overseas Traders, 1550–1653*, Princeton, NJ: Princeton University Press.

—— 1999, 'Reply to Critics', *Comparative Studies of South Asia, Africa and the Middle East*, 19, 2: 62–83.

—— 2002, *The Boom and the Bubble*, London: Verso.

—— 2006, *The Economics of Global Turbulence*, London: Verso.

Brinton, Crane 1967, 'Romanticism', in *The Encyclopaedia of Philosophy*, 7: 206–209, New York: Collier-Macmillan.

Brown, Frederick 2011, *For the Soul of France: Culture Wars in the Age of Dreyfus*, New York: Anchor.

Brown, Louise 2000, *Sex Slaves: The Trafficking of Women in Asia*, London: Virago.

Buber, Martin 1950, *Paths in Utopia*, New York: Beacon Press.

Buchanan, Ian 1988, 'Metacommentary on Utopia, or Jameson's dialectic of hope', *Utopian Studies*, 9, 2: 18–30.

—— (ed.) 2007, *Jameson on Jameson: Conversations on Cultural Marxism*, Durham, NC: Duke University Press.

Buchanan, Patrick 2006, *State of Emergency*, New York: St. Martin's Press.

Budgen, Sebastian, Stathis Kouvelakis and Slavoj Žižek (eds) 2007, *Lenin Reloaded: Towards a Politics of Truth*, Durham, NC: Duke University Press.

Burke, Edmund 2001, *Reflections on the Revolution in France*, edited by J.C.D. Clark, Stanford, CA: Stanford University Press.

Burkett, Paul 1999a, 'Nature's "Free Gifts" and the Ecological Significance of Value', *Capital and Class*, 68: 89–110.

—— 1999b, *Marx and Nature: A Red and Green Perspective*, New York: St. Martin's Press.

Burkholder, Mark A. and Lyman L. Johnson 1994, *Colonial Latin America*, Oxford: Oxford University Press.

Butler, Judith and Joan Scott (eds) 1992, *Feminists Theorize the Political*, New York: Routledge.

Butler, Judith, Ernesto Laclau and Slavoj Žižek 2000, *Contingency, Hegemony, Universality: Contemporary Dialogues on the Left*, London and New York: Verso.

Cain, P.J. and A.G. Hopkins 1986, 'Gentlemanly Capitalism and British Expansion Overseas. I: The Old Colonial System, 1688–1850', *Economic History Review*, second series, 39, 4: 501–525.

—— 1993, *British Imperialism: Innovation and Expansion, 1688–1914*, New York: Longmans.

—— 2002, *British Imperialism, 1688–2000*, New York: Longmans.

Callaghan, John 1997–98, 'Colonies, Racism, the CPGB and the Comintern in the Inter-War Years', *Science and Society*, 61, 4: 513–525.

Callinicos, Alex 1989, 'Bourgeois Revolutions and Historical Materialism', *International Socialism*, 2, 43: 113–171.

—— 2010, 'The Manifesto and the Crisis Today', in *The Communist Manifesto* by Karl Marx and Friedrich Engels, London: Bookmarks.

Carrette, Jeremy (ed.) 1999, *Religion and Culture: Michel Foucault*, London: Routledge.

Césaire, Aimé 2009 [1950], *Discours sur le colonialisme*, Paris: Textuel.

Chakrabarty, Dipesh 1983, 'Conditions of Knowledge for Working-Class Conditions: Employers, Government and the Jute Workers of Calcutta, 1890–1940', in *Subaltern Studies II, Writings on South Asian History & Society*, edited by R. Guha, Delhi: Oxford University Press.

—— 1989, *Rethinking Working-Class History, Bengal 1880–1940*, Princeton, NJ: Princeton University Press.

—— 1992, 'Postcoloniality and the Artifice of History: Who Speaks for "Indian" Pasts?', *Representations*, 37: 1–26.

—— 1993, 'Marx after Marxism: Subaltern Histories and the Question of Difference', *Polygraph*, 6–7: 10–17.

—— 2000, *Provincializing Europe: Postcolonial Thought and Historical Difference*, Princeton, NJ: Princeton University Press.

Chambers, Iain and Lidia Curti (eds) 1996, *The Post-Colonial Question*, London: Routledge.

Chandavarkar, Rajnarayan 1994, *The Origins of Industrial Capitalism in India: Business Strategies and the Working Classes in Bombay, 1900–1940*, Cambridge: Cambridge University Press.

—— 1998, *Imperial Power and Popular Politics: Class, Resistance and the State in India, c. 1850–1950*, Cambridge: Cambridge University Press.

Chandra, Bipan 1984, *Communalism in Modern India*, Delhi: Vikas.

Chang, Ha-joon 2002, *Kicking Away the Ladder: Development Strategy in Historical Perspective*, New York: Anthem Press.

Chari, V. K. 1990, *Sanskrit Criticism*, Honolulu: University of Hawaii Press.

Chatterjee, Partha 1983, 'More on Modes of Power and the Peasantry', in *Subaltern Studies II, Writings on South Asian History & Society*, edited by R. Guha, Delhi: Oxford University Press.

—— 1984, 'Gandhi and the Critique of Civil Society', in *Subaltern Studies III*, edited by R. Guha, New Delhi: Oxford University Press.

—— 1986, *Nationalist Thought in the Colonial World: A Derivative Discourse?*, Delhi: Oxford University Press.

—— 1993, *The Nation and Its Fragments*, Princeton, NJ: Princeton University Press.

—— 1994, 'Secularism and Tolerance', *Economic and Political Weekly*, 29/28: 1768–1777.

—— 1999, 'Partha Chatterjee in Conversation with Anuradha Dingwaney Needham', *Interventions*, 1, 3: 413–425.

—— 2000, 'The Nation and Its Peasants', in *Mapping Subaltern Studies and the Postcolonial*, edited by V. Chaturverdi, London: Verso.

—— 2004, *The Politics of the Governed: Reflections on Popular Politics in Most of the World*, New York: Columbia University Press.

—— 2006, 'India's History from Below', *Le Monde Diplomatique*, March: 12–13.

—— 2008, 'Democracy and Economic Transformation in India', *Economic and Political Weekly*, 43, 16: 53–62.

—— 2010, *Empire and Nation: Selected Essays*, with an introduction by N. Menon, New York: Columbia University Press.

Chaturvedi, Vinayak (ed.) 2000, *Mapping Subaltern Studies and the Postcolonial*, London: Verso.

—— 2000, 'Introduction', in *Mapping Subaltern Studies and the Postcolonial*, London: Verso.

Chew, Sing and Robert Denemark (eds) 1996, *The Underdevelopment of Development: Essays in Honor of Andre Gunder Frank*, Thousand Oaks, CA: Sage Publications.

Chibber, Vivek 2003, *Locked in Place: State-Building and Late Industrialization in India*, Princeton, NJ: Princeton University Press.

—— 2013, *Postcolonial Theory and the Spectre of Capital*, London: Verso.

Chossudovsky, Michel 1998, *The Globalisation of Poverty*, London: Zed Books.

Chrisman, Laura 1994, 'The Imperial Unconscious? Representations of Imperial Discourse', in *Colonial Discourse and Post-colonial Theory*, edited by P. Williams and L. Chrisman, New York: Columbia University Press.

Claudin, Fernando 1975, *The Communist Movement: From Comintern to Cominform*, New York: Monthly Review Press.

Cleary, Joe 2002, 'Misplaced Ideas? Locating and Dislocating Ireland in Colonial and Postcolonial Studies', in *Marxism, Modernity and Postcolonial Studies*, edited by C. Bartolovich and N. Lazarus, Cambridge: Cambridge University Press.

Cliff, Tony 1984, *Class Struggle and Women's Liberation*, London: Bookmarks, <www.marxists.org/archive/cliff/works/1984/women/01-birth.htm#n8>.

Cohen, G.A. 1993, 'Amartya Sen's Unequal World', *Economic and Political Weekly*, 28, 40: 2156–2160.

Cohen, Ralph and Michael S. Roth (eds) 1995, *History and…: Historians within the Human Sciences*, Charlottesville and London: University of Virginia Press.

Collier, Peter and Helga Geyer-Ryan (eds) 1990, *Literary Theory Today*, London: Polity Press.

Coronado, Jorge 2009, *The Andes Imagined: Indigenismo, Society, and Modernity*, Pittsburgh, PA: University of Pittsburgh Press.

Coronil, Fernando 1996, 'Beyond Occidentalism: Toward Nonimperial Geohistorical Categories', *Cultural Anthropology*, 11, 1: 51–87.

Cronin, Edward 1982, 'Eliade, Joyce and "the Nightmare of History"', *Journal of the American Academy of Religion*, 50, 3: 435–448.

Cusset, François 2008, *French Theory: How Foucault, Derrida, Deleuze and Co. Transformed the Intellectual Life of the United States*, Minneapolis, MN: University of Minnesota Press.

Dallmayr, Fred R. 1989, *Margins of Political Discourse*, Albany, NY: SUNY Press.

Dalmia, Vasudha 2003, 'Crossing Borders and Boundaries', in *At Home in Diaspora South Asian Scholars and the West*, edited by J. Assayag and V. Bénéï, Bloomington, IN: Indiana University Press.

Dalrymple, William 2008, *The Last Mughal: The Fall of a Dynasty: Delhi 1857*, New York: Vintage Books.

Das Gupta, Ranajit 1994, *Labour and Working Class in Eastern India: Studies in Colonial History*, Calcutta: K.P. Bagchi and Co.

Datta Gupta, Sobhanlal 1994, 'Gramsci's Presence in India', *International Gramsci Society Newsletter*, 3 (March): 18–21.

Davidson, Basil 1992, *The White Man's Burden*, London: James Currey.

Davidson, Neil 1999, 'In Perspective: Tom Nairn', *International Socialism Journal*, 82, <www.pubs.socialistreviewindex.org.uk/isj82/davidson.htm>.

Davis, Lance and Robert Huttenback 1988, *Mammon and the Pursuit of Empire: The Economics of British Imperialism*, Cambridge: Cambridge University Press.

Davis, Mike 2000, *Prisoners of the American Dream: Politics and Economy in the History of the US Working Class*, second edition, London: Verso.

—— 2001, *Late Victorian Holocausts: El Niño Famines and the Making of the Third World*, London: Verso.

—— 2007, *Planet of Slums*, London: Verso.

De, Barun 1976, 'Susobhan Chandra Sarkar', in *Essays in Honour of Professor S.C. Sarkar*, New Delhi: People's Publishing House.

—— 1983, 'Susobhan Sarkar (1900–1982) – A Personal Memoir', *Social Scientist*, 11, 2: 3–15.

de la Campa, Roman, E. Ann Kaplan and Michael Sprinker (eds) 1995, *Late Imperial Culture*, London: Verso.

Deane, Seamus 1991, 'The Famine and Young Ireland', in *The Field Day Anthology of Irish Writing*, Volume II, Derry: Field Day.

Derrida, Jacques 1978, *Writing and Difference*, Chicago: University of Chicago Press.

—— 1993, *Spectres de Marx*, Paris: Editions Galilée.

—— 1994a, 'Spectres of Marx', *New Left Review*, I/205: 31–58.

—— 1994b, *Spectres of Marx: The State of the Debt, the Work of Mourning and the New International*, London: Routledge.

Desai, A.R. 2006 [1938], *Rural Sociology in India*, fifth edition, Bombay (Mumbai): Popular Prakashan.

Deutscher, Isaac 1984, *The Great Purges*, Oxford: Blackwell Books.

Dews, Peter 1987, *Logics of Disintegration: Post-Structuralist Thought and the Claims of Critical Theory*, London: Verso.

Dhanagare, D.N. 1988, 'Subaltern Consciousness and Populism: Two Approaches in the Study of Social Movements', *Social Scientist*, 16, 11: 18–35.

Digby, William 1901, *'Prosperous' British India: A Revelation from Official Records*, London: George Unwin.

Dirlik, Arif 1994, 'The Postcolonial Aura: Third World Criticism in the Age of Global Capitalism', *Critical Inquiry*, 20, 2: 328–356.

—— 1999, 'Response to the Responses', *Interventions: International Journal of Postcolonial Studies*, 1, 2: 286–290.

—— 2000a, *Postmodernity's Histories: The Past as Legacy and Project*, Lanham, MD: Rowman and Littlefield.

—— 2000b, 'Is There History After Eurocentrism? Globalism, Postcolonialism and the Disavowal of History', in *History after the Three Worlds*, edited by A. Dirlik, V. Bahl and P. Gran, Lanham, MD: Rowman and Littlefield.

Dirlik, Arif, Vinay Bahl and Peter Gran (eds) 2000, *History after the Three Worlds*, Lanham, MD: Rowman and Littlefield.

Djilas, Milovan 1957, *The New Class: An Analysis of the Communist System*, New York: Praeger.

—— 1998, *Fall of the New Class: A History of Communism's Self-Destruction*, New York: A.A. Knopf.

Dobb, Maurice 1947, *Studies in the Development of Capitalism*, London: Routledge.

Driver, Stephen and Luke Martell 1998, *New Labour: Politics after Thatcherism*, Cambridge: Polity Press.

—— 2001, 'From Old Labour to New Labour: A Comment on Rubinstein', *Politics*, 21, 1: 47–50.

Dumont, Louis 1983, *Essais sur l'individualisme: une perspective anthropologique sur l'idéologie modern*, Paris: Editions Seuil.

Duncan, Colin A.M. 1996, *The Centrality of Agriculture: Between Humankind and the Rest of Nature*, Montreal: McGill-Queen's University Press.

During, Simon 1987, 'Postmodernism or Postcolonialism Today', *Textual Practice*, 1, 1: 32–47.

Dutt, Romesh Chunder 1900, *Open Letters to Lord Curzon on Famines and Land Assessments in India*, London: Kegan Paul, Trench, Trübner.

—— 1902, *The Economic History of India Under Early British Rule: From the Rise of the British Power in 1757 to the Accession of Queen Victoria in 1837*, Volume I, London: Kegan Paul, Trench Trübner.

—— 1936 [1910], *The Ramayana and the Mahabharata*, London: J.M. Dent and Sons.

Eagleton, Terry 1996, *The Illusions of Postmodernism*, London: Blackwell.

—— 1998, 'Postcolonialism and "Postcolonialism"', *Interventions: International*

Journal of Postcolonial Studies, 1, 1: 24–6.

—— 2007, 'Lenin in the Postmodern Age', in *Lenin Reloaded: Towards a Politics of Truth*, edited by S. Budgen, S. Kouvelakis and S. Žižek, Durham, NC: Duke University Press.

—— 2011, 'Indomitable' (Review of Eric Hobsbawm's *How to Change the World: Marx and Marxism 1840–2011*), *London Review of Books*, 33, 5: 13–14.

Edwards, Brent Hayes 1998, 'The Ethnics of Surrealism', *Transition*, 78: 84–135.

Eliade, Mircea 1954, *Cosmos and History: The Myth of the Eternal Return*, translated by W.R. Trask, Princeton, NJ: Princeton University Press.

—— 1959, *Myths, Dreams and Mysteries: The Encounter between Contemporary Faiths and Archaic Realities*, translated by P. Mairet, London: Harvill Press.

Ellwood, Robert 1999, *The Politics of Myth: A Study of C.G. Jung, Mircea Eliade, and Joseph Campbell*, Albany, NY: SUNY Press.

Elman, Benjamin A. 2004, 'New Perspectives of the Jesuits and Science in China, 1600–1800', in *Points of Contact: Crossing Cultural Boundaries*, edited by A. Golahny, Lewisburg, PA: Bucknell University Press.

Elson, Diane (ed.) 1979, *Value: The Representation of Labour in Capitalism*, Atlantic Highlands, NJ: Humanities Press.

Emmanuel, Arghiri 1972, *Unequal Exchange: A Study of the Imperialism of Trade*, translated by Brian Pearce, New York and London: Monthly Review Press.

Engels, Friedrich 1940 [1883], *Dialectics of Nature*, translated and edited by C. Dutt with a preface and notes by J.B.S. Haldane, London: Lawrence and Wishart, Ltd.

—— 1989 [1892], *Socialism, Utopian and Scientific*, New York: Pathfinder Press.

—— 2009 [1844], *The Condition of the Working Class in England*, Oxford: Oxford University Press.

Erebon, Didion 1991, *Michel Foucault*, Cambridge, MA: Harvard University Press.

Esteva, Gustavo 1987, 'Regenerating People's Space', in *Towards a Just World Peace*, edited by S.H. Mendlovitz and R.B.J. Walker, London: Butterworths.

—— 1996, 'Hosting the Otherness of the Green Revolution', in *Decolonizing Knowledge: From Development to Dialogue*, edited by F. Apffel-Marglin and S.A. Marglin, Oxford: Clarendon Press.

Fanon, Frantz 1968, *The Wretched of the Earth*, translated by C. Farrington, New York: Grove Press.

Ferguson, Niall 2006, *The War of the World: Twentieth Century Conflict and the Descent of the West*, New York: The Penguin Press.

Forster, E.M. 1992 [1924], *A Passage to India*, New York: Knopf.

Foster, John Bellamy 1998, 'Review of the Month: Malthus' *Essay on Population* at Age 200, A Marxian View', *Monthly Review*, 50, 7: 1–18.

Foucault, Michel 1971, *L'ordre du discours*, Paris: Gallimard.

—— 1972, 'The Discourse on Language', Appendix to *Archaeology of*

Knowledge, translated by A.M. Sheridan Smith, New York: Pantheon.

—— 1978, 'Sexuality and Power', in *Religion and Culture: Michel Foucault*, edited by J. Carette, London: Routledge.

—— 1984a, 'Nietzsche, Genealogy, History', in *Foucault Reader*, edited by P. Rabinow, New York: Pantheon.

—— 1984b, 'Truth and Power', in *Foucault Reader*, edited by P. Rabinow, New York: Pantheon.

Frank, Andre Gunder 1969, *Capitalism and Underdevelopment in Latin America*, New York: Monthly Review Press.

—— 1998, *ReORIENT: Global Economy in the Asian Age*, Berkeley, CA: University of California Press.

Frankel, Boris 1987, *The Post-Industrial Utopians*, Madison, WI: University of Wisconsin Press.

Fukuoka, Masanobu 1978, *The One-Straw Revolution: An Introduction to Natural Farming*, translated by C. Pearce, T. Kurosawa and L. Korn, New York: Rodale Press.

Fukuyama, Francis 1992, *The End of History and the Last Man*, New York: Free Press.

Gadgil, Madhav and Ramachandra Guha 1992, *This Fissured Land: An Ecological History of India*, Delhi: Oxford University Press.

—— 1995, *Ecology and Equity: The Use and Abuse of Nature in Contemporary India*, New Delhi: Penguin Books.

Gadgil, Madhav and V.D. Vartak 1976, 'The Sacred Groves of Western Ghats in India', *Economic Botany*, 30: 152–160.

Galeano, Eduardo 1991, 'A Child Lost in the Storm', in *After the Fall: The Failure of Communism and the Future of Socialism*, edited by R. Blackburn, London: Verso.

Gandhi, Mohandas Karamchand 1947, *India of My Dreams*, with a foreword by R. Prasad, Ahmedabad: Navjivan Publishing House.

—— 1948, *Gandhi's Autobiography: The Story of My Experiments with Truth*, translated by M. Desai, Washington, DC: Public Affairs.

—— 1958–94, *The Collected Works of Mahatma Gandhi*, 100 volumes, New Delhi: Publications Division of the Government of India.

—— 1960, *Trusteeship*, Ahmedabad: Navjivan Publishing House.

—— 1997 [1919], *Hind Swaraj and Other Writings*, edited by A.J. Parel, New York: Cambridge University Press.

Gandhi, Ramachandra 1976, *The Availability of Religious Ideas*, London: MacMillan.

Ganguly, Keya 2002, 'Adorno, Authenticity, Critique', in *Marxism, Modernity and Postcolonial Studies*, edited by C. Bartolovich and N. Lazarus, Cambridge: Cambridge University Press.

Gardet, L. et al. (eds) 1976, *Culture and Time*, Paris: UNESCO Press.

Gentleman, Amelia 2006, 'India's lost daughters: Abortion toll in millions', *International Herald Tribune*, 10 January 2006.

Gerschenkron, Alexander 1962, *Economic Backwardness in Historical Perspective: A Book of Essays*, Cambridge, MA: Belknap Press.

Ghosh, Amitav 2002, *The Glass Palace: A Novel*, New York: Random House.

Ghosh, Peter 2001, 'Gramscian Hegemony: An Absolutely Historicist Approach', *History of European Ideas*, 27: 1–43.

Giddens, Anthony 1981, *A Contemporary Critique of Historical Materialism: Power, Property and the State*, Berkeley, CA: University of California Press.

—— 1994, *Beyond Left and Right: The Future of Radical Politics*, London: Polity Press.

—— 1999, *The Third Way: The Renewal of Social Democracy*, London: Polity Press.

Gillespie, Michael Alan 1984, *Hegel, Heidegger and the Ground of History*, Chicago: University of Chicago Press.

Gilmartin, David 1995, 'Models of the Hydraulic Environment: Colonial Irrigation, State Power and Community in the Indus Basin', in *Nature, Culture, Imperialism, Essays on the Environmental History of South Asia*, edited by D. Arnold and R. Guha, Delhi: Oxford University Press.

Gilmour, David 2007, *The Ruling Caste: Imperial Lives in the Victorian Raj*, New York: Farar, Straus and Giroux.

Ginzburg, Carlo 1980, *The Cheese and the Worms: The Cosmos of a Sixteenth-Century Miller*, translated by A. Tedeschi and J. Tedeschi, Baltimore, MD: Johns Hopkins University Press.

Gitlin, Todd 1995, *The Twilight of Common Dreams*, New York: Henry Holt.

Glaser, Daryl and David M. Walker (eds) 2007, *Twentieth-Century Marxism: A Global Introduction*, Oxford: Routledge.

Gnoli, Raniero 1968, *The Aesthetic Experience According to Abhinavagupta*, Varanasi: Chowkhamba Sanskrit Series Office.

Godelier, Maurice 1973, *Horizon, trajets marxistes en anthropologie*, Paris: Maspero.

—— 1991, 'Les contextes illusoires de la transition au socialisme', in *Fin du communisme? Actualité du marxisme*, edited by J. Bidet and J. Texier, Paris: Presses Universitaires de France.

Golahny, Amy (ed.) 2004, *Points of Contact: Crossing Cultural Boundaries*, Lewisburg, PA: Bucknell University Press.

Golwalkar, M.S. 1939, *We; or Our Nationhood Defined*, Nagpur: Bharat Prakashan.

Gopal, Priyamvada 2002, 'Sex, Space, and Modernity in the Work of Rashid Jahan, "Angareywali"', in *Marxism, Modernity and Postcolonial Studies*, edited by C. Bartolovich and N. Lazarus, Cambridge: Cambridge University Press.

Gorz, André 1982, *Farewell To The Working Class: An Essay On Post-Industrial Socialism*, London: Pluto Press.

Gowan, Peter 1999, *The Global Gamble: Washington's Faustian Bid for Global Dominance*, London: Verso.

Gramsci, Antonio 1968, *The Modern Prince and Other Writings*, New York: International Publishers.

—— 1971, *Selections from the Prison Notebooks of Antonio Gramsci*, edited and translated by Q. Hoare and G. Nowell-Smith, New York: International Publishers.

—— 1985, *Selections from Cultural Writings*, edited by D. Forgacs and G. Nowell-Smith, translated by

W. Boelhower, Cambridge, MA: Harvard University Press.

—— 1990, *Selections from Political Writings 1919–1920*, Minneapolis, MN: University of Minnesota Press.

—— 1994, *Letters from Prison*, 2 Volumes, New York: Columbia University Press.

—— 1994a, *Antonio Gramsci: Pre-Prison Writings*, Cambridge: Cambridge University Press.

—— 1995, *The Southern Question*, translated by P. Verdicchio, West Lafayette, IN: Bordighera, Inc.

Gray, John, *False Dawn: The Illusions of Global Capitalism*, London: Granta Books.

Green, Marcus E. (ed.) 2011, *Rethinking Gramsci*, Oxford: Routledge.

Greenblatt, Stephen and Giles Gunn (eds) 1992, *Redrawing the Boundaries: The Transformation of English and American Literary Studies*, New York: MLA.

Guha, Ramachandra (ed.) 1994, *Social Ecology*, Delhi: Oxford University Press.

—— 2000, *The Unquiet Woods*, Berkeley, CA: University of California Press.

Guha, Ranajit 1963, *A Rule of Property in India: An Essay on the Idea of Permanent Settlement*, Paris: Mouton.

—— 1982, 'Preface', in *Subaltern Studies I, Writings on South Asian History & Society*, Delhi: Oxford University Press.

—— 1983a, *Elementary Aspects of Peasant Insurgency in Colonial India*, Delhi: Oxford University Press.

—— 1983b, 'The Prose of Counter-Insurgency', in *Subaltern Studies II, Writings on South Asian History & Society*, Delhi: Oxford University Press.

—— (ed.) 1984, *Subaltern Studies III*, New Delhi: Oxford University Press.

—— (ed.) 1985, *Subaltern Studies IV*, New Delhi: Oxford University Press.

—— 1988, 'On Some Aspects of the Historiography of Colonial India', in *Selected Subaltern Studies*, edited by R. Guha and G.C. Spivak, New York: Oxford University Press.

—— 1997a, *Dominance Without Hegemony: History and Power in Colonial India*, Cambridge, MA: Harvard University Press.

—— 1997b, *A Subaltern Studies Reader, 1986–95*, Minneapolis, MN: University of Minneapolis Press.

—— 2002, *History at the Limits of World-History*, New York: Columbia University Press.

Guha, Ranajit and Gayatri Chakravorty Spivak (eds) 1988, *Selected Subaltern Studies*, New York: Oxford University Press.

Gupta, Dipankar 1985, 'On Altering the Ego in Peasant History: Paradoxes of the Ethnic Option', *Peasant Studies*, 13, 1: 5–24.

Gurevich, Aaron J. 1976, 'Time as a Problem of Cultural History', in *Culture and Time*, edited by L. Gardet et al., Paris: UNESCO Press.

Habermas, Jürgen 2001, *The Postnational Constellation: Political Essays*, translated and edited by M. Pensky, Oxford: Polity Press.

Habib, Irfan 1995, *Essays in Indian History: Towards a Marxist Perception*, New Delhi: Tulika.

—— 2000, *The Agrarian System of Mughal India, 1556–1707*, Delhi: Oxford University Press.

Hacking, Ian 1995, 'Two Kinds of "New Historicism" for Philosophers,' in *History and...: Historians within the Human Sciences*, edited by R. Cohen and M.S. Roth, Charlottesville and London: University of Virginia Press.

Halbfass, Wilhelm 1988, *India and Europe: An Essay in Understanding*, Albany, NY: SUNY Press.

Hall, John A. 1985, *Powers and Liberties: The Causes and Consequences of the Rise of the West*, Berkeley, CA: University of California Press.

Hall, Stuart 1988, *The Hard Road to Renewal: Thatcherism and the Crisis of the Left*, London: Verso.

—— 1996, 'When was the "Post-Colonial"? Thinking at the Limit', in *The Post-Colonial Question*, edited by I. Chambers and L. Curti, London: Routledge.

Hardiman, David 1981, *Peasant Nationalists of Gujarat: Kheda District, 1917–34*, Delhi: Oxford University Press.

—— 1995, 'Small-Dam Systems of the Sahyadris', in *Nature, Culture, Imperialism, Essays on the Environmental History of South Asia*, edited by D. Arnold and R. Guha, Delhi: Oxford University Press.

Hardt, Michael 2001, 'The Eurocentrism of History' (Review of Dipesh Chakrabarty's *Provincializing Europe*), *Postcolonial Studies*, 4, 2: 243–249.

Harman, Chris 2010, 'The Manifesto and the World of 1848', in *The Communist Manifesto*, by Karl Marx and Friedrich Engels, London: Bookmarks.

Harvey, David 1982, *The Limits to Capital*, Chicago: University of Chicago Press.

—— 1996, *Justice, Nature and the Geography of Difference*, Oxford: Blackwell Publishers.

—— 2000, *Spaces of Hope*, Berkeley and Los Angeles, CA: University of California Press.

—— 2003, *The New Imperialism*, New York: Oxford University Press.

—— 2006, *The Limits to Capital*, new updated edition, London: Verso.

Hay, Douglas, Peter Linebaugh, John Rule, E.P. Thompson and Cal Winslow 1975, *Albion's Fatal Tree: Crime and Society in Eighteenth-Century England*, New York: Pantheon Books.

Hayek, F.A. 1960, *The Constitution of Liberty*, Chicago: University of Chicago Press.

—— 1973–79, *Law, Legislation and Liberty*, 3 volumes, Chicago: University of Chicago Press.

Headrick, Daniel R. 1988, *The Tentacles of Progress: Technology Transfer in the Age of Imperialism 1850–1940*, New York: Oxford University Press.

Hegel, G.W.F. 1890, *Lectures on the Philosophy of History*, translated by J. Sibree, London: George Bell and Sons.

Heidegger, Martin 1962 [1927], *Being and Time*, translated by J. Macquarrie and E. Robinson, New York: Harper Collins.

Heller, Patrick 1999, *The Labor of Development: Workers and the Transformation of Capitalism in Kerala, India*, Ithaca, NY: Cornell University Press.

Heussler, Robert 1968, *The British in Northern Nigeria*, London: Oxford University Press.

Heuzé, Gérard 1996, *Entre émeutes et mafias: L'Inde dans la mondialisation*, Paris: L'Harmattan.

Hill, Christopher 1975, *The World Turned Upside Down: Radical Ideas during the English Revolution*, London: Penguin Books.

—— 1977, *Milton and the English Revolution*, London: Faber.

Hilton, Rodney 1990, *Class Conflict and the Crisis of Feudalism: Essays in Medieval Social History*, London: Verso.

Hobsbawm, Eric 1959, *Primitive Rebels*, New York: W.W. Norton and Company.

—— 1996a [1962], *The Age of Revolution, 1789–1848*, New York: Vintage Books.

—— 1996b [1975], *The Age of Capital, 1848–1875*, New York: Vintage Books.

—— 1996c [1994], *The Age of Extremes, A History of the World, 1914–1991*, New York: Vintage Books.

—— 2011, *How to Change the World: Marx and Marxism 1840–2011*, London: Little, Brown.

Hoggart, Richard 1957, *The Uses of Literacy*, London: Chatto and Windus.

Holloway, John 2010, *Change the World Without Taking Power*, London: Pluto Press.

Holmström, Mark 1984, *Industry and Inequality: The Social Anthropology of Indian Labour*, Cambridge: Cambridge University Press.

Holub, Renate 1992, *Antonio Gramsci: Beyond Marxism and Postmodernism*, London: Routledge.

Hoodbhoy, Pervez 1991, *Islam and Science: Religious Orthodoxy and the Battle for Rationality*, London: Zed Books.

Hopkins, A.G. 2008, 'Rethinking Decolonisation', *Past and Present*, 200, 1: 211–247.

Hudis, Peter 1983, 'The Third World Road to Socialism: New Perspectives on Marx's Writings From His Last Decade', *South Asia Bulletin*, 3, 1: 38–52.

Hughes, Robert 1988, *The Fatal Shore: The Epic of Australia's Founding*, New York: Vintage Books.

Hulme, Peter 1995, 'Including America', *Ariel: A Review of International English Literature*, 26, 1: 117–123.

Huntington, Samuel 1996, *The Clash of Civilizations and the Remaking of World Order*, New York: Simon and Schuster.

Hussey, Andrew 2008, *Paris: A Secret History*, New York: Bloomsbury USA.

IFPRI 2002, 'Green Revolution: Curse Or Blessing', *International Food Policy Research Institute*, Washington, DC: IFPRI.

Inden, Ronald 1986, 'Orientalist Constructions of India', *Modern Asian Studies*, 20, 3: 401–445.

Jackson, Anna and Amin Jaffer 2004, *Encounters: The Meeting of Asia and Europe, 1500–1800*, London: V&A Publications.

Jaffrelot, Christophe 1996, *The Hindu Nationalist Movement in India*, New York: Columbia University Press.

—— 1998, 'The Bahujan Samaj Party in North India: No Longer Just a Dalit Party?', *Comparative Studies of South Asia, Africa and the Middle East*, 28, 1: 35–52.

—— 2003, *India's Silent Revolution: The Rise of the Lower Castes in North*

India, New York: Columbia University Press.

James, C.L.R. 1992, *The C.L.R. James Reader*, edited by A. Grimshaw, Oxford: Blackwell Books.

Jameson, Fredric 1971, *Marxism and Form*, Princeton, NJ: Princeton University Press.

—— 1981, *The Political Unconscious: Narrative as a Socially Symbolic Act*, Ithaca, NY: Cornell University Press.

—— 1986, 'Third-World Literature in the Era of Multinational Capitalism', *Social Text*, 15: 65–88.

—— 1988, *The Ideologies of Theory, Essays 1971–1986*, Vol. II: *Syntax of History*, Minneapolis: University of Minnesota Press.

—— 1991, *Postmodernism, or, The Cultural Logic of Late Capitalism*, Durham, NC: Duke University Press.

—— 1993, 'Actually Existing Marxism', *Polygraph*, 6–7: 170–195.

—— 1994, *The Seeds of Time*, New York: Columbia University Press.

—— 1998, *The Cultural Turn*, London: Verso.

—— 2002, *A Singular Modernity*, London: Verso.

—— 2011, *Representing Capital: A Reading of Volume One*, London, New York: Verso.

Jani, Pranav 2002, 'Karl Marx, Eurocentrism, and the 1857 Revolt in British India', in *Marxism, Modernity and Postcolonial Studies*, edited by C. Bartolovich and N. Lazarus, Cambridge: Cambridge University Press.

Jasanoff, Maya 2005, *Edge of Empire: Conquest and Collecting in the East, 1750–1850*, London: Harper Perennial.

Jay, Martin 2006, 'Taking On the Stigma of Inauthenticity: Adorno's Critique of Genuineness', *New German Critique*, 97, 33, 1: 15–30.

Jones, Eric L. 1981, *The European Miracle*, Cambridge: Cambridge University Press.

Joshi, Chitra 2005, *Lost Worlds: Indian Labour and its Forgotten Histories*, London: Anthem South Asian Studies.

Judt, Tony 2011, *Past Imperfect: French Intellectuals, 1944–1956*, New York: New York University Press.

Kadam, Mansing G. 2006, 'Amitav Ghosh's *The Glass Palace*: A Post-colonial Novel', in *Indian Writings in English*, edited by B. Mishra and S. Kumar, Delhi: Atlantic Publishers.

Kaiwar, Vasant 1989, *Social Property Relations and the Economic Dynamic: The Case of Peasant Agriculture in Western India, ca. mid-Nineteenth to mid-Twentieth Centuries*, Unpublished PhD dissertation: UCLA.

—— 1991, 'On Provincialism and Popular Nationalism: Reflections on Samir Amin's *Eurocentrism*', *South Asia Bulletin: Tenth Anniversary Issue on Nationalism, Populism, and Gender*, 11, 1/2: 69–78.

—— 1992a, 'Property Structures, Demography and the Crisis of the Agrarian Economy of Colonial Bombay Presidency', *Journal of Peasant Studies*, 19, 2: 255–300.

—— 1992b, 'Science, Capitalism and Islam', *South Asia Bulletin*, 12, 2: 39–56.

—— 1994, 'The Colonial State, Capital and the Peasantry in Bombay Presidency', *Modern Asian Studies*, 28, 4: 793–832.

—— 1999, 'The Dilemmas of Late Capitalism', *Comparative Studies of South Asia, Africa and the Middle East*, 19, 2: 47–52.

—— 2000, 'Nature, Property and Polity in Colonial Bombay,' *Journal of Peasant Studies*, 27, 2: 1–49.

—— 2003, 'The Aryan Model of History and the Oriental Renaissance: The Politics of Identity in an Age of Revolutions, Colonialism and Nationalism', in *Antinomies of Modernity: Essays on Race, Orient, Nation*, edited by V. Kaiwar and S. Mazumdar, Durham, NC: Duke University Press.

—— 2004, 'Towards Orientalism and Nativism: The Impasse of Subaltern Studies', *Historical Materialism*, 12, 2: 189–247.

—— 2005a, 'Silences in Postcolonial Thought: The case of *Provincializing Europe*', *Economic and Political Weekly*, 40, 34: 3732–3738.

—— 2005b, 'Des Subaltern Studies comme nouvel orientalisme', *Contre-Temps*, 12: 136–150.

—— 2007a, 'Philosophy and Politics in the *Hind Swaraj* of Mohandas Gandhi', *Journal of South Asian and Middle Eastern Studies*, 31, 1: 50–69.

—— 2007b, 'Review of Surendra Bhana and Goolam Vahed, *The Making of a Political Reformer: Gandhi in South Africa, 1893–1914*', *The Oriental Anthropologist*, 7, 1: 192–197.

—— 2007c, 'Colonialism, difference, and exoticism in the formation of the postcolonial metanarrative', *Littératures, Histoire des Idées, Images, Sociétés du Monde Anglophone*, Université de Caen, 5, 3: 48–71.

—— 2012, 'Famines of Structural Adjustment in Colonial India', in *Nationalism and Imperialism in South and Southeast Asia: Essays in Honour of Damodar R. SarDesai*, edited by R. Long and A. Kaminsky, New Delhi: Manohar.

Kaiwar, Vasant and Sucheta Mazumdar 2003, 'Race, Orient, Nation in the Time-Space of Modernity', in *Antinomies of Modernity: Essays on Race, Orient, Nation*, Durham, NC: Duke University Press.

—— (eds) 2003, *Antinomies of Modernity: Essays on Race, Orient, Nation*, Durham, NC: Duke University Press.

—— 2009, 'Coordinates of Orientalism: Reflections on the Universal and the Particular', in *From Orientalism to Postcolonialism: Asia, Europe and the Lineages of Difference*, edited by S. Mazumdar, V. Kaiwar and T. Labica, London: Routledge.

Kaviraj, Sudipto 1997, 'Filth and the Public Sphere: Concepts and Practices about Space in Calcutta', *Public Culture*, 10, 1: 83–113.

Kelley, Robin D.G. 1999, 'A Poetics of Anti-Colonialism', *Monthly Review*, 51, 6: 1–21.

Kerr, Ian 1995, *Building the Railways of the Raj*, Delhi: Oxford University Press.

Kinealy, Christine 1994, *This Great Calamity: the Irish Famine, 1845–52*, Dublin: Gill and Macmillan.

Kooiman, Dick 1983, 'Rural Labour in the Bombay Textile Industry and the Articulation of Modes of Organization,' in *Rural India, Power and Society under British Rule: Collected Papers on*

South Asia, No. 6, edited by P. Robb, London: Curzon Press.

Koonz, Claudia 1987, *Mothers in the Fatherland: Women, the Family and Nazi Politics*, New York: St. Martin's Press.

Korsch, Karl 1963, *Karl Marx*, New York: Russell and Russell.

Kosa Pan 2002, *The Diary of Kosa Pan, Thai Ambassador to France, June–July 1686*, translated by V. Bisaykul, edited by D. van der Cruysse and M. Smithies, Chiang Mai: Silkworm Books.

Kosambi, D.D. 1972, *The Culture and Civilisation of Ancient India*, Delhi: Vikas Publishing House.

—— 2009, *The Oxford India Kosambi: Combined Methods in Indology and Other Writings*, compiled, edited and introduced by B. Chattopadhyaya, New Delhi: Oxford University Press.

Kothari, Manu and Lopa Mehta 1983, 'The Cancer Conundrum', *The Indian Express*, 11 September 1983.

Kude, U.L. 1986, *Impact of Communism on the Working Class and Peasantry: A Case Study of Maharashtra*, Delhi: Daya Publishing House.

Kumar, Dharma (ed.) 1983, *The Cambridge Economic History of India*, Cambridge: Cambridge University Press.

Kumar, Krishna 1993, 'Mohandas Karamchand Gandhi, 1869–1948', PROSPECTS: *The Quarterly Review of Education*, 23, 3/4: 507–517.

Labica, Georges 2007, 'From Imperialism to Globalization', in *Lenin Reloaded: Towards a Politics of Truth*, edited by S. Budgen, S. Kouvelakis and S. Žižek, Durham, NC and London: Duke University Press.

Labica, Thierry 2009, 'The Cultural Fix? Language, Work, and the Territories of Accumulation', in *From Orientalism to Postcolonialism: Asia, Europe and the Lineages of Difference*, edited by S. Mazumdar, V. Kaiwar and T. Labica, London: Routledge.

Laclau, Ernesto 1977, *Politics and Ideology in Marxist Theory*, London: New Left Books.

Lapidus, Ira Marvin 2002, *A History of Islamic Societies*, Cambridge: Cambridge University Press.

Lardinois, Roland 1996, 'The Genesis of Louis Dumont's Anthropology: The 1930s in France Revisited', *Comparative Studies of South Asia, Africa and the Middle East*, 16, 1: 27–40.

Larsen, Neil 1995, *Reading North by South: On Latin American Literature, Culture, and Politics*, Minneapolis, MN: University of Minnesota Press.

—— 2002, 'Marxism, Postcolonialism, and *The Eighteenth Brumaire*', in *Marxism, Modernity and Postcolonial Studies*, edited by C. Bartolovich and N. Lazarus, Cambridge: Cambridge University Press.

Latin American Subaltern Studies Group 1993, 'Founding Statement', *Boundary 2*, 20: 110–121.

Lavrin, Janko 1960, 'Tolstoy and Gandhi', *Russian Review*, 19, 2: 132–139.

Lawson, Philip 1993, *The East India Company: A History*, London: Longman.

Lazarus, Neil 1999, *Nationalism and Cultural Practice in the Postcolonial World*, Cambridge: Cambridge University Press.

—— 2002, 'The Fetish of the "the West" in Postcolonial Theory,' in *Marxism,*

Modernity and Postcolonial Studies, edited by C. Bartolovich and N. Lazarus, Cambridge: Cambridge University Press.

—— 2011, *The Postcolonial Unconscious*, Cambridge: Cambridge University Press.

Lazzarato, Maurizio 1996, 'Immaterial Labor', in *Radical Thought in Italy: A Potential Politics*, edited by P. Virno and M. Hardt, Minneapolis, MN: University of Minnesota Press.

Lee, Christopher 2005, 'Subaltern Studies and African Studies', *History Compass* 3, 1: 1–13.

Lefebvre, Henri 1957, *Pour connaître la pensée de Lenine*, Paris: Bordas.

Lefkowitz, Mary and Guy MacLean Rogers (eds) 1996, *Black Athena Revisited*, Chapel Hill, NC: University of North Carolina Press.

Lenin, V.I. 1963 [1917], 'Imperialism: The Highest Stage of Capitalism', in *Selected Works*, (Volume I), Moscow: Progress Publishers, <www.marxists.org/archive/lenin/works/1916/imp-hsc/>.

—— 1965, 'Letter to American Workers', in *Collected Works*, Volume 38, Moscow: Progress Publishers.

—— 1974 [1898], *The Development of Capitalism in Russia*, Moscow: Progress Publishers.

Lévi-Strauss, Claude 1966, *The Savage Mind*, Chicago: Chicago University Press.

—— 1970, *The Raw and the Cooked*, translated by J. Weightman and D. Weightman, New York: Harper and Row.

Lewis, Martin and Karen Wigen 1997, *Myth of Continents: A Critique of Metageography*, Berkeley, CA: University of California Press.

Lewontin, Richard and Richard Levins 1987, *The Dialectical Biologist*, Cambridge, MA: Harvard University Press.

—— 2007, *Biology Under the Influence: Dialectical Essays on Ecology, Agriculture, and Health*, New York: Monthly Review Press.

Leys, Colin 1996, *The Rise and Fall of Development Theory*, Bloomington, IN: Indiana University Press.

Li Qiang 2012, 'Beyond Foxconn: Deplorable Working Conditions Characterize Apple's Entire Supply Chain', *China Labor Watch*, <www.chinalaborwatch.org/pdf/2012627-5.pdf>.

Lloyd, David 1999, *Ireland after History*, Cork: Cork University Press.

Long, Roger and Arnold Kaminsky (eds) 2012, *Nationalism and Imperialism in South and Southeast Asia: Essays in Honour of Damodar R. SarDesai*, New Delhi: Manohar.

Loomba, Ania 1998, *Colonialism/Postcolonialism*, London: Routledge.

Losurdo, Domenico 2001, *Heidegger and the Ideology of War: Community, Death and the West*, Amherst, NY: Humanity Books.

—— 2004, *Hegel and the Freedom of Moderns*, translated by M. Morris and J. Morris, Durham, NC: Duke University Press.

—— 2007, 'Lenin and *Herrenvolk* Democracy,' in *Lenin Reloaded: Towards a Politics of Truth*, edited by S. Budgen, S. Kouvelakis and S. Žižek, Durham, NC and London: Duke University Press.

—— 2011, *Liberalism: A Counter-History*, translated by G. Elliott, London: Verso.

Lowe, Lisa and David Lloyd (eds) 1997, *The Politics of Culture in the Shadow of*

Capital, Durham, NC: Duke University Press.

Ludden, David (ed.) 2002, *Reading Subaltern Studies*, London: Anthem Press.

Lukács, Gyorgy 1971, *History and Class Consciousness: Studies in Marxist Dialectics*, translated by R. Livingstone, Cambridge, MA: The MIT Press.

Luxemburg, Rosa 1970, *Rosa Luxemburg Speaks*, New York: Pathfinder Press.

—— 2003 [1913], *The Accumulation of Capital*, translated by A. Schwartzschild, with a new introduction by T. Kowalik, London: Routledge.

MacFarlane, Alan 1987, *The Culture of Capitalism*, Oxford: Basil Blackwell.

Maddison, Angus 1971, *The Economic and Social Impact of Colonial Rule in India*, <www.ggdc.net/maddison/>.

Maharatna, Arup 1996, *The Demography of Famine*, Delhi: Oxford University Press.

Majumdar, R.C. 1961, 'Ideas of History in Sanskrit Literature', in *Historians of India, Pakistan and Ceylon*, edited by C.H. Philips, London: Oxford University Press.

Mallon, Florencia 1994, 'The Promise and Dilemma of Subaltern Studies: Perspectives from Latin American History', *American Historical Review*, 99: 1491–1515.

Mally, Lynn 1990, *Culture of the Future: The Proletkult Movement in Revolutionary Russia*, Berkeley, CA: University of California Press.

Mandel, Ernest 1977, 'Introduction', in *Capital*, Volume I, by K. Marx, New York: Vintage Books.

—— 1983, 'Uneven Development', in *A Dictionary of Marxist Thought*, edited by T. Bottomore, Cambridge, MA: Harvard University Press.

Mandelbaum, Maurice 1971, *History, Man and Reason*, Baltimore, MD: Johns Hopkins University Press.

Mann, Charles 2006, *1491: New Revelations of the Americas before Columbus*, New York: Vintage Books.

Mann, Harold 1917, *Land and Labour in a Deccan Village*, Bombay: University of Bombay Economic Series.

—— 1921, *Land and Labour in a Deccan Village, Study No. 2*, Bombay; University of Bombay Economic Series.

Mansour, Fawzy 1992, *The Arab World: Nation, State and Democracy*, London: Zed Books.

Marglin, Stephen A. 1981, *To Gain the Whole World: The Ends and Means of Economic Development*, Cambridge, MA: Harvard Institute of Economic Research.

—— 2008, *The Dismal Science: How Thinking Like an Economist Undermines Community*, Cambridge, MA: Harvard University Press.

Martin, William and Michael West 1999, *Out of One, Many Africas: Reconstructing the Study and Meaning of Africa*, Champaign, IL: University of Illinois Press.

Marx, Karl 1968, *Karl Marx on Colonialism and Modernization*, edited by S. Avineri, New York: Doubleday.

—— 1969, *Value, Price and Profit*, New York: International Co., Inc.

—— 1970, *A Contribution to the Critique of Political Economy*, Moscow: Progress Publishers.

—— 1971, *Theories of Surplus-Value*, 3 Volumes, Moscow: Progress Publishers.

—— 1972, *The Ethnological Notebooks*, Assen: Van Gorcum.

—— 1973, *Grundrisse*, London: Pelican Books.

—— 1974, *Surveys from Exile*, edited by D. Fernbach, New York: Vintage Books.

—— 1975, *Wages, Prices and Profit*, Peking: Foreign Languages Press.

—— 1975ff., 'Economic Manuscript of 1861–63', in *Collected Works*, Volume 33, by K. Marx and F. Engels, London: Lawrence and Wishart.

—— 1977, *Capital*, Volume I, New York: Vintage Books.

—— 1981, *Capital*, Volume III, New York: Vintage Books.

—— 1995 [1851–52], *The Eighteenth Brumaire of Louis Bonaparte*, translated by S.K. Padover, <www.marxists.org/archive/marx/works/download/pdf/18th-Brumaire.pdf>.

Marx, Karl and Friedrich Engels 1972, *On Colonialism: Articles from the New York Tribune and Other Writings*, New York: International Publishers.

—— 1980, *The Communist Manifesto*, with introduction by L. Trotsky, New York: Pathfinder Press.

Matin-Asgari, Afshin 2004, 'Iranian Postmodernity: The Rhetoric of Irrationality?', *Critique: Critical Middle Eastern Studies*, 13, 1: 113–123.

—— 2009, 'Iranian Modernity in Global Perspective: Nationalist, Marxist, and Authenticity Discourses', in *From Orientalism to Postcolonialism: Asia, Europe and the Lineages of Difference*, edited by S. Mazumdar, V. Kaiwar and T. Labica, London: Routledge.

Max Müller, F. 1883, *India: What Can It Teach Us? A Course of Lectures Delivered Before the University of Cambridge*, New York: Funk and Wagnalls.

Mayer, Arno 1981, *The Persistence of the Old Regime: Europe to the Great War*, New York: Pantheon Books.

Mazumdar, Sucheta 1995, 'Women on the March: Right-Wing Mobilization in Contemporary India', *Feminist Review*, 49: 1–28.

—— 2009, 'Locating China, Positioning America: The Politics of the Civilisational Model of World History', in *From Orientalism to Postcolonialism: Asia, Europe and the Lineages of Difference*, edited by S. Mazumdar, V. Kaiwar and T. Labica, London: Routledge.

Mazumdar, Sucheta, Vasant Kaiwar and Thierry Labica (eds) 2009, *From Orientalism to Postcolonialism: Asia, Europe and the Lineages of Difference*, London: Routledge.

McClelland, David 1961, *The Achieving Society*, Princeton, NJ: Van Nostrand.

—— 1978, 'Managing Motivation to Expand Human Freedom', *American Psychologist*, 33, 3: 201–210.

McClintock, Anne 1994, 'The Angel of Progress: Pitfalls of the Term "Post-colonialism"', in *Colonial Discourse and Post-colonial Theory*, edited by P. Williams and L. Chrisman, New York: Columbia University Press.

McLennan, Gregor 1981, *Marxism and the Methodologies of History*, London: Verso.

Megill, Allan 1985, *Prophets of Extremity: Nietzsche, Heidegger, Foucault, Derrida*, Berkeley, CA: University of California Press.

Mehta, Jarava Lal 1976, *Martin Heidegger: The Way and the Vision*, Honolulu: University of Hawaii Press.

Mehta, Uday Singh 1999, *Liberalism and Empire: A Study in Nineteenth-Century British Liberal Thought*, Chicago: University of Chicago Press.

Meier, Gerald and Dudley Seers (eds) 1984, *Pioneers in Development*, New York: Oxford University Press.

Mendlovitz, Saul H. and R.B.J. Walker (eds) 1987, *Towards a Just World Peace*, London: Butterworths.

Menon, Nivedita 2010, 'Introduction', in *Empire and Nation, Selected Essays*, by P. Chatterjee, New York: Columbia University Press.

Mészáros, István 1995, *Beyond Capital*, London: Merlin Press.

Metcalf, Thomas 1997, *Ideologies of the Raj*, Cambridge: Cambridge University Press.

Mignolo, Walter 2000, *Local Histories/ Global Designs: Coloniality, Subaltern Knowledges, and Border Thinking*, Princeton, NJ: Princeton University Press.

Miliband, Ralph 1978, 'Constitutionalism and Revolution: Notes on Eurocommunism', *Socialist Register*, 15: 158–71.

—— 2009, *Parliamentary Socialism: A Study in the Politics of Labour*, London: Merlin Press.

Mishra, Binod and Sanjay Kumar (eds) 2006, *Indian Writings in English*, Delhi: Atlantic Publishers.

Mishra, Hari Ram 1964, *The Theory of Rasa*, Chattarpur, M.P.: Vindhyachal Prakashan.

Mitchell, Timothy 1998, 'Nationalism, Imperialism, Economism: A Comment on Habermas', *Public Culture*, 10, 2: 417–424.

Mohanty, Chandra Talpade 1994, 'Under Western Eyes: Feminist Scholarship and Colonial Discourses', in *Colonial Discourse and Post-colonial Theory*, edited by P. Williams and L. Chrisman, New York: Columbia University Press.

Moore, Barrington 1993 [1967], *Social Origins of Dictatorship and Democracy*, Boston, MA: Beacon Press.

Moreland, W.H. and A.C. Chatterjee 1953 [1936], *A Short History of India*, London: Longmans, Green and Co.

Mori, Jennifer 2000, *Britain in the Age of the French Revolution*, Harlow: Longman Publishing Group.

Morris, Meaghan 1990, 'Metamorphoses at Sydney Tower', *New Formations*, 11: 5–18.

Morris, R.J. 1981, 'Samuel Smiles and the Genesis of Self-Help; the Retreat to a Petit Bourgeois Utopia', *Historical Journal*, 24, 1: 89–109.

Mosse, George 1985, *Towards the Final Solution: A History of European Racism*, Madison, WI: University of Wisconsin Press.

Mouffe, Chantal (ed.) 1979, *Gramsci and Marxist Theory*, London and Boston: Routledge and Kegan Paul.

Mukherjee, Rudrangshu 2002 [1984], *Awadh in Revolt 1857–1858: A Study of Popular Resistance*, Second Edition, London: Anthem.

Nair, Janaki 1998, *Miners and Millhands: Work, Culture and Politics in Princely Mysore*, Delhi: Sage Books.

Nairn, Tom 1977, *The Break-Up of Britain: Crisis and Neo-nationalism*, London: New Left Books.

Nanda, Meera 1991, 'Is Modern Science a Western, Patriarchal Myth? A Critique of Populist Orthodoxy', *South Asia Bulletin*, 11, 1/2: 32–61.

—— 2003, *Prophets Facing Backward: Postmodern Critiques of Science and Hindu Nationalism in India*, New Brunswick, NJ: Rutgers University Press.

—— 2004, 'Postmodernism, Hindu Nationalism and "Vedic Science"', *Frontline*, 20, 26, <www.flonnet.com/fl2026/stories/20040102000607800.htm>.

Nandy, Ashis 1983, *The Intimate Enemy: Loss and Recovery of Self under Colonialism*, Delhi: Oxford University Press.

—— 1994, *The Illegitimacy of Nationalism: Rabindranath Tagore and the Politics of Self*, Delhi: Oxford University Press.

—— 1995, *The Savage Freud and Other Essays on Possible and Retrievable Selves*, Princeton, NJ: Princeton University Press.

—— 1998, 'The Politics of Secularism and The Recovery of Religious Tolerance', in *Secularism and Its Critics*, edited by R. Bhargava, Delhi: Oxford University Press.

Nayar, Baldev Raj (ed.) 2007, *Globalisation and Politics in India*, New Delhi, Oxford University Press.

Nelson, Cary and Lawrence Grossberg (eds) 1988, *Marxism and the Interpretations of Culture*, Chicago, IL: University of Illinois Press.

Nehru, Jawaharlal 1958, *A Bunch of Old Letters*, Bombay: Asia Publishing House.

Newman, Richard 1981, *Workers and Unions in Bombay, 1918–1929: A Study of Organisation in the Cotton Mills*, Canberra: Australian National University Monographs on South Asia.

Nicolson, I.F. 1969, *The Administration of Nigeria 1900–1960: Men, Methods, and Myths*, London: Oxford University Press.

Nietzsche, Friedrich 1895, *Die Götzen-Dämmerung* [*Twilight of the Idols*], text prepared from the original German and translations by W. Kaufmann and R.J. Hollingdale, <www.handprint.com/SC/NIE/GotDamer.html>.

—— 1967, *The Genealogy of Morals and Ecce Homo*, edited and translated by W. Kaufmann, New York: Vintage.

Nimtz, August 2002, 'The Eurocentric Marx and Engels and Other Related Myths', in *Marxism, Modernity and Postcolonial Studies*, edited by C. Bartolovich and N. Lazarus, Cambridge: Cambridge University Press.

O'Hanlon, Rosalind 2002 [1988], 'Recovering the Subject: *Subaltern Studies* and Histories of Resistance in Colonial South Asia', in *Reading Subaltern Studies*, edited by D. Ludden, London: Anthem Press.

O'Hanlon, Rosalind and David Washbrook 1992, 'After Orientalism: Culture, Criticism, and Politics in the Third World', *Comparative Studies in Society and History*, 34: 141–167.

Olender, Maurice 1992, *The Languages of Paradise. Race, Religion, and Philology in the Nineteenth Century*, translated by A. Goldhammer, Cambridge, MA: Harvard University Press.

Oommen, T.K. (ed.) 2010, *Classes, Citizenship and Inequality*, Delhi: Dorling Kindersley (India) Pvt. Ltd.

Orwell, George 1997 [1934], *Burmese Days*, London: Secker & Warburg.

Pandey, Gyanendra 1978, *Ascendancy of the Congress in Uttar Pradesh 1926–34*, Delhi: Oxford University Press.

—— 1990, *The Construction of Communalism in Colonial North India*, Delhi: Oxford University Press.

—— 1991, 'In Defence of the Fragment: Writing about Hindu-Muslim Riots in India Today', *Economic and Political Weekly*, 26, 11/12: 559–572.

—— 1994, 'The Prose of Otherness', in *Subaltern Studies VIII: Essays in Honour of Ranajit Guha*, edited by D. Arnold and D. Hardiman, Delhi: Oxford University Press.

Panikkar, K.M. 1959, *Asia and Western Dominance*, London: Allen and Unwin.

Parry, Benita 2002, 'Liberation Theory: Variations on Themes of Marxism and Modernity', in *Marxism, Modernity and Postcolonial Studies*, edited by C. Bartolovich and N. Lazarus, Cambridge: Cambridge University Press.

Patnaik, Prabhat 1997, 'The Context and Consequences of Economic Liberalisation in India', *The Journal of International Trade and Economic Development*, 6, 2: 165–178.

Patnaik, Utsa 1976, 'Class Differentiation Within the Peasantry: An Approach to the Analysis of Indian Agriculture', *Economic and Political Weekly* Review of Agriculture, 11: A82–A101.

—— 1978, 'Development of Capitalism in Agriculture', in *Studies in the Development of Capitalism in India*, Lahore: Vanguard Books.

—— 1990, *Agrarian Relations and Accumulation: The 'Mode of Production' Debate in India*, Bombay: Oxford University Press.

Perry, Matt 2002, *Marxism and History*, New York: Palgrave.

Philips, C.H. (ed.) 1961, *Historians of India, Pakistan and Ceylon*, London: Oxford University Press.

Philp, Mark (ed.) 2004, *The French Revolution and British Popular Politics*, Cambridge: Cambridge University Press.

Pilger, John 2003, *The New Rulers of the World*, London: Verso.

Pines, Jim and Paul Willemen (eds) 1989, *Questions of the Third Cinema*, London: BFI Publishing.

Poliakov, Léon 1974, *The Aryan Myth: A History of Racist and Nationalist Ideas in Europe*, New York: Basic Books.

Pollock, Sheldon 1993, 'Deep Orientalism?' in *Orientalism and the Postcolonial Predicament*, edited by C. Breckenridge and P. van der Veer, Philadelphia, PA: University of Pennsylvania Press.

Popper, Karl 1945, *The Open Society and Its Enemies*, 2 Volumes, London: G. Routledge and Sons.

Postone, Moïshe 1996, *Time, Labor and Social Domination: A Reinterpretation* of *Marx's Critical Theory*, Cambridge: Cambridge University Press.

Pouchepadass, Jacques 1999, *Champaran and Gandhi: Planters, Peasants and Gandhian Politics*, Delhi: Oxford University Press.

—— 2002, 'Pluralising Reason (Review of Dipesh Chakrabarty's *Provincializing Europe*)', *History and Theory*, 41, 3: 381–391.

Prakash, Gyan 1990a, *Bonded Histories: Genealogies of Labour Servitude in Colonial India*, Cambridge: Cambridge University Press.

—— 1990b, 'Writing Post-Orientalist Histories of the Third World: Perspectives from Indian Historiography', *Comparative Studies in Society and History*, 32: 383–408.

—— (ed.) 1992a, *The World of the Rural Labourer in Colonial India*, Delhi: Oxford University Press.

—— 1992b, 'Postcolonial Criticism and Indian Historiography,' *Social Text*, 31–32: 8–20.

—— 1992c, 'Reproducing Inequality: Spirit Cults and Labour Relations in Colonial Eastern India', in *The World of the Rural Labourer in Colonial India*, Delhi: Oxford University Press.

—— 1992d, 'Can the "Subaltern" Ride? A Reply to O'Hanlon and Washbrook', *Comparative Studies in Society and History*, 34: 168–184.

—— 1994, 'Subaltern Studies as Postcolonial Criticism', *American Historical Review*, 99, 5: 1475–1490.

Prinja, Nawal K. (ed.) 1996, *Explaining Hindu Dharma: A Guide for Teachers*, London: Religious and Moral Education Press.

Quinet, Edgar 1985 [1845], *Le Christianisme et la revolution française*, Paris: Fayard.

Rabasa, José 1997, 'Of Zapatismo: Reflections on the Folkloric and the Impossible in a Subaltern Insurrection', in *The Politics of Culture in the Shadow of Capital*, edited by L. Lowe and D. Lloyd, Durham, NC: Duke University Press.

Rabinow, Paul (ed.) 1984, *Foucault Reader*, New York: Pantheon.

Rangarajan, Mahesh 1994, 'Imperial Agendas and India's Forests: The Early History of Indian Forestry, 1800–1878', *Indian Economic and Social History Review*, 31, 2: 147–167.

Ray, Rabindra 1992, *The Naxalites and Their Ideology*, Delhi: Oxford University Press.

Raychaudhuri, Tapan 1982, 'Mughal India,' in *The Cambridge Economic History of India, c.1200–c.1750*, edited by T. Raychaudhuri and I. Habib, Cambridge: Cambridge University Press.

—— 1988, *Europe Reconsidered: Perceptions of the West in Nineteenth-Century Bengal*, Delhi: Oxford University Press.

Raychaudhuri, Tapan and Irfan Habib (eds) 1982, *The Cambridge Economic History of India, c.1200–c.1750*, Cambridge: Cambridge University Press.

Report of the Committee on the Riots in Poona and Ahmednagar, 1875–76, Bombay: Central Government Press.

Richards, Eric 1982, *A History of the Highland Clearances: Volume I, Agrarian*

Transformation and the Evictions 1746– 1886, London: Croom Helm.

Richardson, Thomas (ed.) 1996, *Refusal of the Shadow: Surrealism and the Caribbean*, London: Verso.

Robb, Peter (ed.) 1983, *Rural India, Power and Society under British Rule: Collected Papers on South Asia, No. 6*, London: Curzon Press.

Roemer, John (ed.) 1986, *Analytical Marxism*, Cambridge: Cambridge University Press.

Rostow, Walt Whitman 1960, *The Stages of Economic Growth: A Non-Communist Manifesto*, Cambridge: Cambridge University Press.

Rothschild, Emma 2001, *Economic Sentiments: Adam Smith, Condorcet and the Enlightenment*, Cambridge, MA: Harvard University Press.

Roy, Tirthankar 2002, 'Economic History and Modern India: Redefining the Link', *Journal of Economic Perspectives*, 16, 3: 109–130.

Rubenstein, David 2000, 'A New Look at New Labour', *Politics*, 20, 3: 161–167.

Saad-Filho, Alfredo (ed.) 2003, *Anti-Capitalism: A Marxist Introduction*, London: Pluto Press.

Said, Edward 1978, *Orientalism*, New York: Pantheon.

—— 1983, *The World, the Text and the Critic*, Cambridge, MA: Cambridge University Press.

—— 1988, 'Foreword', in *Selected Subaltern Studies*, edited by R. Guha and G.C. Spivak, New York: Oxford University Press.

—— 1993, *Culture and Imperialism*, New York: Knopf.

—— 1994, *Representations of the Intellectual*, London: Vintage.

—— 1995, 'East isn't East', *Times Literary Supplement*, 4792: 2–6.

Samuel, Raphael 1998, 'Four Nations History', in *Island Stories: Unravelling Britain*, London: Verso.

San Juan, Epiphanio 1998, *Beyond Postcolonial Theory*, New York: St. Martin's Press.

—— 2002, 'Postcolonialism and the Problematic of Uneven Development', in *Marxism, Modernity and Postcolonial Studies*, edited by C. Bartolovich and N. Lazarus, Cambridge: Cambridge University Press.

—— 2004, *Working Through the Contradictions: From Cultural Theory to Critical Practice*, Lewisburg, PA: Bucknell University Press.

Sardar, Ziauddin 1984, *The Touch of Midas: Science, Values, and Environment in Islam and the West*, Manchester: Manchester University Press.

Sarkar, Sumit 1983, *Modern India, 1885– 1947*, Bombay: MacMillan and Co.

—— 1994, 'Orientalism Revisited: Saidian Frameworks in the Writings of Modern Indian History', *Oxford Literary Review*, 16: 205–224.

—— 1997, *Writing Social History*, Delhi: Oxford University Press.

—— 2004, 'The Return of Labour to South Asian History', *Historical Materialism*, 12, 3: 285–313.

Sarkar, Susobhan 1968, 'The Thought of Gramsci', *Mainstream*, 2 November 1968.

—— 1972, 'General President's Address', *Indian History Congress: Proceedings of* the Thirty-Third Session, Muzaffarpur, 1–18, New Delhi: Sudha Publications.

Sartre, Jean-Paul 1963, Search for a Method, New York: Random House.

Satya, Laxman 1997, Cotton and Famine in Berar, New Delhi: Manohar Publishers.

Saul, John 2001, Millennial Africa: Capitalism, Socialism, Democracy, Trenton and Asmara: Africa World Press.

Savarkar, Vinayak Damodar 1969 [1923], Hindutva, Who is a Hindu?, Bombay: Veer Savarkar Prakashan.

Schaub, Uta Liebmann 1989, 'Foucault's Oriental Subtext', PMLA: Publications of the Modern Language Association of America, 104, 3: 306–316.

Schott, Robin May 1996, 'The Gender of Enlightenment', in What is Enlightenment?, edited by J. Schmidt, Berkeley, CA: University of California Press.

Schmidt, James (ed.) 1996, What is Enlightenment?, Berkeley, CA: University of California Press.

Schwab, Raymond 1984, The Oriental Renaissance: Europe's Rediscovery of India and the Far East, translated by G. Patterson-Black and V. Reinking, New York: Columbia University Press.

Schwartz, Henry 1997, Writing Cultural History in Colonial and Postcolonial India, Philadelphia, PA: University of Pennsylvania Press.

Schwarz, Roberto 1992, 'Misplaced Ideas', in Misplaced Ideas: Essays on Brazilian Culture, London: Verso.

Scott, Paul 2007 [1966–74], The Raj Quartet, New York: Knopf.

Seavoy, Roland 1986, Famine in Peasant Societies, New York: Greenwood Press.

Sethia, Tara 1996, 'The Rise of the Jute Manufacturing Industry in Colonial India: A Global Perspective', Journal of World History, 7, 1: 71–99.

Shanin, Teodor 1983, Late Marx and the Russian Road: Marx and 'The Peripheries of Capitalism', New York: Monthly Review Press.

Sharpe, Matthew and Geoff Boucher 2010, Žižek and Politics: A Critical Introduction, Edinburgh: Edinburgh University Press.

Shatz, Adam 2012, 'Not in the Mood (Review of Benoît Peeters's Derrida: A Biography)', translated by A. Brown, London: Polity Press.

Shiva, Vandana 1988, Staying Alive: Women, Ecology and Development, London: Zed Books.

—— 1991, Ecology and the Politics of Survival: Conflicts over Natural Resources in India, New Delhi: Sage Publications.

—— 1996, Biopiracy: The Plunder of Nature and Knowledge, Boston: South End Press.

—— 2008, Soil not Oil: Environmental Justice in an Era of Climate Change, Boston: South End Press.

Shohat, Ella 1992, 'Notes on the "Post-Colonial"', Social Text, 31–32: 99–113.

Shohat, Ella and Robert Stam 1994, Unthinking Eurocentrism: Multiculturalism and the Media, London: Routledge.

Siddiqui, Kalim (ed.) 1985, Issues in the Islamic Movement, 1983–84, London: The Open Press.

Simeon, Dilip 1995, The Politics of Labour under Late Colonialism: Workers,

*Unions and the State in Chota Nagpur,
1928–1939*, Delhi: Manohar.

Singh, Navtej 1996, *Starvation and Colonialism: A Study of Famines in the Nineteenth Century British Punjab 1858–1901*, Delhi: National Book Organisation.

Singh, Sangeeta, Minakshi Menon, Pradeep Kumar Datta, Biswamoy Pati, Radhakanta Barik, Radhika Chopra, Partha Dutta and Sanjay Prasad 2002 [1984], 'Subaltern Studies II: A Review Article', in *Reading Subaltern Studies*, edited by D. Ludden, London: Anthem Press.

Smith, Anthony 1995, *Nations and Nationalism in a Global Era*, Cambridge: Polity Press.

Smith, Tony 1990, *The Logic of Marx's Capital: Replies to Hegelian Criticisms*, Albany, NY: SUNY Press.

Smith, Vincent 1958 [1919], *The Oxford History of India*, Third Edition, edited by P. Spear, Oxford: Clarendon Press.

Sohn-Rethel, Alfred 1978, *Intellectual and Manual Labour: A Critique of Epistemology*, Atlantic Highlands, NJ: Humanities Press.

Sonenscher, Michael 2008, *Sans-Culottes: An Eighteenth-Century Emblem in the French Revolution*, Princeton, NJ: Princeton University Press.

Spivak, Gayatri Chakravorty 1985, 'Subaltern Studies: Deconstructing Historiography', in *Subaltern Studies IV*, edited by R. Guha, New Delhi: Oxford University Press.

—— 1988, 'Can the Subaltern Speak?', in *Marxism and the Interpretations of Culture*, edited by C. Nelson and L. Grossberg, Chicago, IL: University of Illinois Press.

—— 1990, 'Poststructuralism, Marginality, Postcoloniality and Value', in *Literary Theory Today*, edited by P. Collier and H. Geyer-Ryan, London: Polity Press.

—— 1992, 'French Feminism Revisited: Ethics and Politics', in *Feminists Theorize the Political*, edited by J. Butler and J. Scott, New York: Routledge.

—— 1993, *Outside in the Teaching Machine*, London: Routledge.

Sprinker, Michael (ed.) 1999, *Ghostly Demarcations: A Symposium on Jacques Derrida's Spectres of Marx*, London: Verso.

Stampe, William 1944, *Planning for Plenty*, Delhi: Government of India Press.

Steiner, George 1987, *Martin Heidegger*, Chicago, IL: Chicago University Press.

Stiglitz, Joseph 2002, *Globalization and Its Discontents*, New York: W.W. Norton.

Stone, Irving 1968, 'British Long-Term Investment in Latin America, 1865–1913', *The Business History Review*, 42, 3: 311–339.

Stunkel, Kenneth R. 1975, 'India and the Idea of a Primitive Revelation in French Neo-Catholic Thought', *Journal of Religious Thought*, 8, 3: 228–239.

Surin, Kenneth 1999, 'Standing Schumpeter on His Head: Robert Brenner's Economics of Global Turbulence', *Comparative Studies of South Asia, Africa and the Middle East*, 19, 2: 53–60.

Suvin, Darko 1976, '"Utopian" and "Scientific": Two Attributes for Socialism from Engels', *The Minnesota Review*, 6: 59–70.

Svallfors, Stefan and Peter Taylor-Gooby (eds) 1999, *The End of the Welfare State? Responses to State Retrenchment*, London: Routledge.

Sweezy, Paul 1942, *The Theory of Capitalist Development: Principles of Marxist Political-Economy*, New York: Oxford University Press.

Tabb, William 1997, 'Globalization may be *an* Issue, the Power of Capital is *the* Issue', *Monthly Review*, 49, 2: 20–30.

Tavakoli-Targhi, Mohamad 2003, 'Orientalism's Genesis Amnesia', in *Antinomies of Modernity: Essays on Race, Orient, Nation*, edited by V. Kaiwar and S. Mazumdar, Durham, NC: Duke University Press.

Terray, Emmanuel 1972, *Marxism and 'Primitive' Societies*, New York: Monthly Review Press.

Terry, Les 1995, 'Not a Postmodern Nomad: A Conversation with Stuart Hall on Race, Ethnicity and Identity', *Arena Journal*, 5: 51–70.

Thapar, Romila 1969, *Communalism and the Writing of Indian History*, Delhi: People's Publishing House.

—— 2002, *Early India: From the Origins to 1300 A.D.*, Berkeley, CA: University of California Press.

Thatcher, Ian D. 2007, 'Left-Communism: Rosa Luxemburg and Leon Trotsky Compared', in *Twentieth-Century Marxism: A Global Introduction*, edited by D. Glaser and D.M. Walker, Oxford: Routledge.

Thomas, Caroline and Peter Wilkin (eds) 1997, *Globalization and the South*, New York: St. Martin's Press.

Thomas, Peter D. 2006, 'Being Max Weber' (Review of Joachim Radkau's *Max Weber: die Leidenschaft des Denkens*), *New Left Review*, 41: 147–158.

—— 2007, 'Absolute Historicism', *Historical Materialism*, 15: 249–256.

—— 2009, *The Gramscian Moment: Philosophy, Hegemony and Marxism*, Leiden: E.J. Brill.

Thompson, E.P. 1966, *The Making of the English Working-Class*, New York: Vintage Books.

—— 1975, 'The Crime of Anonymity', in *Albion's Fatal Tree: Crime and Society in Eighteenth-Century England*, edited by D. Hay, P. Linebaugh, J. Rule and C. Winslow, New York: Pantheon Books.

—— 1978, *The Poverty of Theory and Other Essays*, New York: Monthly Review Press.

—— 1991, *Customs in Common*, London: Merlin Press.

—— 1993, *Witness Against the Beast: William Blake and the Moral Law*, Cambridge: Cambridge University Press.

Thompson, Willie 2004, *Postmodernism and History*, New York: Palgrave-Macmillan.

Tilak, Bal Gangadhar 1919, *Tilak: His Writings and Speeches*, Third Edition, Madras: Ganesh.

—— 1955 [1893], *The Orion, or Researches into the Antiquity of the Vedas*, Poona: Tilak Bros.

—— 1956 [1903], *The Arctic Home in the Vedas, Being also a New Key to the Interpretation of Many Vedic Texts and Legends*, Poona: Tilak Bros.

Tipps, Dean C. 1973, 'Modernization Theory and the Comparative Study of

Societies: A Critical Perspective', *Comparative Studies in Society and History*, 15, 2: 199–226.

Tocqueville, Alexis de 1952, *Oeuvres complètes*, edited by J.P. Mayer, Paris: Gallimard.

Trautmann, Thomas 1997, *Aryans and British India*, Berkeley, CA: University of California Press.

Trotsky, Leon 1991 [1937], *The Revolution Betrayed: What is the Soviet Union and Where is it Going?*, Detroit: Labor Publications.

Tucker, Robert C. 1978, *The Marx-Engels Reader*, Second Edition, New York: W.W. Norton.

Turner, Graeme 2003, *British Cultural Studies: An Introduction*, Third Edition, London: Routledge.

Unger, Roberto 1987, *False Necessity: Anti-necessitarian Social Theory in the Service of Radical Democracy*, Cambridge, MA: Harvard University Press.

Vanaik, Achin 1990, *The Painful Transition: Bourgeois Democracy in India*, London: Verso.

—— 1997, *The Furies of Indian Communalism*, London: Verso.

van Creveld, Martin 1996, 'The Fate of the State', *Parameters*, (Spring): 4–18.

—— 1999, *The Rise and Decline of the State*, Cambridge: Cambridge University Press.

Vermeil, Edmond 1940, *L'Allemagne, Essai d'Explication*, Paris: Gallimard.

Vieira, Else R.P. 1999, 'Postcolonialisms and the Latin Americas', *Interventions: International Journal of Postcolonial Studies*, 1, 2: 273–281.

Virno, Paolo and Michael Hardt (eds) 1996, *Radical Thought in Italy: A Potential Politics*, Minneapolis, MN: University of Minnesota Press.

Visaria, Pravin and Leela Visaria 1983, 'Population, 1757–1947,' in *The Cambridge Economic History of India*, edited by D. Kumar, Cambridge: Cambridge University Press.

Vohra, Ranbir 2001, *The Making of India: A Historical Survey*, New York: M.E. Sharpe.

von Grunebaum, Gustave E. 1953, *Medieval Islam*, Second Edition, Chicago, IL: Chicago University Press.

von Laue, Theodore 1987, *The World Revolution of Westernisation: The Twentieth Century in Global Perspective*, New York: Oxford University Press.

Wallerstein, Immanuel 1974, *The Origins of the Modern World System*, New York: Academic Press.

—— 1991, *Geopolitics and Geoculture: Essays on the Changing World-System*, Cambridge: Cambridge University Press.

—— 2004, *World-systems Analysis: An Introduction*, Durham, NC: Duke University Press.

Washbrook, D.A. 1981, 'The Law, State and Agrarian Society in Colonial India', *Modern Asian Studies*, 15, 3: 649–721.

Weber, Eugen 1976, *Peasants into Frenchmen: The Modernization of Rural France, 1870–1914*, Stanford, CA: Stanford University Press.

Weiss, John 1996, *Ideology of Death*, Chicago, IL: Ivan Dee.

Welsh, Frank 2011, *The Four Nations: A History of the United Kingdom*, New Haven, CT: Yale University Press.

Wheeler, Mortimer 1966, *Civilizations of the Indus Valley and Beyond*, London: Thames and Hudson.

Whitcombe, Elizabeth 1995, 'The Environmental Costs of Irrigation in British India: Waterlogging, Salinity and Malaria', in *Nature, Culture, Imperialism, Essays on the Environmental History of South Asia*, edited by D. Arnold and R. Guha, Delhi: Oxford University Press.

Wiggershaus, Rolf 1994, *The Frankfurt School: Its Histories, Theories, and Political Significance*, Cambridge, MA: MIT Press.

Wilkin, Peter 1997, 'New Myths for the South: Globalization and the Conflict between Private Power and Freedom', in *Globalization and the South*, edited by C. Thomas and P. Wilkin, New York: St. Martin's Press.

Williams, Patrick 1999, 'Totally Ideological', *Interventions: International Journal of Postcolonial Studies*, 1, 2: 282–285.

Williams, Patrick and Laura Chrisman (eds) 1994, *Colonial Discourse and Post-colonial Theory*, New York: Columbia University Press.

Williams, Raymond 1961, *The Long Revolution*, London: Chatto and Windus.

—— 1964, *Second Generation*, London: Chatto and Windus.

—— 1977, *Marxism and Literature*, Oxford: Oxford University Press.

—— 1983, *The Year 2000*, New York: Pantheon.

—— 1989, *Resources of Hope: Culture, Democracy, Socialism*, London: Verso.

—— 1989a, *The Politics of Modernism: Against the New Conformists*, London: Verso.

Winichakul, Thongchai 1997, *Siam Mapped: A History of the Geo-body of a Nation*, Honolulu: University of Hawaii Press.

Wolf, Eric 1984 [1982], *Europe and the People Without History*, Berkeley, CA: University of California Press.

Wolin, Richard 1990, *The Politics of Being: The Political Thought of Martin Heidegger*, New York: Columbia University Press.

Wolpert, Stanley 1962, *Tilak and Gokhale: Revolution and Reform in the Making of Modern India*, Berkeley and Los Angeles, CA: University of California Press.

Wood, Ellen Meiksins 1998, 'The Agrarian Origins of Capitalism', *Monthly Review*, 50, 3: 14–31.

—— 2002, *The Origins of Capitalism: A Longer View*, London: Verso.

—— 2007, 'A Reply to Critics', *Historical Materialism*, 15: 143–170.

Xaxa, Virginius 2011, 'Social Inequality and Peasantry: The Evolving Trajectory', in *Classes, Citizenship and Inequality*, edited by T.K. Oommen, Delhi: Dorling Kindersley (India) Pvt. Ltd.

Young, Robert J.C. 1998, 'Ideologies of the Postcolonial', *Interventions: International Journal of Postcolonial Studies*, 1, 1: 4–8.

—— 2001, *Postcolonialism: A Historical Introduction*, Oxford: Blackwell.

Zeleza, Paul Tiyambe 2009, 'What Happened to the African Renaissance? The Challenges of Development in the

Twenty-First Century', *Comparative Studies of South Asia, Africa and the Middle East*, 29, 2: 155–170.

Žižek, Slavoj 1997, 'Multiculturalism, Or the Cultural Logic of Multinational Capitalism', *New Left Review*, 225: 28–51.

—— 1998, 'A Plea for Left "Eurocentrism"', *Critical Inquiry*, 24, 4: 998–1009.

—— 2000a, *The Ticklish Subject: The Absent Centre of Political Ontology*, London: Verso.

—— 2000b, 'Class Struggle or Postmodernism? Yes, please!', in *Contingency, Hegemony, Universality: Contemporary Dialogues On The Left*, by J. Butler, E. Laclau and S. Žižek, London: Verso.

Index

www.ingramcontent.com/pod-product-compliance
Lightning Source LLC
Chambersburg PA
CBHW060019030426
42334CB00019B/2100